CANADA'S LAWS ON IMPORT AND EXPORT:
AN OVERVIEW

CANADA'S LAWS ON
IMPORT AND EXPORT
AN OVERVIEW

Dr Mohan Prabhu, LLD, QC

Canada's Laws on Import and Export: An Overview
© Irwin Law Inc, 2014

All rights reserved. No part of this publication may be reproduced, stored in a retrieval system, or transmitted, in any form or by any means, without the prior written permission of the publisher or, in the case of photocopying or other reprographic copying, a licence from Access Copyright (Canadian Copyright Licensing Agency), 1 Yonge Street, Suite 800, Toronto, ON, M5E 1E5.

Published in 2014 by
Irwin Law Inc
14 Duncan Street
Suite 206
Toronto, ON
M5H 3G8
www.irwinlaw.com

ISBN: 978-1-55221-361-2
E-BOOK ISBN: 978-1-55221-362-9

Cataloguing in Publication available from Library and Archives Canada

The publisher acknowledges the financial support of the Government of Canada through the Canada Book Fund for its publishing activities.

We acknowledge the assistance of the OMDC Book Fund, an initiative of Ontario Media Development Corporation.

Printed and bound in Canada.
1 2 3 4 5   18 17 16 15 14

Summary Table of Contents

FOREWORD BY JOY NOTT   xxxv
FOREWORD BY CAROL WEST   xxxvii
PREFACE   xxxix

CHAPTER 1: The *Customs Act*   1
CHAPTER 2: The *Customs Tariff*   76
CHAPTER 3: *Special Import Measures Act*   299
CHAPTER 4: The *Export and Import Permits Act*   396
CHAPTER 5: Other Statutes Relating to Import and Export   412
CHAPTER 6: Miscellaneous Federal Statutes   429

TABLE OF CASES   489
TABLE OF CONVENTIONS AND AGREEMENTS   505
TABLE OF CUSTOMS MEMORANDA   509
TABLE OF REGULATIONS   511
TABLE OF STATUTES   521
TABLE OF TARIFFS   537
INDEX   539
ABOUT THE AUTHOR   571

Detailed Table of Contents

FOREWORD BY JOY NOTT   *xxxv*

FOREWORD BY CAROL WEST   *xxxvii*

PREFACE   *xxxix*

CHAPTER 1
The *Customs Act*   *1*

A. Introduction   *1*

B. Obligation to Report   *2*
  1) Who Must Report?   *3*
  2) Failure to Declare and Report   *4*
  3) Movement of Goods after Report   *5*
  4) Release of Goods   *6*
  5) Release Prior to Accounting and Payment of Duties   *6*
  6) Abandoned and Unclaimed Goods   *7*

C. Licences under the *Customs Act* and *Customs Tariff*   *7*
  1) When Is a Licence Needed?   *7*
  2) Licence Requirements   *8*
  3) Warehouse Licences   *8*
      a) Sufferance Warehouse Licence   *9*
      b) Customs Bonded Warehouse Licence   *9*
      c) Highway Frontier Warehouses   *9*
      d) Queen's Warehouses   *10*

D. Accounting and Payment of Duties   *10*
  1) Documentation   *10*

        a) Cargo Control Document 10
        b) Invoice 10
        c) Release on Minimum Documentation 10
        d) Canada Customs Coding Form 11
        e) Other Documents 11
        f) Certificate of Origin 11
            i) Free Trade Partner Certificate 11
            ii) Most-Favoured-Nation, Australia, and New Zealand Tariffs 12
            iii) Other Tariff Beneficiaries 12
            iv) Low Value Shipments 12
        g) Final Accounting Package 13
    2) Customs Self-Assessment Program 13
    3) Advance Rulings 14

E. **Valuation of Imported Goods** 15
    1) Determination of Value for Duty 15
    2) *Ad Valorem* 16
    3) Six Methods of Valuation 16
    4) Primary Method: Transaction Value 17
        a) Sale for Export to Purchaser in Canada 18
        b) Price Paid or Payable Must Be Ascertainable 19
        c) Purchaser in Canada 20
        d) Purchaser and Vendor Not Related 23
        e) Adjustments to Transaction Value of Goods 24
            i) Commissions 26
                a. Buying Commissions 26
                b. Selling Commissions 29
            ii) "Assists" 30
                a. Design Costs 30
                b. Value of Materials Used or Consumed 30
                c. Quota Payments 31
            iii) Royalties and Licence Fees 31
                a. Non-dutiable Payments 31
                b. Dutiable If Condition of Sale 33
            iv) Deductions 35
            v) No Adjustment 36
    5) Transaction Value of Identical Goods 36
        a) Meaning of Identical Goods 36
        b) Same or Substantially Same Trade Level and Quantities 37
        c) Adjustments 37
        d) Two or More Transaction Values 38
        e) Sufficient Information Unavailable 38

      6) Transaction Value of Similar Goods 38
      7) Deductive Value 38
          a) Selling Price under Deductive Value Method 39
              i) Sales at Same or Substantially Same Time 39
              ii) First Trade Level 39
          b) Adjustments 39
      8) Computed Value 40
      9) Residual Method of Valuation 43

F. Marking of Goods 43

      1) Marking Requirement 43
      2) Marking Regulations 43

G. Administrative Determinations and Appeals 44

      1) Marking Determination 44
      2) Determination of Value for Duty, Tariff Classification, and Origin 44
      3) Payment of Duties and Taxes before Appeal 45
          a) Determination by Designated Officer 45
          b) Request for Re-determination by Another Officer 45
          c) Re-determination Following Audit 46
          d) Re-determination and Further Re-determination by President 46
          e) Extension of Time Limit 46
          f) President's Additional Powers 49
      4) Appeals to the Tribunal 49
          a) Filing an Appeal 49
          b) Tribunal's Decision 50
          c) Appeals 50
          d) Appeals to Federal Court of Appeal 51
          e) Disposition 53
      5) References to Tribunal 53
      6) Appeals to Provincial Courts 54
          a) Special Provisions 54
          b) Seizure and Forfeiture of Goods or Conveyances 54

H. Abatement and Refund of Duties 54

      1) Abatement 55
      2) Refund of Duties 55
          a) Deemed Re-determination 56

I. Enforcement 56

      1) Powers of Officers 56
          a) Administrative and Investigative Powers Distinguished 57
      2) Enforcement Powers 58

a) Search of the Person   59
   b) Examination of Goods   60
3) Seizure of Goods and Conveyances   61
4) Forfeiture   61
   a) Effecting Forfeiture   63
   b) *In Rem* Action   63
   c) Limitation   64
5) Ascertained Forfeiture   64
6) Appeals   65
7) Third Party Claims   65
   a) Late Applications   66
   b) Conditions   66
   c) Appeal against Minister's Decision   66
   d) Appeal against Provincial Superior Court's Decision   68
   e) Goods or Conveyance to Be Given to Successful Applicant   68

J. **Penalty for Violation of Designated Provisions**   68

1) Administrative Monetary Penalties   68
2) Appeal   69
   a) Appeal to Minister   70
   b) Appeal to Federal Court   70

K. **Criminal Offences and Punishment**   70

1) General Offences   70
2) Smuggling   72
3) Offences by Corporation   73
4) Punishment for General Offences   73
   a) Obstructing an Officer   74
   b) Punishment for Other Offences   74
5) Limitation Period   74
6) Evidence   74

L. **Protection of Officers**   75

CHAPTER 2
The *Customs Tariff*   76

A. **Introduction**   76

B. **Administration and Enforcement**   77

C. **Imposition of Duties**   78

1) General Provisions   78
2) Goods Taken out of Canada and Subsequently Returned   78

Detailed Table of Contents

D. **Tariff Structure and Commodity Classification** 79
  1) Tariff Structure 79
  2) The Harmonized Commodity Description and Coding System 80
  3) Renumbering Tariff Item or Changing Description of Goods 80
  4) Amendment of the Schedule 81
  5) Tariff Classification Appeals 81
  6) Interpretation of Tariff Items 82
      a) *General Rules* 82
          i) General Rule 1 83
          ii) General Rule 2 83
          iii) General Rule 3 84
          iv) General Rule 4 84
          v) General Rule 5 84
          vi) General Rule 6 85
  7) *Canadian Rules* 85
  8) Summary 86
  9) Application of *General Rules* 86
      a) General Rule 2 86
      b) General Rule 3 87
      c) General Rule 4 88
  10) Classification Decisions of the Tribunal 88
      a) Competing Tariff Classifications 90
          i) Section IV: Chapters 16 to 24 (Foodstuffs, Beverages, Tobacco) 91
              CASE 1: TARIFF ITEM 1806.90.90 (CHRISTMAS ADVENT CALENDARS CONTAINING CHOCOLATES) 91
              CASE 2: TARIFF HEADING 19.02 (RICE NOODLES) 92
              CASE 3: TARIFF HEADINGS 20.09 (FRUIT JUICE) AND 22.02 (OTHER NON-ALCOHOLIC BEVERAGES) 93
              CASE 4: TARIFF HEADING 20.08 (MANGO JUICE) OR 22.02 (NECTAR/BEVERAGE) 95
              CASE 5: TARIFF HEADING 20.09, 20.08, OR 21.06 (CANNED COCONUT MILK) 95
              CASE 6: TARIFF HEADING 21.04 (SOUPS AND BROTHS) 96
          ii) Section VI: Chapters 28 to 38 (Products of the Chemical or Allied Industries) 97
              CASE 1: TARIFF HEADINGS 30.03 AND 30.04 (CERTAIN DEVIL'S ROOT TABLETS, BULK ST. JOHN'S WART OIL, AND GARLIC POWDER TABLETS) 97
              CASE 2: TARIFF HEADING 38.15 OR 38.24 (ALUMINUM PELLETS) 98
          iii) Section VII: Chapters 39 and 40 (Plastics and Rubber) 99

CASE 1: TARIFF ITEM 3916.10.00 (WOOD-PLASTIC COMPOSITE DECKING FOR EXTERIOR FLOORING) 99
CASE 2: TARIFF ITEM 3926.40.10 (GIRL FIGURINES OR DOLLS) 101
CASE 3: TARIFF ITEM 3921.90.91 OR 3921.90.99 (LAMINATED SHEETS) 104
CASE 4: TARIFF HEADING 39.24 (SILICON PLASTIC TEATS (NIPPLES)) 104
CASE 5: TARIFF HEADING 40.08 (VULCANIZED RUBBER) 105
CASE 6: TARIFF HEADING 40.16 (RUBBER CRAWLER TRACKS) 106

iv) Section VIII: Chapters 41 to 43 (Raw Hides, Travel Goods, Handbags) 106

CASE 1: TARIFF ITEM 4202.32.90 (PROTECTIVE COVERS FOR SMART CELLPHONES) 106
CASE 2: TARIFF ITEM 4202.91.90 (CELLPHONE PROTECTIVE COVERS) 107

v) Section X: Chapters 47 to 49 (Pulp and Paper) 108

CASE 1: TARIFF ITEM 4911.99.90 (NHL LOGO FLAGS, BANNERS, AND SIMILAR GOODS) 108

vi) Section XI: Chapters 50 to 63 (Textiles) 110

CASE 1: TARIFF HEADING 55.03 (TUFTS OF SYNTHETIC IMITATING LOCKS OF HAIR) 110
CASE 2: TARIFF HEADINGS 40.16 AND 56.09 (BUNGEE CORDS) 110
CASE 3: TARIFF ITEM 6210.30.00 (WOMEN'S JACKETS) 111
CASE 4: TARIFF HEADING 62.16 (ICE HOCKEY GLOVES) 112
CASE 5: TARIFF ITEM 6307.90.99 (ROLLER COVERS) 114
CASE 6: TARIFF ITEM 6307.20.00 (NEOPRENE PERSONAL FLOTATION DEVICES) 115
CASE 7: TARIFF ITEM 6305.33.00 (ONION BAGS) 115
CASE 8: TARIFF HEADINGS 61.10 AND 61.14 (NECK TOPS AND ONE-PIECE GARMENTS) 116
CASE 9: TARIFF ITEM 6116.93.00 (OVEN MITTS) 117
CASE 10: TARIFF ITEM 6307.90.99 (WEBBING STRAPS) 120
CASE 11: TARIFF ITEM 6307.90.99 (CARGO MATES—WEBBING STRAPS) 121

vii) Section XII: Chapters 64 to 67 (Footwear, Headgear, Others) 122

CASE 1: TARIFF HEADING 64.06 (FOOTWEAR LEATHER UPPERS) 122
CASE 2: TARIFF ITEM 6405.20.90 (CHILDREN'S ANIMAL-SHAPED SLIPPERS) 124

viii) Section XIII: Chapters 68 to 70 (Stone, Plaster, Cement, Asbestos, Ceramic, Glass) 125

CASE 1: TARIFF ITEM 6802.91.00 (MARBLE OR GRANITE TILES) 125

CASE 2: TARIFF ITEM 6807.10.00 (ROOFING SHEETS) *125*

CASE 3: TARIFF ITEM 7323.93.00 (STAINLESS STEEL STEP CANS) *126*

ix) Section XV: Chapters 72 to 83 (Base Metals) *127*

    CASE 1: TARIFF ITEM 7615.19.00 (CHRISTMAS-THEMED CAKE, MUFFIN, AND COOKIE PANS) *127*

    CASE 2. TARIFF ITEM 7308.90.90 (GALLERY GAZEBOS) *128*

    CASE 3: TARIFF ITEM 8208.20.00 (DISPOSABLE SCREW-ON CARBIDE KNIVES) *129*

    CASE 4: TARIFF ITEM 8205.70.90 (RATCHET TIE-DOWNS) *130*

    CASE 5: TARIFF ITEM 8302.42.00 (METAL DRAWER SLIDES) *131*

x) Section XVI: Chapters 84 and 85 (Machinery, Mechanical Appliances, Electrical Equipment, Television Image and Sound Recorders) *133*

    CASE 1: TARIFF HEADING 84.13 (SEROLOGICAL PIPETTES) *133*

    CASE 2: TARIFF ITEM 8415.90.29 (CONDENSERS FOR MOTOR VEHICLES) *134*

    CASE 3: TARIFF ITEM 8467.29.90 (HEAT GUN KITS) *136*

    CASE 4: TARIFF ITEM 8482.80.90 (UNDERMOUNT ROLLER GLIDES OR DRAWER SLIDES) *137*

    CASE 5: TARIFF ITEM 8504.40.90 (PORTABLE BATTERY BOOSTER TO JUMPSTART VEHICLES) *138*

    CASE 6: TARIFF ITEM 8516.79.90 (GLUE GUNS) *139*

    CASE 7: TARIFF ITEM 8516.79.90 (PLUG-IN DEODORIZERS) *140*

    CASE 8: TARIFF ITEM 8517.11.00 (CORDLESS TELEPHONES) *143*

    CASE 9: TARIFF ITEM 8518.30.91 (HEADPHONES OR HEADSETS) *144*

    CASE 10: TARIFF ITEM 8520.90.90 (INTEGRATED CIRCUIT (IC) RECORDERS AND MINIDISK (MD) RECORDERS) *145*

    CASE 11: TARIFF ITEM 8521.90.90 (DIGITAL VIDEO RECORDERS (DVRS) AND MONITORS) *146*

    CASE 12: TARIFF ITEM 8522.90.90 (ARMBAND CASES FOR IPODS) *148*

    CASE 13: TARIFF ITEM 8523.11.00 (HEWLETT-PACKARD DATA CARTRIDGES) *148*

xi) Section XVII: Chapters 86 to 89 (Vehicles, Aircraft, Vessels, and Associated Transport Equipment) *149*

    CASE 1: TARIFF SUBHEADING 8703.21 (ALL-TERRAIN VEHICLES (ATVS)) *149*

    CASE 2: TARIFF ITEM 8703.21.90 (ALL-TERRAIN VEHICLES (ATVS)) *151*

xii) Section XVIII: Chapters 90 to 92 (Optical, Photographic, Cinematographic, Measuring, Medical Instruments; Clocks and Watches; Musical Instruments) *153*

    CASE 1: TARIFF ITEM 9029.20.91 (HEART RATE MONITORS) *153*

    CASE 2: TARIFF ITEM 9105.99.90 (HOLIDAY MELODY CLOCKS) *154*

xiii) Section XX: Chapters 94 to 96 (Miscellaneous Manufactured Articles) 155
    CASE 1: TARIFF ITEM 9401.61.10 (UPHOLSTERED SOFAS, LOVE SEATS, AND SUCH) 155
    CASE 2: TARIFF ITEM 9401.61.00 (GAMING CHAIRS) 156
    CASE 3: TARIFF ITEM 9401.71.10 (UPHOLSTERED FOLDING CHAIRS) 157
    CASE 4: TARIFF ITEM 9401.71.90 (3-IN-1 CREEPER SEATS) 157
    CASE 5: TARIFF ITEM 9401.80.90 (INFANT CAR SEATS/STROLLERS) 158
    CASE 6: TARIFF ITEM 9405.40.90 (3-IN-1 SECURITY LIGHTS) 162
    CASE 7: TARIFF ITEM 9502.10.00 ("FEARLESS RIDER" GIFT SETS) 163
    CASE 8: TARIFF ITEM 9503.00.90 (INFANT SWINGS) 164
    CASE 9: TARIFF ITEM 9503.41.00 (PLUSH ARTICLES) 167
    CASE 10: TARIFF ITEM 9503.90.00 (RED BANDANAS IMPRINTED "DISNEY PIRATES OF THE CARIBBEAN") 168
    CASE 11: TARIFF ITEM 9503.90.00 (INTERACTIVE PLAY MATS) 170
    CASE 12: TARIFF ITEM 9503.90.00 (DRESS UP SETS) 173
    CASE 13: TARIFF ITEM 9505.10.00 (PLASTIC GIFT BOWS) 173
    CASE 14: TARIFF ITEM 9505.90.00 (HALLOWEEN COSTUMES) 174
    CASE 15: TARIFF ITEM 9506.91.90 (TRAMPOLINE) 176
    CASE 16: TARIFF ITEM 9506.99.10 (PLAYGROUND EQUIPMENT) 178
    CASE 17: TARIFF ITEM 9506.99.90 (SLEDS) 178

b) Parts and Accessories 179
  i) Section VII: Chapters 39 and 40 (Plastics and Rubber) 182
    CASE: TARIFF HEADING 40.09 (RUBBER HYDRAULIC HOSE) 182
  ii) Section VIII: Chapters 41 to 43 (Raw Hides, Travel Goods, Handbags) 183
    CASE: TARIFF ITEMS 4202.91.90 (SOFT LEATHER CARRYING CASES FOR CELLPHONES) AND 8504.40.90 (CELLPHONE CAR KITS) 183
  iii) Section XI: Chapters 50 to 63 (Textiles) 184
    CASE: TARIFF ITEM 6307.90.99 (EMERGENCY TOW STRAPS) 184
  iv) Section XV: Chapters 82 and 83 (Base Metals) 185
    CASE: TARIFF ITEM 8212.90.00 (GILLETTE® MACH3® RAZOR BLADE CARTRIDGES) 185
  v) Section XVI: Chapters 84 and 85 (Machinery, Mechanical Appliances, Electrical Equipment, Television Image and Sound Recorders) 187
    CASE 1: TARIFF ITEMS 8436.80.10 (INTEGRATED GREENHOUSE SYSTEM AND FLUE GAS CONDENSER) 187
    CASE 2: TARIFF ITEM 8439.99.90 (ALUMINUM ALLOY WALKWAY SYSTEMS) 188

Detailed Table of Contents

        CASE 3: TARIFF ITEMS 8504.40.99 (RAPID CIGARETTE LIGHTER CHARGERS) AND 8529.90.90 (CELLPHONE BATTERY PACKS) *188*
        CASE 4: TARIFF ITEM 8504.90.91 (BUSHINGS OF ELECTRICAL TRANSFORMERS) *189*
        CASE 5: TARIFF ITEMS 8514.40.90 (ANNEALER) AND 8515.21.10 (WELDER) *190*
        CASE 6: TARIFF ITEM 8520.90.90 (INTEGRATED CIRCUIT (IC) RECORDER AND MINIDISK (MD) RECORDER) *192*
        CASE 7: TARIFF HEADING 85.21 (VIDEO-BASED SECURITY SYSTEM) *194*
    vi) Section XVII: Chapters 86 to 89 (Vehicles, Aircraft, Vessels, and Associated Transport Equipment) *196*
        CASE 1: TARIFF ITEM 8708.29.99 (EXTERIOR LUGGAGE RACKS) *196*
        CASE 2: TARIFF ITEM 8708.99.99 (BICYCLE RACKS) *198*
        CASE 3: TARIFF ITEM 8714.99.10 (BICYCLE RIMS, SPOKES, AND HUBS) *199*
    vii) Section XX: Chapters 94 to 96 (Miscellaneous Manufactured Articles) *199*
        CASE 1: TARIFF ITEM 9403.90.00 (LINEAR BALL-BEARING DRAWER SLIDES) *199*
        CASE 2: TARIFF ITEM 9405.10.00 (RECESSED LIGHTING FIXTURES (POT LIGHTS)) *201*
        CASE 3: TARIFF ITEM 9617.00.00 (COFFEE POTS FOR COMMERCIAL COFFEE MAKERS) *203*
  c) Chapter 99: Duty-Free Treatment *204*
    i) Code 2000 (Article "for use in" goods of tariff item 8436.80.10—agricultural, horticultural, poultry farming, and other machinery) *205*
        CASE: GREENHOUSE SYSTEMS *205*
    ii) Code 2101 (Article "for use in" goods of tariff item 9032.89.20—process control equipment) *205*
        CASE: POWER TRANSFORMERS *205*
    iii) Code 2546 (Article "for use in" goods of tariff headings 90.18 or 90.22—laser imagers) *206*
        CASE: LASER IMAGING FILM *206*
    iv) Code 7934 (Article "for use in" goods of tariff item 3921.90.90—composite goods of plastic sheets) *206*
        CASE 1: POLYSTYRENE *206*
        CASE 2: PLASTIC FILM *207*
    v) Tariff Item 9903.00.00 (Agricultural and horticultural machinery) *207*
        CASE 1: ROCK WOOL *208*

CASE 2: ONION BAGS AND MASTER BAGS 208
CASE 3: GREENHOUSE CARTS 209
CASE 4: HAY BALE WRAPPERS 210
CASE 5: ALUMINUM REFLECTORS IN GREENHOUSES 210

vi) Tariff Item 9908.00.00 (Utility Vehicles for Use in Mining) 211
CASE: DRILL RODS AND COUPLING/SLEEVES 211

vii) Tariff Item 9948.00.00 (Data Processing Machines) 212
CASE 1: CELLPHONE PROTECTIVE COVERS 212
CASE 2: KEYBOARD SYNTHESIZERS 213
CASE 3: MUSIC CDS 214
CASE 4: INTEGRATED CIRCUIT (IC) RECORDERS AND PORTABLE MINIDISK (MD) RECORDERS 214

viii) Tariff Item 9958.00.00 (Passenger Vehicles) 215
CASE 1: COMMERCIAL VANS AND WHEEL RIMS 215
CASE 2: TOP PLATES OR FIFTH-WHEEL CASTINGS 215

ix) Tariff Item 9961.00.00 (Repair of Road Tractors) 217
CASE: DISC BRAKE CALIPERS (REPLACEMENT PARTS) 217

x) Tariff Item 9977.00.00 (Medical Goods) 217
CASE: V-BELTS USED IN CENTRIFUGES 217

xi) Tariff Item 9979.00.00 (Assists for Persons with Disabilities) 218
CASE 1: SUPPORT HOSIERY 218
CASE 2: FORMULA FOR INFANTS AND CHILDREN 220
CASE 3: THERAPEUTIC SPORT SHOES 223

E. **Origin of Goods and Marking** 224

1) Origin of Goods 224
   a) Wholly Produced in Country of Origin 226
   b) Substantially Manufactured or Processed 227
   c) Direct Shipment and Transhipment: Sections 17 and 18 228
   d) Goods in Transit: Section 26 228
2) Marking of Goods 229

F. **Tariff Treatment** 229

1) Introduction 229
2) Most-Favoured-Nation Treatment 229
3) Free Trade Agreements 230
4) GPT, LDCT, and CCCT; AUT and NZT 230
5) Claiming Duty-Free or Preferential Treatment 231
6) General Tariff 231
7) Most-Favoured-Nation Tariff 232
   a) Most Favourable Tariff 232

b) Grant of More Preferred Status 233
8) General Preferential Tariff 233
   a) Tariff Rate Quota 234
   b) Extension and Withdrawal of GPT 234
   c) Expiry Date 234
9) Least-Developed-Country Tariff 234
   a) Tariff Rate Quota 235
   b) Extension and Withdrawal of LDCT 235
   c) Expiry Date 235
10) Commonwealth Caribbean Countries Tariff 235
   a) Tariff Rate Quota 236
   b) Extension and Withdrawal of CCCT 236
11) Australia Tariff and New Zealand Tariff 236
12) United States Tariff, Mexico Tariff, and Mexico–United States Tariff 237
   a) US Tariff 237
   b) Mexico Tariff 237
   c) Mexico–United States Tariff 237
   d) Extension of UST and MT 238
13) Chile Tariff 238
   a) Tariff Rate Quota 238
   b) Extension of Chile Tariff 238
14) Colombia Tariff 238
   a) Extension of Colombia Tariff 239
15) Costa Rica Tariff 239
   a) Application of Costa Rica Tariff 239
   b) Extension of Costa Rica Tariff 239
16) Peru Tariff 240
   a) Application of Peru Tariff 240
   b) Extension of Peru Tariff 240
   c) Tariff Rate Quota 240
17) Canada-Israel Tariff 240
   a) Application of Canada-Israel Tariff 241
   b) Tariff Rate Quota 241
18) Canada-European Free Trade Association Tariff 241
   a) Iceland Tariff 241
   b) Norway Tariff 241
   c) Switzerland-Liechtenstein Tariffs 242
19) Jordan Tariff 242
   a) Application of Jordan Tariff 242
20) Panama Tariff 242
   a) Application of Panama Tariff 243

G. **Special Measures, Emergency Measures, and Safeguards** 243
   1) Introduction 243
   2) Global Emergency Measures 244
      a) Enforcing Rights under Trade Agreements 244
      b) Tribunal Inquiries 245
         INQUIRY 1: IMPORTATION OF CERTAIN STEEL GOODS 245
         INQUIRY 2: BICYCLES AND FINISHED PAINTED BICYCLE FRAMES 246
   3) Surtaxes on Goods from a Free Trade Partner 248
      a) *NAFTA* Partner, Chile, or Peru 248
         i) Goods in Transit 248
         ii) Inquiry by Tribunal 249
         iii) Limitations on Making Second Surtax Order 249
         iv) Exception for Certain Agricultural Goods 249
         v) Order Must Not Contravene *WTO Agreement* 249
         vi) Conditions 250
         vii) Definition of "Contributes Importantly" 250
         viii) Repeal of Order 250
         ix) Exclusion from Surtax Order for Peru Goods 250
      b) Surge of Goods 250
         i) Goods in Transit 251
         ii) Definition of "Surge" 251
         iii) Rate of Surtax 251
         iv) Further Limitation on Order 251
         v) Repeal or Amendment of Surtax Order by Tribunal 251
      c) Extension Order 252
         i) Scope and Rate of Surtax 252
         ii) Conditions 252
         iii) Goods from Peru 252
         iv) Duration and Repeal 252
         v) Cessation of Extension Order 253
      d) Goods in Transit 253
      e) Regulations 253
   4) Safeguard Measures for Agricultural Goods 253
      a) Surtax Order on Agricultural Goods 253
         i) Non-application of Surtax to Goods in Transit 254
         ii) Cessation of Order 254
         iii) Regulations 254
   5) Bilateral Emergency Measures 254
      a) US Goods 254
         i) Imposition of Temporary Duty 254
         ii) Definition of "Principal Cause" 255

- iii) Reference to MFNT Rate in Effect 255
- b) Mexican and MUST Goods 255
  - i) Imposition of Temporary Duty 255
  - ii) Definition of "Principal Cause" 255
  - iii) Reference to MFNT Rate in Effect 256
- c) Republic of Chile Goods 256
  - i) Imposition of Temporary Duty 256
  - ii) Definition of "Principal Cause" 256
  - iii) Reference to MFNT Rate in Effect 256
- d) Colombia 256
  - i) Suspension of Reduction of Tariff Rate; Imposition of Temporary Duty 256
  - ii) Maximum Duty 256
  - iii) Conditions 257
  - iv) Rate of Duty When Order Ceases to Have Effect 257
  - v) Definition of "Principal Cause" 257
- e) Costa Rica 257
  - i) Textile and Apparel Goods Exempt 257
  - ii) Temporary Duty 257
  - iii) Reference to MFNT Rate in Effect 258
  - iv) Application of Measures a Second Time 258
  - v) Rate of Duty When Order Ceases to Have Effect 258
  - vi) Goods in Transit 258
- f) Goods from *EFTA* Countries 258
  - i) Bilateral Emergency Measures 259
  - ii) Suspension of Reduction of Tariff Rate; Imposition of Temporary Duty 259
  - iii) Conditions 259
  - iv) Conditions in Respect of Certain Tariff Items of Chapter 89 260
    - a. Tariff Items 8901.20.90, 8902.00.10, 8905.20.10, 8905.20.20, 8905.90.10, and 8906.90.99 260
    - b. Tariff Items 8901.10.90, 8901.90.99, 8904.00.00, 8905.10.00, and 8905.90.90 260
  - v) Rate of Duty When Order Ceases to Have Effect 261
  - vi) Definition of "Principal Cause" 261
  - vii) Reference to Customs Duty in Effect 261
- g) Goods from Peru 261
  - i) Suspension of Reduction of Tariff Rate; Imposition of Temporary Duty 261
  - ii) Conditions 262
  - iii) Application a Second Time 262
  - iv) Rate of Duty When Order Ceases to Have Effect 262

v) Definition of "Principal Cause" 262
vi) Goods in Transit 263
  h) Jordan 263
     i) Suspension of Reduction of Tariff Rate; Imposition of Temporary Duty 263
     ii) Maximum Rate 263
     iii) Further Orders 263
     iv) Rate of Duty When Order Ceases to Have Effect 264
     v) Definition of "Principal Cause" 264
  i) Goods from Panama 264
     i) Suspending Reduction of Tariff Rate; Imposition of Temporary Duty 264
     ii) Maximum Rate 264
     iii) Conditions 265
     iv) Rate of Duty When Order Ceases to Have Effect 265
     v) Definition of "Principal Cause" 265
     vi) Goods in Transit 265
6) Safeguard Measures in Respect of China 265
  a) Background 265
  b) Meaning of "Domestic Producers": Standing to File Complaint 266
  c) Meaning of "Market Disruption" and "Significant Cause" 267
  d) Market Disruption 268
  e) Rate of Surcharge 268
  f) Maximum Rate 268
  g) Duration and Cessation of Surtax Order 268
  h) Inquiry by Tribunal 269
  i) Extension Order 269
  j) Trade Diversion 269
  k) Meaning of "Action" 269
  l) Rate 270
  m) Duration and Cessation of Surtax Order 270
  n) Expiry 270
  o) Tribunal's China-Specific Investigations 270
7) Surtax When Canada's External Financial Position in Jeopardy 271
  a) General 271
  b) Surtax Order Ceases Unless Approved by Parliament 271

H. Duties Relief Programs 271

1) Introduction 271
2) Traveller's Exemption 272
   a) Returning Residents 273
   b) Bequests 273

Detailed Table of Contents

    c) Settler's Effects   273
    d) Ethno-cultural Groups   273
  3) Duty Deferral   274
    a) Qualifying for Duties Relief   274
    b) Sale or Transfer   275
    c) Customs Bonded Warehouse Option   275
    d) Application to Operate Customs Bonded Warehouse   277
  4) Duties Relief Option: Manufacturing   277
  5) Drawback Program   278
    a) Qualifying for Drawback   278
    b) Application for Drawback   278
  6) Other Duties Relief Programs   278
    a) Temporary Importation Program   278
    b) Temporary Relief on Prescribed Goods   279
    c) Temporary Exportation Program   279
    d) Conditions for Entitlement   280
    e) Emergency Repairs Outside Canada   280
    f) Remission Order   280
    g) *Tariff Items 9971.00.00 and 9992.00.00 Accounting Regulations*   281
    h) Canadian Goods Returned after Being Exported   281
    i) Exporters of Processing Services Program   281
        i) Qualifying for the Program   281
        ii) Application for Relief   281
        iii) Time Limits   282
  7) Refunds for Other Reasons   282
    a) Obsolete or Surplus Goods   282
    b) Waiver   282
    c) Additional Relief   283
        i) Refund under Section 113(1)   283
        ii) Refund on Designated Goods   283
    d) Discretionary Relief   283
    e) Refunds under the *Customs Act*   283
    f) Remissions   284
    g) Clawback   284
    h) General Provisions   284
    i) Further Conditions of Relief   284

I. Prohibited Goods   285

  1) Tariff Item 9897.00.00: Certain Wildlife and Plumage, Copyright, Second-Hand Motor Vehicles, and Others   286
  2) Tariff Item 9898.00.00: Firearms, and Prohibited Weapons and Devices   287

　　　　a) Caselaw on Firearms and Prohibited Weapons　288
　3) Tariff item 9899.00.00: Books and Depictions of Obscenity, Sedition, Violence, Child Pornography, and Others　293

Addendum　294

　A. General Rules for the Interpretation of the Harmonized System　294
　B. Canadian Rules　295

Table 1: Sections and Chapters of the Harmonized System　297

CHAPTER 3
Special Import Measures Act　299

A. Introduction　299
B. Meaning and Occurrence of Dumping and Subsidizing　301
　1) Dumping　301
　　a) Meaning of Dumping and Margin of Dumping　301
　　b) Insignificant Margin　302
　　c) Negligible Volume　302
　2) Subsidizing and Financial Contribution　302
　　a) Meaning of Financial Contribution　303
　　b) Non-actionable Subsidy　303
　　c) Non-specific and Specific Subsidy; Prohibited Subsidy　304
　　d) Amount of Subsidy　305
C. Determination of Normal Value and Export Price　305
　1) Normal Value　305
　　a) Primary Method of Determination　306
　　b) Alternative Methods of Determination　306
　　　i) Where Conditions of Sale Comparison Not Present　306
　　　ii) Where Purchasers Associated with Vendor　307
　　　iii) Where Prices Below Cost of Production　307
　　　iv) Weighted Average of Prices　308
　　　v) Exports to Canada Not Having Trademark　308
　　　vi) Surrogate Countries Sales　308
　　　vii) Prices Determined by Government or Government Monopoly　308
　　　viii) Goods Sold on Credit　310
　　　ix) Ministerial Prescription of Normal Value　310
　　　x) Goods Passing through One or More Countries　311
　　　xi) Calculation during Start-Up Period　311
　2) Export Price　311

      a) Primary Method of Determination *311*
      b) Special Rules Where Price Unreliable *312*
      c) No Deduction for *SIMA* Duties *313*
      d) Undertaking to Pay Anti-dumping Duty *313*
      e) Goods Sold on Credit to Importer in Canada *313*
      f) Exporter Providing Benefits on Resale *313*

D. **Liability for Anti-dumping, Countervailing, and Provisional Duties** *314*

  1) Imposition of Duties *314*
      a) Duties When Massive Importation Causes Injury *314*
      b) Countervailing Duty on Imports from a Specific Country *315*
      c) Provisions in Free Trade Agreements *315*
  2) Liability to Pay *315*
      a) When Liability Arises *315*
          i) Liability Where Undertaking Accepted *316*
          ii) Liability Imposed on Importer *316*
          iii) Payment during Court and *NAFTA* Panel Proceedings *316*
          iv) Duty Reimposed on Referral Back by Binational Panel *317*
          v) General Rules Relating to Payment of Duty *317*
              a. Where Both or Portion of Duties Payable *317*
              b. Duty, Other Than Provisional Duty, Payable by Importer in Canada *317*
              c. Return of Provisional Duty *317*
              d. Return of Duty *318*
              e. Duty When Tribunal Makes a New Order or Finding *318*
              f. Request for Review When Exporter or Producer Establishes Not to Be Associated *318*
          vi) Expedited Review *319*
      b) Undertakings *320*
          i) Acceptance *321*
          ii) Termination of Investigation *321*
          iii) Termination of Undertaking *321*
          iv) Further Undertakings *323*
          v) Expiry, Renewal *323*

E. **Administrative Procedures and Appeals** *324*

  1) Introduction *324*
  2) Investigations and Inquiries *325*
      a) Filing a Complaint *325*
          i) Acknowledgement and Notice *325*
          ii) Where Subsidy Notified to WTO *325*
          iii) No Investigation without Domestic Producers' Support *326*

- b) Initiation and Notice of Investigation by CBSA 326
- c) Preliminary Inquiry by the Tribunal 327
    - i) Termination of Investigation and Preliminary Inquiry 327
    - ii) Goods from Chile 328
    - iii) Tribunal Must Advise CBSA on Reference 328
- d) Determination of Injury, Dumping, or Subsidizing 328
    - i) Preliminary Determination of Injury 328
    - ii) Final Determination 329
    - iii) Reconsideration 330
    - iv) Subsidies Agreement 331
    - v) Investigations Illustrating Section 20 Process 331
        - INVESTIGATION 1: POLYSIO INSULATION BOARD (UNITED STATES) 332
        - INVESTIGATION 2: OIL COUNTRY TUBULAR GOODS (THE PEOPLE'S REPUBLIC OF CHINA) 334
    - vi) Injury Inquiry by the Tribunal 337
        - a. Where Undertaking Terminated 338
        - b. Duties of and Guidance to Tribunal 339
        - c. Tribunal's Order or Finding 339
        - d. Goods of a *NAFTA* Country 340
        - e. Recommencement Following Judicial Review 340
        - f. Illustrative Inquiry Decisions 340
            - INQUIRY 1: WOOD VENETIAN BLINDS AND SLATS FROM MEXICO AND CHINA 340
            - INQUIRY 2: STEEL FUEL TANKS EXPORTED FROM CHINA AND TAIPEI 341
            - INQUIRY 3: FRESH TOMATOES EXPORTED FROM THE UNITED STATES 342
            - INQUIRY 4: CERTAIN GRAIN CORN EXPORTED FROM THE UNITED STATES 343
            - INQUIRY 5: STEEL GRATING EXPORTED FROM CHINA 344
            - INQUIRY 6: GREENHOUSE BELL PEPPERS EXPORTED FROM THE NETHERLANDS 344
            - INQUIRY 7: POLYSIO INSULATION BOARD EXPORTED FROM THE UNITED STATES 345
- e) Public Interest Inquiries 347
    - i) Selected Inquiry Decisions 349
        - INQUIRY 1: CERTAIN PREPARED BABY FOODS 349
        - INQUIRY 2: IODINATED CONTRAST MEDIA 349
        - INQUIRY 3: CERTAIN REFRIGERATORS, DISHWASHERS, AND DRYERS FROM THE UNITED STATES 351
- f) Tribunal Must Advise CBSA 352

Detailed Table of Contents

- g) Termination of Proceedings/Inquiry 353
- 3) CBSA Action on Final Determination, Order, or Finding 353
  - a) Determination by Designated Officer 353
  - b) Goods Subsequently Imported 354
  - c) Re-determination 354
    - i) Re-determination by Designated Officer 354
    - ii) Further Re-determination by the CBSA 355
    - iii) Permissive Re-determination 355
    - iv) Permissive Re-determination of Re-determination 356
    - v) Mandatory Re-determination 356
  - d) Notice of Re-determination 356
  - e) Effect of Re-determination 356
- 4) Appeals 356
  - a) Appeal to the Tribunal 356
    - i) Scope of Tribunal's Findings ("Scope Orders") 357
    - ii) Illustrative Decisions ("Scope Orders") 357
      - CASE 1: FOOTWEAR 357
      - CASE 2: ANCHORING KITS (CONTAINING SHIELDS AND LAG BOLTS) 358
      - CASE 3: HOT-ROLLED STEEL PLATE (CARBON STEEL OR ALLOY STEEL) 359
      - CASE 4: ALUMINUM DOOR FRAME RAILS WITH FITTINGS 360
  - b) Appeal to the Federal Court of Appeal 361
    - i) Judicial Review 361
- 5) Review of Orders and Findings of Injury 362
  - a) Interim Review 362
    - i) Selected Interim Orders 363
      - INTERIM REVIEW 1: FRESH ICEBERG (HEAD) LETTUCE ORIGINATING IN OR EXPORTED FROM THE UNITED STATES OF AMERICA (INJURY INQUIRY) 363
      - INTERIM REVIEW 2: FLAT HOT-ROLLED CARBON AND ALLOY STEEL SHEET PRODUCTS (INJURY INQUIRY) 363
      - INTERIM REVIEW 3: CERTAIN REFRIGERATORS, DISHWASHERS, AND DRYERS FROM THE UNITED STATES (INJURY INQUIRY) 364
      - INTERIM REVIEW 4: WATERPROOF RUBBER FOOTWEAR (EXPIRY REVIEW) 364
      - INTERIM REVIEW 5: LEATHER FOOTWEAR WITH METAL TOE CAPS (EXPIRY REVIEW) 364
  - b) Further Reviews 364
    - i) Review on Referral Back under Part I.1 364
  - c) Expiry Review 365
    - i) Initiation of Expiry Review 365

ii) Determination by CBSA 366
iii) Determination by Tribunal 366
iv) Separate Order or Finding 367
v) Review on Request of Minister of Finance 367
vi) Disputes Resolved by WTO 368
DISPUTE 1: SOFTWOOD LUMBER 368
DISPUTE 2: EUROPEAN UNION BEEF HORMONES BAN (1996) 369
DISPUTE 3: DAIRY PRODUCTS 370
d) Goods of Chile 371
6) **NAFTA Dispute Settlement** 371
a) Binational Panel Review 372
i) Establishment of Binational Panel 372
ii) Request Precludes Application to Federal Court 373
iii) Limitation Periods 373
iv) Binational Panel Decisions 373
v) Action on Binational Panel's Order 374
vi) Illustrative Binational Panel Decisions 374
REVIEW 1: IODINATED CONTRAST MEDIA FROM THE UNITED STATES 374
REVIEW 2: REFRIGERATORS AND DISHWASHERS FROM THE UNITED STATES 375
b) Extraordinary Challenge Proceedings 381
i) Notification of Request 381
ii) Appointment of Extraordinary Challenge Committee 381
iii) Action by and Decision of the Committee 381
c) Orders and Decisions of Panel and Committee 382
d) Stay of Proceedings 382
e) Appointment of Special Committee 382
i) Request for Appointment 382
ii) Stay of Panel Reviews and Extraordinary Challenge Committee Proceedings 383
iii) Stay When Affirmative Finding against Canada 383
iv) Suspension of Time Periods 383
v) Suspension of Article 1904 of *NAFTA* Panel Process 383
vi) Suspension of *NAFTA* Benefits 384
vii) Determination of Special Committee under Paragraph 1905.10(a) of the *NAFTA* 384
viii) Review of Definitive Decision by Federal Court of Appeal 385
ix) Termination of Suspension 385

F. **General Provisions** 385
1) Who Is "Importer in Canada"? 386

Detailed Table of Contents

      a) Tribunal's Ruling   *386*
      b) Illustrative Rulings   *387*
          RULING 1: FRESH GARLIC FROM CHINA   *387*
          RULING 2: BICYCLES FROM CHINA   *389*
      c) Action by CBSA   *391*
      d) Reconsideration of Order or Finding   *392*
      e) Determination Deemed Not Made   *392*
      f) Tribunal's Ruling Binding   *393*
      g) Disclosure of Importer's Name   *393*
  2) Judicial Review: Application to Federal Court of Appeal   *393*
  3) Disclosure of Confidential Information   *395*

CHAPTER 4
The *Export and Import Permits Act*   *396*

A. Introduction   *396*

B. Objectives of the Act   *397*

C. Establishment of Lists   *399*

  1) *Export Control List*   *399* (ECL)
      a) Establishment of the *Export Control List*   *399*
      b) Export Declarations   *400*
      c) Method of Declaration   *401*
  2) *Area Control List*   *401*
  3) *Automatic Firearms Country Control List*   *401*
  4) *Import Control List*   *402*
      a) Inclusion of Goods in *ICL* by Order   *402*
      b) Extension Order   *403*
      c) Exclusion of Goods from Peru and Colombia   *403*
      d) Limitation on Inclusion in the *ICL*   *403*
      e) Inclusion in *ICL* to Facilitate Information Collection   *404*
      f) Removal of Goods from *ICL*   *405*
      g) Goods Originating in the People's Republic of China   *405*
          i) Imports Causing Market Disruption or Trade Diversion   *405*
          ii) Inclusion of Goods for Information Collection   *405*
      h) Bilateral Emergency Measures: Textiles and Apparel Goods *Not* Originating in a Free Trade Partner Country   *406*
          i) Import Access   *406*
          ii) Export Access   *406*
              a. Softwood Lumber Products Export Access   *406*

D. Export and Import Permits and Certificates   *407*

1) Permits That Are Required 407
2) Export Permits 407
3) Import Permits 408
4) General Import or Export Permits 408
5) Permit to Import Access Quantity 409
6) Prohibited Firearms and Weapons 409
7) Import and Export Certificates 409
8) Amendment, Suspension, Cancellation, and Reinstatement 410
9) International Import Certificates 410

E. Offences and Penalties 410

CHAPTER 5
Other Statutes Relating to Import and Export 412

A. The *Export Act* 412

1) Introduction 412
2) Prohibition of Export 413
3) Export of Intoxicating Liquor 413
4) General Note 414

B. The *Wild Animals and Plant Protection Regulation of International and Interprovincial Trade Act* 414

1) Convention on International Trade in Endangered Species of Wild Fauna and Flora 414
2) Classification of Wild Fauna and Flora 415
3) Import and Export 415
4) Interprovincial Transport 416
5) Possession 416
6) Exemptions 416
7) Limitations and Restrictions 417
8) Issue of Permits 417

C. The *Cultural Property Export and Import Act* 418

1) Export of Canadian Cultural Property 418
   a) Export Control List 418
   b) Export Permits 419
      i) General Permits and Open General Permits 420
      ii) Copy of Object to Be Deposited in Public Institution 420
      iii) Objects of Outstanding Significance or National Importance 420
      iv) Review of Permit Decisions 421
         a. Request for Review 421

Detailed Table of Contents

    b. Determination of Fair Offer *421*
  2) Protection of Foreign Cultural Property *422*
    a) Designation *422*
    b) Action to Recover Cultural Property *422*
  3) Convention for the Protection of Cultural Property in the Event of Armed Conflict and Its Protocols *423*
    a) Definition *423*
    b) Offence to Export or Remove Cultural Property *424*
    c) Recovery Action *424*
  4) Offences and Punishment *424*
    a) Offences *424*
    b) Punishment under the Act *425*
    c) Punishment under the *Criminal Code* *425*
D. The *Export and Import of Rough Diamonds Act* *425*
  1) Definition of Rough Diamond *426*
  2) Trade Regulation *426*
    a) Export Control *426*
    b) Import Control *426*
    c) In-Transit Shipment *427*
    d) Regulations *427*
  3) Offences *427*
  4) Punishment *428*

CHAPTER 6
Miscellaneous Federal Statutes *429*

A. The *Canada Consumer Product Safety Act* *429*
  1) Introduction *429*
  2) Purpose, Definitions, and Application *430*
  3) Prohibitions *431*
  4) Duties and Obligations *432*
    a) Incident Reports *432*
    b) Recalls *432*
    c) Regulations *433*
  5) Criminal Penalties *433*
  6) Administrative Monetary Penalties *433*
B. The *Canadian Environmental Protection Act, 1999* *434*
  1) Controlled Ozone-Depleting Substances *434*
    a) Report of Import or Export *434*
    b) Importation *434*

            i) Written Authorization 434
            ii) Exemptions 435
        c) Exportation 436
            i) Written Authorization 436
            ii) Exemptions 436
        d) Maintenance of Records 437
        e) Penalties 437
    2) Export of Other Controlled Substances 437
        a) Export Control List 437
        b) Prohibition 437
        c) Regulations 438

C. The *Consumer Packaging and Labelling Act* 438
    1) Statutory Requirements 439
    2) Offences and Criminal Penalties 440

D. The *Controlled Drugs and Substances Act* 440
    1) Possession and Trafficking 441
    2) Forfeiture of Offence-Related Property 442
    3) *Industrial Hemp Regulations* 442
        a) Definition 442
        b) Importation of Seed, Grain, or Hemp 443
        c) Exportation of Industrial Hemp 444
    4) *Narcotic Control Regulations* 444
        a) Import and Export 445
        b) Permit Required 446
        c) Narcotics Schedule 446
        d) Prohibitions 446
        e) Duties of Licensed Dealer 446
    5) *Precursor Control Regulations* 446
        a) Import and Export of Class A Precursors 447
            i) Permit 447
            ii) Authorization 447
            iii) Dealer Licensing 447
            iv) Importation 448
        b) Exportation 448
            i) Declaration 448
            ii) In-Transit and Transhipment Permits 449
            iii) Authorization Certificate 449
        c) Class B Precursors 450
            i) Limitation on Activities and Exemption 450
            ii) Dealer Registration 450

Detailed Table of Contents

      iii) Export Permit   *450*
      iv) Authorization Certificate   *451*

E. **The *Health of Animals Act***   *451*
  1) Importation   *451*
    a) Statutory Prohibitions   *451*
    b) Regulatory Regime   *453*
      i) Part II: General Provisions, Germplasm, and Regulated Animal   *453*
        a. Definitions   *453*
        b. Prohibition   *453*
        c. False or Misleading Information   *455*
        d. Animal in Contact with Diseased Animals or Things   *455*
        e. Identification and Record Keeping   *455*
      ii) Part III: Animal Products   *455*
        a. Milk and Milk Products from a Country Other than the United States   *455*
        b. Bird Eggs or Egg Products from a Country Other than the United States   *456*
        c. Exemption   *456*
      iii) Part IV: Animal By-products and Animal Pathogens   *456*
        a. Prohibition   *456*
        b. Exemption   *457*
        c. By-products Not Intended as Animal Food   *458*
        d. Raw Wool, Hair, or Bristles, and Hide or Skin   *458*
        e. Animal Glands and Organs   *459*
        f. Cooked Boneless Beef   *459*
        g. Importation of Gluestock   *459*
        h. Rendering Plant Products   *460*
        i. Garbage, Refuse, and Animal Manure   *460*
        j. Ships' Stores   *460*
        k. Carcasses of Game Birds   *460*
        l. Matted or Blood-Stained Wool, Hair, or Bristles   *461*
        m. Animal Pathogens and By-products   *461*
        n. Animal Food with Animal Products or By-products   *461*
      iv) Part V: Fodder   *462*
      v) Part VI: Packing Material, Beehives, and Beeswax   *462*
        a. Packing Material   *462*
        b. Beehives and Beeswax   *463*
      vi) Part XI: Veterinary Biologics   *463*
      vii) Part XIV: Products of Rendering Plants   *463*
        a. Definition   *463*

b. Offence   464
c. Requirements to Facilitate Recall   464
viii) Part XVI: Aquatic Animals   464
   a. Prohibition   464
   b. Aquatic Animals Not in Schedule III   465
   c. Carcasses and Offal   465
ix) Part VII: Quarantine of Imported Animals   466
x) Part XII: Transportation of Animals   466
   a. Prevention of Injury or Undue Suffering   466
   b. Report of Death or Injury of Animal   468
2) Exportation   469
   a) Statutory Provision: Veterinarian's Certificate   469
   b) Regulatory Provisions   469
      i) Livestock, Poultry, Animal Embryo, or Animal Semen   469
      ii) Product of Rendering Plant   470
      iii) Rest Period for Animals   471
3) Permits and Licences   471
4) Offences, Violations, and Penalties   471
   a) Criminal Offences   471
   b) Administrative Monetary Penalties   472

F. The *Pest Control Products Act*   472
   1) Introduction   472
   2) Import Control   473
      a) Prohibition   473
      b) Registration   473
   3) Export Control   474
      a) Pest Control Product Export Control List   474
      b) Regulations   474
   4) Penalties and Punishment   475
      a) Criminal Penalties   475
      b) Administrative Monetary Penalties   475

G. The *Plant Protection Act*   476
   1) Import and Export Control   476
      a) Statutory Provisions   476
         i) Permit   476
         ii) Removal of Imports and Disposal   477
      b) Regulatory Provisions   477
   2) Importation   477
      a) Permits and Phytosanitary Certificates   477
         i) Exemptions   478

   ii) Issue of Permit *479*
  b) Treatment or Processing *479*
  c) Declaration *479*
  d) Packaging and Labelling *479*
  e) Import for Special Purposes *480*
  f) Prohibiting Entry *480*
 3) Exportation *480*
  a) Certificates *480*
  b) Export Permit *481*
  c) Export of Grain by Vessel *481*
 4) Offences and Violations *482*
  a) Offences *482*
  b) Administrative Monetary Penalties *482*

H. The *Precious Metals Marking Act* *483*

 1) Application of Marks *483*
 2) Other Marks *484*
 3) Offences and Criminal Penalties *484*

I. The *Textile Labelling Act* *484*

 1) Prohibition *485*
 2) Regulatory Requirements *485*
 3) Exemptions *486*
 4) Prescribed Consumer Textile Article *487*
 5) Offences and Penalties *487*

TABLE OF CASES *489*

TABLE OF CONVENTIONS AND AGREEMENTS *505*

TABLE OF CUSTOMS MEMORANDA *509*

TABLE OF REGULATIONS *511*

TABLE OF STATUTES *521*

TABLE OF TARIFFS *537*

INDEX *539*

ABOUT THE AUTHOR *571*

Foreword

Dr Prabhu's book takes customs legislation and breaks it down in easy-to-understand language. He takes the unique approach of describing each legislative section of the Act, following it with caselaw along with his explanation of the law. This makes the information accessible and practical for anyone involved in international trade with, and in, Canada. Dr Prabhu brings his expertise to the application of Canada's import and export laws in a way that will help anyone who needs to know the technicalities of trade with Canada.

I have all of Dr Prabhu's books and have used them for many years in my work in customs consulting and with my work with IECanada. They are an extremely valuable resource and are my preferred go-to reference for anything related to trade law. I applaud Dr Prabhu for filling a need in the Canadian marketplace for such books on customs, importing, and exporting.

Joy Nott
President, IECanada

Foreword

Effective border management today involves requirements and obligations beyond traditional customs legislation. These requirements are found in the laws of a number of other departments and agencies, and introduce a significant level of complexity and burden of compliance for Canadian businesses. By bringing his meticulous and thorough analysis to a broader legislative framework for importing and exporting, Dr Prabhu has not only recognized the importance of these requirements, but made an important contribution to our knowledge.

Both the scope and style of this work are impressive. By carefully selecting the most important statutes to include in this work, and by grouping the statutes into three categories, Dr Prabhu has given his readers the gift of accessibility. And by bringing his clear language to this work, he has ensured that it will not only be readily understood, but will have practical value.

Dr Prabhu's previous work, the *Annotated Customs Act*, has been an indispensable resource for Canadian customs practitioners for decades. I have no doubt that this book will prove even more useful to all those in the legal and business communities who want to better understand the major federal statutes affecting the importation and exportation of goods.

Carol West
President, Canadian Society of Customs Brokers
Chair, World Customs Organization Private Sector Consultative Group

Preface

This book provides an overview of Canada's import and export laws and is intended as a primer, in user-friendly language, to assist individuals and firms engaged in Canada's international trade, as well as exporters of goods to Canada and their governments.

While the book does not cover all federal statutes in the field, it does provide a fairly comprehensive description of nearly a score of major ones, grouping them in three categories.

The first group consists of four major statutes, each under its own chapter. The first three, the *Customs Act*, the *Customs Tariff*, and the *Special Import Measures Act*, come within the administration of the Minister of Public Safety and Emergency Preparedness and the Canada Border Services Agency (the CBSA), for which that Minister is political head, while the Minister of Finance has the responsibility for deciding rates of customs tariff. The fourth statute, the *Export and Import Permits Act*, is administered by the Minister of Foreign Affairs and International Trade and is enforced by its officers as well as by officers of the CBSA.

The second group also has four statutes but is covered in a single chapter. These cover exports (the *Export Act*) and both exports and imports (the *Wild Animal and Plant Protection and Regulation of International and Interprovincial Trade Act*, the *Cultural Property Export and Import Act*, and the *Export and Import of Rough Diamonds Act*).

The third is the largest group and is also covered in a single chapter. There are nine statutes in this group, regulating entire sectors of the economy, and all include provisions with respect to both exports and imports. The statutes cover such diverse fields as agriculture, animals and animal products, plant products, consumer protection, controlled substances and drugs, the environment, and pesticides.

The first three statutes covered in the first group come within the definition of "program legislation" of the *CBSA Act*, and hence the Minister of Public Safety and Emergency Preparedness and the CBSA have a direct mandate to enforce them because they relate directly to importation or exportation. The enforcement of the remaining statutes can be and, in respect of some operations relating to export and import, is delegated to the CBSA either by the statute or by a Governor in Council order.

In key areas, such as the *Customs Act* and the *Special Import Measures Act*, the review and appeal mechanism of the regulatory system is described. The same mechanism applies to tariff classification and origin of goods determinations under the *Customs Tariff*.

Many of the statutes have components of international trade agreements (especially free trade agreements) and conventions, and their implementation provisions, where appropriate, are incorporated in the chapters. There are a few other statutes and conventions that have not been included, for example, the *Special Economic Measures Act* and the *Basel Convention* on the export and import of hazardous and toxic wastes, since their inclusion would take the book beyond its intended scope, which is to give a broad overview of international trade law.

Readers may wish to pursue further research by referring to specialized works in the field, such as the author's series on the *Annotated Customs Act* and his chapter on Customs and Excise in Volume 8 of the *Canadian Encyclopedic Digest*.

The author gratefully acknowledges the support provided by Leighton Prabhu in formatting and creating the table of contents in the original manuscript, which greatly facilitated quick and easy review before submission to the publisher.

Dr Mohan Prabhu, LLD, QC
Ottawa, Canada
15 September 2013

To my wife, Clareen, and children, Leighton, Fiona, and Clifton, for their tremendous patience and support

CHAPTER I

The *Customs Act*[1]

A. INTRODUCTION

Customs law, which once included both duty imposition and collection of the revenue thus generated, is among the oldest Canadian laws and is a continuation of English law that governed before Canada received independent legislative authority. The *Customs Act* (enforcement provisions) and the *Customs Tariff*[2] (collection process) are, together, the overarching statutes that govern the importation of all goods into Canada from anywhere outside Canada. Even the English customs law is very ancient and dates from the time of that country's maritime trade and commerce, especially when the earliest *Merchant Shipping Acts* were enacted. Hence, the import systems, procedures, and principles have a long history, some aspects of which continue even to modern times.[3]

Canada adopted the international system of valuation and the harmonized classification and coding system. This resulted in significant changes to earlier statutes and led to the enactment of the current *Customs Act* in 1985 and the *Customs Tariff* in 1996.

This chapter describes the important provisions of the *Customs Act*, with which every person who imports goods into, or removes goods from, Canada must comply. "Goods" are defined by section 2 of the Act to include,

---

1   RSC 1985, c 1 (2d Supp), as am RSC 1985, c 7 (2d Supp), and subsequently.
2   SC 1997, c 36.
3   The *Imperial Customs Act*, 1825 (UK), 6 Geo IV, c 105 had replaced a long list of Customs Acts going back to Richard II, e.g., 1761 (UK), c 24; 1763 (UK), c 19; 1774 and 1808 (UK), c 22.

for greater certainty, "conveyances, animals and any document in any form." The primary function of the Act is to set out ground rules for the determination of the value of goods classified under the thousands of tariff items listed in the Schedule to the *Customs Tariff*, and to prevent the evasion of duties and taxes by elaborate means, ranging from non-declaration of goods when arriving in Canada from outside Canada to undervaluation, smuggling, and similar illegal schemes. The Act is supplemented by several other statutes regulating the importation of specific commodities. The most important of those statutes are covered in subsequent chapters.

While the *Customs Act* is the basic statute regulating imports, the term "import" itself is not defined in it. However, there is settled law enunciated by courts defining its meaning in varying situations. Courts have held that bringing goods into Canada or within Canadian jurisdiction, whether they are landed in Canada or not, or where goods were mistakenly taken out of Canada by a traveller who unwittingly crossed into the territory (or even territorial waters) of another country, such as the United States, amounts to importation, thereby subjecting them and the goods to the requirements and obligations of the Act. The interpretation of this term, however, varies. Regarding liability for duties and taxes, courts have adopted a restrictive interpretation, but when goods, especially drugs, are smuggled or money or monetary instruments in excess of the permissible limits are carried without reporting, a mere crossing of the border suffices.

Customs law imposes three basic obligations: (1) to report goods to customs, (2) to make due entry of them, and (3) to pay duties and taxes that are applicable. These obligations are discussed in the paragraphs that follow.

B. OBLIGATION TO REPORT

The first obligation is to report all goods that are imported into Canada. This obligation is set out in sections 12 to 16. The obligation is so rigorous that courts have gone so far as to hold that goods previously imported and duly reported must be reported each time a traveller returns to Canada with them.[4] If there is no customs office at the point of crossing into Canada, then the traveller must report to the nearest customs office that is open for business at the earliest opportunity before unloading them.[5] Goods must be reported in the prescribed form to the nearest customs office, and when re-

---

4   *Kong v Canada* (1984), 10 DLR (4th) 226 (FCTD) [*Kong*].
5   *Customs Act*, s 11(1).

porting, the person must answer truthfully any question asked by an officer with respect to the goods.[6]

The reporting requirements may be waived by regulations and do not apply if the person has reported at a customs office outside Canada in accordance with the regulations; however, an officer may require the goods to be reported again.

The reporting requirements also do not apply if the person is entering Canadian waters or the airspace over Canada while proceeding directly from a place outside Canada to another place outside Canada, unless required by an officer to report.

1) Who Must Report?

The obligation to report is imposed by sections 11 and 12 on every person who arrives in Canada by any means from a place outside Canada; on every person who is importing goods where the goods do not accompany that person; and on every person in charge of a conveyance (vehicle, aircraft, boat) arriving in Canada, if the goods are in that person's possession, or in accompanying baggage, or are being carried in the conveyance, as the case may be.[7] Section 12 is likely the provision that an individual traveller, whether resident or visitor, is most familiar with and which has generated many administrative and criminal proceedings, because a violation of the reporting requirements can lead to forfeiture of goods and if there is deliberate concealment, even criminal prosecution.

Goods imported by courier or by mail must be reported by the person exporting the goods to Canada.[8]

Section 12 of the *Proceeds of Crime (Money Laundering) and Terrorism Financing Act*[9] (*Proceeds of Crime Act*) contains an analogous provision. If a traveller fails to report money or monetary instruments that he or she carries, as required by the *Cross-Border Currency and Monetary Instruments Reporting Regulations*,[10] where the amount exceeds $10,000, the excess can be

---

6   Ibid.
7   Ibid, s 12; *Reporting of Imported Goods Regulations*, SOR/86-873, am SOR/96-156, am SOR/2005-175.
8   *Accounting for Imported Goods and Payment of Duties Regulations*, SOR/86-1062, am SOR/96-46, SOR/2002-130, SOR/2003-241, SOR/2007-181.
9   SC 2000, c 17.
10 SOR/2002-412, am SOR/2003-358.

forfeited and the traveller can be subject to monetary penalties in addition. The two section 12s are *in pari materiae*.

2) Failure to Declare and Report

Failure to declare and report the goods as required is an offence under section 160 of the *Customs Act*, and the goods may be seized and confiscated. Certain exceptions apply, for example, goods covered by tariff items 9813.00.00 and 9814.00.00 (personal exemptions) when carried in person or in the baggage on arrival, if they are not charged with duties or their importation is not prohibited.[11] The confiscated goods are forfeited to the Crown. The forfeiture consequence is as old as the customs law itself. The law declares that the forfeiture relates back to the time when the offence of failure to report was committed.

A few cases illustrate the hazards of violating the reporting requirements. In *Time Data Recorder International Ltd v Canada (Minister of National Revenue)*,[12] the Federal Court of Appeal pointed out that the forfeiture and a criminal charge are separate consequences of a failure to comply with the reporting requirements; one has no bearing on the other. In *Kong v Canada*,[13] the Federal Court went even further and said that the obligation to declare is not confined to goods acquired abroad, let alone goods acquired on a particular trip from which a traveller has returned. It encompasses all goods in one's possession when entering Canada, including items that a Canadian had acquired in Canada and those owned by him all his life.

The Ontario Court of Appeal in *R v Cook*[14] held that the reporting requirements apply not only to goods acquired from foreign sources but also to goods transported between points in Canada through the United States, because when goods are transported between points in Canada through the United States, they are "imported" within the meaning of section 12(1).

In the case of *Hoang v Canada (Minister of National Revenue)*,[15] Hoang had made a wrong turn and found himself on US territory, so he turned around before going through the US border checkpoint. A Canada Border Services Agency (CBSA) officer stopped his car and found that Hoang had $70,000 in the car, which he had failed to declare. Upholding the validity of the seizure,

---

11 *Customs Act*, s 12(7).
12 (1993), 66 FTR 253 (TD), aff'd (1997), 211 NR 229 (FCA).
13 Above note 4.
14 (1992), 70 CCC (3d) 239 (CA).
15 2006 FC 182.

the court said that inadvertent error or intention of the person in reporting does not affect seizure. The court pointed out that the reporting requirements under section 12 of the *Proceeds of Crime Act* is analogous to the duty to report imported goods under section 12 of the *Customs Act*; caselaw under the *Customs Act* has held that the Act is contravened when an incorrect declaration is made on behalf of the importer even if that error was made with lack of intent to mislead customs. The tracking system is obligatory in order to achieve this purpose.

In the case of *Tourki v Canada (Minister of Public Safety and Emergency Preparedness)*,[16] customs officials removed *Tourki* from an aircraft bound for Paris from the Montreal airport and found undeclared currency of over $100,000 in his possession. The money was seized as forfeit for failure to declare. The court upheld the seizure.

These cases underline the need for travellers to declare all goods in their possession on arrival in Canada and even excess currency before departure, to avoid nasty surprises.

The law of forfeiture is elaborated further in Section I(4), below in this chapter.

3) Movement of Goods after Report

Unless and until the imported goods have been reported, they cannot be taken beyond the customs office or unloaded from a conveyance. Section 19(3) authorizes a customs officer to permit the importer or the carrier (those who carry goods for importers on a regular basis), in accordance with regulations, to deposit the imported goods, without the payment of duties and taxes, at the customs office, or in a duly licensed sufferance or licensed public or private bonded warehouse. See Section C, below in this chapter, for a discussion of these facilities.

Whilst in the warehouse, the goods must be kept in a secure place and no interference with them is permitted except for certain prescribed actions, such as marking and de-consolidating. They can also be exported under customs supervision without the payment of duties, or transferred in bond to another warehouse. Periodic releases may also be authorized if the importer needs them for sale to a purchaser in Canada, upon payment of the duties and taxes.

---

16   2006 FC 50, aff'd 2007 FCA 186.

4) Release of Goods

An importer can obtain release of the goods by going to the nearest customs office and paying the applicable customs duty. When this is done and the customs officer stamps the documents with the word "RELEASED," the goods are formally released and thereafter they are legally in the country.[17]

Certain time limits apply for obtaining release. Goods deposited in a customs office must be removed, reported, and accounted for, and duties must be paid within the time allowed by the customs officer—those deposited in a sufferance warehouse, within fourteen days of their deposit, and those deposited in a public or private bonded warehouse, within four years of their deposit. Only after the goods are formally accounted for and duties and taxes are paid, will their release be authorized by a customs officer.

5) Release Prior to Accounting and Payment of Duties

In accordance with section 32(1), imported goods cannot be released until they are accounted for in the prescribed form and all duties that they are charged with are paid. However, under section 32(2), an importer can request immediate release of the goods, that is, before final accounting and paying duties and taxes, by posting a bond acceptable to customs.

In prescribed circumstances, a customs officer may authorize the removal and delivery of goods to a place of business of the owner or importer or a consignee, after interim accounting. When goods are released after interim accounting, the person who made the interim accounting must account for the goods within the prescribed time and in the prescribed form; if the goods were delivered to a place of business of the owner or importer or consignee, that person must account for them in the prescribed form and within the prescribed time.

Goods imported by courier or by mail may also be released prior to accounting and prior to payment of duties. In that case the accounting and payment of duties is made after delivery but within the prescribed time by

---

[17] *Customs Act*, s 2(1), definition of "release." See *Wirth v Deputy Minister of National Revenue (Customs & Excise)* (1990), 3 TCT 2012 (CITT). (Goods can be said to have been released for customs purposes only after a customs officer has authorized their removal from a customs office, bonded warehouse, etc, for use in Canada. Release does not occur merely on presentation and filing of customs clearance documents.)

the person who was authorized to deliver or if there is no such person, then by the owner or the importer.[18]

6) Abandoned and Unclaimed Goods

With the authorization of a customs officer, the owner of imported goods (other than goods of a prescribed class, for example, tobacco and alcohol) is permitted by section 36 to abandon imported goods to Her Majesty. In that case the goods are no longer charged with customs duties and taxes. They may then be disposed of by sale or otherwise by the CBSA, but the owner may be called upon to pay the disposal costs if the proceeds of the sale are insufficient to cover them.

If goods (not being tobacco and alcohol) that are deposited in a customs office, sufferance warehouse, duty-free shop, or bonded warehouse are not removed within the prescribed time, they may be removed by a customs officer to a designated place of safekeeping. The safekeeping place is deemed by section 37(4) of the Act to be a customs office.

Goods stored in a place of safekeeping remain there at the risk and charge of their owner and importer, and they both are jointly and severally liable for all storage charges and expenses of moving from the place where they had been deposited. They can only be removed by the owner and importer after payment of those charges. If they are not claimed and removed within the prescribed period, they are treated as unclaimed and become forfeit. They may then be disposed of by the CBSA at the expense of the owner and importer.

C. LICENCES UNDER THE *CUSTOMS ACT* AND *CUSTOMS TARIFF*

1) When Is a Licence Needed?

Importers and exporters do not need a licence to conduct their business operations. They can clear goods through customs themselves, use their own agents, or employ licensed customs brokers to act on their behalf. If they import on a regular basis, however, they need to register with the CBSA and obtain a business number. Importers may be required to hold a permit or

---

18   See the *Accounting for Imported Goods and Payment of Duties Regulations*, above note 8. See also *Persons Authorized to Account for Casual Goods Regulations*, SOR/95-418 (these regulations authorize couriers to account for low value goods (under CDN$1,600) in lieu of the importer).

a certificate for certain specified goods controlled or regulated under other statutes, such as the *Export and Import Permits Act*,[19] the *Export Act*, the *Wild Animals and Plant Protection Regulation of International and Interprovincial Trade Act* (which provides the legislative base for the *Convention on International Trade in Endangered Species of Wild Fauna and Flora (CITES)*),[20] and the *Health of Animals Act*.[21]

People or businesses with private conveyances do not need a CBSA licence, but those who carry goods for importers on a regular basis (carriers) can register their conveyances with the CBSA to speed up the clearance process. The same applies to courier companies.

A licence is required for persons conducting business with customs, such as customs brokers, duty-free shop operators, and warehouse operators.

2) Licence Requirements

To get a broker's licence, a person has to follow a prescribed course of study, undergo training, and pass a prescribed examination. The broker also has to post a bond as security for any liability that may be incurred on account of duties and taxes owed to the Crown on goods released, or owed to clients from whom the broker collected duties but had not paid them over to the Crown. These requirements are set out in the *Customs Brokers Licensing Regulations*.[22]

3) Warehouse Licences

There are four types of warehouses operating under specific CBSA programs, policies, and regulations: sufferance, customs bonded, highway frontier examining, and Queen's. Sufferance and customs bonded warehouses are operated by the private sector under a CBSA licence, while highway frontier examining and Queen's warehouses are operated by the CBSA.

Warehouse licences are issued under the authority of the *Customs Act* and/or the *Customs Tariff*, and the operation of the warehouse facilities must adhere to a number of CBSA memoranda and warehouse-specific regulations and policies. Both the *Customs Act* and the *Canada Border Servi-*

---

19 See Chapter 4.
20 See Chapter 5.
21 See Chapter 6.
22 SOR/86-1067, am SOR/98-236.

ces Agency Act[23] authorize border services officers to have access to all warehouse facilities and to examine and seize goods.

a) Sufferance Warehouse Licence

Sufferance and customs bonded warehouses are privately owned and operated and are licensed by the CBSA to store imported goods arriving by truck, rail, or air. The majority arrive by truck, followed by rail and air. Sufferance warehouses (excluding highway frontier sufferance warehouses) are licensed pursuant to regulations prescribed under the *Customs Act*,[24] whereas customs bonded warehouses are licensed under the *Customs Tariff*.[25] The regulations specify the terms and conditions of the licence, the security to be deposited to ensure the payment of any duties payable in respect of the stored goods, how the warehouse is to be operated, and the maintenance of standards.

The CBSA will authorize the deposit of goods in a sufferance warehouse for a temporary period (up to fourteen days) for the purpose of examination before release.

b) Customs Bonded Warehouse Licence

Like sufferance warehouses, customs bonded warehouses are privately owned and operated, and licensed by the CBSA to store imported goods without payment of duties and taxes. They may be either private, that is, used exclusively by a single company, or public, that is, used by a number of companies. Users are charged storage and handling fees. Operators are permitted under the terms of the licence and the *Customs Bonded Warehouses Regulations*[26] to conduct limited processing of goods. Goods can be exported or released for domestic consumption within the four-year maximum period allowed for storage.

In addition to obtaining a licence, a customs bonded warehouse operator must provide a security (bond) in the amount of 60 percent of duties and taxes that would otherwise be payable at any time in the year following the issuance of the licence.

c) Highway Frontier Warehouses

These warehouses are owned and operated by the CBSA and are located at highway points of entry and used by the CBSA for examining incoming goods.

---

23 SC 2005, c 38.
24 SOR/86-1065, am SOR/2002-131, SOR/2005-211.
25 SOR/96-46, am SOR/99-106, SOR/2003-241.
26 *Ibid*.

d) Queen's Warehouses

These are also owned and operated by the CBSA and are used for storage and disposal of unclaimed, abandoned, detained, and seized goods.

D. ACCOUNTING AND PAYMENT OF DUTIES

1) Documentation

In most cases the final accounting package consists of (1) two copies of the Cargo Control Document (CCD); (2) two copies of the invoice; (3) two copies of a completed Form B3 (Canada Customs Coding Form); (4) any import permits, health certificates, or forms that other federal government departments require; and (5) a Form A—Certificate of Origin or Exporter's Statement of Origin in lieu of Form A. Paper copies may be submitted or, if authorized by CBSA, the information may be transmitted electronically.

a) Cargo Control Document

The cargo control document (CCD) is used by the carrier to report a shipment to the CBSA border office. It has a bar-coded cargo control number (CCN), the first four digits of which is the carrier's unique carrier code. The CCD acts as CBSA's initial record of the shipment's arrival. The document is also used for all shipments moved in-bond to an inland CBSA office, sufferance warehouse, or bonded warehouse. The carrier also has to send the importer a copy of the CCD to inform of the shipment's arrival.

b) Invoice

The invoice may be either a Canada Customs Invoice (CCI), which the importer or the vendor can complete, a commercial invoice containing the same information as the CCI, or a commercial invoice that indicates the names of the buyer and seller (exporter), the country of origin, the price paid or payable, a detailed description of the goods, including quantity, and other information required in the CCI.

c) Release on Minimum Documentation

The CBSA may authorize an importer to clear the goods from customs under a Release on Minimum Document (RMD) if the importer has an account with the CBSA. If RMD is used, the invoice must contain the importer's name and the import/export account, the exporter's name, the unit of measure and quantity of goods, the estimated value of the goods in Canadian

Chapter 1: The Customs Act

dollars, a detailed description of the goods, the goods' country of origin, and a bar-coded transaction number that is affixed to the invoice.

d) Canada Customs Coding Form

The Canada Customs Coding Form (Form B3) is used to account for commercial goods and must include the importer name and the import/export account, a description of the goods, the direct shipment date, the tariff treatment or trade agreement, the country of origin, the tariff classification, the value for duty, the appropriate duty or tax rates, and the calculation of duties owing.

e) Other Documents

Import permits, health certificates, or forms may be required by other federal government departments for goods that are subject to their requirements. For example, the Canadian Food Inspection Agency examines and gives permits for some meat products, and all restricted or controlled drugs require an import permit from Health Canada. The Department of Foreign Affairs and International Trade requires import permits for goods such as textiles and clothing, agricultural products, steel products, and some food items such as dairy products, poultry, and eggs that are subject to Tariff Rate Quotas.

f) Certificate of Origin

A certificate of origin is needed to support tariff treatment being claimed by an importer. Various Rules of Origin regulations have been prescribed under the authority of section 35.1.[27]

i) *Free Trade Partner Certificate*

Where goods are imported from a free trade agreement (FTA) partner country, different certificates are required for each of the countries. FTA partner certificates are required for importations from *NAFTA* countries (United States and Mexico),[28] Chile,[29] Colombia,[30] Costa Rica,[31] Israel and *Canada-Israel*

---

27 *Proof of Origin of Imported Goods Regulations,* SOR/98-52, am SOR/2004-186, SOR/2005-164, SOR/2008-78.
28 *NAFTA Rules of Origin Regulations,* SOR/94-14, am SOR/95-382, SOR/98-53, SOR/2001-108, SOR/2003-24, -396, SOR/2007-181, SOR/2008-111.
29 *CCFTA Rules of Origin Regulations,* SOR/97-340.
30 *CCOFTA Rules of Origin Regulations,* SOR/2011-131.
31 *CCRFTA Rules of Origin Regulations,* SOR/2002-395.

Free Trade Agreement (CIFTA) beneficiary countries,[32] Iceland, Liechtenstein, Norway, Switzerland,[33] Jordan,[34] and Panama.[35]

The exporters of the goods must fill out the certificate of origin based on their own knowledge that the goods qualify for a tariff treatment or based on information they have received from the producer of the goods in their country.

ii) Most-Favoured-Nation, Australia, and New Zealand Tariffs

Where a claim of tariff preference for the imported goods is based on the Most-Favoured-Nation Tariff (MFNT),[36] the Australia Tariff (AUT), or the New Zealand Tariff (NZT),[37] the names of the relevant countries may simply be indicated on the invoice or applicable documentation, in English or French, indicating that the goods originated in the applicable beneficiary country.

iii) Other Tariff Beneficiaries

Form A—Certificate of Origin, or the Exporter's Statement of Origin, may be used by an importer to support a claim for goods imported from countries that enjoy a preferential tariff treatment status, namely, goods from the Commonwealth Caribbean Countries Tariff (CCCT),[38] the General Preferential Tariff (GPT), and, with the exception of textile and apparel goods, the Least Developed Country Tariff (LDCT) countries.[39] In the case of textile and apparel goods under the LDCT, Form B255 applies. Form A and the Exporter's Statement of Origin must be completed in English or French.

iv) Low Value Shipments

A formal Certificate of Origin is waived in the case of shipments valued at less than CDN$1,600, provided they are not a part of a series of shipments. Instead, an Exporter's Statement of Origin from the exporter or producer certifying that the goods originate within a *NAFTA, CIFTA, Canada-Chile*

---

32 *CIFTA Rules of Origin Regulations*, SOR/97-63, am SOR/2002-252.
33 *Canada-European Free Trade Agreement Rules of Origin Regulations*, SOR/2009-198.
34 *CJFTA Rules of Origin Regulations*, SOR/2012-179.
35 *CPAFTA Rules of Origin Regulations*, SOR/2013-50.
36 *Most-Favoured-Nation Tariff Rules of Origin Regulations*, SOR/98-33.
37 *Australia Tariff and New Zealand Tariff Rules of Origin Regulations*, SOR/98-35.
38 *Commonwealth Caribbean Countries Tariff Rules of Origin Regulations*, SOR/98-36.
39 *General Preferential Tariff and Least Developed Country Tariff Rules of Origin Regulations*, SOR/98-34, am SOR/2000-335, SOR/2003-19, SOR/2003-20.

Free Trade Agreement (CCFTA), or Canada-Costa Rica Free Trade Agreement (CCRFTA) territory, as the case may be, is sufficient.

g) **Final Accounting Package**

The final accounting package has to be presented no later than five business days after the CBSA releases the goods. Payment can be made in cash, or if RMD (Release on Minimum Documentation) has been authorized, payment can be made by uncertified cheque on a monthly basis upon receipt of the monthly bill from CBSA or by interim payments on the daily statements.

2) Customs Self-Assessment Program

To speed up customs clearance, the CBSA has introduced the Customs Self-Assessment (CSA) Program for Importers under the authority of section 32(2)(b) of the Act. The CSA program is available to firms that qualify for and meet its eligibility criteria. Applicants that are low risk (have a good compliance history) are eligible if the CBSA on a review of their accounting and payment systems is satisfied that they meet the program requirements.

The CSA border clearance option is available only to imported goods arriving from the United States. The vast majority of CSA releases take place in the highway mode. Certain goods are currently excluded from the CSA clearance option, including the following: goods that are subject to regulations by other government departments, goods imported from offshore, and goods imported by a non-resident importer who does not have a branch office in Canada.

To use the CSA clearance option, the goods must be imported by a CSA-approved importer. Goods entering Canada by highway must be transported by a CSA-approved carrier that is using a driver who is registered under the Free and Secure Trade (FAST) Commercial Driver Program (in Canada and the United States) and the Commercial Driver Registration Program (in Canada only). CSA clients, who are also approved as part of the FAST Program, can also benefit by using designated FAST express lanes upon arrival at the border.

Shipments cleared through the CSA process, like all other shipments, may be subject to examination, although in principle CSA shipments are subject to fewer examinations than non-CSA shipments. CSA clients found to be in contravention of any acts or regulations are subject to penalties under the Administrative Monetary Penalty System, removal from the program, or other enforcement actions depending on the severity of the infraction.

Details of the CSA program are provided in Customs D Memorandum D17-1-7.[40]

3) Advance Rulings

Section 43.1 of the Act enables an importer or other persons prescribed under *Advance Rulings Regulations*[41] to request the CBSA for an advance ruling, before the goods are imported, with respect to (1) whether the goods qualify as originating goods and are entitled to the benefit of preferential tariff treatment under a free trade agreement; (2) any matter, other than (1) and (3), concerning the goods set out in the free trade agreements; and (3) the tariff classification of the goods. The regulations require an officer to give consistent rulings with respect to applications for advance rulings that are based on facts and circumstances that are identical in all material respects, along with a full explanation of the reasons for an advance ruling.[42] The Canadian International Trade Tribunal held in *Helly Hansen Leisure Canada v President of the Canada Border Services Agency*[43] that this directive is binding on CBSA officers, not on the Tribunal. Judicial review was rejected by the Federal Court of Appeal which, however, observed that the provision for advance ruling[44] applied to the officer who gives advance rulings, not to the Tribunal. The court added:

> A determination by the Tribunal of whether the CBSA erred in any particular decision cannot be dependent upon a prior decision of the CBSA. In this case, the Tribunal was required to base its decision upon its assessment of the applicable law, and was not bound by prior CBSA decisions. In reaching its decision on this basis, the Tribunal committed no error.[45]

---

40 Customs D Memorandum D17-1-7, 17 December 2010.
41 Three regulations have been enacted under this section: *Free Trade Agreement Advance Rulings Regulations*, SOR/97-72, am SOR/2001-108, SOR/2004-124, and *Tariff Classification Advance Rulings Regulations*, SOR/2005-256.
42 See s 7 of *Free Trade Agreement Advance Rulings Regulations*, ibid, and s 6 of the *Tariff Classification Advance Rulings Regulations*, ibid.
43 (2008), 14 TTR (2d) 53 (CITT), aff'd 2009 FCA 345 [*Helly Hansen*].
44 *Tariff Classification Advance Ruling Regulations*, above note 41.
45 *Helly Hansen*, above note 43 at para 16 (FCA).

E. VALUATION OF IMPORTED GOODS

1) Determination of Value for Duty

Valuation is the centrepiece of the *Customs Act*. It is the first step in the determination of the exact amount of duties and taxes that are payable on the imported goods. Because of the importance of the valuation provisions in determining the amount of duties and taxes, the importers' goal, understandably, is to minimize the amount of duties they are required to pay, which many do by understating the price paid, by claiming duty-free status for additional costs incurred, or by adding many layers in the export-import chain. The government has the opposite goal. As a result, there has been a fair amount of litigation on some of the key concepts embodied in section 48 of the Act, such as "sale for export," "purchaser in Canada," "royalties," "commissions," "assists," and so on. Some of the important decisions have been included in the discussion of the transaction value method (see Section E(4), below in this chapter), which is the primary method of valuation.

The process of valuation begins at the time of reporting the goods and clearing them through customs, simultaneously with the classification of the goods and the determination of the applicable rate of duty. Except for a few classes of goods, all duties are *ad valorem*, that is to say, the duties are computed by applying the rate set out in the *Customs Tariff* to a value determined in accordance with sections 45 to 55 of the *Customs Act*. The importer has to declare the full price that is paid to the exporter, including all costs and charges up to the point of direct shipment from the foreign country.

Simultaneously, the importer must declare the classification of the goods under the appropriate tariff item in which they fall, the country in which they originated, and the tariff rate entitlements of those countries. These steps are described in Chapter 2, which discusses the *Customs Tariff*.

Goods that are prohibited from importation are also covered by that statute. However, all disputes relating to valuation, tariff classification, origin, and tariff treatment that arise between importers and the government go to the Canadian International Trade Tribunal (the Tribunal) for adjudication, pursuant to the procedure specified in the *Customs Act*. The only exceptions are cases where pornographic material is imported and where an importer is charged with an offence relating to an importation. Those cases go to provincial courts.

The following provisions of the *Customs Tariff* must also be noted with respect to the valuation of goods:

1) section 20(2) with respect to goods taken out of Canada and subsequently returned to Canada, if they were repaired, equipment was added, or work was done outside Canada;
2) section 83 with respect to goods exceeding duty-free exemption brought by a traveller (value for duty reduced on goods as provided in tariff headings 9804.10.00, 9804.20.00, and 9804.30.00);
3) section 84 (tariff item 9805.00);
4) section 87 with respect to value of repairs or alterations made to goods in Iceland, Norway, Switzerland, or Liechtenstein (tariff item 9971.00.00);
5) section 88 with respect to goods of tariff item 9937.00 (ethno-cultural exemption); and
6) section 105 with respect to value for duty of work on the goods abroad.

2) Ad Valorem

The general rule established by section 44 is that where duties, other than duties or taxes levied under the *Excise Act, 2001*, are imposed on imported goods at a percentage rate, such duties shall be calculated by applying the rate to a value (*ad valorem*) determined in accordance with sections 45 to 55. Therefore, an accurate valuation is critical when calculating those tariffs. The issue of valuation does not arise in the case of duties and taxes based on weight or volume. For example, specific duty of 1.87 cents per litre is levied on ice-wine, $25.57 per tonne on cane sugar, and 1.9 cents per kilogram on turkey meat. Combined *ad valorem* and specific duty is levied on a few other imports. For example, imported oatmeal cereals in smaller packages are subject to a specific duty rate of 12.6 cents per kilogram, plus an *ad valorem* rate of 8.5 percent.

3) Six Methods of Valuation

Six methods for valuation of imported goods are set out in the *Customs Act*, and their purpose is to determine the fair market value of the goods at the time of their export to Canada. The *Customs Act* gives primacy to the transaction value method. Only when it does not reflect the fair market value are the secondary methods to be employed.

The transaction value method, as specified in section 47(1), calculates the value of the goods in accordance with section 48. This is the price paid for the goods, or price payable if the importer is given credit terms by the vendor. If the value for duty of goods cannot be appraised in accordance with that section, then section 47(2) requires the goods to be appraised by using one of five secondary methods, in sequential order, namely: (1) transaction value of identical goods; (2) transaction value of similar goods; (3) deductive value; (4) computed value; and (5) residual method of valuation. The importer may, however, request the CBSA in writing to reverse the order of the last two methods of valuation before the goods are accounted for.

Each of these six valuation methods is described in greater detail below.

4) Primary Method: Transaction Value

The transaction value method is the primary method of valuation and is of critical importance to importers. It is the method most often used and is designed to capture the fair market value of the imported goods.

Under this method, the value of goods is the price paid or payable by the importer. The importer must produce the vendor's invoice showing all the items of cost charged and the total price.

In order for the transaction value method to be applied, the following six conditions, specified in section 48(1), must be met:

1) The goods must be *sold for export* to Canada to a *purchaser in Canada*.
2) The *price paid or payable* for the goods can be determined.
3) There are *no restrictions* respecting the disposition or use of the goods by the purchaser thereof, other than restrictions that are imposed by law, or that limit the geographical area in which the goods may be resold, or that do not substantially affect the value of the goods.
4) The sale of the goods by the vendor to the purchaser or the price paid or payable for the goods is not subject to some condition or consideration, with respect to the goods, in respect of which a value cannot be determined.
5) When any part of the proceeds of any subsequent resale, disposal, or use of the goods by the purchaser accrues, directly or indirectly, to the vendor, the price paid or payable for the goods includes the value of that part of the proceeds, or the price is adjusted in accordance with section 48(5)(a).
6) The purchaser and the vendor of the goods were *not related to each other* at the time the goods are sold for export or, where the purchaser and the vendor are related to each other at that time, their relationship did not influence the price paid or payable for the goods, or the importer of the goods demonstrates that the transaction value of the goods meets the requirement set out in section 48(3) by establishing that it closely approximates

(a) the transaction value of identical goods or similar goods in a sale of those goods for export to Canada between a vendor and purchaser who are not related to each other at the time of the sale;
(b) the deductive value of identical goods or similar goods; or
(c) the computed value of identical goods or similar goods.

The situations where persons are deemed related to each other are set out in section 45(3).

a) Sale for Export to Purchaser in Canada

The first condition itself has three distinct requirements: (1) there has to be a sale by a vendor; (2) that sale must be for export to Canada; and (3) the sale must be to a purchaser in Canada. The last requirement has been defined in the *Valuation for Duty Regulations*.[46]

The question what constitutes a "sale" and a "sale for export" is critical for the application of the transaction value method. A "sale" occurs when a vendor transfers property in the goods for money consideration to a buyer without any conditions attached to the transaction. That is how it is defined at common law and in the *Sale of Goods Act* of the provinces, all of which except Quebec having adopted the codified United Kingdom *Sale of Goods Act*. Furthermore, a sale occurs at the time when the parties intend to transfer the title.

For the purposes of valuation under section 48 of the *Customs Act*, the relevant sale for export is the sale by which title to the goods passes to the importer. The importer is the party who has title to the goods at the time the goods are shipped to Canada.

The Supreme Court of Canada considered the issue of what constitutes a sale for export to a purchaser in Canada in two important cases. In *Canadian Admiral Corporation v Deputy Minister of National Revenue (Customs and Excise)*,[47] Canadian Admiral, a wholly owned subsidiary of US Admiral, bought refrigerators from Midwest Manufacturing Corporation, also a wholly owned subsidiary of US Admiral, before they were shipped from the United States to Canada for sale in Canada. Canadian Admiral and its parent, US Admiral, also sold refrigerators in their respective countries to their distributors. On the issue of whether there was a sale between the United States and Canadian companies, the Supreme Court held there was a sale, as there was a transfer of property in goods for a money consideration, called

---

46 SOR/86-792, am SOR/95-14, SOR/97-441.
47 [1959] SCR 832.

price. But the matter did not end there. The Court also determined that the sale price was not the only factor to be taken into account in the determination of the fair market value. The price charged was an "arranged" price between a parent company and a wholly owned subsidiary and therefore could not be considered a reflection of fair market value.

In *Canada (Deputy Minister of National Revenue) v Mattel Canada Inc*,[48] the goods were sold in a three-tiered distribution system: the manufacturers sold to the intermediary, the intermediary sold to a second intermediary, and the second intermediary sold to the ultimate purchaser. Because the only party to have title to the goods when the goods were transported into Canada was the ultimate purchaser, the intermediaries were not considered purchasers and so were not subject to any taxes or duties.

In contrast, in *Cherry Stix Ltd v President of the Canada Border Services Agency*,[49] when Cherry Stix Ltd sold women's T-shirts to Wal-Mart under a contract of purchase that provided that the transfer of title from Cherry Stix would occur only when Wal-Mart placed firm purchase orders, the Tribunal held that until the goods were delivered pursuant to the purchase orders, there was no "sale" and that Cherry Stix had title at the time of export of the goods. Cherry Stix, in the Tribunal's view, failed to meet the condition that required the sale to be for export, and, as there was no sale for export, the transaction value method could not be applied.

b) Price Paid or Payable Must Be Ascertainable

This is the fourth element required for the application of the transaction value method of valuation. The price paid or payable is defined by section 45(1) to mean "the aggregate of all payments made or to be made, directly or indirectly, in respect of the goods by the purchaser to or for the benefit of the vendor."

Normally, the invoiced price for goods being exported makes this determination straightforward. However, there are situations where the "final price" is deferred by the parties until after the goods are exported, by the issue of credit notes, for example, to encourage car sales. Consider the appeal to the Federal Court by the Deputy Minister of National Revenue in *Canada (Deputy Minister of National Revenue) v Toyota Canada Inc*[50] of the

---

48   2001 SCC 36 [*Mattel*].
49   (2005), 14 TTR (2d) 435 (CITT).
50   (1996), 1 TTR (2d) 385, rev'd (1999), 247 NR 223 (FCA) [*Toyota*]. Following the reconsideration directed by the FCA, the Tribunal held a hearing on 12 September 2000 at which the parties submitted a jointly concluded agreement asking the Tribunal to dismiss the original appeal.

decision of the Deputy Minister of National Revenue disallowing the credit note issued to Toyota. The Tribunal had found that the purpose of the credit note stipulated on the Canada Customs Invoice was simply to reflect the actual and final selling price of the goods and did not constitute a rebate of, or other decrease in, the "price paid or payable" for the vehicles in issue. The Federal Court of Appeal, however, disagreed because the Tribunal had failed to take into account the time requirements embodied in section 48 of the *Customs Act*, which partly provides that, in order for an importer to avail itself of the transaction value, it must first show that the "price paid or payable" for the goods can be determined when the goods are sold for export to Canada. The Tribunal had therefore to determine whether section 48 is applicable at all and, more specifically, whether the appellant's pricing method allowed for the determination of the "price paid or payable" for the vehicles at the time of importation. When the matter was remitted back to the Tribunal for reconsideration, the Tribunal reversed its original decision and dismissed Toyota Canada's appeal.

c) Purchaser in Canada

In addition to meeting the conditions referred to above (sale for export, price paid or payable), the sale for export must be to a purchaser in Canada as that term is defined by section 2.1 (read with the definitions "resident" and "permanent establishment" in section 2) of the *Valuation for Duty Regulations*.[51] To be a "purchaser in Canada," the person must be ordinarily a resident of Canada or must have a permanent establishment in Canada. In the case of a corporation that carries on business in Canada, to be a resident it must have its management and control in Canada; and in the case of a partnership or other unincorporated organization that carries on business in Canada, to be considered a resident, the member that has the management and control of the partnership or organization, or a majority of such members, must reside in Canada.

If a person is not a resident of Canada, to qualify as a "purchaser in Canada," that person must have a permanent establishment in Canada. If a person is neither a resident nor has a permanent establishment in Canada, that person can import the goods (1) for his or her own consumption, use, or enjoyment in Canada, but not for sale, or (2) for sale, provided that, before the purchase of the goods, the person has not entered into an agreement to sell the goods to a resident. The issue of who is a purchaser in Canada came before the Tribunal in *AAi.FosterGrant of Canada Co v Canada (Customs and Revenue*

---

51 Above note 46.

Agency).⁵² In that case, AAi Canada purchased certain goods from its parent company, AAi US, and asserted that it was a purchaser in Canada on the basis that it had employees in Canada and deposited some funds it generated into its Canadian bank account. The Tribunal found that the employees did not have direct access to funds with which to conduct business as these funds were immediately transferred to an account in the United States, and that AAi Canada performed primarily administrative functions in Canada, such as ordering merchandise, creating and purchasing display racks for placement in stores, and showing merchandise to customers. The Tribunal dismissed the appeal, ruling that AAi US was so significantly involved in the appellant's affairs that the business was really being conducted by the parent. This ruling was set aside by the Federal Court of Appeal, which held that there was no legal authority in the *Customs Act* or in the *Valuation for Duty Regulations* that would suggest that the meaning of the phrase "carrying on business" should be interpreted in a manner that was not consistent with the established legal definitions for the proposition that the Canadian subsidiary did not carry on business in Canada because it was subject to significant outside control. The court followed the reasoning of McLachlin J (as she then was) in the Supreme Court of Canada decision in *Shell Canada Ltd v Canada*,⁵³ a tax case. The Federal Court was of the opinion that the reasons in the Supreme Court decision were equally valid in *Customs Act* cases.

The Tribunal had arrived at the same conclusions in the earlier case of *Brunswick International* and in the later case of *The Pampered Chef, Canada*, which was decided on the basis of *AAi.FosterGrant*.

At issue in *Brunswick International (Canada) Ltd v Canada (Deputy Minister of National Revenue)*⁵⁴ was whether the value for duty of bowling equipment should be based on the price at which it allegedly purchased the goods from Brunswick America, as it claimed, or whether the value for duty should be based on the (higher) price at which Brunswick America allegedly sold to the Canadian end user, as determined by the Deputy Minister. In holding that the transaction value should be used to determine the value for duty, the Tribunal noted that Brunswick Canada and Brunswick America were distinct legal entities, and the Canadian company was not the agent of the latter. There was a sale between them and there was also a sale between Brunswick Canada and the Canadian end user. The sale between Brunswick America and Brunswick Canada was a sale for export to Canada. On the

---

52   (2003), 8 TTR (2d) 51 (CITT), rev'd 2004 FCA 259 [*AAi.FosterGrant*].
53   [1999] 3 SCR 622.
54   (1999), 4 TTR (2d) 279 (CITT) [*Brunswick International*].

issue whether Brunswick Canada was a "purchaser in Canada," the Tribunal had no doubt that it was. Brunswick Canada had a permanent establishment in Canada. It had a number of fixed places of business in Canada, including a warehouse, a main sales office in Mississauga, and three other sales offices located throughout Canada. It also carried on business in Canada from those locations. Furthermore, (1) Brunswick Canada's employees solicited customers for orders in Canada; (2) its employees had authority to negotiate the terms of sale of the bowling capital equipment without seeking confirmation from Brunswick America and to enter into contracts on its behalf; (3) invoices were issued in Brunswick Canada's name, and all payments by the Canadian customers were received by it and deposited in its Canadian bank accounts; (4) the Canadian customers dealt with Brunswick Canada in respect of warranty claims; and (5) Brunswick Canada filed Canadian income tax returns. In the Tribunal's view, therefore, Brunswick Canada had a permanent establishment in Canada, and it was not necessary to consider whether Brunswick Canada was or was not a resident. In either event, it would be a purchaser in Canada as defined in the Regulations.

In *The Pampered Chef, Canada Corporation v President of the Canada Border Services Agency*,[55] the Tribunal found that the Canadian company met the test of a purchaser in Canada as set out in the *Value for Duty Regulations*.[56] While conceding that it did not qualify as a "resident" within the meaning of the Regulations, its premises *did* qualify as a "permanent establishment," which is defined as "a fixed place of business of the person and includes a place of management, a branch, an office, a factory or a workshop through which the person carries on business." Pampered Chef, Canada had an office in Ontario, had employees, a warehouse, and bank accounts, and could be said to manage its operations from those premises. The Tribunal relied on the test for "carrying on business" enunciated by the Federal Court of Appeal in *AAi.FosterGrant* discussed above, which was: Is the company buying and selling goods on its own account for a profit in Canada? Pampered Chef, Canada sold goods to customers in Canada, as evidenced by order forms used at the sales parties and by payments that were either sent to Pampered Chef, Canada directly or deposited by the consultant in an account to which the company had access. It was also clear, in the Tribunal's opinion, that Pampered Chef, Canada bought goods from Pampered Chef, US, which it resold in Canada for profit. The CBSA had conceded that, if the sale for ex-

---

55   (2008), 12 TTR (2d) 284 (CITT) [*The Pampered Chef, Canada*].
56   Above note 46.

d) Purchaser and Vendor Not Related

Section 45(3) defines "related persons," and Customs D Memorandum D13-3-2 explains the provision further. As indicated above in this section, if a purchaser and a vendor in the country of export were related to each other at the time of export, the transaction method of appraising the value of goods would only be acceptable to the CBSA if the purchaser can satisfy that it meets one of the two conditions set out in section 48(1)(d), namely, (1) their relationship did not influence the price paid or payable for the goods or (2) the transaction value meets the requirement set out in section 48(3) by establishing that it closely approximates (a) the transaction value of identical goods or similar goods in a sale of those goods for export to Canada between a vendor and purchaser who are not related to each other at the time of the sale; (b) the deductive value of identical goods or similar goods; or (c) the computed value of identical goods or similar goods.

To use the transaction value method, under the first condition, the importer must examine how the price between the vendor and the purchaser was determined and provide to the CBSA the evidence to support the claim. The *Customs Act* does not detail the information to be used in establishing that the relationship has not influenced the price, nor does the *Customs Valuation Agreement* adopted by the World Trade Organization (WTO), on which the valuation provisions of the *Customs Act* are based, detail such information. However, paragraph 16 of Customs D Memorandum D13-3-2[57] provides several examples of ways to establish that a price is not influenced by the relationship. These examples were drawn by the CBSA from a report entitled *Transfer Pricing Guidelines for Multinational Enterprises and Tax Administrations*, published by the Organisation for Economic Co-operation and Development (OECD).[58]

It is the view of the CBSA that importers will be able to satisfy themselves more easily and more often of the acceptability of prices between related persons than they will be able to demonstrate that the transaction value meets one of the test values mentioned in section 48(3) above, which is the alternative to section 48(1)(d)(i). The test values reflect the results drawn from the other three methods of appraising the value for duty, namely, the

---

57 Related Persons (9 August 2013).
58 (Paris: OECD, 2001).

transaction value of identical or similar goods, the deductive value of identical or similar goods, and the computed value of identical or similar goods. The time element for determination of the test values as well as the comparison of values must take into account the relevant factors and differences, including those set out in section 3 of the *Valuation for Duty Regulations*.

The appeal in *Nu Skin Canada Inc v Canada (Deputy Minister of National Revenue)*[59] against the decision of the Deputy Minister of National Revenue illustrates the application of transfer pricing by the Tribunal in transactions where the appellant and its US parent (Nu Skin International) were regarded by it as well as by the Deputy Minister as a single business entity, which was not contested by the appellant. The US parent had placed separate purchase orders with various third-party producers over which, the evidence indicated, it did not exercise sufficiently close supervisory control, and some of those orders were for goods to be shipped to Canada and clearly distinguished as such (in that they used metric sizing and bilingual labels that indicated the appellant's name and address); they were also acquired by a distinct purchase order and were shipped directly to the appellant's warehouse in Ontario from their place of manufacture.

The Deputy Minister had argued that the transactions between the US parent and the third parties were not sales but rather contracts for services or, if they were sales, they did not qualify as sales for export under section 48. The Tribunal disagreed and concluded that (1) the US parent and the appellant were a single business entity and (2) the sales by third party manufacturers to the US parent constituted sales for export for purposes of section 48.

The US parent of Nu Skin had used a transfer pricing formula based on the "resale price methods" for goods shipped to the Canadian entity.

In view of its finding that the transactions between the third parties and the US parent were sales and those sales were for export to Canada, the Tribunal concluded that the value for duty of the imported goods should be determined on the transaction value method and should be based on the price paid to the third party manufacturers by the US parent.

e) Adjustments to Transaction Value of Goods

Section 48(5) requires the price shown on the invoice to be revised up or down, depending on what the total price is comprised of. Section 48(5)(a) requires the following amounts to be added to the price paid or payable if they are not already included in the invoice:

---

59   (1997), 3 TTR (2d) 95 (CITT).

1) commissions and brokerage in respect of the goods incurred by the purchaser thereof, other than fees paid or payable by the purchaser to his agent for the service of representing the purchaser abroad in respect of the transaction;
2) packing costs and charges incurred by the purchaser in respect of the goods, including the cost of cartons, cases, and other containers and coverings that are treated for customs purposes as being part of the imported goods, and all expenses of packing incident to placing the goods in the condition in which they are shipped to Canada;
3) "assists," that is, the value of any of the following goods and services, determined in the manner prescribed by regulations, that are supplied, directly or indirectly, by the purchaser of the goods free of charge or at a reduced cost for use in connection with the production and sale for export of the imported goods, apportioned to the imported goods in a reasonable manner and in accordance with generally accepted accounting principles:
    a) materials, components, parts, and other goods incorporated in the imported goods;
    b) tools, dies, moulds, and other goods utilized in the production of the imported goods;
    c) any materials consumed in the production of the imported goods;
    d) engineering, development work, artwork, design work, plans, and sketches undertaken elsewhere than in Canada and necessary for the production of the imported goods;
4) royalties and licence fees, including payments for patents, trademarks, and copyrights, in respect of the goods that the purchaser of the goods must pay, directly or indirectly, *as a condition of the sale* of the goods for export to Canada, exclusive of charges for the right to reproduce the goods in Canada;
5) subsequent proceeds, that is, the value of any part of the proceeds of any subsequent resale, disposal, or use of the goods by the purchaser thereof that accrues or is to accrue, directly or indirectly, to the vendor; and
6) transportation costs and insurance costs (including the loading, unloading, and handling charges and other charges and expenses associated with the transportation) of the goods *to the place* within the country of export from which the goods are shipped directly to Canada.

If, however, the information provided by the importer for the above items is not sufficient or the appraising officer believes that it is inaccurate, the transaction value method cannot be used in determining the value of the imported goods.

What type of commissions, "assists," and royalties are to be excluded from value for duty has been the subject of a number of decisions at all levels of adjudication. The following are some examples.

i) Commissions

a. Buying Commissions

Both the Tribunal and the Federal Court on appeal have uniformly held that certain commissions are not dutiable. In *Chaps Ralph Lauren, a Division of 131384 Canada Inc v Canada (Deputy Minister of National Revenue)*[60] and *Brown's Shoe Shops Inc v Canada (Customs and Revenue Agency)*,[61] the Tribunal, following its earlier decision in *Woodward Stores Ltd v Deputy Minister of National Revenue (Customs and Excise)*,[62] held that commissions paid under a legitimate buying agency agreement, where the purchaser exercised control over choice, specification, and price of goods, and directed the agent to manage quality control and logistics, were not part of the value for duty. In the latter case the payment was made directly to the manufacturer, but the Tribunal found no conflict of interest in that arrangement. The Federal Court affirmed the Tribunal's decisions in *Signature Plaza Sport Inc v Minister of National Revenue (Customs & Excise)*[63] and held that the 15 percent agency commission was not to be added to value for duty, approving the Tariff Board's decision in *Woodward Stores*, as well as in *Canada v Kay Silver Inc*,[64] where a 10 percent commission paid by the importer to its foreign agent was upheld. The Federal Court of Appeal similarly upheld the non-dutiability of the fees paid to an agent in *Utex Corporation v Canada (Deputy Minister of National Revenue)*.[65] A buying or agency commission is not dutiable provided it is not paid to the vendor in order to hide the true price paid or payable.

The Tribunal has similarly held in *Simms Sigal & Co Ltd v Canada (Customs and Revenue Agency)*[66] that distribution fees paid by the appellant to Ann Klein & Co pursuant to a distribution agreement did not become part of the price paid or payable, rejecting the CCRA's argument that all payments

---

60 (1997), 1 TTR (2d) 781 (CITT).
61 (2004), 8 TTR (2d) 574 (CITT).
62 (1974), 6 TBR 184 (Tariff Bd) [*Woodward Stores*].
63 (1990), 32 FTR 287 (TD).
64 [1981] 2 FC 436 (TD).
65 2001 FCA 54.
66 (2003), 8 TTR (2d) 20 (CITT).

made by the purchaser for the benefit of the vendor where the goods are sold for export to Canada were dutiable and that the fees were not paid "in respect of the goods."

In *Sherson Marketing Corporation v Canada (Deputy Minister of National Revenue) (Sherson No 3)*,[67] the issue was whether the 13 percent Free on Board (FOB) factory cost fee paid by the appellant for the Plaza Suite brand shoes to Jervin, a company related to the Nine West Group Inc, were dutiable and should be added to the price paid or payable. The appellant claimed that the fee was a buying commission and not dutiable. It made a similar claim respecting the Enzo Angiolini brand name where it paid 13.5 to 15 percent to Enzo Angiolini, Division of Nine West Group Inc. The Deputy Minister of National Revenue (DMNR) (Customs and Excise) determined that these fees were dutiable. The Tribunal did not accept the respondent's proposition that an agent, simply by virtue of its size or, in this case, by virtue of the size of a related company, cannot act in the best interest of its principal. In this case, no convincing evidence was presented to the Tribunal indicating that, in any specific instance or transaction, Jervin did not act in the appellant's best interest. The Tribunal therefore found that FOB factory cost commissions were *bona fide* buying commissions and were not dutiable.

In the second appeal in *Sherson Marketing Corporation v Canada (Deputy Minister of National Revenue) (Sherson No 4)*,[68] the issue was the same: whether the 5 percent FOB factory cost fee paid by it to its consultants with respect to the Prevata shoes and Repeat shoes were non-dutiable buying commissions. However, the Tribunal was not convinced by the evidence that the fees paid by the appellant were for the service of representing the appellant abroad in respect of the sale. Therefore, it found that the fees were dutiable commissions.

The non-dutiability of buying commissions was raised by Sherson Marketing in yet another appeal, in *Sherson Marketing Corporation v Canada (Deputy Minister of National Revenue) (Sherson No 2)*.[69] It had paid a 10 percent FOB factory cost fee to Chang's Imports Inc for the Apropos, Margaret J, and Margaret Jerrold brand-name shoes, and claimed that it was a *bona fide* buying commission and, therefore, was non-dutiable. The respondent determined that the 10 percent fee was a dutiable design fee. The Tribunal allowed Sherson Marketing's appeal in part, finding that with respect to shoes bearing the Margaret J and Margaret Jerrold brand names, an amount of US$3,000 per year of the 10 percent FOB factory cost fee paid to Chang's

---

67 (2000), 4 TTR (2d) 832 (CITT).
68 (2000), 4 TTR (2d) 842 (CITT).
69 (2000), 4 TTR (2d) 821 (CITT).

Imports Inc was a dutiable design fee and that the remaining portion of the fee was a *bona fide* buying commission and was not dutiable. With respect to the 10 percent FOB factory cost fee paid in respect of the shoes bearing the Apropos brand name, the Tribunal found that it was a *bona fide* buying commission and was not dutiable.

In the appeal in *Clothes Line Apparel, division of 2810221 Canada Inc v Canada (Border Services Agency)*[70] (discussed under royalties in Section E(4)(e)(iii)(b.), below in this chapter), one of the issues raised by the appellant was whether the CBSA correctly disallowed its claim for deduction of the amounts paid by it as commissions to Diesel US, which held the Diesel trademark licence from its Italian parent, Diesel SpA, and had sub-licensed it to the appellant for use in Canada. According to the witness for Diesel US, the exporter, Diesel US simply acted as a facilitator or a buying agent, and did not buy and resell the goods in issue. The Tribunal found that the evidence indicated that the payments of commission were not made at the same time as the payments for the goods and the royalties. They were invoiced to the appellant separately, on a monthly basis, by Diesel US and represented 20 to 25 percent of the total purchases made by the appellant in a given month, but in some cases they were included in the cost of the goods purchased by the appellant in the same invoice. Furthermore, Diesel US was designated in the appellant's insurance policy for the goods received directly from the manufacturers as an insured party, which suggested that Diesel US had an insurable interest in the goods and bore some of the risk concerning the goods if they were damaged or lost.

The Tribunal found the testimony of the witnesses for the appellant that Diesel US was only a buying agent not to be credible, in view of the other evidence before it, and that, on the facts of the appeal, the relationship between Diesel US and the appellant was that of a vendor and purchaser; therefore, by definition, Diesel US cannot be the appellant's buying agent and the commissions cannot be fees paid or payable by the purchaser to its agent for the service of representing the purchaser abroad in respect of the sale. In view of this, the Tribunal held that the commissions must be added to the price paid or payable for the goods as determined by the CBSA.

In the case of *The Pampered Chef, Canada*,[71] a multi-level marketing company, the appellant bought products from its parent, Pampered Chef, US, in an elaborate, complex intercompany arrangement, and sold them in Canada

---

70 (2008), 12 TTR (2d) 967 (CITT), aff'd 2009 FCA 366 [*Clothes Line Apparel*].
71 Above note 55.

during "at-home" parties through independent sales consultants. The format for a home show was the following: after finding someone to host and arrange the show, the consultant arrived at the host's home on the appointed day, visited with the guests, handed out individual order forms, and then demonstrated Pampered Chef products. Guests could purchase some articles of the product line before the end of the evening. In the Tribunal's view, the commissions paid to consultants should not have been added to the invoiced value of the goods because the context of section 48(5) of the *Customs Act* makes it clear that this requirement related to the sale for export, that is, the related-company transfer, not some subsequent sale within Canada.

b. Selling Commissions

For a selling commission to be added to the value for duty, the CBSA must first determine that the importer was not in reality the purchaser of the goods, but acted as a selling agent for the exporter. In *DMG Trading Company v Canada (Deputy Minister of National Revenue)*,[72] the Deputy Minister of National Revenue determined that the appellant, although the importer of the goods, was in reality bringing the goods for sale on behalf of the exporter, and that the value for duty of the goods must be the price paid by the Canadian purchaser from the importer plus the selling commission. The Tribunal upheld the Deputy Minister's decision in the appeal filed by DMG Trading Company. In reaching its conclusion that the importer was acting as the selling agent, the Tribunal relied, in particular, on the following factors: (1) the terms for the sale of goods in issue were determined by the exporter; (2) in most cases, the appellant secured customers and orders before importing the goods from that exporter; (3) the goods were shipped directly to the Canadian purchaser; (4) the appellant had no choice of suppliers; (5) under certain circumstances, in order to service warranties, goods had to be returned to the appellant, which, in turn, would return them to the exporter; (6) in most circumstances, the appellant did not remit payment to the exporter until it had received payment from the Canadian purchaser; and finally (7) the appellant did not, and could not, mark up the price charged by the Canadian exporter for the goods in issue after having been set by the exporter.

On the basis of the above evidence, and the definition of "selling agent" found in Customs D Memorandum D13-4-12,[73] the Tribunal found that the appellant acted for the account of the exporter. The Tribunal also noted that

---

72 (1997), 1 TTR (2d) 104 (CITT).
73 D13-4-12 Commissions and Brokerage (*Customs Act*, s 48), (13 June 2008).

the exporter delivered the goods to the Canadian purchaser in pursuance of orders placed through the appellant and that the price quoted on the invoice sent to the appellant included an amount for the appellant's services. Since the trade discount or selling commission had already been included in the price, the Tribunal concluded that it should not have been deducted by the appellant when calculating the value for duty.

ii) "Assists"

a. Design Costs

In *Capital Garment Co v Canada (Deputy Minister of National Revenue)*,[74] the appellant, as part of the process ultimately leading to the manufacture of textile garments, provided, free of charge, the foreign manufacturer with graded paper patterns (GPPs) produced in Canada for each garment size. The issue in this appeal was whether the GPPs constituted "assists" under section 48(5)(a)(iii) of the *Customs Act* as determined by the respondent and, if so, whether their value must be added to the transaction value of the imported goods in order to determine the value for duty of the apparel. The Tribunal was of the view that grading was but one step in the design process, albeit one that took place towards the end of that process, and that the dictionary definitions of the term "design" that referred to "an outline, sketch, or plan" would encompass the grading element in the manufacture of garments. It agreed with counsel for the respondent that the GPPs constituted "design work" necessary for the production of the imported goods and, accordingly, they fell within section 48(5)(a)(iii)(D) of the Act. However, since the work associated with the GPPs was undertaken in Canada, they were not dutiable under section 48(5)(a).

On the other hand, in *Fritz Marketing Inc v Canada (Border Services Agency)*,[75] the Tribunal held that the design costs on goods imported from India were dutiable, because from the evidence, it was clear that they were part of the full cost of the goods, and that the parties had created design service invoices with a view to avoiding customs duty.

b. Value of Materials Used or Consumed

While materials, components, parts, and other goods incorporated in the imported goods or those consumed in the production of the imported goods are to be included in the full cost of the goods (if those materials were

---

74   (1997), 2 TTR (2d) 466 (CITT).
75   (2006), 1 TTR (2d) 954 (CITT), aff'd (*sub nom Fritz Marketing Inc v Canada (Border Services Agency, President)*) (2010), 14 TTR (2d) 447 (CITT) [*Fritz Marketing*].

supplied by the importer), the Tribunal has held, in *Charley Originals Ltd, division of Algo Group Inc v Canada (Deputy Minister of National Revenue)*,[76] that the cost of unused fabric that was not waste and was not "consumed" in the production of the imported goods nor incorporated into the imported clothing, should not be added to the price paid or payable.

c. Quota Payments

Payments for the quota allotted to manufacturers/vendors by Canada and included in the price paid or payable by an importer are payments to or for the benefit of the vendor within the meaning of section 45(1). In *Charley Originals*,[77] the appellant had made payments for the quotas to two different parties, one to Taiwan factories producing apparel and the other, on its behalf, to manufacturers/vendors from Hong Kong. The Tribunal held that the value of the quota must be added to the price paid or payable for the textiles. On the other hand, it was not persuaded that the quota payment to export clothing from Hong Kong should have been included in the price paid or payable for the goods, as the evidence indicated that the quota payments were made by Colby & Staton Fashions Ltd, on the appellants' behalf, to the owners of the quota that were unrelated to the manufacturers/vendors of the clothing. There was also evidence in this case which indicated that purchases of such quota were sometimes made in advance of the purchase of clothing.

iii) Royalties and Licence Fees

To be dutiable, the royalties and licence fees must be paid "as a condition of the sale of goods for export to Canada" (section 48(5)(a)(iv)). In other words, the vendor must have a right to refuse to sell the goods if the royalties and licence fees are not paid.

a. Non-dutiable Payments

Prior to the Supreme Court decision in *Mattel*,[78] there were a number of decisions of the Tribunal and the Federal Court on the deductibility of royalties paid by an importer when the goods were shipped to Canada. A brief review of those cases would clarify the issue. In *Canada v Mondev Corp Ltd*,[79] the importer had paid royalties to three separate owners of trademarks, "Lanvin," "Cardin," and "Hermes," under a royalty agreement. In the appeal

---

76   (1997), 2 TTR (2d) 106 (CITT), aff'd (2000), 257 NR 104 (FCA) [*Charley Originals*].
77   *Ibid*.
78   Above note 48.
79   (1974), 33 CPR (2d) 193 (FCTD) [*Mondev*].

against duties and taxes on the royalties, the Federal Court Trial Division rejected the Crown's claim, saying the royalties had nothing to do with the value for duty as they were for use of names on the boutique, which sold many other goods, including those made in Canada.

In *Triton Industries Ltd v Canada (Deputy Minister of National Revenue for Customs and Excise)*,[80] the Tariff Board, following *Mondev*, held that where an importer contracted with a third party who is unrelated to the exporter, authorizing the importer to apply the trademark owned by the third party on imported goods as well as Canadian goods, the royalty agreement under which the authorization was given did not have any bearing on the value for duty and therefore did not enhance their value; hence, royalty was not dutiable.

In *Nike Canada Ltd v Canada (Deputy Minister of National Revenue)*,[81] the Federal Court of Appeal arrived at a similar conclusion with respect to royalties paid to athletes for services provided by them. The court held that these royalties were not paid as a direct or indirect condition of sale of goods, and, therefore, were not dutiable. On the other hand, royalties paid to Nike Ireland as a condition of the sale of the goods for export were dutiable and came within section 48(5)(a)(iv).

In *Mattel*,[82] the Supreme Court of Canada specifically dealt with the issue of the dutiability of royalties and licence fees, among others. In that case, the goods were invoiced in three stages: the foreign manufacturers invoiced the intermediary, the intermediary invoiced Mattel US, and Mattel US invoiced Mattel Canada. The goods were sold at progressively higher prices. The intermediary and Mattel US took title to the goods before the title was transferred to Mattel Canada. The goods were shipped directly from the foreign manufacturers to Mattel Canada. Mattel Canada had title to the goods when the goods were transported into Canada.

The Court held that the royalty payments were not caught by the words "paid or payable" because the royalty payments were not made for the benefit of Mattel US, the vendor. Rather, they were made for the benefit of the recipient of the payments, Licensor X.

Further, the Court held that the royalty payments were not caught by section 48(5)(a)(iv) merely because the section used the words "directly or indirectly." While these adverbs did modify the verb "pay" and therefore indicated that royalties paid to third parties may be captured by that clause,

---

80 (1980), 2 CER 34, 7 TBR 33 (Tariff Bd).
81 (1999), 85 ACWS (3d) 820 (FCA).
82 Above note 48.

adverbs cannot modify nouns such as "condition." Therefore, the words "directly or indirectly" did not modify the requirement that royalties must be paid "as a condition of the sale of the goods for export to Canada" to be dutiable.

Mattel Canada had also made periodic payments to Mattel US in respect of agreements Mattel US had made with various licensors ("Master Licensors"). The Deputy Minister sought to include these payments in the value for duty of the imported goods. The Tribunal had held that neither the royalties nor the periodic payments were dutiable because they were not paid "as a condition of the sale of the goods for export to Canada" in accordance with section 48(5)(a)(iv) of the Act. The Federal Court of Appeal reversed that decision in part, finding that the periodic payments fell within the ambit of that clause.

With respect to these periodic payments, the Supreme Court held that they did not fall within the ambit of section 48(5)(a)(iv). They were not dutiable because Mattel US would not be entitled to refuse to sell licensed goods to Mattel Canada or repudiate the contract of sale if Mattel Canada refused to pay licence fees to the Master Licensors. Mattel Canada's obligation to pay licence fees to the Master Licensors was distinct from its obligation to purchase goods from Mattel US. Since these payments were not caught by the section, the Court found no need to consider whether they were caught by section 48(5)(a)(v).

b. Dutiable If Condition of Sale

To be dutiable, the royalties and licence fees have to be paid to the vendor as a condition of the sale for export to Canada. If they are not paid, the vendor could refuse to sell the licensed goods.

In *Mattel*,[83] the Supreme Court of Canada noted that the words "condition of the sale" in section 48(5)(a)(iv) were clear and unambiguous. The Court pointed out that it has repeatedly held that where clear and unambiguous statutory provisions can be applied directly to the facts, it is not necessary to resort to an analysis of the economic realities of a transaction.

The words, according to the Court, incorporate traditional concepts found in sale of goods legislation and the common law of contract. Unless a vendor is entitled to refuse to sell licensed goods to the purchaser or repudiate the contract of sale where the purchaser failed to pay royalties or licence fees, section 48(5)(a)(iv) was inapplicable.

---

83   *Ibid.*

The Federal Court of Appeal, which had reserved its decision in *Reebok Canada, a division of Avrecan International Inc v Canada (Deputy Minister of National Revenue, Customs and Excise)*[84] pending the Supreme Court's judgment in *Mattel*, followed the latter. In this case, Reebok Canada had purchased goods from a foreign supplier and paid royalties pursuant to a separate licence agreement. Here, the vendor and the licensor were the same person, but Reebok's purchase orders did not make reference to the royalty, nor did the royalty agreement expressly refer to the purchase orders. The issue before the court was whether Reebok's obligation to make the royalty payment was a condition of the sale for export of the goods to Reebok Canada. It was the court's opinion that if Reebok did not pay royalties, the vendor would probably add a condition to pay them into future orders, but held that with respect to the current contract of sale, the vendor's prior obligation to sell was not affected. Furthermore, the fact that the vendor and the licensor were the same person did not mean that Reebok's obligations under the licence agreement automatically became obligations under the contract.

In *Clothes Line Apparel*,[85] which came up before the Tribunal after the landmark decision of the Supreme Court in *Mattel*, the issue was whether payments made to the vendor by the Canadian importer of Diesel brand women's clothing, operating under a sub-licence from Diesel US, which held exclusive licence to use the trademark in North America from its parent, Diesel SpA, were dutiable. Even though the goods were ordered directly from the manufacturers, the appellant was provided with copies of original invoices for the sale. It was clear from the evidence that the sale for export actually took place between the manufacturers and Diesel US, which billed the appellant for the exact same price it paid and added an amount for royalties. There was no dispute that the payments were royalties, but the disagreement was on the issue whether the royalties were paid as a condition of the sale of the goods for export to Canada. The appellant relied on *Mattel* and the Federal Court of Appeal decision in *Reebok* when arguing that the royalties were not paid as a condition of the sale of the goods for export to Canada.

The Tribunal examined all the circumstances surrounding the payment of royalties and found that it was an integral part of the business arrangements between Diesel US and the appellant. In particular, the Tribunal found that (1) the royalties were billed to the appellant on the same invoices from

---

84 2002 FCA 133 [*Reebok*].
85 Above note 70.

Diesel US as the cost of the goods themselves; (2) all the invoices that were filed by the appellant in evidence referred to Diesel brand goods, and with the exception of invoices from Diesel SpA (the Italian clothier) for advertising purposes and promotional material, included royalties; (3) there was a significant amount of evidence to confirm the payment of royalties and that the royalty payments were part of the same financial transaction as the payment of the goods bought from Diesel US; and (4) it was clear from the testimony that it was routine to pay the royalties. The written contract clearly indicated that the royalties be paid. It distinguished *Reebok*, where the contract did not expressly state that the royalties were to be paid as a condition of the sale for export to Canada. On the basis of the evidence, therefore, the Tribunal concluded that the royalty payments were a condition of the sales and, pursuant to section 48(5)(a)(iv) of the Act, they must be added to the price paid or payable for the goods, as was determined by the CBSA.

iv) Deductions

Section 48(5)(b) requires the following costs to be deducted from the price paid or payable if they are already included in the invoice:

1) the cost of transportation, loading, unloading, and handling charges and other charges and expenses associated with the transportation of, and the cost of insurance relating to the transportation of, the goods "from the place" within the country of export from which the goods are shipped directly to Canada; and
2) any of the following costs, charges, or expenses, if they are identified separately from the price paid or payable for the goods:
   a) reasonable cost, charge, or expense that is incurred for the construction, erection, assembly, or maintenance of, or technical assistance provided in respect of, the goods after the goods are imported, and
   b) duties and taxes paid or payable by reason of the importation of the goods or sale of the goods in Canada, including any duties or taxes levied on the goods under the *Customs Tariff*; *Excise Act, 2001*; *Excise Tax Act*; *Special Import Measures Act*; or any other law relating to customs.

If goods were sold by a vendor for export on a Free on Board (FOB) basis, the transportation costs; the loading, unloading, and handling costs; and other charges and expenses associated with the transportation are not dutiable, as these costs and charges are already included in the FOB terms, and if they are included in the vendor's invoice, they are to be deducted. On the other hand, if freight and insurance are itemized in the invoice for goods sold on a Cost, Insurance, and Freight (CIF) basis, they are to be deducted from the value for duty. It was so held by the Tribunal in *Fritz Marketing*.[86]

v) No Adjustment

If after importation the vendor gives any rebate or reduces the price paid or payable, section 48(5)(c) requires that rebate or price reduction to be disregarded. In *Nordic Laboratories Inc v Canada (Deputy Minister of National Revenue, Customs and Excise)*,[87] the Tribunal held that a credit note issued by the vendor after importation was correctly disregarded by the Deputy Minister because the conditions precedent to the issuance of the note had not been met. The Federal Court, however, set aside that decision, holding that the value of the goods should have been based on the reduced price because the credit note was not a rebate or discount in price but an adjustment, or, alternatively, if the credit note was a rebate or price reduction, it was effected before, not after, the product was imported into Canada.[88]

5) Transaction Value of Identical Goods

If the value for duty of goods cannot be appraised under section 48, the next method of valuation, provided in section 49, is the transaction value of identical goods.

a) Meaning of Identical Goods

"Identical goods" is defined in section 45(1) as imported goods that (1) are the same as the goods being appraised in all respects, including physical characteristics, quality, and reputation, except for minor differences in appearance that do not affect value; (2) were produced in the same country as the country in which the goods being appraised were produced; and (3) were produced by or on behalf of the same person who produced the goods being appraised. They do not include imported goods where engineering, development work, artwork, design work, and so on were supplied directly or indirectly by the purchaser of the imported goods free of cost or at a reduced cost for use in connection with the production and sale for export of those imported goods.

---

86 Above note 75.
87 (1992), 10 TTR 13 (CITT), rev'd (1996), 113 FTR 168 (TD).
88 Compare to *Toyota*, above note 50.

In *R & H Products Ltd v Deputy Minister of National Revenue (Customs and Excise)*,[89] the Tariff Board (the predecessor to the Tribunal) held that "like goods" means *identical* goods, not *similar* goods. Allowing the appeal of R & H Products, the Board was of the opinion that colour and chrome films are not like goods because they did not function in the same manner in the camera, nor were they designed to be transported (that is, moved forward within the camera) in the same manner.

On the other hand, in *Triple-A Specialty Co v Deputy Minister of National Revenue (Customs and Excise)*,[90] the appellant had imported battery chargers, accessories, and parts from its parent company in Chicago without a trademark applied to them, with the intention of applying it or a different trademark after importation. Rejecting the appeal, the Board held that the application of a different trademark to "like goods" did not have the effect of changing "like" goods into *unlike* goods.

If the purchaser had supplied free of cost, or at a reduced cost, engineering and development work, artwork, design work, plans, or sketches ("assists") undertaken in Canada for use in connection with the production and sale for export of the imported goods, then those costs are not included in determining whether the goods are identical to the goods being appraised.

If there are no goods identical to the goods being appraised, but there are goods that would be identical as defined above if they were produced by or on behalf of the same producer, then the latter are deemed to be identical.

b) Same or Substantially Same Trade Level and Quantities

In addition to meeting the definition of identical goods, in order for this method of valuation to be applied, section 49(1) requires that the sale of identical goods to other purchasers must satisify two conditions: (1) the purchaser of the identical goods must be at the same or substantially the same trade level as the purchaser of the goods being appraised, and (2) the quantities sold to that purchaser must be the same or substantially the same as those sold to the purchaser whose goods are being appraised.

c) Adjustments

The transaction value of identical goods may be adjusted by adding or deducting commercially significant differences in prescribed costs, charges, and expenses between the identical goods and the goods that are being appraised

---

[89] (1978), 6 TBR 257 (Tariff Bd).
[90] (1978), 6 TBR 701 (Tariff Bd).

that are attributable to differences in distances and modes of transport, as well as amounts that take account of differences in trade level or quantities, or both.

d) Two or More Transaction Values

Section 49(5) states that where there are two or more transaction values of identical goods, the value for duty of the goods being appraised is to be determined on the basis of the lowest transaction value.

e) Sufficient Information Unavailable

If sufficient information is not available to determine these adjustments, section 49(4) does not permit the imported goods to be appraised on the basis of the transaction value of identical goods.

6) Transaction Value of Similar Goods

The transaction value of identical goods method and the transaction value of similar goods method are applied in the same way. Conditions relating to trade level and quantities sold also apply, and the same adjustments relating to supply of construction or design work and so on ("assists") have to be made.

The difference between the two methods lies in the definitions of "identical" and "similar." The identical goods method must be applied before the similar goods method, and then only if the transaction value method does not apply.

Goods are considered "similar" under section 45(1) if, in respect of their component materials and characteristics, they closely resemble the goods being appraised; are capable of performing the same functions as and are commercially interchangeable with the goods being appraised; and are produced by or on behalf of the same person, and in the same country as, the goods being appraised.

7) Deductive Value

If the value for duty of goods cannot be appraised under sections 48 to 50, the value for duty of the goods is required by section 51(1) to be calculated using the deductive value. The deductive value is calculated by determining the importer's most common selling price of the goods to Canadian customers and then deducting certain expenses from that selling price. Section 51(2) specifies the calculation for arriving at the selling price.

a) Selling Price under Deductive Value Method

The calculation of selling price and the adjustments that may be needed are discussed below.

i) Sales at Same or Substantially Same Time

1) If there are sales in Canada at the "same or substantially same time" as goods that are being appraised, or identical or similar goods, in the condition in which those goods were imported, the deductive value is the price per unit, determined and adjusted as prescribed by regulations, at which the greatest number of units of the goods being appraised, identical goods, or similar goods are so sold.

2) If there were no sales in Canada of goods being appraised, or identical or similar goods, but there have been sales in the condition in which those goods were imported within ninety days from the date that the goods being appraised were imported, the deductive value is the price per unit, determined and adjusted as prescribed by regulations, at which the greatest number of units of the goods being appraised, identical goods, or similar goods were sold at the earliest of the ninety-day period.

3) If conditions in neither (1) nor (2) are met, but within a period of 180 days after the importation of the goods being appraised there were sales of those goods after being assembled, packaged, or further processed, and the importer of the goods being appraised requests that this provision be applied in the determination of the value for duty of those goods, the deductive value is the price per unit of the goods so sold, determined, and adjusted as prescribed by regulations, of the greatest number of units so sold.

ii) First Trade Level

The sales referred to in the list above must be to purchasers from the importer at the first trade level, provided (1) those purchasers are not related to the importer, (2) those purchasers have not supplied free of charge or at a reduced cost any of the prescribed goods or services for use in connection with the production and sale for export of the goods, and (3) the CBSA determines that there were sufficient number of sales to permit a determination of the unit price.

b) Adjustments

After determining the deductive value in accordance with the conditions referred to above, the following amounts may be deducted from the unit price thus arrived:

1) the amount of
   (a) the commission determined in the prescribed manner and
   (b) the profit and general expenses, including all costs of marketing the goods, considered together as a whole, in connection with sales in Canada of goods of the same class or kind;
2) the costs of transportation and insurance of the goods within Canada and those generally incurred in connection with the sales of the goods in Canada, if not already deducted under (1)(a) and (b) above;
3) the cost, charges, and expenses for transportation from the place of export from where the goods were directly exported to Canada, provided those costs have not already been included in the price paid or payable and were not deducted under the preceding paragraphs;
4) any duties and taxes paid or payable by reason of the importation of the goods or sale of the goods in Canada, including any duties or taxes levied on the goods under the *Customs Tariff*; the *Excise Act, 2001*; the *Excise Tax Act*; the *Special Import Measures Act*; or any other law relating to customs, if not already deducted; and
5) where section 51(2)(c) applies, the amount of the value added to the goods that is attributable to the assembly, packaging, or further processing of the goods in Canada.

8) Computed Value

Under this method, the value of the imported goods is arrived at by aggregating the following amounts: (1) the costs, charges, and expenses incurred in respect of, or the value of materials employed in producing, the goods being appraised; (2) the production and other processing costs of the goods being appraised, determined in the prescribed manner; and (3) the amount, determined in the manner prescribed, for profit and general expenses considered together as a whole, that is generally reflected in sales for export to Canada of goods of the same class or kind as the goods being appraised made by producers in the country of export.

The appropriate method of valuation was in issue in the appeal of *Patagonia International, Inc v Canada (Deputy Minister of National Revenue)*.[91] The appellant claimed that if neither the transaction value method nor the deductive value method was appropriate, the respondent should have used the computed value method to appraise the goods in issue. The respondent determined that

---

91 (2000), 5 TTR (2d) 74 (CITT).

the residual method should be used. In this case, the appellant was the wholly owned subsidiary of Patagonia Inc US, which was, on the basis of the business operations in the United States, found by the Tribunal to be the "producer" of the goods, since it bought all the input material and subcontracted all the operations of putting together the finished clothing, retaining only quality control.

The Tribunal found the first three valuation methods to be inapplicable in this case. In the Tribunal's view, even if there was a buyer-seller relationship between the US parent and its subcontractors in the United States, those sales were not for export to Canada. The evidence indicated that the clothing was not earmarked for Canada, nor were the goods received in the US parent's warehouse segregated for further export to Canada. There was also no buyer-seller relationship between the US parent and the appellant under the circumstances of this case, particularly because of the very high degree of control exercised by the US parent over the appellant; the transactions between it and Patagonia International was rather one of agency. Because no sale took place between the two, the transaction value method could not be used to appraise the value of the clothing in issue.

The deductive value method was also not appropriate since there was no clearly ascertainable method to apportion the appellant's profits between the US and Canadian companies as had been proposed by the appellant. Under those circumstances, the Tribunal agreed with the respondent that the deductive value method could not be applied to appraise the clothing in issue.

With respect to the computed value method claimed by the appellant, the Tribunal was of the view that, for the purpose of the application of that method, the "producer" must be the person that was responsible for bringing the goods into existence, which the Tribunal found was the US parent of the appellant.

The selling price from the US parent to the appellant was set at the former's acquisition cost, plus additional expenses and a markup for profit. According to the testimony, the transfer price between the US parent and the appellant was based on a draft transfer pricing report prepared by an accounting firm. Although it was never formally issued, the appellant's witness testified that the methodology that it laid out was used by the parties to establish transfer prices.

The respondent submitted that, in order to apply the computed value method, the goods appraised must be sold for export. The Tribunal disagreed. In its opinion, section 52(2) of the Act and the Regulations did not comprise such a requirement. Under the Regulations, the costs, charges, and expenses, or the value referred to in section 52(2), must be determined on the basis of the commercial accounts of the producer of the goods being appraised or other sufficient information relating to the production of the goods.

As regards the amount to be added for profit and general expenses, the Regulations provided that it shall be calculated on a percentage basis and determined from sufficient information that is prepared in a manner consistent with generally accepted accounting principles of the country of production of the goods being appraised and is supplied by the producer of the goods being appraised. There was no requirement that the goods produced by the producer be sold for export.

The Tribunal noted that the percentage arrived at, using the information provided by a producer who is *not selling its goods for export*, may or may not be consistent with the amount generally reflected in sales for export to Canada of goods of the same class or kind as the goods being appraised made by producers in the country of export in *sales for export to Canada*. This must be determined on the facts of the specific transactions. The Tribunal did not find any prohibition against using information supplied by a producer that related to sales that were not for export, as long as the amount for profit and general expenses was reflective of the amount for profit and general expenses relating to sales for export to Canada of goods of the same class or kind as the goods being appraised by producers that deal with importers in a manner consistent with that of persons who are not related.

In the Tribunal's view, the clothing in issue should be appraised using the computed value method. The appellant had provided the costing data for the clothing in issue. In order to arrive at a proper value for duty, an amount must be added for profit and general expenses. Nothing indicated, and the respondent did not show, that those numbers were not consistent with the amount for profit and general expenses generally reflected in sales for export to Canada of goods of the same class or kind as the goods being appraised by producers that deal with importers in a manner consistent with that of persons who are not related. Therefore, for the purpose of adding an amount for profit and general expenses pursuant to section 52(2)(b) of the Act, the Tribunal directed the respondent to use those numbers, and returned the matter to the respondent for re-appraisal of the value for duty of the clothing in issue in a manner consistent with these reasons.

Customs D Memorandum D13-8-1 elaborates on this method of valuation.[92]

---

92   D13-8-1 Computed Value Method (*Customs Act*, s 52) (22 March 2001).

9) Residual Method of Valuation

If none of the five foregoing methods of valuation is appropriate, the imported goods must be appraised by using the residual method. Under this method, the value to be used is any one that is derived from among those five methods that, when flexibly applied, conforms closer to the requirements with respect to that method than any other method so applied, provided the information for such determination is available in Canada.

Customs D Memorandum D13-9-1 elaborates on the residual method of valuation.[93]

F. MARKING OF GOODS

1) Marking Requirement

Marking of the origin of goods is an essential element in the determination of the tariff classification and tariff rates. A secondary objective is to protect consumers. Both the *Customs Act* and the *Customs Tariff* require all imported goods to be marked on their containers with the country or geographical origin of the goods at the time of importation. If goods were not marked at the time of importation, with the authorization of the CBSA, they may be marked in a customs office, bonded warehouse, or sufferance warehouse, before they are released by the CBSA.

Other government departments, such as Agriculture and Agri-Food Canada and Industry Canada, have their own requirements. The *Precious Metals Marking Act*[94] and the *Textile Labelling Act*,[95] discussed in Chapter 6, make specific provisions with respect to goods covered by those statutes.

The country or geographical origin of the goods is the country or place where the goods were produced or manufactured.

2) Marking Regulations

Regulations made under section 19 of the *Customs Tariff* require that the marking of origin be sufficiently prominent, must not be deceptive, and must be in characters that remain sufficiently permanent, that is, until the goods reach the ultimate purchaser or the ultimate recipient in Canada. If

---

93 D13-9-1 Residual Basis of Appraisal Method (*Customs Act*, s 53) (19 November 2013).
94 RSC 1985, c P-19.
95 RSC 1985, c T-10.

the goods are from *NAFTA* countries, the marking should appear in one of the three official languages (English, French, or Spanish); if they are from non-*NAFTA* countries, the marking should be only in English or French. If the words "Canada" or "Canadian" appears on the container, the country or geographical area of origin must clearly show the words "Made in" or "Produced in" or "Printed in" as the case may be, so that there is no confusion where the goods originated from.

It is the importer's responsibility to ensure that the goods are marked as required by the legislation.

G. ADMINISTRATIVE DETERMINATIONS AND APPEALS

1) Marking Determination

The marking requirements found in section 35.01 of the Act and the Regulations were noted in Section F(1), above in this chapter. An officer of the CBSA is authorized to make a determination whether imported goods from a *NAFTA* country have been marked before or at the time they are accounted for pursuant to sections 32(1), (2), or (5). If this determination is not made at that time, it is deemed by section 57.01(2) to have been made on the basis of the representations made by the importer.

2) Determination of Value for Duty, Tariff Classification, and Origin

The *Customs Act* empowers the CBSA to determine the value for duty of goods, their tariff classification, and their country of or geographical origin. The value for duty is to be determined in accordance with sections 47 to 55 of the *Customs Act* and section 87 of the *Customs Tariff*, the tariff classification in accordance with sections 10 and 11 of the *Customs Tariff*, and the origin of the goods under section 16 of the *Customs Tariff* and any regulations enacted under that section. This administrative determination can be appealed only in accordance with the procedure set out in the Act and cannot be sidestepped by going directly to the Tribunal or the courts. The Federal Court, in *Abbott Laboratories, Ltd v Canada (Minister of National Revenue)*,[96] dismissed the application of the plaintiff for judicial review of a customs officer's decision that the imported goods did not qualify for NAFTA benefits

---

[96] 2004 FC 140.

on the basis that the privative clause of the Act ousted judicial review by the court and section 18.5 of the *Federal Courts Act* was inapplicable. Similarly, the Federal Court of Appeal rejected an application in *CB Powell Ltd v Canada (Border Services Agency)*[97] when the applicant went to the court directly from a decision of the President of the CBSA. The court pointed out that Parliament had established an administrative process of adjudication and appeal under the *Customs Act* that did not allow the courts, absent exceptional circumstances, to become involved before that process is completed. In its view, the presence of jurisdictional issues was not an exceptional circumstance justifying early recourse to the courts.

3) Payment of Duties and Taxes before Appeal

It is important to note that whether or not an importer pursues the appeal rights given by the *Customs Act*, duties and taxes demanded by the CBSA and owing as a result of the determination, re-determination, or further re-determination have to be paid within the time allowed, or security that is acceptable to the CBSA has to be deposited in lieu of payment, before proceeding to the next appeal level. Until the duties and taxes are secured, the importer will not be allowed to go further.

a) Determination by Designated Officer

The CBSA makes the determination of the value for duty, the tariff classification, and the country or geographical area of origin of the goods that are being imported at the time when, or at any time before, the goods are accounted for. At the first level this is done by a designated CBSA officer. If the officer does not make a determination at that time, section 58(2) of the Act deems that the value for duty, tariff classification, and origin are as declared by the person accounting for the goods. This provision has important implications, as discussed in Section H(2)(a), below in this chapter.

b) Request for Re-determination by Another Officer

If the designated officer made a determination but the importer disagrees with that officer's decision, the importer has ninety days after the determination to seek a re-determination by another designated officer of the CBSA.

---

97 2010 FCA 61, rev'g 2009 FC 528.

c) Re-determination Following Audit

Section 59 empowers the CBSA to make a re-determination of a determination under sections 57.01 (marking of *NAFTA* goods) or 58 (origin, value for duty, or tariff classification) at any time within four years of the determination, or deemed determination, on the basis of an audit, examination, or verification, or if the Minister considers it advisable to do so. If the importer was granted a refund, or was allowed to make a correction to the declaration made at the time of importation or accounting for the goods, the granting of a refund or permission to make the correction is deemed to be a re-determination, in which case the CBSA is given a right to make a further re-determination within four years from the date of deemed re-determination following audit, examination, or verification, or if the Minister deems it advisable, within such further time as may be prescribed.

d) Re-determination and Further Re-determination by President

The importer is given a further right to request a re-determination, this time by applying to the President of the CBSA under section 60. The importer has ninety days to seek that re-determination but can request an extension. The President may extend the ninety-day period if satisfied with the reasons for requesting it.

The President must, without delay, communicate his or her decision to the importer on the request for extension if made, and on the re-determination, as the case may be.

e) Extension of Time Limit

A request for extension of the ninety-day time limit may be granted by the President only if satisfied that, within those ninety days, (1) the application was made within one year after the expiry of the time limit set out in section 60; (2) the importer was unable to act or give instructions to an agent to act on the importer's behalf, or that the importer had a *bona fide* intention to make a request; (3) it is just and equitable to grant the request; (4) the application was made as soon as the circumstances permitted; and (5) there are reasonable grounds for the appeal. If the request is rejected by the President, or if the applicant has not heard from the President regarding the decision, the applicant has a right to appeal the rejection within ninety days of rejection or the President's failure to notify the applicant of the decision within that period, to the Tribunal under section 60.2. Section 60.2(4) requires the Tribunal to apply the same four-pronged test when an application is made to it for granting an extension.

In *Bernard Chaus Inc (Re)*,[98] after the CCRA denied Bernard Chaus Inc its request for an extension of time under section 60.1 on the basis that it missed the ninety-day time limit for requesting a re-determination and that it did not make the application as soon as circumstances permitted, the applicant applied to the Tribunal for an extension of time under section 60.2, which sets out the same four-pronged test as in section 60.1. This was the first such application received by the Tribunal. It granted the application after determining that the applicant met all four parts of the test for the application to succeed.

The Tribunal (1) noted that the applicant had met the first test, that is, it had made the application within one year of the time allowed to make a request under section 60.1; (2) found that the applicant had a *bona fide* intention to make a request within the ninety-day period prescribed by section 60.2(4)(b)(i); (3) found that it would be just and equitable to grant the application because the applicant demonstrated that it would be unfair for it to potentially pay a much higher assessment as a result of missing the deadline by only two days. According to the Tribunal, this was a "minor, technical breach of the Act" that called for relief, especially in light of the fact that the CCRA took a long time (three years) to make the initial re-determination. And (4), the Tribunal was satisfied that the application to the CCRA was made as soon as circumstances permitted within the meaning of section 60.2(4)(b)(iii). During the ninety-two days that elapsed between the CCRA's re-determination and the appellant's application to the CCRA for an extension of time, the appellant ceased Canadian operations, sought professional advice, notified the CCRA of the grounds for its request for a further re-determination, carefully considered the strategy proposed by its advisors, and sought a second opinion. By this evidence, the applicant had demonstrated that it had prepared the application and presented it to the CCRA as early as could reasonably be expected.

IPSCO Inc (Re)[99] was similar to *Bernard Chaus*. The applicant had missed just one day in seeking re-determination. The CCRA denied the extension on the basis that the applicant had not met all four tests set out in section 60.1 to be entitled to an extension. The Tribunal disagreed and granted the extension. It was of the opinion that it would be just and equitable to grant the application since the CCRA's decision would have a significant impact on the applicant, the goods were custom-made and, as such, others would not be unfairly disadvantaged by the extension, and it would not have been

---

98 [2003] CITT No 99 [*Bernard Chaus*].
99 [2005] CITT No 10.

equitable for the applicant to lose its opportunity to argue its case because its request was just one day late. The Tribunal also found that the application was made to the CCRA as soon as circumstances permitted in light of the relative complexity of the matter and a potentially relevant Federal Court of Appeal decision that was rendered after the CCRA's re-determination.

On the other hand, the Tribunal rejected the request in *Volpak Inc v Canada (Border Services Agency)*[100] for an extension of time under section 60.2 because the applicant did not meet the fourth condition for the grant of extension. The CBSA had denied the request for extension because the applicant did not meet the third and fourth condition, namely (1) it would be just and equitable to grant the application and (2) the application was made as soon as circumstances permitted. The applicant contended that the uncertainty and complexity surrounding the Tribunal's jurisdiction to review the rejection of its security proposal required the filing of three discrete legal proceedings, namely: an appeal to the Tribunal, an application for judicial review, and an action in the Federal Court. On this issue, the Tribunal agreed with the CBSA that nothing prevented the applicant from filing an application for an extension of time with the CBSA under section 60 of the Act in order to protect its interests at the same time as the other proceedings. It noted that even if the applicant was faced with uncertainty and complexity, it was definitely capable of filing an application for an extension of time with the CBSA at the same time as it pursued the other three legal avenues. Instead, it waited for eight months. Furthermore, the Tribunal noted that Volpak waited for three months after receiving the Tribunal's order and reasons settling the question of jurisdiction before filing the application for an extension of time with the CBSA.

A similar test was applied by the Federal Court of Appeal with respect to the motion to file an application for judicial review by *Pacific Shower Doors (1995) Ltd v Canada (Canadian International Trade Tribunal)*[101] (a decision under the *Special Import Measures Act*). In denying the motion, the court said that the applicant did not meet all four requirements laid down in *Canada (Minister of Human Resources Development) v Hogervest*,[102] which were (1) a continuing intention on the part of the person presenting the motion to pursue the appeal; (2) the subject matter of the appeal disclosed an arguable case; (3) there is a reasonable explanation for the defaulting party's delay; and (4) there is no prejudice to the other party in allowing the extension. These tests are similar to those in sections 60.1 and 60.2 of the *Customs Act*. This Federal

---

100 (2010), 15 TTR (2d) 52 (CITT).
101 2009 FCA 317.
102 2007 FCA 41.

Court of Appeal decision is an endorsement of the Tribunal's reasoning and is likely to be quoted by the Tribunal in customs cases in the future.

f) President's Additional Powers

Section 61 of the Act empowers the CBSA President to re-determine a determination, re-determination, or further re-determination of (1) the value for duty, tariff classification, and origin of the goods; and (2) the marking on the goods.

With respect to value for duty, tariff classification, and origin, the grounds are

1) on the recommendation of the Attorney General of Canada, if the re-determination would reduce the duties payable, *at any time* but before an appeal is heard by the Tribunal under section 67;
2) where an importer had failed to comply with the customs laws and regulations or had committed an offence in respect of the goods, *at any time*;
3) to give effect to a decision of the Tribunal, the Federal Court of Appeal, or the Supreme Court of Canada, *at any time*; and
4) to give effect to a decision of the Tribunal or the courts that relates to the origin or tariff classification of other like goods imported by the same importer, or that relates to the determination of the value for duty of other goods previously imported by the same importer or owner, *at any time*.

With respect to marking of country of origin, the grounds are

1) if the Minister considers it advisable to do so, within four years after the determination was made;
2) where the importer has failed to comply with the customs laws and regulations or has committed an offence in respect of the goods, *at any time*;
3) to give effect to a decision of the Tribunal, the Federal Court of Appeal, or the Supreme Court of Canada in respect of the goods, *at any time*; and
4) on the recommendation of the Attorney General of Canada, *at any time* but before an appeal is heard by the Tribunal under section 67.

4) Appeals to the Tribunal

a) Filing an Appeal

An appeal from the President's decision lies to the Tribunal if it is filed within ninety days of the President's decision or within such extended time requested by the applicant and granted by the Tribunal. The Tribunal has held, in *GFT Mode Canada v Canada (Deputy Minister of National Revenue)*,[103] that in an appeal the appellant may raise alternative arguments that had not been raised during re-determination by the CBSA, as the Tribunal is not an appellate court but a court of "first instance."

Section 67.1 allows an appeal to be filed within one year after the expiration of the ninety days prescribed for filing the appeal if a request is made to the Tribunal and the request is supported with reasons, that (1) the applicant was unable to act within the prescribed time or to give a mandate to an agent to act on the applicant's behalf, or the applicant had a *bona fide* intention to appeal; (2) it would be just and equitable to grant the extension; (3) the application was made as soon as circumstances permitted; and (4) there are reasonable grounds for the appeal. The caselaw under sections 60.1 and 60.2 referred to in Section G(3)(e), above in this chapter, applies to applications under this section as well.

b) Tribunal's Decision

After publishing a notice in the *Canada Gazette* at least twenty-one days prior to the hearing, the Tribunal must hold a hearing at which any person who enters an appearance with the secretary of the Tribunal on or before the day of the hearing may be heard on the appeal. The Tribunal may make such order, finding, or declaration as the nature of the matter may require.

c) Appeals

The Act contains a privative clause as in the case of appeals to the CBSA. An order, finding, or decision of the Tribunal is not subject to review, and is not to be restrained, prohibited, or removed, set aside, or otherwise dealt with except as provided in the *Customs Act*, namely, by way of an appeal on any question of law to the Federal Court of Appeal. As decided by the Federal Court in *Jockey Canada Co v Canada (Minister of Public Safety and Emergency Preparedness)*,[104] judicial review can only be sought after the statutory procedures have been exhausted and only thereafter can the Federal Court of Appeal exercise its jurisdiction.

---

103 [2000] CITT No 35.
104 2010 FC 396.

d) Appeals to Federal Court of Appeal

An appeal may be filed against the decision of the Tribunal with the Federal Court of Appeal on any question of law within ninety days after its decision, by any of the parties, namely the person who appealed to the Tribunal, the CBSA President, and any person who entered an appearance with the secretary of the Tribunal.

There are several decisions of the Federal Court (and its predecessor the Exchequer Court) as well as of the Supreme Court on the issue of what is a "question of law" as opposed to a "question of fact." The issue frequently arises in tariff classification disputes, and a few of these decisions follow.

In *General Supply Co of Canada v Deputy Minister of National Revenue (Customs and Excise)*,[105] the issue was whether the Tariff Board correctly concluded that a certain power shovel imported by the appellant from the United States fell under tariff item 427 ("machinery") or should, as contended by the appellant, be classified under tariff item 431 ("shovel") or under 438 ("conveyance," and therefore a "vehicle" under the *Customs Act* definition). The Tariff Board did not make an express reference to the statute for its conclusion, but its conclusion necessarily involved the construction of certain portions of the statute, namely tariff items 427, 431, and 438, and section 2(r) of the *Customs Act* [1927]. The Deputy Minister of National Revenue submitted that all that the Tariff Board did was to make a finding on the basis of the evidence before it. The court said that in interpreting the tariff items and the section of the *Customs Act*, the Board was determining a question of law, which gave the appellant a right to appeal under the Act.

In *Dominion Engineering Works Ltd v A B Wing Ltd*,[106] the respondent imported a power shovel of 2½ cc dipper capacity, which it entered under tariff item 427. The Deputy Minister of National Revenue confirmed that classification, but the respondent appealed, claiming that the power shovel should have been classified under tariff item 427a. The Tariff Board reversed the Deputy Minister's classification. On the question of whether the Board erred as a matter of law in holding that the power shovel came under tariff item 427a, the court concluded that it was within the Board's competence to settle where the line of difference of class or kind of power shovels, according to the differences in nominal dipper capacities, should be drawn. In drawing that line, the Board's decision was a decision of fact, with which the court had no jurisdiction to interfere.

---

105 (1952), [1953] Ex CR 185.
106 [1956] Ex CR 379.

The Supreme Court clarified the distinction between a question of law and a question of fact in *Deputy Minister of National Revenue (Customs and Excise) v Ferguson Industries Ltd*.[107] In this case, the respondent had imported two electrically driven motor winches through a Belgium firm, but the electric motors and other control equipment for those winches were supplied directly through a firm in England. The motors and control equipment arrived before the winches. The motors were entered under tariff item 44516-1, and the control equipment under tariff item 44022-1. The latter did not attract duty, but the motors did. The Deputy Minister confirmed the classification of the motors under tariff item 44516-1. The respondent appealed to the Tariff Board, which allowed the appeal. The Exchequer Court dismissed the appeal, holding that the Board did not err as a matter of law.

The Supreme Court allowed the Deputy Minister's appeal, holding that this was a question of law and not of fact. The *facts* were that the motors and control equipment were, as the Board said, *parts* of an original installation ordered from one company and designed as a unit to perform one function. The *question of law* was whether on those facts the motors should be regarded for customs classification as parts of winches rather than as motors. The Court determined that the Board erred *in law* when it held that parts are to be regarded as falling within the classification of the whole thing rather than as parts.

In *Utex Corporation v Canada (Deputy Minister of National Revenue)*,[108] the Federal Court of Appeal held that the Tribunal erred in law as its decision was not supported by the weight of evidence.

The Federal Court of Appeal applied the reasonableness simpliciter standard in *Richards Packaging Inc v Deputy Minister of National Revenue*[109] when it rejected a request for review of the Tribunal's decision, as it was satisfied that the Tribunal's decision was reasonable and supported by evidence.

In *Mattel*,[110] the Supreme Court of Canada ruled that the appropriate standard of review applicable to the Tribunal's decisions is correctness with respect to questions of law. It characterized the standards of review as points occurring on a spectrum of curial deference that ranges from patent unreasonableness at one end of the continuum—that of greatest deference—through reasonableness simpliciter, to correctness at the other end of the spectrum, where the least deference is accorded the decision of the administrative tribunal.

---

107 [1973] SCR 21.
108 2001 FCA 54.
109 (2000), 266 NR 352.
110 Above note 48.

e) Disposition

In disposing of an appeal under section 68(1), the court may make such order or finding as the nature of the matter requires, or refer the matter back to the Tribunal for a rehearing. In a leading case, *Sable Offshore Energy Inc v Canada (Customs and Revenue Agency)*,[111] the Federal Court of Appeal, while setting aside the decision of the Tribunal because the specific reasons it had given for the conclusion it reached were legally flawed, substituted the decision that the Tribunal ought to have given and allowed the appellant's appeal on the tariff classification. That decision is further discussed in Section D(10) in Chapter 2.

Further appeal lies to the Supreme Court of Canada under the *Federal Courts Act*[112] and the *Supreme Court Act*.[113]

5) References to Tribunal

Section 70 of the Act allows the CBSA President to refer to the Tribunal for an opinion on any question relating to the value for duty of any goods or class of goods, tariff classification, and origin. The word "opinion" is not defined, but section 70(2) provides that sections 67 and 68 apply in respect of a reference as if it were an appeal taken pursuant to section 67. In a reference made by the Deputy Minister in 1998,[114] the Tribunal noted that (1) the referral to sections 67 and 68 is unreserved; (2) there were no words in these sections that limited or altered their application in the context of a reference; (3) elsewhere in the Act, where a section incorporated by reference other sections and there was an intention that the incorporated sections were to be limited or altered, Parliament had made that intention clear; and (4) Parliament, in referring to sections 67 and 68 in section 70, elected not to include words altering or limiting their application, suggesting, thereby, that it intended those sections to apply, without restriction, to a proceeding initiated pursuant to section 70. The Tribunal, therefore, held that its opinion given under section 70 is binding on the Deputy Minister.

---

111 (2002), 6 TTR (2d) 567 (CITT), rev'd 2003 FCA 220.
112 RSC 1985, c F-7.
113 RSC 1985, c S-26.
114 *Reference by the Deputy Minister of National Revenue under section 70 of the Customs Act, RSC 1985, c 1 (2nd Supp), regarding the tariff classification of certain butteroil blends*, AP-98-055 (unreported). The Federal Court of Appeal in *Dairy Farmers of Canada v Canada (Deputy Minister of National Revenue)*, 2001 FCA 77, held that the Tribunal did not err in its conclusion that its opinion is binding on the Deputy Minister of National Revenue, as indicated in the text above.

6) Appeals to Provincial Courts

a) Special Provisions

Goods prohibited from importation have been classified under three tariff items of Chapter 98 of the *Customs Tariff*: 9897.00.00, 9898.00.00, and 9899.00.00. The first two are discussed in Chapter 2.

Tariff item 9899.00.00 covers books, printed paper, drawings, paintings, prints, photographs, or representations of any kind that under the *Criminal Code* (1) are deemed to be obscene; (2) constitute hate propaganda; (3) are of a treasonable character; (4) are of a seditious character; (5) are posters and handbills depicting scenes of crime or violence; and (6) are photographic, film, video, or other visual representations, including those made by mechanical or electronic means, or written material, that are child pornography within the meaning of section 163.1 of the *Criminal Code*.[115]

Section 71 of the *Customs Act* provides a special appeal procedure with respect to goods falling within this tariff item if they have been refused entry into Canada by an administrative determination. The Tribunal does not have jurisdiction to hear an importer's appeal; that jurisdiction is conferred only on a superior court of the province in which the goods were imported.

The leading case, in which the constitutionality of the prohibition provisions of section 71 was upheld, is *Little Sisters Book and Art Emporium v Canada (Minister of Justice)*.[116] The Supreme Court upheld the decision of the trial judge that the provisions that incorporate the definition of "obscene material" in section 163(8) of the *Criminal Code* were a justifiable intrusion into the citizen's rights guaranteed by the *Canadian Charter of Rights* since it was directed to the prevention of harm, and the fact that customs officials applied the provisions in a differential manner did not vitiate the legislation itself.

b) Seizure and Forfeiture of Goods or Conveyances

This topic is dealt with under the discussion of enforcement, in Sections I(2) and I(3), below in this chapter.

H. ABATEMENT AND REFUND OF DUTIES

Part IV of the *Customs Act* contains provisions for abatements and refunds for reasons set out in sections 73 to 81.

---

115 RSC 1985, c C-46 (as amended).
116 (1996), 131 DLR (4th) 486 (BCSC), aff'd (1998), 109 BCAC 49, rev'd 2000 SCC 69.

1) Abatement

Abatement of duties is provided for in section 73 and is subject to the *Abatement of Duties Payable Regulations*[117] prescribed pursuant to section 81.

Subject to the Regulations, an abatement of duties can be claimed of the whole or part of the duties if (1) after shipment but before release the goods suffered damage or deterioration, and (2) if goods that were deposited in a bonded warehouse suffered a loss in volume or weight arising from natural causes while in the warehouse.

2) Refund of Duties

Section 74 sets out the circumstances under which an importer can claim a refund of all or part of the duties that were paid on imported goods under the *Customs Tariff*, but those paid under the other statutes (the *Special Import Measures Act;* the *Excise Act, 2001;* and the *Excise Tax Act*) are not refundable.

A refund can be claimed in the following situations:

1) after shipment but before release, the goods had suffered damage, deterioration, or destruction;
2) the quantity released is less than the quantity on which duties were paid;
3) the quality of goods released is inferior to those on which duties were paid;
4) the calculation of the duties owing was based on a clerical, typographical, or similar error;
5) no claim had been made for preferential rate of tariff on goods exported from a *NAFTA* country or from Chile at the time the goods were accounted for;
6) no claim had been made for preferential rate of tariff on goods imported from Costa Rica, Columbia, Peru, a *CIFTA* beneficiary, or from a European Free Trade Association (EFTA) state under the respective trade agreements, at the time of accounting;
7) in compliance with the conditions set out in the *Customs Tariff*, the imported goods, or the imported goods incorporated into other goods, were sold or otherwise disposed of to a person coming within the terms of the *Customs Tariff* or regulations made under the *Customs Tariff* (in this last case, the refund has to be claimed before any other use is made of the goods); and

---

117 SOR/86-946.

8) the duties were overpaid or paid in error for any reason that may be prescribed.

Section 74(6) gives a general power to the Minister to refund the whole or part of the duties paid in error, without an application, for any reason referred to in items (1) to (3), (4), and (8) above.

A claim for refund must be made within the prescribed time, but in certain circumstances the Minister may authorize a refund without an application, within four years after the goods were accounted for.

Detailed requirements for making an application for refund are set out in the *Refund of Duties Regulations*.[118]

a) Deemed Re-determination

The grant of a refund, or the denial of a claim for refund, is required by sections 74(1.1), (4), and (5) to be treated as if it were a re-determination of the origin, tariff classification, and value for duty of the imported goods pursuant to section 59(1)(a). This was found to create unintended consequences for recovery of a refund once made, when the CBSA makes a re-determination after the expiration of four years from the time of refund, as the CBSA realized in *Grodan Inc v President of the Canada Border Services Agency*.[119] The Tribunal held in that case that if a refund was granted between the thirty-seventh and forty-eighth month after the claim was made, the CBSA has a further year to make a re-determination, but if the refund was made after the forty-eighth month expired, it ceases to have jurisdiction to make a re-determination.

I. ENFORCEMENT

1) Powers of Officers

Wide-ranging powers of officers are scattered throughout the *Customs Act* by which CBSA officials perform their duties and carry out their responsibilities. As every person arriving in Canada from anywhere outside the country knows, his or her first encounter is with a CBSA official. In fact, if a person has arrived by air or sea, his or her profile is known in advance by the CBSA, as the carrier is required by section 11(3) and the *Presentation of Persons (2003)*

---

118 *Refund of Duties Regulations*, SOR/98-48, am SOR/2004-126, SOR/3005-213; SOR/2005-386, SOR/2006-222.
119 AP-2011-030 (20 June 2012).

Regulations[120] to provide passenger information well before landing. In the case of imports and exports, the CBSA officers' powers begin from the time goods or vehicles enter or at the time they are about to leave Canada. If they discover a non-compliance situation, the Act empowers them to resolve it, whether by way of seizure and forfeiture of goods and vehicles or by resorting to administrative action, penalties, or prosecution, according to the seriousness of the contraventions.

Administrative actions can take various forms. They include termination of privileges given under special programs to frequent travellers; suspension and revocation of licences issued to customs brokers, warehouses, and duty-free shops; as well as suspension of special privileges accorded to regular CBSA customers such as importers, carriers, and couriers who were allowed fast clearance of their goods and their accounting at a later date. As the Act allows a "self assessment" privilege to importers under which the CBSA is deemed to have accepted the valuation and tariff classification as declared by an importer,[121] as in income tax collection, the CBSA is given a right to audit importers at a subsequent date and issue what are called "Detailed Adjustment Statements," or DASs. DASs may lead to demands to pay up additional duties and taxes that were avoided, and in some cases may lead to administrative monetary penalties and even criminal proceedings.

If non-compliance is handled administratively, the Act gives a person whose privileges are terminated or licence withdrawn, or whose goods are seized and forfeited, an administrative recourse that, after it has gone through the various specified levels of appeal, can be the subject of judicial review. Imposition of administrative monetary penalties, too, is subject to the same recourse. The latter process is described in Section J(1), below in this chapter.

a) Administrative and Investigative Powers Distinguished

The distinction between administrative powers, which include auditing, and investigation powers has to be borne in mind by CBSA officials since, occasionally, the two areas intersect, bringing into focus the rights guaranteed by the *Canadian Charter of Rights and Freedoms*.[122] Similarly, some travellers who report the goods they had imported, on arrival, may be referred to a secondary process (the secondary) whereby they may be subjected to probing questions, examination of baggage, and even body search. Courts

---

120 SOR/2003-323, am SOR/2005-385, SOR/2006-154, SOR/2008-24, SOR/2008-27.
121 See s 4.5 Customs Self-assessment (CSA) Program, Customs D Memorandum D17-1-7.
122 *Canadian Charter of Rights and Freedoms*, Part I of the *Constitution Act, 1982*, being Schedule B to the *Canada Act 1982* (UK), 1982, c 11, s 1.

have insisted that when a routine inspection (or audit) crosses over into investigation of wrongdoing with a view to laying criminal charges, *Charter* guarantees have to be accorded to the person being investigated.

The line between the purely administrative processes of audit and inspection, and investigation has been clarified by the Supreme Court in *Comité Paritaire de l'Industrie de la Chemise v Potash*[123] as follows:

> An inspection is characterized by a visit to determine whether there is compliance with a given statute. The basic intent is not to uncover a breach of the Act; the purpose is rather to protect the public. On the other hand, if the inspector enters the establishment because he has reasonable grounds to believe that there has been a breach of the Act, there is no longer inspection but a search as the intent is then essentially to see if those reasonable grounds are justified and seize anything which may serve as proof of the offence.

The Supreme Court has further clarified when an inspection (or audit in customs cases) crosses into investigation because, in the latter situation, the safeguards provided by the *Charter* become available and evidence obtained in violation of those safeguards will be excluded by the courts, though in some cases the court has looked the other way and allowed it. In *R v Jarvis*,[124] the Court set out seven factors that would assist in ascertaining whether an inquiry's purpose is to investigate penal liability, and if the predominant purpose of an inquiry is to determine the latter, all *Charter* protections that are relevant in the criminal context must apply. The same issue arose in the companion case *R v Ling*,[125] and the Court, reiterating the judgment in *Jarvis*, pointed out that all evidence gathered subsequent to the point in time when an inquiry turns to investigation will be excluded if prior warning is not given to the person that the purpose is to further the investigation or prosecution for an offence.

2) Enforcement Powers

Powers of the CBSA officers under sections 98 to 105 of the Act include search of the person (sections 98 and 99.2 to 99.4) and examination of goods (section 99); power to stop anyone who evades presentation of himself or herself as required by section 11(1) (section 99.1); detention of controlled goods, in-

---

123 [1994] 2 SCR 406 at para 5, La Forest J (translated from Lucie Angers).
124 2002 SCC 73.
125 2002 SCC 74.

cluding those about to be exported and disposal of goods illegally imported (sections 101 and 102); and power to call other persons to assist them in the exercise of their powers of search, seizure, or detention (section 104).

a) Search of the Person

Section 98 authorizes a customs officer to detain a person for the purposes of search of his or her person and accompanying baggage. A mere suspicion is enough to send a person to the secondary for such search. Experienced officers are wary about travellers who arrive from certain countries that are known to be narcotic or smuggling sources. Certain itineraries or a sudden unexplained change in them can arouse suspicion. On the other hand, some travellers, fatigued after a long flight, encounter these wary officials and may not be able to grasp some probing questions asked by them. Numerous cases are brought before the courts to challenge the treatment they received at the hands of officials. While courts are sympathetic with the travellers' plight, they understand that officials have a difficult job to do and that they do it in the best possible way they know.

In the case of *Kelly v Palazzo*,[126] the Ontario Court of Appeal held that a senior officer only has to review the decision of the customs officer who referred the traveller to the secondary. A review, in its view, connotes a process wherein senior supervisory personnel assess the fitness of decisions made by subordinate customs officers; it does not suggest a *de novo* investigation as to whether the reviewing officer reasonably believed that the person to be searched is carrying drugs.

Border searches are often conducted taking into account certain factors that are known to cause suspicion, such as the country of origin of the traveller. In *R v Simmons*,[127] the accused had been detained at the border for search. While his argument that his *Charter* rights were violated when he was detained was successful at the Federal Court level, the Supreme Court held that border searches for contraband fell into a special category and that it would be wrong to conclude that a brief restraint involved in the ordinary progressive border search pursuant to the *Customs Act* is detention within the meaning of section 10 of the *Charter*. In its judgment, the term "detention" for the purposes of section 10 did not apply to routine questioning, but it did apply when referred to the secondary officer for intrusive search. At that stage there was a violation of his rights, which rendered the purpose of

---

126 2008 ONCA 82, leave to appeal to SCC refused, [2008] SCCA No 152.
127 (1984), 45 OR (2d) 609 (CA), aff'd [1988] 2 SCR 495.

the search unreasonable, and that violation cannot be justified by section 1 of the *Charter*. Despite this, the Court admitted the evidence, holding that the cannabis discovered in the search was real evidence as opposed to evidence extracted by confession and its admission would not tend to affect adversely the fairness of the trial. Therefore, it should not be excluded under section 24(2). Furthermore, in the Court's opinion, the customs officers acted in good faith in accordance with the existing statutory requirements.

A body search is considered very intrusive and courts have tried to rein in that power when officers disregarded basic human rights of a traveller. In *R v Monney*,[128] the search involved a passive "bedpan vigil," which the Supreme Court held not to be as invasive as a body cavity search or medical procedure such as the administration of emetics. The Court also held that the phrase "on or about the person" occurring in section 98 included "inside" the person, and therefore the section applied to travellers suspected of ingesting narcotics. The Court restored the conviction of the accused, which had been set aside by the Federal Court of Appeal.

The Supreme Court has not been consistent with its decisions. *R v Therriens*[129] is a case in point. The accused in this case was asked to give a breath sample. At no time was he informed of the right to retain and instruct counsel and he was never placed under arrest. The Court held that the accused was "detained" within the meaning of section 10 of the *Charter*. "Detention" refers to restraint of liberty other than arrest. While detention required some form of compulsion or coercion, such compulsion or coercion is not limited to physical restraint; it is sufficient if the officer assumed some control over the movement of a person by demand or direction. On the question whether evidence obtained in violation of the *Charter* right of the accused should be excluded, the Court held that the evidence was properly excluded because the police officer flagrantly violated the *Charter* without any statutory authority for so doing. It said that to admit the evidence on the facts and circumstances of this case would be to invite police officers to disregard the *Charter* rights of the citizen and to do so with assurance of impunity; it would bring the administration of justice into disrepute.

b) Examination of Goods

Section 99 of the Act gives the CBSA officers extensive powers to gain access to goods imported or exported, including mail that weighs over 30 grams,

---

128 (1997), 153 DLR (4th) 617 (Ont CA), rev'd [1999] 1 SCR 652.
129 [1985] 1 SCR 613.

with certain exceptions; to open any packages, coverings, and containers; to take samples; and to examine the goods or mail, for the purpose of verifying their origin, tariff classification, and value for duty, as well as to ensure their admissibility (or export) under the various federal laws relating to customs. The exception is of mail weighing less than 30 grams, which can be opened only if the addressee consents or there is attached to it a label from the sender in Form RE 601 of the *Letter Post Regulations* of the *Universal Postal Convention*.

This power to examine goods must be exercised before or at the time the imported goods are released or the goods are exported from Canada. However, the goods may be examined after they have been released if, on reasonable grounds, a CBSA officer suspects that an error was made with respect to the origin, tariff classification, value for duty, or quantity of goods released, or a drawback (refund of duty), or with respect to a refund claimed by an applicant, or where goods or conveyance might have contravened any laws relating to importation or exportation. The officer may direct that the goods or conveyance be moved to a place where they can properly be examined. Samples can be taken or drawn in the case of liquid cargo.

3) Seizure of Goods and Conveyances

Seizure of goods is the first step in the enforcement process when an officer finds illegally imported goods or goods the importation of which is prohibited by law. If those goods are found in a vehicle, the vehicle too is liable to seizure. Even if the goods found their way illegally into the country, if they are subsequently found in a vehicle, goods as well as the vehicle are liable to seizure. In *Sandness v Canada*,[130] the Exchequer Court held that the penalty of forfeiture is independent of the guilt or innocence of the owner of the vehicle, and in *Gosselin v Canada*,[131] it held that the subsequent transportation of smuggled cigarettes need not be directly associated with the importation.

4) Forfeiture

The most potent enforcement tool in the arsenal of the CBSA is the penalty of forfeiture, a right enjoyed by the Crown from the inception of customs law, which is matched only by the decade-old administratively imposed monetary

---

130 [1933] Ex CR 78.
131 [1954] Ex CR 658.

penalty for violations that have been designated in the *Designated Provisions (Customs) Regulations*.[132] Together, and even independently, these two types of penalty render recourse to the criminal law largely unnecessary, and the latter is reserved by the CBSA for serious breaches of the *Customs Act*.

Section 122 embodies the old common law rule that forfeiture accrues from the time of contravention of the Act in respect of the goods and the conveyance used in respect of those goods.

The law of forfeiture was eloquently summarized by Sedgwick J in *"Frederick Gerring Jr" (The) v Canada*[133] more than a century ago, this way:

> In the eye of the statute the vessel itself is the offender. The statute gives to it a moral consciousness—a personality—a capacity to act within or without the law, and imposes upon it the liability of forfeiture in the event of a transgression .... If I bring dutiable goods into Canada without paying duty, I am liable to penalty although ignorant of the tariff. The goods themselves, endowed by law as they are with faculty and right of speech, cannot plead my ignorance either of law or fact as a bar to forfeiture.

As Rand J pointed out in *Industrial Acceptance Corp v Canada*,[134] forfeiture of property used in violation of revenue laws has for several centuries been one of the characteristic features of their enforcement. He added:

> Smuggling, illegal manufacture of liquor, illegal sales of narcotics and like activities, because of their high profits and demand, in certain sections of society, for them, take on the character of organized action against the forces of the law. The necessity to strike against not only the persons but everything that has enabled them to carry out their purposes has been universally recognized.

In that case, the Supreme Court held that the forfeiture was constitutionally within the power of the federal government and is an integral part of the criminal law; therefore, the seizure was not in conflict with the property and civil rights jurisdiction of the provinces.

Section 122 expressly states that all goods seized by customs under the Act, including goods that have been prohibited from importation, and any conveyance that has been used to carry the goods, with respect to which the importer or the carrier has contravened the Act, are forfeited to the Crown,

---

132 SOR/2002-336, am SOR/2005-304, SOR/2006-149, SOR/2008-23, SOR/2009-267.
133 (1897), 27 SCR 271 at 284–85 [*The "Frederick Gerring Jr"*].
134 [1953] 2 SCR 273 at 277.

and this penalty of forfeiture accrues from the time of the contravention, that is, from the time the goods are brought into Canada, or from the time the conveyance is used to carry them into Canada.

a) Effecting Forfeiture

Section 122 further provides that no act or proceeding by the Crown is necessary subsequent to the contravention to effect the forfeiture.

b) *In Rem* Action

Forfeiture is an *in rem* action against the goods or the conveyance, in which the goods or the conveyance is the defendant, as Sedgewick J indicated in *The "Frederick Gerring Jr."*[135]

In that case, customs officers had seized the ship for fishing outside the three-mile limit when it had drifted into the three-mile limit in violation of the Imperial statute 59 Geo III, c38 and the *Convention of 1818* between the United Kingdom and the United States. The Court held that the ship was rightly condemned and forfeited.

Two other Supreme Court decisions illustrate the law of forfeiture further. In *R v Mason*[136] customs officers seized a vessel that was hovering within Canadian waters with cargo of contraband liquors on board. The Court held that the schooner became forfeited by operation of law. Proof of the forfeiture itself was established after the offence had been committed. The Court pointed out that when the presence of the liquor was established as a fact, forfeiture, which followed as a matter of law, related back to the time of hovering in territorial waters. "The forfeiture itself is not brought about by any act of the customs officials or officers of the Department, but it is the legal unescapable consequence of the unlawful importation."[137]

In *R v Krakowec*,[138] excise officials seized a truck that was used for removing spirits unlawfully manufactured, contrary to section 181 of the *Excise Act*, which has provisions similar to section 122 of the *Customs Act*. The truck was forfeited, even though it belonged not to the owner of the contraband spirits but to a finance company that had sold it to the owner under a conditional sales contract. In holding that the truck was rightly seized and forfeited, Rinfret J observed,

---

135 Above note 133.
136 [1935] SCR 513.
137 *Ibid* at 518.
138 [1932] SCR 134.

[I]t is not assuming too much to say that it must have been known to the legislature, when it passed the *Excise Act* that a great many drivers of motor vehicles are not the owners thereof.... If section 181 was meant to apply only to vehicles driven by the owners thereof, it is obvious with what ease the provision respecting forfeiture could be evaded.[139]

c) Limitation

Section 122 provides that it is subject to section 113, which expressly bars any seizure or ascertained forfeiture under the Act more than six years after the contravention.

5) Ascertained Forfeiture

The ascertained procedure is used when goods or conveyances that contravened the *Customs Act*, and thereby incurred the penalty of forfeiture, cannot be found or it is impractical to seize them, for example, where the imported material is incorporated into another article. In cases where this procedure is used, the CBSA officer determines the value of goods and the amount of duties, if any, that would have been payable on them and demands payment which, if not paid or contested, becomes a debt owing to the Crown.

The ascertained forfeiture process is a four-step administrative process: (1) precondition set out in section 124; (2) review under sections 129(1)(d) and 130(1), (2), and (3); (3) Minister's decision under section 131 (which is not subject to review except in the manner provided by section 135(1); and (4) appeal by way of action under section 135(1). The Supreme Court of Canada described this procedure in *Martineau v Canada (Minister of National Revenue)*[140] as a civil collection mechanism, and that it cannot properly be classified as a penal proceeding. The fact that a single violation can result in both a notice of ascertained forfeiture and a criminal proceeding is irrelevant. According to the Court, the proper test is the nature of the proceeding, not the nature of the act. It upheld the judgment of the Federal Court, which had ruled that while the administrative penalty under the section was serious, it was not a true penal consequence required by section 11(d) of the *Canadian Charter of Rights and Freedoms*.[141]

---

139 *Ibid* at 142–43.
140 2004 SCC 81.
141 Above note 122. See also http://globalnews.ca/news/1042861/supreme-court-strikes-down-canadas-anti-prostitution-laws.

6) Appeals

Appeals against forfeiture, ascertained forfeiture, and other administrative penalties lie to the Minister of Public Safety and Emergency Preparedness, and from the Minister to the Federal Court. Appeals against penalties under the Administrative Monetary Penalties System (AMPS) of the *Customs Act* (discussed in Section J(1), below in this chapter) follow the same appeal route as that under the *Agriculture and Agri-Food Administrative Monetary Penalties Act*[142] with the exception that an appeal from the Minister is heard by the Federal Court and not by the Agriculture Review Tribunal.

7) Third Party Claims

Since a person may have used vehicles that belonged to innocent third parties to transport illegal goods, relief against forfeiture is provided to those parties by sections 138 to 141. The procedure is not available to persons in whose possession the goods or conveyance was when seized or detained.

Sections 138 to 141 establish a procedure for persons who claim an interest in the goods or conveyance seized as forfeit as owner, mortgagee, hypothecary creditor, lien-holder, or holder of any like interest, to apply to the Minister of Public Safety and Emergency Preparedness for a decision that the applicant's interest in the goods or conveyance is not affected by the seizure or detention. The application must be made by giving notice in writing within ninety days after the seizure or detention to the officer who seized or detained the goods or conveyance or to an officer at the customs office closest to the place where the seizure or detention took place. The application must be supported by evidence proving the person's interest in the goods or conveyance seized, and any other evidence the Minister requests; such evidence may be proffered by affidavit.

If the application is made within ninety days of seizure or detention, or if extended, within the extended time, and the Minister is satisfied that the conditions set out in section 139 have been met (for example, good faith, absence of complicity, or collusion), the Minister must make a determination that the applicant's interest in the goods or conveyance is not affected by the seizure or detention. The Minister must further determine the nature and extent of the applicant's interest at the time of the contravention or use.

---

142 SC 1995, c 40.

a) Late Applications

If an applicant has missed the ninety-day time limit prescribed by section 138(1), a late application may be accepted by the Minister, provided the person makes an application within one year after the expiration of that time limit and satisfies the Minister that (1) within the ninety-day period the person was unable to act or to instruct another person to act in the person's name, (2) the person had a *bona fide* intention to apply within the ninety-day period, (3) it would be just and equitable to grant the application, and (4) the application was made as soon as circumstances permitted.

b) Conditions

For an applicant to succeed, section 139 requires the following conditions to be met: (1) the interest in the goods or conveyance was acquired in good faith before the contravention or use; (2) the applicant was innocent of any complicity or collusion in the contravention or use; and (3) the applicant exercised all reasonable care in respect of any person permitted to obtain possession of the goods or conveyance that satisfied the applicant that it was not likely to be used in the contravention, or, if the applicant is a mortgagee, hypothecary creditor, or lien-holder, the applicant exercised that care in relation to the mortgagor, hypothecary debtor, or lien-giver.

c) Appeal against Minister's Decision

If an applicant is dissatisfied with the Minister's determination with respect to the nature and extent of its interest in the seized or forfeited goods or conveyance, it can resort to the civil procedure provided in section 139. The applicant must apply for an order to the superior court of the province within ninety days after the Minister has notified the applicant of the decision under section 138. To be successful, the applicant must satisfy the conditions set out in section 139.1(6), which are identical to those specified under section 139 above with respect to the application made to the Minister.

> A few decisions will illustrate the interpretation of this section. In *Beach v Deputy Minister of National Revenue (Customs and Excise)*,[143] the applicant alleged that the property that was seized by customs belonged to the returning resident and that he was carrying it on the latter's behalf, without complicity with him. Believing the story, the Ontario court declared there was no basis for forfeiture and that the returning resident is entitled to its

---

143 (1992), 8 TTR 55 (Ont Ct Gen Div), rev'd in part on costs (1992), 10 OR (3d) 572 (CA).

return without penalty. In *Coombs v Canada (Deputy Minister of National Revenue, Customs and Excise)*,[144] the Newfoundland Supreme Court pointed out that the applicant had the onus to establish that she acted as a reasonable person would in the circumstances in lending the vehicle to the person from whom it was seized, but that onus can be discharged in some cases by reliance on personal knowledge; a positive inquiry is not mandated in every case. The Court declared that the applicant's interest as owner was not affected by the seizure as she had exercised all reasonable care. The same court pointed out in *Evan's Sales & Service Ltd v Canada (Minister of National Revenue, Customs and Excise)*[145] that section 139.1(6)(c) requires an applicant to make some positive attempt to satisfy himself that the person permitted to obtain possession of the goods that were seized was not likely to use them in contravention of the *Customs Act*.

In *Down East Toyota v Canada (Minister of National Revenue, Customs and Excise)*,[146] the New Brunswick Court of Appeal upheld the decision of the lower court that the applicant had satisfied the requirements of section 139 when it believed that the person from whom its truck was seized had falsely declared to the applicant in a credit application completed by phone that he was a US resident, whereas he was in reality a Canadian resident; the court declared that the applicant's interest was not affected by the seizure.

The decision of the Federal Court, Trial Division, in *McGregor v Canada (Minister of National Revenue, Customs and Excise)*[147] went against the applicant. The applicant had lent her truck to her spouse, who had previously used it to transport contraband alcohol. The court held that the applicant did not exercise all reasonable care as required by the section to prevent the use of the truck to commit a violation of the law. Her application was dismissed. Similarly, in *El Khoury v Canada (Minister of National Revenue, Customs and Excise)*,[148] the court held that the applicant was not entitled to the declaration as he had failed to make any inquiries. That, the court said, amounted to failure to exercise due diligence; the onus placed by the section was not met by the mere absence of complicity in the offence.

---

144 (1992), 10 TTR 235 (NL SCTD).
145 (1990), 3 TTR 270 (NL SCTD).
146 (1994), 145 NBR (2d) 116 (CA).
147 (1994), 93 FTR 247 (TD).
148 (1996), 207 NR 311 (CA).

d) Appeal against Provincial Superior Court's Decision

An applicant who fails to obtain an order in its favour from the provincial superior court can appeal to the court of appeal of the province and the ordinary procedure of the court applies.

e) Goods or Conveyance to Be Given to Successful Applicant

Where an applicant succeeds in getting a declaration from the court that his or her interest in the goods or conveyance is not affected by the seizure, the Minister is directed by section 141 to surrender it to the applicant. If the CBSA has sold or disposed of the goods or conveyance, the Minister is directed to pay the applicant an amount calculated on the basis of the applicant's interest, but the maximum amount of payment must not exceed the proceeds of the sale or disposition less the cost incurred by the CBSA in respect of those goods or conveyance. If there is no surplus left after the costs of disposition, the applicant is not entitled to any payment.

J. PENALTY FOR VIOLATION OF DESIGNATED PROVISIONS

1) Administrative Monetary Penalties

The *Customs Act* was amended in 2001 to provide for an administratively imposed monetary penalty system (AMPS) for contraventions that are considered by the CBSA as not warranting prosecution under the criminal law. Section 109.1 created a special category of offences from among the contraventions of the Act, as well as breaches of a term or condition of a licence issued under the Act, or failure to comply with an undertaking given by an importer or carrier, terming them as *designated provisions,* the designation being made by the *Designated Provisions (Customs) Regulations*[149] prescribed under the authority of section 109.1(3).

Instead of prosecuting a contravention, section 109.1 authorizes the Minister of Public Safety and Emergency Preparedness to impose a monetary penalty of up to $25,000 or such lesser sum as the Minister may direct. This provision has proved very effective, saving the CBSA considerable financial and human resources. Prior to the AMPS, the only tool available was a licence revocation or other sanction such as forfeiture or prosecution. If the contravention was minor, usually prosecution was not resorted to and the contravention was ignored. The CBSA data indicate that over

---

149 Above note 132.

a period of five years since the AMPS was utilized, it issued nearly 60,000 penalties (amps) for contravention of the designated provisions. Amps were most frequently resorted to for the contravention of sections 7.1, 11(3), 12(1), 13, 31, 32(3), 32.2, 33, 35.01, 95, and 107.1, and for breaches of section 12 of the *Customs Bonded Warehouse Regulations*,[150] sections 12 and 17 of the *Customs Sufferance Warehouse Regulations*,[151] section 41 of the *Accounting for Imported Goods and Payment of Duties Regulations*,[152] section 5 of the *Reporting of Exported Goods Regulations*,[153] and section 118 of the *Customs Tariff*.[154]

The largest monetary penalty issued was for $522,000 for contraventions of the Low Value Shipment Program in *United Parcel Service Canada Ltd v Canada (Minister of Public Safety and Emergency Preparedness)*.[155] An application by UPS for judicial review was dismissed by the Federal Court since the Minister did not exceed the statutory authority and the decision was transparent and supported by the evidence. In this case, 173 contraventions had been consolidated into one administrative proceeding. Even though the maximum penalty in the *Agriculture and Agri-Food Administrative Monetary Penalties Act (AAAMP Act)*[156] was $25,000, that penalty was to be assessed for each contravention and the court said there was nothing in that Act that required notices of penalty to be conflated with penalty.

Section 127.1 allows the Minister to correct clerical errors in the computation of penalties and also to withdraw a penalty if no contravention was found.

2) Appeal

Although section 109.1 was modelled on the *AAAMP Act*, unlike the latter, section 109.1 does not expressly eliminate the defence of due diligence, and there is no definitive judicial pronouncement on the question whether liability is absolute. This issue arose in *Canada (Attorney General) v Consolidated Canadian Contractors Inc*,[157] decided ten years earlier than the *UPS* case, and the court was of the view that the presumption in favour of strict liability was

---

150 SOR/96-46, am SOR/2002-130, SOR/2003-241, SOR/2007-181.
151 SOR/86-1065, as amended several times, more recently by SOR/2002-131, SOR/2005-211.
152 SOR/86-1062, as amended several times, more recently by SOR/2005-202, SOR/2005-210, SOR/2005-383, SOR/2006-152, SOR/2011-208.
153 SOR/2005-23, as am SOR/2007-181.
154 Above note 2.
155 2011 FC 204 [*UPS*].
156 Above note 142.
157 (1998), 165 DLR (4th) 433, [1999] 1 FC 209 (CA).

not rebutted in that case, and said that an implied due diligence in the context of administrative monetary penalties is neither incompatible with the legislative scheme nor does it frustrate or undermine the purposes underlying that scheme. The decision involved section 280 of the *Excise Tax Act*,[158] which the court characterized as an amps provision. On the other hand, in *Doyon v Canada (Attorney General)*,[159] the Federal Court of Appeal reluctantly sustained the defence in the *AAAMP Act*, Letourneau J voicing serious concerns. However, the decision in *UPS*[160] implicitly recognizes the soundness of this provision.

a) Appeal to Minister

Sections 129 to 133 of the Act provide an aggrieved person a right to appeal the monetary penalty first to the Minister of Public Safety and Emergency Preparedness, and from the Minister to the Federal Court. The person has ninety days to appeal.

b) Appeal to Federal Court

A person whose penalty has been confirmed by the Minister in accordance with section 131 has a right to appeal the Minister's decision within ninety days of being notified of it, to the Federal Court by way of an action. The *Federal Courts Act*[161] and the rules applicable to ordinary actions in that court apply.

K. CRIMINAL OFFENCES AND PUNISHMENT

1) General Offences

Section 160(1) declares that a contravention of the following sections of the *Customs Act* is an offence, which can be prosecuted summarily or by indictment, and prescribes the punishment.

1) section 11: person failing to present himself or herself on arrival in Canada at the nearest customs office that is open for business; carrier failing to ensure that passengers and crew on arrival are transported to the nearest customs office that is open for business;

---

158 RSC 1985, c E-15, as amended.
159 2009 FCA 152.
160 Above note 155.
161 Above note 112.

2) section 12: failing to report imported goods at the nearest customs office designated for that purpose that is open for business;
3) section 13: failing to answer truthfully any questions asked by an officer or to present the goods, inside or outside Canada (where goods are presented for pre-clearance) and to present those goods for examination;
4) section 15: failing to report illegally imported goods;
5) section 20(1): transporting imported goods that have not been released without complying with the conditions of bond or security given by the carrier;
6) section 31: removing imported goods from a customs office, sufferance warehouse, bonded warehouse, or duty-free shop prior to their release by an officer;
7) section 40: importer failing to keep prescribed records and produce or give access to them to an officer when requested;
8) section 43(2): failing to produce records with respect to collection of duties, and so on, as required; in this case, under section 160(2), a court convicting the accused has power to make an appropriate order to effect compliance with the section;
9) section 95(1): failing to report exported goods as required;
10) section 95(3): exporter failing to answer truthfully any questions asked by an officer with respect to goods being exported, or failing to present those goods when asked;
11) section 103(3): unauthorized use of customs information by an official; and
12) section 107(2): prohibition against disclosing or giving access to customs information.

Section 160(1) also enumerates the offences created by sections 153 to 157, 159, 159.1, and 160.1, namely,

1) section 153: making false or deceptive statements and entries in records, and so on;
2) section 153.1: obstructing an officer in the performance of the officer's duties;
3) section 154: misdescribing goods in accounting documents;
4) section 155: keeping, acquiring, or disposing of illegally imported goods. It was the Exchequer Court's view in *Marun v Canada*[162] that this section is intended to protect a person who innocently comes into possession

---

162 [1965] 1 Ex CR 280.

of unlawfully imported goods without means of knowing they were unlawfully imported, from prosecution, and that it does not vest the title to unlawfully imported goods in that person because the title is already in the Crown by operation of law;

5) section 156: possessing blank documents;
6) section 157: opening and unpacking goods, or breaking seals on containers, that have not been formally released;
7) section 159: smuggling; this is a serious offence that has generated several prosecutions, a few of which are summarized separately in Section K(2), below in this chapter; and
8) section 159.1: failing to mark imported goods as required, or marking them in a deceptive manner, or concealing the information given by or contained in the mark, or altering, defacing, or destroying a mark as required by regulations made under the *Customs Tariff*.

As indicated under the section on administrative monetary penalties, many of these offences can be proceeded with under the AMPS procedure as violations.[163]

2) Smuggling

Smuggling, including attempted smuggling, is the most serious offence in the *Customs Act*.

Smuggling can be done clandestinely or openly, and can include both dutiable goods and goods whose importation is prohibited or controlled by any law of the Parliament of Canada. A person cannot be charged with smuggling if goods are not dutiable, but may be charged with the offence of failure to report contrary to section 12.

The Supreme Court acquitted the accused of smuggling in *Canada v Bureau*[164] as the accused had not taken the goods past the line of customs, though it sustained the forfeiture for various breaches of the *Customs Act*. The Court said that the line of customs may perhaps vary in differing circumstances; "[i]t may be that the mere crossing of the border with no intention of clearing the goods at any custom house, whether there be one at the point of crossing or not, would, in certain circumstances, be sufficient."[165]

---

163 See Sections J(1) & J(2), above in this chapter.
164 [1949] SCR 367.
165 *Ibid* at 384.

Early cases decided by the Exchequer Court, for example, *Canada (Attorney-General) v JC Ayer Co*[166] and *Canada (Attorney-General) v Racicot*,[167] required clandestine introduction of imported goods with a view to defrauding the revenue. The element of secrecy was emphasized by the Federal Court of Appeal in *Canada v Sun Parlor Advertising Company*,[168] but this requirement has now been dispensed with by section 159. However, being a criminal offence, the law now requires knowledge or intent to smuggle, as laid down by the *Reference Re Section 94(2) of the Motor Vehicle Act (BC)*[169] case. In this regard, the decision of the House of Lords in a recent English case (*R v Taafe*[170]) may be relevant; the UK House of Lords held that in order to be convicted of the offence of smuggling drugs, the accused should have knowledge not only of the existence of a smuggling operation, but also that the substance being smuggled into the country was one the importation of which was prohibited by statute.

Smuggling is a hybrid offence; the accused may be charged with a summary conviction offence or an indictable offence. The punishment is the same as for the general offences and is specified in section 161.

3) Offences by Corporation

Under section 158, officers of a corporation that has committed an offence are guilty of the offence if they directed, authorized, acquiesced in, or participated in its commission, and are liable to the punishment provided in sections 160 and 160.1, even where the corporation has not been prosecuted for the offence.

4) Punishment for General Offences

The general offences enumerated in section 160 are hybrid offences that can be prosecuted either by way of summary conviction or by indictment. If prosecuted summarily, the punishment is a fine of up to $50,000, or a prison term of up to six months, or both; if prosecuted by indictment, the punishment is ten times the amount (up to $500,000), or a prison term of up to five years, or both.

---

166   (1887), 1 Ex CR 232.
167   (1913), 14 Ex CR 214.
168   [1973] FC 1055 (CA).
169   (1983), 4 CCC (3d) 243 (BCCA), aff'd [1985] 2 SCR 486.
170   [1984] AC 539 (HL).

a) Obstructing an Officer

Hindering an officer who is carrying out his or her duties is, under section 153.1 of the *Customs Act*, a separate offence and is punishable by a minimum fine of $1,000 and a maximum fine of $25,000 on summary conviction, or both the fine and a prison term of up to twelve months. This punishment is in addition to any other penalty that is provided in the Act.

b) Punishment for Other Offences

Any contravention that is an offence and is not enumerated in section 160 is punishable by summary conviction and the penalty is a fine of a minimum of $1,000 and a maximum of $25,000, or a prison term of up to six months, or both.

5) Limitation Period

Section 163 specifies that the prosecution of an offence by way of summary conviction may only be instituted within three years of its commission. The Crown can choose between the two procedures, but if the limitation period bars prosecution of summary offences, it can opt for the indictment procedure, which has no limitation bar.

6) Evidence

Sections 151 and 152 cast the burden of proof in any proceeding, including a criminal prosecution, as follows:

1) section 151: Where two or more documents, such as invoices, were made or sent by or on behalf of the same person in which the same goods are shown as having different prices, names, or descriptions, it is *prima facie* evidence that the documents were intended to evade compliance with the Act, or to evade the payment of duties.
2) section 152: In any proceeding or prosecution, if the Crown proves the foreign origin of imported goods, it is *prima facie* evidence. In all other matters, except in a prosecution where the identity or origin of the goods is in issue, the onus lies on the defendant or the accused. This reverse onus may be problematic in light of the Supreme Court's judgment in *R v Oakes*,[171] where the Court held that the reverse onus placed by this section on the accused in so far as it related to a criminal pro-

---

171 [1986] 1 SCR 103.

ceeding violated an accused's right to be presumed innocent guaranteed by section 11(d) of the *Canadian Charter of Rights and Freedoms* since it is possible for the accused to be convicted despite the existence of a reasonable doubt in the mind of the judge.

L. PROTECTION OF OFFICERS

Section 106 of the Act shields a customs officer against any actions or judicial proceedings for anything done by the officer in the performance of his duties under the *Customs Act* or any other federal statute, as well as a person called on by an officer to assist in the performance of such duties, if such action is instituted more than three months after the cause of action or the subject matter of the proceedings arose.

The same time limitation is provided in section 106(2) for action or judicial proceeding for the recovery of goods that were seized, detained, or held in custody or safekeeping by the Crown or an officer. Under section 106(3), if an action is brought under the *Federal Courts Act* or other Act, where substantially the same issues are involved, the Minister is authorized to file a stay of those proceedings.

In *Kearns & McMurchy Inc v Canada*,[172] the Federal Court dismissed the action of the plaintiff for damages against the officers for the tort of conversion with respect to prohibited goods because the plaintiff had a remedy under sections 67 and 68, which it should have pursued. In *Ingredia SA v Canada*,[173] the plaintiff sued for $27 million in damages based on the ground that customs officers had classified the product imported by it under a wrong tariff item. The court granted summary judgment to the Crown because the action was brought after the three-month limitation period had expired. The court said that section 106(1) applies to Crown servants for negligently applying a wrong tariff item.

---

[172] 2003 FCT 814.
[173] 2009 FC 389, aff'd 2010 FCA 176.

CHAPTER 2

The *Customs Tariff*[1]

A. INTRODUCTION

Tariff rate is the second of two components in the computation of customs duties, the first being value for duty. Customs duties are the product of the two. The first component was the subject of Chapter 1. It should be noted that the primary basis of valuation, namely, the transaction value, and the five subsidiary bases, have to be modified when imported goods are shipped from a country of export but had been processed, partly manufactured, or added on in another country without losing their origin status. The value for duty of components, additions, and combinations that give the product a new character from what it was before undergoing such operations may also have to be separately calculated.

This chapter describes the process of classifying the goods before or at the same time as they have been appraised in accordance with the valuation provisions of the *Customs Act*.[2] Duties of customs are imposed on goods imported into Canada, pursuant to the *Customs Tariff*, at the rates shown opposite the tariff item under which they are classified in the Schedule to that Act, and those rates are further determined by their country of origin. These three additional factors, namely, the determination of the appropriate classification, the rate of duty that is based on that classification, and the country of origin of the goods on which basis a specific tariff treatment is accorded, are described in this chapter. Even where goods are entitled to the

---

1 SC 1997, c 36.
2 RSC 1985, c 1 (2d Supp), as am RSC 1985, c 7 (2d Supp), and subsequently.

preferential or other rates set out in the Schedule, those rates are increased when importers of goods that are subject to tariff rate quotas exceed the quotas allotted, thus making "over access" imports prohibitively expensive in many cases.

Chapters 1 and 2 cover the revenue-raising and collection processes. However, in addition to customs duties, duties and taxes are levied under other federal statutes, such as the *Excise Act*, the *Excise Act, 2001*, Part IX of the *Excise Tax Act* (General Sales Tax/Harmonized Sales Tax), and the *Special Import Measures Act*, unless they are specifically excluded.

Chapter 2 also describes the various incentives that the Canadian government provides to manufacturers, such as the Duty Deferral Program and the Duties Relief Program. These incentives are independent of the duty-free treatment given under Chapter 98 for goods imported for use in the manufacture or production of other goods in Canada, and are designed to encourage entrepôt businesses and re-exporters of imported goods that are processed, or consumed in the processing of other imported goods, for the purpose of exportation. The *Customs Tariff* also accords duty-free allowances to Canadians returning from travel abroad after being away for certain specified lengths of time. Some of the provisions in the *Customs Tariff* provide safeguards in the form of surtaxes and tariff rate quotas which, to some extent, protect Canadian manufacturers, textiles, agriculture, and dairy farmers from unfair competition. They are further reinforced by measures taken under the *Special Import Measures Act*. By the same token, Canada cannot violate the principles of fair trade agreed to in the *World Trade Organization Agreement* and embodied in the *World Trade Organization Agreement Implementation Act*[3] when taking restrictive or protective actions, and those principles are embodied in all three customs-related statutes.

Five principal topics are dealt with in this chapter. They are (1) imposition of duties; (2) tariff classification; (3) origin of goods; (4) tariff treatment; and (5) duties relief. A separate section deals with prohibited goods classified under tariff items 9897.00.00, 9898.00.00, and 9899.00.00, to which the international harmonized coding system (HCS) and rules do not apply.

B. ADMINISTRATION AND ENFORCEMENT

The Minister of Public Safety and Emergency Preparedness, through the Canada Border Services Agency (CBSA), is responsible for the administration

---

[3] SC 1994, c 47.

and enforcement of the *Customs Tariff* and the various regulations and orders prescribed under it. The provisions of the *Customs Act* apply. Any contravention of the *Customs Tariff* or regulations, or a failure to comply with a condition to which relief or remission, drawback, or refund under the duties relief provisions, is subject or to which classification under a tariff classification is subject, is deemed to be a contravention of the *Customs Act*. Sections 153 to 163 of that Act apply.

C. IMPOSITION OF DUTIES

1) General Provisions

Unless otherwise indicated in Chapter 98 or 99 of the List of Tariff Provisions, a customs duty is imposed by section 20(1) of the *Customs Tariff* on all goods set out in the List of Tariff Provisions at the time those goods are imported, and the duty must be paid in accordance with the *Customs Act*, at the rates set out in that List, the "F" Staging List, or section 29 that are applicable to those goods. This levy is in addition to (1) any other duties imposed under the *Customs Tariff* (namely, duty under section 21 on tobacco, wine, beer, spirits, and so on, equivalent to the excise tax) and (2) a surtax or temporary duty, if levied under section 22, or any other Act of Parliament relating to customs (for example, the *Special Import Measures Act* and goods and services tax/harmonized sales tax (GST/HST) under the *Excise Tax Act*).

For most importations, customs duties are based on the value of goods, that is, on an *ad valorem* basis, but in several cases a specific duty, or in combination with *ad valorem*, is payable. The *ad valorem* rate is expressed as a percentage, and duties are calculated in accordance with the valuation sections 45 to 55 of the *Customs Act* described in Chapter 1. Where a rate is based in whole or in part on weight or volume, duties imposed are calculated on the basis of the net weight or volume of the goods, unless another basis is provided in the Schedule.

2) Goods Taken out of Canada and Subsequently Returned

Under section 20(1), the value for duty of goods that were taken out of Canada for the purpose of repairs, or to add equipment or to do work on them outside Canada, and are subsequently returned to Canada, is the value of the goods at the time of the subsequent return.

D. TARIFF STRUCTURE AND COMMODITY CLASSIFICATION

1) Tariff Structure

Canada adheres to the *International Convention on the Harmonized Commodity Description and Coding System*[4] (*HS Convention*), which was developed by the World Customs Organization (WCO) and was adopted in 1983, and entered into force in 1988. The *HS Convention* governs the Harmonized Commodity Description and Coding System (HCDCS), generally referred to as the Harmonized System, or simply, the HS, which is a nomenclature for the coding, description, and classification of goods/products in international trade. It consists of over 5,000 commodity groups that are structured into twenty-one sections (I to XXI), 97 chapters (1 to 97), four-digit headings, six-digit subheadings, and eight-digit tariff items. Chapters 98 and 99 are reserved for national use to each country. The Contracting Parties are obliged to base their tariff schedules on the HS nomenclature, but they are free to set their own rates of duty.

To achieve uniform classification of goods, the HS also contains Section, Chapter, and Subheading Notes, as well as *General Interpretative Rules*. The official interpretation of the HS is given in the Explanatory Notes published by the WCO. These Explanatory Notes are part of a commodity database giving the HS classification of more than 200,000 commodities actually traded internationally.

The HS is binding on Contracting Parties. The *HS Convention* and any disputes are administered by the WCO HS Committee. The HS Committee also prepares amendments updating the HS every five to six years. The latest HS edition now in force is the 2012 edition, following those of 2002 and 2007. By the end of the 2007 edition the HS had 143 Contracting Parties (142 countries and the European Union (EU)). As of July 2012 there were 143 Contracting Parties. Many more countries and territories actually apply the HS without being a Contracting Party. As of July 2012, over 206 countries, territories, and economic or customs unions were applying HS in practice. Over 98 percent of the merchandise in international trade is classified in terms of the HS.

The *HS Convention* was implemented by Canada in the new *Customs Tariff*, enacted in 1996. The new Act adopts the *HS Convention* and its commodity classification and eight-digit coding system, and applies the *General Interpretative Rules* of that system.

---

4   1503 UNTS 167 (done at Brussels 14 June 1983).

The Schedule to the *Customs Tariff* is organized into five parts: (1) the *General Rules for the Interpretation of the Harmonized System*; (2) a list of countries and applicable tariff treatments; (3) a table of the sections and chapters of the Harmonized Coding System (see Table 1); (4) List of Tariff Provisions in ninety-nine chapters; and (5) a list of intermediate and final rates for tariff items of the "F" staging category with respect to countries that have a free trade agreement with Canada.

The *Customs Tariff* gives specific regulation-making authority to the Governor in Council, such authority to be exercised on the recommendations of the Minister of Finance, and in some cases, if expressly named, the Minister of Public Safety and Emergency Preparedness.

2) The Harmonized Commodity Description and Coding System

Section 10(1) of the *Customs Tariff* requires classification of goods to be determined in accordance with the *General Rules for the Interpretation of the Harmonized System* and the *Canadian Rules* set out in the Schedule to the *Customs Tariff* unless expressly provided otherwise. It further provides that where a tariff item contains the phrase "within access commitments," goods are not to be classified under that tariff item unless they are imported under the authority of a permit issued pursuant to the *Export and Import Permits Act*[5] and in compliance with the conditions of the permit. Tariff rate quotas (TRQs) are established under that statute by the Department of Foreign Affairs and International Trade.

Section 11 stipulates that in interpreting the headings and subheadings, regard shall be had to the Compendium of Classification Opinions and the Explanatory Notes to the HS, published by the World Customs Organization (WCO), as amended from time to time.

The *General Rules* of the HS and the *Canadian Rules* are discussed in Sections D(6)(a) and D(7), below in this chapter, and are reproduced in full in the Addendum at the end of this chapter.

3) Renumbering Tariff Item or Changing Description of Goods

Renumbering a tariff item and changing the description of goods can be done by the Minister of Finance under the authority of sections 13 and 15 of the

---

5   RSC 1985, c E-19.

Customs Tariff, respectively, if by so doing the rate of customs duty applicable to the goods is not affected. The Minister can also change the name of a country in the List of Countries to reflect a country's change of name, but the change does not affect the tariff treatment accorded to that country.

4) Amendment of the Schedule

The Governor in Council is given authority under section 14 of the *Customs Tariff* to amend the Schedule, other than tariff items 9898.00.00 and 9899.00.00 (prohibited goods and publications or other materials). Under certain circumstances, the Governor in Council is also authorized to amend the List of Tariff Provisions and the "F" Staging List in order to reduce a rate of customs duty on goods imported from any specific country.

5) Tariff Classification Appeals

Tariff classification appeals constitute a major part of the work of the Tribunal where the importer disputes the decision of the customs agency, the Canada Border Services Agency (CBSA)—the successor to the Canada Customs and Revenue Agency (CCRA) in 2006, whose predecessor was the Minister of National Revenue represented by the Deputy Minister of National Revenue, Customs and Excise. The dispute procedure is outlined in the *Customs Act*. While generally a dispute is centred on the tariff item itself, it inevitably involves the scope of the chapter, its headings, and subheadings under which the tariff item falls.

General Rules of the HS form the basis of interpretation. They are further elaborated by the *Canadian Rules*. Their success can be measured by the small fraction of appeals that are taken to the Tribunal by importers, compared to the large number of transactions, many involving very large import volumes. That said, many appeals are filed to preserve the strict limitation period provided in the *Customs Act*, but are subsequently withdrawn by the importer before they reach the hearing stage. The clarity of the *General Rules*, aided by the Explanatory Notes to each chapter, heading and subheading, which indicate what is and what is not covered under them and what conditions apply to them, and the clarity of the nomenclature and description of commodities under each tariff item, have reduced the number of disputes to a minimum.

Appeals are further minimized by the operation of section 58(2) of the *Customs Act*, which expressly provides that if the origin, tariff classification, and value for duty are not determined by a designated officer at or before the time the importer accounts for the goods under section 32(1), (3), or (5) of that Act, the origin, tariff classification, and value for duty are deemed to have been determined by the CBSA on the basis of the importer's declaration. The CBSA is, however, authorized by section 59(1) to make a re-determination within four years after the deemed determination.

6) Interpretation of Tariff Items

It is well established in Canadian customs law that the tariff classification of goods is to be determined at the time of their entry into Canada, on the basis of examination of the goods as a whole in the manner in which they were presented at the time of their importation. This was authoritatively stated over half a century ago by the Supreme Court of Canada in *Deputy Minister of National Revenue (Customs and Excise) v Macmillan & Bloedel (Alberni) Ltd*[6] and reiterated several times since, by that and other courts. This rule is still valid today under the new *Customs Tariff* legislation, which was enacted in 1996.[7]

Commodity nomenclature and description is the core of the *Customs Tariff* because it is the sole determinant of customs duty rates, which is the reason why both the importer and the revenue collection agency vigorously pursue their positions, in order to ensure that the correct tariff item is assigned for each importation. Rules and the jurisprudence interpreting them are, therefore, critical to the resolution of differences between the two parties, and these rules are now internationally agreed under the *HS Convention*.

Section 10(1) of the *Customs Tariff* requires that classification, unless otherwise provided, be determined in accordance with the *General Rules* and the *Canadian Rules* set out in the Schedule.

a) *General Rules*

The *General Rules* (GR) comprise six rules (Rules 1 to 6), which are structured in a hierarchical order, so that if the classification of goods cannot be determined in accordance with GR 1, then the remaining rules in sequence must be followed. Rule 1 is crucial to the classification of goods, since most disputes can be and are resolved by its application, with the remaining rules called in aid where necessary.

In considering whether GR 1 can be used to classify goods, one has to look at the Explanatory Notes. They provide a commentary on the scope of

---

6   [1965] SCR 366; reaffirmed in *Deputy Minister of National Revenue (Customs and Excise) v Ferguson Industries Ltd*, [1973] SCR 21.

7   *Tiffany Woodworth v President of the Canada Border Services Agency*, AP-2006-035 (2007) (CITT).

each heading (and, where applicable, each subheading) and give illustrative examples of goods that are included in or excluded from that heading or subheading. The Explanatory Notes also provide technical descriptions of the products wherever necessary.

Section 11 of the *Customs Tariff* provides as follows:

> In interpreting the headings and subheadings, regard shall be had to the Compendium of Classification Opinions to the Harmonized Commodity Description and Coding System and the Explanatory Notes to the Harmonized Commodity Description and Coding System, published by the Customs Co-operation Council (also known as the World Customs Organization), as amended from time to time.

Although the Explanatory Notes (EN) are not legally binding, the Federal Court of Appeal emphasized in *Canada (Customs and Revenue Agency) v Suzuki Canada Inc*[8] that they are intended to be an interpretive guide to tariff classification and, therefore, must be considered within that context, and that they should be respected, unless there is a sound reason to do otherwise, to satisfy their interpretive purpose and to ensure harmony within the international community.

i) General Rule 1

General Rule 1 states:

> The titles of Sections, Chapters, and Sub-Chapters are provided for ease of reference only. For legal purposes, classification shall be determined according to the terms of the headings and any relative Section or Chapter Notes and, provided that such headings or notes do not otherwise require, according to the following provisions ... [These are *General Rules* (GR) 2 to 6, set out below.]

Once a determination is made pursuant to GR 1 (and GR 2 to 5 where applicable) as to the heading in which the goods should be classified, the next step is to determine the proper subheading by applying GR 6.

ii) General Rule 2

General Rule 2 states:

> (a) Any reference in a heading to an article shall be taken to include a reference to that article incomplete or unfinished provided that, as presented,

---

8   2004 FCA 131.

the incomplete or unfinished article has the essential character of the complete or finished article. It shall also be taken to include a reference to that article complete or finished (or falling to be classified as complete or finished by virtue of this Rule), presented unassembled or disassembled.

(b) Any reference in a heading to a material or substance shall be taken to include a reference to mixtures or combinations of that material or substance with other materials or substances. Any reference to goods of a given material or substance shall be taken to include a reference to goods consisting wholly or partly of such material or substance. The classification of goods consisting of more than one material or substance shall be according to the principles of Rule 3.

iii) General Rule 3

General Rule 3 states:

When by application of Rule 2 (b), or for any other reason, goods are, *prima facie*, classifiable under two or more headings, classification shall be effected as follows:

(a) The heading which provides the most specific description shall be preferred to headings providing a more general description.

(b) Mixtures, composite goods consisting of different materials or made up of different components, and goods put up in sets for retail sale, which cannot be classified by reference to Rule 3 (a) shall be classified as if they consisted of the material or component which gives them their essential character insofar as this criterion is applicable.

(c) When goods cannot be classified by reference to Rules 3 (a) or 3 (b), they shall be classified under the heading which occurs last in the numerical order among those which equally merit consideration.

iv) General Rule 4

General Rule 4 provides as follows:

Goods which cannot be classified in accordance with the above Rules shall be classified under the heading appropriate to the goods to which they are most akin.

v) General Rule 5

Additional rules for packing cases, containers, and other packing materials provide as follows:

In addition to the foregoing provisions, the following Rules shall apply in respect of the goods referred to therein:

(a) Camera cases, musical instrument cases, gun cases, drawing instrument cases, necklace cases and similar containers, specially shaped or fitted to contain a specific article or set of articles, suitable for long-term use and presented with the articles for which they are intended, shall be classified with such articles when of a kind normally sold therewith. This Rule does not, however, apply to containers which give the whole its essential character.

(b) Subject to the provisions of Rule 5 (a) above, packing materials and packing containers presented with the goods therein shall be classified with the goods if they are of a kind normally used for packing such goods. However, this provision is not binding when such packing materials or packing containers are clearly suitable for repetitive use.

vi) General Rule 6

General Rule 6 governs the classification of goods in subheadings. The Rule states:

> For legal purposes, the classification of goods in the subheadings of a heading shall be determined according to the terms of those subheadings and any relative subheading Notes and, *mutatis mutandis*, to the above Rules on the understanding that only subheadings at the same level are comparable.
>
> For the purpose of this Rule, the relative Section and Chapter Notes also apply, unless the context otherwise requires.

7) Canadian Rules

The *Canadian Rules* apply to the classification of tariff items. They provide as follows:

1. For legal purposes, the classification of goods in the tariff items of a subheading or of a heading shall be determined according to the terms of those tariff items and any related Supplementary Notes and, *mutatis mutandis*, to the *General Rules* for the Interpretation of the Harmonized System, on the understanding that only tariff items at the same level are comparable. For the purpose of this Rule the relative Section, Chapter and Subheading Notes also apply, unless the context otherwise requires.

2. Where both a Canadian term and an international term are presented in this Nomenclature, the commonly accepted meaning and scope of

the international term shall take precedence.

3. For the purpose of Rule 5 (b) of the *General Rules* for the Interpretation of the Harmonized System, packing materials or packing containers clearly suitable for repetitive use shall be classified under their respective headings.

8) Summary

As stated in Sections D(6) and (7), above in this chapter, under General Rule 1, classification is determined according to the terms of the headings and any relative Section or Chapter Notes and, provided that such headings or notes do not otherwise require, according to the *General Rules* 2 to 6. General Rule 6, which applies to the determination of the classification of goods coming under subheadings, goes hand in hand with General Rule 1 because in many cases headings are divided into subheadings. These two Rules are predominantly used when there is no dispute at the heading or subheading level, but disagreement arises only at the tariff item level.

The nomenclature of goods in a tariff item is critically important because it is the key to determining all disputes. The *Canadian Rules* require that a tariff item should be interpreted according to its terms, paying close attention to its meaning and scope and any qualifications that are contained in it, and in light of the notes to the chapter, heading, and subheading under which it appears.

A lot is riding on the correct determination of a tariff item because the rate of customs duty is shown only opposite that tariff item and that rate could be anywhere from zero (that is, free), upwards. Therefore, underlying every dispute is the possible financial loss or gain to both parties to a dispute if the Tribunal, which is the final arbiter, barring judicial review, decides in favour of or against either of them. Compared to the daily volume of goods flowing into Canada, it is surprising that there should be so few disputes going to the Tribunal, even fewer appeals from the Tribunal to the Federal Court of Appeal, and far fewer still from the latter to the Supreme Court.

9) Application of *General Rules*

a) General Rule 2

If goods cannot be classified in accordance with General Rule 1, then regard must be had to General Rule 2. The application of GR 2 is illustrated by the decision of the Tribunal in *Renelle Furniture Inc v President of the Canada*

Border Services Agency[9] with respect to unassembled metal futon frames for futon sofa beds. The appellant and the CBSA were in agreement on the classification at the heading level, but not at the subheading level. The CBSA classified the unassembled futon bunk beds under tariff item 9401.40.00 as "seats, convertible into beds," and the unassembled metal futon frames under tariff item 9403.20.00 as "other metal furniture," whereas the importer claimed that they should have been classified under tariff items 9401.90 and 9403.90 as parts for seats and parts for other furniture, respectively.

The Tribunal dismissed the appeal because, although unassembled, the goods in issue were imported in a finished state, that is, not requiring further fabrication or finishing, with all the parts necessary for assembly into complete frames. It noted that the goods in issue were not imported with either futon mattresses or futon mattress covers and, therefore, cannot be said to form complete futon sofa beds or futon bunk beds. Therefore, pursuant to GR 2(a), because the goods when imported had the essential character of a complete or finished article, the Tribunal held that they were properly classified under tariff items 9401.40.00 and 9403.20.00, respectively.

In contrast, in the *Tai Lung (Canada) Ltd v President of the Canada Border Services Agency*[10] appeal, discussed in Section D(10)(a)(vii), below in this chapter, the Tribunal concluded that GR 2 did not apply where footwear components were imported together but had to undergo further processing.

b) General Rule 3

If goods are classifiable in two headings, General Rule 3(a) must be applied. The first sentence of GR 3(a) states that "[t]he heading which provides the most specific description shall be preferred to headings providing a more general description." In *Calego International Inc v Deputy Minister of National Revenue*,[11] the Tribunal was faced with this issue. In that case, the goods in issue functioned both as rucksacks having a carrying function, and as toys having an amusement function. Because the description in each of the headings under consideration mentioned only one of these functions, the Tribunal considered that both headings were equally descriptive for the purposes of GR 3(a) and, therefore, GR 3(b) did not apply. Accordingly, as directed by GR 3(c) to classify the goods in the heading "which occurs last in the numerical order" among those which equally merit consideration, it concluded that the goods in issue should be classified under tariff item 9503.41.00 as

---

9   AP-2005-028 (2007), 11 TTR (2d) 531.
10 AP-2006-034 (2007), 11 TTR (2d) 684.
11 AP-98-102 (2000), 4 TTR (2d) 672.

"other stuffed toys representing animals or non-human creatures" as claimed by the appellant.

c) General Rule 4

General Rule 4 is unique. It is called in aid when goods cannot be classified in accordance with GR 1, 2, and 3. There are very few reported decisions applying this Rule. The appeal of *Coloridé Inc v Deputy Minister of National Revenue (Customs and Excise)*[12] provides a good example. In that case, the Deputy Minister of National Revenue determined the classification of small tufts of nylon hair, called *"mèches"* in French, under heading 55.03, which covered synthetic staple fibres of nylon, while the appellant claimed that they should be classified under heading 67.03, which included textile materials prepared for use in making wigs and the like. In allowing the appeal, the Tribunal was of the view that, contrary to the Deputy Minister's position, the textile materials in issue were not of the type contemplated in heading 55.03. The Tribunal noted that the goods in issue were unique and, not surprisingly, were not provided for in the nomenclature. The textile materials that were used for making wigs or the like, or for making doll's hair, ultimately represented human hair, which was the true character and purpose of those materials. The same could be said of the textile materials in issue, that is, the tufts so arranged as to imitate locks of hair and then fixed onto displays and books that were sold to producers of hair colour dyes for use by hairstylists to demonstrate to their clients the results that could be achieved by the dyeing process. The evidence in this case revealed that the goods in issue had no other use or purpose but to be used in displays and books. They had lost their usefulness as staple fibres for use in making fabrics.

10) Classification Decisions of the Tribunal

The application by the Tribunal of the *General Rules of Interpretation* is illustrated in detail below by cases under three headings: (1) competing tariff classifications; (2) parts and accessories; and (3) duty-free treatment for goods imported "for use in" other goods and for specifically designed goods.

The Tribunal has ruled in past cases that a decision on tariff classification binds only the parties in respect of a particular importation and goods of the same class imported by the litigant. It has even gone a step further by holding that once a classification is determined and the appeal period

---

12 AP-99-037 (2000) [*Coloridé Inc*].

is time-barred, it cannot be re-opened with respect to future importations, even if the original classification was erroneous.

In the important decision of the Federal Court of Appeal in *Sable Offshore Energy Inc v Commissioner of the Canada Customs and Revenue Agency*,[13] the court set aside the decision of the Tribunal, which had justified its decision on a variety of grounds having to do with the need for consistency in the classification of imported goods. These grounds were,

1) components may not be classified under a heading appropriate to a functional unit as that would permit the reclassification of goods that had already been classified and were time-barred from reclassification;
2) classifying a component as belonging to a functional unit when the other components had been classified otherwise and were statute-barred from reclassification would lead to absurd results and create uncertainty in the marketplace;
3) classifying the pipe (one of the components) as a component belonging to a functional unit would result in dual classification; and
4) it could not have been Parliament's intention that goods be reclassified once the limitation period had expired or that there be a regime of dual classification.

The court examined each ground and characterized the reasoning to be without merit and contrary to the intention of Parliament in prescribing limitation periods. The court said that the reasoning ignored the purpose of limitation periods, which was "to put an end to the revisiting of past errors," in recognition that, at some point, the achievement of the "correct" resolution of a problem must give way to the need for finality. The court was of the view that absurdity, if any, would lie in refusing to classify the goods under its proper tariff heading simply to maintain consistency with previous, erroneous classifications that cannot be revisited due to the limitation period.

The Tribunal had further stated that classifying the goods under the functional unit heading would result in "a regime of dual classification" based on the fact that "components or parts not yet classified would benefit from a classification from which other parts or components of the same machine that were already classified and time-barred would not benefit."[14] The court pointed out that this reasoning ignored the fact that the subject matter of the classification was not the functional unit *per se* but the components

---

13   AP-2000-040 (2002), 6 TTR (2d) 567 (CITT), rev'd 2003 FCA 220.
14   *Ibid* at para 22 (FCA).

thereof. The fact that other components of the functional unit were individually classified elsewhere and that some of the components remained eligible for reclassification under the correct item did not create dual classification for those goods.

Finally, the Tribunal had expressed the view that classifying some components of a functional unit as such while the other components were classified under different headings and were time-barred from review would be contrary to Parliament's intent. Inherent in this view was the belief that Parliament did not intend that separate components of a functional unit be treated differently on account of the expiration of the limitation period. However, the court said that the Tribunal pointed to no such expression of Parliamentary intent, and the very nature and purpose of limitation periods pointed in the other direction. Subject to the expiration of the limitation period, Parliament had granted both the taxpayer and the Commissioner the right to rectify improperly classified entries.

It was, therefore, clear that as long as the time period within which goods may be reclassified had not expired, Parliament's intent would be best respected by giving those goods the classification that was most appropriate in fact and in law. As there can be no doubt in the case under appeal, having regard to the Tribunal's initial conclusion that the goods in issue (the pipe) properly came within tariff item 8479.89.99, and as the time limitation for applying this item to those goods had not expired, the Tribunal was bound to give effect to it.

The court, therefore, allowed the appeal with costs, set aside the decision of the Tribunal to the effect that it was no longer open to it to classify the pipe in issue under tariff item 8479.89.99, and, rendering the decision that ought to have been rendered by the Tribunal, ordered that the pipe in issue be so classified.

a) Competing Tariff Classifications

Several decisions of the Tribunal have been selected below to illustrate how the Tribunal has applied Rules 1 and 6. The decisions are arranged in the order of Chapter numbers, indicating the results of any application for judicial review of the Tribunal's decision to the Federal Court of Appeal. A Table of Sections and Chapters is reproduced in Table 1 at the end of this chapter.

i) **Section IV: Chapters 16 to 24 (Foodstuffs, Beverages, Tobacco)**

CASE 1: TARIFF ITEM 1806.90.90 (CHRISTMAS ADVENT CALENDARS CONTAINING CHOCOLATES)

The appeal in *Morris National Inc v President of the Canada Border Services Agency*[15] was with respect to the decision of the CBSA that the goods in issue, Christmas Advent calendars containing chocolates, were incorrectly classified by the CBSA as "other chocolate and other food preparations containing cocoa" under tariff item 1806.90.90 and that they should be classified as "articles for Christmas festivities" under tariff item 9505.10.00.

The goods in issue were wrapped in plastic cellophane. They consisted of a thin cardboard box decorated with Christmas themes. The box had twenty-four perforated openings, one for each calendar day from December 1 to 24. It was commonly known that Advent calendars were intended to count down the last twenty-four days until Christmas. Small pieces of chocolate were hidden behind each of the twenty-four openings. The chocolates were set in a plastic tray that was inserted into the box.

The appellant did not dispute that chocolates were properly classified in heading 18.06, but it contended that the goods in issue cannot be classified as such because they were presented in an Advent calendar, which included puzzles, games, and cut-outs, all of which were associated with the Christmas season. In support of this contention, the appellant indicated that parents purchased this product for their children at the specific time of the year that marked the beginning of the Christmas season, not at any other time of the year. The appellant argued that, pursuant to Rule 1 of the *General Rules*, the goods in issue had a "festive" nature that imparted upon the whole their essential character. It disagreed with the contention that they were merely chocolates in Christmas-themed packaging. In the alternative, the appellant argued that the goods should be classified according to Rule 3 (b) or (c).

In the Tribunal's view, the evidence showed that the goods in issue were predominantly (in weight and in number) an assortment of twenty-four food products made of chocolate. In addition to these considerations, it found that their essential character could not be said to be derived from the packaging component, since the testimony that it heard confirmed that an Advent calendar was not sold on its own, that is, without chocolates. The Tribunal also noted that the weight indication on the packaging pertained to the chocolate only and the ingredients listed were those of the chocolate only.

---

15   AP-2005-039 (2007).

The Tribunal therefore agreed with the CBSA's position that the goods in issue were described in the terms of heading 18.06. It was of the view that the evidence clearly indicated that they were not festive packaging, but chocolates put up in packages with a festive design.

The Tribunal also noted that the Explanatory Notes to heading 95.05 did not allow goods to be classified in that heading based on "festive design" alone; on the contrary, certain goods presenting festive designs were expressly excluded from classification in that heading. Therefore, the Tribunal did not believe that the festive nature of the packaging of the chocolates made the goods anything other than what they were, that is, chocolates in seasonally appropriate packaging used for marketing and sales purposes.

The Tribunal was also of the view that its conclusion with respect to the classification of the goods in issue pursuant to Rule 1 of the *General Rules* was supported by the provisions of Rule 5 (b), which reads "packing materials and packing containers presented with the goods therein shall be classified with the goods if they are of a kind normally used for packing such goods. However, this provision is not binding when such packing materials or packing containers are clearly suitable for repetitive use."

Finally, the Tribunal recalled its decision in *Regal Confections Inc v Deputy Minister of National Revenue*[16] in which it remarked that novelty packaging is not usually determinative of classification. In the Tribunal's view, the goods in issue were chocolates packaged in novelty Christmas Advent calendars and held that they were properly classified by the CBSA under tariff item 1806.90.90 as "other chocolate and other food preparations containing cocoa." The appeal was dismissed.

CASE 2: TARIFF HEADING 19.02 (RICE NOODLES)
The appellant in *New Asia (Brampton) Food Centre v President of the Canada Border Services Agency*[17] had imported rice stick noodles, which the CBSA classified under tariff item 1902.30.40 as "other pasta without meat." The appellant contended that the goods should have been classified under tariff item 1902.19.29 as "other uncooked pasta not stuffed or otherwise prepared, containing flour and water only." The Tribunal allowed the appeal. It agreed with the appellant that when a product has been steamed it does not necessarily mean that it has been cooked. It was not convinced that the World Customs Organization's ruling provided by the CBSA in support of its argument applied to this case, as it was not clear whether the nature of

---

16 AP-98-043, AP-98-044 and AP-98-051 (1999) [*Regal Confections*].
17 AP-2006-042 (2007), 11 TTR (2d) 709.

the "pre-cooking" of dried rice noodles packed in plastic bags was comparable to the steaming of the goods which the rice noodles imported by the appellant had been subjected to.

CASE 3: TARIFF HEADINGS 20.09 (FRUIT JUICE) AND 22.02 (OTHER NON-ALCOHOLIC BEVERAGES)

The products in issue in the appeal of Excelsior in *Excelsior Foods Inc v Commissioner of the Canada Customs and Revenue Agency*[18] were Yoga® nectars in peach, pear, and apricot flavours, and the issue in the appeal was whether the products were properly classified by the CCRA under tariff item 2202.90.90 as "other non-alcoholic beverages" or should be classified under tariff item 2009.80.19 as "other juice of any other single fruit" as claimed by the appellant. The competing headings in this case were the following:

> 20.09 Fruit juices (including grape must) and vegetable juices, unfermented and not containing added spirit, whether or not containing added sugar or other sweetening matter.
>
> 22.02 Waters, including mineral waters and aerated waters, containing added sugar or other sweetening matter or flavoured, and other non-alcoholic beverages, not including fruit or vegetable juices of heading 20.09.

The appellant argued that the products in issue were reconstituted to the point where the proportion of water that was present before the start of the process had been restored, but not beyond that level. That was why, in its view, the products were still fruit juices.

The CCRA pointed out that the Explanatory Notes to heading 22.02 provide that the heading covers, among other things, tamarind nectar, which is akin to the products in issue. It also referred to the Compendium of Classification Opinions, which classified peach and apricot nectars in heading 22.02.

Pursuant to Rule 1 of the *General Rules*, the Tribunal concluded that the products in issue were classifiable under heading 22.02 as "other non-alcoholic beverages." The juices of this heading may be concentrated (whether or not frozen) or in the form of crystals or powder provided that, in the latter case, they were entirely or almost entirely soluble in water. Such products are usually obtained by processes involving either heat (whether or not in a vacuum) or cold (lyophilization). Certain concentrated juices can be distinguished from their corresponding non-concentrated juices on the basis of their Brix value (sugar content).

---

18 AP-2002-113 (2004), 9 TTR (2d) 295 [*Excelsior Foods*].

The Tribunal considered the opposing arguments of the CCRA and the appellant with respect to the addition of water, sugar, acid, and other additives to the product with regard to the sugar component, and the implications of the addition of water and other components to the products. It took careful note of the Explanatory Notes to the competing chapters in order to determine the intent of the language of the headings in the classification system. The Explanatory Notes to heading 20.09 contained a number of details, whereas the Explanatory Notes to heading 22.02 were very limited in scope.

The term "reconstituted" had a particular meaning. Reconstituted juices are defined in the Explanatory Notes to heading 20.09 as "products obtained by the addition, to the concentrated juice, of a quantity of water not exceeding that contained in similar non-concentrated juices of normal composition." Given that the products in issue had never been in concentrated form, the Tribunal was of the view that they were not "reconstituted juices" in accordance with the terms of the Explanatory Notes to heading 20.09.

On the basis of the evidence presented, it was the Tribunal's view that, once the purée was diluted by the addition of water, the proportions of certain other constituents of the fruit or the purée, such as sugar and acids, would be reduced by the dilution. Starting with this new base material, that is, the combined water and purée, it would be only by the addition of ingredients such as sugar and acids that the balance of constituents could be restored and a juice simulated. The "original character" of the juice that might have been produced was simulated by the product that resulted from the further processing of the purée, particularly the addition of water, sugars, and acids.

With regard to the acceptable additives and their levels, the Tribunal saw no reason to disqualify the products in issue as juices simply on the basis of the addition to the purée of sugar or acid.

The Tribunal noted that, in establishing the benchmark for comparisons, the Explanatory Notes consistently referred to juices rather than to the fruits from which they were extracted. The Tribunal was of the view that the appellant failed to make the comparisons required to satisfy the terms of the Explanatory Notes.

Having concluded that the products in issue were not classifiable in heading 20.09, the Tribunal then looked at the only other competing heading, which was heading 22.02. This heading covered, among other things, other non-alcoholic beverages. Both the terms of the heading and the Explanatory Notes to that heading specifically excluded fruit juices of heading 20.09.

In light of the above, the Tribunal was of the view that the products in issue were properly classified under tariff item 2202.90.90 as "other non-alcoholic beverages." Therefore, it dismissed the appeal.

In its application to the Federal Court of Appeal for review, the appellant argued that a product was still fruit juice if the amount of water added to reconstitute juice concentrate did not exceed the amount removed when the concentrate was prepared. The court did not accept that argument and held that the Tribunal was not unreasonable in classifying the goods as "other non-alcoholic beverages" under tariff item 2202.90.90 rather than fruit juices under heading 20.09.

CASE 4: TARIFF HEADING 20.08 (MANGO JUICE) OR 22.02 (NECTAR/BEVERAGE)
In *Sy Marketing Inc v President of the Canada Border Services Agency*,[19] the appellant, Sy Marketing, imported cans of mango juice nectar from the Philippines (the goods in issue) and entered them under tariff item 2008.80.19 as "other juice of any other single fruit" or, in the alternative, claimed that they came under tariff item 2008.99.30 as "other fruit otherwise prepared or preserved." The label on the cans stated that the product is "NOT from Concentrate" and that it "Contains 37% Juice." The list of ingredients on the label read as follows: "Water, Mango Juice Nectar, Sugar, Citric Acid, Ascorbic Acid (Vitamin C)." The CBSA redetermined the classification of the juice under tariff item 2202.90.90 as "other non-alcoholic beverages." The Tribunal dismissed the appeal, finding that the goods in issue were properly classified under tariff item 2202.90.90 as "other non-alcoholic beverages."

The appellant argued that, while the goods in issue were produced and marketed as nectars, they met the terms of the Explanatory Notes to heading 20.09 since they had, within allowable standards, the same constituents, in the same proportions, as found in the natural fruit; their composition was consistent with that of a mango; when mangoes are processed, water was lost due to evaporation and enzymatic activity; and when the goods in issue were produced, no more water was added than what was proportionate in the natural fruit. Although the appellant conceded that sugar was perhaps added, it submitted that it was allowed by the terms of the headings and the Explanatory Notes. The Tribunal dismissed the appeal, following *Excelsior Foods*, which had been upheld by the Federal Court of Appeal.

CASE 5: TARIFF HEADING 20.09, 20.08, OR 21.06 (CANNED COCONUT MILK)
The product in issue in the appeal by Intersave in *Intersave West Buying and Merchandising Service v Commissioner of the Canada Customs and Revenue*

---

19   AP-2006-040 (2008), 12 TTR (2d) 1024.

Agency[20] was canned coconut milk. The issue was whether this product was properly classified by the CCRA under tariff item 2106.90.99 as "other food preparations not elsewhere specified or included" or whether it should be classified under tariff item 2009.80.19 as "other juice of any other single fruit" or, in the alternative, under tariff item 2008.99.90 as "other fruit, nuts and other edible parts of plants" as claimed by the appellant.

The Tribunal allowed the appeal, holding that the product in issue should be classified under tariff item 2008.99.90 for the following reasons:

1) The evidence indicated that the coconut milk was not a concentrated juice, nor was it drinkable as a beverage.
2) Heading 20.09 covered fruit juices and vegetable juices. The Explanatory Notes to that heading made it clear that, for a normal fruit juice to be classified under heading 20.09, it must not contain added water. As the product in issue contained added water, even if the Tribunal were to consider the coconut milk a normal fruit juice, it would not meet the requirements of the Explanatory Notes to the heading. Accordingly, the product in issue was not classifiable under heading 20.09.
3) Heading 21.06 was residual in character. The Explanatory Notes to that heading excluded preparations made from fruit and nuts, provided the essential character of the preparation was given by such fruit or nuts. It was clear from the evidence that the essential character of the canned coconut milk was given by the coconut itself. Therefore, heading 21.06 did not apply.
4) That left heading 20.08. The product in issue should, therefore, be classified under this tariff item.

CASE 6: TARIFF HEADING 21.04 (SOUPS AND BROTHS)

The product in issue in the appeal in *Eurotrade Import-Export Inc v Commissioner of the Canada Border Services Agency*[21] was described as "VEGETA," which was generally based on vegetable products (flour, starches, tapioca, macaroni, spaghetti and the like, rice, plant extracts, and so on), meat, meat extracts, fat, fish, crustaceans, molluscs or other aquatic invertebrates, peptones, amino acids, or yeast extract. It might also contain a considerable proportion of salt. The product was generally put up as tablets, cakes, cubes, or in powder or liquid form. The issue was whether the product was properly classified by the CCRA under tariff item 2104.10.00 as "soups and broths and

---

20 AP-2000-057 (2002), 6 TTR (2d) 357.
21 AP-2001-090 (2003), 7 TTR (2d) 645.

preparations therefor" or whether it should have been classified under tariff item 2103.90.20 as "mixed condiments and mixed seasonings," as claimed by the appellant.

The Tribunal noted that the fact that the packaging of the product no longer contained any mention of soup mix or directions to prepare a soup did not prevent its classification as a preparation for broths.

The Tribunal dismissed the appeal. Although the product in issue was used extensively as a seasoning, the essential question was whether it also constituted a preparation for broths. On the basis of the testimony of the expert witness and the fact that the main characteristics of broths referred to in the Explanatory Notes to heading 21.04 were found in the product in issue, the Tribunal found that it was properly classified under heading 21.04 as "soups and broths and preparations therefor."

ii) Section VI: Chapters 28 to 38 (Products of the Chemical or Allied Industries)

CASE 1: TARIFF HEADINGS 30.03 AND 30.04 (CERTAIN DEVIL'S ROOT TABLETS, BULK ST. JOHN'S WART OIL, AND GARLIC POWDER TABLETS)

In the appeal filed in *Yves Ponroy Canada v Deputy Minister of National Revenue*,[22] the appellant claimed that the goods in issue, which were certain devil's root tablets, bulk St. John's wart oil, and garlic powder tablets, should be classified as "medicaments" under tariff headings 30.03 and 30.04 (which carried "zero" tariff rate) and that the respondent Deputy Minister of National Revenue incorrectly determined that they were "food preparations not elsewhere specified or included" under tariff subheading 2106.90, which attracted a duty of 14.4 percent.

It was common ground that if the products in issue were not "medicaments," they would fall within subheading 2106.90. The Tribunal referred to the Explanatory Notes and other relevant provisions, and interpreted the language of headings 30.03 and 30.04 as requiring only an indication of the use of the product in the prevention or treatment of a disease or ailment, not proof of medical efficacy. The evidence presented to the Tribunal indicated that the products were so used. In the view of the Tribunal, the tariff headings did not require proof of medical efficacy of the goods in issue.

The respondent appealed the Tribunal's decision to the Federal Court of Appeal on a point of law, that the Tribunal made an error in deciding that the tariff headings did not require scientific proof of medical efficacy. The

---

22   AP-96-117 (1997), 4 TTR (2d) 779.

respondent suggested that unless that precondition was adopted, a product may be classified as a medicament based on nothing more than unsubstantiated claims.

The court upheld the Tribunal's decision and refused to disturb its classification of the products in issue on the ground that the Tribunal's interpretation of "medicaments" was not unreasonable and there was no reviewable error of law.

In another case, in the appeal by Flora in *Flora Manufacturing & Distributing Ltd v Deputy Minister of National Revenue*,[23] the Tribunal had taken the view that deficiency of vitamins or iron was not a disease but merely a condition that may lead to a disease and, therefore, the fact that vitamin and iron supplements were taken to prevent or reverse such a deficiency did not indicate a use for the prevention or treatment of a disease. The Federal Court of Appeal reversed that decision. In giving the court's judgment, Sharlow JA said that the Tribunal's reasoning was flawed.

> If, as the CITT accepted, the ingestion of vitamins and minerals prevents or reverses a deficiency that may lead to a disease or an ailment, it must follow that the purpose of ingesting vitamins and minerals is to prevent that disease or ailment. It is suggestive, though of course not conclusive, that vitamin products intended for human use are expressly included in sub-subheadings as 'medicaments' in Schedule I of the *Customs Tariff*.[24]

The *Flora* decision has been followed by the Tribunal in several subsequent decisions, for example, *DSM Nutritional Products Canada Ltd v President of the Canada Border Services Agency*,[25] where the appellant had imported Vitamin B12 1% for animal nutrition and claimed the benefit of tariff item 3003.90.00 as "other medicaments." The Tribunal allowed the appeal with one member strongly dissenting. In that member's opinion, the *Flora* decision should be treated as applying to vitamins for treating human conditions only, that vitamin B12 1% was a preparation of a kind used in animal feeding and was therefore properly classified by the CBSA under tariff item 2309.90.99.

CASE 2: TARIFF HEADING 38.15 OR 38.24 (ALUMINUM PELLETS)
The goods in issue in the appeal in *Criterion Catalysts & Technologies Canada Inc v President of the Canada Border Services Agency*[26] were small extruded aluminum pellets consisting of mixtures of various oxides, which were

---

23   AP-97-002 (1998) (CITT), rev'd A-720-98 (2000), 4 TTR (2d) 791 (FCA) [*Flora*].
24   *Ibid* at para 17 (FCA).
25   AP-2007-012 (2007).
26   AP-2009-061 (2010), 15 TTR (2d) 165.

intermediate products used in the manufacture of hydro-treating catalysts that were required in the processing of petroleum products. Both parties agreed that, at the time of importation, the pellets were incomplete catalysts, since they did not contain all of the ingredients necessary to function so as to serve their purpose. The issue was whether the pellets were properly classified by the CBSA under tariff item 3824.90.10 as "oxide preparations to be employed in the removal of sulphide compounds" or whether they should be classified under tariff item 3815.90.90 as "other catalytic preparations not elsewhere specified or included."

The appellant, Criterion, contended that heading 38.15 provided the most specific description of the goods in issue and should therefore be preferred over heading 38.24 by virtue of Rule 3(a) of the *General Rules*. The CBSA, in response, submitted that the goods in issue did not constitute catalytic preparations and, thus, were not classifiable under heading 38.15; therefore it was not necessary to consider Rule 3(a) to determine tariff heading for the goods. According to the CBSA, the goods were not covered by the terms of heading 38.15 and were properly classified in heading 38.24 through the application of Rule 1 of the *General Rules*.

The central issue in the appeal, therefore, was whether the goods in issue were *prima facie* classifiable under heading 38.15. The Tribunal concluded that they could not be, because of the clear language of the Explanatory Note to that heading, which stated that it only covered compounds containing active substances and specific types of catalysts. According to the evidence, the goods in issue did not constitute such compounds.

The Tribunal, therefore, dismissed the appeal. It concluded that the goods in issue were properly classified by the CBSA under tariff heading 38.24. With regard to the subheading level, on the basis of the terms of the relevant subheadings, the Tribunal agreed with the CBSA that subheading 3824.90 was the only subheading in heading 38.24 that could cover the goods in issue, and the goods in issue met the terms of tariff item 3824.90.10, which covered oxide preparations to be employed in the removal of sulphide compounds.

iii) Section VII: Chapters 39 and 40 (Plastics and Rubber)

CASE 1: TARIFF ITEM 3916.10.00 (WOOD-PLASTIC COMPOSITE DECKING FOR EXTERIOR FLOORING)

In its appeal in *Monterra Lumber Mills Ltd v President of the Canada Border Services Agency*,[27] Monterra submitted that the CBSA incorrectly classified the

---

27   AP-2011-055 (2012), 17 TTR (2d) 57.

goods in issue, namely, certain wood-plastic composite decking marketed under the trade name Trex®, under tariff item 3916.10.00, by its advance ruling, and that they should be classified under tariff item 4410.11.90 as "other particle board, oriented strand board (OSB) and similar board (for example waferboard) of wood, whether or not agglomerated with resins or other organic binding substances" or, alternatively, under tariff item 4410.19.90 as "other similar board of wood, whether or not agglomerated with resins or other organic binding substances." The goods in issue were used as flooring elements for exterior decking installed over traditional structural wood framing.

The appellant submitted that the goods in issue were *prima facie* classifiable under both heading 39.16 and heading 44.10, and invoked Rules 1, 2 (b), 3 (a), and 3 (c) of the *General Rules*. It argued that, according to Rule 1, the goods should be classified under heading 44.10 as boards similar to particle boards, of wood particles, agglomerated with polyethylene resins. It then argued that the goods in issue were also *prima facie* classifiable under both headings 39.16 and 44.10 and that, therefore, they should be classified by the application of Rules 2 (b) and 3. The appellant, however, took the position that heading 44.10 was more specific because, by contrast to heading 39.16, it described both components of the goods in issue, that is, both the wood component and the plastic component of "resins" or "polyethylene." In addition, the term "boards" of heading 44.10 provided a more precise description of the goods than the more generic term "profile shapes" of heading 39.16. Accordingly, it suggested that the goods should be classified under heading 44.10 on the basis of Rule 3 (a).

In the alternative, the appellant suggested that the classification proceed by application of Rule 3 (c), under which the heading that occurs last in the numerical order among those that equally merit consideration should govern, which, in this instance, would be tariff heading 44.10.

The CBSA took the position that the goods in issue were properly classified as profile shapes of plastics under heading 39.16 pursuant to Rule 1 of the *General Rules* or, alternatively, in accordance with Rule 3 (b). The goods in issue met both requirements of that heading: (1) to be composed of plastics, and (2) to consist of a profile shape. It submitted that, if the Tribunal determined that the goods in issue were *prima facie* classifiable under both heading 39.16 and heading 44.10, they should remain classified under heading 39.16 because the plastic component imparted the essential character to the whole of the goods in issue. It added that, despite the weight of the wood component (which represented 60 percent of the total weight of the goods in issue), the other factors outlined by the Explanatory Notes to Rule 3 (b) and the Tribunal's caselaw (such as physical properties, function, shape, and price) pointed to the plastic as being the component that gave the goods in issue their essential character.

The Tribunal was of the view that, in light of the evidence presented before it, this appeal could be resolved on the basis of Rule 1 of the *General Rules*, and that, therefore, recourse to the other *General Rules* was not necessary. It was also of the view that the goods in issue did not share important characteristics and functions associated with the goods described in heading 44.10.

On the basis of its analysis of heading 39.16, the Tribunal accepted that the term "plastics" in heading 39.16 included a polymer, and was of the opinion that the goods were classifiable under heading 39.16. In light of the evidence on the record, it was uncontestably the plastic that imparted the essential character to the whole of the goods in issue. However, in this particular case, the Tribunal saw no need to have recourse to any rule other than Rule 1 of the *General Rules*.

The parties agreed that the plastic used to form the goods in issue was "polymer of ethylene." As there were no further breakdowns of subheading 3916.10, in accordance with Rule 6 of the *General Rules* and Rule 1 of the *Canadian Rules*, the Tribunal concluded that the goods in issue were properly classified by the CBSA under tariff item 3916.10.00. Accordingly, the appeal was dismissed.

CASE 2: TARIFF ITEM 3926.40.10 (GIRL FIGURINES OR DOLLS)
The goods in issue in the appeal in *NC Cameron & Sons Ltd v President of the Canada Border Services Agency*[28] were girl figurines, described as "All About Dance BLONDE JAZZ GIRL Figurine," and the issue was whether the goods in issue were properly classified by the CBSA under tariff item 3926.40.10 as "a statuette and other ornamental article" or whether they should be classified under tariff item 9502.10.00 as "a doll representing only a human being, whether or not dressed," as claimed by the appellant.

The appellant argued that heading 95.02 for "[d]olls representing only human beings" was more descriptive than heading 39.26 for "[o]ther articles of plastics and articles of other materials of headings 39.01 to 39.14." It also argued that the justification for the goods in issue being classified under heading 95.02 was found in the Explanatory Notes to Chapter 95, which read as follows: "[Chapter 95] covers toys of all kinds whether designed for the amusement of children or adults .... The articles of [Chapter 95] may, in

---

28   AP-2006-022 (2007), 11 TTR (2d) 634.

general, be made of any material." The appellant also relied on the Explanatory Notes to heading 95.02, which read as follows: "[Heading No. 95.02] includes not only dolls designed for the amusement of children, but also dolls intended for decorative purposes.... Dolls are usually made of rubber, plastics...."

The Tribunal acknowledged that, although the figurines may have an amusement value, that factor was not determinative and did not make them toys for the purpose of tariff classification. "Play value" was an identifying aspect of toys. The goods were not sold as toys, were usually not played with by children, and were not designed to be manipulated. This was particularly true of the bell jars. Moreover, the testimony of the appellant's witness indicated that the goods were marketed as collector's items rather than toys in order to fetch a higher price in the market.

In support of its position, the appellant also invoked the fact that the Explanatory Notes to heading 95.02 stated that goods of that heading included "not only dolls designed for the amusement of children, but also dolls intended for decorative purposes" and that any such "[d]olls are usually made of rubber, plastics...."

Although the Tribunal accepted the proposition that the goods in issue may have a certain decorative element considering its aesthetic value, on balance, it believed that their construction and design were such that it was clearly not meant to be played with in the same way as a doll would normally be or meant to provide amusement.

The goods in issue were permanently rigid because they were cast from a moulding and were mounted on a base. As such, the goods in issue were not dolls. Whether they were intended for decorative purposes or not was therefore irrelevant for the purpose of the Explanatory Notes. Consequently, the Tribunal was of the view that the goods in issue did not fall under heading 95.02.

The Tribunal considered its decision in *Franklin Mint Inc v Commissioner of the Canada Customs and Revenue Agency*,[29] where the issue was whether figurines that evoked the memory of particular scenes in the movie *The Wizard of Oz* should be classified as "other toys" under tariff item 9503.90.00 or whether they were properly classified as statuettes of plastics and other materials under tariff item 3926.40.10. The Tribunal in *Franklin Mint* con-

---

29   AP-2003-013 (2004), 8 TTR (2d) 766 [*Franklin Mint*].

sidered the description of a toy in *Zellers Inc v Deputy Minister of National Revenue*[30] as

> ... something from which one derives amusement or pleasure. Toys can replicate things or animals or have forms of their own. They can be of hard or stiff construction, or be soft and cuddly. They can be designed for manipulation or for display on a shelf. They can be cute and friendly in presentation, or be fierce and frightening. They can be designed for rough and tumble use or require careful handling. Their value is often small in cash terms, although some toys, such as miniature electric train sets, can easily cost thousands of dollars. This is all to say that toys cover a world of products, some of which are readily identified as toys and some of which are recognizable as toys only upon closer inspection.[31]

The Tribunal in *Franklin Mint* had also considered the reasoning in *Regal Confections Inc v Deputy Minister of National Revenue*,[32] which included the following:

> Regarding toys generally, and in light of *Zellers*, the Tribunal notes that, in *Zellers*, the Tribunal referred to the essence of a toy as being amusement. That did not mean, however, that merely because a product provided amusement value, it should necessarily be classified as a toy. It is common knowledge that a child will play for hours with an empty cardboard box, a paper bag or a stick. Thus, the Tribunal was of the view that amusement alone does not make an object a toy for the purpose of tariff classification.[33]

With respect to the application of heading 39.26, the Tribunal observed that the Explanatory Notes to that heading specified that it includes "[s]tatuettes and other ornamental articles." The Tribunal noted that the manufacturer of the good in issue described the good as a figurine and that the dictionary definition of "figurine" referred to by the CBSA defined that word as "a small moulded or carved figure; a statuette." As such, the Tribunal concluded that the good in issue fell under the description of heading 39.26; that, at the subheading level, it fell under subheading 3926.40 for "[s]tatuettes and other ornamental articles"; and that it was classifiable under tariff item 3926.40.10 because it was a statuette. Accordingly, the Tribunal dismissed the appeal.

---

30   AP-97-057(1998) [*Zellers*].
31   Above note 28 at para 13.
32   Above note 16.
33   Above note 28 at para 14.

The Federal Court of Appeal dismissed the appellant's application for judicial review of the Tribunal's decision.

CASE 3: TARIFF ITEM 3921.90.91 OR 3921.90.99 (LAMINATED SHEETS)

The disagreement between the parties in *Formica Canada Inc v Commissioner of Canada Customs and Revenue Agency*[34] was at the tariff item level only. The appellant had imported rigid non-cellular laminated sheets, which the CCRA classified under tariff item 3921.90.99. It claimed that the CCRA should have classified the goods under tariff item 3921.90.91 as "other sheets of plastics of polymers of heading No. 39.09, excluding of formaldehyde resins, of melamine-formaldehyde resins, of phenol-formaldehyde resins or of polyurethanes." Based on evidence that the phenol-formaldehyde monomer units predominated by weight over the melamine-formaldehyde monomer units, and hence they were excluded from tariff item 3921.90.91, the Tribunal concluded that the CCRA had properly classified them under tariff item 3921.90.99 and dismissed the appeal.

CASE 4: TARIFF HEADING 39.24 (SILICON PLASTIC TEATS (NIPPLES))

The goods in issue in *Philips Electronics Ltd v President of the Canada Border Services Agency*[35] were Philips AVENT Airflex Teats (Model No. SCF632/27), which were clear silicone plastic teats (nipples) intended for use with Philips AVENT baby bottles. The baby bottles were sold separately. When in use, the nipples were attached to the bottle by means of a locking collar. A skirt at the bottom of the nipples slid into the neck of the bottle and flexed as the baby sucked, allowing air to flow into the bottle. The nipples were suitable for use by babies aged one month or over. The issue was whether the goods in issue were properly classified by the CBSA under tariff item 3924.90.00 as "other hygienic articles of plastic" or whether they should have been classified under tariff item 8481.30.00 as "check (nonreturn) valves" or under tariff item 8481.80.00 as "other appliances," as claimed by the appellant. In the alternative, the appellant submitted that the goods in issue should be classified under tariff item 8479.90.90 as "parts of machines and mechanical appliances having individual functions, not specified or included elsewhere in Chapter 84."

The Tribunal dismissed the appeal. It concluded that the goods in issue were properly classified by the CBSA under tariff item 3924.90.00 as "other hygienic articles of plastic," applying Rule 6 of the *General Rules* and Rule 1

---

34 AP-2000-041 (2002), 6 TTR (2d) 417.
35 AP-2011-042 (2012), 16 TTR (2d) 722.

of the *Canadian Rules*. They were not classifiable in any of the tariff headings claimed by the appellant, which were 8479.90 and 8481.80. They were not "machines and mechanical appliances having individual functions, not specified or included elsewhere in this Chapter" (heading 84.79), nor were they "(a) taps, cocks, valves or similar appliances and (b) for use on or in pipes, boiler shells, tanks, vats or the like" (heading 84.81). On the other hand, the nipples being made of plastic, they squarely fell under Chapter 39, which covered plastics and articles thereof, among others, and specifically by 39.24. This was confirmed by the relevant Explanatory Notes to heading 39.24, which listed among the examples, "teats for baby bottles (nursing nipples)."

CASE 5: TARIFF HEADING 40.08 (VULCANIZED RUBBER)

The goods in issue in *GCP Elastomeric Ltd v President of the Canada Border Services Agency*[36] were three models of flexible, non-cellular, vulcanized compounded rubber in sheets of various sizes. The issue was whether the rubber mats and sheets were properly classified by the CBSA under tariff item 4008.21.90 as "other plates, sheets and strip of non-cellular rubber," or they should be classified under tariff item 4003.00.00 as "reclaimed rubber in primary forms or in plates, sheets or strip," as submitted by the appellant.

To justify its claim of classification in heading 40.03, the appellant argued that the goods in issue were vulcanized reclaimed rubber sheets, referring to the definition of "reclaimed rubber" found in the Explanatory Notes to heading 40.03. It argued that, since the goods in issue were manufactured from used tires and were subjected to a devulcanization process, they had the essential character of reclaimed rubber. In support of that argument, the appellant submitted a document from the producer of the goods, the Beijing Rubber Company, which detailed the manufacturing process of the goods, and argued that the goods had been manufactured by a process using reclaimed rubber tires, stripped of their steel and fabric elements, shredded and reduced to a fine crumb, and subjected to a devulcanizing process.

There was no dispute between the parties that *prima facie* only one heading was applicable in this case. Therefore the resolution of the appeal turned on whether the goods were made of vulcanized rubber as claimed by the CBSA or whether they were made of reclaimed rubber as claimed by the appellant. The Tribunal examined the terms of the competing headings and any relative notes to Section VII or Chapter 40 in order to determine the heading in which the goods were classifiable.

---

36   AP-2010-011 (2011), 15 TTR (2d) 553.

The Tribunal noted that, according to the terms of heading 40.08, in order for the goods in issue to be classified in that heading, they must, at the time of importation into Canada, be (1) plates, sheets, strip, rods, or profile shapes; (2) of vulcanized rubber; and (3) other than hard rubber.

The Tribunal found that the goods in issue were made of vulcanized rubber. It followed that they were correctly classified under tariff item 4008.21.90 as "other plates, sheets and strip of non-cellular vulcanized rubber, other than hard rubber." The appeal was therefore dismissed.

CASE 6: TARIFF HEADING 40.16 (RUBBER CRAWLER TRACKS)
The goods in issue in *Rollins Machinery Ltd v Deputy Minister of National Revenue*[37] were rubber crawler tracks, composed of vulcanized rubber containing a cord and canvas, as well as steel components within the vulcanized material. They were used as tracks for vehicles. The issue in this appeal was whether the goods in issue were properly classified by the Deputy Minister of National Revenue under tariff item 4016.99.90 as "other articles of vulcanized rubber other than hard rubber" or whether they should be classified under heading 40.10 as "conveyor or transmission belts or belting, of vulcanized rubber" as claimed by the appellant.

The Tribunal had originally concluded that the goods in issue constituted conveyor belting and found that they should be classified under tariff item 4010.19.90 as "other conveyor belting." On appeal to the Federal Court of Appeal, that decision was set aside and the matter remitted to the Tribunal because of an error of law regarding the application of a tariff item that was not in force at the time that the goods were imported into Canada.

Because the matter was returned to the Tribunal for reconsideration on the record as it stood, the Tribunal's decision was based on the expert evidence and the written submissions on the record in the original appeal. The Tribunal was not persuaded by the evidence that the goods in issue can be characterized as "[c]onveyor or transmission belts or belting." Consequently, it reaffirmed its decision to classify the goods in issue under 4016.99.90.

iv) **Section VIII: Chapters 41 to 43 (Raw Hides, Travel Goods, Handbags)**

CASE 1: TARIFF ITEM 4202.32.90 (PROTECTIVE COVERS FOR SMART CELLPHONES)
The goods in issue in *Curve Distribution Services Inc v President of the Canada Border Services Agency*[38] were protective cases for smart cellphones, which

---

37 AP-99-073 (2000), 2 TTR (2d) 348, appeal allowed and remand to Tribunal (*sub nom Deputy Minister of National Revenue v Rollins Machinery Limited*), A-3-98 (1999), 4 TTR (2d) 177 (FCA).
38 AP-2011-023 (2012), 16 TTR (2d) 742.

were specifically designed and shaped to accommodate particular models and to protect them from dust, knocks, and scratches. The CBSA classified the goods under tariff item 4202.32.90 as "articles of a kind normally carried in the pocket or in the handbag with outer surface of sheeting of plastics." The appellant claimed that they should have been classified either under tariff item 4202.99.90 as "other containers" or under tariff item 4202.12.90 as "trunks, suitcases, vanity cases, executive cases, briefcases, school satchels and similar containers with outer surface of plastics."

The Tribunal dismissed the appeal, finding that the protective cases without armbands were properly classified under tariff 4202.32.90 as "articles of a kind normally carried in the pocket or in the handbag with outer surface of sheeting of plastics" and those with armbands under tariff item 4202.92.90 as "other containers with outer surface of sheeting of plastics." It based the decision on the following grounds:

1) The goods were not "containers" similar to the articles specifically named in heading 42.02.
2) They were obviously not trunks, suitcases, vanity cases, and so on, nor handbags, which come under the first two first-level (that is, one-dash) subheadings.
3) That left the other two first-level subheadings, namely, (1) "articles of a kind normally carried in the pocket or in the handbag" and (2) "other." Protective cases without armbands were clearly intended to hold, protect, and carry cellphones while in a pocket or handbag and should therefore be classified as such (that is, under subheading 4202.32), and those with armbands would not normally be carried in a pocket or handbag and should be classified as "other containers" under subheading 4202.92.

CASE 2: TARIFF ITEM 4202.91.90 (CELLPHONE PROTECTIVE COVERS)
In *Nokia Products Limited & Primecell Communications Inc v Commissioner of the Canada Customs and Revenue Agency*,[39] the appellant imported two different cellphone products, which were the subject of separate appeals. The goods in issue in two appeals were soft leather carrying cases and, in the third appeal, car kits. The Tribunal heard all three appeals together.

The appellant had entered the soft leather carrying cases for cellphones under tariff item 8529.90.90 (as "other parts suitable for use solely or prin-

---

39 AP-2001-073 (car kits), AP-2001-074, AP-2001-084 (soft leather cases) (2003), 9 TTR (2d) 314 [*Nokia*].

cipally with the apparatus of heading 85.25 to 85.28"). The CCRA re-determined their classification under tariff item 4202.91.90.

The appellants had entered the car kits for cellphones under 8529.90.90 as "other parts suitable for use solely or principally with the apparatus of headings 85.25 to 85.28" or, in the alternative, under tariff item 8504.40.90 as "other static converters," but the CCRA re-determined their classification under tariff item 8518.30.99 as "other combined microphone/speaker sets." The reasons for allowing the latter appeal are to be found under "Parts and Accessories."

The Tribunal rejected the appellant's argument with respect to the classification of soft leather carrying cases. It was of the view that while a carrying case could be considered as a part, as in the case of a remote-controlled converter that was classified as a part of a television by the Tribunal in a previous case, it said that regard should primarily be given to the Explanatory Note, which specifically provided for the classification of cases in heading 85.29. It accepted the CCRA's argument that carrying cases were not a part but an accessory to the cellphone; they were decorative and protective, and were used to transport and protect the cellphone. In support, the CCRA cited the Federal Court of Appeal's decision in *Deputy Minister of National Revenue for Customs and Excise v Androck Inc*[40] in which the court had held that, to be considered a part, goods had to be related to the entity with which they would be used as a necessary and integral part thereof and not simply be an optional accessory.

The Tribunal noted that, although not explicitly named in the list, the goods in issue were very similar in design and function to a number of items listed in tariff heading 42.02. While the evidence indicated that the leather cases were fitted to the shapes of the cellphone and were physically connected in that manner, the cellphones were complete without the cases; the leather cases were not essential to the operation of the cellphones that they encased and, therefore, were not functionally joined. Rule 1 of the *General Rules*, therefore, applied. The Tribunal dismissed the appeal.

v) *Section X: Chapters 47 to 49 (Pulp and Paper)*

CASE 1: TARIFF ITEM 4911.99.90 (NHL LOGO FLAGS, BANNERS, AND SIMILAR GOODS)
The goods in issue in *Future Product Sales Inc v President of the Canada Border Services Agency*[41] were flags, banners, and car antenna flags. All were made of

---

40   (1987), 74 NR 255 (FCA).
41   AP-2009-056 (2010), 14 TTR (2d) 561.

100 percent woven polyester fabric and were hemmed, folded, and sewn on all edges. The flags were fitted with grommets and the banners with Velcro® strips. They were all screen-printed with NHL team logos on one side of the fabric.

The tariff classification of the goods was in issue. The CBSA classified the flags under tariff item 6307.90.99 as "other made-up articles, including dress patterns, of other textile materials." The appellant submitted that they should be classified under tariff item 4911.99.90 as "other printed matter, including printed pictures and photographs."

The Tribunal allowed the appeal. It was of the view that the printed NHL team logos provided the essential nature or *raison d'être* of the goods in issue; that a distinction must be made between decorative and essential printing. In this case, if the logo is removed, the goods in issue were "blank" made-up textile articles. Put simply, in the case of the goods in issue, the printing was the product and the product was the printing. In the Tribunal's view, further to the Explanatory Notes to Chapter 49, the textile material in this case was the medium on which the NHL team logo was printed. The Explanatory Notes to heading 63.07 indicated that the heading includes "[f]lags, pennants and banners ... ," whereas they specifically excluded "printed matter," directing classification for such goods to Chapter 49. These provisions were not contradictory. Rather, they required the Tribunal to read them as directing classification of made-up textile flags in heading 63.07, whereas certain "printed matter" was redirected to Chapter 49.

The Tribunal agreed with the CBSA's argument that a textile flag or banner with printed decorative pictures or designs may be made-up textile articles of Chapter 63. For example, in the Tribunal's view, a flower design on a textile made-up article was decorative and did not necessarily change the essential nature of the article. However, this argument was not acceptable in the case of the goods in issue, because the evidence showed that the NHL team logos had an importance that was well beyond that of a decoration.

The Tribunal noted:

1) The pictorial representations of NHL team logos were protected registered trademarks, the use of which was closely controlled by the NHL.
2) As was the case in *Éditions Panini du Canada Ltée v Deputy Minister of National Revenue for Customs and Excise*,[42] it was the printed pictorial content of a sports card or, in this case, the printed NHL team logo on

---

42 AP-92-018 (1993).

the flags, that conferred the essential nature and use of the goods. The appellant would not sell plain white flags and banners.

For the foregoing reasons, in accordance with Rule 1 of the *General Rules* and the applicable tariff, the Tribunal concluded that the goods in issue should be classified under heading 49.11. Pursuant to the *Canadian Rules*, it followed that the goods in issue should be classified under tariff item 4911.99.90 as "other printed matter, including printed pictures and photographs."

vi) Section XI: Chapters 50 to 63 (Textiles)

CASE 1: TARIFF HEADING 55.03 (TUFTS OF SYNTHETIC IMITATING LOCKS OF HAIR)

The decision of the Tribunal in the appeal of *Coloridé Inc*[43] with respect to the classification of *"mèches"* (small tufts of synthetic material, being nylon) is found in Section D(9)(c), above in this chapter, in the discussion of General Rule 4.

CASE 2: TARIFF HEADINGS 40.16 AND 56.09 (BUNGEE CORDS)

The appeal in *Innovak DIY Products Inc v President of the Canada Border Services Agency*[44] related to the tariff classification of bungee cords of various lengths with hooks at each end (the goods in issue), which the CBSA had classified under tariff item 5609.00.00 or, in the alternative, under tariff item 6307.90.99. The appellant claimed that they should be classified under heading 40.16.

Tariff heading 40.16 covered "Other articles of vulcanized rubber other than hard rubber" and tariff item 4016.10.00 read "Of cellular rubber."

In contrast, the three relevant tariff headings, 56.04, 56.07, and 56.09 provided as follows:

> 56.04: Rubber thread and cord, textile covered; textile yarn, and strip and the like of heading 54.04 or 54.05, impregnated, coated, covered or sheathed with rubber or plastics

> 56.07: Twine, cordage, ropes and cables, whether or not plaited or braided and whether or not impregnated, coated, covered or sheathed with rubber or plastics

> 56.09: Articles of yarn, strip or the like of heading 54.04 or 54.05, twine, cordage, rope or cables, not elsewhere specified or included

---

43 Above note 12.
44 AP-2006-009 (2006), 10 TTR (2d) 674.

The appellant submitted that the goods that are described in Chapters 50 to 63 of Section XI were textile goods. Various textile goods may contain some rubber, as do the elastic of socks or briefs, but this rubber played a minor role, and such goods still remained identifiable as textile goods.

The CBSA argued that the goods in issue were cords of man-made fibres and rubber, cut to length and fitted with hooks, and were properly classified under tariff item 5609.00.00.

The Tribunal noted that, although the goods in issue were referred to as bungee cords, dictionary definitions appear to require that the strands of a cord be twisted or woven together in order to be a cord. Nevertheless, in the case of the goods in issue, that distinction made no difference as heading 56.04 covered both thread and cord.

However, the goods in issue were not just textile-covered rubber thread or cord, but were cut-to-length materials of heading 56.04 with hooks at each end. Accordingly, as properly advanced by both parties, once a material of heading 56.04 underwent further manufacturing, it became an "article," and the Tribunal must look to a heading that provides for the classification of "articles." Two headings were suggested to the Tribunal: heading 56.09 by the CBSA and heading 40.16 by the appellant.

The Tribunal examined both headings 56.09 and 40.16. It noted that heading 56.09 covered "[a]rticles of yarn, strip or the like of heading 54.04 or 54.05, twine, cordage, rope or cables, not elsewhere specified or included." In the Tribunal's view, the word "includes" in the Explanatory Notes to the heading were meant to provide for the inclusion of goods such as those in issue.

Given that the semi-finished goods (the cord without the hooks) would fall under heading 56.04 and, as a result, could not, in their finished form, fall under heading 40.16, the Tribunal concluded that, by application of Rule 1 of the *General Rules* giving consideration to the Explanatory Notes, the goods in issue were properly classified under heading 56.09 and under tariff item 5609.00.00. Given that conclusion, the Tribunal found no need to address the alternative classification advanced by the CBSA. Consequently, it dismissed the appeal.

CASE 3: TARIFF ITEM 6210.30.00 (WOMEN'S JACKETS)
The goods in issue in the appeal of *Helly Hansen Leisure Canada v President of the Canada Border Services Agency*[45] were two styles of women's jackets, both hooded with Helly Hansen logos and a right-over-left closure. The outer shell of these jackets consisted of two layers—a layer of uniformly dyed textile

---

45   AP-2006-054 (2008), 14 TTR (2d) 53. aff'd 2009 FCA 345.

fabric woven from yarns of nylon filaments and a layer of plastics. The layer of fabric formed the exterior surface of the jackets, and the layer of plastics formed the interior of the jackets. The textile fabric was completely laminated on one side with the layer of plastics. There was a visible pattern within the textile fabric used in both jackets. Each fabric had its own distinctive pattern. In the case of the *Lyric* jacket, the pattern consisted of squares of different sizes. In the case of the *Sunrise* jacket, it consisted of a series of T-shaped lines on the surface of the textile fabric. The goods in issue were worn for recreational activities, such as skiing.

The CBSA, by an advance ruling, classified the goods in issue under tariff item 6210.30.00 as "women's jackets made of fabrics of heading 59.03."

The issue in this appeal was whether the two styles of women's jackets (*Sunrise* and *Lyric*) were properly classified by the CBSA under tariff item 6210.30.00 as "other garments made up of fabrics of heading 59.03, of the type described in subheading 6202.11 to 6202.19" or whether they should have been classified under tariff item 3926.20.95 as "other articles of apparel and clothing accessories, of plastics combined with knitted or woven fabrics, bolducs, nonwovens or felt," as claimed by the appellant.

The Tribunal dismissed the appeal. It concluded that the goods in issue were properly classified pursuant to Rule 6 of the *General Rules* and Rule 1 of the *Canadian Rules* under tariff item 6210.30.00 as "other garments made up of fabrics of heading No. 59.03 of the type described in subheading Nos. 6202.11 to 6202.19."

The appellant's application for judicial review was dismissed by the Federal Court of Appeal with costs.

CASE 4: TARIFF HEADING 62.16 (ICE HOCKEY GLOVES)

The goods in issue in *Sher-Wood Hockey Inc v President of the Canada Border Services Agency*[46] were two models of ice hockey gloves, HG 5030 and HG PMP-X. The gloves were designed to be worn by forwards and defencemen to protect the hands; both models were very similar and made of the same materials.

The issue in the appeal was whether the goods were correctly classified by the CBSA under tariff item 6216.00.00 as "gloves of textile materials not knitted or crocheted" or whether they should be classified under tariff item 3926.20.92 as "articles of apparel (non-disposable gloves) of plastics," as claimed by the appellant.

---

46 AP-2009-045 (2011), 15 TTR (2d) 336, appeal to Federal Court of Appeal discontinued, file no A-167-11.

The Tribunal dismissed the appeal. It concluded that the goods in issue were properly classified by the CBSA under tariff item 6216.00.00 as "gloves of textile materials not knitted or crocheted."

The parties had agreed that the goods in issue were gloves specifically designed and used for the sport of ice hockey. They had also agreed that the gloves could be classified in Chapter 95, which generally covered sports requisites, including sports or athletic equipment. The Tribunal accepted the parties' submissions and found that note 1(u) to Chapter 95, which excluded the goods, applied. Since they were excluded, it followed that the goods must be classified elsewhere, according to their constituent material.

Both parties accepted the laboratory analysis, according to which the ice hockey gloves consisted of two major components sewn together: (1) The component that covered the greater surface area consisted of black sheets of cellular plastics (polyurethane) combined with textile fabrics woven from yarns of different colours (mixture yarns blended from black fibres; grey fibres; and clear, colourless fibres). The fabric was not bleached, unbleached, or uniformly dyed. (2) The component that covered the lesser surface area consisted of an off-white nonwoven fabric consisting of man-made (nylon) fibres impregnated with plastics (polyurethane). The first component covered the back of the hand, the wrist, and part of the forearm, whereas the second component covered only the palm of the hand. Thus, the composition of the material on the back of the gloves was different from that of the material on the palm portion. Together, these components formed the exterior of the goods in issue. According to the evidence, the gloves also contained high-density foam padding and hard plastic padding enclosed inside the outer surface material or back portion.

As it was not disputed that the goods in issue were gloves, the question remained whether they were gloves fitting the description in heading 62.16.

The Explanatory Notes to heading 62.16 provided that the heading covered "gloves, mittens and mitts, of textile fabrics (including lace) other than knitted or crocheted fabric." Thus, heading 62.16 clearly included gloves that were (1) "made-up" articles, (2) of any textile fabric, (3) other than knitted and crocheted fabric. If certain conditions were met, gloves of heading 62.16 might also contain parts or accessories of other materials.

The appellant contended that the ice hockey gloves should be classified in Chapter 39 on the basis of Rule 1 of the *General Rules*. The Tribunal did not accept that argument. In its opinion, the Explanatory Notes to Chapter 62 did not state that goods were necessarily excluded from classification in Chapter 62 (and thus in heading 62.16) where the presence of non-textile materials constituted more than mere trimming.

In light of the above, and based on Rules 1 and 2 (b) of the *General Rules*, the Tribunal concluded that the goods in issue were gloves of textile materials classifiable under heading 62.16. As heading 62.16 was not divided at the subheading or tariff item level, the Tribunal held that the goods in issue were properly classified by the CBSA under tariff item 6216.00.00.

CASE 5: TARIFF ITEM 6307.90.99 (ROLLER COVERS)

The goods in issue in the appeal in *BMC Coaters Inc v President of the Canada Border Services Agency*[47] were roller covers, which were either open at both ends or open at one end with a cap on the other end; they were replaceable and provided different finishes to paint applications, depending on the type of textile material used and its pile or thickness. According to the appellant, the goods were sold individually or in packages of two to six. The parties agreed that, when the roller covers were mounted on a handle, they formed "paint rollers." The goods in issue were imported without handles. The parties also agreed that the roller covers consisted of plastic, nylon, or polypropylene tubes and in standard lengths. The tubes were covered with knitted or woven textile material consisting of polyester, microfibre, wool, mohair, velour, acrylic, or fabric mixtures.

The parties disputed the tariff classification of the goods in issue, which the CBSA determined as "replacement rollers" or "roller covers" under tariff item 6307.90.99 ("other made-up articles, including dress patterns, of other textile materials") and the appellant claimed that they should be classified under tariff item 9603.40.10 as "paint pads and rollers of textile materials."

The Tribunal dismissed the appeal. It determined that the goods did not come under tariff item 9603.40.10 as claimed by the appellant, but were properly classified by the CBSA under heading 63.07.

With respect to the subheading in which the goods in issue fell, there were three subheadings to choose from, namely 6307.10, 6307.20, and 6307.90. Subheading 6307.10 covered "Floor-cloths, dish-cloths, dusters and similar cleaning cloths," 6307.20 covered "Life-jackets and life-belts," and 6307.90 covered "Other." As the goods in issue obviously did not fit the terms of the first or second subheading, the Tribunal found that the third subheading applied. In that subheading there were numerous items with tariff item 6307.90.99 being the default. Since the first two tariff items did not apply, the Tribunal held, applying Rule 1 of the *General Rules* and Rule 1 of the *Canadian Rules*, that the goods in issue were covered by the default tariff item, namely, 6307.90.99.

---

47   AP-2009-071 (2010), 15 TTR (2d) 171.

CASE 6: TARIFF ITEM 6307.20.00 (NEOPRENE PERSONAL FLOTATION DEVICES)

The goods in issue in *Canadian Tire Corporation Ltd v President of the Canada Border Services Agency*[48] were neoprene personal flotation devices (PFDs). The issue in the appeal was whether these PFDs were properly classified by the CBSA under tariff item 6307.20.00 as "life jackets" or whether they should be classified under tariff item 3926.90.90 as "other articles of plastics and articles of other materials of headings 39.01 to 39.14," as claimed by the appellant. Both parties had agreed that the goods in issue met the common definition of a life jacket and were essentially the same as life jackets. They had also agreed that the life jackets were *prima facie* classifiable under heading 63.07 as "other made up articles." However, they disagreed as to the importance of the plastic sheets, in regard to the classification of the life jackets.

The Tribunal dismissed the appeal. It held that the goods were classifiable under heading 63.07, which was part of Section XI, and by virtue of Note 2(p) to Chapter 39, which excluded goods of Section XI (textiles and textile articles), they were excluded from classification under heading 39.26. Therefore, Rules 2 (b) and 3 (b) of the *General Rules* could not be applied and Rule 1 was sufficient to determine the classification of the life jackets in only one heading, which was *prima facie* heading 63.07 ("other made up articles"). Therefore, the Tribunal concluded that the CBSA correctly classified the goods in issue under tariff item 6307.20.00 as "life jackets."

CASE 7: TARIFF ITEM 6305.33.00 (ONION BAGS)

The appellant in *Agri-Pack v Commissioner of the Canada Customs and Revenue Agency*[49] imported eight kinds of onion bags, which it entered under tariff item 5608.19.90 as "other made up fishing nets and other made up nets of textile material." The CCRA re-determined them under tariff item 6305.33.00 as "other sacks and bags of polyethylene or polypropylene strip or the like."

Referring to the Explanatory Notes to heading 56.08 as claimed by the appellant, the Tribunal was of the view that that heading could not cover the goods in issue as the Explanatory Notes expressly state that goods cannot fall under heading 56.08 if they are more specifically covered under another heading. That was the case in this instance. As the bags were woven from polypropylene strip, the Tribunal held that under Rule 1 of the *General*

---

48   AP-2009-019 (2010), 14 TTR (2d) 631, aff'd 2011 FCA 242 [*Canadian Tire #1*].
49   AP-2003-010, (2004), 9 TTR (2d) 462, var'd 2005 FCA 414, remand to CITT AP-2003-010R (2006), 10 TTR (2d) 86.

Rules and Rule 1 of the *Canadian Rules*, the goods were properly classified by the CCRA under tariff item 6305.33.00, as "other sacks and bags of polyethylene or polypropylene strip or the like." The appeal was, therefore, dismissed.

The Federal Court of Appeal dismissed the appellant's application for judicial review. It also dismissed the CCRA's cross-appeal and referred the matter back to the Tribunal, asking it to address the CCRA's argument, so that it may determine whether Chapter 63 Note 2(a) had the effect of excluding the application of heading 63.05. The court agreed with the Tribunal that the test "for use in another good" was whether it was "physically connected and functionally joined to that other good."

CASE 8: TARIFF HEADINGS 61.10 AND 61.14 (NECK TOPS AND ONE-PIECE GARMENTS)
In *Bauer Hockey Corporation v President of the Canada Border Services Agency*,[50] the appellant imported two hockey products, namely, (1) premium and core short- and long-sleeved integrated neck tops, and (2) one-piece garments. It entered their classification under tariff heading 95.06, which the CBSA re-determined under headings 61.10 and 61.14. The latter tariff items specifically covered jerseys, pullovers, cardigans, waistcoats, and similar articles, knitted or crocheted.

The Tribunal analyzed the nomenclature of heading 95.06 as well as of headings 61.10 and 61.14 before coming to the conclusion that the CBSA had correctly classified the products under tariff items 61.10 amd 61.14. It noted that Chapter 95 covered "toys, games and sports requisites, and parts and accessories thereof" and that heading 95.06 specifically covered the residual category of "articles and equipment for general physical exercise, gymnastics, athletics, other sports (including table-tennis) or outdoor games, not specified or included elsewhere in this Chapter." On the other hand, heading 61.14 specifically covered "other garments, knitted or crocheted" and tariff item 6114.30.00, paragraph (e) covered "sports clothing or fancy dress, of textiles, of Chapter 61 or 62." However, Note 1 to Section XI, which includes Chapter 61, provided that the Section did not cover ". . . (t) Articles of Chapter 95 (for example, toys, games, sports requisites and nets)."

The Tribunal agreed with the shared view of the parties that to be classified under heading 61.10, the goods in issue must incorporate "incidentally protective components," such as elbow pads sewn on sleeves and used for certain sports, for example, soccer goalkeeper jerseys. The issue, therefore, turned on the meaning of the term "incidentally protective component."

---

50   AP-2011-011 (2012), 16 TTR (2d) 611.

The Tribunal was satisfied that the protection afforded by the integrated neck guard and by the removable plastic groin cup was incidental to the primary function of the goods in issue, which was that of a base-layer hockey garment. Similarly, the Explanatory Notes to heading 61.14 provided that "(5) Special articles of apparel, whether or not incorporating incidentally protective components such as pads or padding in the elbow, knee or groin areas, used for certain sports . . . (e.g. fencing clothing, jockeys' silks . . .) are included in this tariff heading, but protective equipment for sports or games (e.g. masks and breast plates, ice hockey pants, etc.) are excluded."

Therefore, on the basis of Rule 1 of the *General Rules*, the Tribunal concluded that the goods were properly classified by the CBSA and dismissed the appeal.

CASE 9: TARIFF ITEM 6116.93.00 (OVEN MITTS)
The appellant in *VGI Village Green Imports v President of the Canada Border Services Agency*[51] imported oven mitts, which it entered under tariff item 3926.20.92 as "mittens or non-disposable gloves" or, in the alternative, under tariff item 4015.90.10 as "protective suits and parts thereof, to be employed in a noxious atmosphere," or, in the further alternative, under tariff item 4015.90.20 as "diving suits." The CBSA re-determined their classification under tariff item 6116.93.00 as "gloves, mittens and mitts, knitted or crocheted, other than impregnated, coated or covered with plastics or rubber, of synthetic fibres." The parties disputed the tariff classification and also disagreed as to the construction and composition of the oven mitts.

The appellant argued that the goods in issue should be classified under heading 39.26 as "other articles of plastics and articles of other materials of headings 39.01 to 39.14" because they were composed of neoprene, which is the "needed, major, useful component" of the goods in issue. It claimed that, since neoprene is a synthetic polymer, it was a plastic. It described the composition of the goods in issue in the same manner as its supplier, 30 percent polyester and 70 percent styrene-butadiene rubber (SBR); that the polyester textile contained in the goods in issue was used to give comfort on the inside and for decorative purposes on the outside; and that the polyester textile was used for reinforcing purposes only.

The appellant argued that the decorative layer of polyester found on the goods in issue did not impact their function and should therefore not affect their classification.

---

51   AP-2010-046 (2012), 16 TTR (2d) 333.

In the alternative, the appellant argued that the goods in issue should be classified under tariff item 4015.90.10 as "protective suits and parts thereof." It preferred tariff item 4015.90.10 over tariff item 4015.90.20 (diving suits) because the former had a lower rate of duty than the latter.

The CBSA argued that the goods in issue were properly classified under heading 61.16 as "gloves, mittens and mitts, knitted or crocheted," which heading applied, *inter alia*, to articles made up of fabrics of heading 59.06. It relied on two laboratory reports that indicated that the goods in issue consisted of knitted textile fabrics of yarns of synthetic fibres (polyester). In support of that position, the CBSA relied on the definition of "textile fabric" in Chapter 59 and in Note 1 to that Chapter.

The CBSA also submitted that the goods in issue met the definition of a rubberized textile fabric set out in Note 4 to Chapter 59, as well as the weight condition set out in Note 4(a)(i) (not more than 1,500 g/m^2). It also relied on the Explanatory Notes to Section XI, which indicated that the section "covers ... man-made ... made up articles" of the textile industry, with the condition for "made up" articles of Note 7(e) to Section XI being met in this instance.

On the basis of the evidence on the record of this matter, the Tribunal concluded that the goods in issue contained SBR and that, in accordance with the Explanatory Notes to Chapter 40, that material is a synthetic rubber. Therefore, the goods in issue were not made of plastic, and therefore they were not classifiable under heading 39.26.

With regard to the appellant's alternative position, that the goods in issue should be classified under heading 40.15 as "articles of apparel and clothing accessories (including gloves, mittens and mitts), for all purposes, of vulcanized rubber other than hard rubber," the Tribunal noted that as per the Explanatory Notes to heading 40.15, in order for the goods in issue to be classifiable in that heading they need to meet two conditions: (1) they must be articles of apparel and clothing accessories (including gloves, mittens, and mitts), assembled by sewing; the Tribunal found that the goods in issue met these requirements—both parties agreed that these articles were oven mitts; and (2) they must also be either (a) wholly of rubber; (b) of knitted fabrics laminated with rubber, other than those falling under Section XI as per Note 4 to Chapter 59; or (c) of rubber, with parts of textile fabric, when the rubber is the constituent giving the goods their essential character.

The Tribunal found that the goods in issue were not wholly of rubber, according to both the laboratory reports and the appellant's description of those goods.

On the balance of the evidence before it, the Tribunal found that component 2 of the goods in issue was a sheet of vulcanized rubber where the textile fabric was present on one surface only. It did not have an important role and was there merely for reinforcing purposes. However, to conclude that the palm area of the goods in issue was of vulcanized rubber was not sufficient for the goods in issue to be classifiable under heading 40.15; it needed to meet the condition in Note 3 of the Explanatory Notes to heading 40.15. The test under Note 3 was whether the rubber (that is, component 2, which was the palm area of the mitt, made of vulcanized rubber), with parts of textile fabrics (that is, component 1, which was the back and underside of the mitt and the back of the thumb, made of rubberized textile fabrics), was the constituent giving the goods their essential character. The Tribunal was unable to reach such a conclusion in this instance.

On balance, in considering all the elements above, the Tribunal could not conclude that the vulcanized rubber (component 2) provided the goods in issue their essential character. Rather, both the rubberized textile fabric (component 1) and the vulcanized rubber (component 2) contributed equally to giving the goods in issue their essential character.

The Tribunal found that the goods in issue failed to meet the condition set out in Note 3 of the Explanatory Notes to heading 40.15 and that, therefore, the goods in issue were not classifiable under heading 40.15.

With respect to the CBSA's argument that the goods in issue were classifiable under Chapter 61 (articles of apparel and clothing accessories, knitted or crocheted) and, more precisely, under heading 61.16 (gloves, mittens and mitts, knitted or crocheted), the Tribunal found that the goods in issue were made up of two components, one of vulcanized rubber and one of rubberized textile fabrics where the textile fabric was not present merely for reinforcing purposes. Accordingly, the rubberized textile fabric was not excluded from heading 59.06 in conformity with Note 4 to Chapter 59.

Under Rule 1 of the *General Rules*, the classification is to be determined according to the terms of the headings, and relevant Section and Chapter notes. In the Tribunal's view, the terms of heading 61.16 squarely described the goods in issue. Indeed, the goods in issue were "mitts" made of knitted rubberized textile fabric. In addition, Note 1 to Chapter 61 directs that the chapter "applies only to made up ... articles." The goods in issue were articles as described above. Finally, Note 7(e) to Section XI defines the expression "made up," among others, as "[a]ssembled by sewing." The goods in issue met that requirement as well, that is, the three components of the goods in issue had been stitched together.

As to the subheading and tariff item levels, in accordance with Rules 1 and 6 of the *General Rules*, the Tribunal noted that, according to the laboratory reports, the knitted textile fabrics were of polyester yarns and that polyester was a synthetic fibre. Consequently, the Tribunal found that the goods in issue were properly classified by the CBSA under tariff item 6116.93.00 as knitted mitts of synthetic fibres. Accordingly, it dismissed the appeal.

CASE 10: TARIFF ITEM 6307.90.99 (WEBBING STRAPS)

The appellant in *Kinedyne Canada Limited v President of the Canada Border Services Agency*[52] imported straps, described as webbing, which consisted of a resin-coated polyester. It claimed that the goods in issue were correctly entered by it on importation under tariff item 8431.10.00 as "parts suitable for use solely or principally with the machinery of heading No. 84.25" but the CBSA re-determined them under tariff item 6307.90.99 as "other made up articles of other textile materials."

The Tribunal analyzed heading 63.07 to determine if the goods in issue could be brought under that heading. It noted that, in order to be classifiable under that heading, the goods in issue must be (1) "made up" articles, (2) of any textile fabric, (3) webbing carrier straps or similar articles, and (4) not included more specifically elsewhere in the nomenclature.

On the basis of the evidence presented at the hearing and Note 16 of the Explanatory Notes to heading 63.07, the Tribunal concluded that the goods in issue closely resembled, and were similar to, webbing carrier straps. It also found that the goods in issue were textile articles similar to webbing carrier straps, which were specifically included in the list of articles found in the Explanatory Notes to heading 63.07; the goods in issue were, therefore, classifiable in that heading.

Turning next to heading 84.31, which the appellant claimed was the proper heading, the Tribunal found that, as the goods in issue were articles of textile materials, the Explanatory Notes to Section XVI, Note I(B), precluded their classification in Section XVI. It also found that the goods cannot be more specifically included in a heading from which they are explicitly excluded.

Since heading 84.31 was eliminated for possible classification, the Tribunal concluded that the goods in issue came under heading 63.07 as determined by the CBSA. With regard to their classification at the subheading level, the Tribunal noted that there were eight tariff items in 6307.90, but the first seven were clearly inapplicable to the goods in issue; therefore,

---

52 AP-2010-027 (2011), 15 TTR (2d) 790.

pursuant to Rule 1 of the *Canadian Rules*, they must be classified under 6307.90.99 as "other made up articles of other textile materials." As a result of this analysis, the appeal was dismissed.

CASE 11: TARIFF ITEM 6307.90.99 (CARGO MATES—WEBBING STRAPS)
In *Rui Royal International Corp v President of the Canada Border Services Agency*,[53] the appellant imported "Crawford Cargo Mates" emergency tow straps, the goods in issue, which it entered under tariff item 8708.99.90 as "other parts and accessories of the motor vehicles of heading Nos. 87.01 to 87.05." The CBSA re-determined their classification under tariff item 6307.90.99 as "other made up articles of other textile materials."

The Tribunal dismissed the appeal and affirmed the CBSA's decision. It gave the following reasons for the decision:

1) The goods in issue were not classifiable under heading 87.08 as "parts and accessories of the motor vehicles of headings 87.01 to 87.05." The effect of Note 3 to the Chapter was that when a part or accessory could fall in one or more other Sections as well as in Section XVII, its final classification was determined by its principal use. Thus, the steering gear, braking systems, road wheels, mudguards, and so on, used on many of the mobile machines falling within Chapter 84, were virtually identical to those used on the lorries of Chapter 87, and since their principal use was with lorries, such parts and accessories were classified in this Section. The goods in issue were not specifically mentioned in the list of examples provided in Note (III)(C) of the General Explanatory Notes to Section XVII and, in particular, they were not towing ropes.

2) Heading 63.07 more specifically described the goods in issue than heading 87.08. The goods in issue met the terms of heading 63.07 and the related Chapter Note and Explanatory Notes, which specified four conditions in order for the goods to be classified in that heading, namely: (a) they must be articles; (b) they must meet the definition of "made up"; (c) they must be of any textile fabric; and (d) they must satisfy the proviso that they not be more specifically described in other Chapters of Section XI or elsewhere in the nomenclature. The evidence indicated that the goods in issue shared sufficient characteristics with webbing carrier straps in both make and functionality to allow them to be classified in heading 63.07. They closely resembled webbing carrier straps in

---

53 AP-2010-003 (2011), 15 TTR (2d) 485, appeal dismissed, A-229-11 (28 October 2011) (FCA) [*Rui Royal International*].

that both products were made of strong, narrow woven fabric and both were capable of withstanding strain. In addition, the goods in issue and webbing carrier straps performed similar functions.

3) On the basis of the evidence referred to in (2), the Tribunal found that the goods in issue were articles similar to webbing carrier straps. Accordingly, they were included under heading 63.07 as "articles similar to webbing carrier straps" and were not more specifically included in heading 87.08.

4) Therefore, in accordance with Rule 1 of the *General Rules* and the applicable tariff nomenclature identified above, the goods were properly classified under heading 63.07. Pursuant to Rule 6 of the *General Rules* and Rule 1 of the *Canadian Rules*, it followed that they should be classified under tariff item 6307.90.99 as "other made up articles of other textile materials."

vii) Section XII: Chapters 64 to 67 (Footwear, Headgear, Others)

CASE 1: TARIFF HEADING 64.06 (FOOTWEAR LEATHER UPPERS)
The goods in issue in the appeal of *Tai Lung (Canada) Ltd v President of the Canada Border Services Agency*[54] were footwear components, specifically, leather uppers incorporating a metal toecap and plastic outer soles. The issue in the appeal was whether the footwear components were correctly classified by the CBSA under heading 64.03 as "complete footwear" or whether they should be classified under heading 64.06 as "parts of footwear," as claimed by the appellant.

The Tribunal allowed the appeal. For the following reasons, it found that the goods in issue should be classified under heading 64.06 as "parts of footwear."

The appellant argued that the goods in issue must be classified according to Rule 1 of the *General Rules* and that there was no need to consider Rule 2(a). In this regard, the appellant referred to the Chapter Notes of Section XII, which defined the term "outer sole" as used in headings 64.01 to 64.05 to mean that part of the footwear (other than the attached heel) that, when in use, was in contact with the ground. It was the appellant's submission that it was the middle sole that was attached to the upper and that, when the two imported components, that is, the upper attached to the middle sole and the outer sole, were put together, it was only the outer sole that was in contact

---

54   Above note 10.

with the ground. Since heading 64.06 specifically named parts of footwear (including uppers, whether or not attached to soles other than outer soles), the appellant argued that, on the basis of the *General Rules*, the goods in issue, that is, the upper attached to the sole other than the outer sole and the outer sole, were included in that heading.

The appellant also argued that the processes that occurred at its factory were more than mere assembly operations and that the goods produced took on a new form and possessed different qualities and properties. In other words, further working operations were performed to render the goods in issue safety footwear. Consequently, the goods did not satisfy the requirements of the Explanatory Notes to Rule 2(a) of the *General Rules* regarding articles presented unassembled or disassembled.

The CBSA argued that the *eo nomine* principle no longer applied, as it was used to determine the way goods were classified prior to 1 January 1988. The *General Rules* superseded the *eo nomine* principle, and tariff classification is determined according to these rules.

The CBSA further argued that at the time of importation the main features of the upper were present, such as hang tags describing the product and indicating the price, labels (for example, CSA label), and laces. The CBSA also argued that, in the context of provision (VII) of the Explanatory Notes to Rule 2(a) regarding unassembled or disassembled articles, the processes undertaken in Tai Lung's plant only served to "finish" the product for retail sale. According to the CBSA, the principal feature of footwear, that is, to cover the foot, the ankle, and part of the leg, was maintained regardless of the processes being applied.

On the basis of the evidence, and having considered the arguments of both parties, it was the Tribunal's view that heading 64.06 correctly described the goods in issue. In advancing the contrary position, the CBSA contended that, because the uppers and the outer soles in issue were imported together, they formed complete footwear and cannot be considered as "parts of footwear." It also submitted that the goods in issue had the "essential character" of the finished and assembled product and that they should therefore be classified as such pursuant to Rule 2(a) of the *General Rules*.

The Tribunal did not accept the CBSA's arguments. In its view, the language of heading 64.06 was clear with regard to its application to the goods in issue, in that it precisely covered parts of footwear, including uppers, whether or not attached to soles other than outer soles. Consequently, Rule 1 of the *General Rules* resolved the classification, and there was no need to consider Rule 2.

As for the CBSA's argument with regard to the application of Rule 2(a), the Tribunal agreed with the applicant that the processes to which the goods in issue were subjected went beyond "assembly" to constitute "further working" and therefore fell outside the scope of Rule 2(a).

In the Tribunal's opinion, the goods in issue were imported in an unfinished state, that is, requiring further working, and therefore failed to qualify as articles that merely required assembly, as envisaged by provision (VII) of the Explanatory Notes to Rule 2(a).

CASE 2: TARIFF ITEM 6405.20.90 (CHILDREN'S ANIMAL-SHAPED SLIPPERS)

The goods in *Laxus Products Ltd v Commissioner of the Canada Customs and Revenue Agency*[55] were slippers in the shape of animals that were designed to be worn by children. The issue in the appeal was whether the goods were properly classified by the CCRA under tariff item 6405.20.90 as "other footwear, with uppers of textile materials" or whether they should be classified under tariff item 9503.41.00 as "stuffed toys representing animals or non-human creatures" or, in the alternative, under tariff item 9503.49.00 as "other toys," as claimed by the appellant.

The Tribunal dismissed the appeal. It found that the goods in issue were *prima facie* footwear of heading 64.05. They were also *prima facie* toys of heading 95.03. The Explanatory Notes to Chapter 95 provided that this chapter covered "toys of all kinds whether designed for the amusement of children or adults." The Explanatory Notes to heading 95.03 provided that the heading covered "toys intended essentially for the amusement of persons (children or adults)." The Explanatory Notes to heading 95.03 also provided that goods remained "toys" even if they were capable of a limited "use." The Tribunal pointed out that a toy was generally distinguishable from the "real" item by its size and limited capacity. In both *Zellers* and *Regal*, it had stated that, in essence, a toy was something from which one derived pleasure or amusement—"an object intended to amuse and with which to play." The goods in issue had an amusement function, and therefore, they can be considered as toys.

However, the Tribunal considered that both headings were not equally descriptive for the purposes of Rule 3(a). It was of the view that, while the term "toy" covered a wide variety of goods, the term "footwear" was limited to goods that were worn on the feet. Therefore, heading 64.05 provided a more specific description of the goods in issue, as "other footwear," than did heading 95.03 as "toy."

---

55 AP-99-117 (2001), 5 TTR (2d) 372.

Given the foregoing, the Tribunal held that the goods in issue were correctly classified under tariff item 6405.20.90 as "other footwear, with uppers of textile materials." Consequently, the appeal was dismissed.

viii) Section XIII: Chapters 68 to 70 (Stone, Plaster, Cement, Asbestos, Ceramic, Glass)

CASE 1: TARIFF ITEM 6802.91.00 (MARBLE OR GRANITE TILES)

The goods in issue in *Active Marble & Tile Ltd v Commissioner of the Canada Customs and Revenue Agency*[56] were marble and granite tiles. The issue in the appeal was whether the goods were correctly classified by the CCRA under tariff item 6802.91.00 as "worked monumental or building stone ... Other: ... Marble, travertine and alabaster" and tariff item 6802.93.00 as "worked monumental or building stone ... Other: ... Granite," or whether they should be classified under tariff item 6802.21.00 as "worked monumental or building stone ... Other monumental or building stone and articles thereof, simply cut or sawn, with a flat or even surface: ... Marble, travertine and alabaster" and tariff item 6802.23.00 as "worked monumental or building stone .... Other monumental or building stone and articles thereof, simply cut or sawn, with a flat or even surface: ... Granite," as claimed by the appellant.

The Tribunal dismissed the appeal. In its view, the granite and marble tiles in issue were not "simply cut or sawn." It was clear from the evidence that the edges of the tiles were cut and sawn and further processed by bevelling. The tiles in issue were therefore correctly classified under tariff item 6802.91.00 and 6802.93.00, since they were more than "simply cut or sawn" and, therefore, could not be classified under tariff item 6802.21.00 and 6802.23.00.

CASE 2: TARIFF ITEM 6807.10.00 (ROOFING SHEETS)

The goods in issue in two appeals in *Convoy Supply Ltd v Commissioner of the Canada Customs and Revenue Agency*[57] were roofing sheets that were imported from the United States in eleven shipments under the brand names GlasPly IV and GlasPly Premier. The goods were thin roofing sheets (voiles), coated or impregnated with asphalt. The issues in the appeals related both to jurisdiction and to classification. The jurisdictional issue was settled during the hearing.

---

56   AP-2001-017 (2002), 6 TTR (2d) 631.
57   AP-99-015 to AP-99-025 (2000), 4 TTR (2d) 423.

The classification issue was whether the goods in issue were correctly classified by the CCRA under tariff item 7019.32.10 as "thin sheets (voiles), coated or impregnated with asphalt, of a kind used as roofing," or whether they should be classified under tariff item 6807.10.00 as "articles of asphalt or of similar material (for example, petroleum bitumen or coal tar pitch) in rolls," as claimed by the appellant.

According to the evidence, the goods in issue were roofing boards within the meaning of Note (2) of the Explanatory Notes to heading 68.07, as roofing felts were flat thin pieces of fabric of raw fibreglass used as part of a roofing system. Exclusion (d) for "thin sheets (voiles)" as per subheading 7019.32 did not apply, as the goods did not meet the description for voiles found in the Explanatory Notes to heading 70.19. The fibre distribution was not random, and its orientation was in both the machine and cross-machine directions. Further, the glass fibres were not pressed or compacted, and it was possible to remove the glass fibres, albeit with difficulty, without damaging the ply sheet; they were, therefore, not "thin sheets (voiles)." On the basis of this evidence, and relying on Rule 1 of the *General Rules*, the Tribunal held that the goods in issue should be classified under tariff item 6807.10.00 as "articles of asphalt or of similar material (for example, petroleum bitumen or coal tar pitch) in rolls," as claimed by the appellant.

CASE 3: TARIFF ITEM 7323.93.00 (STAINLESS STEEL STEP CANS)
The goods in issue in *Canadian Tire Corporation Ltd v President of the Canada Border Services Agency*[58] were stainless steel step cans. The appeal was against the CBSA's advance ruling by which it classified the goods under tariff item 7323.93.00 as "household articles of iron or steel." The appellant claimed that the goods in issue should be classified under tariff item 8479.89.99 "mechanical appliances."

The Tribunal dismissed the appeal. It concluded that the goods in issue were not machines or mechanical appliances, and held that they were correctly classified by the CBSA under tariff item 7323.93.00.

In arriving at its decision, the Tribunal considered Note 1(f) to Section XV in which Chapter 73 fell, as well as Section XVI (machinery, mechanical appliances and electrical equipment) in which Chapter 84 fell, as the appellant claimed that the goods in issue came under tariff heading 84.79. In addition, the Tribunal considered Supplementary Note to Section XVI, which stated that the term "mechanically operated" referred to those goods that are comprised of a more or less complex combination of moving and sta-

---

58   AP-2006-041 (2007), 12 TTR (2d) 135 [*Canadian Tire #2*].

tionary parts and do work through the production, modification, or transmission of force and motion.

The Tribunal was of the opinion that, in order to determine the proper classification of the goods in issue, it must look at the goods in their entirety. The question to be resolved by the Tribunal was whether the step can performed work, and not whether some part of the step can acts on some other part of the step can to do work. In the Tribunal's view, this inquiry was supported by the wording of heading 84.79, which read: "Machines and mechanical appliances having individual functions . . . ." The phrase "having individual functions" and its French equivalent clearly indicated that it was the goods in their entirety that must perform a function on their own, as opposed to part of them.

Accordingly, it was necessary to determine whether the goods in issue produced, modified, or transmitted force to an external body (that is, the trash) and not only to the lid. The goods in issue were designed to contain waste. Both parties agreed that the lid-lifting mechanism had no effect on the trash. No force was applied to the trash, and the trash was not displaced.

For the foregoing reasons, the Tribunal concluded that the goods in issue were not machines or mechanical appliances. Accordingly, the Tribunal found that the CBSA had correctly classified the goods in issue under tariff item 7323.93.00.

ix) Section XV: Chapters 72 to 83 (Base Metals)

CASE 1: TARIFF ITEM 7615.19.00 (CHRISTMAS-THEMED CAKE, MUFFIN, AND COOKIE PANS)

The goods in issue in *Wilton Industries Canada Ltd v Commissioner of the Canada Customs and Revenue Agency*[59] were Christmas-themed cake, muffin, and cookie pans. The issue in the appeal was whether the goods were correctly classified by the CCRA under tariff item 7615.19.00 as "other aluminum kitchen articles" or whether they should be classified under tariff item 9505.10.00 as "articles for Christmas festivities," as claimed by the appellant.

The Tribunal dismissed the appeal. It agreed with the CCRA that (1) to allow heading 95.05 to cover all articles primarily or exclusively used during the celebration of a festivity would give too broad a meaning to that heading and would ignore its plain meaning; and (2) to be consistent with the Tribunal's previous findings with respect to heading 95.05, the Explanatory Notes, and the heading itself, the articles classified in that heading must be

---

59   AP-2001-088 (2002), 6 TTR (2d) 802.

decorative as well as festive in nature and must not have a primarily utilitarian function.

The Tribunal was of the opinion that the goods in issue were used for baking at Christmas time; they were not, in and of themselves, "[f]estive, carnival or other entertainment articles." Therefore, they did not fall under Chapter 95. Nor were they "decorative" as specified in the Explanatory Note to that Chapter. As the goods in issue were made of aluminum, and since they were accurately described by the terms of heading 76.15 as well as by the Explanatory Notes to that heading, the Tribunal found that the goods were correctly classified under tariff item 7615.19.00.

CASE 2: TARIFF ITEM 7308.90.90 (GALLERY GAZEBOS)
The goods in issue in *Rona Corporation Inc v President of the Canada Border Services Agency*[60] were gallery gazebos with bug nets. They were composed of a synthetic fabric roof, synthetic fabric bug-screen sides, a steel frame that included four corner posts, and steel rods that supported the textile roof. The frame came with two planter holders, and the steel base was equipped with holes so that the gazebo could be secured to a deck or concrete pad. The goods in issue were imported and sold in an unassembled form.

The issue in this appeal was whether the gallery gazebos were correctly classified by the CBSA under tariff item 6306.22.00 as "tents of synthetic fibres" or whether they should be classified under tariff item 7308.90.90 as "other structures (excluding prefabricated buildings of heading 94.06) and parts of structures of iron or steel," as claimed by the appellant.

The Tribunal allowed the appeal. It found that the goods in issue properly fell under tariff item 7308.90.90 as "other structures (excluding prefabricated buildings of heading 94.06) and parts of structures of iron or steel," for example, bridges and bridge-sections, lockgates, towers, lattice masts, roofs, roofing frame-works, doors and windows and their frames and thresholds for doors, shutters, balustrades, pillars, and columns.

The CBSA had classified the goods in issue under heading 63.06 as "tents" because, in its view, they met the description of a tent found in the Explanatory Notes to heading 63.06, as well as in dictionary and encyclopaedic definitions of the term "tent." It submitted that the goods in issue possessed many of the characteristics of a tent. Based on the examples of tents listed in the Explanatory Notes, it submitted that tents included in heading 63.06 may have different shapes and sizes, may or may not have sides or walls, and, depending on their type, may be used for short or extended periods of time.

---

60 AP-2006-033 (2008), 12 TTR (2d) 295.

In its view, a tent was basically a product that provided shelter. The goods in issue were tents, since they were essentially designed to provide shelter. According to the CBSA, this was evidenced by the fact that the goods were purchased and used to protect the users from the sun and insects.

The Tribunal did not accept the CBSA's arguments. The goods were gazebos, which are commonly found in yards and gardens. The mere fact that they provided basic shelter from the sun and insects was not sufficient to conclude that gazebos were tents. While the relevant Explanatory Notes provided that "tents are shelters," that did not mean that all "shelters," or goods that provide shelter, are tents. The Explanatory Notes and the definitions provided by the CBSA indicated that tents have other characteristics that gazebos do not possess. Accordingly, the Tribunal found that the goods in issue were not properly classified under heading 63.06.

The Tribunal accepted the appellant's arguments that the goods in issue were classifiable under heading 73.08 as "structures of steel," assembled primarily of metal panels and bars, bolted or clipped together, and generally designed to be permanent and free-standing on the ground. According to the dictionary, and in common parlance, a gazebo is a structure with open or screen sides, designed for decorative or sunshade purposes. They are not tents. Pursuant to Rule 6 of the *General Rules* and the *Canadian Rules*, the goods in issue should be classified under tariff item 7308.90.90.

CASE 3: TARIFF ITEM 8208.20.00 (DISPOSABLE SCREW-ON CARBIDE KNIVES)

In *Outils Gladu Inc v President of the Canada Border Services Agency*,[61] the appellant imported disposable screw-on carbide knives for use with a Spiramax device for woodworking. The CBSA re-determined their classification under tariff item 8208.20.00, whereas the appellant claimed that they should be classified under heading 82.09 for use with hand tools of heading 82.07. The Tribunal dismissed the appeal and held that the goods in issue were correctly classified by the CBSA under tariff item 8208.20.00.

The appellant's application for judicial review of the Tribunal's decision was granted by the Federal Court of Appeal. The court set aside the Tribunal's decision. It found that, although the goods in issue met the definition of cermets (ceramic metal alloy), in subheading 8209.00, the word "cermet" was used exclusively in the metal machining industry. This led the Tribunal to construe the Explanatory Notes to heading 82.09 as excluding wood from the description of "hard materials." The court found that the Tribunal erred in its interpretation of heading 82.09 and referred the matter back to the

---

61   AP-2004-018 (2005) (in French), rev'd 2007 FCA 213, remand to CITT AP-2004-18R (2008).

Tribunal to determine the proper classification on the basis that both heading 82.08 and subheading 82.09 were *prima facie* applicable to the goods in issue. In the court's view, although not specifically mentioned like the metal and other hard materials in the Explanatory Notes to heading 82.09, the Tribunal took too narrow an interpretation of those Notes by holding that wood was not a hard material; according to the Tribunal, the approximation of "materials" and "hard materials" by means of the words "and other" prevents wood from being included as a hard material. The court added that, although this construction would have been plausible if the Explanatory Notes were read in isolation, it became implausible when regard was had to the tariff items that they explained, and in particular, tariff item 8209.00.91, which referred to sawmills.

CASE 4: TARIFF ITEM 8205.70.90 (RATCHET TIE-DOWNS)
The goods imported in *Canadian Tire Corporation Ltd v President of the Canada Border Services Agency*[62] were ratchet tie-downs that operated by attaching the plastic-coated steel hooks to an anchor point and wrapping the textile strap around a load or articles to be held or transported. The textile strap was drawn tightly by the ratchet handle to create sufficient tension to constrict or press the load or articles to the anchor points to hold them firmly in place. The parties appeared to agree that the goods in issue were generally described as ratchet tie-downs consisting of a textile strap, plastic-coated steel hooks, and a ratchet handle, which functioned to constrict or hold items in place.

The issue in the appeal was whether the goods in issue were correctly classified by the CBSA under tariff item 6307.90.99 as "other made-up articles of other textile materials, including dress patterns" in its advance ruling, or whether they should be classified under tariff item 8205.70.90 as "other vices, clamps and the like," as claimed by the appellant or, in the alternative, under heading 73.26 as "other articles of iron or steel."

The Tribunal allowed the appeal. It found that the goods in issue were in fact used "to bind or constrict or to press two or more parts together so as to hold them firmly in their relative position" for "strengthening or fastening things together" or for "holding or compressing." This was in accord with the underlying end use suggested by both definitions of "clamp," namely, that a clamp holds or maintains items together. As such, the goods in issue met the description of "clamps or the like" as required by heading 82.05.

---

62 AP-2011-024 (2012), 16 TTR (2d) 675 [*Canadian Tire #3*].

Accordingly, the goods in issue could be classified under heading 82.05 as "vices, clamps and the like."

It was the Tribunal's view that the Explanatory Notes to Chapter 63 and heading 63.07 provided useful guidance to determine the proper tariff classification of the goods in issue, and found no reason not to apply them in this appeal. The Tribunal therefore determined first whether the goods in issue could be *prima facie* classified in heading 82.05 and, if so, whether they were more specifically described in that heading than in heading 63.07. In that event, they could not be classified in both headings, as heading 82.05 would take precedence over heading 63.07 on the basis of Rule 1 of the *General Rules*, having regard to the relevant Explanatory Notes.

Heading 82.05 was not limited to clamps, but may also include clamps "and the like." The Tribunal accepted the appellant's contention that those additional words were intended to identify goods that should also be classified in heading 82.05 as a result of their close association with or resemblance to clamps. The use of the word "and" in the phrase "clamps and the like" denotes a further descriptor. In other words, "and" was used to indicate that the heading was meant to include not only clamps but also goods that were "like" clamps. The test to determine whether goods were "like" or similar was not strict, and the goods need not be identical. Rather, the test will be met if such goods shared important characteristics and had common features. The Tribunal concluded that the goods in issue may be classified under heading 82.05 if they were determined to be "like" clamps. As the goods in issue were in fact used "to bind or constrict or to press two or more parts together so as to hold them firmly in their relative position," for "strengthening or fastening things together" or for "holding or compressing," they fell within the definitions of "clamp." Therefore, the goods met the description of "clamps and the like" as required by heading 82.05.

On the basis of the foregoing analysis, the Tribunal concluded that the goods in issue should be classified under heading 82.05 as "vices, clamps and the like." As a result of this conclusion, it allowed the appeal. It saw no need to deal with the appellant's alternative submission that the goods in issue may be classified under heading 73.26.

CASE 5: TARIFF ITEM 8302.42.00 (METAL DRAWER SLIDES)
The goods in *Canmade Furniture Products Inc v Commissioner of the Canada Customs and Revenue Agency*[63] were metal drawer slides, which functioned

---

63 AP-2003-025 (2004), 8 TTR (2d) 10 [*Canmade Furniture*].

to permit drawers to slide smoothly into and out of furniture. The issue was whether the goods were correctly classified by the CCRA under tariff item 8302.42.00 as "other base metal mountings, fittings and similar articles suitable for furniture" or whether they should be classified under tariff item 9403.90.00 as "other furniture and parts thereof" or in heading 84.82 as "ball or roller bearings," as submitted by the appellant. The appellant further submitted that if the goods in issue were determined to be parts of furniture, then they should be classified under tariff item 9403.90.00, or in the alternative, if the goods can be considered to be bearings, they should be classified as bearings under tariff item 8482.80.90. If the goods cannot be classified under either of these tariff items by virtue of Rule 1 of the *General Rules*, then they should be classified pursuant to Rule 3, in accordance with the essential character of the goods.

The CCRA argued that the goods in issue should be classified according to Rule 1 of the *General Rules* under tariff item 8302.42.00 as other base metal mountings, fittings, and similar articles suitable for furniture. It argued that the Explanatory Notes to heading 83.02 state, in part: "This heading covers general purpose classes of base metal accessory fittings and mountings." The goods were of "general use," given that they may be mounted on a variety of furniture articles, and were specifically identified in the Explanatory Notes to heading 83.02.

The CCRA argued that the word "accessory," as used in the Explanatory Notes to heading 83.02, did not mean "secondary to the function," as it would if the word had been included in the heading itself. The word "accessory" simply meant that it was added to an item. It should be read in light of the examples in the tariff item, which included such things as door hinges, pegs, and castors. None of these items would qualify as "accessories" if that word were to be given the meaning of "secondary to the function." It added that the goods in issue did not provide the drawer its essential character, nor were they essential to the structure of the drawer and, hence, they were accessories to the drawer. It further argued that the goods in issue did not form an essential part of furniture and, therefore, were not excluded by the wording of the Explanatory Notes to heading 83.02; it contended that it was possible to make fully functional furniture with drawers without the metal slides and that the structural integrity of the drawers and furniture was the same with or without the goods in issue.

The CCRA further argued that the goods in issue cannot be classified under heading 94.03 since they were not committed by design for use with any specific furniture, and are classified under heading 83.02 being "parts of general use." Since Note 1(d) of Chapter 94 excludes "[p]arts of general use" from that chapter, the goods cannot be classified under heading 94.03.

The CCRA also argued that the goods in issue cannot be classified under heading 84.82 as proposed by the appellant in the alternative. They were not bearings, given that the tracks into which the rollers were fixed comprised the essential character of the goods. The rollers only allowed for a smoother movement along the tracks.

The Tribunal was of the view that the goods in issue were supplementary to the drawers to an extent similar to the examples from the tariff items and Explanatory Notes referred to above. Accordingly, the Tribunal considered that the goods in issue are "accessory" to furniture, as contemplated in the Explanatory Notes.

In the Tribunal's view, the goods in issue were not "an essential part of the structure" of drawers or cabinets containing drawers. According to the testimony of both parties, cabinets with drawers can function without the goods in issue and their absence would not compromise the structural integrity of the drawers or the cabinets.

The Tribunal also considered whether the goods in issue were referred to as bearings in the industry. It concluded that, in industry usage, these drawer slides were not generally referred to as bearings and that, given the type of goods, the industry usage should be applied in preference to the technical definition in this instance.

In light of the foregoing, the Tribunal dismissed the appeal and held that the goods in issue were correctly classified under heading 83.02 and under tariff item 8302.42.00. Therefore, they should not be classified under heading 94.03.

This decision should be contrasted with that in *Groupe Cabico Inc v President of the Canada Border Services Agency*,[64] discussed in section D(10)(a)(x) (Case 4), below in this chapter, where the Tribunal reached a different conclusion.

x) **Section XVI: Chapters 84 and 85 (Machinery, Mechanical Appliances, Electrical Equipment, Television Image and Sound Recorders)**

CASE 1: TARIFF HEADING 84.13 (SEROLOGICAL PIPETTES)
The goods in issue in *Sarstedt Canada Inc v President of the Canada Border Services Agency*[65] were serological pipettes and pipette tips, which varied in

---

64 AP-2006-004 (2007), 12 TTR (2d) 51 [*Groupe Cabico Inc*].
65 AP-2008-011 (2010), 14 TTR (2d) 401.

size and were used for a range of laboratory applications. They were manufactured from clear polystyrene plastic. The issue was whether the CBSA was correct in classifying both products under tariff item 3926.90.90 as "other articles of plastics and articles of other materials of headings 39.01 to 39.14," or whether they should have been classified under tariff item 8413.91.30 as parts of the goods of tariff item 8413.20.00 (pipettes) and 8413.19.90 (pipette tips), respectively, as submitted by the appellant.

It was not disputed by the parties that the pipettes in issue were made of plastic. The Tribunal agreed with this conclusion and, consequently, it was of the view that they were correctly classified under heading 39.26.

The Tribunal did not agree with the CBSA's position that the pipettes should be classified under tariff item 3926.90.90.94 because it specifically named laboratory ware and, since the serological pipettes were regularly used in a laboratory environment, they should be considered as laboratory ware. The classification number at the ten-digit level argued by the CBSA was not part of the legal regime for tariff classification; rather, it was an administrative code that has been established for gathering information under the Statistics Act.[66] The Tribunal was of the view that none of the specific subheadings under heading 39.26 applied to the pipettes and, therefore, they were classifiable, and should be classified in the residual subheading 3926.90 as "other articles of plastics." The appellant was successful on the classification of pipettes.

The CBSA, however, succeeded on the classification of pipette tips. The Tribunal was of the view that pipette tips could not be considered to be "capacity measures" since they were not used for measuring a volume of liquid on their own. Therefore, they came under tariff subheading 8414.10, which covered parts of vacuum pumps of heading 84.14, and as they were used with vacuum pumps, they were classifiable under tariff item 8414.90.90 as "other parts of vacuum pumps."

CASE 2: TARIFF ITEM 8415.90.29 (CONDENSERS FOR MOTOR VEHICLES)

The goods in issue in the appeal of *Spectra/Premium Industries Inc v President of the Canada Border Services Agency*[67] were condensers, which were used as repair or replacement parts for motor vehicle air conditioning machines and sold to automotive parts distributors and professional installers. They were one of the various components of an air conditioning machine. Other components included the evaporator, the compressor, and the blower. The

---

66   RSC 1985, c S-19.
67   AP-2006-053 (2008), 12 TTR (2d) 912.

condensers were connected to the other components by way of piping and tubing. They resembled a flat grill unit, and their location in motor vehicles was usually in front of the radiator.

The issue in the appeal was whether the condensers were properly classified by the CBSA under tariff item 8415.90.29 as "parts of air conditioning machines of a kind used for persons, in motor vehicles, not presented in complete 'kits'" or whether they should be classified under tariff item 8419.60.00 as "machinery for liquefying air or other gases," as claimed by the appellant.

Both parties acknowledged that the goods in issue were used only as parts of air conditioning machines in motor vehicles.

The Tribunal pointed out that when classifying goods as either parts of something or as entities in their own right, the application of Rule 1 of the *General Rules* was of utmost importance. Under Rule 1 "classification is first determined by the wording of the tariff headings and any relevant legal note." Therefore, if the goods were named or generically described in a particular heading of the tariff schedule, they were classified in that heading, subject to any relevant legal note. If not, consideration should be given to the heading of the product for which the goods were claimed to be a part.

Note 2 of Section XVI provided additional rules for the classification of parts of articles within that section. Note 2(a) provided that, in the case of goods covered by Section XVI, when parts of machines were themselves goods included in a particular heading of Chapter 84 or 85, they are to be classified as goods of that heading and not as parts of something else. In addition, Note 2(b) indicated that "[o]ther parts" (that is, parts that are not goods included in any of the headings of Chapters 84 and 85) that were suitable for use "solely or principally" with a particular kind of machine are to be classified with the machine of that kind or in certain specifically identified headings, as appropriate.

The Tribunal found that the goods in issue did not fall under heading 84.19 and, therefore, they were not classifiable under tariff items of that heading or under tariff item 8419.60.00 as machinery for liquefying air or other gases, as claimed by the appellant.

On the other hand, there was no doubt that heading 84.15 covered air conditioning machines. As Rule 1 of the *General Rules* required that the goods in issue must be classified with air conditioning machines, the Tribunal was of the opinion that the goods in issue were properly classified in heading 84.15.

With respect to classification at the subheading and tariff item levels, the evidence indicated that the goods in issue were parts of air conditioning machines of a kind used for persons, in motor vehicles. Such air conditioning machines are to be classified under subheading 8415.20, which includes two tariff items, the first (8415.20.10) covering air conditioning machines of a kind used for persons, in motor vehicles, presented in complete kits, and the second (8415.20.90) covering other air conditioning machines of a kind used for persons, in motor vehicles.

Accordingly, air conditioning machines of a kind used for persons, in motor vehicles, not presented in complete kits, are to be classified under tariff item 8415.20.90. Applying the *General Rules* and the *Canadian Rules*, the Tribunal found that air conditioning machines of which the goods in issue were parts were properly classified under tariff item 8415.20.90.

In addition, heading 84.15 included a specific subheading that applied to parts of certain goods classified under certain tariff items of that heading, namely, subheading 8415.90. Under that subheading, there were four tariff items that can potentially apply to parts of the type of motor vehicle air conditioning machines that are relevant in this appeal, that is, those of tariff item 8415.20.90. The goods in issue were not goods named in the first three listed tariff items. Therefore, pursuant to Rule 1 of the *General Rules* and the *Canadian Rules*, they were to be classified in the residual category "other" (tariff item 8415.90.29). The Tribunal dismissed the appeal, holding that the goods in issue were correctly classified under tariff item 8415.90.29 as "parts of goods of tariff item 8415.20.90."

CASE 3: TARIFF ITEM 8467.29.90 (HEAT GUN KITS)

The goods in *Canadian Tire Corporation Ltd v President of the Canada Border Services Agency*[68] were Mastercraft® heat gun kits. The issue was whether the goods were properly classified by the CBSA under tariff item 8516.79.90 as "other electro-thermic appliances of a kind used for domestic purposes" or whether they should be classified under tariff item 8467.29.90 as "other tools for working in the hand, pneumatic, hydraulic or with self-contained electric motor," as claimed by the appellant. Should the Tribunal determine that the goods in issue constituted electro-thermic appliances, but not of a kind used for domestic purposes, the CBSA suggested that they be classified under tariff item 8419.89.90 as "other machinery, plant or laboratory equipment, whether or not electrically heated (excluding furnaces, ovens and other equipment of heading No. 85.14), for the treatment of materials by a process involving a change of temperature such as heating, other than of a kind used for domestic purposes."

---

68 AP-2006-038 (2007), 12 TTR (2d) 39 [*Canadian Tire #4*].

The parties agreed the goods were electro-thermic and electro-mechanical and that they were mechanically operated as defined in the supplementary note of Section XVI of the *Customs Tariff*.

The Tribunal noted that the goods in issue were "kits" and were therefore put up for retail sale in "sets." They contained a number of articles that had their own classification. According to Rule 3(b) of the *General Rules*, such goods must be classified as if they consisted of the component that determined the essential character of the kits when they cannot be classified according to Rule 3(a).

The evidence was clear that it was the heat gun that played the most important role in relation to the use of the goods in issue. The other articles in the kit were merely accessories to the heat gun. It was the heat gun component that provided this basic feature and, therefore, it was the heat gun that gave the kit its essential character. In consequence, Rule 3(b) required the Tribunal to classify the goods in issue as if they consisted of the heat gun.

The Tribunal allowed the appeal. Applying Rule 1, the Tribunal held that the goods in issue should be classified under heading 84.67 and under subheading 8467.29. Subheading 8467.29 included tools with a self-contained electric motor "other" than certain "drills" and "saws." The subheading was subdivided into two tariff items, namely, 8467.29.10, which covered certain "angle sanders" and "angle grinders," and 8467.29.90, which included "other" tools. As the goods in issue were not "angle sanders" or "angle grinders," they ultimately fell under tariff item 8467.29.90 as "other tools for working in the hand, with a self-contained electric motor." Accordingly, the Tribunal concluded that the goods in issue should be classified under tariff item 8467.29.90 and allowed the appeal.

This decision may be contrasted with that in *Rona Corporation Inc v President of the Canada Border Services Agency*,[69] below in Case 6 in this section, where the Tribunal reached a different conclusion with respect to glue guns.

CASE 4: TARIFF ITEM 8482.80.90 (UNDERMOUNT ROLLER GLIDES OR DRAWER SLIDES)

The goods in issue in *Groupe Cabico Inc*[70] were undermount roller glides, also described as drawer slides. The tracks, rails, or runners (rails) were made of base metal and the internal mechanisms (rollers and roller housings) were made of plastic. Each slide was designed so that its rails can move parallel to each other. The plastic rollers were held in place by plastic roller housings

---

69   AP-2009-072 (2011) [*Rona Corporation Inc*].
70   Above note 64.

that separated the rails, maintained a constant distance between them, bore weight, and facilitated the movement of the rails relative to each other.

The CBSA classified the undermount roller glides under tariff item 8302.42.00, whereas the appellant claimed that they should be classified under tariff item 8482.80.90. The Tribunal, applying Rule 1 of the *General Rules*, allowed the appeal, finding that the goods in issue should be classified as "other ball or roller bearings" under tariff item 8482.80.90. In its view, the undermount roller glides were better described as linear roller bearings because of their construction and the direction of movement of their rails relative to each other. It rejected the CBSA's submission that the goods in issue were fittings for furniture and accepted the appellant's argument that since the essential character of the components (plastic rollers and housing) were not the base metal, it was the plastic rollers and their plastic housing, not the base metal, that gave the goods their essential character, even though the base metal predominated by weight.

Note that the Tribunal came to a different conclusion on metal drawer slides in the appeal of *Canmade Furniture*[71] (see Section D(10)(a)(ix)(Case 5), above in this chapter).

CASE 5: TARIFF ITEM 8504.40.90 (PORTABLE BATTERY BOOSTER TO JUMPSTART VEHICLES)

The good in issue in *Costco Wholesale Canada Ltd v President of the Canada Border Services Agency*[72] was a portable battery booster system that was used for jumpstarting motor vehicles and that could also be used as a source of power to charge or operate various 12-volt electronic devices (for example, cellphones, laptop computers, and camcorders) equipped with a direct current (DC) male plug. The parties were agreed on this; their difference arose at the heading level.

The issue was whether the good in issue was correctly classified by the CBSA in its advance ruling, under tariff item 8507.20.90 as "other lead-acid accumulators, other than for use as the primary source of electrical power for electrically powered vehicles of subheading 8703.90" or whether it should be classified under tariff item 8504.40.90 as "other static converters," as claimed by the appellant.

The Tribunal allowed the appeal. It found that the good in issue was covered as such in heading 85.04 and that it should be classified under tariff item 8504.40.90. The Tribunal was satisfied that, as a rectifier that converted AC into DC with a resulting change in voltage, the good in issue fell

---

71   Above note 63.
72   AP-2011-009 (2012), 16 TTR (2d) 380.

under subheading 8504.40 as a static converter, in accordance with Rule 6 of the *General Rules*. More specifically, in accordance with Rule 1 of the *Canadian Rules*, it fell under tariff item 8504.40.90 as an emergency power pack, the "as such" description of which necessarily included a battery for the purpose of storing the electrical power for the purpose of jumpstarting motor vehicles and powering certain 12-volt devices.

CASE 6: TARIFF ITEM 8516.79.90 (GLUE GUNS)

The goods in issue in *Rona Corporation Inc*[73] consisted of SUREBONDER® glue guns, manufactured in the People's Republic of China and subsequently imported from the United States into Canada by the appellant. The glue guns used electricity to power an internal heating element that melted the glue and allowed it to be applied or deposited in a specific location. Glue sticks were inserted in the back of the glue guns and were mechanically moved forward through the nozzle by using the trigger.

The issue was whether the glue guns were correctly classified by the CBSA under tariff item 8516.79.90 as "other electro-thermic appliances of a kind used for domestic purposes" or whether they should be classified under tariff item 8465.99.90 as "other machine-tools (including machines for nailing, stapling, glueing or otherwise assembling) for working wood, cork, bone, hard rubber, hard plastics or similar hard materials," as claimed by the appellant. The parties had agreed that the glue guns were electro-thermic, had no motor, and, in certain circumstances and for certain purposes, could be used for glueing wood.

The appellant argued that the glue guns were not appliances but were tools, and that they were not for domestic purposes, claiming that they were very similar to the heat guns that were in issue in the *Canadian Tire #4*[74] appeal. In that case, the Tribunal had decided that the heat guns were not "of a kind used for domestic purposes." The CBSA made the opposite argument, that they were appliances and were "of a kind used for domestic purposes" since they were primarily used by individuals performing domestic chores, such as do-it-yourself tasks, minor household repairs, and crafts in domestic settings. The CBSA relied on the Tribunal's decision in *Evenflo Canada Inc v President of the Canada Border Services Agency*.[75]

The Tribunal considered whether the goods in issue could also be classified under heading 84.65, which the appellant had claimed. To be classified

---

73   Above note 69.
74   Above note 68.
75   AP-2009-049 (2010), 14 TTR (2d) 470.

under that heading, they must be (1) machine-tools; (2) for glueing; and (3) for working wood, cork, bone, hard rubber, hard plastics, or similar hard materials. The parties had agreed that, in certain circumstances, the goods in issue could be used for glueing wood. The parties seemed to have accepted that the goods in issue can be used for glueing wood and other hard materials. While the first test was met, the Tribunal was not satisfied that they were "machine-tools" of the type intended to be covered by heading 84.65. In the Tribunal's view, the Explanatory Notes to heading 84.65 made it clear that machine-tools "worked by hand" were different from "hand tools" and from "tools for working in the hand" in that they are usually designed to be mounted on the floor, on a bench, on a wall, or on another machine. The Tribunal was of the view that heading 84.65 was intended to cover such types of machines. The evidence in this case plainly indicated that the goods in issue were not designed to be mounted on a solid surface or structure so as to be fixed or stationary. Instead, they are small glue-dispensing machines (or appliances) that were designed to be held in the hand for working on crafts and hobbies.

The Tribunal, therefore, concluded that the glue guns were not classifiable in heading 84.65. Accordingly, pursuant to Rule 1 of the *General Rules*, it held that they were correctly classified under heading 85.16.

The Tribunal next determined the proper classification at the subheading and tariff item levels. Heading 85.16 had nine first-level subheadings, of which only one, the first-level, specifically pertained to the glue guns. This first-level subheading, "Other electro-thermic appliances," was subdivided into three second-level subheadings as follows: "Coffee or tea makers," "Toasters," and "Other." As the goods in issue were not coffee or tea makers or toasters, they must be classified in the only remaining subheading, "Other." Therefore, pursuant to Rule 6 of the *General Rules*, the goods in issue were properly classified in subheading 8516.79.

Subheading 8516.79 had two tariff items. As the glue guns were not fabric steamers of tariff item 8516.79.10, they must be classified under the only other tariff item, "Other." Therefore, pursuant to Rule 1 of the *Canadian Rules*, the goods in issue were properly classified under tariff item 8516.79.90. Therefore, the Tribunal dismissed the appeal.

CASE 7: TARIFF ITEM 8516.79.90 (PLUG-IN DEODORIZERS)
In *SC Johnson & Son, Limited v President of the Canada Border Services Agency*,[76] the goods involved were plug-in deodorizers that used eletricity to heat fragrances in order to disperse them and, hence, deodorize an area. They

---

76 AP-2005-015 (2006), 11 TTR (2d) 77.

consisted of two components packaged together for retail sale: an electrical heating unit and a fragrance unit. The issue was whether the goods were correctly classified by the CBSA under tariff item 8516.79.90 as "other electro-thermic appliances of a kind used for domestic purposes," or whether they should be classified under tariff item 3307.49.00 as "other prepared room deodorizers," as claimed by the appellant.

Tariff heading 33.07 covered "pre-shave, shaving or after-shave preparations, personal deodorants, bath preparations, depilatories and other perfumery, cosmetic or toilet preparations, not elsewhere specified or included; prepared room deodorizers, whether or not perfumed or having disinfectant properties; . . . preparations for perfuming or deodorizing rooms, including odoriferous preparations used during religious rites." Tariff item 3307.49.00 covered "Other."

Note 2 to Section VI provided that "(s)ubject to Note 1 . . . , goods classifiable in heading 30.04, 30.05, 30.06, 32.12, 33.03, 33.04, 33.05, 33.06, 33.07, 35.06, 37.07 or 38.08 by reason of being put up in measured doses or for retail sale are to be classified in those headings and in no other heading of the Nomenclature." Explanatory Notes to Note 2 to Section VI provided that goods (other than those described in headings 28.43 to 28.46) that are covered by heading 30.04, 30.05, 30.06, 32.12, 33.03, 33.04, 33.05, 33.06, 33.07, 35.06, 37.07, or 38.08 by reason of being put up in measured doses or for retail sale, are to be classified in those headings notwithstanding that they could also fall in some other heading of the Nomenclature. For example, sulphur put up for retail sale for therapeutic purposes is classified in heading 30.04 and not in heading 25.03 or 28.02, and dextrin put up for retail sale as a glue is classified in heading 35.06 and not in heading 35.05.

The Explanatory Notes to heading 33.07 were also relevant as they applied to prepared room deodorizers, whether or not perfumed or having disinfectant properties. Prepared room deodorizers consisted essentially of substances (such as lauryl methacrylate) that acted chemically on the odours to be overcome or other substances designed to physically absorb odours by, for example, Van der Waal's bonds. When for retail sale, they were generally put up in aerosol cans. Products, such as activated carbon, put up in packings for retail sale as deodorizers for refrigerators, cars, and so on were also classified in that heading.

The competing tariff heading 85.15 covered "Electric instantaneous or storage water heaters and immersion heaters; electric space heating apparatus and soil heating apparatus; electro-thermic hair-dressing apparatus (for example, hair dryers, hair curlers, curling tong heaters) and hand dryers;

electric smoothing irons; other electro-thermic appliances of a kind used for domestic purposes; electric heating resistors, other than those of heading 85.45; and "Other electro-thermic appliances." Tariff subheading 8516.79 covered "Other" and tariff item 8516.79.90 covered "Other."

Explanatory Notes (E) to heading 85.16 ("Other electro-thermic appliances of a kind used for domestic purposes") stated that "the group includes all electro-thermic machines and appliances provided they are normally used in the household." Certain of these have been referred to in previous parts of this Explanatory Note (for example, electric fires, geysers, hair dryers, smoothing irons, and so on). Others include "(19) Perfume or incense heaters, and heaters for diffusing insecticides."

It was clear from the information found on the packaging that the fragrance unit in the goods in issue, whether they contained oil or gel, dealt with odours as contemplated in the Explanatory Notes to heading 33.07. Accordingly, if considered independently from the electrical unit, the fragrance unit would be classifiable under heading 33.07. Both parties agreed with that view.

It was also clear that the electrical heating unit, when considered on its own, was classifiable under heading 85.16 as an electro-thermic appliance of a kind used for domestic purposes.

As a result, when the electrical heating unit and the fragrance unit were put up in a set for retail sale, the set was *prima facie* classifiable under both heading 85.16 and heading 33.07. Rule 3 of the *General Rules* provided directions as to how to effect classification in such a case. Rule 3 (a) provided that, when two or more headings each refer to part only of the items in a set put up for retail sale, those headings were to be regarded as equally specific in relation to those goods. The Explanatory Notes to Rule 3 (a) provided that, when such is the case, classification of the goods shall be determined according to Rule 3 (b) or 3 (c).

Rule 3 (b) provided that goods put up in sets for retail sale shall be classified as if they consisted of the component that gave them their essential character. The Explanatory Notes to Rule 3 (b) provided that, for the purposes of that rule, the term "goods put up in sets for retail sale" shall be taken to mean goods that (a) consist of at least two different articles that are *prima facie* classifiable in different headings; (b) consist of products or articles put up together to meet a particular need or carry out a specific activity; and (c) are put up in a manner suitable for sale directly to users without repacking. In the Tribunal's opinion, the goods in issue constituted goods put up in sets for retail sale, as they consisted of two articles that were *prima facie* classifiable under different headings. The two articles or components were put up together to meet a particular need or carry out a specific activity, that is, to deodorize an area, and were packaged together in the way in which consumers would buy them.

The Explanatory Notes to Rule 3 (b) of the *General Rules* further provided that "[t]he factor which determines essential character will vary as between different kinds of goods. It may, for example, be determined by the nature of the material or component, its bulk, quantity, weight or value, or by the role of a constituent material in relation to the use of the goods."

Considering the roles of the constituent units, the evidence indicated that the electrical heating unit lasted approximately two years, while the fragrance unit only lasted approximately one or two months. According to the appellant, a consumer who bought a set comprising an electrical heating unit and a fragrance unit would typically buy fragrance unit refills for the electrical heating unit once the fragrance was used up, rather than buy a new set of both units. In the Tribunal's view, given that the fragrance was used up and the fragrance unit was replaced, the fragrance unit played a role that was subsidiary to that of the electrical heating unit.

The Tribunal also considered that the electrical heating unit played a key role in the functioning of the goods in issue, because the heat provided by the electrical heating unit was essential to dispersing the fragrance and making it effective. The addition of a fan to certain models increased the efficiency of the diffusion. These were important characteristics of the goods in issue and constituted a considerable evolution over the traditional aerosol can that dispersed only a single dose of fragrance at a time.

Based on the foregoing, the Tribunal found that the electrical heating unit gave the goods in issue their essential character.

Therefore, applying Rule 3 (b), the Tribunal concluded that the goods in issue should be classified as if they consisted of the electrical heating unit, that is, under heading 85.16, more specifically under tariff item 8516.79.90 as electro-thermic appliances of a kind used for domestic purposes. It therefore dismissed the appeal.

CASE 8: TARIFF ITEM 8517.11.00 (CORDLESS TELEPHONES)
The goods in *Sanyo Canada Inc v Deputy Minister of National Revenue*[77] were cordless telephones, and the issue was whether the Deputy Minister of National Revenue correctly classified them under tariff item 8517.11.00 as "line telephone sets with cordless handsets" or whether they should be classified

---

77   AP-99-029 and AP-99-046 (2000), 4 TTR (2d) 770.

under tariff item 8525.20.90 as "other transmission apparatus for radio-telephony incorporating reception apparatus," as claimed by the appellant.

It was not contested that the telephones were electrical apparatus. It was also clear from the evidence that the base unit of the telephones in issue had to be connected to the public switched telephone network to effect communications over that network. Therefore, the telephones were properly characterized as line telephone sets. Given the fact that they were equipped with cordless handsets, which communicated with the base unit using radio waves, they were line telephone sets with cordless handsets.

Even if the Tribunal were to accept that the telephones in issue were *prima facie* classifiable under heading 85.25 as transmission apparatus for radio-telephony incorporating reception apparatus, as well as under heading 85.17, the Tribunal said it would still classify the telephones under heading 85.17 by application of Rule 3(a) of the *General Rules*, since heading 85.17 provided a more specific description of the telephones than heading 85.25. The expression "[t]ransmission apparatus for radio-telephony incorporating reception apparatus" covered a variety of goods as indicated by the list found in the Explanatory Notes to heading 85.25. On the other hand, heading 85.17 provided a precise description of the products, namely, "[l]ine telephone sets with cordless handsets." The Tribunal therefore dismissed the appeal and held that the telephones in issue were electrical apparatus for line telephony.

CASE 9: TARIFF ITEM 8518.30.91 (HEADPHONES OR HEADSETS)

The goods in *Ingram Micro Inc v President of the Canada Border Services Agency*[78] were headphones or headsets. The parties described them differently in their submissions, using the terms "headsets" and "headphones" interchangeably. There were two models. The first was the Plantronics Encore® model, which had, at the end of an adjustable headband, a voice tube that extended from the receiver to the wearer's mouth. It appeared that the microphone was not located at the end of the voice tube, but rather within the "receiver" itself. The function of the voice tube, therefore, was only to carry the sound to the microphone. The second was the Encore® NC model, which had a click-stop turret at one end of an adjustable headband, plus a boom, which seemed to be designed to extend over the wearer's mouth and was fitted with a noise-cancelling microphone at the end. Both models were equipped with headset cables, a Quick Disconnect™ connector, and a clothing clip.

---

78   AP-2009-073 (2011), 15 TTR (2d) 323.

The issue was whether Plantronics Encore® and Encore® NC headphones or headsets were correctly classified by the CBSA under tariff item 8518.30.99 as "other headphones and earphones, whether or not combined with a microphone" or whether they should be classified under tariff item 8518.30.91 as "headphones, including earphones," as claimed by the appellant. The parties did not dispute the heading and subheading classification, but differed as to the tariff item.

It was the Tribunal's finding that the goods in issue met the terms of tariff item 8518.30.91, which expressly referred to "headphones," rather than tariff item 8518.30.99, which provided a more general description. In the Tribunal's view, the presence of the microphone did not change the fact that the goods in issue were headphones.

Applying Rule 1 of the *General Rules* and Rule 1 of the *Canadian Rules*, the Tribunal concluded that the goods in issue should be classified in tariff item 8518.30.91 as "headphones, including earphones" and allowed the appeal.

CASE 10: TARIFF ITEM 8520.90.90 (INTEGRATED CIRCUIT (IC) RECORDERS AND MINIDISK (MD) RECORDERS)

The appellant in *Sony of Canada Ltd v Commissioner of the Canada Customs and Revenue Agency*[79] imported integrated circuit (IC) recorders and portable minidisk (MD) recorders. The IC recorder was a battery-operated portable recording and playing device with a built-in microphone that recorded messages on one of two types of media: a built-in memory or a removable memory card (memory stick). The MD recorder was also a battery-operated portable music recording and playing device, which used MDs that are similar to 3½ inch floppy discs but are smaller in diameter, and was used for storing data.

The appellant entered the goods in issue under tariff item 8471.70.00 as "storage units of automatic data processing machines and units thereof; magnetic or optical readers, machines for transcribing data onto data media in coded form and machines for processing such data, not elsewhere specified or included," claiming, as an alternative, their classification as "compact disc players," which came under tariff item 8519.99.10. It also claimed the benefit of tariff relief under tariff item 9948.00.00, claiming that the goods were "for use in automatic data processing machines and units thereof, or as parts and accessories of those machines."

The CCRA re-determined the tariff classification of the goods in issue under tariff item 8520.90.90 as "other magnetic tape recorders and other

---

79   AP-2001-097 (2004), 8 TTR (2d) 554 [*Sony Canada*].

sound recording apparatus, whether or not incorporating a sound reproducing device."

The Tribunal dismissed the appeal in respect of the classification of the goods in issue, but in respect of the IC recorders, it found that they qualified for the benefit from tariff relief under item 9948.00.00 because, in its view, they were physically connected and functionally joined to a computer and, as such, were "for use in . . . [a]utomatic data processing machines."

With respect to classification, the Tribunal was of the opinion that the goods in issue were correctly classified by the CCRA, according to Rule 1 of the *General Rules*, under heading 85.20, on the basis that they were sound recording apparatus and they incorporated sound recording devices. The fact that they had other functions, such as storing sound, did not, for purposes of classification, make them other than articles that fell under heading 85.20. As no other subheading or tariff item described the goods in issue, they were classified under the residual tariff item 8520.90.90.

CASE 11: TARIFF ITEM 8521.90.90 (DIGITAL VIDEO RECORDERS (DVRS) AND MONITORS)

The goods in *Pelco Worldwide Headquarters v President of the Canada Border Services Agency*[80] were certain models of digital video recorders (DVRs) and certain models of black and white and colour monitors that can be used in video surveillance and security applications.

There were two classifiction issues in the appeal, the first with respect to the DVRs, the second with respect to the monitors. With respect to the DVRs, the issue was whether they were correctly classified by the CBSA under tariff item 8521.90.90 as "other video recording or reproducing apparatus, whether or not incorporating a video tuner," or whether they should be classified under tariff item 8525.10.00 as "transmission apparatus, whether or not incorporating reception apparatus" or, in the alternative, under tariff item 8471.10.00 as "analog or hybrid automatic data processing machines and units thereof, not elsewhere specified or included," as claimed by the appellant.

With respect to the monitors, the issue was whether they were correctly classified by the CBSA under tariff item 8528.22.00 (for the black and white monitors) and tariff item 8528.21.82 (for the colour monitors) or they should be classified under tariff item 9948.00.00 as "articles for use in automatic data processing machines" (to the extent that the DVRs are classified under

---

80   AP-2006-016 and AP-2006-018 (2007), 12 TTR (2d) 15.

heading 84.71 as "automatic data processing machines"), as claimed by the appellant.

The Tribunal dismissed the appeal and upheld the CBSA's classification of both the DVRs and the monitors.

With respect to the DVRs, the evidence was clear that they were digital disc recorders, not laser disc players. Heading 8521.90 was subdivided into two tariff items, 8521.90.10 ("laser video disc players") and 8521.90.90 ("other"). As the DVRs did not utilize a magnetic tape and were not laser video disc players, they ultimately fell under tariff item 8521.90.90. Therefore, they were correctly classified under tariff item 8521.90.90.

The evidence was clear that the recording and reproduction of visual images were the basic requirements for which the DVRs provided a solution. Without the recording, storing, and reproduction of information that began as visual images and later reconstituted as visual images, the DVRs would not be capable of providing that solution. The Tribunal acknowledged that multiplexing was a significant part of the solution. However, in the Tribunal's view, single-channel functionality would still permit surveillance and recording. Multiplexing was a process function, which was used to organize the information that was the substantive content of both the input and output of the units, and, in the DVRs, was integral to their proper functioning. Multiplexing was a means of responding to the need for complexity in information management, and it enhanced the sophistication of the goods, but it did not determine the identity of the goods. The goods existed to capture, record, and reproduce the substantive information. The Tribunal therefore regarded the principal function as the recording and reproduction of visual images.

Turning to the appellant's alternative position that the DVRs in issue should be classified under heading 84.71, because the Tribunal had already determined that the principal function of the DVRs was the recording and reproduction of visual images and was not that performed by an automatic data processing machine, they cannot be classified as automatic data processing machines, but must be classified in the heading appropriate for such a function. Therefore, the DVRs were not classifiable under tariff item 8471.10.00.

Subheading 8521.90 was subdivided into two tariff items, 8521.90.10 ("laser video disc players") and 8521.90.90 ("other"). Again, the evidence was clear that the DVRs in issue were digital disc recorders, not laser disc players. Applying that Rule 1, because the DVRs in issue did not utilize a magnetic tape and were not laser video disc players, they ultimately fell under tariff item 8521.90.90. The Tribunal therefore concluded that the DVRs were properly classified by the CBSA under tariff item 8521.90.90.

With respect to the monitors, since the Tribunal had determined that the DVRs were correctly classified under tariff item 8521.90.90, it did not find it necessary to examine the question of their reclassification, which would have been a consideration only if the DVRs had been classifiable under heading 84.71.

CASE 12: TARIFF ITEM 8522.90.90 (ARMBAND CASES FOR IPODS)
The goods in *Rlogistics Limited Partnership v President of the Canada Border Services Agency*[81] were Digital Lifestyle Outfitters fourth/fifth generation iPod nano sport armband cases. They consisted of a padded neoprene case (with a clear plastic screen), an adjustable elastic armband, and a clip. The neoprene case held the iPod nano, and the clip permitted attachment of the case to the armband, which fitted on a wearer's arm or directly on clothing. The evidence indicated that the goods in issue were protective cases that allowed individuals to carry and use an iPod nano while exercising or performing other activities that required them to have their hands free.

The issue was whether the goods were properly classified by the CBSA under tariff item 4202.99.90 as "other trunks, suitcases, vanity cases, executive cases, briefcases, school satchels, spectacle cases, binocular cases, camera cases, musical instrument cases, gun cases, holsters and similar containers" or whether they should be classified under tariff item 8522.90.90 as "other accessories suitable for use solely or principally with the apparatus of headings 85.19 to 85.21," as claimed by the appellant. There was no dispute between the parties that the goods in issue were for use solely or principally with an iPod nano.

The Tribunal allowed the appeal. It concluded that the relevant terms of heading 85.22 provided the most specific description of the goods in issue compared to the relevant terms of heading 42.02. Therefore, pursuant to Rule 3(a) of the *General Rules*, the goods should be classified under heading 85.22.

CASE 13: TARIFF ITEM 8523.11.00 (HEWLETT-PACKARD DATA CARTRIDGES)
The goods in *Canadisc Inc v Commissioner of the Canada Customs and Revenue Agency*[82] were Hewlett-Packard data cartridges with a 4-millimetre-wide tape. The issue was whether the goods were correctly classified by the CCRA under tariff item 8523.11.00 as "prepared unrecorded media" or whether they should be classified under tariff item 8524.51.90 as "other records, tapes and other recorded media," as claimed by the appellant. The parties had agreed

---

81   AP-2010-057 (2011), 16 TTR (2d) 94.
82   AP-99-086 (2000), 5 TTR (2d) 111.

that the goods in issue were covered in Chapter 85 as "parts and accessories suitable for use with sound or other similarly recorded phenomena."

The disagreement between the parties was at the heading level. Heading 85.23 covered "[p]repared unrecorded media for sound recording or similar recording of other phenomena, other than products of Chapter 37." Heading 85.24 covered "[r]ecords, tapes and other recorded media for sound or other similarly recorded phenomena, including matrices and masters for the production of records, but excluding products of Chapter 37."

The Tribunal accepted the evidence that formatting was a process used to write a layout on the magnetic tape of a cartridge so that data could be stored and retrieved at a later time and that formatting was not meant for later retrieval or reproduction. It also accepted the evidence that the goods in issue, at the time of sale, were sold as blank tapes, as they did not contain additional information or data beyond that of the formatting.

In the Tribunal's view, formatting was a method of preparing the cartridges for use and not a recording intended for later retrieval, and that the formatting marks contained within the cartridge could not be considered recorded information. In the context of computer science and data cartridges, the Tribunal was persuaded that the term "recorded" meant more than "formatted" since, unlike formatted marks, recorded information could be reproduced or retrieved. In the Tribunal's view, the evidence was clear that the goods in issue had been assembled and formatted, but not yet recorded.

In light of the foregoing, the Tribunal concluded that as the goods in issue can be described as formatted data cartridges, they must be considered prepared unrecorded media and, therefore, they were correctly classified by the CCRA under heading 85.23. On the basis of Rule 1 of the *General Rules*, they came under tariff item 8523.11.00. Therefore, it dismissed the appeal.

xi) Section XVII: Chapters 86 to 89 (Vehicles, Aircraft, Vessels, and Associated Transport Equipment)

CASE 1: TARIFF SUBHEADING 8703.21 (ALL-TERRAIN VEHICLES (ATVS))
In *Yamaha Motor Canada Ltd v Commissioner of the Canada Customs and Revenue Agency*,[83] the goods were seven all-terrain vehicles, also referred to as utility ATVs. The issue was whether these ATVs were correctly classified by the CCRA under subheading 8703.21 as "other motor vehicles principally designed for the transport of persons" or whether they should be classified under subheading 8701.90 as "other tractors," as claimed by the appellant.

---

83   AP-99-105 (2000), 4 TTR (2d) 108, aff'd 2002 FCA 34 [*Yamaha Motor Canada*].

The Explanatory Notes to heading 87.01 stated: "For the purposes of this heading, tractors means wheeled or track-laying vehicles constructed essentially for hauling or pushing another vehicle, appliance or load. They may contain subsidiary provision for the transport, in connection with the main use of the tractor, of tools, seeds, fertilisers or other goods, or provision for fitting with working tools as a subsidiary function."

The evidence showed that the utility ATVs performed a wide variety of functions for a diverse buying public. In light of this, the Tribunal was not persuaded that they were "constructed essentially for" pushing or hauling and, therefore, it was not convinced that they were tractors. In order to succeed in this appeal, the appellant had to demonstrate that the pushing or hauling functions constituted the essence of the ATVs in issue. While the evidence clearly demonstrated that they were capable of fulfilling those functions, these, in the Tribunal's view, did not constitute their "essence" or "*raison d'être.*"

The evidence also showed that some of the ATVs may be purchased primarily as personal or corporate workhorses to perform pushing or hauling functions. On the other hand, others may be purchased by individuals primarily for recreational purposes, such as hunting and trail riding. The latter may gravitate towards the higher-priced utility ATVs simply because they were more rugged and reliable, important features when being used in the back country. People may even use them from time to time to push loads (for example, snow) or to haul things (for example, cut wood). In other words, the evidence showed that the ATVs had many different uses, some of which had nothing to do with pushing or hauling, some of which did. In the Tribunal's opinion, the appellant failed to show that the goods in issue were "constructed essentially for" pushing or hauling and that they are tractors.

In arguing the distinction between "essentially" and "principally," the CCRA submitted that, by saying that something is principally designed for some purpose, one recognizes that there may be other secondary uses. However, if something was constructed essentially for some purpose, that purpose constituted its very essence. Less was required to characterize the goods as principally designed. Since the appellant had not provided the Tribunal with adequate information and evidence as to the design or construction, the CCRA argued that the appeal should be dismissed. In response to this argument, the Tribunal cautioned the parties not to think that it had interpreted "constructed essentially for" to mean that, for a vehicle to be classified in this heading, it must perform only pushing or hauling functions. Other subsidiary functions, such as transporting tools, seeds, fertilizer, and so on may be performed by a tractor according to the Chapter Notes to Chapter 87. However, it was clear that the threshold for "constructed essentially for" was a more demanding one than "principally designed for," the latter phrase permitting a wider range of functions. On the basis of the foregoing analysis, the Tribunal dismissed the appeal.

CASE 2: TARIFF ITEM 8703.21.90 (ALL-TERRAIN VEHICLES (ATVS))
The goods in *Suzuki Canada Inc and Canadian Kawasaki Motors Inc v Commissioner of the Canada Customs and Revenue Agency*[84] were all-terrain vehicles (ATVs). The issue was whether the ATVs were correctly classified by the CCRA under tariff item 8703.21.90 as "other motor vehicles principally designed for the transport of persons" or whether they should be classified under the applicable tariff item of heading 87.11 as "motorcycles and cycles fitted with an auxiliary motor," as claimed by the appellants.

The Tribunal allowed the appeals. It was of the view that the goods in issue were more correctly described in heading 87.11 as "motorcycles" than in heading 87.03 as "motor cars and other motor vehicles principally designed for the transport of persons." The Tribunal accepted the appellants' argument, among others, that the ATVs could not be classified under heading 87.03, given that they did not have "a motor-car type steering system," even though their steering system was based on the Ackerman principle. The CCRA's contrary argument, among others, was that the ATVs were classified under heading 87.03, given that they were described in the Explanatory Notes to that heading by the inclusion of item (6): "Four-wheeled motor vehicles with tube chassis, having a motor-car type steering system (e.g., a steering system based on the Ackerman principle)."

In this case, item (6) of the Explanatory Notes to heading 87.03 appeared to indicate that any four-wheeled vehicle with a tube chassis, having a steering system based on the Ackerman principle, fell under heading 87.03. The Tribunal did not see why the fact that ATVs had a steering system based on the Ackerman principle would determine their exclusion from heading 87.11 and their inclusion under heading 87.03. The Tribunal acknowledged that ATVs, like motor cars and many other motor vehicles, had a steering system based on the Ackerman principle. Steering systems based on that principle were used in almost all three-wheeled and four-wheeled vehicles, including golf carts, tractors, and quadricycles, but were not used in two-wheeled motorcycles. Given the evidence before the Tribunal, to rely on the fact that

---

84   AP-99-114, AP-99-115, and AP-2000-008 (2003), 8 TTR (2d) 1 (CITT), rev'd (*sub nom Suzuki Canada Inc v Canada (Customs and Revenue Agency)*), 2004 FCA 131 [*Suzuki*].

ATVs have a steering system based on the Ackerman principle as a determinative factor for classification would be erroneous.

The CCRA had argued that the Tribunal's decision in *Yamaha Motor Canada*[85] should stand, because, among other things, the Tribunal could have classified the goods under a different heading at that time, but chose not to do so. Although it was well established that the Tribunal was not bound by its jurisprudence, the Tribunal noted that classification under heading 87.11 was neither argued nor contemplated by the parties in *Yamaha* and that it was not presented with any evidence in support of classification under that heading at the hearing.

The CCRA applied for judicial review of the Tribunal's decision to the Federal Court of Appeal. The court set aside the Tribunal's decision. It said that on a proper interpretation of the Explanatory Notes to heading 87.03 and heading 87.11, and based on the undisputed evidence that the steering system utilized the Ackerman principle, the Tribunal acted unreasonably in concluding that the ATVs could be classified other than under heading 87.03. The mere fact that ATVs did not have three components of a motor car steering system as that term was used by industry engineers did not demonstrate that ATVs did not belong under heading 87.03, especially in view of the fact that these vehicles possessed the components that had been identified in the Explanatory Notes as determinative for classification purposes.

The court defined ATVs as follows:

> An ATV is a four-wheeled, motorized, off-road vehicle with a tube chassis, and is used to transport a person and goods over rough terrain. Like virtually all other four-wheeled vehicles, the steering system on an ATV turns the inside wheels at a slightly sharper angle than the outside wheels so that the wheels track a straight line. This is known as the "Ackerman principle". Handlebar movement and operator weight shift also contribute to steering an ATV.[86]

Note, the Tribunal followed the *Suzuki* decision of the Federal Court of Appeal in the appeal of *Arctic Cat Sales Inc v Deputy Minister of National Revenue*.[87] Arctic Cat had imported all-terrain vehicles. The CCRA classified them under tariff item 8703.21.90 as "motor vehicles principally designed for the transport of persons," whereas the appellant claimed that they should

---

85 Above note 83.
86 *Suzuki*, above note 84 at para 3 (FCA).
87 AP-2005-005, A9-2005-010, AP-2005, 011, and AP-2005-020 (2006), 10 TTR (2d) 693, aff'd 2007 FCA 277.

be classified under heading 87.11 as "motorcycles and cycles fitted with an auxiliary motor." The Tribunal held that it was bound by the *Suzuki* decision and, as the ATVs were essentially the same, it dismissed the appeal.

xii) **Section XVIII: Chapters 90 to 92 (Optical, Photographic, Cinematographic, Measuring, Medical Instruments; Clocks and Watches; Musical Instruments)**

CASE 1: TARIFF ITEM 9029.20.91 (HEART RATE MONITORS)
In *Sport Dinaco Inc v Deputy Minister of National Revenue*,[88] the goods under appeal were heart rate monitors (HRMs) and related items and kits consisting of a wrist receiver and a monitoring belt, with an elastic strap, to be worn around the torso. The related items and kits included monitoring belts, elastic straps, computer interface systems, speed sensor kits, cadence sensor kits, bike mount kits, and pulse simulators. The main issue was whether the various models of HRMs were correctly classified by the Deputy Minister of National Revenue under tariff item 9102.12.00 as "wristwatches, electrically operated, whether or not incorporating a stopwatch facility" or whether they should be classified under tariff item 9029.20.91 as "tachometers," as claimed by the appellant. The second issue related to the correct classification of the related items and kits.

The Tribunal allowed the appeal. It held that the HRMs were tachometers under tariff item 9029.20.91 for the following reasons:

1) Heading 90.29 specifically mentions tachometers. Note (B) of the Explanatory Notes to that heading described tachometers as instruments that indicate the number of revolutions, speed, output, and so on per unit of time. A measurement of time was, therefore, inherent in a tachometer, and thus the mere fact that the HRM receivers also told the time did not render the HRMs wristwatches.

2) Furthermore, General Note (I) of the Explanatory Notes to Chapter 90 provided, among other things, that "this chapter covers a wide variety of instruments and apparatus which are, as a rule, characterized by their high finish and high precision, most of them being used mainly for specialized technical purposes, such as measuring." The HRMs were precision instruments with a level of accuracy comparable to that of electrocardiograms in measuring the rate of heartbeat, and they were used for the specialized technical purpose of monitoring the heart rate

---

88 AP-99-061 (2000), 4 TTR (2d) 524.

during exercise. Consequently, the HRMs were tachometers under tariff item 9029.20.91.

3) Given the Tribunal's conclusion, and the respondent's acceptance to classify the related items and kits as parts and accessories of tachometers under tariff item 9029.90.92 should the Tribunal agree with the appellant on the main issue, these goods were so classified.

CASE 2: TARIFF ITEM 9105.99.90 (HOLIDAY MELODY CLOCKS)

The goods in *Avon Canada Inc v Commissioner of the Canada Customs and Revenue Agency*[89] were holiday clocks, referred to as "Holiday Melody Clocks." The clocks were in the shape of a snow-covered Victorian period house decorated in a Christmas motif. The decoration included human figures that appeared to be carolling, standing in front of the house. The timepiece dial of the clocks was set in the middle of a large Christmas wreath on the front of the house. Each of the twelve hours on the time dial was shown by four Roman numerals, four golden dots, and four lights. The clocks had hour, minute, and seconds hands. They had a music box that played different Christmas tunes every hour on the hour, and, at the same time, the lights in the wreath flashed. The music could be turned off without affecting the timing operation. The clocks were electronically operated and regulated by a piezo-electric quartz crystal that ran on three AA batteries.

The issue was whether melody clocks were correctly classified by the CCRA under tariff item 9105.99.90 as "other clocks" or whether they should be classified under tariff item 9505.10.00.10 as "articles for Christmas festivities," as claimed by the appellant.

In the Tribunal's view, although the melody clocks had a decorative or ornamental role during the Christmas season, they also served a very utilitarian function. Their predominant feature was the timekeeping component. As the Explanatory Notes to Chapter 91 indicated, the products included in the chapter were "designed mainly for measuring time." They specifically excluded "(c) Toy clocks and watches and Christmas tree accessories in the form of clocks or watches, such as those without clock or watch movements (heading 95.03 or 95.05)," which the goods in issue were clearly not.

The melody clocks certainly carried a decorative or ornamental quality particularly relevant to the Christmas season. That said, they were marketed as clocks, albeit festive ones. The appellant's marketing literature featured the seasonal nature of the clocks. For all those reasons, the Tribunal dismissed the appeal.

---

89 AP-99-074 (2000), 5 TTR (2d) 11.

Chapter 2: The Customs Tariff

xiii) Section XX: Chapters 94 to 96 (Miscellaneous Manufactured Articles)

CASE 1: TARIFF ITEM 9401.61.10 (UPHOLSTERED SOFAS, LOVE SEATS, AND SUCH)
In *6572243 Canada Ltd o/a Kwality Imports v President of the Canada Border Services Agency*,[90] the appeal concerned twenty decisions of the CBSA with respect to the tariff classification of various models of upholstered sofas, loveseats, rockers, recliners, chairs, and ottomans with wooden frames. The issue was whether the goods in issue were correctly classified by the CBSA under tariff item 9401.61.10 as "other upholstered seats with wooden frames for domestic purposes" or whether they should be classified under tariff item 9401.61.90 as "other upholstered seats with wooden frames," as claimed by the appellant.

There was no disagreement about the classification of the goods at either the heading or the subheading level. The dispute was focussed on the tariff item level. Disputes of this nature are governed by Rule 1 of the *Canadian Rules*. The only issue before the Tribunal was whether the goods in issue were upholstered seats with wooden frames "for domestic purposes."

Because the words "for domestic purposes" do not create an end-use provision, actual use of the goods in issue was not the dispositive factor to be considered for classification purposes. The end-use requirement was eliminated when the current wording of the tariff item came into force. Previously, the tariff item read "of a kind used for domestic purposes." It is the intended, and not actual, use that matters.

In the Tribunal's body of past decisions, evidence of items being primarily intended for domestic purposes created a rebuttable presumption in favour of classification under tariff item 9401.61.10. However, the Tribunal had never accepted evidence of mere occasional or potential use in a non-domestic situation, as was the case here, as being sufficient to rebut the presumption.

Based on the evidence, the Tribunal found that the goods in issue were primarily used for household purposes but could incidentally also be used in commercial settings calling for comfortable seating.

In summary, in the instant case, it was clear that the goods in issue possessed none of the additional qualities needed to make them suitable or destined for the commercial market. Rather, their generic construction, greater comfort, lower price points, and targeted marketing approach made them particularly attractive to domestic buyers. The fact that other market segments,

---

90   AP-2010-068 (2012), 17 TTR (2d) 1.

to some extent, effectively "borrowed" such goods from the domestic market did not as such change their overall nature.

On the basis of Rule 1 of the *General Rules* and Rule 6 of the *Canadian Rules*, the Tribunal decided that the goods in issue were correctly classified by the CBSA under tariff item 9401.61.10 as "other upholstered seats with wooden frames for domestic purposes" and dismissed the appeal.

CASE 2: TARIFF ITEM 9401.61.00 (GAMING CHAIRS)

The goods under appeal in *Wal-Mart Canada Corporation v President of the Canada Border Services Agency*[91] were X Rocker II gaming chairs, vinyl upholstered and made of a hardwood frame and brushed aluminum arms. The chairs were designed to be placed directly on the floor and had a convex base that allowed them to rock. They were equipped with an internal subwoofer (to simulate rumbling) and internal mid-range and high-range speakers whose volumes were adjustable from a control panel located on the side of the seat. They could be connected to video game consoles and DVD, music CD, MP3, and video cassette players, as well as television and satellite receivers.

The issue was whether the gaming chairs were correctly classified by the CBSA under tariff item 9401.61.10 as "other upholstered seats, with wooden frames, for domestic purposes," or whether they should be classified under tariff item 9504.10.00 as "articles for video games of a kind used with a television receiver," as claimed by the appellant.

The Tribunal was satisfied on the basis of the evidence and the testimony that the goods in issue were furniture. The evidence did not indicate that the goods in issue were constructed expressly or particularly for video game consoles, nor did it indicate that they were suitable for use principally with articles of Chapter 95, namely, video game consoles of a kind used with a television receiver, nor were they specially constructed for games. Therefore, the goods in issue were not classifiable under heading 95.04.

The Tribunal was of the view that the balance of the evidence indicated that the goods in issue were classifiable under heading 94.01 as "[s]eats (other than those of heading 94.02), whether or not convertible into beds, and parts thereof." The Tribunal reached this conclusion on the basis that the appellant failed to discharge its onus to establish that the CBSA's tariff classification of the goods in issue was incorrect.

Having determined that the goods in issue were correctly classified under heading 94.01, the Tribunal next determined the proper classification at the subheading and tariff item levels. Subheading 9401.61 had two tariff items.

---

91 AP-2010-035 (2011), 15 TTR (2d) 726.

The goods in issue were used to equip private dwellings. In addition, they were marketed and distributed by retail stores such as the appellant and were marketed towards individuals for gaming, listening to music, and watching movies in their homes. The Tribunal considered these to be "for domestic purposes." Therefore, pursuant to Rule 1 of the *Canadian Rules*, the Tribunal concluded that the goods in issue were correctly classified under tariff item No. 9401.61.10. The Tribunal, therefore, dismissed the appeal.

CASE 3: TARIFF ITEM 9401.71.10 (UPHOLSTERED FOLDING CHAIRS)

The goods under appeal in *Alliance Ro-Na Home Inc v Commissioner of the Canada Customs and Revenue Agency*[92] were padded steel folding chairs. The issue was whether these goods were correctly classified by the CCRA under tariff item 9401.71.10 as "other upholstered seats with metal frames for domestic purposes" or whether they should be classified under tariff item 9401.71.90 as "other upholstered seats with metal frames other than for domestic purposes," as claimed by the appellant. The parties were agreed at the subheading level; their disagreement was at the tariff item level.

The Tribunal examined the inherent characteristics of the folding chairs in trying to determine whether they were used for purposes other than domestic purposes. It was of the view that (1) there was no evidence to demonstrate that the folding chairs, because of their physical characteristics, their design, and their price were primarily made to be used in a domestic setting; (2) the evidence showed that the folding chairs closely resembled the chairs advertised in the catalogues as commercial furniture; (3) it was also clear from the evidence that the folding chairs may be of a lesser quality, but were in fact used in non-domestic sites, such as hotels and conference centres, for different events; and (4) price was merely an indicator of quality but was not determinative of whether the folding chairs were used primarily for domestic purposes. For all these reasons, the Tribunal allowed the appeal.

CASE 4: TARIFF ITEM 9401.71.90 (3-IN-1 CREEPER SEATS)

The goods under appeal in *Costco Wholesale Canada v President of the Canada Border Services Agency*[93] were 3-in-1 creeper seats made with metal frames, upholstered with leather, fitted with castor wheels, and equipped with trays. These multi-function goods could be converted into roller seats with trays, seat-style creepers, and lay-down creepers (birthing beds). The issue was whether the goods were correctly classified by the CBSA in its advance ruling as "other

---

92   AP-2001-065 (2002), 6 TTR (2d) 794.
93   AP-2008-031 (2010), 14 TTR (2d) 215.

metal furniture" under tariff item 9403.20.00 or whether they should be classified under tariff item 9401.71.90 as "other upholstered seats with metal frames" or, in the alternative, under tariff item 8716.80.10 as "other vehicles, not mechanically propelled, for the transport of persons," as claimed by the appellant.

The Tribunal allowed the appeal. The birthing beds were *prima facie* classifiable under two or more tariff items. Such a situation was governed by Rule 3(a) of the *General Rules*, which stated that the heading that provides the most specific description is to be preferred to headings providing a more general description. In the Tribunal's view, "operating table" was a more specific description than "other medical or surgical furniture."

Therefore, pursuant to Rule 3(a) of the *General Rules*, the most specific description of the goods in issue was found in heading 94.01, "Seats (other than those of heading 94.02), whether or not convertible into beds, and parts thereof" and therefore the goods in issue should be classified under tariff item 9401.71.90 as "other upholstered seats with metal frames, for other purposes."

CASE 5: TARIFF ITEM 9401.80.90 (INFANT CAR SEATS/STROLLERS)

The goods under appeal in *Evenflo Canada Inc v President of the Canada Border Services Agency*[94] consisted of five models of infant/child travel systems manufactured by Evenflo Company, Inc US. They were prepackaged sets that comprised an infant car seat, a car seat base, and a full-size stroller. The infant car seat, which could be used for infants weighing up to 22 pounds, was designed to snap into the car seat base, which was itself installed in a motor vehicle by means of an anchoring system or seat belts. In addition, the infant car seat was equipped with a handle that allowed it to be used independently as an infant carrier. Finally, the infant car seat was designed to snap into the stroller. The stroller, which could also be used without the infant car seat, could, depending on the exact model, accommodate infants and children weighing up to 50 pounds.

The issue in this appeal was whether the infant car seat/stroller combinations were correctly classified by the CBSA under tariff item 8715.00.00 as "baby carriages and parts thereof" or under tariff item 9401.80.10 as "other seats, for domestic purposes" or whether they should be classified under tariff item 9401.80.90 as "other seats, other than for domestic purposes," as claimed by the appellant.

---

94 AP-2009-049 (2010), 14 TTR (2d) 470.

Both parties agreed that the infant car seats should be classified under subheading 9401.80. The Tribunal also agreed. Both parties agreed that the goods in issue should be classified at the heading level pursuant to Rule 3 of the *General Rules*.

However, the CBSA submitted that classification at the heading level can be done through the application of Rule 3(b), while the appellant submitted that such classification could only be done through the application of Rule 3(c).

The Tribunal dealt with the parties' arguments as follows:

1) The CBSA submitted that the essential character of the goods in issue was conferred by the stroller and that, as such, the goods in issue were correctly classified under heading 87.15 as baby carriages. It further submitted that, as a result, there was no need to proceed to Rule 3(c) of the *General Rules*; that the stroller made up the largest portion of the goods in issue (that is, it was the larger and heavier of the items and occupied more space); that the stroller could bear more weight than the infant car seat and could thus be used for a longer duration of time; that the stroller was the more costly component of the set (that is, when purchased separately, the stroller had a higher retail value than the infant car seat); and that, at several major distributors, the appellant marketed the goods in issue as strollers and even emphasized their weight capacity.

   It was the Tribunal's view that the fact that goods were presented to consumers in the market as a "set" was not dispositive of whether they should be treated as such for classification purposes. However, it was satisfied that the goods in issue met each of the three requirements. Specifically, the goods in issue (1) consisted of at least two different articles that were *prima facie* classifiable under different headings (that is, an infant car seat and a full-size stroller); (2) consisted of articles put up together to carry out the specific activity of infant/child transportation; and (3) were imported into Canada in packaged form suitable for sale directly to consumers. Accordingly, the goods in issue were correctly considered "goods put up in sets for retail sale." That point was not contested by the parties.

2) The appellant submitted that neither the infant car seat nor the stroller conferred their essential character to the goods in issue. In its view, both components added equal functional value to the goods in issue, which precluded the Tribunal from considering Rule 3(b) of the *General Rules* and required that classification be done pursuant to Rule 3(c). In

response, the CBSA argued that the essential character of the goods in issue was conferred by the stroller because it was that component which independently provided all the "end uses" of the goods in issue. As for specific factors, it argued that the relative weight, bulk, value, and useful life of the stroller, as well as the marketing of the goods in issue, all militated in favour of the Tribunal finding that the stroller conferred on the goods in issue their essential character.

3) On the issue of "essential character," the Tribunal referred to the Federal Court of Appeal's decision in *Mon-Tex Mills Ltd v Commissioner of the Canada Customs and Revenue Agency*,[95] in which the court had explained that the purpose of an analysis under Rule 3(b) of the *General Rules* "(was) not merely to weigh the various elements of *Explanatory Note* VIII against one another, but rather to determine the essence or fundamental nature of the goods." The court added that, "to be essential, a characteristic must pertain to the essence of something. It must be fundamental." The Tribunal pointed out that it had taken a similar approach in its own decision in *Oriental Trading (MTL) Ltd v Deputy Minister of National Revenue*,[96] where it had to determine which component of cotton swabs—the cotton wadding or the polypropylene stem—gave the goods their essential character. Despite the evidence that the polypropylene stem weighed more, was bulkier, and accounted for more of the cost of the cotton swabs than the cotton wadding, the Tribunal found that, based on the role that the cotton wadding played in contributing to the personal hygiene nature of the product, the essential character of the product was conferred by the cotton wadding.

Examining each of these factors in turn to see how they weighed upon the essential character of the goods in issue, the Tribunal accepted that the relatively lighter weight and lower bulk of the infant car seat, which was also used as a hand-held infant carrier, was a design feature intended to respond to a specific and understandable demand of consumers. On the issue of value, the Tribunal noted that, depending on the specific model of the goods in issue, the value of the stroller was either comparable to, or higher than, that of the infant car seat.

While the stroller component may predominate to a certain degree in terms of such factors as relative weight, bulk, value, useful life, and marketing, it could also be reasonably argued that it was the functional compatibil-

---

95 AP-2002-103 (2003), 8 TTR (2d) 419, rev'd 2004 FCA 346.
96 AP-91-081 and AP-91-223 (1992), 10 TTR 347.

ity of the infant car seat with both the car seat base on the one hand, and the stroller on the other, that connected the individual articles to create a multi-modal travel "system" during the period of child infancy. In this regard, the fact that the stroller and infant car seat were purchased as a set rather than separately evinced an intention on the part of the consumer to use them as part of an integrated travel system, which further underscored the importance of the infant car seat as the common denominator across all three modes of transport covered by the goods in issue.

The Tribunal was therefore inclined to agree with the appellant that the respective contributions of the infant car seat and stroller to the overall functionality of the goods in issue were such that no single component can be said to confer essential character. Consequently, the classification of the goods in issue at the heading level cannot be effected under Rule 3 (b) of the *General Rules*.

The Tribunal, in support, also referred to the WCO Classification Opinions, which contained the following opinion with regard to subheading 9401.80: "1. Car safety seats suitable for use for the carriage of infants and toddlers in motor vehicles or other means of transport. They are removable and are attached to the vehicle's seats by means of the seat belt and a tether strap."

Therefore, pursuant to Rules 1 and 6 of the *General Rules*, the Tribunal concluded that the appropriate subheading was 9401.80.

With regard to the appropriate tariff item, the appellant submitted that infant car seats should be classified under tariff item 9401.80.90 as "other seats, other than for domestic purposes," while the CBSA submitted that they were correctly classified under tariff item 9401.80.10 as "other seats, for domestic purposes." In the CBSA's submission, the definition of the word "domestic" indicated that it referred to the normal, everyday actions of a family or household, and that the primary purpose of infant car seats was the transportation of children by their parents—an activity relating to the family and therefore domestic in nature.

The Tribunal disagreed with the CBSA's definition of "domestic purposes." In its opinion, the decisions in *Black & Decker Canada Inc v Deputy Minister of National Revenue for Customs and Excise*[97] and *Costco Canada Inc v Commissioner of the Canada Customs and Revenue Agency*[98] made it clear that, in order to be considered as goods used for "domestic purposes," goods must

---

97   AP-2003-007 (2004) (CITT) [*Black & Decker*].
98   AP-2000-050 (2001) (CITT).

be primarily for domestic or household use. These decisions made it equally clear that, in order for goods to be for domestic or household use, they must be used in the home or its direct surroundings. While the Tribunal's decision in *Black & Decker* appears, at first glance, to be inconsistent with these statements, a careful reading revealed that the activity that was being performed in that case took place in a motor home, which the Tribunal equated to a house. In light of the above, the Tribunal saw no reason why it should depart from previous decisions and, accordingly, it was clear that the infant car seats were not primarily used in and around the home.

As the infant car seats were designed to facilitate the transportation of infants, be it by car, by stroller, or by hand, it was self-evident that any use of the infant car seats would primarily occur away from the home or in the transportation of infants at a distance from the home. While the infant car seats may be used in the home or its direct surroundings, such use would generally be limited to transferring the infant to and from the car. Accordingly, the Tribunal concluded that the infant car seats, and, by implication, the goods in issue, are not used for "domestic purposes." Therefore, pursuant to the *Canadian Rules* and Rule 1 of the *General Rules*, the appropriate tariff item was 9401.80.90.

CASE 6: TARIFF ITEM 9405.40.90 (3-IN-1 SECURITY LIGHTS)

The goods in *Globe Electric Company Inc v President of the Canada Border Services Agency*[99] were 3-in-1 security lights. They were lightweight, circular-shaped electric lights with a retractable plug, equipped with a rechargeable battery, and had three different functions: (1) used as night lights, plugged into a wall outlet and automatically turned on at dusk and off at dawn; (2) served as security lights, providing light for a period of time by means of the rechargeable battery when no power is sensed in the outlet; and (3) used as portable lights when pulled out from the wall outlet, using the power from the rechargeable battery. According to the evidence, although the goods in issue technically had these three functions, the appellant viewed them as night lights and marketed them as such. This approach was consistent with the fact that their performance capability as flashlights or security lights was very minor in comparison to their capability as night lights.

The issue in the appeal was whether the goods were correctly classified by the CBSA under tariff item 9405.40.90 as "other electric lamps and light-

---

99 AP-2008-022 (2010), 14 TTR (2d) 394. A similar decision had been reached by the Tribunal in the appeal of *Supertek Canada Inc v Commissioner of the Canada Customs and Revenue Agency*, AP-2001-095 (2003), 7 TTR (2d) 931 in respect of the classification of battery-operated push-on lights.

ing fittings" or whether they should be classified under tariff item 8513.10.10 as "flashlights," as submitted by the appellant.

The Tribunal analyzed heading 85.13, which read: "Portable electric lamps designed to function by their own source of energy (for example, dry batteries, accumulators, magnetos), other than lighting equipment of heading 85.12." The Explanatory Notes to that heading provided as follows:

> The term "portable lamps" refers only to those lamps . . . which are designed for use when carried in the hand or on the person . . . . They usually have a handle or a fastening device and may be recognised by their particular shapes and their light weight. The term therefore excluded . . . lamps which are connected to a fixed installation (heading 94.05).

The appellant submitted that the goods in issue fell within the scope of heading 85.13 because they were "portable electric lamps, designed to function using their own source of energy"; equipped with a rechargeable internal battery, composed of lightweight material; and shaped to be comfortably carried in the hand, and thus met the conditions set out in the Explanatory Notes to heading 85.13. It further submitted that the fact that the goods in issue had features that allowed them to be used as security lights or night lights did not change the fact that they conformed to the requirements of tariff item 8513.10.10.

The CBSA, on the other hand, submitted that because an electrical outlet was a fixed installation, the goods in issue were excluded from classification under heading 85.13 by the Explanatory Notes to that heading.

The Tribunal agreed with the CBSA and classified the goods in issue as night lights under tariff item 9405.40.90, and not as flashlights or security lights, and dismissed the appeal.

CASE 7: TARIFF ITEM 9502.10.00 ("FEARLESS RIDER" GIFT SETS)
The goods under appeal in *Intersave West Buying and Merchandising Service v Commissioner of the Canada Customs and Revenue Service Agency*[100] consisted of a doll representing either Mulan or Li Shang, the two characters from a Walt Disney movie entitled *Mulan*, a horse designed to be "ridden" by the doll, and a sword that was the doll's "weapon." All items were packaged together and were made of plastic.

The CCRA classified the doll under tariff item 9503.70.10 (as "other toys of plastics, put up in sets or outfits"), whereas the appellant claimed that they should be classified under tariff item 9502.10.00 (as "dolls representing only

---

100 AP-2000-017 (2001), 5 TTR (2d) 386.

human beings") or, in the alternative, under tariff item 9503.49.00 (as "other toys representing animals or non-human creatures").

The Tribunal dismissed the appeal. It was of the view that the goods in issue satisfied the definition of a set found in the Explanatory Notes to Rule 3(b) of the *General Rules*. The goods in issue consisted of at least two different articles, which were *prima facie* classifiable under different headings; they consisted of articles put up together to carry out the specific play activity of a rider going into battle on his/her horse, and they were put up in a manner suitable for sale directly to users without repacking. Given that two headings, heading 95.02 and 95.03, each referred to part only of the items in the set, those headings were to be regarded as equally specific in relation to the goods in issue.

The Tribunal found that neither the doll nor the horse gave the goods in issue their essential character and, therefore, Rule 3(b) was not determinative. Since heading 95.03 occurred last in numerical order, the goods were correctly classified, pursuant to Rule 3(c) in that heading. Within heading 95.03, the goods in issue were correctly classified in subheading 9503.70 (as "other toys put up in sets") and because the goods were made of plastic, they were correctly classified under tariff item 9503.70.10.

CASE 8: TARIFF ITEM 9503.00.90 (INFANT SWINGS)

In *Elfe Juvenile Products v President of the Canada Border Services Agency*,[101] the appellant was contesting five decisions of the CBSA classifying Graco Lovin' Hug™ infant swings under tariff item 9401.71.10 as "other upholstered seats with metal frames for domestic purposes," claiming that the goods in issue should have been classified under tariff item 9503.00.90 as "other toys."

The infant swing was mounted on a metal frame and could be placed in four positions of different reclining angles. It was equipped with a head support, an electric motor, and an overhead mobile with three soft toys. It was capable of swinging (six variable speeds), playing music (ten classical melodies or songs), and reproducing nature sounds (five different sounds). Mix 'n Move® toys, for use with the tray, were sold separately. The swing was intended for babies weighing from 5.5 to 30 pounds (2.5 to 13.6 kilograms), aged from zero to six months.

The relevant provisions of Chapter 94 covered "Furniture; bedding; mattresses"; heading 94.01 covered "Seats (other than those of heading 94.02) whether or not convertible into beds, and parts thereof"; subheading 9401.71

---

101   AP-2011-029 (2012), 16 TTR (2) 830.

covered "Upholstered seats"; and tariff item 9401.71.10 covered "upholstered seats for domestic purposes."

The relevant notes to Chapter 94 provided that the Chapter did not cover "(l) Toy furniture or toy lamps or lighting fittings (heading 95.03)." The relevant Explanatory Notes to Chapter 94 and heading 94.01 provided that the Chapter covered, subject to the exclusions listed in the Explanatory Notes to the Chapter, "(1) All furniture and parts thereof (headings 94.01 to 94.03)." They defined the term "furniture" to mean,

> (A) Any "movable" articles (not included under other more specific headings of the Nomenclature), which have the essential characteristic that they are constructed for placing on the floor or ground, and which are used, mainly with a utilitarian purpose, to equip private dwellings . . . .

Subject to the exclusions mentioned below, heading 94.01 covered all seats (including those for vehicles, provided that they complied with the conditions prescribed in Note 2 to this Chapter), for example, "19. Lounge chairs, arm-chairs, folding chairs, deck chairs, infants' high chairs and children's seats designed to be hung on the back of other seats (including vehicle seats) . . . ."

The relevant provisions of Chapter 95 covered "toys, games and sports requisites; parts and accessories thereof"; subheading 9503.00 covered "tricycles, scooters, pedal cars and similar wheeled toys; dolls' carriages; dolls; other toys; reduced size ('scale') models and similar recreational models, working or not; puzzles of all kinds." Tariff item 9503.00.90 covered "Other" (toys, and so on).

The relevant Explanatory Notes to Chapter 95 and heading 95.03 provided that the Chapter covered "toys of all kinds whether designed for the amusement of children or adults"; and heading 95.03 covered "(D) Other toys."

The appellant submitted that the goods in issue were classifiable, on the basis of Rule 1 of the *General Rules*, under heading 95.03 as other toys, relying on note 1(l) to Chapter 94, which provided that "[t]his Chapter does not cover . . . (l) [t]oy furniture or toy lamps or lighting fittings (heading 95.03)" and were expressly excluded from the ambit of heading 94.01, and directed classification under heading 95.03. In support of its position that the goods in issue were toys, the appellant relied on the Explanatory Notes to Chapter 95, which provide for ". . . toys of all kinds whether designed for the amusement of children or adults" and also referred to the dictionary definition of the term "amuse": "to divert the attention of so as to deceive . . . to entertain or occupy in a light, playful, or pleasant manner," and argued that the goods in issue fell within the meaning of the term "toy" as the swing occupied the attention of the babies that it was designed to hold.

The CBSA submitted that the goods in issue were correctly classified, on the basis of Rule 1 of the *General Rules*, under heading 94.01 as other upholstered seats with metal frames for domestic purposes.

In several previous decisions, the Tribunal had outlined the factors that the amusement and the play value can be ascertained by examining the actual and intended use of the goods. Among them were the design of the goods and the manner in which they were marketed, packaged, and advertised. Consequently, the Tribunal examined the amusement value of the goods in issue, as well as their intended and actual uses.

The Tribunal accepted that the swinging motion, the sounds, and the plush toys of the goods in issue provided some measure of amusement or distraction for babies. It also noted that the product literature, packaging, and marketing of the goods in issue emphasized the ways in which babies will purportedly be amused and entertained. The Tribunal further observed that the goods in issue were distributed mainly in retail toy stores, such as Toys "R" Us and Babies "R" Us, as well as in other general merchandise retail stores, such as Wal-Mart, in their infant and baby gear sections.

The CBSA recognized that the goods in issue provided amusement for babies. However, it insisted that the goods had mainly a practical, utilitarian purpose of providing a "seat" for babies. It submitted that amusement was not the fundamental element of the essential characteristics and functions of the goods in issue.

The Tribunal did not agree with CBSA's assertion. It was of the view that the amusement value was provided not only by the visual and audio inputs but also by the movement of the swing itself. On the basis of the evidence, the Tribunal considered that the vibration mechanism, the swing motion, the mobile, and their play value were fundamental elements of the goods in issue.

Given that the electrical and mechanical components were incorporated in the goods, they were an intrinsic part of them; therefore, in the Tribunal's opinion, the goods must be viewed as a whole because they interacted with the baby in swinging (stimulating the moving sensory system), playing music, and making noises (hearing stimulation), moving the toy mobile (visual stimulation), and overall entertaining and amusing the baby. All of these amusements and stimulations may be used alone or in combination with others.

As the Tribunal has found in the past, even if goods had some incidental utilitarian functions, classification under heading 95.03 as "other toys" was not precluded. In this instance, the Tribunal found that the overarching reason for which the goods in issue existed was for the amusement of babies through the stimulation of their sensory systems and that this stimulation provided entertainment to them, in addition to hopefully giving a break to their caregivers. Moreover, the goods in issue were marketed and advertised as toys.

Having regard to the above considerations, the Tribunal was satisfied that the goods in issue were correctly described as toys that were intended essentially for the amusement of infants. Therefore, it found that the goods in issue were classifiable under heading 95.03 as other toys.

On the basis of the evidence on the record, the Tribunal determined that even if the seats were essential parts of the goods in issue, they were more than seats. Even if the goods may be used incidentally to hold a baby, without swinging, moving, playing music and making sounds, and rotating the mobile toys, that was not sufficient to qualify the goods as mere infant seats and thereby ignore their inherent swinging properties and amusement value.

Therefore, while the goods in issue may have the characteristics to meet part of the definition of "furniture" found in Explanatory Note (A) to Chapter 94, they did not meet the proviso included in the definition of "furniture" that the goods in issue are "not included under other more specific headings of the Nomenclature." Therefore, they were not classifiable under heading 94.01.

Consequently, in accordance with Rule 1 of the *General Rules*, the goods in issue were properly classifiable under heading 95.03. Pursuant to Rule 6 of the *General Rules*, the goods in issue must be classified under subheading 9503.00 as other toys because no other first-level subheading under heading 95.03 described them. By virtue of Rule 1 of the *Canadian Rules*, the goods in issue were properly classifiable under tariff item 9503.00.90 (subheading 9503.00 not being otherwise subdivided). The Tribunal, therefore, allowed the appeal.

CASE 9: TARIFF ITEM 9503.41.00 (PLUSH ARTICLES)

The goods in the appeal in *Calego International Inc v Deputy Minister of National Revenue*[102] were plush articles with an outer surface of textile materials. The issue was whether the goods were properly classified by the Deputy Minister of National Revenue under tariff item 4202.92.11 as "tool bags, haversacks, knapsacks, packsacks and rucksacks, with an outer surface of textile

---

102   Above note 11.

materials" or whether they should be classified under tariff item 9503.41.00 as "other stuffed toys representing animals or non-human creatures," as claimed by the appellant.

The Tribunal found that the goods in issue were *prima facie* rucksacks of heading 42.02. It also found that the goods were *prima facie* other toys of heading 95.03. Because the description in each of the two headings under consideration related to only one of the two functions of the goods in issue, the Tribunal was of the opinion that both headings were equally descriptive for the purposes of Rule 3(a) of the *General Rules*. As the goods consisted of different materials, regardless of whether the essential character of the goods was found to be a rucksack or a toy, no single material gave the goods either character. Therefore, Rule 3(b) did not apply. Accordingly, as directed by Rule 3(c) to classify the goods in the heading that occurs last in numerical order among those that equally merit consideration, the Tribunal concluded that the goods should be classified under tariff item 9503.41.00 as "other stuffed toys representing animals or non-human creatures," as claimed by the appellant.

CASE 10: TARIFF ITEM 9503.90.00 (RED BANDANAS IMPRINTED "DISNEY PIRATES OF THE CARIBBEAN")

In this appeal, *Havi Global Solutions (Canada) Limited Partnership v President of the Canada Border Services Agency*[103] contested the advance ruling of the CBSA with respect to the goods in issue, which were red bandanas imprinted with a movie logo, being a pirate's head superimposed on two crossed swords with the words "Disney Pirates of the Caribbean" printed below the logo, and with a piece of fabric hanging from the bandana to cover the back of the neck. The bandanas were imported in plastic bags that also contained a pirate card. They were part of a promotion created for the McDonald's Corporation, called the "Pirates of the Caribbean 2: Dead Man's Chest Happy Meal." The promotion consisted of eight different items, each with a different pirate card, and when collected and put together, these cards formed a treasure map.

The CBSA classified the goods in issue under tariff item 6505.90.90. Tariff heading 65.05 read "Hats and other headgear, knitted or crocheted, or made up from lace, felt or other textile fabric, in the piece (but not in strips), whether or not lined or trimmed; hair-nets of any material, whether or not lined or trimmed." Tariff subheading 6505.90 read "Other" and tariff item 6505.90.90 read "Other."

103   AP-2007-014 (2008), 13 TTR (2d) 23.

The appellant claimed that the goods in issue should be classified under tariff item 9503.90.00 as other toys. Tariff head 95.03 read: "Other toys; reduced-size ('scale') models and similar recreational models, working or not; puzzles of all kinds." Tariff item 9503.90.00 covered "Other."

Both parties submitted that the tariff classification of the goods in issue can be effected by reference to Rule 1 of the *General Rules*.

The Explanatory Notes to heading 95.03 stated that the heading covered toys intended essentially for the amusement of persons (children or adults). It included: "(A) All toys not included in headings 95.01 and 95.02 . . . (C) Puzzles of all kinds."

Both parties cited the Tribunal's decisions in *Zellers*[104] and *Regal Confections*,[105] in which the Tribunal emphasized four factors in its determination as to whether the goods in issue were toys (collectability; marketing and distribution; design and best use; and appearance). The CBSA submitted that the Tribunal, in *Regal Confections*, specifically noted that merely because a product provided amusement value, it did not mean that it should necessarily be classified as a toy.

As indicated in previous cases, the Tribunal was of the view that a toy was something from which one derived amusement or pleasure and that the play value of an object was an identifying aspect of it being a toy. The determination of whether an item constituted a toy was a factual issue to be determined on a case-by-case basis.

The evidence indicated that the goods in issue were specifically designed to be played with by children pretending to be pirates, based on the Pirates of the Caribbean characters. The Pirates of the Caribbean logo, which was printed on the bandana, was intended to associate the bandana with the movie, the movie character Jack Sparrow, and pirate role playing. The bandana was the eighth toy in the series, all of which were clearly identified as toys, and which together were intended to convey the image of a child engaging in fantasy play as the pirate Jack Sparrow. The Tribunal noted that the Pirates of the Caribbean Happy Meal promotion was carefully planned to be launched at about the same time as the movie was released in theatres.

Based on the evidence, the Tribunal was satisfied that, although the goods in issue can be worn as hats, in their essence, they were things from which a child derived amusement and pleasure. They were items with play value. Therefore, they were classifiable under tariff item 9503.90.00 as toys.

---

104 Above note 30.
105 Above note 16.

With regard to the CBSA's assertion that the goods in issue were properly classified under tariff item 6505.90.90 as other headgear, the Tribunal considered that, in their essence, the goods in issue were toys, not headgear. Therefore, it allowed the appeal.

CASE 11: TARIFF ITEM 9503.90.00 (INTERACTIVE PLAY MATS)

In *Korhani Canada Inc v President of the Canada Border Services Agency*,[106] the goods were various styles and sizes of interactive play mats, and the issue was whether the Canada Border Service Agency correctly classified them under tariff item 5703.20.10 as "machine tufted carpets of nylon" in its advance ruling, or whether they should have been classified under tariff item 9503.90.00 as "other toys," as claimed by the appellant.

The play mats were made of 100 percent nylon filament loop pile tufts with an anti-slip gel foam backing, and ranged in size from 1.0 metre by 1.2 metres to 1.0 metre by 2.0 metres. The top surface of the goods was printed with various designs, which divided the mats into two categories: generic (unlicensed) play mats and licensed play mats. The generic play mats were the "City Life," "Canadian Tire City Life," and "Rona Warehouse City Life" play mats. Each play mat was printed to depict a city setting with features such as roads, houses, a hospital, a police station, and an airport. The "Canadian Tire City Life" and the "Rona Warehouse City Life" play mats also depicted their respective stores in the centre of the mat. The licensed play mats featured characters from Disney (Winnie the Pooh, Cinderella, and Cars), Nickelodeon (SpongeBob SquarePants and Dora the Explorer), and Marvel Comics (Spider-Man). Each play mat was printed with a map-like setting consisting of pathway or roadway scenes with licensed characters. The play mats showed various locations relating to the television show, movie, and so on in which the characters appear.

With respect to the appellant's claim that the goods in issue should be classified under tariff item 9503.90.00, which read "Other toys; reduced-size ('scale') models and similar recreational models, working or not; puzzles of all kinds." "Other," the Tribunal pointed out that the notes relating to Section XI (which included Chapter 57) and to Chapter 57 were relevant for the purposes of determining under which heading the goods in issue are to be classified. Note 1(t) to Section XI states that the Section did not cover ... articles of Chapter 95 (for example, toys, games, sports requisites and nets); and Note 1 to Chapter 57 reads: "For the purpose of this Chapter, the term 'carpets and other textile floor coverings' means floor coverings in which

---

106 AP-2007-008 (2008), 13 TTR (2d) 63.

textile materials serve as the exposed surface of the article when in use and includes articles having the characteristics of textile floor coverings but intended for use for other purposes."

While agreeing that the goods in issue were made of nylon filament loop pile tufts with an anti-slip gel foam backing and were thus *prima facie* classifiable under heading 57.03 as tufted carpets, the appellant argued that, on the basis of Note 1(t) to Section XI, it was necessary to first determine whether the goods in issue were considered articles of Chapter 95. In other words, it submitted that the goods in issue cannot be classified under Section XI unless it was first determined that they cannot be classified under Chapter 95. It also submitted that there were no notes to Section XX (which included Chapter 95) and that the notes to Chapter 95 did not exclude the goods in issue from classification therein.

With respect to tariff item 5703.20.10, under which the CBSA classified the goods in issue, that heading read: "Carpets and other textile floor coverings, tufted, whether or not made up ... [o]f nylon and other polyamides ... machine tufted."

In defending its determination, the CBSA took the position that the design of the goods in issue should not result in their classification under heading 95.03 as "other toys" as that would be contrary to Note 1 to Chapter 57. It argued that, even if the goods in issue were intended for use for other purposes, the application of Note 1 to Chapter 57 meant that they must still be considered textile floor coverings and should thus be classified under heading 57.03 as tufted carpets.

In the Tribunal's view, it was clear that Note 1(t) to Section XI precluded articles of Chapter 95 from being classified under Section XI (that is, under Chapters 50 to 63). Although Note 1 to Chapter 57 was relevant for the purposes of determining whether goods can be classified in that chapter, it must be interpreted in a manner that gives effect to Note 1(t) to Section XI.

Accordingly, the Tribunal first determined whether the goods in issue were articles of Chapter 95 and, in particular, whether they could be classified under heading 95.03 as other toys. If the goods were in fact such "other toys," they would be precluded from classification under Chapters 50 to 63. The Tribunal then determined the proper classification at the subheading and tariff item levels. If the goods in issue did not constitute "other toys," it would then determine whether they could be classified under heading 57.03.

In the Tribunal's opinion, the Explanatory Notes to Chapter 95 and heading 95.03, as well as dictionary definitions of the word "toy," helped delineate the scope of application of heading 95.03. The Explanatory Notes to Chapter 95 read: "This Chapter covers toys of all kinds whether designed for the amusement of children or adults." The Explanatory Notes to heading 95.03 are similar and read: "This heading covers toys intended essentially for the amusement of persons (children or adults)."

Although the goods in issue had various themes, each was essentially a floor mat that depicted either a city setting (for example, the urban area near a Canadian Tire store) or a map-like setting consisting of pathway or roadway scenes with licensed characters (for example, Winnie the Pooh's 100 Acre Wood). According to Korhani, the goods in issue were designed to allow children to interact with the printed designs by manoeuvring or positioning various toys on the pathways, roadways, or other identifiable locations printed on the goods in issue.

On the basis of the appellant's evidence, the Tribunal was of the opinion that the goods in issue provided play value and should thus be considered toys. The evidence clearly demonstrated that the goods in issue had been both designed and marketed with the specific intent that they be used by children as objects to play with. There was also some evidence to confirm that this objective was in fact achieved, in that children had actually been using the goods in issue to play with.

In addition to being used as toys, the goods in issue can be used as carpets in the traditional sense. However, the fact that the goods in issue may also have a utilitarian function did not, in the Tribunal's view, preclude them from being classified as toys. Because the goods in issue satisfied the terms of heading 95.03, Note 1(t) to Section XI automatically precluded them from classification under heading 57.03.

In light of the foregoing, the Tribunal found that the goods in issue were correctly classified under heading 95.03 as other toys, and Note 1(t) to Section XI precluded them from classification under heading 57.03.

Having determined that the goods in issue were correctly classified under heading 95.03, the Tribunal then turned to the classification at the subheading and tariff item levels. Heading 95.03 had nine first-level subheadings, but as eight of those subheadings pertained to specific types of toys or toy sets that did not include the play mats, the mats must be classified in the remaining subheading as "other toys." Therefore, pursuant to Rule 6 of the *General Rules*, the goods in issue were classified under subheading 9503.90. As subheading 9503.90 was not further divided at the tariff item level, the goods were classified under tariff item 9503.90.00. Accordingly, the Tribunal allowed the appeal.

CASE 12: TARIFF ITEM 9503.90.00 (DRESS UP SETS)

The appeal in *Toys "R" Us (Canada) Ltd v Deputy Minister of National Revenue*[107] related to Buzz Lightyear Dress Up Sets, which the Deputy Minister of National Revenue had classified under tariff item 9503.70.10 as "other toys of plastics put up in outfits." The appellant claimed that they should have been classified under tariff item 9503.90.00 as "other toys."

The Tribunal allowed the appeal. In its view, the goods were not outfits, which under tariff subheading 9503.70 must be composed of two or more different articles, as required by the Explanatory Notes to the subheading. Rather, they constituted one article, one single toy, albeit composed of three different components, which were clearly interdependent, as shown by the presence of clips that served to connect the chest plate and the backpack, and by the fact that the wings could only be worn with the backpack. The packaging of the goods in issue, although referring to them as a "dress up set," clearly showed that the components were part of a single toy. The chest plates, the backpack, and the wings did not have the required degree of independence that was required by the Explanatory Notes to constitute different articles.

CASE 13: TARIFF ITEM 9505.10.00 (PLASTIC GIFT BOWS)

The goods in *Danson Décor Inc v President of the Canada Border Services Agency*[108] were eleven models of gift bows, which consisted of multiple layers of plastics that had been formed into flexible metallized strips or metallized die-cut shapes. The bows were metallic in appearance and came in a variety of sizes (small or large), colours (red, green, blue, gold, or silver), finishes (shiny, dull, or with a holographic image), and shapes (rosette or florist bow, narrow curly streamers, or starburst). The bows were held together by a pin, staple, or thread and were attached to a paperboard backing with a disposable release paper. They were either attached to a paperboard holder for hanging from a hook or enclosed in bags held together at the top by a piece of folded paperboard, which were all prepared for retail sale. The front side of the paperboard was printed with the words "Décorations de Noël" and "Christmas Decorations" or "Une Tradition de Noël" and "A Holiday Tradition." The reverse side of the paperboard was printed with Danson Décor's address, a computer barcode, and instructions for removing the disposable release paper.

---

107 AP-99-067 (2001).
108 AP-2009-066 (2011), 15 TTR (2d) 646.

The issue was whether the gift bows were correctly classified by the CBSA under tariff item 3926.90.90 as "other articles of plastics" or whether they should be classified under tariff item 9505.10.00 as "articles for Christmas festivities," as claimed by the appellant.

The Tribunal concluded that the goods in issue should be classified under tariff item 9505.10.00 as articles for Christmas festivities. According to the evidence, the goods were predominantly used to decorate gifts exchanged during the Christmas period and were labelled as Christmas items. Heading 95.05 had a specific subheading and tariff item pertaining to articles for Christmas festivities. Although the goods in issue were not specifically named in the Explanatory Notes to heading 95.05, the Tribunal was of the view that the use of the word "etc." in the Explanatory Notes to heading 95.05 allowed for a broad interpretation of the phrase "festive decorations" and that these Notes could be interpreted to encompass the goods in issue, since they were festive articles used to decorate gifts.

On the basis of the dictionary definitions, the Tribunal took the view that bows such as the goods in issue were not a type of packaging, nor were they listed as examples of articles that may be used to package or wrap a gift. According to the evidence, the bows were used to decorate a gift that had been wrapped or packaged. They were festive decorations for gifts and the exclusionary Note (c) in the Explanatory Notes to heading 95.05 did not cover them. Therefore, they should be classified under heading 95.05 as festive articles. Consequently, the goods in issue were excluded from classification under Chapter 39 by virtue of Note 2(y) to Chapter 39. Pursuant to Rule 6 of the *General Rules* and Rule 1 of the *Canadian Rules*, it followed that the goods in issue should be classified under tariff item No. 9505.10.00 as articles for Christmas festivities.

CASE 14: TARIFF ITEM 9505.90.00 (HALLOWEEN COSTUMES)

The appeal in *Loblaws Companies Limited v President of the Canada Border Services Agency*[109] was in regard to various types of full-body or partial-coverage Halloween costumes for children and adults, manufactured from either knitted or woven synthetic, polyester, nylon, or nylon/polyester textile material. They were made to resemble animals, super heroes, and fictional and historical characters. Some of the costumes included plastic or textile accessories to be worn with the costume or carried by the wearer.

---

109 AP-2010-022 (2011), 15 TTR (2d) 853.

The issue was whether the goods were correctly classified by the CBSA under tariff item 6104.43.00 as "women's or girls' knitted or crocheted dresses of synthetic fibres"; tariff item 6114.30.00 as "other knitted or crocheted garments of man-made fibres"; tariff item 6115.93.00 as "knitted socks of synthetic fibres"; tariff item 6204.43.00 as "women's or girls' woven dresses of synthetic fibres"; or tariff item 6211.33.90 as "other men's or boys' woven garments," or whether they should be classified under tariff item 9505.90.00 as "other festive articles," as claimed by the appellant.

The CBSA argued that the goods were fancy dresses composed of either knitted or woven synthetic, polyester, nylon, or nylon/polyester textile material, and, therefore, were excluded from classification under Chapter 95. The CBSA also argued that they were goods of Chapter 61 or 62 because they were clothing that was worn on the body whether over or under any other clothing, as described in those chapters. In further support of its argument, the CBSA referred to the *Canadian Oxford Dictionary*, which defined "fancy dress" as a "costume."

The appellant argued that Halloween costumes were festive articles and not fancy dresses, as found by the Tribunal in *Thinkway Trading Corporation v Deputy Minister of National Revenue*; they were flimsy, non-durable textile costumes sold only for Halloween and worn for festive purposes or as disguises. It referred to the Federal Court of Appeal's decision in *Shaklee Canada Inc v The Queen* to support its position that the language of Chapters 61 and 62, such as "apparel or clothing," should be given its common and ordinary meaning as perceived by the consumer. It also referred to the Tribunal's decision in *Trudell Medical Marketing Limited v Deputy Minister of National Revenue*, arguing that Chapters 61 and 62 were reserved for traditional clothing, whereas other clothing, such as disposable clothing (surgeons' masks and gowns) worn once or twice and discarded, worn clothing, and rags that did not exhibit the characteristics attributable to clothing, were not classified under Chapter 61 or 62 but under headings 63.07, 63.09, and 63.10 respectively.

The Tribunal analyzed Chapter 95 in the context of its exclusionary Note 1(e), which sets out three conditions in order for goods to be excluded from classification in Chapter 95: the goods must be (1) fancy dress, (2) composed at least in part of textiles, and (3) apparel or clothing accessories of Chapter 61 or 62.

In the case at bar, it was uncontested that the goods in issue were costumes and fancy dress; however, neither Chapter 95 nor the Explanatory Note to it defined the term "fancy dress." In the absence of a definition, the Tribunal turned to dictionary definitions for assistance and found that "fancy dress" was defined as "costume." The Tribunal was satisfied that the terms "fancy dress" and "costume" were synonymous and concluded that the goods in issue were fancy dress and met the first condition of Note 1(e) to Chapter 95. They also met the second condition, as it was not contested that the goods in issue were composed of textile materials.

The third and final condition of the exclusionary Note 1(e) referred to apparel "of Chapter 61 or 62." The Explanatory Notes to Chapters 61 and 62 indicated that the chapters covered men's, women's, or children's articles of apparel; however, the Notes did not define "apparel." The common and ordinary meaning as found in dictionaries as well as Canadian and US caselaw, which the Tribunal referred to, were of no assistance.

On the basis of the foregoing, the Tribunal found that the goods in issue were not "of Chapter 61 or 62," and, thus, did not meet the third condition of Note 1(e) to Chapter 95. As the goods in issue had not met all three conditions, the Tribunal concluded that the goods were not excluded from classification under Chapter 95.

The Tribunal concluded that the Halloween costumes should be classified under heading 95.05 as "festive, carnival or other entertainment articles." According to the evidence, the costumes were primarily marketed, sold, and worn for Halloween. As heading 95.05 had no specific subheading and tariff item pertaining to articles for Halloween, pursuant to Rule 6 of the *General Rules* and Rule 1 of the *Canadian Rules*, it followed that the costumes should be classified under tariff item 9505.90.00 as "other festive articles." It, therefore, allowed the appeal.

CASE 15: TARIFF ITEM 9506.91.90 (TRAMPOLINE)

The good in *Canadian Tire Corporation Limited v President of the Canada Border Services Agency*[110] was described as a round 55-inch (140-centimetre) band trampoline with a mesh enclosure, a zippered entrance, and a powder-coated, rust-resistant steel tube frame, designed for use by children aged three to six years, with a maximum user weight of 100 pounds (45.36 kilograms). It was offered in either a Dora or Diego theme associated with the Nickelodeon cartoon shows *Dora the Explorer* and *Go, Diego, Go!*

The issue was whether the trampoline was correctly classified by the CBSA under tariff item 9506.91.90 as "other articles and equipment for general physical exercise, gymnastics or athletics" or whether it should be classified under tariff item 9503.00.90 as "other toys," as claimed by the appellant.

---

110 AP-2011-020 (2012), 16 TTR (2d) 511 [*Canadian Tire #5*].

Both parties acknowledged that the good in issue was a trampoline and referred to it as such in their respective submissions. A "trampoline" is defined as "an apparatus for performing acrobatic tumbling and jumping feats, consisting of a sheet of strong canvas attached to a frame by springs and held tautly stretched above the floor" or as "a strong fabric sheet connected by springs to a horizontal frame, used by gymnasts, etc. for somersaults, as a springboard, etc."[111] It is not defined as a toy. The Tribunal concluded that the good in issue was designed to be used by children as a trampoline and not merely as a toy for amusement. On the basis of the evidence, the Tribunal was not convinced that, for the purposes of the tariff classification, the good in issue was considered "other toys" within the meaning of the terms of heading 95.03, and found that it was not classifiable under that heading.

It was clear that the good in issue provided amusement and play value, as the appellant contended. It was also clear that the good in issue was designed for use by and marketed towards children. However, in the Tribunal's view, that was not sufficient to describe the trampoline as a "toy."

If amusement or play value alone were sufficient, all kinds of articles and equipment for sport and games would necessarily be classified as "toys" per se, when clearly this was not the intention of Parliament as demonstrated by, *inter alia*, the express terms of heading 95.06. In focusing on the pleasure-giving element, the appellant in fact omitted that the essential purpose of the trampoline was to enable children to perform the physical activity of jumping and bouncing. It was this physical action of jumping and bouncing that provided the amusement.

On the other hand, the good in issue was covered in heading 95.06, which read: "[a]rticles and equipment for general physical exercise, gymnastics, athletics, other sports (including table-tennis) or outdoor games, not specified or included elsewhere in this Chapter." Since the good met the terms of the heading, it was classifiable therein, since the relevant section or chapter notes and the Explanatory Notes did not provide otherwise. Therefore, in accordance with Rule 1 of the *General Rules* and the applicable tariff nomenclature identified above, the good in issue was correctly classified under heading 95.06.

Subheadings of heading 95.06 did not specifically name trampolines. Therefore, pursuant to Rule 6 of the *General Rules*, the good in issue should be further classified under the residual subheading 9506.91 that included

---

111   *Ibid* at para 13.

"articles and equipment for general physical exercise, gymnastics or athletics other than those that are specifically covered by other subheadings."

In regard to the relevant tariff item, there were two tariff items of subheading 9506.91. Tariff item 9506.91.10 covered "Exercise bicycles; Parts for use in the manufacture of physical exercise machines; Stair climbing machines" and was therefore not applicable to trampolines. Therefore, the trampoline was classifiable under tariff item 9506.91.90, which covered all "other" articles and equipment for general physical exercise, gymnastics or athletics." Accordingly, under Rule 1 of the *Canadian Rules*, it followed that the trampoline was correctly classified under tariff item 9506.91.90. For the above reasons, the Tribunal dismissed the appeal.

CASE 16: TARIFF ITEM 9506.99.10 (PLAYGROUND EQUIPMENT)

The appellant in *Dynamo Industries, Inc v President of the Canada Border Services Agency*[112] had imported playground equipment that the CBSA classified under tariff item 9506.99.90 (as "other articles and equipment for general physical exercise"). It claimed that the goods should have been classified by the CBSA under tariff item 9506.99.10 as "other articles and equipment for general physical exercise or outdoor games not elsewhere specified or included elsewhere in Chapter 95, for climbing or mountaineering."

The Tribunal allowed the appeal. It concluded that, for goods to be correctly classified under tariff item 9506.99.10, it was sufficient that they be used for either climbing or mountaineering, within the normal meaning of either of those terms. The Tribunal was of the opinion that the wording of that tariff item did not require non-exclusive use. All that was required for classification in this instance was that the goods be used either for "climbing" or for "mountaineering." Because the evidence indicated a significant degree of use for climbing, that was sufficient to satisfy the requirement of the tariff item.

CASE 17: TARIFF ITEM 9506.99.90 (SLEDS)

The goods in *HBC Imports c/o Zellers Inc v President of the Canada Border Services Agency*[113] were "sleds," 39 inches (99 centimetres) long, with two handles, a soft foam core, and a slick skin, designed for riding down snow-covered hills.

The issue was whether the sleds were correctly classified by the CBSA under tariff item 9506.99.90 as "other articles and equipment for general

---

112   AP-2008-007 (2009), 13 TTR (2d) 500.
113   AP-2011-018 (2012), 16 TTR (2d) 530.

physical exercise, gymnastics, athletics, other sports (including table-tennis) or outdoor games, not specified or included elsewhere in Chapter 95" or whether they should be classified under tariff item 9503.00.90 as "other toys" as claimed by the appellant.

The Tribunal dismissed the appeal. It was clear that the goods in issue provided amusement and play value, as the appellant contended. However, this factor alone was not sufficient to describe it as a "toy." The Tribunal's jurisprudence had interpreted the term "toy" broadly as encompassing a wide range of articles that provided amusement or play value. On that basis, and on the evidence, the Tribunal was not convinced that, for the purposes of tariff classification, the sleds can be qualified as "other toys" within the terms of heading 95.03.

The Tribunal was satisfied that sledding or sliding on snow was indeed an outdoor game. Note 1(n) of Chapter 95 stated that the chapter did not cover "[s]ports vehicles (other than bobsleighs, toboggans and the like) of Section XVII." In turn, Note 1 to Section XVII expressly excluded "bobsleighs, toboggans or the like of heading 95.06." Read together, it was clear that heading 95.06 must then include "toboggans and the like." Therefore, in accordance with Rule 1 of the *General Rules* and the applicable tariff nomenclature identified above, the sled was correctly classified in heading 95.06. Pursuant to Rule 6 of the *General Rules*, the goods in issue were correctly classified under subheading 9506.99. The other subheadings did not apply.

b) Parts and Accessories

The terms "parts," "parts of general use," "parts of the foregoing," "parts suitable for," "parts for use in the manufacture or production of," "parts and accessories," and like terms can be found in many sections and chapters of the List of Tariff Provisions in the Schedule to the Act, most often in Chapters 84 and 85 (machinery and parts thereof). These sections and headings, as well as the latter's subheadings, explain the meaning of the terms by way of Explanatory Notes. Therefore, it is essential to fully analyze them before classifying an article as a part or as an accessory, and even as to competing host articles. The following are a few of the more important notes to be considered:

1) Section XV, Note 2 defines the expression "parts of general use" to mean:

   (A) Articles of heading 73.07, 73.12, 73.15, 73.17 or 73.18 and similar articles of other base metals;
   (B) Springs and leaves for springs, of base metal, other than clock or watch springs (heading 91.14); and

(C) Articles of heading 83.01, 83.02, 83.08 or 83.10 and frames and mirrors, of base metal, of heading 83.06.

2) In chapters 73 to 76 and 78 to 82 (but not in heading 73.15), references to parts of goods do not include references to "parts of general use" as defined above.

3) Subject to the preceding paragraph and to Note 1 to Chapter 83, the articles of Chapters 82 or 83 are excluded from Chapters 72 to 76 and 78 to 81.

4) The Explanatory Note to Section XV states:

In general, identifiable parts of articles are classified as such parts in their appropriate headings in the Nomenclature. However, parts of general use (as defined in Note 2 to this Section) presented separately are not considered as parts of articles, but are classified in the headings of this Section appropriate to them.

5) Sections XVI and XVII and numerous chapters in the HS include notes explicitly excluding parts of general use from classification within their provisions. See Section XVI, Note 1(g); Section XVII, Note 2(b); Chapter 90, Note 1(f); Chapter 91, Note 1(c); Chapter 92, Note 1(a); Chapter 93, Note 1(b); Chapter 94, Note 1(d); Chapter 95, Note 1(k); and Chapter 96, Note 1(d).

6) Section XVI, Note 1(k) also excludes articles of Chapters 82 or 83 from classification within this section. Thus, articles of heading 83.02 are parts of general use, as per Section XV, Note 2(c). Accordingly, a good that falls within heading 83.02 will be classified under that heading, regardless of whether it may also be covered by another heading in the tariff. Some examples are the following: A door handle for a car, although a part of a vehicle, is classified under 83.02 as a mounting or fitting suitable for motor vehicles, not in Chapter 87. Base metal drawer knobs and handles are not classified under Chapter 94 as parts of furniture; instead they are classified under heading 83.02 as mountings and fittings suitable for furniture.

On the other hand, it has to be remembered that if a tariff item does not expressly provide for "parts" or "accessory," and there are no relevant notes in the Sections, Chapters, Headings, or Subheadings, an imported good that is obviously a part of some other good has to be classified according to the nature of the good at the time of import, under the tariff item most appropriate to it. The decision of the Supreme Court of Canada in

Deputy Minister of National Revenue v Ferguson Industries Ltd[114] under the old *Customs Tariff* is still relevant. In that case, winches and electrically-driven motors were ordered from different manufacturers located in two different European countries, and they arrived in Canada earlier than the mechanical parts of the winches. The motors had been designed for the winches and were intended to be built into them. The Tariff Board, agreeing with the importer, classified the motors with the winches, and the Deputy Minister appealed to the Exchequer Court, which dismissed the appeal. On further appeal, the Supreme Court of Canada held that the Tariff Board erred in law by holding that parts are to be regarded as falling within the classification of the whole thing rather than as such. It pointed out that what was important was the nature of the goods at the time of import. Parts cannot correctly be considered as included in items in which they are not mentioned; to do so would render meaningless the mention of parts or of complete parts in a great many items.

The CBSA's Customs D Memorandum D10-0-1[115] sets out the following criteria for determining whether goods are parts. Parts:

1) form a complete unit with the machine of which they are a part,
2) have no alternative function,
3) are marketed and shipped as a unit,
4) are necessary for the safe and prudent use of the unit, and
5) are committed to the use of the unit.

According to the CBSA, the Memorandum was developed on the basis of criteria established through Tribunal and Federal Court of Canada caselaw. As the Customs Memorandum states, these criteria have no particular order of precedence and can be used singly or in combination.

There is thus a further issue, in addition to competing classifications of a given product, being whether an article is a part or an accessory of the machine or machinery specified in the List of Tariff Provisions in the Schedule. Decisions that resolve competing classifications are dealt with in Section D(10)(a), above in this chapter. Those dealing specifically with parts and accessories are discussed below in this section, a few of which are also found in the example cases under Section D(10)(a), above in this chapter. As in the examples above, the decisions regarding parts and accessories are arranged by chapters and tariff items.

---

114 Above note 6.
115 "Classification of Parts and Accessories in the *Customs Tariff*" (24 January 1994).

i) Section VII: Chapters 39 and 40 (Plastics and Rubber)

CASE: TARIFF HEADING 40.09 (RUBBER HYDRAULIC HOSE)

The appellant in *Komatsu International (Canada) Inc v President of the Canada Border Services Agency*[116] imported rubber hydraulic hose assemblies, which included customized fittings manufactured to its specifications that were specifically committed by design for attachment to other components of the hydraulic systems of front-end wheel loaders, which Komatsu manufactured. The appellant claimed that the goods in issue should be classified under tariff heading 84.12 as "other engines and motors" or, in the alternative, under heading 84.31 as "parts suitable for use solely or principally with the machinery of headings 84.25 to 84.30." The CBSA re-determined their classification under tariff heading 40.09 as "hoses of vulcanized rubber other than hard rubber, with or without fittings."

The Tribunal considered the appellant's primary position that the goods in issue were parts suitable for use solely or principally with a particular kind of machine and, therefore, should be classified in the same heading as the machine itself. The appellant also claimed that the goods in issue also met the conditions of note 2(b) of Section XVI. In that regard, the Tribunal found that the goods in issue were "parts" of hydraulic systems, which were themselves classifiable in heading 84.12. It noted, however, that they were not excluded from Chapter 40 or from the ambit of heading 40.09, as being of hard rubber. Thus the goods in issue were *prima facie* classifiable under both headings 40.09 and 84.12.

Following the Supreme Court decision in *Accessories Machinery Ltd v Canada (Deputy Minister of National Revenue, Customs and Excise)*,[117] wherein it was determined that a tariff provision that more specifically describes goods overrides a basket provision in respect of parts, the Tribunal found that the goods in issue were not classifiable under heading 84.12 on the basis that they were parts of engines and motors, which were more specifically described in heading 40.09.

The Tribunal then turned to the appellant's alternative submission that the goods in issue should be classified under heading 84.31 (and, more specifically, under tariff item 8431.49.00) as other parts suitable for use solely or principally with the machinery of headings 84.25 to 84.30. In this regard, the appellant claimed that the front-end wheel loaders, of which the goods in issue formed part, fell under heading 84.29. The Tribunal accepted the ap-

---

116   AP-2010-006 (2012), 16 TTR (2d) 479.
117   [1957] SCR 358.

pellant's claim. However, it noted that the Explanatory Note to heading 84.31 expressly stated that classification under that heading was subject to the general provisions regarding the classification of parts, that is to say, the heading covered parts for use solely or principally with the machinery of headings 84.25 to 84.30. Under Part II of the Explanatory Notes to Section XVI in respect of the treatment of "parts," goods covered more specifically in other sections were properly classified under those other sections. Furthermore, the Explanatory Notes to heading 84.31 indicated that "many parts do not fall in this heading since they are: (a) Specified elsewhere in the Nomenclature."

The appellant's alternative submission was, therefore, not acceptable to the Tribunal for the same reason as its primary position that the goods in issue came under heading 84.12. Therefore, the Tribunal found that the goods in issue were not *prima facie* classifiable under either heading 84.12 or 84.31, as they were more specifically described in heading 40.09.

ii) Section VIII: Chapters 41 to 43 (Raw Hides, Travel Goods, Handbags)

CASE: TARIFF ITEMS 4202.91.90 (SOFT LEATHER CARRYING CASES FOR CELLPHONES) AND 8504.40.90 (CELLPHONE CAR KITS)

The decision of the Tribunal in the *Nokia* case,[118] which involved the classification of two different products under two different tariff items, is noteworthy as it clarifies the distinction between parts and accessories. The products were the subject of separate appeals, which were heard together. This decision with respect to soft leather carrying cases was summarized earlier in Section D(10)(a)(iv) (Case 2), above in this chapter.

With respect to the car kits, the CCRA argued that to be considered a part, a component must be essential to the functioning of a product. A car kit was a feature that expanded the time or the ability of a person to use the cellular phone, but was not, in any way, integral to the design nor essential to the function of the cellular phone. The evidence, according to the CCRA, showed that a car kit was an optional device that must be described as an accessory and not as a part and, thus, cannot be classified under tariff item 8529.90.90.

The Tribunal, however, took a different view. It first considered that the parts classification was inappropriate in the case of car kits. Unable to classify them according to Rule 1 of the *General Rules*, it moved to Rule 3 (b), as the car kits consisted of more than one component.

---

118   Above note 39.

Rule 3(b) provided that, where goods are *prima facie* classifiable in two or more headings and those headings each refer to part only of the materials contained in composite goods, the goods shall be classified as if they consisted of the material or component that gives them their essential character, insofar as this criterion is applicable. The Explanatory Notes to Rule 3(b) provided that the factors, which determine essential character, will vary as between different kinds of goods. It may, for example, be determined by the nature of the material or component, its bulk, the quantity, its weight, or its value, or by the role of a constituent material in relation to the use of the goods.

Thus, the Tribunal had to determine the essential character of the goods as the basis for classifying them as either static converters under heading 85.04 or as microphone/speaker sets under heading 85.18. In its view, the factor that determined the essential character of the car kits was the role of one particular component in relation to the use of the cellphone. This essential character of the goods was provided by its static conversion capacity.

It was clear from the evidence that the junction box that contained the static converter was the main component of the car kit—that the primary function of the junction box was to adapt the voltage of the vehicle's electrical system to the correct voltage that was required to power the cellular phone. It was the Tribunal's view that the additional functionality provided by the static converter through the junction box component of the car kits was a feature that differentiated the car kits from simple microphone/speaker sets. In terms of value, the evidence indicated that the most costly component in the car kit was the junction box.

For the above reasons, the Tribunal concluded that the car kits should be classified under tariff item 8504.40.90 as other static converters. Consequently, it allowed the appeal of the appellant on car kits.

iii) Section XI: Chapters 50 to 63 (Textiles)

CASE: TARIFF ITEM 6307.90.99 (EMERGENCY TOW STRAPS)

The goods in *Rui Royal International*[119] were "Crawford Cargo Mates" emergency tow straps. This decision has been covered under the discussion of competing tariff items in Section D(10)(a)(vi) (Case 11), above in this chapter. Here, only the arguments relating to parts and accessories, which the appellant had claimed to be the appropriate classification, are analyzed.

The Tribunal pointed out that in order for the emergency tow straps to be classified as parts and accessories of a motor vehicle of heading 87.01 to 87.08,

---

119 Above note 53.

they must qualify under the Explanatory Notes to Section XVII, Chapter 87 and heading 87.08, which provide that those headings apply *only* to those parts or accessories that comply with *all three* of the following conditions:

1) They must not be excluded by the terms of Note 2 to this Section.
2) They must be suitable for use solely or principally with the articles of Chapters 86 to 88.
3) They must not be more specifically included elsewhere in the Nomenclature.

The Tribunal found that the towing straps did not meet the last condition, that is, that they were not "more specifically included elsewhere in the Nomenclature." It concluded that heading 63.07 more specifically described the goods than did heading 87.08 and that, by virtue of Note (III)(C) of the Explanatory Note to Section XVII, they were not classifiable under heading 87.08.

iv) Section XV: Chapters 82 and 83 (Base Metals)

CASE: TARIFF ITEM 8212.90.00 (GILLETTE® MACH3® RAZOR BLADE CARTRIDGES)

The goods in *Commonwealth Wholesale Corp v President of the Canada Border Services Agency*[120] were packages of five Gillette® Mach3® razor blade cartridges for retail sale, designed to be used with Gillette® Mach3® razor handles. They were imported without razor handles. They were composed of blades, end caps, plastic devices to hold the blade in place, a plastic frame, a plastic device that allowed the head to pivot, a lubricating strip, and other parts. The sole issue was whether the razor blade cartridges were correctly classified by the CBSA under tariff item 8212.20.00 as safety razor blades, including razor blade blanks in strips, or whether they should be classified under tariff item 8212.90.00 as other parts of razors, as claimed by the appellant.

The parties submitted, and the Tribunal agreed, that only Rule 1 of the *General Rules* and Rule 1 of the *Canadian Rules* were applicable to the classification.

According to the appellant, the term "safety razor blades," as used in tariff item 8212.20.00, designated exclusively the old-fashioned double-edged blades, and that such old-fashioned double-edged blades were for use in an original safety razor. Accordingly, it argued that the goods in issue were different from the safety razor blades described in tariff item 8212.20.00.

---

120   AP-2011-010 and AP-2011-019 (2012), 16 TTR (2d) 402.

Indeed, it submitted that the goods in issue were an evolution of the cartridge-type product that began entering the marketplace in the early 1970s.

For its part, the CBSA submitted that the goods in issue were sold as replacement razor blades for the Gillette® Mach3® and were referred to in the industry as "safety razor blade units" or "safety razor blades." It relied on dictionary definitions of the terms "safety razor" and "blade." It also pointed to patent applications filed by the Gillette Company where it used the term "safety razor blade units" to describe the goods in issue.

The Tribunal noted that the term "safety razor" was not used on its own in the schedule to the *Customs Tariff*, but only with the word "blades." Accordingly, the *Customs Tariff* did not provide for the classification of safety razors. In fact, it only provided for the classification of "razors" on the one hand and of "safety razor blades" on the other, and, finally, of "[o]ther parts." Indeed, tariff item 8212.10.00 made no distinction between razors; accordingly, all razors, including the so-called safety razors, would be classified under that tariff item.

The Tribunal was of the view that too great a focus on the word "safety" in classifying the goods in issue could be unnecessarily confusing; and that the focus must remain squarely on the goods in issue, which were not mere exposed razor blades, such as is the case with the safety razor blades, but rather blade units, cartridge units, or shaving cartridges, composed of various parts, such as a casing of plastic with strips of metal that each had a single sharp-blade edge.

The Tribunal was of the view that tariff item 8212.20.00 was limited to (1) the old-fashioned double-edged blades, which were the (potentially dangerous) razor blades of the type to be used in the original safety razor; and (2) razor blade blanks in strips. The Explanatory Notes to heading 82.12 provided that "razor blade blanks in strips" were nothing more than sheets of old-fashioned double-edged blades that had yet to be separated from one another; in other words, their outline was there, and they may be broken off from the strip.

The Tribunal concluded that the terms of tariff item 8212.20.00 were not broad enough to comprise the same type of blade units or cartridge units as the goods in issue because they were goods altogether different from the simple safety razor blade. The evidence indicated that the goods in issue were especially committed for use with Gillette® Mach3® shavers and were essential to their function. As such, they should be classified under tariff item 8212.90.00 as "other parts of razors." Accordingly, the appeal was allowed.

v) Section XVI: Chapters 84 and 85 (Machinery, Mechanical Appliances, Electrical Equipment, Television Image and Sound Recorders)

CASE 1: TARIFF ITEMS 8436.80.10 (INTEGRATED GREENHOUSE SYSTEM AND FLUE GAS CONDENSER)

The goods in *Prins Greenhouses Ltd v Deputy Minister of National Revenue*[121] were (1) an integrated greenhouse system and (2) a flue gas condenser. The Deputy Minister of National Revenue classified the first item under tariff item 8403.10.10 as "central heating boilers other than those of heading 84.02" and the second item under tariff item 8403.90.00 as "parts of central heating boilers other than those of heading 84.02."

The appellant claimed that the two items were incorrectly classified by the CCRA and that they should be classified as follows: (1) the integrated greenhouse system under tariff item 8436.80.10 as "other agricultural or horticultural type of machinery" and (2) the flue gas condenser under 8421.31.90 as "other filtering or purifying machinery and apparatus for gases."

With respect to the first item, the evidence and testimony clearly indicated that it was marketed and sold as a complete climate and environmental control system for greenhouses and not as individual components. The climate and environmental control system regulated carbon dioxide and heat to maximize plant growth and productivity. The components could not fulfill this function without each other and were functionally linked within the system to ensure plant growth. The Tribunal was persuaded that they formed an integrated greenhouse system that was a "functional unit" as described in Part VII of the Explanatory Notes to Section XVI and should be classified under tariff item 8436.80.10 as "other agricultural or horticultural type of machinery."

On the other hand, the Tribunal was not convinced that the flue gas condenser was essential to the functioning of the central heating boiler. Therefore, while the flue gas condenser may be attached to the central heating boiler, it was not a part of the boiler. However, it was a component whose activity was essential to the basic functioning of the integrated greenhouse system, and, therefore, given Note 2(a) of the Explanatory Notes to Section XVI, which provides, in part, that "[p]arts which are goods included in any of the headings of Chapters 84 and 85 (except in certain headings) are in all cases to be classified in their respective headings," the Tribunal determined that the flue gas condenser should be classified under tariff item 8436.80.10.

---

121 AP-99-045 (2001), 5 TTR (2d) 553 [*Prins Greenhouses Ltd*].

CASE 2: TARIFF ITEM 8439.99.90 (ALUMINUM ALLOY WALKWAY SYSTEMS)

The appellant in *GL&V/Black Clawson-Kennedy v Deputy Minister of National Revenue*[122] imported aluminum alloy walkway systems, which it entered under tariff item 8439.99.90 as "other parts of machinery for making pulp of fibrous cellulosic material" but the Deputy Minister of National Revenue re-determined their classification under tariff item 7610.90.00 as "other aluminum structures." The evidence presented in this case led the Tribunal to the conclusion that the walkway systems were an integral part of the paper-making machines, and as parts were specifically provided for in heading 84.39, which was key to determining whether the walkway systems qualified as parts.

Based on a review of the jurisprudence and guided by Customs D Memorandum D10-0-1 (Classification of Parts and Accessories in the Customs Tariff), the Tribunal was of the view that the evidence clearly indicated that the walkway systems met the established criteria for parts. It, therefore, allowed the appeal.

CASE 3: TARIFF ITEMS 8504.40.99 (RAPID CIGARETTE LIGHTER CHARGERS) AND 8529.91.90 (CELLPHONE BATTERY PACKS)

The appellant in *Nokia Products Limited v Deputy Minister of National Revenue*[123] imported rapid cigarette lighter chargers and battery packs for cellphones. Cigarette lighter chargers were entered under tariff item 8504.40.99 as "other static converters" and battery packs, under tariff item 8529.90.99 as "other parts suitable for use solely or principally with the apparatus of headings 85.25 to 85.28."

The Deputy Minister of National Revenue re-classified the rapid cigarette lighter chargers under tariff item 8544.41.10 as "other insulated electric conductors, for a voltage not exceeding 80V, fitted with connectors, of a kind used for telecommunications" and the battery packs under tariff item 8507.30.90 as "other nickel-cadmium electric accumulators, including separators therefor, whether or not rectangular (including square)."

The Tribunal considered that the "rapid cigarette lighter chargers" should be classified under tariff item 8504.40.99 as "other static converters" and allowed the appeal.

With respect to the second product, the battery packs for cellphones, the Tribunal held that they were parts of cellular telephones, as they formed a complete unit with the cellular telephone, had no alternative function,

---

122 AP-99-063 (2000), 5 TTR (2d) 59, aff'd 2002 FCA 43.
123 AP-99-082 (2000), 4 TTR (2d) 797.

were committed for use with one particular model of cellular telephone, and were marketed and sold for use with cellular telephones. Therefore, they did not belong under heading 85.07.

The Tribunal next considered the appellant's submission that the battery packs fell under heading 85.29. Heading 85.29 provided for "parts suitable for use solely or principally with the apparatus of headings 85.25 to 85.28." Note 2(a) to Section XVI, which includes Chapter 85, provided that parts of machines that are goods included in any of the headings of Chapters 84 and 85 are in all cases to be classified under their respective headings. Note 2(b) provided that other parts, if suitable for use solely or principally with a particular kind of machine, are to be classified with that machine. The Tribunal had, therefore, to determine whether the goods in issue were parts.

From the evidence adduced in the appeal, it was the Tribunal's view that the battery packs were parts of cellular telephones. They were ergonomically designed to form a complete unit with a cellular telephone because the plastic housing formed the back of the telephone. Cellular telephones cannot work without a battery pack attached, as the battery pack provides them with power. The battery packs had no alternative function than that of supplying power to a cellular telephone. It was not safe or prudent for a user to power a cellular telephone by other means. By design, the battery packs were committed for use with a particular model of Nokia cellular telephone. Cellular telephones were also marketed and sold with battery packs, and the battery packs were marketed and sold for use with cellular telephones. Therefore, they were parts of cellular telephones. The fact that the battery packs were not imported with the cellular telephones or necessarily sold with the cellular telephones did not change their characterization as parts of cellular telephones. For the foregoing reasons, the Tribunal allowed the appeal.

CASE 4: TARIFF ITEM 8504.90.91 (BUSHINGS OF ELECTRICAL TRANSFORMERS)

The bushings imported in *Asea Brown Boveri Inc v Commissioner of the Canada Customs and Revenue Agency*[124] were entered under tariff item 8504.90.91 as "parts of the goods of tariff items 8504.21.20, 8504.22.00, 8504.23.00 or 8504.34.00 (electrical transformers)." The CCRA re-determined their classification under tariff item 8544.60.00 as "other insulated electric conductors, for a voltage exceeding 1,000 V, whether or not fitted with connectors." Allowing the appeal, the Tribunal was of the opinion that the bushings were more complex than the conductors contemplated by heading 85.44, under

---

124 AP-98-001 (2000) [*Asea Brown Boveri Inc*].

which the CCRA had classified the bushings. The Tribunal found that the bushings were parts, that they formed a complete unit with the power transformer and were necessary for its use, and also that they were committed for use solely or principally with the power transformers, being specifically designed for them and having no other use. For those reasons, the Tribunal, applying the Notes to Section XVI under which Chapter 85 falls, held that the bushings should be classified with the power transformers under heading 85.04 and allowed the appeal.

CASE 5: TARIFF ITEMS 8514.40.90 (ANNEALER) AND 8515.21.10 (WELDER)
The goods in *IPSCO Inc v President of the Canada Border Services Agency*[125] were a 600-kilowatt seam annealer system (the annealer) and a Weldac G2 1200-kilowatt electric resistance welding (ERW) system (the welder). The CBSA determined that the goods in issue came under separate tariff items—the annealer under tariff item 8514.40.90 as "other industrial or laboratory electric furnaces for the heat treatment of materials by induction or dielectric loss" and the welder under tariff item 8515.21.10 as a "high frequency or ultra high frequency ERW apparatus."

The appellant claimed that the goods should be classified under tariff item 8455.10.00 as "components of a functional unit" or, in the alternative, under tariff item 8455.90.90 as "other parts of metal-rolling mills and rolls therefor." Metal-rolling mills and rolls therefor came under heading 84.55.

Tariff heading 85.14 covered "Industrial or laboratory electric (including induction or dielectric) furnaces and ovens." Other industrial or laboratory induction or dielectric heating equipment, and other induction or dielectric heating equipment came under 8514.40. Tariff heading 85.15 covered "Electric (including electrically heated gas), laser or other light or photon beam, ultrasonic, electron beam, magnetic pulse or plasma arc soldering, brazing or welding machines and apparatus, whether or not capable of cutting; electric machines and apparatus for hot spraying of metals or cermets" and "fully or partly automatic machines and apparatus" came under subheading 8515.21.

The Tribunal also referred to Notes 4 and 5 to Section XVI of the *Customs Tariff*.

The goods in issue were part of a single purchase of equipment, sourced in Norway; it took place in February 2001. There were no subsequent importations. The appellant had imported the goods in issue to incorporate them into its existing pipe mill in Regina, Saskatchewan, in order to produce pipe to new specifications for the oil industry.

---

125   AP-2005-041 (2007), 11 TTR (2d) 676.

The Tribunal agreed that the appellant's tube mill was made up of individual interconnected components, two of which were the welder and the annealer. All the components, including the goods in issue, taken together, served a clearly defined function, that is, to work together as a rolling mill and, more specifically, as a tube mill.

The appellant submitted that the goods in issue were essential components of the "functional unit," that is, its tube mill, and that they should be classified in the same manner as the tube mill itself, namely, under tariff item 8455.10.00 or 8455.90.90. It argued that Note 4 to Section XVI of the *Customs Tariff* did not preclude the goods in issue from being classified in the same manner as the "functional unit" that, together, they contributed to create, even if the goods in issue were imported subsequently to that existing host machinery.

The CBSA argued that the goods in issue cannot be considered a "functional unit" of a metal-rolling mill because they were intended to be integrated into an existing system. At the time of importation, the goods in issue were two separate machines, and the existing system was not a system in the process of being built. It submitted that Note 4 to Section XVI of the *Customs Tariff* applied only when all the machines, apparatus, and other components of the resulting "functional unit" were imported at the same time. It conceded that it allowed, in certain cases, a "functional unit" to be imported in a number of separate and discrete shipments, provided the goods were named in a single contract and were part of a single purchase.

The Tribunal agreed that the evidence indicated that the goods in issue were upgrades to an existing mill and that, at the time of importation, the goods in issue were intended and perceived as parts of a tube mill. It was clear to the Tribunal that, together, the components constituted a tube mill, whose operation constituted "a clearly defined function" that is covered by heading 84.55, which is "one of the headings in Chapter 84." However, it noted that, in this instance, the "whole" could not have been classified together because the goods in issue were only two components of that whole. The other components of the tube mill, with which the goods in issue were "intended to contribute together to a clearly defined function" were not before the Tribunal, nor were they included in the same importation or series of importations.

The Tribunal carefully considered *Sable Offshore Energy Inc v Commissioner of the Canada Customs and Revenue Agency*[126] and *Windsor Wafers, Division*

---

126 Above note 13.

of *Beatrice Foods v Deputy Minister of National Revenue.*[127] However, in the Tribunal's view, both those cases dealt with factual situations that were different from those in the present case. In each of those cases, there was a question whether the goods, which were components that were required in order to complete a system in its original form, could be classified with that system, despite being imported separately from its other components. In contrast, the present case concerned a machine that already existed as a total system (a tube mill) and the issue was whether parts that were imported to upgrade it can be classified together with that original system as if the whole were now to be seen as a functional unit.

On this point, the Tribunal's view was consistent with its earlier position in *Windsor Wafers,* that is, that the framework in the *Customs Tariff* for the classification of goods as a functional unit "is not intended to allow future additions, upgrading or replacement of equipment ordered under the original importation." Whether the existing tube mill as a whole was an "original importation" under the *Customs Tariff* or whether it could have been classified as a functional unit at the time of its original construction was not of concern to the Tribunal here. Whatever the classification of the original machinery may have been, it was the Tribunal's view that the conditions that the *Customs Tariff* established for the classification of goods as a functional unit were not intended to extend to later upgrades or replacements of existing components of that machinery.

In light of these observations, the Tribunal was of the view that, in the given circumstances, the goods in issue were not classifiable as components of a functional unit. The Tribunal concluded that the annealer and the welder were correctly classified under tariff item 8514.40.90 and 8515.21.10 respectively and, accordingly, dismissed the appeal.

CASE 6: TARIFF ITEM 8520.90.90 (INTEGRATED CIRCUIT (IC) RECORDER AND MINIDISK (MD) RECORDER)

The appeal of *Sony Canada*[128] concerning the tariff classification of the integrated circuit recorder and portable minidisk recorder has been covered in Section D(10)(a)(x)(Case 10), above in this chapter. Here, the discussion is of the Tribunal's disposition of the appellant's argument that the goods in issue were storage units of automatic data processing machines and units thereof, which came under tariff item 8471.70.00, and as parts and acces-

---

127 AP-89-281 (1991) [*Windsor Wafers*].
128 Above note 79.

sories of those machines, they were entitled to the benefits of tariff item 9948.00.00.

Sony had argued that the goods, themselves, were parts and accessories of the automatic data processing machines (in this case, a computer). This assertion involved the interpretation of the phrase "[p]arts and accessories of the foregoing." Did this phrase mean that the goods can benefit from tariff relief if they were articles for use *in* parts and accessories of an automatic data processing machine, or did it mean that the goods can benefit from tariff relief if they, *themselves*, were parts and accessories of such machine? The appellant argued the latter. On this issue, the Tribunal agreed with the CCRA's position. The punctuation used in the tariff item led the Tribunal to interpret the description to mean that articles can benefit from tariff relief if they are articles for use *in* parts and accessories of an automatic data processing machine, and not if they, themselves, were parts and accessories of such machine.

The Tribunal, therefore, turned its attention to whether the goods in issue were for use *in* automatic data processing machines or units thereof. Section 2 of the *Customs Tariff* defined the term "for use in" as follows: "Wherever it appears in a tariff item, in respect of goods classified in the tariff item, ["for use in"] means that the goods must be wrought or incorporated into, or attached to, other goods referred to in that tariff item."

The Tribunal was of the opinion that the goods in issue were not "wrought or incorporated into" the automatic data processing machines. Were they "attached to" the computers? Previous Tribunal decisions had interpreted the expression "attached to" to mean that the goods are "physically connected and are functionally joined" to, in this case, a computer. But, does that connection need to be permanent in order to meet the requirement of "for use in"? The CCRA argued that the goods in issue could not be considered "attached to" computers, given that they were portable devices. The Tribunal did not agree. It relied upon Customs Notice N-278, which clearly stated that, regarding the interpretation of "for use in," specifically the interpretation of physical connection, "[p]hysical connection need not be permanent (e.g., cables)."

The Tribunal noted that models ICD-R100PC and ICD-70 were imported with the cables and necessary software to be attached to a computer. This cable and the software provided for the downloading of files from the IC recorder to the computer, and the transfer of the saved sound files from the computer back to the IC recorder. It was the Tribunal's view that these models passed the first hurdle in the interpretation of "attached to," in that they may be considered "physically connected" to computers *via* the PC Link cable, even though that physical connection was not permanent. Furthermore, in the Tribunal's opinion, these models actually contributed to the function of an automated data processing machine, in that they allowed the computer to input or download sound files. Based on the testimony of the witnesses and the evidence, the Tribunal found that the ICD-R100PC and ICD-70 were "functionally joined" to the computer. Furthermore, the Tribunal accepted the appellant's argument that there would be little reason, if any, to purchase an IC recorder *with* a PC Link cable and PC Link software, rather than a normal dictaphone, magnetic or digital, if it was not going to be used with a computer. The evidence before the Tribunal was that these models were more expensive than voice recorders not intended for use with computers.

With respect to the issue of primary function, the Tribunal had addressed it in *PHD Canada Distributing Ltd v Commissioner of the Canada Customs and Revenue Agency*,[129] where it considered the argument that the music CDs must play a "primary function" or must be "actually used" in the CD-ROM drive in order for the goods in issue to be "for use in" and qualify for tariff relief." In that case, the Tribunal found that there was no merit to those arguments, and its decision did not turn on whether the music CDs played a "primary function" or were "actually used" in the CD-ROM drive. The Tribunal found, in the present case, as in *PHD Canada*, that the arguments concerning "primary function" had no merit.

On the basis of the foregoing analysis, the Tribunal found that the ICD-R100PC and ICD-70 were "for use in" "automatic data processing machines" and, as a result, should benefit from tariff relief under tariff item 9948.00.00.

However, the same thing cannot be said about models MZ-R70, MZ-R90, and OCD-MS1. While they can be connected to a computer *via* a USB port and PC Link cable, they were not sold with the computer cable attachment and, in fact, such a cable attachment may not even have been available when the goods were imported. Therefore, those models were correctly classified under tariff item 8520.90.90.[130]

CASE 7: TARIFF HEADING 85.21 (VIDEO-BASED SECURITY SYSTEM)
In *Tyco Safety Products Canada Ltd v President of the Canada Border Services Agency*,[131] Tyco imported video-based security systems. They consisted of four EDVR models and nine Intellex models.

---

129 AP-99-116 (2002), 7 TTR (2d) 254 [*PHD Canada*].
130 *Sony Canada*, above note 79.
131 AP-2010-055 (2011), 16 TTR (2d) 29.

The appellant claimed that the goods in issue formed a complete microprocessor-based closed-circuit television (CCTV) system (excluding cameras) and should be classified according to their principal function. While it acknowledged that the goods had a recording function, it submitted that recording was not their principal function, as the design capabilities of the goods included multiplexing for the transmission of live video CCTV signals, live CCTV video transmission over the Internet, video decoding and encoding, video camera control (pan, tilt, and zoom), and recording security events with alarm-triggered dome positioning. Therefore, it claimed that the transmission capabilities of the goods took functional precedence over any recording or video-playback features, and that the goods in issue ought to be classified under heading 85.25 as "transmission apparatus." That definition, in its view, corresponded to their principal function. In the alternative, the appellant submitted that the goods would be covered by heading 84.71 and, more specifically, under tariff item 8471.49.00, as "other automatic data processing machines and units thereof, not elsewhere specified or included, presented in the form of systems."

The CCRA, on the other hand, re-determined the goods under heading 85.21 as "other video recording or reproducing apparatus." It argued that the goods were multi-function or composite machines and that, in accordance with Note 3 to Section XVI, they were to be classified under the heading that described their principal function. The CCRA claimed that the marketing, design, and best usage of the goods pointed to recording as their principal function, which rendered them properly classifiable under heading 85.21.

After analyzing Note 3 to Section XVI and the Explanatory Notes to that section, the Tribunal was of the opinion that the EDVR models were correctly classified by the CCRA under tariff item 8521.90.90 as other video recording or reproducing apparatus, and that the nine Intellex models should be classified under tariff item 8525.50.00 as "transmission apparatus for radio-broadcasting or television, whether or not incorporating reception apparatus or sound recording or reproducing apparatus." Tyco's appeal was allowed in part.

The Tribunal also considered, pursuant to Note 2(b) of the Explanatory Notes to Section XVI, whether the goods in issue were suitable for use solely or principally with a particular kind of machine and, if so, whether to classify them with the machines of that kind. In this regard, the Tribunal found that the goods in issue were suitable "principally" for use with "[e]lectro-mechanical tools for working in the hand, with self-contained electric motor," as found in heading 85.08. Given that there was evidence on the record that indicated that the battery packs may be used with other devices, such as flashlights and radios, they were not suitable "solely" for machines of this kind; however, they were used predominantly with the tools of heading 85.08 (for example, drills and saws) and that any portion used with the machines that were not covered by that heading was minuscule in comparison. In any case, the Tribunal said that its finding that these goods were suitable "principally" for use with the tools in heading 85.08 sufficiently satisfied Note 2(b) of the Explanatory Notes to Section XVI.

vi) Section XVII: Chapters 86 to 89 (Vehicles, Aircraft, Vessels, and Associated Transport Equipment)

CASE 1: TARIFF ITEM 8708.29.99 (EXTERIOR LUGGAGE RACKS)

In *Uvex Toko Canada Ltd v Deputy Minister of National Revenue*,[132] the appellant imported containers for storing luggage and ski equipment, which were used with the luggage rack system produced by Yakima in the United States, for whom it was a distributor. The issue was whether these storage containers were correctly classified by the Deputy Minister of National Revenue under tariff item 3923.10.00 as articles of plastic for the conveyance or packing of goods, or whether they should be classified under tariff item 8708.29.99 as other accessories of bodies of motor vehicles, as claimed by the appellant.

Pointing to the reference to "exterior luggage racks" in the Explanatory Notes to heading 87.08, the appellant argued that it was unreasonable to hold that this term covered only the bars and clips that attach to the vehicle and not the other components of the "rack system." Citing a statement in the respondent's brief that the goods in issue might be considered accessories to exterior luggage racks, it argued that such accessories are also accessories for motor vehicles within the terms of heading 87.08, as they were solely or principally used with motor vehicles and were not more specifically named elsewhere in the nomenclature. In essence, it argued, the boxes were themselves exterior luggage racks for motor vehicles or, at least, components of exterior luggage racks. They could not be used for anything else, even though sold separately from other components of the rack system. Although not arguing for classification in heading 86.09, it suggested that it would be more logical to classify the goods under that heading rather than under heading 39.23.

The respondent submitted that the goods in issue were not exterior luggage racks, but rather distinct goods that sit on top of such racks. They were not advertised as "racks" in the appellant's sales brochures; rather, they were illustrated under the heading "luggage." They were sold separately from

---

132 AP-95-269 and AP-95-285 (1996) [*Uvex Toko Canada*].

goods described as "racks"; accessories, other than the goods in issue could be, and were, attached to the racks; and the goods in issue could be fitted to at least one other brand of rack. Thus, they were not part of a "luggage rack system." While the Yakima rack, by itself, was an accessory to a motor vehicle, this did not mean that anything that connected to the rack was also an accessory to a motor vehicle. Although the goods in issue may be used principally with motor vehicles, it submitted that this was not a sufficient ground to classify them under heading 87.08. They must fall under heading 39.23 because, in the words of Note III(C) of the Explanatory Notes to Section XVII, they were "covered more specifically" in that heading.

Rule 1, which is of the utmost importance when classifying goods, stated that classification is first determined by the wording of the tariff headings and any relative Section or Chapter Notes. The Tribunal, therefore, first considered the wording of headings 39.23 and 87.08. In considering the wording of heading 39.23, the Tribunal acknowledged that the goods in issue may be described as being made of plastic and used for conveying goods. However, it said it was persuaded by the evidence that the goods in issue were more clearly or specifically described as being accessories of motor vehicles. Note III(B)(1) of the Explanatory Notes to Section XVII states that "when a part or accessory can fall in one or more other Sections as well as in Section XVII, its final classification is determined by its *principal use*."

The Tribunal accepted the argument of the appellant that the goods in issue were, themselves, accessories of motor vehicles, even though they must be combined with a rack to be used with a vehicle. It was clear from Yakima's sales brochure that the company saw itself as a supplier of a "roof rack system" and that the "base rack" was designed to be combined with other components to form a "customized system" suitable for the model of car driven by the user and the load to be carried. Different components are added to the basic rack to carry bikes, canoes, skis, and luggage. In the Tribunal's view, the rack itself was not, strictly speaking, a "luggage rack." It was a "roof rack," which became a luggage rack only when a container such as a "luggage box" was mounted on it. Both parts of the combination, or system, were accessories for motor vehicles because they were designed specifically to be attached to and carried by such vehicles. Taken together, the rack and the goods in issue were an "exterior luggage rack" as provided for in Note (B) of the Explanatory Notes to heading 87.08. The Tribunal was of the view that the goods in issue were parts of exterior luggage rack systems for passenger automobiles and, therefore, should be classified under tariff item 8708.29.99, and allowed the appeal.

The Tribunal came to the opposite conclusion in the *Accessories Sportracks Inc* case, discussed next.

CASE 2: TARIFF ITEM 8708.99.99 (BICYCLE RACKS)

The issue in *Accessories Sportracks Inc de Thule Canada Inc v President of the Canada Border Services Agency*[133] was whether the bicycle racks that it imported should be classified as "accessories of bicycles" under tariff heading 87.14, as it claimed, or whether they were correctly classified by the CBSA as "accessories of motor vehicles" under tariff heading 87.08 and tariff item 8708.99.99. The nub of the dispute was whether the bike racks were accessories to motor vehicles or to bicycles.

The Explanatory Notes to heading 87.08 provided that the heading covered "parts and accessories of the motor vehicles of headings 87.01 to 87.05, *provided* the parts and accessories fulfilled both the following conditions: (i) They must be identifiable as being suitable for use solely or principally with the above-mentioned vehicles; and (ii) they must not be excluded by the provisions of the Notes to Section XVII." On the other hand, the Explanatory Notes to heading 87.14 provided that

> the heading covered parts and accessories of a kind used with motorcycles (including mopeds), cycles fitted with an auxiliary motor, side-cars, non-motorised cycles, or carriages for disabled persons, provided the parts and accessories fulfill both the following conditions: (i) They must be identifiable as being suitable for use solely or principally with the above-mentioned vehicles; and (ii) they must not be excluded by the provisions of the Notes to Section XVII . . . .

After analyzing both headings 87.08 and 87.14, and after considering its previous decision in *Uvex Toko Canada*,[134] where it had held that luggage carriers were accessories of motor vehicles, the Tribunal held that Rule 1 of the *General Rules* directs that the bike racks were accessories of motor vehicles and not bicycles. Their chief purpose was to carry the bicycles on a motor vehicle from the point of origin to the point of destination in order to enhance its use, and not the other way round. The Tribunal accepted the CBSA's contention that bike racks not only did not enhance the use of the bike for transporting persons, but they were altogether useless for that purpose; that although bike racks may have some uses to carry bicycles on trailers, as contended by the appellant, that use was secondary; the primary use was to carry bikes on motor vehicles.

---

133 AP-2010-036 (2012), 16 TTR (2d) 320.
134 Above note 132.

CASE 3: TARIFF ITEM 8714.99.10 (BICYCLE RIMS, SPOKES, AND HUBS)

In *Outdoor Gear Canada v President of the Canada Border Services Agency*,[135] the dispute was over the classification of assembled bicycle rims, spokes, and hubs, without tubes, valves, nipples, or tires. The appellant claimed that these goods should be classified as bicycle parts under tariff item 8714.99.90 as "other parts and accessories of bicycles" under headings 87.12 to 87.13, whereas the CBSA had classified them as "bicycle wheels," which were specifically mentioned in tariff item 8714.99.10. The Tribunal upheld the CBSA's decision, accepting its argument that the term "bicycle wheels" was not limited in the tariff item to bicycle wheels with tires and tubes, and that the goods were known as bicycle wheels in the bicycle industry. In coming to the decision, the Tribunal also cited the dictionary definition of a "wheel," which referred to hubs and spokes, not to tires and tubes.

vii) Section XX: Chapters 94 to 96 (Miscellaneous Manufactured Articles)

CASE 1: TARIFF ITEM 9403.90.00 (LINEAR BALL-BEARING DRAWER SLIDES)

The appeal in *JIT Industrial Supply & Distribution Ltd v President of the Canada Border Services Agency*[136] concerned the classification of ten models of custom-designed linear ball-bearing drawer slides, used in the manufacture of metal filing cabinets. The goods were used exclusively in the manufacture of metal filing cabinets for attaching the drawers to allow them to slide in and out. The issue was whether they were correctly classified by the CBSA under tariff item 8302.42.00 as "other base metal mountings, fittings and similar articles suitable for furniture" or whether they should be classified under tariff item 9403.90.00 as "other furniture and parts thereof" or, in the alternative, under tariff item 8482.80.90 as "linear ball bearings," as submitted by the appellant.

The Tribunal noted that heading 83.02 covered general purpose classes of base metal accessory fittings and mountings, such as those used largely on furniture, doors, windows, coachwork, and so on, but did not extend to goods used on furniture that formed an essential part of the structure of the article of furniture. In the present appeal, both parties agreed that the goods in issue were made of base metal and were used in furniture, and that they facilitated the in and out movement of the drawer. The Tribunal agreed that the evidence so indicated.

---

135 AP-2010-060 (2011), 16 TTR (2d) 155.
136 AP-2008-015 (2010), 14 TTR (2d) 244. See also *Canmade Furniture*, above note 63.

The disagreement between the parties, however, was over whether the goods in issue were an essential part of the structure of the filing cabinets and whether the goods in issue were "general mountings and fittings." The CBSA submitted that, despite their support function, the goods in issue were not an "essential" part of the structure. The appellant submitted that the goods in issue were specifically designed for and essential to the structural functionality of the filing cabinets and, consequently, were classifiable under heading 94.03 as parts of other furniture, namely, metal filing cabinets.

In the Tribunal's opinion, the essentiality as to structure included essentiality as to the intended function of the article. There was ample evidence before it to indicate that the goods were essential parts of the structural framework of filing cabinets, considering the crucial role that they play in the functionality of the cabinets.

In addition, the goods were affixed to the cabinet in a way to counter deflection from side to side. They also had to allow for the full extension of the drawer and sustain weights of up to 200 pounds with repeated use. Another important feature of the goods was the anti-rebounding feature, which ensured that, when a drawer was closed, it stayed in that position and was prevented from opening.

The Tribunal was of the opinion, based on the evidence, that the goods in issue were essential to the structure of the filing cabinet, and, accordingly, in light of the Explanatory Notes to heading 83.02, they were not classifiable under that heading.

On the basis of the testimony of the appellant's witnesses, the Tribunal also concluded that the goods in issue were ball bearings within the meaning of heading 84.82. However, in order to determine whether the goods in issue were classifiable under that heading, the Tribunal had also to consider whether the goods were "general-purpose goods" as required by the Explanatory Notes to that heading. The evidence on this indicated that the goods in issue were not intended for use in cabinets generally, but rather were intensively engineered for use in metal filing cabinets designed to carry heavy loads, with each set of slides committed by design to a specific model of filing cabinet.

That left heading 94.03 for consideration. Parts of furniture came under subheading 9403.90.00. The notes to Chapter 94 that were relevant to heading 94.03 read that the Chapter did not cover "(d) Parts of general use as defined in Note 2 to Section XV, of base metal (Section XV), or similar goods of plastics (Chapter 39), or safes of heading 83.03." Similarly, the Explanatory Notes to Chapter 94 read that the Chapter covered, subject to the exclusions listed in the Explanatory Notes to that Chapter "(1) All furniture and parts thereof (headings 94.01 to 94.03)." The term "furniture" was defined as: "(A) Any 'movable' articles (not included under other more specific headings of the Nomenclature), which have the essential characteristic that they are constructed for placing on the floor or ground, and which are used, mainly with a utilitarian purpose, to equip ... offices." The Chapter covered

> only [p]arts of headings 94.01 to 94.03 and 94.05 ..., when identifiable by their shape or other specific features as parts designed solely or principally for an article of those headings. They are classified in this Chapter when not more specifically covered elsewhere. Heading 94.03 covered furniture and parts thereof that are not covered by previous headings.

Accepting the appellant's submission, the Tribunal concluded that the goods in issue were designed solely for an article of heading 94.03, that is, a filing cabinet; they were intensively engineered for use in metal filing cabinets designed to carry heavy loads and were not used for general purposes. Based on the foregoing, the goods in issue should be classified under tariff item 9403.90.00 as parts of other furniture.

CASE 2: TARIFF ITEM 9405.10.00 (RECESSED LIGHTING FIXTURES (POT LIGHTS))

The appellant in *Ulextra Inc v President of the Canada Border Services Agency*[137] imported three models of ceiling-mounted recessed lighting fittings ("pot lights" or "recessed lighting fixtures") that were designed to be permanently installed in a ceiling for room illumination. The models contained a junction box, a lamp socket, mounting brackets, and electrical wiring, and one model included a junction box, metal brackets, and a flexible conduit that connected the junction box to a cone in which a lamp socket was embedded. The main difference between this last model and the other two models in terms of physical appearance was that its various components were not enclosed in a metal box. The evidence indicated that this last model was intended for installation in a ceiling that was completely built or finished, whereas the other two were designed to be fixed on wood beams before a ceiling was finished. For all three models, additional components that were necessary to form a complete lighting fitting, including the glass shield, trim, and bulb, were imported separately.

The appellant argued that the lamp-holders in issue came under heading 85.37 as part of an assembly that included a junction box to allow an electrical connection. In the alternative, it submitted that the goods fell within

---

137 AP-2010-024 (2011), 15 TTR (2d) 765.

the scope of heading 85.36, as they were lamp-holders/sockets (that is, goods provided for in heading 85.36) and were not complete lighting fixtures or fittings as described in heading 94.05.

The CBSA, on the other hand, re-determined the tariff classification under heading 94.05 as the goods met the definition of "lighting fittings," and, more specifically, tariff item 9405.10.00, as "other electric ceiling ... lighting fittings." In addition, the CBSA argued that the goods in issue are not "assemblies" of the kind described in the Explanatory Notes to heading No. 85.37.

Thus, the dispute arose at the heading level, that is, whether the goods fall under heading 85.36, 85.37, or 94.05.

The Tribunal analyzed the nomenclatures of the tariff items and the relevant Explanatory Notes to Section XVI, in which Chapter 85 belonged, since it was the appellant's position that the goods in issue fell within that Chapter, and, in particular, heading 85.37, which was primarily relied upon by the appellant. The Tribunal then analyzed the classifications submitted by the CBSA, namely, those under Chapter 94, on which it had relied for re-determining the classification of the goods in issue.

Heading 94.05 covered "lamps and lighting fittings including search-lights and spotlights and parts thereof, not elsewhere specified or included; illuminated signs, illuminated name-plates and the like, having a permanently fixed light source, and parts thereof not elsewhere specified or included." Tariff item 9405.10.00 specifically covered "chandeliers and other electric ceiling or wall lighting fittings, excluding those of a kind used for lighting public open spaces or thoroughfares."

With respect to the appellant's claim that the goods came under tariff heading 85.36, or, in the alternative, heading 85.37, the Tribunal found, on the basis of the evidence, that they were indeed assemblies (other than simple switch assemblies) of two apparatus of heading 85.36, namely, a lamp-holder/socket and a junction box. Accordingly, they could not be classified under heading 85.36. They were also not properly classifiable under heading 85.37 as the models failed to meet all three elements of heading 85.37, in particular, they did not form part of the requirement that they must be boards, panels, consoles, desks, cabinets, or other bases (the first element).

The Tribunal then turned to the remaining classification, the one on the basis of which the CBSA had made its re-determination of the goods in issue, namely heading 94.05 and, in particular, tariff item 9405.10.00, as "other electric ceiling lighting fittings." It noted that the terms of heading 94.05 required that the goods in issue be (1) lighting fittings and (2) not elsewhere specified or included. General Note 3 of the Explanatory Notes to Chapter 94 confirmed that this chapter provides for "[l]amps and lighting fittings . . . not elsewhere specified or included." More specifically, the Explanatory Notes to heading 94.05 provided that the heading covered, in particular, "(1) Lamps and lighting fittings normally used for the illumination of rooms, e.g.: hanging lamps; bowl lamps; ceiling lamps; chandeliers; wall lamps; standard lamps; table lamps; bedside lamps; desk lamps; night lamps; water-tight lamps."

On the basis of the foregoing, the Tribunal concluded that the goods fell within the generic description of lighting fittings.

Having found that the goods in issue were not *prima facie* classifiable under heading 85.36 or 85.37, and being satisfied that they were not *prima facie* classifiable under any other heading, the Tribunal found that the goods in issue met the requirement of heading 94.05 as lighting fittings "not elsewhere specified or included."

Therefore, applying Rule 6 of the *General Rules* and Rule 1 of the *Canadian Rules*, the Tribunal held that the goods in issue were correctly classified by the CBSA under heading 94.05 and, in particular, they fell under tariff item 9405.10.00 as "other electric ceiling or wall lighting fittings."

CASE 3: TARIFF ITEM 9617.00.00 (COFFEE POTS FOR COMMERCIAL COFFEE MAKERS)

The appellant in *Newtech Beverage Systems Ltd v Commissioner of the Canada Customs and Revenue Agency*[138] imported coffee pots for commercial coffee makers. It claimed that the coffee pots should have been classified by the CCRA under tariff item 8419.90.00 as "parts of commercial coffee makers" or, alternatively, under headings 82.10, 84.13, or 84.79, not under tariff item 9617.00.00 as "other vacuum vessels," as determined by the CCRA. The evidence indicated that the commercial coffee makers were an entire coffee brewing system, consisting of coffee-making, storing, and dispensing functions.

The Tribunal first considered the appellant's primary position that the coffee pots came under tariff item 8419.90.00. It noted that heading 84.19 had two subheadings, 8419.81 and 8419.90. The nomenclature of tariff item 8419.81.10, which came in the first subheading, excluded coffee making and dispensing machines, but included espresso or cappuccino machines and combination roasting, milling, and brewing machines. However, in the Tribunal's view, coffee makers were covered by tariff item 8419.81.90, which described "other machinery, plant and equipment for making hot drinks or

138 AP-2003-029 (2004), 9 TTR (2d) 62.

for cooking or heating food" and this nomenclature would cover commercial coffee making and dispensing machines.

The Tribunal next considered tariff item 9617.00.00 under which the CBSA had re-determined the classification of the coffee pots. That tariff item covered "vacuum flasks and other vacuum vessels, complete with cases; parts thereof other than glass inners." The majority of the Tribunal was of the view that the coffee pots were classifiable *prima facie* under this tariff item as well. Therefore, the majority resorted to Rule 1 of the *Canadian Rules* and Rule 3(a) of the *General Rules*, the latter of which states that "3. When ... goods are *prima facie*, classifiable under two or more headings, classification shall be effected as follows: (a) The heading which provides the most specific description shall be preferred to headings providing a more general description."

The Tribunal, by a majority, held that tariff item 9617.00.00 ("other vacuum vessels") provided a more specific description of the coffee pot.

c) Chapter 99: Duty-Free Treatment

Several decisions of the Tribunal follow that deal with tariff benefits under the tariff codes 2000 onwards that were in effect before 1997, when the new *Customs Tariff* came into force. These cases have been chosen because they elucidate important principles that govern the entitlement of importers to tariff benefits that are continued in the new Schedule under the corresponding tariff items of Chapter 99. Furthermore, the definition of "for use in," which is key to the entitlement contained in Section 4 of the old *Customs Tariff* remained virtually unchanged in the current Act. That definition stated:

> The expression "for use in", wherever it occurs in a tariff item in Schedule I or a code in Schedule II in relation to goods, means, unless the context otherwise requires, that the goods must be wrought into, attached to or incorporated into other goods as provided for in that tariff item or code.

Chapter 99 (Special classification provisions—commercial) of the Schedule to the current *Customs Tariff* (as well as Chapter 98) is reserved to States for national use. The Notes to Chapter 99 state that

1. The provisions of this Chapter are not subject to the rule of specificity in General Interpretative Rule 3(a).
2. Goods which may be classified under the provisions of Chapter 99, if also eligible for classification under the provisions of Chapter 98, shall be classified in Chapter 98.

3. Goods may be classified under a tariff item in this Chapter [99] and be entitled to the Most-Favoured-Nation Tariff or a preferential tariff rate of customs duty under this Chapter that applies to those goods according to the tariff treatment applicable to their country of origin only after classification under a tariff item in Chapters 1 to 97 has been determined and the conditions of any Chapter 99 provision and any applicable regulations or orders in relation thereto have been met.
4. The words and expressions used in this Chapter have the same meaning as in Chapters 1 to 97.

The Tribunal's decisions below appear in numerical order of the Codes contained in Schedule II to the former *Customs Tariff* and the tariff items in the Schedule to the new *Customs Tariff*.

i) *Code 2000 (Article "for use in" goods of tariff item 8436.80.10—agricultural, horticultural, poultry farming, and other machinery)*

CASE: GREENHOUSE SYSTEMS

Prins Greenhouses Ltd[139] had imported an integrated greenhouse system consisting of a heater and flue gas condenser to keep the temperature in the greenhouse consistent. The tariff classification of the goods was determined in favour of the appellant under tariff item 8436.80.10, as noted in Section D(10)(b)(v)(Case 1), above in this chapter. That would entitle the appellant to the tariff benefit of Code 2000 if the goods satisfied the conditions set out in tariff item 8436.80.10. The CCRA had rejected the claim, but the Tribunal allowed the appeal, holding that the goods in issue were functionally part of the greenhouse system, which was listed under that Code, and, therefore, they satisfied all three conditions for tariff benefit, namely: (1) they must be "articles," (2) they must be "for use in," and (3) they must be "articles for use in" an item listed in that code.

ii) *Code 2101 (Article "for use in" goods of tariff item 9032.89.20—process control equipment)*

CASE: POWER TRANSFORMERS

Asea Brown Boveri Inc[140] claimed duty-free benefit of Code 2101 for the goods in issue, namely, power transformers and other parts of process control equipment, which it had imported. Its appeal against the decision of the

---

139 Above note 121.
140 Above note 124.

Deputy Minister of National Revenue was allowed in respect of the tariff classification of the goods in issue, as noted in Section D(10)(b)(v)(Case 4), above in this chapter. The Deputy Minister had also rejected the claim for tariff benefit of Code 2101, following re-determination. As the Tribunal had held that the goods fall under tariff item 9032.89.20, and as the goods in issue were imported for use in process control apparatus listed in that tariff item, the Tribunal held that they qualified for duty relief under Code 2101.

iii) **Code 2546 (Article "for use in" goods of tariff headings 90.18 or 90.22—laser imagers)**

CASE: LASER IMAGING FILM

The appellant in *Imation Canada Inc v Commissioner of the Canada Customs and Revenue Agency*[141] claimed the tariff benefit of Code 2546 for laser imaging films, a claim which the CCRA had rejected. As the Tribunal had held that the laser imaging films were "for use in" in the laser imagers, which came under tariff heading 90.18, they qualified for the tariff benefit of the Code, which listed, *inter alia*, "articles for use in the goods of heading 90.18."

The Tribunal was of the view that the concept of "functionally joined" simply meant that the goods "for use in" the host goods had a functional relationship (be it active or passive) with the host goods. In this case, the film was integral to the functioning of the laser imagers. The technical functions of the laser imager existed only to make an image on the film; conversely, the film existed for the exclusive benefit of the laser imager. Further, the evidence was that each had been designed specifically for use with the other. Without being joined, the goods were virtually useless; on the one hand, the film remained blank and, on the other, the laser imager could not produce an image. As the film was integral to the functioning of the laser imagers, Code 2546 applied to the films and they were eligible for the tariff benefit.

iv) **Code 7934 (Article "for use in" goods of tariff item 3921.90.90—composite goods of plastic sheets)**

CASE 1: POLYSTYRENE

The claim of *EM Plastic & Electric Products Ltd v Deputy Minister of National Revenue*[142] for the benefits of Code 7934 for the multi-layer GATORFOAM®, composed of polystyrene (the goods in issue), had been rejected by the

---

141 AP-2000-047 (2001), 6 TTR (2d) 239 [*Imation Canada*].
142 AP-98-012 (2000).

Deputy Minister of National Revenue as a result of its re-determination, although both parties had agreed that the goods came under tariff item 3921.90.90. The appeal against the rejection was allowed by the Tribunal, which held that the goods in issue were not excluded under Code 7934. Reiterating its decision in *Formica Canada Inc v Deputy Minister of National Revenue*[143] as it related to the application of the tariff code, the Tribunal held that (1) the goods were classified under one of the tariff items covered by the tariff code, and (2) the goods did not fall within the exclusions of the Code.

The Tribunal expressed two important views regarding the application of the *General Rules* to tariff benefit Codes (by extension, to the tariff benefits under the current *Customs Tariff*): (1) nowhere do section 10(1) of the *Customs Tariff* and the *General Rules* say these rules apply to the interpretation of tariff codes, and, even if they do apply, the rules would not apply differently at the tariff item and tariff code levels; and (2) the goods in issue cannot have two essential elements, one for tariff item and one for tariff code interpretation. It rejected the DMNR's arguments in that regard.

CASE 2: PLASTIC FILM

The appellant in *Transilwrap of Canada Ltd v Commissioner of the Canada Customs and Revenue Agency*[144] had imported plastic film made by lamination of polyethylene terephthalate and polyethylene, which came under both subheadings 3920.10 and 3920.62, as film of polymers of ethylene. The two subheadings referred to part only of the material contained in composite goods. Pursuant to Rule 3 (b) of the *General Rules*, the Tribunal had ruled that subheading 3920.62 was more appropriate, because the goods consisted of the material that gave them their essential character and that material came under subheading 3920.62. Given that the goods in issue were more than 15 centimetres in width, the Tribunal held that they are entitled to the benefits of tariff Code 7934.

[Note: The following tariff items are in the Schedule to the new *Customs Tariff*.]

v) *Tariff Item 9903.00.00 (Agricultural and horticultural machinery)*
This tariff item provides duty-free benefit for all articles and materials that enter into the cost of manufacture or repair of, and articles *for use* in, among others, agricultural or horticultural elevators or conveyors; agricultural or horticultural machinery for soil preparation or farm, and pneumatic tires

---

143   AP-96-205 (1998).
144   AP-2000-018 (2001), 6 TTR (2d) 220.

and inner tubes for use therewith; continued combination machinery for bagging or boxing and weighing, or machinery for filling, for use with fresh fruit or vegetables; chassis fitted with engines therefor, cabs therefor, and parts and accessories thereof, other than bumpers and bumper parts, safety seat belts and suspension shock-absorbers; and windmills.

The following are a few of the decisions of the Tribunal interpreting this tariff item.

CASE 1: ROCK WOOL

The appellant in *AMA Plastics Ltd v President of the Canada Border Services Agency*[145] claimed the benefits of tariff item 9903.00.00 for the goods in issue, which were blocks of rock wool impregnated with a wetting agent to allow water absorption and retention and to enhance plant growth. The goods were classified under tariff heading 68.06 as slag wool, rock wool, and so on, which was conceded by the CBSA. The CBSA, however, had rejected the appellant's claim for the benefits of tariff item 9903.00.00, which provided relief if the articles were for use in machines of heading 84.36 or as sprinkler or trickle irrigation. Allowing the appeal, the Tribunal held that the evidence clearly established that the goods in issue enhanced the host good (in this case, the integrated greenhouse systems or trickle irrigation systems) for use in greenhouses. The primary function of the systems was for use in greenhouses designed for the production of vegetables or flowers and was complemented and enhanced by the presence of the goods in issue, which ensured that water and nutrients were absorbed directly by the roots of the plants. That being the case, the Tribunal found that the goods in issue were entitled to the benefits of tariff item 9903.00.00.

CASE 2: ONION BAGS AND MASTER BAGS

The appellant in *Agri-Pack v Commissioner of the Canada Customs and Revenue Agency*[146] claimed the benefits of tariff item 9903.00.00 for the goods in issue (onion bags and master bags). The tariff classification issue was decided by the Tribunal (see Section D(10)(a)(vi) (Case 7), above in this chapter—the goods in issue came under tariff item 6305.33.00 ("other sacks and bags") or 5608.19.90 ("other made up nets")). The further issue was whether the goods in issue qualified for duty relief under tariff item 9903.00.00 as articles "for use in" combination machinery for bagging or boxing and weighing, or machinery for filling, for use with fresh fruit or vegetables, or

---

145 AP-2009-052 (2010), 15 TTR (2d) 149.
146 Above note 49.

for use in machinery for packing fresh fruit or vegetables from the dumper, feed table, bin, or hopper stage to the box or bag closing stage.

The CBSA had rejected the tariff benefit claim on the basis that the goods were subsequently diverted contrary to section 32.2 of the *Customs Act*, and therefore they became ineligible. The Tribunal rejected the CBSA's argument, holding that there was nothing in the tariff item that indicated that the declared use of the imported articles must continue throughout the full four years. If the articles had to be used in the machinery on a permanent basis, they would ordinarily be considered to be machinery parts, which the CBSA admitted the tariff item did not require. Therefore, the Tribunal only had to decide, for classification under the "for use in" tariff relief provisions of Chapter 99, whether the goods in issue were, in point of fact, sufficiently integrated into the above-described machinery as to constitute a single system, however brief the integration of each individual imported article may be. If the goods in issue were fully integrated into bagging machines, the fact that they would be used, once they were run through the machine, for the sole purpose of storing onions, was irrelevant for classification purposes, since tariff item 9903.00.00 did not use the words "solely" or even "principally." The fact that the bags were only temporarily attached to the machinery was not an impediment to classification under Chapter 99. The Tribunal cited the decision of the Federal Court of Appeal in *Entrelec Inc v Canada (Minister of National Revenue)*,[147] in which the court had decided that such dual use did not prevent an article from falling within the meaning of the tariff relief qualifications. The Tribunal reiterated its previous determination (in *Imation Canada*[148]) that "the concept of 'functionally joined' simply meant that the goods 'for use in' the host goods have a functional relationship (be it active or passive) with the host goods."[149] The Tribunal held that only the onion bags qualified for tariff benefits (but not the "master" bags, which had also been imported).

CASE 3: GREENHOUSE CARTS
The goods imported by *Contech Holdings Canada Inc v President of the Canada Border Services Agency*[150] consisted of greenhouse carts and their parts, which were classified under tariff heading 84.36, a classification agreed to by both parties. The appellant claimed the benefits of tariff item 9903.00.00 for

---

147   2004 FCA 159.
148   Above note 141.
149   *Ibid* at para 19.
150   AP-2010-033 and AP-2010-042 (2012).

these goods as it claimed they were "for use in agricultural or horticultural conveyors, or agricultural or horticultural machines of heading 84.36." This claim was dismissed by the CBSA, and the CBSA's decision was upheld by the Tribunal. Its rationale was as follows: (1) It was not possible for the carts to constitute an essential part of a conveyor or machine and, at the same time, be "for use in" that conveyor or machine. (2) If goods that are "for use in" host goods and the host goods are distinct, then it logically followed that the host goods must exist independently of the other goods. (3) Goods that constitute an essential part of host goods should only be regarded as enabling the existence of the host goods rather than enhancing or complementing their function.

CASE 4: HAY BALE WRAPPERS

The appellant in *Kverneland Group North America Inc v President of the Canada Border Services Agency*[151] imported hay bale wrappers, which were classified under tariff item 8422.40.91. It claimed the benefits of tariff item 9903.00.00 on the basis that the goods in issue were "articles for use in tractors ... for use on the farm," but the CBSA rejected that claim on the ground that the goods were not "for use in" tractors. The Tribunal upheld the CBSA's decision, as the goods, although attached to the tractor, were not functionally joined to the tractor because the tractor could function on its own without them. By being attached to the tractor, they were pulled by the tractor to the hay bale wrapping site. The tractor ("host") complemented the function of the wrapper, and not *vice versa*.

CASE 5: ALUMINUM REFLECTORS IN GREENHOUSES

The goods in *PL Light Systems Canada Inc v President of the Canada Border Services Agency*[152] were aluminum reflectors for supplementary lighting fixtures specially designed for integrated greenhouse systems. There was no disagreement between the parties as to the tariff classification; they agreed that the goods were agricultural or horticultural machines of heading 84.36 and, therefore, came under tariff item 9405.99.00. The appellant's claim for the tariff benefits of tariff item 9903.00.0 was, however, rejected by the CBSA, and the appeal concerned that rejection. The Tribunal allowed the appeal. It held that, as the aluminum reflectors were physically attached to and functionally joined to the lighting fixtures, which were for use in in-

---

151 AP-2009-013 (2010), 14 TTR (2d) 422.
152 AP-2008-012 (2009), 13 TTR (2d) 739, remand to Tribunal by FCA, AP-2008-012R (2011), 16 TTR (2d) 127.

tegrated systems, they fell under tariff item 9403.00.00. Consequently, the appellant was entitled to the benefits of that tariff item.

vi) *Tariff Item 9908.00.00 (Utility Vehicles for Use in Mining)*
This tariff item covers

> Utility vehicles of heading 87.03 and lorries (trucks) or shuttle cars of heading 87.04, for use underground in mining or in developing mineral deposits; Articles (excluding tires and inner tubes) for use in the foregoing equipment, or for use in loading machinery for loading coal or for loading minerals directly from the working face of a mine, or for use in extracting machinery for extracting minerals directly from the working face of a mine.

CASE: DRILL RODS AND COUPLING/SLEEVES

In *Sandvik Tamrock Canada Inc v Commissioner of the Canada Customs and Revenue Agency*,[153] the goods in issue were drill rods and coupling/sleeves, for which the appellant claimed the benefit of tariff item 9908.00.00. This claim was rejected by the CCRA on the basis that tariff item 9908.00.00 required goods to be for use in extracting machinery for extracting minerals directly from the working face of a mine, and the goods in issue did not qualify.

The Tribunal upheld the CCRA's decision for the reason that the goods did not meet the three conditions specified in the tariff item, all of which had to be met: (1) they must be articles, (2) they must be for use in extracting machinery, and (3) the extracting machinery must be for extracting minerals directly from the working face of a mine. The Tribunal noted that the goods in issue were predominantly for use in jumbo drills, which were not extracting machinery, and the jumbo drills and bolters performed the function of a drill, not the extraction function.

The appellant applied to the Federal Court of Appeal for judicial review of the Tribunal's decision. The court reversed the Tribunal's decision because, in its opinion, the reasoning of the Tribunal for excluding the articles in issue from the ambit of tariff item 9908.00.00 was clearly flawed and could not withstand the type of scrutiny that the "reasonableness *simpliciter*" standard of review called for. It was not open to the Tribunal to hold that the "Continuous Mover" was the only kind of machine that qualified. Therefore, it held that the drill rods and coupling sleeves must be classified under tariff item 9908.00.00.

---

153   AP-99-083 (2000), 4 TTR (2d) 759, rev'd 2001 FCA 340.

vii) Tariff Item 9948.00.00 (Data Processing Machines)

The following decisions interpret eligibility for duty relief under this tariff item 9948.00.00, which covers

> Articles for use in the following: Automatic banknote dispensers; Automatic data processing machines and units thereof, magnetic or optical readers, machines for transcribing data onto data media in coded form and machines for processing such data; Automatic word-processing machines; Chart recorders and other instruments for measuring or checking electrical quantities, designed for use with automatic data processing machines; Electronic calculating machines; Magnetic discs; Numerical control panels with built-in automatic data processing machines; Power supplies of automatic data processing machines and units thereof; Process control apparatus, excluding sensors, which converts analog signals from or to digital signals; Video games used with a television receiver, and other electronic games; Parts and accessories of the foregoing.

CASE 1: CELLPHONE PROTECTIVE COVERS

In *Curve Distribution Services Inc v President of the Canada Border Services Agency*,[154] the appellant imported cellphone protective covers, entering them under tariff item 4302.92.90 as "parts and accessories for use in telecommunications network." It claimed entitlement to the duty-free benefit provided by tariff item 9948.00.00 because, it claimed, they were "articles for use in . . . automatic data processing machines and units thereof . . . [or] parts and accessories of the foregoing."

The CBSA rejected the duty-free benefit entitlement. The Tribunal dismissed the appeal because the goods in issue did not qualify for the benefit of tariff item 9948.00.00; they did not meet all three conditions specified in the tariff item. According to the terms of tariff item 9948.00.00 the "articles" themselves must be "for use in" the automatic data processing machines or parts and accessories thereof.

The Tribunal was of the view that, in the context of this appeal, it was irrelevant whether cellphones were "for use in" telecommunications networks, or whether the cellphone covers were accessories for cellphones. The reference in tariff item 9948.00.00 to "[p]arts and accessories of the foregoing" means parts and accessories of the items listed in that tariff item (for example, parts and accessories of automatic data processing machines) and *not* parts and accessories of articles that are for use in the items listed in

---

154 AP-2011-023 (2012), 16 TTR (2d) 742.

that tariff item. Even if cellphones may themselves be automatic data processing machines or, alternatively, parts and accessories of automatic data processing machines, and even though the cellphone covers are physically connected to and specifically designed and shaped to fit the cellphones, they did not enhance or complement the function of the cellphones and therefore could not be considered as being functionally joined to the cellphones. Cellphones performed the same functions, regardless of whether they were covered by the goods in issue. In other words, cellphones were equally capable of transmitting or receiving voice, images, or other data, or running software applications, with or without being covered by the goods in issue. Although the goods in issue held, protected, and carried cellphones, there was no functional interaction between the two.

CASE 2: KEYBOARD SYNTHESIZERS

The appellant in *Jam Industries Ltd v President of the Canada Border Services Agency*[155] imported keyboard synthesizers, digital pianos and digital organs; expansion boards for synthesizers; and non-keyboard synthesizers. It entered the keyboard synthesizers, digital pianos, and digital organs under tariff item 9207.10.00, the expansion boards for synthesizers under tariff item 9209.94.90, and the non-keyboard synthesizers under tariff item 8543.89.99. All the instruments except the expansion boards were enabled by Musical Instrument Digital Interface (MIDI). Further, it claimed entitlement to the benefit of tariff item 9948.00.00. The CBSA re-determined the tariff classifications, which the appellant did not dispute.

The dispute was with respect to the entitlement to the benefit of tariff item 9948.00.00, which the CBSA had rejected. The appellant argued that the goods were for use in automatic data processing machines (that is, computers) and were therefore entitled to duty-free benefits of tariff item 9948.00.00. The Tribunal rejected this argument, holding that the goods were not "for use" in a data processing machine within the meaning of tariff item 9948.00.00 for the reason that (1) the goods did not complement the function of a computer by being connected to it; rather, the reverse appeared to be true: connection to a computer enabled the goods to have additional capability; and (2) it was the instrument's function that was expanded or improved and not that of the computer.

---

155 AP-2005-006 (2006), 10 TTR (2d) 748, aff'd 207 FCA 20.

CASE 3: MUSIC CDS

The appellant in *PHD Canada*[156] imported audio music compact discs, some before 1 January 1998 under tariff item 8513.99.91, when Code 2101 was in force, and some after 1 January 1998 under tariff item 8524.32.90, when the new tariff item 9948.00.00 came into effect.

The CCRA re-determined the classification of the goods imported prior to 1 January 1998 under 8524.99.91 and those imported after 1 January 1998 under tariff item 8524.22.90 as "other discs for laser reading systems for sound only." Code 2101 had accorded duty-free benefits for articles for use in goods of tariff item 8471.70 ("disc drives; drums storage memories"). Tariff item 9948.00.0, which replaced that Code, provided for "articles for use in automatic data processing machines and units thereof, but not including the goods themselves."

The Tribunal allowed the appeal. It found that the goods imported prior to 1 January 1998 should be classified under 8524.32.00 as "discs for laser reading systems for reproducing sound only" and those imported after that date should be classified under 8524.32.90 as "other discs for laser reading systems for reproducing sound only." Both importations were entitled to tariff benefits during the relevant periods, the earlier under Code 2101 and the later under tariff item 9948.00.00.

CASE 4: INTEGRATED CIRCUIT (IC) RECORDERS AND PORTABLE MINIDISK (MD) RECORDERS

In the case of *Sony Canada*,[157] which dealt with integrated circuit (IC) recorders and portable minidisk (MD) recorders, Sony had entered their classification under tariff items 8520.90.90 or 8471.70.00 as storage units of automatic data processing machines and units thereof, or, alternatively, under tariff item 8519.99.10 as compact disc players. It further claimed the benefit of tariff item 9948.00.00. The CCRA re-determined the tariff classification under 8520.90.90, which was the first position of the appellant, but rejected its claim for duty-free benefit of tariff item 9948.00.00 on the basis that the goods in issue were not solely or principally used in those machines.

The Tribunal dismissed the appeal in respect of the classification of the goods in issue. However, it held that the IC recorders qualified for benefit under tariff item 9948.00.00 as they were physically connected and functionally joined to a computer and, as such, were "for use in . . . [a]utomatic data processing machines." The two minidisk models, however, did not

---

156 Above note 129.
157 Above note 79.

qualify. The Tribunal's interpretation of the term "parts and accessories" in tariff item 9948.00.00 was discussed in Section D(10)(b)(v)(Case 6), above in this chapter.

viii) Tariff Item 9958.00.00 (Passenger Vehicles)
This tariff item covers:

> Parts, accessories and articles, excluding tires and tubes, for use in the manufacture of original equipment parts for passenger automobiles, trucks or buses, or for use as original equipment in the manufacture of such vehicles or chassis therefor.

CASE 1: COMMERCIAL VANS AND WHEEL RIMS
The appellant in *Great West Van Conversions Inc v President of the Canada Border Services Agency*[158] imported Sprinter commercial vans and wheel rims, the goods in issue. Commercial vans can be and were manufactured into motor homes. The claim for duty-free benefit of either tariff item 9958.00.00 or 9959.00.00 was rejected by the CBSA, and this rejection was appealed to the Tribunal. The Tribunal allowed the appeal and held that the appellant was entitled to the duty-free benefits because the goods in issue fell under tariff item 9958.00.00. Its reasons were as follows: (1) Wheel rims with caps and so on and wheels each equally qualified as parts and so on. Thus, they met the first condition. (2) Motor homes, having a function that was additional to that of transporting persons, could still be considered as automobiles. The appellant's Class B motor homes met the dictionary definition of a road vehicle and a road vehicle as a "car or automobile." (3) The appellant did manufacture Class B motor homes. (4) Because the appellant was the original manufacturer of Class B motor homes, all goods, whether parts, accessories, or articles that were specifically designed by the appellant to be installed or incorporated into them, could be considered original equipment.

Since the appellant received duty-free benefit under tariff item 9958.00.00, there was no need to consider tariff item 9959.00.00. Both parties agreed that the goods did not qualify under that tariff item, and the Tribunal concurred.

CASE 2: TOP PLATES, OR FIFTH-WHEEL CASTINGS
In *Holland Hitch of Canada Limited v President of the Canada Border Services Agency*,[159] the goods in issue were eight models of top plates, or fifth-wheel

---
158 AP-2010-037 (2011) [*Great West Van*].
159 AP-2012-004 (2013), 17 TTR (2d) 349.

castings, imported by the appellant from a casting supplier in France for further processing, including machining, facing, drilling, and the installation of other components to produce fifth-wheel assemblies. The end product was used as fifth wheels on highway tractors for pulling semi-trailers.

The issue in this appeal was whether the fifth-wheel assemblies, which the parties agreed were correctly classified under tariff item 8708.99.99 were entitled to the benefits of tariff item 9958.00.00 as parts, accessories, and articles for use in the manufacture of original equipment parts for trucks or for use as original equipment in the manufacture of trucks or chassis, or, in the alternative, under tariff item 9959.00.00 as materials of Section XV for use in the manufacture of trucks or parts, accessories, or parts thereof, or, in the further alternative, under tariff item 9962.00.00 as parts of chassis frames for use in the repair of road tractors for semi-trailers. The CBSA accepted that the fifth-wheel assemblies were parts for use in the manufacture of parts for trucks, but disagreed that they qualified as "original equipment." In fact, the parties defined this term differently. The CBSA also contended that in its view, the proper construction of the "for use in" phrase excluded original equipment from the scope of tariff item 9958.00.00, because the disjunctive "or" used in the section was a variation of the phrase preceding "or for use as." The appellant contended the opposite.

The Tribunal found that the goods in issue qualified for the benefits of tariff item 9958.00.00 and allowed the appeal. They were parts or articles for use in the manufacture of original equipment for trucks, to the extent that "original equipment" referred to fifth wheels destined for use in original vehicle manufacture, "first fit" assembly, or for aftermarket replacement for trucks originally equipped with the same fifth-wheel product and covered by vehicle warranty.

The Tribunal rejected the conjunctive approach argued by the CBSA, stating that the phrase following "or for use as" was merely a variation of the preceding phrase and, thus, the goods in issue were eligible for duty relief under this tariff item only in cases where their end use was original truck manufacture. The CBSA argued that if Parliament had intended a disjunctive approach, it would have used a semicolon to separate the two phrases. The Tribunal took the disjunctive approach, referring to its decision in *Great West Van*,[160] in which it had taken a similar approach, even though the CBSA attempted to discredit that decision.

---

160 Above note 158.

ix) Tariff Item 9961.00.00 (Repair of Road Tractors)

This tariff item covers a long list of articles for use in the repair of road tractors for semitrailers, motor vehicles principally designed for the transport of persons or goods, or firefighting vehicles, and parts thereof, including "Vacuum, hydraulic or air control assemblies" and "Parts of the foregoing."

CASE: DISC BRAKE CALIPERS (REPLACEMENT PARTS)

The appellant in *Fenwick Automotive Products Limited v President of the Canada Border Services Agency*[161] imported disc brake calipers (replacement parts) for Ford Mustang motor vehicles. There was no dispute as to the tariff classification of the goods under tariff item 8708.39.90, but the dispute was about the entitlement to duty-free benefit of tariff item 9961.00.00. The CBSA rejected the duty-free claim on the basis that tariff item 9961.00.00 did not cover the goods in issue.

The Tribunal upheld the CBSA's determination on the basis of the wording of tariff item 9961.00.00, which read: "The following for use in the repair of road tractors ... motor vehicles ... and parts thereof: ... Vacuum, hydraulic or air control assemblies." In the Tribunal's opinion, the goods in issue controlled neither the brakes and vehicle movement, nor the hydraulic pressure. Such control instead originated upstream from the goods in issue, with the driver of the vehicle and with various hydraulic control assemblies, such as the master cylinder. For their part, the goods in issue were actuators that responded to hydraulic pressure. Therefore, they were not parts of a hydraulic control assembly for use in the repair of motor vehicles principally designed for the transport of persons or goods, and, as a result, they were not entitled to the duty-free treatment provided by tariff item 9961.00.00.

x) Tariff Item 9977.00.00 (Medical Goods)

This tariff item covers articles for use "in ... [i]nstruments and appliances used in medical, surgical, dental or veterinary sciences, including scintigraphic apparatus, other electromedical apparatus and sight-testing instruments."

CASE: V-BELTS USED IN CENTRIFUGES

The appeal in *Beckman Coulter Canada Inc v President of the Canada Border Services Agency*[162] concerned the CBSA's rejection of the appellant's claim for the benefits of tariff item 9977.00.0 for the V-belts that were actually used in the J6 centrifuges. The CBSA did not dispute that the V-belts were so

---

161 AP-2006-063 (2009), 13 TTR (2d) 316.
162 AP-2010-065 (2012), 16 TTR (2d) 365.

used, nor did it dispute that, when that was the case, the V-belts were incorporated into or attached to the J6 centrifuges. However, the reason for rejecting the claim was its interpretation of the definition of "for use in" in section 2(1) of the *Customs Tariff*. The CBSA considered that the term "for use in" required that the goods be wrought or incorporated into, or attached to, other goods for which they have been specifically designed, and asked the Tribunal to read this requirement into the section.

The Tribunal allowed the appeal and found that the goods were in fact incorporated into the centrifuges and, therefore, "for use in" them. It also found that the centrifuges were "appliances used in medical sciences," considering that they satisfied the dictionary definition of "appliance," and that there was evidence that they were designed for the market comprising customers such as the Canadian Blood Services. It rejected the CBSA's interpretation, stating that, on its face, the definition did not require that goods be for the sole or exclusive use in the other goods. If that was Parliament's intention, it could easily have made that intention express. Furthermore, as the appellant pointed out, the CBSA itself treated some goods as being "for use in" goods referred to elsewhere in Chapter 99 (for example, tariff item 9948.00.00), even where they can be used with other goods not referred to in the tariff item, as long as an importer showed that they were actually used in the other goods that are referred to in the tariff item.

xi) *Tariff Item 9979.00.00 (Assists for Persons with Disabilities)*

Tariff item 9979.00.00 provides duty-free benefits for goods specifically designed to assist persons with disabilities in alleviating the effects of those disabilities, and articles and materials for use in such goods.

There are only a few recent decisions interpreting this tariff item. Three are reported below, the leading decision being *Sigvaris Corporation v President of the Canada Border Services*.[163]

CASE 1: SUPPORT HOSIERY

In *Sigvaris*, the goods in issue were graduated compression (or support) hosiery imported from the United States, and the issue was whether, in addition to being classified under tariff item 6115.12.00, the goods should be classified under tariff item 9979.00.00 as articles and materials specifically designed to assist persons with disabilities and alleviate those disabilities, and thereby be entitled to preferential tariff treatment. The CBSA rejected the appellant's claim.

---

163 AP-2007-009 (2009), 13 TTR (2d) 291 [*Sigvaris*].

There was no dispute that the support hosiery fell under tariff item 6115.12.00. However, in order to qualify for the benefits under tariff item 9979.00.00, two conditions set out in the tariff item had to be met: (1) the goods must be specifically designed to assist persons with disabilities, and (2) they must be specifically designed to assist such persons in alleviating the effects of those disabilities.

The CBSA argued that the conditions that were treated with the goods in issue were not "disabilities," but rather less severe conditions. The point of contention, therefore, was the meaning to be ascribed to the word "disabilities." Once that was determined, it would be necessary to examine the second condition.

The CBSA argued that "disabilities" were different from "diseases" and that a "disability" must lead to a significant limitation in some aspect of people's lives.

The Tribunal considered both dictionary and WHO definitions of the word "disability." Those definitions referred to the condition of disability as one of a particular degree of severity, one that affected the performance of the individual concerned. The Supreme Court of Canada in *Granovsky v Canada*[164] also considered the definition of "disability" provided by the WHO, although in a different context. The Court equated the concept of "disability" used by the WHO in the medical context with that of "functional limitations," thereby suggesting that not all physical or mental impairments gave rise to functional limitations. To illustrate its thinking, the Supreme Court used the example of an individual who is slightly colour-blind and who, unless he or she chooses to undertake employment where an ability to differentiate colours precisely is important, may not notice any functional limitations. In other words, there may be a restriction or lack of ability (that is, impairment) that does not necessarily constitute a disability.[165]

Neither the tariff item nor Chapter 99 contained a definition of the word "disability." In the Tribunal's view, if Parliament wanted to restrict the meaning given to the term "disability," it would have said so in explicit and precise terms as it had done, for example, in the Canada Pension Plan. Therefore, the ordinary meaning of the word should be applied. In light of dictionary definitions and in the context of the provision that is being examined, it was the Tribunal's view that it was reasonable to conclude that the ordinary

---

164 2000 SCC 28.
165 *Ibid* at para 36.

meaning of the word "disability" was that of "a physical condition that made progress or success difficult."

Because the goods in issue were specifically designed to assist persons with achy legs, tired itchy legs, beginning stages of edema, and beginning stages of chronic venous insufficiency, and because such conditions could translate into restrictions or inabilities for certain individuals who suffered from those conditions with regard to performing their normal daily activities, the Tribunal was convinced that the goods in issue were "specifically designed to assist persons with disabilities" within the meaning of tariff item 9979.00.00.

The second condition required the determination whether the goods in issue were designed to alleviate the effects of those disabilities. To examine this issue, it was relevant to consider whether doctors, in treating patients, did in fact use the goods in issue for that purpose.

The Tribunal concluded that there was sufficient evidence that the goods in issue could be used and were being used to alleviate the symptoms of less severe chronic venous insufficiency conditions that were causing disabilities and, in some circumstances, more severe conditions of chronic venous insufficiency.

Since both conditions of tariff item 9979.00.00 were met by the goods in issue, the Tribunal held that the goods were entitled to the duty-free treatment provided by that tariff item.

CASE 2: FORMULA FOR INFANTS AND CHILDREN

In *Nutricia North America v President of the Canada Border Services Agency*,[166] the appellant claimed that the goods in issue, namely Neocate® formulas for infants and children, were incorrectly classified by the CBSA under tariff item 2106.90.99 as "other food preparations." The appellant submitted that they should be classified under tariff item 3004.50.00 as "medicaments consisting of mixed products for therapeutic or prophylactic uses, put up in measured doses, containing vitamins." If they were so classified, they would be entitled to the duty-free benefit of tariff item 9979.00.00.

In order for the goods in issue to be classified under tariff item 3004.50.00, they must be medicaments as defined in that item. Chapter 30, in which the tariff item fell, covered pharmaceutical products, and heading 30.04 covered "medicaments excluding those of headings 30.02, 30.05 and 30.06, consisting of mixed or unmixed products for therapeutic or prophylactic uses, put up

---

166 AP-2009-017 (2011).

in measured doses (including those in the form of transdermal administration systems) or in forms or packings for retail sale."

In support of its claim that the goods in issue were medicaments of heading 30.04, the appellant referred to the Tribunal's decision in *Hilary's Distribution Ltd v Deputy Minister of National Revenue*,[167] in which the Tribunal interpreted the term "medicament" as referring to substances used to treat or prevent human diseases, ailments, or disorders. In this regard, it submitted that the goods in issue were fed to infants and children to prevent or reverse the signs and symptoms associated with various gastrointestinal diseases, ailments, and disorders, including eosinophilic esophagitis, gastroesophageal reflux, multiple food protein allergies, and protein intolerance. The appellant submitted that Hilary's Distribution demonstrated that proof of efficacy was not required in order for the goods in issue to be classified as medicaments. It also referred to *Pfizer Canada Inc v Commissioner of the Canada Customs and Revenue Agency*[168] in support of its argument that marketing, packaging, and actual use of a product is relevant in determining whether it is a medicament.

The appellant also referred to Customs D Memorandum D10-14-30,[169] which explained the CBSA's policy in respect of the classification of medicaments. The Memorandum provided as follows:

> (c) Medicaments are generally not included in the common understanding of the term food. However, certain nutritional dietary supplements, sometimes considered food preparations, can be classified in heading 30.04 as a medicament. This is the case when the supplement is expressly for use in the prevention or treatment of a disease, illness or ailment and put up in a form specified in that heading.

In addition to the assertion that the Memorandum supported its position, the appellant submitted that it clearly demonstrated that the CBSA's policy was such that gastrointestinal disorders constituted a form of disorder or ailment.

In response to the CBSA's classification of the goods in issue as "other food preparations not elsewhere specified or included," the appellant noted Note 1(f) to Chapter 21, which excluded from heading 21.06 "[y]east put up as a medicament or other products of heading 30.03 or 30.04." In this regard,

---

167   AP-97-010 (1998) [*Hilary's Distribution*].
168   AP-2002-038 to AP-2002-090 (2003).
169   Customs D Memorandum D10-14-30, "Tariff Classification of Medicaments including Natural Health Products" (20 August 2004).

it argued that, because the goods in issue were specifically indicated for use in the prevention and treatment of certain gastrointestinal diseases, they were "elsewhere specified or included" as a medicament of heading 30.04.

Finally, the appellant argued that the goods in issue, not being a "food supplement" or used to "maintain general health or well-being," were not described by Note 16 of the Explanatory Notes to heading 21.06.

The CBSA submitted that the goods in issue were dietetic foods or nutritional preparations other than for intravenous administration, which were correctly classified under heading 21.06. It contended that Note 1(a) to Chapter 30 excluded all foods "other than nutritional preparations for intravenous administration" from classification in Chapter 30. It noted that "dietetic foods" were expressly excluded from classification in that chapter and argued that the goods in issue, being dietetic foods, were therefore excluded from classification in Chapter 30.

In that regard, the CBSA submitted that the term "dietetic food" was not limited to food for weight loss and included food for people with special medical conditions, such as the gastrointestinal conditions that the goods in issue were used to treat.

The CBSA argued that the goods in issue contained no medicinal substances or active ingredients, were available without a prescription, and were ingested by mouth or through a tube rather than being administered intravenously.

The Tribunal noted, and it was uncontested, that the use of amino acid–based nutritional formulations such as the goods in issue was widely recognized in medical circles as an effective treatment for certain gastrointestinal diseases and ailments in infants and children. It was also uncontested that the goods in issue were intended for use under the supervision of a medical health care professional, were not available in grocery stores, and could be purchased only by direct order from behind the counter at pharmacies and from hospital specialty stores. They were also not suitable for the general infant and child population, and were covered under certain public and private health care plans.

The Tribunal therefore concluded that, with regard to their marketing and intended use, the goods in issue possessed characteristics consistent with those of goods in the nature of medicaments.

However, the Tribunal found that the goods in issue did not meet the two conditions specified in tariff item 9979.00 as they were not "specifically designed to assist persons with disabilities in alleviating the effects of those disabilities" within the meaning of that phrase in that tariff item. Indeed, to suggest that this tariff item captured food preparations such as the goods in issue would, in the Tribunal's view, expand the scope of that provision well beyond what was intended.

For all the above reasons, the Tribunal determined that the goods in issue were correctly classified under tariff item 2106.90.99 as other food preparations not elsewhere specified or included, and that the goods in issue were not classifiable under tariff item 9979.00.00, and thus not entitled to the benefits of that tariff item.

CASE 3: THERAPEUTIC SPORT SHOES

The issue in *Masai Canada v President of the Canada Border Services Agency*[170] was whether the white therapeutic sport shoes imported by the appellant, in addition to being classified under tariff item 6404.11.99, should be classified under tariff item 9979.00.00 as goods specifically designed to assist persons with disabilities in alleviating the effects of those disabilities, thereby benefiting from duty-free treatment.

As in the *Sigvaris* decision,[171] the Tribunal examined the two conditions that the goods in issue must meet in order to qualify for the duty-free benefits: (1) whether the goods in issue were specifically designed to assist persons with disabilities, and (2) whether they alleviated the effects of those disabilities.

The Tribunal explained that its decision in *Sigvaris* stood for the proposition that there must be evidence that a design is purposefully related to the alleviation of the effect of disabilities and that there was some evidence that the goods lived up to the claim that they made. It added that the claim must not simply be a disguised attempt to gain the benefit of duty-free treatment.

The Tribunal concluded that the first requirement was met. It was also of the view that, even if the shoes were in fact marketed and used by individuals who did not suffer from disabilities, that did not negate the fact that the goods in issue were designed specifically to address a condition that may be associated with the cause of various disabilities. With respect to the second condition, the Tribunal did not believe, as a matter of logic, that it was necessary nor helpful to dissociate a disability from its effects when inquiring into the specific intent of the designer of the goods in issue. Even though it was anecdotal, the Tribunal found the evidence to be credible and to show a convincing nexus between the disabilities and their effects, and the objective of the goods in issue of alleviating their effects with the view

---

170 AP-2010-025 (2011).
171 Above note 163.

of assisting persons by making them more functional in their daily activities. In the Tribunal's view, although the matter was not settled as a matter of science, there was evidence that suggested that the goods in issue may alleviate some of the effects caused by the disabilities associated with walking on hard flat surfaces. Therefore, the Tribunal found that the goods in issue met the second requirement of tariff item 9979.00.00.

Since the goods in issue met both conditions of tariff item 9979.00.00, the Tribunal concluded that they were entitled to the duty-free benefits of that tariff item.

E. ORIGIN OF GOODS AND MARKING

1) Origin of Goods

Origin of goods is the third essential factor that determines tariff rate and the entitlement to tariff preferences. "Origin" means the country in which the goods originate, that is, the country in which the whole of the value of those goods is produced. Section 16(1) of the *Customs Tariff* states that, "subject to any regulations made under section 16(2), goods originate in a country if the whole of the value of the goods is produced in that country." In order to determine origin, section 35.01 of the *Customs Act* makes special provision for the marking of goods.[172]

Section 24(1) of the *Customs Tariff* stipulates that goods are entitled to a tariff treatment, other than the General Tariff, only if proof of origin of the goods is given in accordance with the *Customs Act*;[173] and only if the goods are

---

172 See Chapter 1, Section G(1).
173 The following Proof of Origin and/or Certificate of Origin Regulations have been prescribed by the Governor in Council under s 35.01 of the *Customs Act*: (1) *Proof of Origin of Imported Goods Regulations*, SOR/98-52, as am SOR/2004-186, SOR/2005-164, SOR/2008-78; s 4 relates to countries that are beneficiaries of the General Preferential Tariff [GPT], Commonwealth Caribbean Countries Tariff [CCCT], or Least Developed Country Tariff [LDCT]); s 5 relates to countries that are beneficiaries of the Most-Favoured-Nation Tariff [MFN], Australia Tariff [AUT], or New Zealand Tariff [NZT]; ss 6 to 9 relate to countries entitled to the benefit of preferential tariff treatment under the *North American Free Trade Agreement* [NAFTA], *Canada-Chile Free Trade Agreement* [CCFTA], or *Canada-Costa Rica Free Trade Agreement* [CCRFTA]; s 10 relates to countries entitled under the *Canada-Israel Free Trade Agreement* [CIFTA]; (2) *Canada-European Free Trade Association Free Trade Agreement* [CEFTA FTA] *Rules of Origin Regulations*, SOR/2009-198; (3) *Canada-Colombia Free Trade Agreement* [CCOFTA] *Rules of Origin Regulations*, SOR/2011-131; (4) *Canada-Jordan Free Trade Agreement* [CJFTA] *Rules of Origin Regulations*, SOR/2012-179; and (5) *Canada-Panama Free Trade Agreement* [CPAFTA] *Rules of Origin Regulations*, SOR/2013-50.

entitled to that tariff treatment in accordance with regulations made under section 16 or an order made under section 16(2) of the *Customs Tariff*.[174]

Therefore, the origin of goods is particularly important where an importer claims preferential treatment under the GPT, LDCT, CCCT, AUT, or NZT, or under any of the free trade agreements (FTAs). It may also be important where goods receive the MFNT treatment, or if the MFNT status is withdrawn through an order of the Governor in Council, or if the goods partly, wholly, or substantially originated in a country that has only a General Tariff status.

For instance, when the benefit of the Least-Developed-Country Tariff (LDCT) is claimed for imported goods, they must be certified as originating under a wholly produced rule or a cumulative manufacturing process in an LDC beneficiary with value-added inputs or cumulations from other LDCs or Canada. Similarly, when the *NAFTA* preferential tariff treatment is claimed for imported goods, a *NAFTA* certificate of origin is needed.

The decision of the Tribunal in *Jan K Overweel Limited v President of the Canada Border Services Agency*[175] interpreted the word "originate" in the *European Union Surtax Order* SOR/99-317 restrictively so as not to affect the MFNT status for canned meat produced in Brazil (a country enjoying MFNT status), which were then further processed and finished in Italy, a member of the European Union (EU). The Tribunal held that, having regard to the purpose of the surtax order as set out in the Preamble to that Order, the Order applied only to products wholly produced in a member state of the EU, and as the goods in issue were partly produced in Brazil and partly in Italy, the retaliatory Order did not apply to the goods. The Tribunal reasoned that the *MFNT Rules of Origin Regulations*[176] did not distinguish between partly and wholly produced goods when they were produced in any country with MFNT status. The Tribunal noted that the legislator (the Governor in Council) did not focus the Order squarely on products originating in an EU member state, perhaps due to inadvertence or perhaps deliberately.

---

174 See, for example, *CIFTA Tariff Preference Regulations*, SOR/97-64; *CCFTA Tariff Preference Regulations*, SOR/97-322; *CEFTA Tariff Preference Regulations*, SOR/2009-200; *CJFTA Tariff Preference Regulations*, SOR/2012-181; and *CPAFTA Tariff Preference Regulations*, SOR/2013-52.
175 AP-2011-075 (2013), 17 TTR (2d) 406. This decision was rendered after the Surtax Order was repealed in 2011 by SOR/2011-157.
176 SOR/98-33.

a) Wholly Produced in Country of Origin

No problem arises when a good is produced wholly in one country. For instance, a mineral extracted from the soil or the seabed of a country, or a vegetable good grown and harvested in, a live animal born and raised in, a good obtained from hunting or fishing in the same country, fulfils the requirement of the rule that goods must be wholly produced in the country of origin. In the case of goods originating in a LDC, however, the goods will be eligible for the LDCT rate even if a primary product has undergone further processing in another LDC.

Similarly, if goods originated in the United States or Mexico but were processed in the other country, they continue to be eligible for the duty-free benefits accorded by *NAFTA*. Generally, disputes are easily resolved, and are related to the furnishing of the certificate or declaration of origin as required by the *NAFTA* provisions or the related *Rules of Origin Regulations*. This was the situation in the appeals of *Buffalo Inc v Commissioner of the Canada Customs and Revenue Agency*,[177] *MRP Retail Inc v President of the Canada Border Services Agency*,[178] and *Western RV Coach v President of the Canada Border Services Agency*.[179] In *Buffalo Inc*, laces were produced in the United States from materials originating in Mexico. In *MRP Retail*, the fabric for women's T-shirts, tank tops, singlets, and other vests was provided by California Sunshine of the United States but the garments were sewed and finished by Alimex of Mexico, who returned the finished product to California Sunshine, who then sold them to MRP Retail. The Tribunal had no problem in deciding in favour of the appellants. On the other hand, in *Western RV Coach*, Western failed to produce a certificate of origin for the used motor home that it imported from the United States, and its appeal was dismissed by the Tribunal. In the last case, the Tribunal, following its earlier decision in *Duhamel & Dewar Inc v President of the Canada Border Services Agency*,[180] said that it was no excuse that the exporter refused to certify the goods and failed to submit supporting documentation for the preferential treatment. The Tribunal interpreted the phrase "reasons beyond its control" used in section 15 of the *NAFTA Rules of Origin Regulations*, to include bankruptcy, financial distress, business reorganization, fire, flooding, or other natural causes leading to the loss of records.

---

177 AP-2002-023 (2004), 8 TTR (2d) 787 [*Buffalo Inc*].
178 AP-2006-005 (2007), 12 TTR (2d) 1 [*MRP Retail*].
179 AP-2006-002 (2007), 11 TTR (2d) 576 [*Western RV Coach*].
180 AP-2005-046 (2007), 11 TTR (2d) 372.

In contrast to the above three appeals, the situation in *Tara Materials Inc v President of the Canada Border Services Agency*[181] was somewhat different. The goods, finished artist canvases, originated in the United States but the materials used in making them originated partly in the United States (72 percent) and the rest in a non-*NAFTA* country. The CBSA allowed *NAFTA* benefit only for the 72 percent and denied the claim for the remaining 28 percent. The appeal was dismissed by the Tribunal. On further appeal by Tara Materials to the Federal Court of Appeal, the court directed the Tribunal to investigate what proportion of materials used could be proved by Tara to have originated in a *NAFTA* country. Unable to prove more than 72 percent, the Tribunal confirmed its original decision.

Provisions on rules of origin set out in bilateral or free trade agreements are incorporated in various *Rules of Origin Regulations* specific to those countries.[182]

b) Substantially Manufactured or Processed

If the goods exported to Canada from a country were produced in that country but processed or manufactured, or further processed and manufactured, in another country or group of countries, regulations under the *Customs Tariff* prescribe special rules to determine their origin so as to accept or deny claim of special tariff treatment for them.

Specific Rules of Origin apply in respect of textile and apparel goods from LDC countries. Fabrics that are spun or extruded in a LDC and that do not undergo further processing outside any LDC, and goods produced from yarns originating in a LDC or Canada, but do not undergo further processing outside any LDC or Canada, are considered fabrics originating in a least developed country. Similarly, goods are considered originating in a LDC if they are assembled in a LDC from fabric cut in that country or in Canada, or from parts knit to shape, provided the fabric or the parts knit to shape are produced in any LDC or Canada from yarns originating in a LDC, a beneficiary country, or Canada, and provided the yarns or fabric do not undergo further processing outside any LDC or Canada.

In the case of materials, including packing, that are used in the manufacture of the goods and that originate outside a LDC in which the goods are assembled, their value must be no more than 75 percent of the ex-factory price of the goods as packed for shipment to Canada.

---

181   AP-2009-016 (2010), 14 TTR (2d) 609.
182   Above note 173.

Determination of the country of origin is governed by regulations prescribed under the *Customs Tariff*. There is some overlap in the legislative authority to make regulations between the *Customs Act* and the *Customs Tariff*; therefore, both statutes are cited when enacting regulations.

c) Direct Shipment and Transhipment: Sections 17 and 18

Sections 17(1) and 18(1) of the *Customs Tariff*, as well as section 54 of the *Customs Act*, contain special provisions that deal with the situation where goods are exported to Canada from a country but pass in transit through another country. If the goods are conveyed to Canada on a through bill of lading to a consignee in Canada, they are deemed to have been directly shipped to Canada.[183] If they are not so shipped, conveyed, or consigned, they may be deemed by regulations to have been shipped directly to Canada if certain authorized activities occurred in the intermediate country, namely: (1) the goods remained under customs control; (2) they did not undergo operations other than unloading, reloading, splitting up of loads, or other operations to keep the goods in good condition; (3) they did not enter into trade or consumption; and (4) they remained in temporary storage under prescribed conditions and for a prescribed period.[184]

The decision of the Exchequer Court, affirmed by the Supreme Court of Canada, in *Carter, Macy & Co v Canada*[185] illustrates the issue. In that case, tea had been imported from Japan and shipped to New York where it remained in a bonded warehouse for several months. It was entered for exportation to Canada in New York. The invoice for one shipment was marked "in transit to Canada"; in the consular invoice for another shipment, the tea appeared to be consigned to the plaintiff's brokers in New York for transhipment to Canada. The issue was whether this was a direct importation into Canada from Japan via New York, and therefore free from customs duty, or whether the goods were imported from the United States, and therefore dutiable. The court held that this was tea from the United States, that is, tea imported from the United States, even though not the growth and produce of the United States.

d) Goods in Transit: Section 26

If goods with a preferential tariff treatment are already in transit to Canada when the Governor in Council, under sections 31(1)(b), 38(1)(b), or 42(1)(b),

---

183 *Direct Shipment of Goods Regulations*, SOR/86-876 (enacted under the *Customs Act*).
184 Ibid; *Haiti Deemed Direct Shipment (General Preferential Tariff and Least Developed Country Tariff) Regulations*, SOR/2010-58 (enacted under the *Customs Tariff*).
185 (1890), 2 Ex CR 126, aff'd (1890), 18 SCR 706.

changes the tariff treatment of those goods to remove the preferential treatment, those goods are entitled to retain the tariff treatment that was applicable immediately before that time.

2) Marking of Goods

Marking complements the rules on the origin of goods. Both the *Customs Tariff* and the *Customs Act* contain provisions requiring imported goods to be marked. For marking purposes, regulations authorized by section 19(1) of the *Customs Tariff* prescribe the country or geographic area of origin of imported goods, the manner in which the goods must be marked, and when they must be marked, that is to say, whether before or after importation.[186]

If imported goods are not marked as required by the regulations, section 35.02(2) of the *Customs Act* empowers a designated CBSA officer to require the importer to mark the goods within the time stipulated in the notice.

F. TARIFF TREATMENT

1) Introduction

Bilateral trade accords and free trade partner agreements constitute a key element of the *Customs Tariff*. A significant part of the Act is concerned with these and other tariff treatments, such as agreements with Australia and New Zealand, and unilateral concessions to Commonwealth Caribbean countries, developing countries, and least developed countries. The *Customs Tariff* deals with the implementation of those accords, agreements, and concessions, as well as safeguard measures that are designed to protect Canadian industries, workers, and consumers, and the economy as a whole. These agreements and accords are summarized in the following paragraphs.

2) Most-Favoured-Nation Treatment

The *World Trade Organization Agreement*, under which the Most-Favoured-Nation treatment is accorded, is a multilateral treaty. This status is given to 222 countries, which include 150 of the 153 current members of the World Trade

---

186 *Marking of Imported Goods Regulations*, SOR/94-10, am SOR/96-302, SOR/98-83; *Determination of the Country of Origin for the Purposes of Marking of Goods (NAFTA Countries) Regulations*, SOR/94-23, am SOR/95-447, SOR/98-28, SOR/2002-129, SOR/2013-100. See also Customs D Memorandum D11-3-3, "NAFTA Country of Origin Marking Rules" (23 March 2007).

Organization (WTO). They are, *ipso jure*, entitled to MFN treatment under the *WTO Agreement*. In addition to the 150 WTO members, Canada has extended the MFN status to 72 non-WTO members through bilateral agreements.

3) Free Trade Agreements

Within the MFNT group, there is currently a small group of thirteen with whom bilateral free trade agreements have been concluded by Canada, and a few more agreements are in the pipeline. These, with the symbol denoting them in the Schedule to the *Customs Tariff* shown in brackets, are: United States and Mexico (*NAFTA*, with which the earlier *Canada-US Free Trade Agreement* was rolled over), Chile (*CCFTA*), and Israel and beneficiaries (*CIFTA*) (this first group of four has been designated in the *Customs Tariff* as "free trade partners"); Colombia (*CCOFTA*), Costa Rica (*CCRFTA*), Panama (*CPAFTA*), and Peru (*CPFTA*); the four European Free Trade Association members (*EFTA*): Iceland (IT), Norway (NT), Liechtenstein, and Switzerland (SLT); and Jordan (JT). Perhaps when goods from each of this second group of nine has reached the final rate of "free" at the end of the "staging categories," they too may be designated as "free trade partners."

Free trade negotiations have been concluded with Honduras and are ongoing with the CARICOM member countries, Dominion Republic, India, Japan, Korea, Morocco, Ukraine and the European Union, as well as countries of the Trans-Pacific region, such as Australia, Brunei Darussalam, Malaysia, New Zealand, Singapore, and Vietnam.

4) GPT, LDCT, and CCCT; AUT and NZT

Within the MFNT, a large group of over 100 countries are accorded, unilaterally by Canada, General Preferential Tariff (GPT) treatment. Just under half of them are least-developed countries and get further preference under the Least-Developed-Country Tariff (LDCT). Their preferential tariff was scheduled to expire in June 2014, but has now been extended by ten years.

Commonwealth Caribbean countries are accorded preferred tariff status under the Commonwealth Caribbean Countries Tariff (CCCT).

Canada also grants preferential treatment for certain specified goods from Australia (AUT) and New Zealand (NZT). Trade relations with Australia have been governed by a special trade agreement since 1925, and while there is no such agreement with New Zealand, the British Preferential Tariff (BPT) given to it since 1904 continues under the NZT.

Most of the above preferred arrangements are a historical legacy from the British colonial era, when dominions and colonies, including Canada, were granted preferential status by Britain to goods under imperial and colonial tariffs. Canada extended the preferential treatment to India, South Africa, the British West Indies, and New Zealand by 1904 and to practically the whole of the dependent Empire by 1913. Until recently, it was called the British Preferential Tariff.

5) Claiming Duty-Free or Preferential Treatment

To receive duty-free or reduced tariffs under preferential treatment, goods must be eligible, and the goods must be shipped directly from the beneficiary country with or without transhipment. To be eligible, sufficient manufacturing must be performed in the country of origin, and the importer must possess valid proof of origin, normally a certificate of origin signed by the exporter in the beneficiary country.[187] However, this condition is relaxed in the case of certain textile goods originating in North America under the *NAFTA* tariff treatment, and in Costa Rica.

Even if the rules of origin are not met, duty-free treatment may still be available under other tariff items, such as those that allow goods imported "for use in" goods being manufactured in Canada (Chapter 99) or under tariff item 9979.00.00 for goods specifically designed to assist persons with certain disabilities in alleviating the effects of those disabilities.[188]

Section 25 of the *Customs Tariff* stipulates that if under the Act goods are entitled to both the MFNT and another tariff (other than the General Tariff) and the amount of customs duty imposed under the MFNT is lower than the amount imposed under the other tariff, the rate of customs duty under the MFNT applies to those goods in lieu of the rate under the other tariff.

6) General Tariff

Where there is no trade accord or agreement between Canada and another country, under section 29(1) of the Act, those countries are entitled only to the General Tariff (GT) rate of 35 percent, which rate is indicated by the abbreviation "N/A" in the List of Tariff Provisions. North Korea is one of the countries subject to GT rates by default.

---

187 See Section E(1), above in this chapter, and above note 174 (proof of origin).
188 See Section D(10)(c), above in this chapter.

The GT rate also applies to goods that originate from countries not mentioned in the List of Countries in the Schedule to the *Customs Tariff* and to goods that originate from countries set out in that list but that fail to meet the requirements for entitlement to any other tariff treatment. It also applies to goods in respect of which the MFNT is withdrawn by an order made under section 31(1)(b).

An exception to the application of the GT is provided by section 29(2). If the MFNT is equal to or greater than the GT, or if a Note or Supplementary Note to a Chapter of the List of Tariff Provisions or a tariff item so provides, then the MFNT applies.

7) Most-Favoured-Nation Tariff

MFNT rates are accorded to WTO members and to the non-WTO members that are named in the List of Countries set out in the Schedule to the *Customs Tariff*—to the WTO members as required by the *WTO Agreement*, and to the non-WTO members by virtue of the bilateral agreement that Canada has signed with them.

To be entitled, section 24(1) requires that (a) the goods should originate in the country from which they are exported and proof of origin of the goods be given in accordance with the *Customs Act*; and (b) the goods should be entitled to that tariff treatment in accordance with regulations made under section 16 of the *Customs Tariff* or under an order of the Governor in Council made under section 16(2).

The MFNT rates are set out opposite a tariff item in the Schedule to the *Customs Tariff*. If a rate is denoted by the letter "A," the rate that is set out is the final rate. If it is denoted by letters "B" to "E," and "G," the rate under each became final on or before 1 January 2004, as indicated in section 30. If it is denoted by the letter "F," the MFNT rate that applies to those goods is the initial rate reduced as provided in the "F" Staging List.

a) Most Favourable Tariff

In accordance with section 26, if under the Act goods are entitled to both the MFNT and another Tariff (not being the General Tariff) and the amount of customs duty imposed under the MFNT is lower than the amount imposed under the other Tariff, the rate of customs duty under the MFNT applies to those goods in lieu of the rate under the other Tariff.

MFNT treatment is critically important for smaller economies that do not get special tariff treatment from Canada, because it lowers the cost of their exports and makes them more competitive and, in turn, increases their exports and their country's economic growth.

b) Grant of More Preferred Status

The *WTO Agreement* permits countries to accord a more preferred status than MFNT, subject to the conditions specifically set out therein. Canada has accorded preferred status under bilateral free trade agreements or by unilateral grants, such as the GPT, LDCT, and CCCT, but if a country fails to meet its commitments under the FTAs or unilateral grants, it becomes ineligible to receive the lower rates, which may be withdrawn for a period of time, or in respect of certain goods, but the goods would still enjoy the MFNT treatment except in specified cases. Nevertheless, the new tariff rate cannot exceed the GT rate of 35 percent.

Section 31 of the *Customs Tariff* empowers the Governor in Council to make an order extending the MFNT rate to countries not entitled to it, and to withdraw the MFNT rate from those who are entitled to it. A legislated procedure, involving Parliamentary approval, has to be complied with before making such an order.

8) General Preferential Tariff

The General Preferential Tariff (GPT) was introduced in 1974 by Canada and by other developed economies, including the United States, the European Union, and Japan following a recommendation by the United Nations Conference on Trade and Development. Under the GPT, developing countries designated in the List of Countries in the Schedule to the *Customs Tariff* are entitled to duty-free or preferential tariff rates that are lower than the standard MFNT rates until June 2014, when the program expires and will be reviewed.

Duty-free benefit under the GPT is given to most goods (about 67 percent of tariff items), but dairy products, poultry, eggs, refined sugar, and most textiles, clothing, and footwear are not eligible.

The GPT applies to goods that originate from those countries. Goods originate in a beneficiary country if the value of the materials, parts, or products is 60 percent of the ex-factory price of the goods as packed for shipment to Canada.

The GPT rate is set out under the Preferential Tariff Rate column and denoted by the abbreviation "GPT." By section 33, if the letter "A" is set out in the column, it is the final rate. If the rate is denoted by the letter "F," the initial rate is reduced as provided in the "F" Staging List. If "J" is set out, the GPT rate that applies to those goods is the initial rate, reduced by one percentage point on January 1 of each year after 1998, until the difference between the reduced rate and the final rate is less than one percentage point, at which time the final rate applies.

a) Tariff Rate Quota

The Governor in Council is authorized by section 35 to set a tariff rate quota (TRQ) in respect of particular goods for a specified period. If goods are imported in excess of the TRQ, they are ineligible for the GPT, in which case the rate otherwise applicable would be charged on the excess quantities, but that rate will not be more than the MFNT. The TRQs are administered by the Department of Foreign Affairs and International Trade under the *Export and Import Permits Act*.

b) Extension and Withdrawal of GPT

Section 34 authorizes the Governor in Council to extend entitlement to the GPT to any goods that originate in a country that is a beneficiary of the MFNT if, in the opinion of the Governor in Council, that country is a developing country, and to withdraw such entitlement.

c) Expiry Date

Section 36 stipulates that the GPT rate expires on 30 June 2014 or on such earlier date as may be fixed by order of the Governor in Council. The Government has announced that it will be reviewing the continued need of granting general preferential tariff rates. This date was extended by ten years, to 30 June 2024, by an amendment to the section in 2013.

9) Least-Developed-Country Tariff

Canada has granted to forty-eight of the forty-nine countries considered by the United Nations as least developed, the LDCT treatment. The LDCT provides duty-free access for most imports from these countries. Following the Market Access Initiative, which came into effect in January 2003, close to 99 percent of exports to Canada of LDCT goods are eligible for duty-free and quota-free treatment. The remaining 1 percent is subject to either the GPT or the MFNT; the latter rate also applies to dairy, poultry, and egg products, which have been excluded from preferential treatment under the LDCT.

To qualify for LDCT duty-free treatment, at least 60 percent of the ex-factory price of the goods packed for shipment to Canada must originate in one or more LDCT beneficiary countries. Goods must also satisfy legal requirements respecting rules of origin, certification, and direct shipment described in Section E(1)(c), above in this chapter.

The LDCT rate is set out under the Preferential Tariff Rate column and denoted by the abbreviation "LDCT." Under section 37, if the letter "A" is set out in the column, it is the final rate. If the rate is denoted by the letter "F," the initial rate is reduced as provided in the "F" Staging List.

a) Tariff Rate Quota

The Governor in Council is authorized by section 39 to set a TRQ in respect of particular goods for a specified period. If goods are imported in excess of the TRQ, they are ineligible for the LDCT, in which case the rate otherwise applicable would be charged on the excess quantities. That rate will not be more than the MFNT.

b) Extension and Withdrawal of LDCT

Section 38 authorizes the Governor in Council to make an order extending entitlement to the LDCT to any goods that originate in a country that is a beneficiary of the GPT or MFNT if, in the opinion of the Governor in Council, that country is a least-developed country, and to withdraw entitlement to the LDCT from such goods.

c) Expiry Date

Section 40 stipulates that the LDCT rate expires on 30 June 2014 or on such earlier date as may be fixed by order of the Governor in Council. This date was extended by ten years, to 30 June 2024, by an amendment to the section in 2013.

10) Commonwealth Caribbean Countries Tariff

Fourteen Commonwealth Caribbean countries have been granted by section 41 the CCCT rate in respect of certain goods. The tariff is shown under the Preferential Tariff column in the List of Tariff Provisions, by the abbreviation "CCCT."

Under section 41(2), if the letter "A" is set out in the column, it is the final rate. If the rate is denoted by the letter "F," the initial rate is reduced as provided in the "F" Staging List.

To qualify for the duty-free or reduced tariffs, at least 60 percent of the ex-factory price of the goods as packed for shipment to Canada must originate in one or more beneficiary countries or Canada. The 60 percent qualifying content may be cumulated from various beneficiary countries or Canada. The goods must be finished in the beneficiary country in the form in which they were imported into Canada.

a) Tariff Rate Quota

The Governor in Council is authorized by section 43 to set a TRQ in respect of particular goods for a specified period. If goods are imported in excess of the TRQ, they are ineligible for CCCT, in which case the rate otherwise applicable would be charged on the excess quantities. That rate will not be more than the MFNT.

b) Extension and Withdrawal of CCCT

Section 42 authorizes the Governor in Council to extend the entitlement to the CCCT to any goods that originate in a country that is a beneficiary of that rate; to reduce the tariff rate in the "F" Staging List, and to withdraw entitlement to the CCCT from any such goods.

11) Australia Tariff and New Zealand Tariff

In accordance with section 44, qualifying goods that originate in Australia or New Zealand are entitled to the Australia Tariff (AUT) and the New Zealand Tariff (NZT), respectively.

The AUT and NZT rates are shown under the Preferential Tariff column in the List of Tariff Provisions by the abbreviation "AUT" or "NZT," as the case may be.

Goods are considered to originate in Australia or New Zealand if not less than 50 percent of the cost of production of those goods was incurred by the industry of Australia or New Zealand, as the case may be, or Canada, and the goods were finished in Australia or New Zealand in the form in which they were imported into Canada. Goods must also be shipped directly to Canada, without transhipment.

Under section 44(3), if the letter "A" is set out in the column, it is the final rate. If the rate is denoted by the letters "B" or "E," the rates shown under those columns became final effective 1 January 2000 and 1 January 2004, respectively. If the letter "F" is shown, the initial rate is reduced as provided in the "F" Staging List.

12) United States Tariff, Mexico Tariff, and Mexico–United States Tariff

The *North American Free Trade Agreement* (*NAFTA*) was signed in January 1994 with the aim of eliminating customs duties on most goods traded amongst the three trade partners, the United States, Canada, and Mexico. There was a ten-year transition period during which the rates were progressively reduced to zero, some in equal stages over five, six, and ten years; others in unequal stages over eight years. Since the *Canada-US Free Trade Agreement*, signed five years earlier, was rolled into the *NAFTA*, it was agreed that the phase-out of rates under the original agreement would not be affected; the phase-out was completed on 1 January 1998. As of that date, virtually all tariffs on Canada-US trade in originating goods were eliminated. Some tariffs remain in place for certain products in Canada's supply-managed sectors (for example, eggs, dairy, and poultry products). In the United States, tariffs remain in place for certain products such as sugar, dairy, peanuts, and cotton.

During the ten-year transition period (ending 1 January 2003), there were three different rates: the US Tariff (UST) for goods originating exclusively from the United States; the Mexico Tariff (MT) for goods exclusively originating from Mexico; and the Mexico-US Tariff (MUST), where it was uncertain whether goods originated exclusively from either country.

a) US Tariff

The UST rates apply to goods originating in the United States where the goods are wholly obtained or produced in the US or the goods have been processed or assembled in the US such that sufficient transformation has occurred to result in a change in tariff classification. On 1 January 2003, the final phase-out of tariffs was completed.

b) Mexico Tariff

The MT rates were incorporated in the *NAFTA* Tariff when Mexico became the third partner to the *NAFTA*, in 1994. The MT rates followed the same pattern as the UST rates, being progressively reduced to zero. On 1 January 2003, the final phase-out of tariffs was completed.

c) Mexico–United States Tariff

The MUST rate applies to goods that qualify under the *NAFTA* but fail to meet the requirements for either rate. The MUST is the default *NAFTA* treatment. On 1 January 2003, the final phase-out of tariffs was completed.

d) Extension of UST and MT

Section 45(13) authorizes the Minister of Finance by an order to extend entitlement to the UST or the MT to any imported goods under such conditions as may be specified in the order for the purpose of giving effect to Appendix 6 of Annex 300-B of Chapter Three of the *North American Free Trade Agreement*, notwithstanding any other provision of the *Customs Tariff*.

13) Chile Tariff

The *Canada-Chile Free Trade Agreement* (CCFTA) was signed on 5 July 1997. It covers mainly agricultural and food products, which became duty free either immediately or within five to ten years. The Chili Tariff (CT) rate applies to goods originating in Chile. By 1 January 2003, duties on all qualifying goods were eliminated.

a) Tariff Rate Quota

Section 49(1) provided for tariff rate quotas, but they were eliminated on 31 December 2002, when the CT rate of "Free" came into effect the next day.

b) Extension of Chile Tariff

Section 48 authorizes the Minister of Finance by an order to extend entitlement to the CT rate to any goods under such conditions as may be specified in the order for the purpose of giving effect to Appendix 5.1 of Annex C-00-B of the *CCFTA*, notwithstanding any other provision of the *Customs Tariff*.

14) Colombia Tariff

The *Canada-Colombia Free Trade Agreement* (CCOFTA) was signed on 21 November 2008. Section 49.01 eliminated tariffs on most goods exported to Canada from Colombia, some immediately and others progressively over a period of seventeen years.

The initial Colombia Tariff (COLT) rate becomes the final rate of "Free" if the letter "A" appears in relation to the goods concerned. If the letter "F" appears, the reduction is as provided in the "F" Staging List.

There were three further stages of reduction: "S1," "S2," and "S3." The reduction in the "S1" and "S2" stages to zero rate is now complete; the reduction in the "S3" stage to the final rate of "Free" will be completed in 2025.

a) Extension of Colombia Tariff

Section 49.08 authorizes the Minister of Finance by an order to extend entitlement to the COLT to any goods under such conditions as may be specified in the order for the purpose of giving effect to Article 317 of the *CCOFTA*, notwithstanding any other provision of the *Customs Tariff*.

15) Costa Rica Tariff

The *Canada-Costa Rica Free Trade Agreement* (*CCRFTA*) was signed on 23 April 2001. The Agreement covers mainly some key Canadian export interests such as automotive goods, environmental goods, pre-fabricated buildings, and some construction products such as steel structures. Most of the industrial products covered in the Agreement became duty free.

a) Application of Costa Rica Tariff

Section 49.1 provides that goods originating in Costa Rica are entitled to the Costa Rica Tariff (CRT) rate of customs duty, subject to proof of origin and other requirements set out in section 24. By section 49.1(2), if the letter "A" is set out in the List of Tariff Provisions, the CRT rate that applies to those goods is the final rate of "Free." By section 49.1(3), if the letter "F" is set out, the CRT rate that applies to those goods is the initial rate, reduced as provided in the "F" staging list.

There were four stages in the Staging List: "M," "N," "O," and "P." For goods where "M" is set out, the CRT rate that applied was the initial rate reduced to a final rate of "Free" when the Minister is satisfied that Costa Rica has eliminated all business income tax exemptions and other export subsidies in respect of goods produced wholly or partially within a geographic area, as defined in section 16(2.1). Section 49.4 authorized the Governor in Council to reduce the rate in this staging period. By 1 January 2011, the final rate of "Free" on all qualifying goods became effective.

b) Extension of Costa Rica Tariff

Section 49.2 authorizes the Minister of Finance by an order to extend entitlement to the CRT to any goods under such conditions as may be specified in the order, for the purpose of giving effect to Appendix III.1.6.1 of Annex III.1 of the CCRFTA, notwithstanding any other provision of the *Customs Tariff*.

16) Peru Tariff

The *Canada-Peru Free Trade Agreement* (*CPFTA*) was signed on 1 August 2009. Section 49.5 of the *Customs Tariff* eliminates tariffs on most goods exported to Canada from Peru, some immediately and others progressively over a period of five years.

a) Application of Peru Tariff

Goods imported from Peru are entitled to the Peru Tariff (PT) if they originate in Peru and proof of origin and other requirements of section 24 are met.

The initial PT rate becomes the final rate of "Free" if the letter "A" appears in relation to the goods concerned. If the letter "F" appears, the reduction is as provided in the "F" Staging List.

There are two further stages of reduction: "R1" and "R2." The "R1" rate became the final rate of "Free" on 1 January 2011; "R2" rates will become the final rate of "Free" on 1 January 2015.

b) Extension of Peru Tariff

Section 49.08 authorizes the Minister of Finance by an order to extend entitlement to the PT to any goods, under such conditions as may be specified in the order for the purpose of giving effect to Article 317 of the *CPFTA*, notwithstanding any other provision of the *Customs Tariff*.

c) Tariff Rate Quota

Section 49.5(9) authorizes the Governor in Council to pass an order on the recommendation of the Minister of Finance imposing a TRQ on tariff items 1701.91.10, 1701.99.10, 1702.90.21, 1702.90.61, 1702.90.70, and 1702.90.81 that are entitled to the PT rates, and the limits apply during the periods and subject to the conditions that may be specified in the order.

17) Canada-Israel Tariff

The preferential tariff accorded to Israel and territories over which it exercises *de facto* control is the result of the *Canada-Israel Free Trade Agreement* (*CIFTA*), implemented on 1 January 1997. The Agreement covers mainly agrifood products, most of which are duty free, but not the dairy and poultry sectors, which are sensitive to both countries.

a) Application of Canada-Israel Tariff

Section 50 provides that goods originating in Israel or another *CIFTA* beneficiary, subject to their meeting proof of origin and other requirements specified in section 24, are entitled to the Canada-Israel Agreement Tariff (CIAT) rates of customs duty. Pursuant to section 52, the Governor in Council, on the recommendation of the Minister of Finance, may define the expression "Israel or another *CIFTA* beneficiary" and "imported from Israel or another *CIFTA* beneficiary." Currently, the beneficiaries are the Israeli occupied territories of East Jerusalem, the Golan Heights, the West Bank, and the Gaza Strip.

For products listed under the letter "A" in the List of Tariff Provisions, the CIAT rate that applies is the final rate. If the goods come under letter "F," the CIAT rate is reduced as provided in the "F" Staging List.

b) Tariff Rate Quota

Section 51 authorizes the Governor in Council to make an order on the recommendation of the Minister of Foreign Affairs, to set a TRQ on roses under tariff item 0603.10.11 that are entitled to the CIAT rate during the periods that may be specified in the order.

18) Canada-European Free Trade Association Tariff

The *Canada-European Free Trade Association Free Trade Agreement* (CEFTA FTA) was signed on 1 July 2009. CEFTA FTA contains three separate agreements, one each with Iceland and Norway, and the third with Switzerland and Liechtenstein. As the provisions in all three agreements are identical, they are treated together in this and later sections. Goods from these four countries are entitled, respectively, to (1) the Iceland Tariff (IT) under section 52.1, (2) the Norway Tariff (NT) under section 52.2, and (3) the Switzerland-Liechtenstein Tariff (SLT), under section 52.3, if the goods originate in those countries, proof of origin is given, and the other requirements of section 24 are met.

a) Iceland Tariff

The IT rates of customs duty for goods imported from Iceland are set out in the List of Tariff Provisions under the abbreviation "IT," against which an "A" rate, an "F" Staging List, and "Q1" and "Q2" staging are shown.

b) Norway Tariff

The NT rates of customs duty for goods imported from Norway are set out in the List of Tariff Provisions under the abbreviation "NT," against which an "A" rate, an "F" Staging List, and "Q1" and "Q2" staging are shown.

c) **Switzerland-Liechtenstein Tariffs**
The SLT rates of customs duty for goods imported from Switzerland and Liechtenstein are set out in the List of Tariff Provisions under the abbreviation "SLT," against which an "A" rate, an "F" Staging List, and "Q1" and "Q2" staging are shown.

If "A" is set out, the IT, NT, and SLT rates that apply are the final rates. If "F" is set out, the rates that apply are the initial rates reduced as provided in the "F" Staging List.

If "Q1" is set out, effective on the day that is three years after the day on which sections 52.1(4) to 52.4(4) come into force, the rates are reduced to ⅞ths of the initial rates, and thereafter progressively each year by ⅛th until ten years after that day, to the final rate of "Free." If "Q2" is set out, effective on the day that is three years after the day on which sections 52.1(4) to 52.4(4) come into force, the rates are reduced to 12⁄13ths of the initial rates, and thereafter progressively each year by 1⁄16th until fifteen years after that day, to the final rate of "Free."

19) Jordan Tariff

The *Canada-Jordan Economic Growth and Prosperity Act* was enacted in 2012 to give effect to the free trade and side agreements signed by the two countries on 28 June 2009. Section 54.5 was added to the *Customs Tariff* eliminating tariffs on most goods exported to Canada from Jordan, some immediately and others progressively over a period specified in the "F" staging category. Goods of tariff items specified in Schedule 3 to that Act are excluded.

a) **Application of Jordan Tariff**
Goods imported from Jordan are entitled to the Jordan Tariff (JT) rates if they originate in Jordan and proof of origin and other requirements of section 24 are met.

20) Panama Tariff

The *Canada-Panama Economic Growth and Prosperity Act* was enacted in 2012 to give effect to the free trade and side agreements signed by the two countries on 13 and 14 May 2010. Section 49.41 was added to the *Customs Tariff* eliminating tariffs on most goods exported to Canada from Panama, some immediately and others progressively over a period of fourteen years after the agreement comes into force. Goods of tariff items specified in Schedule 4 to the *Canada-Panama Economic Growth and Prosperity Act* are excluded, but the goods specified in tariff items listed in Schedule 5 have "free" status as of the dates shown in the letters T1, T2, or T3 and set out against them in the List of Tariff Provisions of the Schedule to the *Customs Tariff*.

a) Application of Panama Tariff

Goods imported from Panama are entitled to the Panama Tariff (PAT) rates if they originate in Panama and proof of origin and other requirements of section 24 are met.

G. SPECIAL MEASURES, EMERGENCY MEASURES, AND SAFEGUARDS

1) Introduction

This section describes the safeguard provisions of the *Customs Tariff* through which the government is authorized to (1) suspend or withdraw rights or privileges granted by Canada under trade agreements, including free trade agreements; (2) impose surtaxes or tariff rate quotas on imports from those countries; (3) take bilateral measures provided for in free trade agreements against free trade partners; and (4) impose specific safeguard measures against market disruption and trade diversion by the People's Republic of China. It also describes the provisions relating to surtaxes on any goods that are designed to safeguard Canada's financial position, a measure that is rarely used. The safeguard measures under the *Customs Tariff* are independent of the special measures taken under the *Special Import Measures Act* to combat dumping and subsidizing of exported goods, which are the subject of the next chapter.

Common to all safeguard measures are the following statutory requirements. The government must use its power only through an order of the Governor in Council, which must,

1) adhere to the prescribed procedure, such as a recommendation from the designated Minister, an Inquiry, or an Investigation by the Tribunal and approval by Parliament, within the period set out in the *Customs Tariff*;
2) not breach Canada's obligations under free trade agreements; and
3) not breach Canada's obligations under the *General Agreement on Tariffs and Trade (GATT 1994)* and the *World Trade Organization Agreement*. The

WTO Agreement and the *Protocol on the Accession of the People's Republic of China to the WTO* (the Protocol) permit Canada to impose China-specific measures, respectively. The Protocol expired on 11 December 2013.

Any domestic producer of goods that are like or directly competitive with goods being imported into Canada, or any person or association acting on behalf of any such domestic producer, may file a written complaint with the Tribunal alleging that the imported goods are being imported in such increased quantities and under such conditions as to cause or threaten serious injury to domestic producers of like or directly competitive goods. With respect to imports from China, the complaint must allege (1) that the imports cause or threaten to cause market disruption, or that (2) an action taken by China affecting imports of its goods into the market of another WTO country causes or threatens to cause a significant diversion of trade into Canada.

The government may also direct the Tribunal by way of an order in council to commence an inquiry and make recommendations as to the most appropriate remedy that would address the effects of dumping, or, in the case of dumping by China, of market disruption or trade diversion. However, the government does not have to accept those recommendations.

The following measures are described in this section:

1) Special measures against goods imported from any country (Global Emergency measures),
2) Surtaxes against goods imported from a free trade partner,
3) Safeguard measures for agricultural goods,
4) Bilateral emergency measures,
5) safeguard measures against goods imported from China, and
6) surtaxes to safeguard Canada's external financial position.

There have been only a few inquiries under these provisions. A few relevant ones are reported in this section to illustrate the process.

2) Global Emergency Measures

a) Enforcing Rights under Trade Agreements

Section 53(1) of the *Customs Tariff* authorizes the Governor in Council to make an order against any country with which Canada has signed a trade agreement, on the recommendation of the Minister of Finance and the Minister of Foreign Affairs, if the acts, policies, or practices of the government of that country; of a state, regional, or local government of that country; or of an association of countries of which the country is a member adversely affect, directly or indirectly, trade in goods and services of Canada, to take one or more of the following measures in order to enforce Canada's rights under the trade agreement:

1) suspend or withdraw the rights or privileges granted by Canada under the trade agreement;
2) impose a surtax on the goods, or class of goods, that originate in the country or that are entitled to a preferential tariff treatment, in addition to the applicable customs and other duties;
3) include the goods on the Import Control List established under section 5 of the *Export and Import Permits Act*; and
4) levy a duty on the goods at a rate that varies from time to time as the quantity of those goods imported during a period specified in the order equals or exceeds totals set out in the order.

The Minister of Finance is required to table a copy of the order containing the above-noted measures before Parliament on any of the first fifteen days after the making of the order that either House of Parliament is sitting.

b) Tribunal Inquiries

INQUIRY 1: IMPORTATION OF CERTAIN STEEL GOODS

This Global Safeguard Inquiry on Certain Steel Goods[189] was commenced by the Tribunal on 21 March 2002 on a reference by the Governor in Council pursuant to the recommendation of the Ministers of Finance and for International Trade. Its purpose was to determine whether certain steel goods were being imported into Canada since the beginning of 1996 from all sources in such quantities and under such conditions as to be a principal cause of serious injury or threat thereof to domestic producers of like or directly competitive goods. If the Tribunal made injury determinations with respect to a product, it was directed to make recommendations as to the most appropriate remedy, over a period of three years, to address the injury caused or threatened to be caused by increased imports of that product. In addition, the Tribunal was directed to provide recommendations to exclude, from any remedy, goods that were not available from domestic producers.

---

189 Reference GC-2001-001, Tribunal's recommendation (4 July 2002).

Nine different steel products were subject to the Inquiry. Four free trade partners and several other developed and developing countries were included. The top five exporters were the United States (the largest exporter), Germany, the People's Republic of China, and Brazil. Over 175 interested parties participated in the Inquiry, and more than 100 witnesses testified at the two public hearings that the Tribunal held, the first dealing with injury and the second with remedies.

The Tribunal found that increased imports were a principal cause of serious injury to domestic producers of discrete plate, cold-rolled sheet and coil, reinforcing bar, angles, shapes and sections, and standard pipe. Of the four free trade partners, the Tribunal found that Mexico, Israel and its dependent territories, and Chile were not contributing importantly to the serious injury, but the United States was, except in respect of the fifth product, reinforcing bars. The Tribunal also determined that with respect to the remaining four steel products, increased imports were not a principal cause of serious injury or threat of serious injury to domestic producers.

In its report to the Governor in Council dated 19 August 2002, the Tribunal recommended that tariff rate quotas were the most appropriate remedy that would address the effects of dumping of the four steel products by the United States, but in respect of the fifth product, as no serious injury was caused or threatened, a tariff rate would be the most appropriate remedy. It also recommended the exclusion from any safeguard remedy of imports from countries considered to be developing countries by the Development Assistance Committee of the Organisation for Economic Co-operation and Development (OECD) that met the volume criteria for developing countries as set out in the WTO *Agreement on Safeguards*. The Tribunal further recommended that the government grant, in full or in part, 215 requests that certain goods be excluded from any safeguard remedy.

The government, however, decided not to implement the recommendations.

INQUIRY 2: BICYCLES AND FINISHED PAINTED BICYCLE FRAMES
These two Global Safeguard Inquiries[190] were combined by the Tribunal. Their purpose was to determine whether bicycles (assembled and unassembled) and bicycle frames (finished painted) were being imported into Canada from all sources in such increased quantities under such conditions as to be the principal cause of serious injury, or threat thereof, to domestic produ-

---

190 Global Safeguard Inquiry into the Importation of Bicycles and Finished Painted Bicycle Frames, GS-2004-001, GS-2004-002 (2005), 10 TTR (2d) 1.

cers of like or directly competitive goods. The predominant exporters were the People's Republic of China, the Republic of China (Taiwan), and the United States. The inquiry was initiated on the basis of a complaint by the Canadian Bicycle Manufacturers. The subject of the complaint were those bicycles with a wheel diameter of 15 inches (38.1 centimetres) or greater, assembled or unassembled, and finished painted bicycle frames.

Fifty parties filed notices with the Tribunal indicating that they wished to participate.

The Tribunal found that there had been a recent, sharp, sudden, and significant increase in the importation of bicycles, both in absolute terms and relative to the production in Canada of like or directly competitive goods, and that the increased imports were a principal cause of serious injury to domestic producers of bicycles in the form of a serious deterioration in production, capacity utilization, sales volume, market share, sales revenue, cash flow, employment, and ability to invest.

The Tribunal also examined several other factors alleged to have caused injury to domestic producers but found that none was a principal cause of the injury.

The Tribunal determined that the quantity of bicycles imported from each of Canada's free trade partners did not account for a substantial share of total imports, and concluded that its finding was not changed by the exclusion of imports from those countries.

With respect to Canada's obligations under the *GATT 1994*, the Tribunal found that the significant increase in imports of bicycles was due to unforeseen developments and resulted from the effect of the obligations incurred by Canada under the *GATT*.

As to the most appropriate remedy, the Tribunal considered that a surtax over three years at 30 percent in the first year, 25 percent in the second, and 20 percent in the third should be applied to imports of bicycles, assembled or unassembled, with a wheel diameter greater than 15 inches (38.1 centimetres), with Free on Board (FOB) value of $225 or less. It recommended the exclusion of certain products for which it had received requests, as well as bicycles from Canada's free trade partners and certain developing countries.

With respect to finished painted bicycle frames, although there had been a recent, sharp, sudden, and significant increase in imports of those products in absolute terms and relative to the production in Canada of like or directly competitive goods, because no serious injury was alleged by the complainant, nor did the evidence indicate that such injury had occurred, and after deducting imports by domestic producers, the Tribunal determined that the remaining volume and increase in imported finished painted bicycle frames were insufficient to threaten serious injury to domestic producers of finished painted bicycle frames.

The government, however, announced in a 29 May 2006 news release that, after considering all the representations it received, it would not impose a surtax on bicycles, assembled or unassembled.

3) Surtaxes on Goods from a Free Trade Partner

Sections 55, 60, and 68 of the *Customs Tariff* authorize the levy of surtaxes on goods imported from a free trade partner country; sections 55 and 60 on goods other than prescribed agricultural goods, and section 68 on prescribed agricultural goods. In addition, a surtax can also be levied by way of an extension order under section 63. The conditions for the levy are specified below.

a) NAFTA Partner, Chile, or Peru

A surtax under section 55(1) can be levied by an order of the Governor in Council on goods being imported from a *NAFTA* partner country, Chile, or Peru on the basis of a report of the Minister of Finance, or as a result of an inquiry made by the Tribunal under section 20 or 26 of the *Canadian International Trade Tribunal Act*[191] (*CITT Act*), that goods are being imported under such conditions as to cause or threaten serious injury to domestic producers of like or directly competitive goods, when imported into Canada or a region or part of Canada specified in the order.

The rate specified in the order (1) may vary from time to time as the quantity of those goods imported into Canada or that region or part of Canada during a period specified in the order equals or exceeds quantities specified in the order, and (2) may not exceed the rate that, in the opinion of the Governor in Council, is sufficient to prevent or remedy serious injury to domestic producers of like or directly competitive goods.

Before making the report to the Governor in Council, the Minister must be of the opinion that critical circumstances exist or that the report relates to perishable agricultural goods.

i) Goods in Transit

An Order made under section 55(1) may provide that goods that are in transit to Canada at the time the Order comes into force are entitled to the

---

191 RSC 1985, c 47 (4th Supp).

tariff treatment that was applicable to those goods immediately before that time.[192]

ii) Inquiry by Tribunal

If an Order imposing the surtax is made on the basis of the Minister's report, the Governor in Council is required immediately to refer the matter to the Tribunal for an inquiry under section 20(a) of the *CITT Act*.[193]

iii) Limitations on Making Second Surtax Order

An order made under section 55 has effect for a maximum of four years. If it was effective for a period of less than four years, a second surtax order may not be made within two years of the lapsing of the first order. If it was effective for a period of 180 days, a further order may be made with respect to the goods if at least one year has elapsed since the previous order took effect and not more than two orders have been made with respect to the same goods within the period of five years before the further order takes effect.

An order made on the basis of a report of the Minister ceases to have effect at the end of the 200th day after the day on which the order was made, unless, before the order ceases to have effect, an inquiry made by the Tribunal under section 20 or 26 of the *CITT Act* confirms that the goods are being imported from a country named in the report under such conditions as to cause or threaten serious injury to domestic producers of like or directly competitive goods.

iv) Exception for Certain Agricultural Goods

Section 57 excludes from a surtax order made under section 55 prescribed agricultural goods that may be subject to a surtax under section 68(1).

v) Order Must Not Contravene WTO Agreement

A surtax order made under section 55(1) is subject to Article 6 of the *Agreement on Safeguards* in Annex 1A of the *World Trade Organization Agreement*.[194] If it is found to be in contravention, Canada is obligated to refund any surtaxes collected.

---

192 *Customs Tariff*, above note 1, s 79.
193 Above note 191.
194 Above note 3.

vi) Conditions

In accordance with section 59(1), a surtax order under section 55(1) must satisfy three conditions:

1) The quantity of the imported goods represents a substantial share of total imports of goods of the same kind.
2) In the case of goods imported from a *NAFTA* country, the quantity of those goods, alone or, in exceptional circumstances, together with the quantity of goods of the same kind imported from the other *NAFTA* country, contributes importantly to serious injury or threat of serious injury to domestic producers of like or directly competitive goods.
3) In the case of goods imported from any other free trade partner country, the quantity of those goods contributes importantly to serious injury or threat of serious injury to domestic producers of like or directly competitive goods.

vii) Definition of "Contributes Importantly"

Section 54 defines the term "contribute importantly" with respect to goods from *NAFTA* or Chile to mean an important cause, but not necessarily the most important cause.

viii) Repeal of Order

The Governor in Council must repeal a surtax order if the above conditions no longer continue. However, a surtax order may be made under section 60 if there is a surge of imports from a free trade partner country. This is discussed below in this chapter.

ix) Exclusion from Surtax Order for Peru Goods

Pursuant to section 59.1, goods of any kind imported from Peru may be excluded from a surtax order made under section 55(1) if the Governor in Council is satisfied from the Minister's report or the Tribunal's report under section 20 or 29 of the *CITT Act* that the quantity of those goods being imported is not a principal cause of serious injury or threat of serious injury to domestic producers of like or directly competitive goods. "Principal cause" in respect of goods from Peru is defined by section 54 to mean "an important cause that is no less important than any other cause."

b) Surge of Goods

If a surtax order made under section 55(1) or 63(1) has excluded goods from a free trade partner because those goods did not meet the conditions set out in section 59(1) or 63(4), the Governor in Council may make a surtax order on any such goods under section 60 if satisfied by the Minister's recommendation or as a result of an inquiry by the Tribunal that there has been a surge of those goods from a free trade partner on or after the coming into force of the order and that, as a result of that surge, the effectiveness of the imposition of the surtax is being undermined. The Order may specify the rate and provide that that rate may vary from time to time as the quantity of those goods equals or exceeds the quantities specified in the Order.

i) Goods in Transit

An order made under section 60 may provide that goods that are in transit to Canada at the time the order comes into force are entitled to the tariff treatment that was applicable to those goods immediately before that time.[195]

ii) Definition of "Surge"

Section 54 stipulates that the term "surge" in section 60, in respect of goods imported from a *NAFTA* country or from Chile, has the meaning given that word by Article 805 of the *NAFTA* or Article F-05 of the *CCFTA*, as the case may be.

iii) Rate of Surtax

By section 61(1), the rate of a surtax imposed under section 55(1), section 60, or section 63(1) on goods imported from a free trade partner need not be the same as, but must not exceed, that imposed under section 55(1) or 63(1) on goods of the same kind imported from any other country.

iv) Further Limitation on Order

In making an order under sections 55(1), 60, or 63(1) in respect of a free trade partner, section 61(2) requires the Governor in Council to be guided by subparagraph of Article 802 of the *NAFTA*, subparagraph 5(b) of Article F-02 of the *CCFTA*, or subparagraph 5(b) of Article 4.6 of the *CIFTA*, as the case may be.

v) Repeal or Amendment of Surtax Order by Tribunal

If the Governor in Council is satisfied as a result of a mid-term review by the Tribunal under section 19.02 of the *CITT Act* that a surtax order under section 55(1), section 60, or section 63(1) should be repealed or amended, the Governor in Council may, pursuant to section 62, repeal or amend the order.

---

195   Above note 1, s 79.

c) Extension Order

If the Governor in Council is satisfied as a result of an inquiry made by the Tribunal under section 30.07 of the *CITT Act* that (1) an order continues to be necessary to prevent or remedy serious injury to domestic producers of like or directly competitive goods, and (2) there is evidence that the domestic producers of like or directly competitive goods are adjusting, as determined in accordance with any regulations made under section 40(b) of the *CITT Act*, the Governor in Council may, on the recommendation of the Minister, make an extension order under section 63 imposing a surtax on any goods specified in the previous order imported from any country specified in the extension order.

i) Scope and Rate of Surtax

The rate of surtax imposed by the extension order may vary from time to time as the quantity of the goods imported into Canada or that region or part of Canada during a period specified in the order equals or exceeds totals specified in the order, but the rate must not exceed (1) the lowest of any rates previously imposed with respect to the goods under sections 63(1), 55(1), or 60; and (2) the rate that, in the opinion of the Governor in Council, is sufficient to prevent or remedy serious injury to domestic producers of like or directly competitive goods and to facilitate the adjustment of the domestic producers.

ii) Conditions

The same three conditions imposed on the making of a surtax order under section 59(1) (see Section G(3)(c)(ii), above in this chapter) apply to the making of an extension order under section 63(1).

iii) Goods from Peru

An extension order under section 63(1) may, pursuant to section 63(4.1) exclude goods of any kind imported from Peru if the Governor in Council is satisfied, on the basis of a report under the *CITT Act*, that the quantity of those goods being imported is not a principal cause of serious injury or threat of serious injury to domestic producers of like or directly competitive goods.

iv) Duration and Repeal

Section 63(5) limits the total periods specified in an extension order and in related orders made under sections 63(1), 55(1) or 60, or under section 5(3.2) or (4.1) of the *Export and Import Permits Act*, to eight years. However, it authorizes the Governor in Council on the recommendation of the Minister, at any time before the eight years, to amend or repeal the order, unless, before that time, a resolution directing that it cease to have effect has been adopted by both Houses of Parliament under section 64.

v) Cessation of Extension Order

Section 64 provides that Parliament may, by a resolution, direct that an order made under section 55(1), section 60, or 63(1) cease to have effect immediately or on another day. The order thereupon ceases to have effect on the day that the resolution is adopted or, if another day is specified in the resolution, on that specified day. The resolution of Parliament must be published in the *Canada Gazette*.

d) Goods in Transit

An order made under section 63(1) may provide that goods that are in transit to Canada at the time the order comes into force are entitled to the tariff treatment that was applicable to those goods immediately before that time.[196]

e) Regulations

The Governor in Council is authorized by section 66 to make regulations for carrying out the purposes of sections 55 to 65 and, by an order, to suspend a surtax or rate in whole or in part from applying to goods of any country or any class of such goods.

The decision of the Governor in Council is, by virtue of section 67, final on any question that may arise regarding the application of the surtax or rate imposed under sections 55 to 66.

4) Safeguard Measures for Agricultural Goods

a) Surtax Order on Agricultural Goods

Section 68 of the Act authorizes the Governor in Council, by an order made under section 68(1), to impose a surtax on any prescribed agricultural goods at a rate and on conditions specified in the order. The surtax is in addition to any other duty authorized by the Act or by any other Act of Parliament, and the order imposing the surtax must comply with the following two conditions: (1) It must be recommended by the Minister of Finance; and (2) The

---

196 *Ibid.*

Governor in Council must be satisfied, on the basis of a report by the Minister of Agriculture and Agri-Food, that the conditions set out in Article 5 of the *Agreement on Agriculture* in Annex 1A of the *WTO Agreement* for the imposition of a surtax on the prescribed agricultural goods have been met.

i) Non-application of Surtax to Goods in Transit

Goods that were purchased by an importer in good faith prior to the coming into force of the order, and that were in transit when the order came into force, may be relieved from payment of the surtax by the CBSA.

ii) Cessation of Order

A surtax order ceases to have effect if Parliament adopts a resolution and specifies a day for its cessation or, if no day is specified, on the day the resolution is adopted. The resolution of Parliament must be published in the *Canada Gazette*.

iii) Regulations

The Governor in Council is authorized by section 68(6), on the recommendation of the Minister, to prescribe agricultural goods and the terms and conditions for the purposes of section 68 in respect of any country, and generally for carrying out the purposes and provisions of this section. The order must be published in the *Canada Gazette* and is exempt from the requirements of the *Statutory Instruments Act*.

5) Bilateral Emergency Measures

a) US Goods

i) Imposition of Temporary Duty

Section 69(2) authorizes the Governor in Council to impose, by an order, a temporary duty, in addition to any other duty specified in the *Customs Tariff* or in any other Act of Parliament, on goods imported from the United States and entitled to the UST, under the following conditions:

1) There must have been an Inquiry conducted by the Tribunal under section 19.01 or section 19.1(2) of the *CITT Act* or as a result of a complaint filed with it under section 23 of that Act.
2) The Governor in Council must be satisfied as a result of the Tribunal's Inquiry that the goods entitled to the UST are, as a result of that entitlement, being imported in such increased quantities and under such

conditions as to alone constitute a principal cause of serious injury to domestic producers of like or directly competitive goods.
3) The rate of temporary duty, when added to the rate in effect that is applicable to those goods, must not exceed the lesser of (a) the MFNT rate that was in effect in respect of those goods on 31 December 1988, and (b) the MFNT rate that is in effect in respect of those goods at the time the order is made.

Fresh fruits and vegetables are covered separately under section 68.

A temporary duty order may be made only if it is based on an agreement between the Government of Canada and the Government of the United States.

ii) Definition of "Principal Cause"

The term "principal cause" is defined in section 69(4) to mean, in respect of a serious injury, an important cause that is not less important than any other cause of the serious injury.

iii) Reference to MFNT Rate in Effect

The MFNT rate for fresh vegetables is that set out in the applicable tariff item referred to in Supplementary Note 2(b) in Chapter 7 of the List of Tariff Provisions; and the MFNT rate for fresh fruit is that set out in the applicable tariff item referred to in Supplementary Note 4(b) in Chapter 8 of the List of Tariff Provisions.

b) Mexican and MUST Goods

i) Imposition of Temporary Duty

Section 70(2) authorizes the Governor in Council to impose, by an order, a temporary duty, in addition to any other duty specified in the *Customs Tariff* or in any other Act of Parliament, on goods imported from Mexico and entitled to the MUST rates, under the same conditions as in section 69(2) with respect to US goods. The references to the sections of the *CITT Act* in the case of Mexico are to sections 19.01(3) and 23(1.02). Fresh fruits and vegetables are covered by section 68.

A temporary duty order may be made only if it is based on an agreement between the Government of Canada and the Government of Mexico.

ii) Definition of "Principal Cause"

The term "principal cause" is defined as in section 69(4) with respect to US goods.

iii) Reference to MFNT Rate in Effect

This is the same reference as in section 69(5) with respect to US goods.

c) Republic of Chile Goods

i) Imposition of Temporary Duty

Section 71(2) authorizes the Governor in Council to impose, by an order, a temporary duty, in addition to any other duty specified in the *Customs Tariff* or in any other Act of Parliament, on goods imported from Chile and entitled to the CT rates, under the same conditions as in section 69(2) with respect to US goods. The references to the sections of the *CITT Act* in the case of Chile are to sections 19.012(2) and 23(1.05).

A temporary duty order may be made only if it is based on an agreement between the Government of Canada and the Government of the Republic of Chile.

ii) Definition of "Principal Cause"

This is identical to the definition of the term in section 69(4) with respect to US goods.

iii) Reference to MFNT Rate in Effect

This is the same reference as in section 69(5) with respect to US goods.

d) Colombia

i) Suspension of Reduction of Tariff Rate; Imposition of Temporary Duty

Section 71.01(1) of the *Customs Tariff* authorizes the Governor in Council to make an order against goods entitled to the Colombia Tariff,

1) suspending during the period that the order is in effect, any reduction of the rate of customs duty with respect to those goods that would otherwise be made after that time by virtue of section 49.01; and
2) subjecting those goods to a temporary duty, in addition to any other duty specified in this Act or in any other Act of Parliament relating to customs, at a rate set out in the order.

ii) Maximum Duty

The temporary duty imposed under section 71.01, when added to the rate of customs duty specified in the Colombia Tariff that is in effect in respect of those goods at the time of making the order, may not exceed the lesser of (1) the MFNT rate that is in effect in respect of those goods at the time the order is made, and (2) the MFNT rate that was in effect in respect of those goods on 1 January 2007.

iii) Conditions

An order under section 71.01(1) may not be made more than once in respect of goods of any particular kind, may be in effect for a maximum period of three years, and may only be made during the period beginning on the day on which this section comes into force and ending (1) if the period of reduction to final rate of "Free" on the goods covered by the order is less than ten years, on the day that is ten years after the day on which section 71.01(1) comes into force, and (2) if the period of reduction to the final rate of "Free" on those goods is ten years or more, on the day after the expiry of the tariff staging period in respect of those goods.

iv) Rate of Duty When Order Ceases to Have Effect

If an order made under section 71.01(1) ceases to have effect in a particular calendar year, the rate of customs duty applicable to the goods after the order ceases to have effect is the rate of customs duty that is applicable in accordance with section 49.01.

v) Definition of "Principal Cause"

This is identical to the definition of the term in section 69(4) with respect to US goods.

e) Costa Rica

i) Textile and Apparel Goods Exempt

In accordance with section 71.1(1), section 71 does not apply in respect of textile and apparel goods set out in Appendix III.1.1.1 of Annex III.1 of the *Canada-Costa Rica Free Trade Agreement*.

ii) Temporary Duty

Under section 71.1(2), a temporary duty may be imposed on goods imported from Costa Rica and entitled to the CRT rates only after complying with the same conditions as under section 69(4) with respect to US goods, but the references to the sections of the *CITT Act* are to sections 19.013(2) and 23(1.07). A temporary duty order may be made only if it is based on an agreement between the Government of Canada and the Government of the Republic of Costa Rica relating to the application of section 71.1(2).

iii) Reference to MFNT Rate in Effect

The reference in section 71.1(4) to the MFNT rate in effect is the same as in section 69(5) in respect of US goods.

iv) Application of Measures a Second Time

A temporary duty may be applied a second time if

1) the period of time that has elapsed since the initial application ended is equal to at least one-half the initial period of application;
2) the rate of duty for the first year of the second action is not greater than the rate that would be in effect in accordance with the Schedule of Canada referred to in Annex III.3.1 of the *Canada-Costa Rica Free Trade Agreement*, entitled "Tariff Elimination," at the time the first action was imposed; and
3) the rate of duty applicable to any subsequent year is reduced in equal steps such that the duty rate in the final year of the action is equivalent to the rate provided for in the Schedule of Canada referred to in Annex III.3.1 of the *Canada-Costa Rica Free Trade Agreement*, entitled "Tariff Elimination," for that year.

v) Rate of Duty When Order Ceases to Have Effect

After the temporary duty order ends, the rate prior to reduction continues, and the reduction again continues until December 31 of that year, and thereafter, in accordance with the phased reduction, in accordance with section 49.1 of the *Customs Tariff*. The Minister of Finance must notify the importer of the applicable rates after the Governor in Council order ceases to have effect.

vi) Goods in Transit

An order made under section 71.1(2) may provide that goods that are in transit to Canada at the time the order comes into force are entitled to the tariff treatment that was applicable to those goods immediately before that time.

f) Goods from *EFTA* Countries

The bilateral measures set out in sections 71.2 (Iceland), 71.3 (Norway), and 71.4 (Switzerland and Liechtenstein) are identical. The FTA with these countries specifically provides that,

1) an emergency action shall only be taken upon clear evidence that increased imports have caused or are threatening to cause serious injury

pursuant to an investigation conducted in accordance with definitions and procedures equivalent to those of Articles 3 and 4 of the WTO *Agreement on Safeguards*;
2) before taking an action, notification will be given to the other Parties and the Joint Committee giving all pertinent information, including evidence of serious injury or threat thereof caused by increased imports, a precise description of the product involved, and the proposed action, as well as the proposed date of introduction, and expected duration of, the action; and
3) each Party retains its rights and obligations under Article XIX of the GATT 1994 and the WTO *Agreement on Safeguards*.

i) Bilateral Emergency Measures

The bilateral emergency measures against the EFTA partners consist of the suspension of the reduction of the tariff rates under the free trade agreement and the imposition of a temporary duty in conformity with sections 71.2, 71.3, and 71.4 of the *Customs Tariff*.

ii) Suspension of Reduction of Tariff Rate; Imposition of Temporary Duty

The reduction of the IT, NT, and SLT rates applicable to goods imported from any of these *EFTA* countries pursuant to sections 52.1, 52.2, and 52.3, respectively, of the *Customs Tariff* may be suspended by an order of the Governor in Council for a specified period and, in addition to any other duty specified in the *Customs Tariff* or any other Act of Parliament, a temporary duty may be imposed on those goods. The following conditions must be complied with before making the order:

1) An inquiry must have been conducted by the Tribunal under sections 19.014(2) to 19.016(2) of the *CITT Act* or further to a complaint filed with it under section 23(1.09) to (1.11) of that Act.
2) The Governor in Council must be satisfied as a result of the Tribunal's Inquiry that the goods entitled to the IT, NT, or SLT rate, as the case may be, are, as a result of that entitlement, being imported in such increased quantities and under such conditions as to alone constitute a principal cause of serious injury to domestic producers of like or directly competitive goods.

iii) Conditions

The following conditions apply:

1) The rate of temporary duty, when added to the rate in effect that is applicable to those goods may not exceed the lesser of

a) the MFNT rate of customs duty that was in effect in respect of those goods immediately before the coming into force of sections 71.2(3) to 71.4(3), and
   b) the MFNT rate that is in effect in respect of those goods at the time the order is made.
2) For tariff items other than those referred to in subparagraphs (3) and (4) (see next paragraph, below), an order under sections 71.2(1)(a) to 71.4(1)
   a) may not be made more than once during the period beginning on the day on which sections 71.2 to 71.4 came into force and ending on the day before the day that is five years after the day on which those sections came into force in respect of goods of a particular kind and, if made during that period remains in effect for the period, not exceeding three years, specified in the order; and
   b) may be made *after the expiry of the period* referred to in (a) only if it is based on an agreement between the Government of Canada and the Government of the Republics of Iceland, Norway, or Liechtenstein and Switzerland, as the case may be, relating to the application of the section.

iv) Conditions in Respect of Certain Tariff Items of Chapter 89

Chapter 89 of the List of Tariff Provisions in the Schedule covers ships, boats, and floating structures, including cruise ships, cargo ships, ferry boats, fishing vessels, drilling ships, and barges.

a. Tariff Items 8901.20.90, 8902.00.10, 8905.20.10, 8905.20.20, 8905.90.10, and 8906.90.99

An order under sections 71.2(1) to 71.4(1) may not be made more than once during the period beginning on the day that is three years after the day on which sections 71.2(3) to 71.4(3) came into force and ending on the day before the day that is *ten* years after the day on which those sections came into force in respect of any goods of tariff items 8901.20.90 (tankers—other), 8902.00.10 (fishing vessels), 8905.20.10 (drilling platforms), 8905.20.20 (production platforms), 8905.90.10 (other vessels), and 8906.90.99 (other vessels—other), and, if made during that period, remains in effect for the period specified in the order, but that period must not exceed three years.

b. Tariff Items 8901.10.90, 8901.90.99, 8904.00.00, 8905.10.00, and 8905.90.90

An order under sections 71.2(1) to 71.4(1) may not be made more than once during the period beginning on the day that is three years after the day on which those sections came into force and ending on the day before the day that is *fifteen* years after the day on which they came into force in respect of goods of Tariff items 8901.10.90 (cruise ships, etc—other), 8901.90.99 (other vessels—other), 8904.00.00 (tugs and pusher craft), 8905.10.00 (dredgers), and 8905.90.90 (other platforms) and, if made during that period, remains in effect for the period specified in the order, but that period must not exceed three years.

v) **Rate of Duty When Order Ceases to Have Effect**
After the temporary duty order ends, the rate prior to reduction continues and the reduction again continues until December 31 of that year, and thereafter, in accordance with the phased reduction, in accordance with section 52.1 of the *Customs Tariff*. The Minister of Finance must notify the importer of the applicable rates after the Governor in Council order ceases to have effect.

vi) **Definition of "Principal Cause"**
The term "principal cause" used in sections 71.2 to 71.4 has the same meaning as in section 69(4) with respect to US goods.

vii) **Reference to Customs Duty in Effect**
The reference in section 71.4(4) to customs duty in effect is in the same terms as in section 69(5) with respect to US goods.

g) **Goods from Peru**

i) **Suspension of Reduction of Tariff Rate; Imposition of Temporary Duty**
The reduction of the PT rates applicable to goods imported from Peru pursuant to section 49.5 of the *Customs Tariff* may be suspended by an order of the Governor in Council for a specified period and, in addition to any other duty specified in the *Customs Tariff* or any other Act of Parliament, a temporary duty may be imposed on those goods. The following conditions must be complied with before making the order:

1) There must have been an inquiry conducted by the Tribunal under section 19.017(2) of the *CITT Act* or as a result of a complaint filed with it under section 23(1.09) of that Act.
2) The Governor in Council must be satisfied as a result of the Tribunal's inquiry that the goods entitled to the PT rates are, as a result of that entitlement, being imported in such increased quantities and under such

conditions as to constitute a principal cause of serious injury, or a threat of serious injury, to domestic producers of like or directly competitive goods.
3) The rate of temporary duty when added to the Peru Tariff in effect that is applicable to those goods must not exceed the lesser of
   a) the MFNT rate that is in effect in respect of those goods at the time the order is made, and
   b) the MFNT rate that was in effect in respect of those goods on 1 January 2007.

With respect to fresh vegetables and fresh fruits, the MFNT rate referred to above is the rate set out for those goods in the applicable tariff items referred to in Supplementary Notes 2(b) of Chapter 7 and 4(b) of Chapter 8, respectively.

ii) Conditions

An order under section 71.5(1)(a) may not be made more than twice during the period beginning on the day on which section 71.5(1) came into force and ending on the day that is seven years after the day on which that section came into force in respect of goods of a particular kind and, if made during that period, remains in effect for a maximum period of three years, specified in the order; and may not be made after the day that is seven years after the day on which the section came into force.

iii) Application a Second Time

A measure referred to in an order made under section 71.5(1) may be applied a second time if the period that has elapsed since the initial application of the measure ended is equal to at least one-half of the initial period of application.

iv) Rate of Duty When Order Ceases to Have Effect

If an order made under section 71.5(1) ceases to have effect in a particular calendar year, the rate of customs duty applicable to the goods after the order ceases to have effect is the rate of customs duty that is applicable in accordance with section 49.5.

v) Definition of "Principal Cause"

The term "principal cause" used in section 71.5(1) has the same meaning as in section 69(4) with respect to US goods.

vi) Goods in Transit

An order made under sections 71.5(1) and 71.6(1) may provide that goods that are in transit to Canada at the time the order comes into force are entitled to the tariff treatment that was applicable to those goods immediately before that time.

h) Jordan

i) Suspension of Reduction of Tariff Rate; Imposition of Temporary Duty

The reduction of the JT rates applicable to goods imported from Jordan pursuant to section 52.4 of the *Customs Tariff* may be suspended by an order of the Governor in Council for a specified period and, in addition to any other duty specified in the *Customs Tariff* or any other Act of Parliament, a temporary duty may be imposed on those goods. The following conditions must be complied with before making the order:

1) There must have been an inquiry conducted by the Tribunal under section 19.018(2) of the *CITT Act* or as a result of a complaint filed with it under section 23(1.094) of that Act.
2) The Governor in Council must be satisfied as a result of the Tribunal's inquiry that the goods entitled to the JT rates are, as a result of that entitlement, being imported in such increased quantities and under such conditions as to constitute a principal cause of serious injury, or a threat of serious injury, to domestic producers of like or directly competitive goods.

ii) Maximum Rate

In respect of goods imported on a seasonal basis, the rate of temporary duty on goods, when added to the JT in effect that is applicable to those goods, must not exceed the MFNT rate that is in effect in respect of those goods at the time the order is made, and in respect of other goods, the lesser of the rate that was in effect immediately before the order was made and the MFNT rate that was in effect in respect of those goods on the date of the order imposing the temporary duty.

With respect to fresh vegetables and fresh fruits, the MFNT rate referred to above is the rate set out for those goods in the applicable tariff items referred to in Supplementary Notes 2(b) of Chapter 7 and 4(b) of Chapter 8, respectively.

iii) Further Orders

An order under section 71.6(1)(a) may not be made more than twice during the period beginning on the day on which section 71.6(1) comes into force and ending on the day that is ten years after the day on which that section comes into force in respect of goods of a particular kind and, if made during that period, remains in effect for a maximum period of three years, specified in the order; but if Jordan and Canada agree, it may be made after the ten year period.

A measure suspending reduction of JT rates of duty or imposing a temporary duty, referred to in section 71.6(1), may be applied a second time if at least two years have elapsed since the initial order ended.

iv) Rate of Duty When Order Ceases to Have Effect

If an order made under section 71.6(1) ceases to have effect in a particular calendar year, the rate of customs duty applicable to the goods after the order ceases to have effect is the rate of customs duty that is applicable in accordance with section 52.4.

v) Definition of "Principal Cause"

The term "principal cause" used in section 71.6(1) has the same meaning as in section 69(4) with respect to US goods.

i) Goods from Panama

i) Suspending Reduction of Tariff Rate; Imposition of Temporary Duty

The reduction of the PAT rates applicable to goods imported from Panama pursuant to section 49.41 of the *Customs Tariff* may be suspended by an order of the Governor in Council for a specified period and, in addition to any other duty specified in the *Customs Tariff* or any other Act of Parliament, a temporary duty may be imposed on those goods. The following conditions must be complied with before making the order:

1) There must have been an inquiry conducted by the Tribunal under section 19.0131(2) of the *CITT Act* or as a result of a complaint filed with it under section 23(1.081) of that Act.
2) The Governor in Council must be satisfied as a result of the Tribunal's inquiry that the goods entitled to the PAT rates are, as a result of that entitlement, being imported in such increased quantities and under such conditions as to constitute a principal cause of serious injury, or a threat of serious injury, to domestic producers of like or directly competitive goods.

ii) Maximum Rate

The rate of temporary duty, when added to the Panama Tariff in effect that is applicable to those goods must not exceed the lesser of (1) the MFNT rate that is in effect in respect of those goods at the time the order is made, and (2) the MFNT rate that was in effect in respect of those goods on 1 January 2009.

iii) Conditions

An order under section 71.41(1)(a) may not be made more than twice during the period beginning on the day on which section 71.41(1) comes into force and ending on the day that is ten years after the day on which that section comes into force in respect of goods of a particular kind and, if made during that period, remains in effect for a maximum period of three years specified in the order; but may be made after the day that is ten years after the day on which the section comes into force if Panama and Canada so agree. Such a measure may be applied a second time if a period of at least two years has elapsed since the expiration of the initial order.

iv) Rate of Duty When Order Ceases to Have Effect

If an order made under section 71.41(1) ceases to have effect in a particular calendar year, the rate of customs duty applicable to the goods after the order ceases to have effect is the rate of customs duty that is applicable in accordance with section 49.41.

v) Definition of "Principal Cause"

The term "principal cause" used in section 71.41(1) has the same meaning as in section 69(4) with respect to US goods.

vi) Goods in Transit

An order made under section 71.41(1) may provide that goods that are in transit to Canada at the time the order comes into force are entitled to the tariff treatment that was applicable to those goods immediately before that time.

6) Safeguard Measures in Respect of China

a) Background

Of all the countries to which MFNT treatment has been accorded by Canada through the *Customs Tariff*, China has attracted special safeguard measures. This was permitted by a bilateral agreement signed in 1999 under which, as a condition of Canada agreeing to support China's membership in the WTO, China committed to reduce its tariffs on Canadian goods and to improve market access to Canadian firms. These tariff reductions and commitments were implemented with China's accession to the *WTO Agreement* in 2001. Earlier, in 1973, Canada and China had signed a bilateral agreement by which each country agreed to give the other a trade status equivalent to MFNT, and in 1980, Canada granted GPT status to China, reducing tariffs on imports from China by over one-third from the regular MFNT rate.

As a result of the accession of China to the Agreement establishing the WTO, the *CITT Act* was amended in 2002 by adding sections 30.2 to 30.26 under the heading "Safeguard Measures in Respect of China." The *Customs Tariff* was correspondingly amended by adding sections 77.1 to 77.8, reflecting the same regime of safeguards.

Safeguard inquiries in respect of China are commenced in one of two ways: by referral of a matter from the Governor in Council to the Tribunal for inquiry pursuant to section 30.21(1) of the *CITT Act*, or by the direct filing of a complaint with the Tribunal by a domestic producer of goods that are like or directly competitive with the subject goods, or by any person or association acting on behalf of any such domestic producer, pursuant to section 30.22(1) or 30.23(1) of that Act.

b) Meaning of "Domestic Producers": Standing to File Complaint

The "domestic producers" who matter for the purposes of the complaint are those who are not importers of, nor related to, an exporter or importer of the alleged dumped or subsidized goods; similarly, "domestic industry" must comprise domestic producers who are not related to an exporter or importer of alleged dumped or subsidized goods.

The terms "domestic producer" and "domestic industry" have not been defined in the *Customs Tariff*, nor in the *Special Import Measures Act* or the *CITT Act*, but in a decision rendered under the *Customs Tariff* with respect to safeguard measures, the Tribunal held that the terms must be construed in the context of the provisions in the legislation and not on the basis of its ordinary sense.

In Textile and Apparel Goods Safeguard Inquiry No CS-2005-002,[197] the Tribunal rejected the complaint filed by Unite Here Canada for lack of standing because the complainant did not represent "domestic producers," nor was it acting on behalf of domestic producers, even though it had claimed support from them. It was the Tribunal's view that the concept of "producer"

---

197 (2006), 11 TTR (2d) 326 (CITT).

in section 30.22 of the *CITT Act* required a more direct economic interest in the production of like or directly competitive goods, and that "employees" who were represented by the complainant did not qualify as "producers." With regard to the argument of Unite Here that the complaint had the support from certain manufacturers of textile and apparel products, the Tribunal did not equate support for a complaint with "acting on behalf of" the producers, as none of the manufacturers had indicated that Unite Here was authorized to act on their behalf. In its view, there was a significant difference between a party expressing support for another person's actions and that party authorizing the person to act on the party's behalf.

c) Meaning of "Market Disruption" and "Significant Cause"

Section 77.1(1)(a) of the *Customs Tariff* defines the term "market disruption" to mean a rapid increase in the importation of goods that are like, or directly competitive with, goods produced by a domestic industry, in absolute terms or relative to the production of those goods by a domestic industry, so as to be a significant cause of material injury, or threat of material injury, to the domestic industry.

The same section also defines the term "significant cause" to mean, in respect of a material injury or threat thereof, an important cause that need not be as important as, or more important than, any other cause of the material injury or threat.

The *CITT Act* has the corresponding definitions of "market disruption" and "significant cause."

In the market disruption–type inquiry, the *CITT Regulations* direct the Tribunal, in assessing whether there is market disruption, to consider the volume of imports, the effect of the imported goods on prices of like goods in Canada, and the impact of the goods on domestic producers.

In the trade diversion–type inquiry, the Tribunal determines if trade actions affecting imports of goods from China into the market of another WTO country have caused or are threatening to cause a significant "trade diversion" of the goods into the Canadian market.

The Tribunal does not have authority to impose safeguard measures. It can only make a determination of serious injury, market disruption, or trade diversion. Its role is to make findings and submit them to the government, which may then choose to ignore them or to apply safeguard measures through an order in council. These measures are applied on the recommendation of the Minister of Finance in the form of surtaxes under section 77.1(2) of the *Customs Tariff* or in the form of quotas or tariff rate quotas under the

Export and Import Permits Act[198] on the recommendation of the Minister of Foreign Affairs and International Trade.

d) Market Disruption

If goods imported from China cause market disruption, the Governor in Council may, pursuant to section 77.1(2), by order made on the recommendation of the Minister of Finance, impose a surtax on any goods originating in that country that are being imported into Canada or a region or part of Canada in such increased quantities or under such conditions as to cause or threaten to cause market disruption to domestic producers of like or directly competitive goods.

e) Rate of Surcharge

Subject to the maximum rate authorized by section 77.1(3), the rate is as specified in the order or is a rate that varies from time to time as the quantity of those goods imported into Canada or that region or part of Canada during a period specified in the order equals or exceeds the quantities specified in the order.

f) Maximum Rate

The rate specified in the order may not exceed a rate that, in the opinion of the Governor in Council, is sufficient to prevent or remedy market disruption to domestic producers of like or directly competitive goods.

g) Duration and Cessation of Surtax Order

The order of the Governor in Council imposing a surtax, if based on the Minister's report, has effect for a period of 200 days unless, before the end of the 200th day,

1) a resolution has been adopted by both Houses of Parliament under section 77.4 directing that the order cease to have effect; or
2) the Tribunal reports to the Governor in Council, on the basis of an inquiry made under section 30.21 or 30.22 of the *CITT Act*, that the goods described in the report of the Minister are being imported in such increased quantities or under such conditions as to cause or threaten to cause market disruption to domestic producers of like or directly competitive goods; or

---

198 Above note 5.

3) an extension order has been made by the Governor in Council pursuant to section 77.3.

h) Inquiry by Tribunal

Upon making an order under section 77.1(2) on the basis of the Minister's report, the Governor in Council must immediately refer the matter to the Tribunal for an inquiry under section 30.21(1) of the *CITT Act*.

i) Extension Order

Before the expiry of the surtax order, the Governor in Council may make an extension order imposing a surtax on any goods specified in the previous order if satisfied, as a result of an inquiry made by the Tribunal under section 30.25(7) of the *CITT Act* or under section 5.4(2) or (4) of the *Export and Import Permits Act*, that an order continues to be necessary to prevent or remedy market disruption to domestic producers of like or directly competitive goods.

The scope, the rate, and the cessation of the extension order are identical to those for the previous order that is being extended. Parliament may, pursuant to section 77.4, direct that the extension order cease to have effect immediately or on a specified day.

j) Trade Diversion

Under the authority of section 77.6(2), the Governor in Council may, by an order made on the basis of an inquiry made by the Tribunal under section 30.21 or 30.23 of the *CITT Act*, impose a surtax on any goods originating in the People's Republic of China that are being imported into Canada or a region or part of Canada in such increased quantities, as a result of an "action" taken by that country or by another WTO member (other than Canada), or any combination of the two actions, and such action causes or threatens to cause a significant diversion of trade into the domestic market in Canada.

k) Meaning of "Action"

The term "action" means any action, including a provisional action, taken by the People's Republic of China to prevent or remedy market disruption in a WTO member other than Canada, or taken by a WTO member other than Canada to withdraw concessions under the *WTO Agreement* or otherwise to limit imports to prevent or remedy market disruption in that member caused or threatened by the importation of goods originating in the People's Republic of China. It also includes any combination of such actions.

l) Rate

Subject to the maximum rate authorized by section 77.6(3), the rate is as specified in the order or is a rate that varies from time to time as the quantity of those goods imported into Canada or that region or part of Canada during a period specified in the order equals or exceeds quantities specified in the order. In accordance with section 77.6(3), the rate may not exceed that which, in the opinion of the Governor in Council, is sufficient to prevent or remedy diversion of trade into the domestic market in Canada.

m) Duration and Cessation of Surtax Order

The order of the Governor in Council imposing a surtax may be amended or repealed on the recommendation of the Minister. If not repealed, it ceases to have effect if a resolution has been adopted by both Houses of Parliament under section 77.4 directing that the order cease to have effect.

n) Expiry

Sections 77.1 to 77.8, which authorize surtax orders, ceased to have effect on 11 December 2013.

o) Tribunal's China-Specific Investigations

A market disruption investigation was initiated by the Tribunal on the basis of a complaint filed by the Onward Manufacturing Company Limited[199] in May 2005 that there was a significant increase in the imports of outdoor barbeques from China. The Tribunal also received a directive from the Governor in Council on 10 August 2005 to recommend a remedy to deal with the market disruption in the event that it made an affirmative determination. The directive asked the Tribunal to ensure that any remedy it recommended was in accordance with Canada's rights and obligations under international trade agreements.

The products under investigation were self-standing barbeques for outdoor use. They consisted of a metal lid, base, and frame, fuelled by either propane or natural gas, and had a primary cooking space between 200 and 1,500 square inches (1,290 and 9,675 square centimetres), in assembled or knocked-down condition.

The Tribunal found that the allegations of the complainant and its submission, as well as that of Fiesta, another primary producer of barbeques, concerning lost sales volumes, price suppression, and price erosion suffered by domestic producers, as well as reduced margins and net income and de-

---

199 Certain Outdoor Barbeques Safeguard Inquiry No. CS-2005-001 (2005), 10 TTR (2d) 463 (CITT).

creases in capacity utilization, were substantiated by the evidence.

The Tribunal reviewed other factors that may have had an impact on the performance of the domestic industry, but found that none of those factors was pervasive or of such magnitude as to explain the loss of market value.

Accordingly, the Tribunal was satisfied that there was a reasonable indication that the subject goods were being imported from China in such increased quantities and under such conditions as to cause or threaten market disruption to domestic producers of like or directly competitive goods.

With respect to the appropriate remedy, the Tribunal recommended that the government impose a surtax of 15 percent for a period of three years on the imports.

On 29 May 2006, the government announced that, after considering all the representations it had received, it would not impose a surtax as recommended by the Tribunal.

7) Surtax When Canada's External Financial Position in Jeopardy

a) General

Section 78 authorizes the Governor in Council to impose a surtax that is in addition to the duties imposed under the *Customs Tariff* if satisfied on a report of the Minister of Finance that Canada's external financial position and its balance of payments are such as to require special measures respecting Canadian imports. The order may impose a surtax on goods that originate in a country or that are entitled to any tariff treatment under regulations pursuant to section 16, or any class of such goods. The surtax may differ in amount for different goods or classes of goods. This power has not been used in recent memory.

b) Surtax Order Ceases Unless Approved by Parliament

If a surtax order is for a period longer than 180 days, it ceases to have effect on the 180th day after it is made unless, before it expires, the order is approved by a resolution adopted by both Houses of Parliament.

H. DUTIES RELIEF PROGRAMS

1) Introduction

Relief from duties and taxes plays a significant role (though diminishing in importance because of the growing free trade in a vast number of commodities, especially under the *NAFTA* and other FTAs) in assisting importers and entrepôt operators when goods are not for home consumption, but for use in the manufacture or processing of goods for export. The program offers Canadian businesses many of the same duty and tax incentives as those found in free trade zones around the world, giving them competitive advantage. For example, importers do not have to pay duties and taxes on imported goods that they plan to export, even if those goods undergo a wide range of processing and manufacturing activities while they are in warehouses.

Quite apart from the Duty Deferral Program described in Section H(3), below in this chapter, two sections in Division 1 of the *Customs Tariff*—sections 81 and 82—authorize the Governor in Council, on the recommendation of the Minister of Finance, to make an order lowering the duties set out in the List of Tariff Provisions and in the "F" Staging List in respect of goods used in the production of other goods or the provision of services, subject to any conditions and for any period that may be specified in the order.

In addition, five sections of Division 2 of Part 3 authorize the Governor in Council to make regulations, on the recommendation of the Minister of Finance, to permit the importation of goods under tariff headings 98.04, 98.05, 98.06, 98.07, and 99.37 without the full payment of duties.

2) Traveller's Exemption

Tariff heading 98.04 comprises four tariff items (9804.10.00, 9804.20.00, 9804.30.00, and 9804.40.00) and relates to goods acquired abroad by a resident or temporary resident of Canada or by a former resident who is returning to Canada to resume residence after a short period of absence, for the personal or household use of that person or as souvenirs or gifts, provided they are not bought on commission or as an accommodation for any other person or for sale, and provided they are reported by that person at the time of return to Canada. The duty-free allowance varies according to the number of days the traveller spends away from Canada. Currently, it is $50 after an absence of a minimum of twenty-four hours, $300 (not including wine or alcoholic beverages and tobacco) or $400 (including wine or alcoholic beverages and tobacco) after an absence of a minimum of forty-eight hours, and $750 (including wine or alcoholic beverages and tobacco) after an absence of a minimum of seven days. Quantity limitations on wine or alcoholic beverages and tobacco, as well as age restrictions, apply.

a) Returning Residents

Canadian residents or former residents, members of the Canadian Forces, and employees of the Canadian government who return to Canada to resume residence after an absence of a minimum of one year are allowed duty-free importation under tariff item 9805.00.00. The goods must have been acquired by that person for personal or household use; were actually owned, possessed, and used by them for at least six months prior to returning to Canada; and the goods must accompany that person at the time of their return to Canada. The goods must not be sold or otherwise disposed of within twelve months after importation. Quantity limitations on wine or liquor and tobacco, as well as age restrictions, apply.

b) Bequests

Tariff item 9806.00.00 relates to personal and household effects bequeathed by a resident of Canada who has died, on the condition that such goods were owned, possessed, and used abroad by the deceased resident. The tariff item also includes bequests received by a resident of Canada as a result of the death or in anticipation of the death of a person who is not a resident of Canada, on condition that such goods were owned, possessed, and used by the deceased non-resident. There is no minimum time limit for ownership, possession, or use under the tariff item, unlike the returning resident's exemption under tariff item 9805.00.00.

c) Settler's Effects

Goods imported by a settler for the settler's household or personal use are allowed duty free under tariff item 9807.00.00. Here, too, the goods must be actually owned, possessed, and used abroad by the settler prior to arrival in Canada and imported as accompanying baggage at the time of arrival in Canada. There is no minimum time limit for ownership, possession, or use under the tariff item.

d) Ethno-cultural Groups

Pursuant to section 88, recognized ethno-cultural groups can apply for duty-free importation of goods classified under tariff item 9937.00.00 if they meet the criteria set out in that tariff item. The goods include costumes, and parts and accessories thereof, designed or decorated in a manner reflecting a specific ethno-cultural heritage when for the use of the group that requires the costumes for the public manifestation of its heritage. The goods must not be sold or otherwise disposed of within twelve months after importation. The ethno-cultural group must have at least five persons, each of whom is at least eighteen years of age and is either a Canadian citizen or permanent resident of Canada. Furthermore, to be recognized, the group must be voluntary, non-profit, and constituted for the purpose of preserving its ethno-cultural heritage and sharing that heritage with Canadians; and is supported by, and is a representative of, the ethnic community to which it belongs.

3) Duty Deferral

The remaining twenty-six sections of Division 2 of Part 3 contain provisions that give relief from duties, which are comprised in the Duty Deferral Program. The Program is portable and has no geographic restrictions. Each has particular advantages. Persons who participate in it may pick the most competitive and advantageous location for their business needs.

The following three options are available:

- The Customs Bonded Warehouse Program enables the importer to defer paying all duties and taxes on goods until the goods are released for consumption in Canada or exported.
- The Duties Relief Program relieves the importer from having to pay duties if the goods are eventually re-exported, either in the same condition or after having been used, consumed, or expended to process other goods.
- The Drawback Program has the same advantages as the Duties Relief Program and the only difference is that the Drawback Program is for people who have already paid the duty and are asking for a refund.

In addition, there are remission programs under a variety of legislation, through orders and orders in council.

a) Qualifying for Duties Relief

An importer, exporter, processor, owner, or producer of the goods can apply for duties relief under section 89 of the *Customs Tariff* if they meet one of the following criteria:

1) the applicant is directly or indirectly involved in importing goods that are later exported, or deemed to have been exported, in the same condition as they were imported;
2) the applicant uses the goods to produce other goods for export;

3) if the goods are directly consumed or expended in the processing in Canada of goods that are subsequently exported; or
4) if the same quantity of domestic or imported goods of the same class is directly consumed or expended in the processing in Canada of goods that are subsequently exported.

No relief is granted on tobacco products or designated goods from duties or taxes levied or imposed under sections 21.1 to 21.3 of the *Excise Act, 2001*[200] or under the *Excise Tax Act*.[201]

Exportation is deemed to occur if goods are,

1) designated as ships' stores by regulations and supplied for use on board a conveyance of a prescribed class;
2) used for the equipment, repair, or reconstruction of ships or aircraft of a prescribed class;
3) delivered to a telegraph cable ship of a prescribed class; or
4) supplied for exportation to a department or agency of, or a corporation owned, controlled, or operated by, the Government of Canada or the government of a province, that is designated by the Minister of Public Safety and Emergency Preparedness.

In most cases, the goods imported under the Duties Relief Program have to be exported no later than four years after their import.

If goods that are exported to the United States or Mexico were further processed, they may be subject to restrictions under the *NAFTA*.[202]

b) Sale or Transfer

Imported goods can be sold or transferred before they are exported without paying duties, as long as the receiving company is also an authorized Program participant. The latter assumes all liability, such as paying duties and reporting non-compliance.

c) Customs Bonded Warehouse Option

A customs bonded warehouse is a facility licensed under section 91 of the *Customs Tariff* and regulated by the CBSA to store imported goods before they are released, as well as to store imported and domestic goods destined

---

200   SC 2002, c 22.
201   RSC 1985, c E-15.
202   Customs D Memorandum D7-4-3, "NAFTA Requirements for Drawback and Duty Deferral" (12 April 1996).

for export. The facility is operated by the private sector. It can be a conference room in a hotel or convention centre, part of an existing office building, or part of a complex of buildings. An annual licensing fee applies. The option permits storage on a site even if the site is licensed to others.[203]

The customs bonded warehouse option provides flexibility in moving imported goods, whether they are destined for the international or domestic marketplace. This option permits handling, storage, and minor manipulation of goods before they are exported or sold domestically. It benefits importers by lowering their transaction costs, improving cash flow, and simplifying the importing process.

The option provides the following benefits:

- relief from all duties, including anti-dumping and countervailing duties, and excise duties and taxes, including GST/HST, until the goods enter the Canadian marketplace;
- exemption from duties and taxes if the goods are sold abroad (duties and taxes are payable only on the portion of goods entering the Canadian market); and
- the ability to take advantage of just-in-time inventory practices by buying goods in bulk and removing them from the warehouse in required quantities.

An importer who wants to claim relief from duties and taxes under this option must apply for a certificate from the Minister of Public Safety and Emergency Preparedness under section 90, and if the certificate is issued and the number on the certificate is disclosed at the time of importation, the goods will be released without payment of duties and taxes whilst they are in storage in the licensed customs bonded warehouse. Section 92 does not require the importer to pay duties and taxes on the goods until they are removed from the bonded warehouse. The section does not, however, relieve manufactured tobacco that is manufactured in Canada and imported manufactured tobacco that is stamped in accordance with the *Excise Act, 2001* from the duty imposed under the latter Act.

While the goods are in the warehouse they can be stored for up to four years, and whilst in storage, the following are some of the activities that are permitted: reassembling goods that were disassembled for transport; displaying; inspecting; marking, labelling, tagging, or ticketing; packing, unpacking, packaging, or repackaging; sampling, testing, cleaning, and di-

---

203 *Customs Bonded Warehouse Regulations*, SOR/96-46.

luting; usual maintenance and servicing; preserving; separating defective goods from those of prime quality; sorting or grading; and trimming, filing, slitting, or cutting. A manufacturer or producer who imports fabrics, for instance, can tailor the program to its particular business requirements. While the fabrics are in the warehouse, the producer can cut and mark them, and then export them to foreign countries, all without paying duties and taxes.

An importer can use the services of an existing licensed bonded warehouse operator in order to take advantage of this program. Conventions, exhibitions, and trade shows can also take advantage of the customs bonded warehouse option to license their event sites. Participants can then display and handle imported goods in authorized ways without incurring the cost of duties and taxes.

d) Application to Operate Customs Bonded Warehouse

A licence to operate a customs bonded warehouse may be issued by the Minister of Public Safety and Emergency Preparedness under section 91 of the *Customs Tariff* if the applicant meets the qualifications prescribed by regulations and pays the required fees as well as deposits security considered sufficient by the Minister. The application is submitted to the CBSA, and when approved, the CBSA issues a unique customs bonded warehouse licence number. Both residents and non-residents can apply to operate a customs bonded warehouse.

4) Duties Relief Option: Manufacturing

If a person imports goods for storage, manufacturing, or processing and for eventual export, the duty relief option gives their business a competitive edge by lowering costs, since the goods are relieved of their duties.

As with the customs bonded warehouse program, the option is not restricted to a specific geographical site.

Under this option, a wide range of processing functions can be performed—everything from minor adjustments, to repair, to full-fledged manufacturing. Domestic and export production do not have to be separated, and imported and domestic raw materials can be used interchangeably. Even goods that are consumed or expended in a manufacturing process are eligible under the program.

Persons who use this option do not have to post a bond to financially secure their liability; have up to four years to identify their export markets; can substitute Canadian-made parts for imported ones, thus allowing flexibility to meet changing market conditions; and can sell or transfer the goods to other program participants without having to pay the duties.

5) Drawback Program

A drawback is a full or partial refund of customs duties on imported goods that are eventually exported. Goods can be exported in the same condition they were imported or, before export, they may be further manufactured by a full range of processes in Canada, or they may be consumed or expended in production processes without affecting the refund amount.

The drawback program provides for drawbacks on consumable and expendable goods used in production processes, as well as on scrap materials. In addition, it allows for the assignment of drawback rights using a waiver system. Through the program, an exporter can claim a drawback on imported goods that were sourced from a supplier in the domestic market.

a) Qualifying for Drawback

An importer, exporter, processor, owner, or producer of goods qualifies for a drawback if one of the following applies: (1) it is directly or indirectly involved in importing goods that are later exported in the same condition they were imported, or (2) it further manufactures or uses imported goods in a limited manner to produce other goods for export.

b) Application for Drawback

To obtain a drawback, a drawback claim has to be filed with the local CBSA office, along with documents establishing that the goods qualify for refund of duties and that they have been exported. A claim has to be filed no later than four years after the goods in respect of which the refund is claimed were imported. If more than one person is eligible to file a drawback claim, waivers must be submitted by the other eligible claimants before the CBSA can process the claim.

6) Other Duties Relief Programs

There are a number of other duties relief programs, some of which provide relief from excise taxes and GST/HST. A few of these are described below.

a) Temporary Importation Program

Goods that are temporarily imported for a trade show can enter duty free. Similarly, goods temporarily exported to the United States for warranty repair can re-enter duty and tax free. Also, goods temporarily imported for use in an emergency can enter duty free. In the last case, any goods not consumed or destroyed during the emergency when they are no longer required must be exported.[204]

Temporary importations have to be documented on a Temporary Admission Permit Form[205] and a security deposit may be required. However, as an alternative, the importer may obtain an ATA Carnet (a document used to clear customs without paying duties and import taxes on merchandise that will be re-exported within twelve months) issued by the national chamber of commerce in the country of export. The issuing authority posts security. In Canada, the guaranteeing association is the Canadian Chamber of Commerce.[206]

b) Temporary Relief on Prescribed Goods

The Schedule to the *Customs Tariff* and the *Temporary Importation (Excise Levies and Additional Duties) Regulations*[207] made under section 106 of the *Customs Tariff* prescribe the purposes for which goods may be imported into Canada and then exported after they have been used for those purposes. Duties and taxes that are relieved include excise duties and taxes, but not GST/HST. The goods must be exported within one year after their release, but an extension for up to six months may be granted where it is impracticable or impossible to export the goods within the time allowed.

c) Temporary Exportation Program

When Canadian goods are exported for repair, alteration, additions, or further processing, the *Customs Act* generally requires that they be subject to duties and taxes on the full value of those goods at the time of their return to Canada. However, under section 101 of the *Customs Tariff*, the Canadian Goods Abroad Program allows for the relief of duties on the "Canadian" portion of the value of the goods. Under this program, the duty is payable only on the value added to the Canadian goods in the form of labour or additional material. Similarly, under the *Value of Imported Goods (GST/HST) Regulations*,[208] the GST/HST is payable only on the value of the processing

---

204 *Temporary Importation Tariff Item 9993.00.00 Regulations*, SOR/98-58. Details are provided in Customs D Memorandum D8-1-1, "Temporary Importation" (22 January 2010).
205 Customs D Memorandum D8-1-4 (7 November 2005).
206 Customs D Memorandum D8-1-7, "Use of ATA Carnets and Canada-China-Taiwan Carnets for the Temporary Admission of Goods" (8 June 2007).
207 *Temporary Importation (Excise Levies and Additional Duties) Regulations*, SOR/89-427.
208 SOR/91-30.

performed outside of Canada. The following conditions apply: (1) the goods must be repaired outside Canada after being exported for the declared purpose of being repaired, (2) equipment must have been added to the goods outside Canada, or (3) the goods must have been the product of Canada and work was done outside Canada on them.

d) Conditions for Entitlement

To be entitled, the claimant must produce evidence that,

1) the repairs could not have been made in Canada at the place the goods were located before their exportation or within a reasonable distance of that place;
2) if equipment was added, it could not have been added in Canada;
3) if the goods were a product of Canada, it would not have been practicable to do the work in Canada; and
4) the goods must be returned within one year from the date of exportation or within such further time as may be prescribed.

e) Emergency Repairs Outside Canada

Section 101(2) provides relief from duties for emergency repairs of aircraft, vehicles, or vessels outside Canada as a result of an unforeseen contingency that occurred outside Canada if the repairs were necessary to ensure their safe return to Canada. The application for relief must be made with the prescribed information and in the prescribed manner at the time of the return of the goods to Canada.[209] An application for relief must be submitted to the CBSA in accordance with section 102 with evidence that supports the claim for relief. The value for duty of the work done abroad is calculated on the basis of section 105 of the *Customs Tariff* and not under section 46 of the *Customs Act*.

f) Remission Order

The *Repair Abroad of Canadian Civil Aircraft, Canadian Aircraft Engines, and Flight Simulators Order* outlines and explains the conditions under which remission is granted on the difference between the tax paid or payable and the duty paid or payable on the value of the repair for the aircraft, engines, and flight simulators exported for repair.

---

209 See additional details in Customs Memoranda D8-2-1, "Canadian Goods Abroad Program" and 8-2-4, "Canadian Goods Abroad Program—Emergency Repairs" (22 June 2009).

g) Tariff Items 9971.00.00 and 9992.00.00 Accounting Regulations[210]

The above Regulations set out the customs duty rates that are levied on goods, regardless of origin, that are returned to Canada after being exported to the United States, Mexico, Chile or Israel or another *CIFTA* beneficiary, for alteration, or warranty or non-warranty repairs. The goods covered under these tariff items are ships, boats, barges, fishing vessels, factory ships, light vessels, and so on regardless of their country of origin or tariff treatment.

h) Canadian Goods Returned after Being Exported

Goods originating in Canada, or goods which have been accounted for and released that have been exported, may be returned to Canada under tariff items 9813.00.00 or 9814.00.00, respectively, if they have not been advanced in value or combined with any other article abroad. The duties are payable only on the value added to the Canadian goods in the form of labour or additional material. Similarly, the GST/HST is payable only on the value of the processing performed outside of Canada (*Value of Imported Goods (GST/HST) Regulations*).[211]

i) Exporters of Processing Services Program

Under the Exporters of Processing Services (EOPS) program, companies that perform manufacturing services, such as assembly and alteration services for the benefit of a non-resident person, for which they charge a fee, can import certain goods that they do not own but will eventually re-export, without paying the GST/HST.

i) Qualifying for the Program

The following criteria have to be met in order to participate in the EOPS program: (1) the participant must be a GST/HST-registered company, (2) it must have no ownership interest in the imported or processed goods, and (3) it must not be closely related to the non-resident person on whose behalf it is doing the processing.

ii) Application for Relief

To participate in the EOPS program, a written application has to be submitted to the local Canada Revenue Agency (CRA) tax services office, which will process the application and conduct a field verification if necessary, following

---

210 SOR/98-47, am SOR/2004-127.
211 Above note 208.

which it will give a written confirmation acknowledging that the applicant is authorized to participate in the program. This letter of authorization must then be filed at the local CBSA office, which will issue a certificate number that is needed to account for the goods when importing. Those who are already participants in the duties relief program and hold a duties relief certificate must apply to the CRA through the CBSA office.

iii) Time Limits

All authorizations for relief under the EOPS program are valid for three years. The export of the imported goods being processed in Canada has to occur within four years of the date the goods were released by the CBSA.

7) Refunds for Other Reasons

a) Obsolete or Surplus Goods

Under sections 109 to 111 of the *Customs Tariff*, imported goods that are found to be obsolete or surplus, and goods processed from imported goods that become obsolete or surplus as a result of processing, are eligible for relief by way of full refund of duties and taxes other than GST/HST. Included in the relief provision are imported goods, other than fuel or plant equipment, directly consumed or expended in the processing in Canada of goods that become obsolete or surplus. The claimant for refund must be the importer or owner if the imported goods are obsolete or surplus, and if goods processed from imported goods become surplus as a result of processing, the claimant must be the manufacturer, producer, or owner. Application for refund must be made within five years after the release of the imported goods.

The ordinary and acceptable meaning of goods refers to "merchantable" items, and, therefore, if the goods are scrap and have no value, they are not eligible for refund. In *A & R Dress Co Inc v Canada (Minister of National Revenue)*,[212] the Tribunal held that as the claimant produced no evidence that the textile leftovers had any value, it was not eligible for a refund under section 110(b).

b) Waiver

If any other person is eligible to claim a refund of the duties in respect of which the application is made, the application must be accompanied by a

---

212 2006 FCA 298.

waiver, in the prescribed form, from those persons waiving their right to apply for the refund.

c) Additional Relief

i) Refund under Section 113(1)

Section 113(1) authorizes the grant of refund of all or a portion of duties if a relief or a refund could have been but was not granted, under sections 89 to 101. The application must be made in the form and manner prescribed under section 119. Regulations made under section 113(4) may prescribe several conditions for entitlement to the relief or refund. A claim must be submitted within four years after the goods in respect of which it is made were released.

ii) Refund on Designated Goods

Section 113(5) allows the grant of refund of duties and taxes on goods designated by regulations prescribed under the authority of section 113(4). Tobacco products are excluded from this section, but they may be eligible under other sections of Division 3 detailed above. If any other person is eligible to claim a refund of the duties in respect of which the application is made, the application must be accompanied by a waiver, in the prescribed form, from those persons waiving their right to apply for the refund.

d) Discretionary Relief

Section 115 of the *Customs Tariff* authorizes the Governor in Council to grant relief in respect of the whole or any portion of the duties that may be applicable regardless of whether any liability to pay the duties has arisen. The relief is granted by way of a remission order. If duties have been paid, they may be refunded by such an order.

e) Refunds under the *Customs Act*

Quite apart from the *Customs Tariff*, refunds can also be obtained under sections 74(1), 75, 76.78 to 79.1, 80, 80.1, 80.2, and 81 of the *Customs Act* and Regulations.[213] Under these sections and the Regulations, refunds can be obtained of full or partial duties paid on imported goods that have suffered

---

213 *Abatement of Duties Payable Regulations,* SOR/86-946 ("Regulations Respecting the Abatement of Duties on Imported Goods that Have Suffered Damage, Deterioration or Destruction, or a Loss in Volume or Weight"); *Refund of Duties Regulations,* SOR/98-48, am SOR/2004-126, SOR/2005-165, SOR/2005-213, SOR/2005-386, SOR/2006-222.

damage, deterioration, or destruction; for shortages; or that are inferior in quality, or on equipment removed from the goods and returned to the manufacturer for credit.

f) Remissions
In addition to the remission programs under section 115 of the *Customs Tariff*, remissions can also be obtained under the *Financial Administration Act*.[214] These remissions are also administered by the CBSA.

g) Clawback
Where goods in respect of which relief is granted under the *Customs Tariff* enter into a process that produces a by-product in respect of which relief could not have been granted, section 121 requires the processor to refund a proportionate amount of duty relieved, based upon the value of the by-product. If a refund or drawback was not paid previously on the imported goods, the amount of refund or drawback will be reduced by the duties payable on the by-product. Similarly, section 122 requires the processor to refund a proportionate amount of duties on merchantable scrap or waste produced by the processing of imported goods.

h) General Provisions
Where it is difficult to determine the exact amount of relief, refund, or drawback, or a remission of duties under the *Customs Tariff* or under the *Financial Administration Act*, the Minister of Public Safety and Emergency Preparedness may, with the consent of the applicant, grant to the applicant a sum in lieu of the relief, refund, drawback, or remission.

i) Further Conditions of Relief
The following conditions are laid down by sections 116 to 127 of Division 5 in respect of the grant of relief, refunds, drawbacks, or remissions ("relief"):

1) If an applicant is indebted to the federal or provincial government (the latter in respect of taxes, provided there is an agreement with the federal government) at the time the applicant applies, relief may be refused (section 116).
2) If the relief is subject to a condition and the condition has not been complied with, and the person who did not comply with the condition failed to report the non-compliance within ninety days after the failure to com-

---

214 RSC 1985, c F-11.

ply, the relief would have to be refunded, with interest, unless the failure to comply can be excused for legitimate reasons (sections 118(1) and (2)).
3) If a drawback has been granted by reason of a deemed exportation under section 89(3) and the goods are not subsequently exported but diverted to a use other than a use set out in that section, the person who diverted the goods must, within ninety days after the day of the diversion, report the diversion to an officer at a customs office and repay the amount of the drawback, with interest (section 118(2)).
4) Amounts required to be returned to the Government, and interest on those amounts, constitute a debt owing to Her Majesty in right of Canada under the *Customs Act*, and are recoverable under that Act (sections 121(2) and 122(2)).
5) Compound interest must be paid on amounts that have to be returned, while they are unpaid, in situations such as overpayments to a person who was granted relief, or because of failure to comply with a condition, or for diversion of the goods for uses not authorized (sections 95(2), 98(2), 114(2), 118(3), 121(2), and 122(2)).

The Federal Court, in an important decision, held that section 118 cannot be applied retroactively so as to cancel a certificate of exemption issued under section 89 and collect duties and taxes, as well as interest, because no condition had existed at the time of issuing the certificate and, therefore, there was no non-compliance. While the certificate can be cancelled because it was erroneously issued, it can only be done prospectively. Justice Blais, in *Dominion Sample Limited v Canada (Customs and Revenue Agency)*,[215] when granting judicial review of the CBSA's decision, said he had "no hesitation in concluding that the part of the Minister's decision which retroactively claim[ed] duties, penalties and interest [was] unlawful, unfair and arbitrary, and based on an erroneous finding of fact and law."

I. PROHIBITED GOODS

Section 136 of the *Customs Tariff* prohibits the importation of goods of tariff items 9897.00.00, 9898.00.00, and 9899.00.00. These tariff items include pornographic materials that are considered "obscene" under the *Criminal Code*;[216] firearms (except those that qualify in the limited circumstances discussed under "Firearms" in Section I(2), below in this chapter); and certain pets, plants, and foodstuffs prohibited under various Canadian agriculture

---

215 2003 FC 1244, Blais J at para 70.
216 RSC 1985, c C-46.

laws and endangered species laws. In addition, the *Copyright Act*[217] enables the interdiction of foreign-made copies of work that if produced in Canada would infringe copyright of the owner. Upon written notification of the copyright owner that it desires that the copies not be imported, the CBSA may deem the works to be included in the prescribed tariff item, and the relevant prohibited goods provision of the *Customs Tariff* applies accordingly.

The provisions relating to classification in accordance with the *General Rules for the Interpretation of the Harmonized System* and the *Canadian Rules* set out in the Schedule, do not apply to such goods.

1) Tariff Item 9897.00.00: Certain Wildlife and Plumage, Copyright, Second-Hand Motor Vehicles, and Others

The goods prohibited under this tariff item include certain wildlife species and plumage, such as live specimens of the mongoose family, certain live birds of the starling family, non-game birds, aigrettes, egret plumes, so-called osprey plumes; base or counterfeit coins; used or second-hand mattresses, with exceptions; reprints of Canadian copyrighted works and British copyrighted works that have been copyrighted in Canada; and any goods in association with which there is used any description that is false in a material respect as to the geographical origin of the goods, or the importation of which is prohibited by an order made under the *Trade-marks Act*; goods manufactured or produced wholly or partly by prison labour; used or second-hand motor vehicles of all kinds manufactured prior to the calendar year in which the importation into Canada is sought to be made, subject to certain exceptions when imported by the Department of National Defence, or by a settler on the settler's first arrival, or left by bequest, or when imported from the United States or Mexico to which the UST, MT, or MUST rates apply and manufactured during the calendar years 2009 to 2018, progressively reduced in age to one year old in 2018; smoke-screen apparatus for use on motor vehicles or certain vessels; white phosphorous matches; and used or second-hand aircraft, with certain exceptions.

---

217   RSC 1985, c C-42.

2) Tariff Item 9898.00.00: Firearms, and Prohibited Weapons and Devices

Firearms and prohibited weapons and devices are strictly regulated by both the *Criminal Code* and the *Customs Tariff*. An impressive body of caselaw has been generated by the import prohibitions of tariff item 9898.00.00, with the individual seldom achieving any success at the Tribunal level and even less at the appeals level. Most of these cases have dealt with the import of replica firearms by individuals who often advance frivolous arguments why they consider the imported items are not covered by the *Criminal Code* and, as a result, by tariff item 9898.00.00. There are also a few decisions relating to the importation of knives, especially those designated as "push daggers."

In tariff item 9898.00.00, the words "firearms," "weapons," "automatic firearm," "licence," "prohibited ammunition," "prohibited device," "prohibited firearm," "prohibited weapon," "restricted firearm," and "restricted weapon" have the same definitions as in sections 2 and 84 of the *Criminal Code*; "public officer" has the same definition as in section 117.07(2) of the *Criminal Code*. The terms "authorization to transport," "business," "carrier," and "non-resident" have the same meanings as in section 2(1) of the *Firearms Act*;[218] and "visiting force" has the same meaning as in section 2 of the *Visiting Forces Act*.[219]

The tariff item contains a long list of exceptions to the prohibitions. They include,

- imports by public officers in the course of their duties or employment, businesses that are licensed to acquire and possess goods, and weapons exempted by the *Criminal Code*;
- firearms, not being restricted or prohibited firearms, imported by
  » a non-resident who meets the requirements of section 35 of the *Firearms Act* or who holds a licence to acquire and possess that kind of firearm,
  » an individual who holds a licence to acquire and possess that kind of firearm, who is a resident of Canada and who acquired the firearm outside Canada, or
  » an individual who is a resident of Canada and who did not acquire the firearm outside Canada;
- any restricted firearm imported by

---

218 SC 1995, c 39.
219 RSC 1985, c V-2.

> a non-resident who meets the requirements of section 35 of the *Firearms Act* or who holds a licence to acquire and possess that kind of firearm and an authorization to transport,
> an individual who holds a licence to acquire and possess that kind of firearm and an authorization to transport, who is a resident of Canada and who acquired the firearm outside Canada, or
> an individual who is a resident of Canada, who holds an authorization to transport, and who did not acquire the firearm outside Canada;

- any prohibited firearm imported by an individual who is a resident of Canada, who holds an authorization to transport, and who did not acquire the firearm outside Canada;
- arms; ammunition; implements or munitions of war; army, naval, or air stores; and any articles deemed capable of being converted into any such things or made useful in the production of any such things, imported with a permit issued under section 8 of the *Export and Import Permits Act*;[220]
- arms, military stores, munitions of war, and other goods eligible for entry under tariff item 9810.00.00 or 9811.00.00; and
- arms, military stores, munitions of war, or classes thereof that, under regulations made by the Governor in Council, are exempted from the provisions of this tariff item.

a) Caselaw on Firearms and Prohibited Weapons

The Supreme Court of Canada in *R v Hasselwander*[221] elaborated what has since been known as the "*Hasselwander* test," interpreting the term "capable" as it relates to being an "automatic firearm" within section 84(1)(c) of the *Criminal Code* in the definition of a "prohibited weapon" in section 84(1)(c) of the *Criminal Code*. In its judgment, the Court declared that this term includes an aspect of potential capability for conversion, and given a reasonable interpretation, should be defined as meaning "capable of conversion to an automatic weapon in a relatively short period of time with relative ease."[222] Justice Cory added: "Where a weapon can be quickly and readily converted to automatic status, then that weapon must fall within the defin-

---

220 Above note 5.
221 [1993] 2 SCR 398.
222 *Ibid* at 416.

ition of 'prohibited weapon.' To come to any other conclusion would undermine the very purpose of the legislation."[223]

In *R v Vaughan*,[224] a criminal case that did not involve tariff item 9898.00.00, a butterfly knife that was in issue opened automatically through centrifugal force, and the accused was convicted by the trial judge, but was acquitted by the Quebec Court of Appeal. The Supreme Court of Canada restored the conviction, upholding the dissenting opinion of Beauregard JA, who would have dismissed the appeal against conviction on the basis of section 84(1) of the *Criminal Code*. In Beauregard JA's dissenting opinion at the Court of Appeal approved by the Supreme Court, "(t)he fact that two additional operations, the raising of the bar of the case and the joining of the two parts of the handle are required, does not take away from the fact that the knife blade can be opened automatically by centrifugal force; the opening of the blade is brought about automatically by the application of centrifugal force."[225]

The Federal Court of Appeal, setting aside the decision of the Tribunal and remitting it back to the Tribunal, ruled in *M Miner v President of the Canada Border Services Agency*[226] that the burden of proof of whether a weapon or device (in that case, two wooden tubes) was prohibited is not on the CBSA, as the Tribunal had imposed contrary to section 152(3)(d) of the *Customs Act*, but on the importer who brings an article into Canada. The Tribunal, on referral back of its decision by the court, dismissed the appeal of Mike Miner because, as the court had concluded, Mr Miner had failed to establish that the goods in issue were, at the time of importation, incapable of allowing a dart or arrow to be shot.

The Tribunal has, time and again, rejected all arguments of importers that weapons and devices of the same kind or even more dangerous are readily available in Canada and that they were not intercepted by customs[227] or other agencies, and has adopted a strict interpretation of the tariff item. In *Wayne Ericksen v Commissioner of the Canada Customs and Revenue Agency*[228] and *Romain L Klaasen v Commissioner of the Canada Customs and Revenue*

---

223 *Ibid* at 419.
224 [1991] 3 SCR 691.
225 (1990), 60 CCC (3d) 87 at 88.
226 AP-2009-080 (2011), rev'd 2012 FCA 81, remand to CITT AP-2009-080R (2012), 15 TTR (2d) 310.
227 *Ivan Hoza v President of the Canada Border Services Agency*, AP-2009-002 (2010), 14 TTR (2d) 435.
228 AP-2000-059 (2002).

Agency,[229] and several other decisions[230] where such an argument was advanced by the importer, the Tribunal pointed out that it is not a court of equity and must apply the law as it is. The administrative action, or inaction, of the CBSA cannot change the law.

Several importations have involved replica firearms, and both the CBSA and its predecessors have been extremely successful in refusing to allow entry and their decisions have in most cases been upheld by the Tribunal. If a replica firearm meets the three-part test set out in the *Criminal Code*, that is the end of the matter. For a device to be considered a "replica firearm" under section 84(1) of the Code, it must fulfil three conditions: (1) it must be designed or intended to exactly resemble, or to resemble with near precision, a firearm; (2) it must not itself be a firearm; and (3) it must not be designed or intended to exactly resemble, or to resemble with near precision, an antique firearm. To be considered as an "antique firearm," it must have been manufactured before 1898 and not have been designed to discharge rim-fire or centre-fire ammunition, and not have been re-designed to discharge such ammunition, or be prescribed to be an antique firearm. A long list of antique firearms has been prescribed by the *Regulations Prescribing Antique Firearms*.[231]

If a prohibited article falls squarely within the tariff item, that is enough for its detention and confiscation. The importers in *Gordon Schebek v President of the Canada Border Services Agency*[232] and *Jonathan Bell v President of the Canada Border Services Agency*[233] were two of a very small number of importers who succeeded in convincing the Tribunal that the devices they imported were not prohibited weapons. Gordon Schebek convinced the Tribunal that the knife he imported was significantly larger than the type of knife, commonly known as a push-dagger, which came within the prohibition of section 9 of the Regulations. The knife he imported was approximately 15-½ inches (39 centimetres) in length, with a blade approximately 8 inches (20 centimetres) in length. While allowing the appeal, the Tribunal pointed out that its determination applied only to the particular knife in issue, and that it did not draw any conclusions on whether "Katars" in general were prohibited weapons.

---

229 AP-2004-007 (2005), 10 TTR (2d) 542.
230 For example, *Allen Zerr v President of the Canada Border Services Agency*, AP-2006-057 (2008), 12 TTR (2d) 272.
231 SOR/98-464.
232 AP-2005-009 (2006), 10 TTR (2d) 877 [*Gordon Schebek*].
233 AP-2007-021 (2008) [*Jonathan Bell*].

In the *Jonathan Bell* case, Bell had imported an MP-5 Destron Leader Megatron action figure made of plastic that transformed from a toy robot with moveable parts to a purported replica of a Walther model P-38 semi-automatic pistol with optical sight. After examining both the action figure in issue and the authentic Walther P-38 pistol provided by the CBSA, the Tribunal was of the view that the action figure in issue was significantly larger than the Walther P-38 pistol. Consequently, it was satisfied that the action figure did not fulfil the first condition of the definition of "replica firearm" as set out in section 84(1) of the Code, that is, it was not designed or intended to exactly resemble, or to resemble with near precision, a firearm.

Even where an appeal was allowed in exceptional situations, such as in *Gordon Schebek* and *Jonathan Bell*, if a gun, weapon, or other device is thought to be dangerous, the government has the ability to include it specifically in regulations authorized under the Code, as it did, for instance, when the Regulations were amended in 1978 to include "Yaqua" blowguns in the list of prohibited weapons.[234] The inclusion of this weapon did not, however, stop the importer in *Walter Seaton v Commissioner of the Canada Customs and Revenue Agency* from successfully challenging the decision of the CCRA's determination that a blowgun, similar to the "Yaqua" blowgun, but just over half the latter's size and incapable of discharging anything other than toothpicks or matchsticks, was a prohibited weapon.[235] Seaton testified that he bought the wooden blowgun in issue from a street vendor in an Amazon village, as a toy for his grandson. The Tribunal examined the blowgun and agreed with Seaton that it was a toy and that it was not a weapon as defined in section 2 of the Code. In its view, the definition of weapon in section 2 is deemed to have been included in the schedule to the regulations which had listed "Yaqua" blowgun as a prohibited weapon. Walter Seaton's case can be distinguished from Mike Miner's, discussed earlier, where the Federal Court of Appeal had set aside the Tribunal's decision on a different ground, namely, that it had cast the burden of proof on the CBSA. A reading of the Tribunal's decision did not suggest that; all that it said was that the evidence adduced by the CBSA was weak. There was no such issue in Walter Seaton's case, as the CCRA did not challenge the evidence presented by the appellant and had asked the Tribunal to interpret only the words "or a similar device" (to the "Yaqua" blowgun) liberally.

---

234   *Criminal Code* amended by *Firearms Act*, SC 1995, c 39, s 139, adding s 117.15; *Regulations Prescribing Certain Firearms and Other Weapons, Components and Parts of Weapons, Accessories, Cartridges, Magazines, Ammunitions and Projectiles as Prohibited Weapons*, SOR/98-462, Sched, Part 3, Item 12.

235   (2003) AP-2002-020.

On the other hand, the Tribunal held in *Rebecca Wigod v Commissioner of the Canada Customs and Revenue Agency*[236] that the two hollow pieces of wood that were attached together to form a tube with openings at each end, one designed to receive a dart and be brought to the mouth for blowing, the other to allow the dart to exit, came within the description of a blowgun within the meaning of the Regulations and was a prohibited weapon. While accepting the appellant's submission that she purchased the item as a souvenir while on a vacation in Borneo as a decorative ornament for display purposes and not as a weapon, the Tribunal found that the product met the statutory definition and therefore was prohibited.

The Tribunal invariably rejects frivolous arguments, such as that (1) the guns or weapons were bought as souvenirs or as toys or playthings and are not dangerous items, (2) they do not cause as much harm as those already in the country,[237] (3) they have historical and personal sentimental value,[238] (4) they were intended to be a collector's item to be appreciated for their artistic merit and aesthetic beauty,[239] (5) they were destined for secure display as part of a small personal collection of wartime memorabilia,[240] and (6) they were imported to conduct simulated training, purely for entertainment purposes.[241] While politely rebuking appellants that it does not question their claims, the Tribunal firmly points out that those consideratons have no bearing on its determination of whether an imported article is a "prohibited" article within the meaning of tariff item 9898.00.00. For instance, in *Robert Gustas v Deputy Minister of National Revenue*,[242] there was no doubt that the knife in issue fell squarely within the definition of knives that are "prohibited weapons." In his written pleadings, the appellant submitted that he had been a knife collector for many years and regarded the knife in issue more as a work of art or a tool than as a weapon. The Tribunal pointed out that there were no exemption provisions for *bona fide* collectors and, regrettably for the appellant, there were also no dimensional limitations that would exempt knives as small and apparently inoffensive as the one in issue.

---

236 AP-2000-013 (2002), 6 TTR (2d) 366.
237 *R Joschko v President of the Canada Border Services Agency*, AP-2011-012 (2011), 16 TTR (2d) 155 [*Joschko*].
238 *Ibid*.
239 *Tiffany Woodworth v President of the Canada Border Services Agency*, AP-2006-035 (2007), 11 TTR (2d) 718.
240 *Joschko*, above note 237.
241 *Serge Poirier v President of the Canada Border Services Agency*, AP-2006-012 (2007), 11 TTR (2d) 439.
242 AP-96-006 (1997), 1 TTR (2d) 904.

The Tribunal commented, however, that the only feature that distinguished the knife in issue from garden-variety pocket knives was the automatic opening feature, a feature that would come in handy for many practical uses where the other hand was engaged.

3) Tariff item 9899.00.00: Books and Depictions of Obscenity, Sedition, Violence, Child Pornography, and Others

This tariff item prohibits the importation of (1) books, printed paper, drawings, paintings, prints, photographs, or representations of any kind that (a) are deemed to be obscene, (b) constitute hate propaganda, (c) are of a treasonable character, or (d) are of a seditious character, within the meaning of sections 163(8), 320(8), and 46 of the *Criminal Code*, respectively; (2) posters and handbills depicting scenes of crime or violence; or (3) photographic, film, video, or other visual representations, including those made by mechanical or electronic means, or written material, that are child pornography, within the meaning of sections 163.1, 59, and 60 of the *Criminal Code*, respectively.

If goods contravene the *Criminal Code*, penalties provided in it apply. If entry into Canada is denied because the goods have been determined by CBSA to be prohibited goods, an appeal would lie under section 71 of the *Customs Act* to a superior court of the province in which the goods were imported, and not to the Tribunal.

The leading case in which the constitutionality of the prohibition provisions of section 71 was upheld, is *Little Sisters Book and Art Emporium v Canada (Minister of Justice)*.[243] The Supreme Court of Canada upheld the decision of the trial judge, that the provisions which incorporate the definition of "obscene material" in section 163(8) of the *Criminal Code* are a justifiable intrusion into the citizen's rights guaranteed by the *Canadian Charter*, since they were directed to the prevention of harm, and the fact that customs officials applied the provisions in a differential manner did not vitiate the legislation itself.

---

243   (1996), 131 DLR (4th) 486 (BCSC), aff'd (1998), 109 BCAC 49 (CA), rev'd 2000 SCC 69.

ADDENDUM

A. *General Rules for the Interpretation of the Harmonized System*

Classification of goods in the Nomenclature shall be governed by the following principles:

1. The titles of Sections, Chapters and sub-Chapters are provided for ease of reference only; for legal purposes, classification shall be determined according to the terms of the headings and any relative Section or Chapter Notes and, provided such headings or Notes do not otherwise require, according to the following provisions.

2. (a) Any reference in a heading to an article shall be taken to include a reference to that article incomplete or unfinished, provided that, as presented, the incomplete or unfinished article has the essential character of the complete or finished article. It shall also be taken to include a reference to that article complete or finished (or falling to be classified as complete or finished by virtue of this Rule), presented unassembled or disassembled.

    (b) Any reference in a heading to a material or substance shall be taken to include a reference to mixtures or combinations of that material or substance with other materials or substances. Any reference to goods of a given material or substance shall be taken to include a reference to goods consisting wholly or partly of such material or substance. The classification of goods consisting of more than one material or substance shall be according to the principles of Rule 3.

3. When by application of Rule 2(b) or for any other reason, goods are, *prima facie*, classifiable under two or more headings, classification shall be effected as follows:

    (a) The heading which provides the most specific description shall be preferred to headings providing a more general description. However, when two or more headings each refer to part only of the materials or substances contained in mixed or composite goods or to part only of the items in a set put up for retail sale, those headings are to be regarded as equally specific in relation to those goods, even if one of them gives a more complete or precise description of the goods.

    (b) Mixtures, composite goods consisting of different materials or made up of different components, and goods put up in sets for retail sale, which cannot be classified by reference to Rule 3 (a), shall be classified as if they consisted of the material or component which gives them their essential character, insofar as this criterion is applicable.

(c) When goods cannot be classified by reference to Rule 3(a) or 3(b), they shall be classified under the heading which occurs last in numerical order among those which equally merit consideration.

4. Goods which cannot be classified in accordance with the above Rules shall be classified under the heading appropriate to the goods to which they are most akin.

5. In addition to the foregoing provisions, the following Rules shall apply in respect of the goods referred to therein:

(a) Camera cases, musical instrument cases, gun cases, drawing instrument cases, necklace cases and similar containers, specially shaped or fitted to contain a specific article or set of articles, suitable for long-term use and presented with the articles for which they are intended, shall be classified with such articles when of a kind normally sold therewith. This Rule does not, however, apply to containers which give the whole its essential character.

(b) Subject to the provisions of Rule 5(a) above, packing materials and packing containers presented with the goods therein shall be classified with the goods if they are of a kind normally used for packing such goods. However, this provision is not binding when such packing materials or packing containers are clearly suitable for repetitive use.

6. For legal purposes, the classification of goods in the subheadings of a heading shall be determined according to the terms of those subheadings and any related Subheading Notes and, *mutatis mutandis*, to the above Rules, on the understanding that only subheadings at the same level are comparable. For the purpose of this Rule the relative Section and Chapter Notes also apply, unless the context otherwise requires.

B. *Canadian Rules*

1. For legal purposes, the classification of goods in the tariff items of a subheading or of a heading shall be determined according to the terms of those tariff items and any related Supplementary Notes and, *mutatis mutandis*, to the *General Rules* for the Interpretation of the Harmonized System, on the understanding that only tariff items at the same level are comparable. For the purpose of this Rule the relative Section, Chapter and Subheading Notes also apply, unless the context otherwise requires.

2. Where both a Canadian term and an international term are presented in this Nomenclature, the commonly accepted meaning and scope of the international term shall take precedence.
3. For the purpose of Rule 5 (b) of the *General Rules* for the Interpretation of the Harmonized System, packing materials or packing containers clearly suitable for repetitive use shall be classified under their respective headings.

TABLE 1

Sections and Chapters of the Harmonized System

Section	Items	Chapters
I	Live Animals; Animal Products	1–5
II	Vegetable Products	6–14
III	Animal or Vegetable Fats and Oils and Their Cleavage Products; Prepared Edible Fats; Animal or Vegetable Waxes	15
IV	Prepared Foodstuffs; Beverages, Spirits and Vinegar; Tobacco and Manufactured Tobacco Substitutes	16–24
V	Mineral Products	25–27
VI	Products of the Chemical or Allied Industries	28–38
VII	Plastics and Articles Thereof; Rubber and Articles Thereof	39–40
VIII	Raw Hides and Skins; Leather, Furskins and Articles Thereof; Saddlery and Harness; Travel Goods, Handbags and Similar Containers; Articles of Animal Gut (Other Than Silkworm Gut)	41–43
IX	Wood and Articles of Wood; Wood Charcoal; Cork and Articles of Cork; Manufactures of Straw, of Esparto or of Plaiting Materials; Basketware and Wickerwork	44–46
X	Pulp of Wood or of Other Fibrous Cellulosic Material; Recovered (Waste and Scrap) Paper or Paperboard; Paper and Paperboard and Articles Thereof	47–49
XI	Textile and Textile Articles	50–63
XII	Footwear, Headgear, Umbrellas, Sun Umbrellas, Walking-Sticks, Seat-Sticks, Whips, Riding-Crops and Parts Thereof; Prepared Feathers and Articles Made Therewith; Flowers, Articles of Human Hair	64–67
XIII	Articles of Stone, Plaster, Cement, Asbestos, Mica or Similar Materials; Ceramic Products; Glass and Glassware	68–70
XIV	Natural or Cultured Pearls, Precious or Semi-Precious Stones, Precious Metals, Metals Clad with Precious Metal and Articles Thereof; Imitation Jewellery; Coin	71
XV	Base Metals and Articles of Base Metal	72–83
XVI	Machinery and Mechanical Appliances; Electrical Equipment; Parts Thereof; Sound Recorders and Reproducers; Television Image and Sound Recorders and Reproducers, and Parts and Accessories of Such Articles	84–85
XVII	Vehicles, Aircraft, Vessels and Associated Transport Equipment	86–89

Section	Items	Chapters
XVIII	Optical, Photographic, Cinematographic, Measuring, Checking, Precision, Medical or Surgical Instruments and Apparatus; Clocks and Watches; Musical Instruments; Parts and Accessories Thereof	90–92
XIX	Arms and Ammunition; Parts and Accessories Thereof	93
XX	Miscellaneous Manufactured Articles	94–96
XXI	Works of Art, Collectors' Pieces and Antiques	97
XXII	Special Classification Provisions; Temporary Legislation; Temporary Modifications Proclaimed Pursuant to Trade Agreements Legislation; Additional Import Restrictions Proclaimed Pursuant to Section 22 of the Agricultural Adjustment Act, As Amended	98–99

Table 1 | Sections and Chapters of the Harmonized System

CHAPTER 3

Special Import Measures Act[1]

A. INTRODUCTION

The primary purpose of the *Special Import Measures Act (SIMA)* is to protect Canadian manufacturers and producers by levelling the playing field between exporting countries with which Canada has trade relations and Canadian manufacturers and producers of goods and merchandise, by counteracting unfair and aggressive competition that materially injures or threatens to cause material injury resulting in disruption of Canadian markets, through the special measures provided by the Act. Unfair competition is caused not only by below-normal pricing but also by the consequence of various forms of government subsidy that enable foreign manufacturers, producers, and exporters to reduce their production costs and sell at lower prices in domestic as well as foreign markets. An analysis of facts in various investigations conducted by the Canadian Border Services Agency (CBSA) and the Tribunal reveals that financial subsidies granted to manufacturers, producers, and exporters take various forms, both financial and non-financial, including tax preferences; write-off of research and development costs against income; cheap leases of government lands that enable extraction of timber, minerals, oil, and gas; and state trading, especially in grains.

The process begins with a preliminary investigation into dumping or subsidizing, or both, by the CBSA on the basis of valid complaints from the Canadian industry or producers, followed simultaneously by an inquiry by the Tribunal. If the CBSA's investigation finds that the complaints are valid,

---

1   RSC 1985, c S-15 [*SIMA*].

it is authorized to impose provisional duties on all imports from the exporters concerned as of the date the investigation commenced. The provisional duties, as the term implies, are only temporary, though payable immediately, and must be confirmed by the Tribunal through a finding of injury. When that finding is made, and it has become final, the *SIMA* dumping or countervailing duties, or both, are payable by the importer of the goods as from the date of the finding. If the Tribunal does not find injury, the provisional duties have to be refunded. The obligation to pay the duties is imposed on the importers who will, if they can, pass them on to Canadian manufacturers and producers, who will ultimately raise the prices of their products. If the imported goods continue to be cheaper than similar goods produced in Canada, the ultimate losers are Canadians, hurting both the consumer and the economy. To mitigate the effects of the levy, however, the Tribunal may conduct a public interest investigation and, at the conclusion of its inquiry, may, and usually does, invite Canadian manufacturers who were dependant on the imports, and public interest groups, to make submissions, following which the Tribunal may make a recommendation to the Minister of Finance to reduce or eliminate the levies.

The *SIMA* applies to goods imported from any country. Specific Parts of the Act apply to goods imported from the United States (Part II) and from the *NAFTA* countries (Part I.1), but the operation of Part II (goods imported from the United States) is suspended while Part I.1 (goods imported from a *NAFTA* country) is in operation.[2] The Governor in Council, on the recommendation of the Minister of Finance, may by regulations prescribed under section 14, exempt any goods or class of goods imported from any country from the application of the *SIMA*, and, specifically, goods imported from Chile, the latter during a period and subject to conditions specified in the regulations.

Canadian exporters are not immune from similar protective measures taken by other countries, including free trade partners, if they too engage in unfair competition or receive financial or non-financial subsidies from various levels of the Canadian government. A few of the significant measures imposed on Canadian exporters, especially on softwood lumber exports, are referred to in this chapter.

Safeguard measures taken under the *Customs Tariff* that result in the imposition of surtaxes and tariff rate quotas have a similar purpose. They have been discussed in Chapter 2. Unlike those measures, the *SIMA* anti-dumping and countervailing duties are applied when there is evidence that the dump-

---

[2] *Ibid*, s 77.1(2).

ing or subsidizing by exporters has caused, or is likely to cause, injury to, or retardation of, production in Canada of like goods. Unlike the *Customs Tariff* safeguard measures, there is no limitation on the amount of anti-dumping and countervailing duties so long as they do not exceed the margins of dumping or subsidy, and those margins or volumes of export to Canada are not insignificant or negligible.

Anti-dumping and countervailing duties are authorized by Article VI of the *General Agreement on Tariffs and Trade (GATT)* as a *quid pro quo* to globalization of trade advocated by the World Trade Organization (WTO), of which Canada and over 150 other countries are members. The *SIMA* inquiries and investigations must be consistent with the *GATT* Article VI procedures; if they are not adhered to and the facts are disputed, the aggrieved country can appeal to the appeals body of the WTO, whose decisions are binding.

In this chapter, except in respect of the Dispute Settlement provisions of Parts I.1 and II, the word "Minister" is defined by the Act to mean the Minister of Public Safety and Emergency Preparedness, who acts through the CBSA. In some provisions of the Act, another Minister is named, who may be the Minister of Finance or the Minister of International Trade. The latter is specifically named in a few provisions of Part I.1. If the word "Minister" is used alone in the Act, other than in Parts I.1 and II, it stands for the Minister of Public Safety and Emergency Preparedness.

Section 98 of the Act expressly authorizes the Governor in Council, by order, to modify or suspend the application, with respect to any country, of any provision of the *SIMA*, in whole or in part, for the purpose of ensuring that the *SIMA* procedures comply with the *GATT* Subsidies Agreement.

B. MEANING AND OCCURRENCE OF DUMPING AND SUBSIDIZING

1) Dumping

Dumping and subsidizing are two concepts that are central to the *SIMA*. Dumping is counteracted by levying an anti-dumping duty to offset its effects, subsidizing by levying a countervailing duty to offset the amount of subsidy granted to exporters by their governments.

a) Meaning of Dumping and Margin of Dumping

According to section 2(1), dumping occurs when an exporter sells goods to an importer in Canada at prices that are lower than those the exporter charges for "like" goods in its home market or at unprofitable prices. "Like goods" in relation to any other goods means goods that are identical in all respects to the other goods. If there are no like goods, goods the use and other characters of which closely resemble the other goods are deemed to be "like" goods.

"Margin of dumping" is defined by section 2(1) as the amount by which the normal value of the goods exceeds the export price. The normal value is generally the selling price of the goods in the country where they were produced or from which they were exported.

b) Insignificant Margin

A margin of dumping that is less than 2 percent is deemed by section 2(1) to be "insignificant." Sections 30.1 and 30.2 provide for weighting of export prices and the normal values; the greater of the two is the margin of dumping. If it is impracticable to determine a margin of dumping where many exporters have dumped goods and are under dumping investigation, then the CBSA, under the authority of section 30.4, may use either the largest percentage of goods of each of the countries that, in its opinion, can reasonably be investigated, or statistically valid samples.

c) Negligible Volume

Dumping is deemed by section 2(1) to be "negligible" if the volume of goods of a country that are exported to Canada is less than 3 percent of the total volume of goods of the same description that emanate from all countries. However, if the total volume of three or more countries, each of whose dumped goods is less than 3 percent of the total volume but exceeds 7 percent in totality then dumping is not deemed to be negligible.

2) Subsidizing and Financial Contribution

Subsidizing, according to section 2(1), occurs when a country gives financial assistance to its industries or producers and the goods exported from that country to Canada benefit from that assistance. "Subsidy" means a financial contribution by an exporting country that confers benefit to persons engaged in the production, manufacture, growth, processing, purchase, distribution, transportation, sale, export, or import of goods, in any of the circumstances set out in section 2(1.6). Any form of income or price support within the meaning of Article VI of the *GATT 1994* that confers a benefit, comes within that section. If the financial assistance has not been exempted under Article VI (and by the *SIMA*), goods exported to Canada that benefited from that assistance become liable to a countervailing duty.

a) Meaning of Financial Contribution

Under section 2(1.6), there is deemed to be a financial contribution where:

1) the practices of the government involve direct transfer of funds or liabilities;
2) the amounts that would otherwise be owing and due to the government are exempted, deducted, forgiven, or not collected;
3) the government provides goods or services, other than general government infrastructure, or purchases goods; or
4) the government permits or directs a non-governmental body to do any of the things referred to in points (1) to (3) above if the right or obligation to do the thing is normally vested in the government and the manner in which the non-governmental body acts does not differ in any meaningful way from the manner in which the government does it.

There is, however, deemed to be no financial contribution in the following situations:

1) a financial contribution made by Canada;
2) the amount of any duty or internal tax imposed by the exporting country or country of origin on goods that have been exempt or have been or will be relieved by means of remission, refund, or drawback because of their exportation from that country;
3) energy, fuel, oil, and catalysts that are used or consumed in the production of exported goods and that have been exempted or have been or will be relieved by means of remission, refund, or drawback; and
4) goods that are incorporated into exported goods that have been exempted or relieved or will be relieved by remission, refund, or drawback.

b) Non-actionable Subsidy

The following subsidies are not actionable if they meet prescribed criteria:

1) a subsidy that is not specific as determined by sections 2(7.1) to (7.4),
2) subsidies for industrial research,
3) pre-competitive development assistance,
4) assistance to disadvantaged regions,
5) assistance for the adaptation of existing facilities to new environmental standards, and

6) assistance for research activities conducted by institutions of higher education and independent research bodies.

In addition to the above non-actionable situations, the *SIMA* expressly excludes a domestic support measure for agriculture products listed in Annex 1 to the *Agreement on Agriculture*, which is part of Annex 1A to the *World Trade Organization Agreement*, that conforms to the provisions of Annex 2 of that *Agreement*. However, this exclusion expires, and the domestic support measure ceases to be non-actionable, on the day on which the implementation period in respect of the *Agreement on Agriculture* expires.

A subsidy is deemed to be insignificant if the amount is less than 1 percent of the export price.

c) Non-specific and Specific Subsidy; Prohibited Subsidy

A non-specific subsidy is made non-actionable by sections 2(7.1), as above stated, only if the criteria or conditions governing eligibility for, and the amount of the subsidy, are

1) objective;
2) set out in a legislative, regulatory, or administrative instrument, or other public document; and
3) applied in a manner that does not favour, or is not limited to, a particular enterprise. If it is so limited, or if it is a prohibited subsidy, it is deemed to be a specific subsidy by section 2(7.2).

A prohibited subsidy is an export subsidy or a portion of a subsidy that is contingent in whole or in part on the use of goods that are produced or that originate in the country of export.

Section 2(7.3) authorizes the CBSA to determine that a subsidy is specific, but in so doing, it must have regard to the following factors:

1) whether there is exclusive use of the subsidy by a limited number of enterprises,
2) whether there is predominant use of the subsidy by a particular enterprise,
3) whether disproportionately large amounts of subsidy are granted to a limited number of enterprises, and
4) whether the manner in which discretion is exercised by the granting authority indicates that the subsidy is not generally available.

If any of the above four factors is present, the CBSA must consider whether the presence of those factors is due to (1) the extent of diversification of economic activities within the jurisdiction of the granting authority, or (2) the length of time that the subsidy program has been in operation. And where any of these two conditions exist, the CBSA may find the subsidy to be specific.

d) Amount of Subsidy

Taking into account the foregoing rules relating to the definition of subsidy and the manner of its administration by the government of an exporting country, the amount of subsidy is to be determined in the manner prescribed by regulations. Part II of the *Special Import Measures Regulations*[3] provides for the determination of subsidy in various situations where the government of an exporting country gives financial advantages in the form of a grant (section 27); direct transfer of funds or liabilities (section 27.1); loan at a preferential rate (sections 28 to 31); loan guarantee (section 31.1); income tax credits, refunds, and exemptions (section 32); deferral of income taxes (sections 33 and 34); excessive relief on duties and taxes on exported goods (section 35) and on inputs (section 35.01); and acquisition of shares (section 35.1), purchase of goods (section 35.2), and provision of goods and services by government (section 36).

In accordance with section 36.001, where there is a significant difference between the amount of subsidy in relation to goods as otherwise determined under Part III and the future value, on the date of sale of the goods, of the amount of subsidy so determined, the CBSA must calculate the amount of subsidy on the basis of the future value of that subsidy on the date of sale.

Where a regulation has not been enacted to govern the calculation, or in the opinion of the CBSA sufficient information is not available or has not been provided to enable the determination of the amount, the Minister may, in accordance with section 30.4, specify the manner in which the subsidy should be determined. However, a non-actionable subsidy, as defined above by section 2(1), cannot be included in the computation of the subsidy.

C. DETERMINATION OF NORMAL VALUE AND EXPORT PRICE

1) Normal Value

The normal value is used to calculate the margin of dumping or amount of subsidy, as the case may be. "Normal value" is defined by section 2(1) to mean

---

[3] SOR/84-927 [*SIMR*].

normal value as determined under sections 15 to 23, 29, and 30. It is generally the selling price of the goods in the exporter's home market.

a) Primary Method of Determination

Section 15 specifies the primary method for determining the normal value. Under this method, the normal value is the price of like goods (that is, identical goods or goods closely resembling them) when sold by the exporter to purchasers in the country of export

1) who are not, at the time of the sale, associated with the exporter;
2) who are at the same or substantially the same trade level as the exporter;
3) in the same or substantially the same quantities as the sale of goods to the importer;
4) in the ordinary course of trade for use in the country of export under competitive conditions;
5) during such period of sixty days that ends in the interval commencing with the first day of the year preceding the date of sale of the goods to the importer and ending on the forty-ninth day after such sale, as is selected by the CBSA. If goods are sold for future delivery, the CBSA may choose another period during that interval; and
6) at the place from which the goods were shipped directly to Canada under normal conditions of trade.[4]

b) Alternative Methods of Determination

The *SIMA* specifies other methods of determining the normal value where the primary method is not appropriate. These methods are described below:

i) Where Conditions of Sale Comparison Not Present

If the CBSA is of the opinion that,

1) there was not such a number of sales of like goods made by the exporter at the place of export to enable comparison, the Minister may choose any other place nearest to the place where there were sales of like goods;
2) the purchasers from the exporter in the home market are not at the same or substantially the same trade level as the importer, the Minister may choose sales to purchasers who are at a trade level nearest and sub-

---

4 *Shaw Industries v Deputy Minister of National Revenue (Customs and Excise)* (1992), 53 FTR 15 (TD) [*Shaw Industries*]. The Federal Court held that in preliminary determination of dumping, the Minister is permitted to use *SIMA* s 19 to determine normal value where identical goods were sold at a loss in a foreign country, and s 15 where goods were sold at a profit in a foreign country.

sequent to that of the importer, if there was a sufficient number of sales at that trade level;
3) the exporter sold the like goods solely or primarily for export, or the sale of like goods during the prescribed period were solely or primarily to prescribed persons, the Minister may choose sales of like goods for use in the country of export by other vendors;
4) the quantity of goods sold to the importer in Canada is larger than the largest quantity of like goods sold by the exporter for use in the country of export, the latter sales are to be used; and
5) if the quantity of goods sold to the importer is smaller than the smallest quantity of goods sold to purchasers in the country of export, the latter sales are to be used.

ii) Where Purchasers Associated with Vendor

Section 2(1.2) of the Act provides that a domestic producer is associated with the exporter or importer if,

1) the producer either directly or indirectly controls, or is controlled by, the exporter or importer;
2) the producer and the exporter or importer are directly or indirectly controlled by a third person; or
3) the producer and the exporter or importer directly or indirectly control a third person, and there are grounds to believe that the producer behaves differently towards the exporter or importer than does a non-related person.

Section 2(1.3) further clarifies that there is deemed to be control where a person is legally or operationally in a position to exercise restraint or direction over another person.

Where the producer and the exporter or importer are associated, the CBSA may not take into account sales made by a producer or exporter to a purchaser of like goods in the country of export if the vendor did not at the same or substantially the same time sell like goods in the ordinary course of trade to other purchasers in that country who are at the same trade level as and not associated with the purchaser.

iii) Where Prices Below Cost of Production

If, in the opinion of the Minister, any sale of like goods forms part of a series of sales at prices that are below the cost of production, marketing, and profit, the Minister may not take into account such sales.

iv) Weighted Average of Prices

The price of goods sold to purchasers during a prescribed period is the price at which the preponderance of sales of like goods that comply with the requisite terms and conditions were made by the exporter to purchasers throughout that period. When there is no such preponderance of sales at a single price throughout the prescribed period, the weighted average of the prices at which like goods were sold during the said period must be used.

v) Exports to Canada Not Having Trademark

If goods imported into Canada do not bear a trademark that is applied to like goods in home sales, and the goods like the imported goods are not sold for use in the home market, the goods imported into Canada and the goods sold for use in the home market are deemed to be like goods if the CBSA is of the opinion that the goods are being imported into Canada in order to avoid the operation of the *SIMA* and it is probable that the trademark or another closely resembling trademark will be applied to the goods subsequent to their importation.

vi) Surrogate Countries Sales

If, in the opinion of the Minister, there were not sufficient numbers of sales of like goods to permit a proper comparison, normal value is to be determined under section 19, at the option of the CBSA, as (1) the price at which the exporter sold like goods to importers in any country other than Canada during a prescribed period as in the opinion of the CBSA fairly reflects the market value of the goods, adjusted in the prescribed manner and circumstances to reflect differences in terms and conditions of sale, taxation, and other differences relating to price comparability between the goods sold to the importer in Canada and like goods sold by the exporter to the importers in the other country; or (2) the aggregate of the cost of production of the goods; a reasonable amount for administrative, selling, and all other costs; and a reasonable amount for profits.

vii) Prices Determined by Government or Government Monopoly

The normal value of imported goods is to be determined pursuant to section 20(1) of the *SIMA* where the goods sold to an importer in Canada and shipped directly to Canada (a) from a prescribed country where, in the opinion of the CBSA, domestic prices are substantially determined by the government of that country and there is reason to believe that they are not substantially the same as they would be if they were determined in a competitive market, or

(b) in the case of any other country, (i) the government of that country has a monopoly or substantial monopoly of its export trade and (ii) where, in the opinion of the CBSA, there is reason to believe that they are not substantially the same as they would be if they were determined in a competitive market.

Section 20(1)(a) can be applied only to a prescribed country, whereas section 20(1)(b) can be applied to any country. The section can only be applied to a particular sector within a country, and not to the entire country.

Only two countries, the People's Republic of China and the Socialist Republic of Vietnam, have been prescribed under section 20(1)(a) by sections 17.1 and 17.2, respectively, of the *Special Import Measures Regulations* (*SIMR*);[5] hence condition (a) only applies to them.

For all other countries, the above two conditions specified in section 20(b) must exist.

Most typically, the normal values in the "non-market" situation are determined by using prices and costs of like goods in a third country (that is, a "surrogate" country). For the purpose of determining the normal value, section 16 of the *SIMR* specifies as follows:

1) Where like goods are sold by producers in any country other than Canada designated by the CBSA for use in that country, the normal value is
    a) the price of such goods at the time of the sale of the goods to the importer in Canada, adjusted in the prescribed manner and circumstances to reflect the differences in terms and conditions of sale, taxation, and other differences relating to price comparability between the goods sold to the importer in Canada and the like goods sold in the designated country, or, at the option of the CBSA,
    b) the aggregate of the cost of production of the like goods; a reasonable amount for administrative, selling, and all other costs; and a reasonable amount for profits.
2) Where sufficient information has not been furnished to the CBSA, or is not available, to determine the normal value as provided above, the normal value is the price of like goods in any country other than Canada, designated by the CBSA, or the country from which the goods were directly shipped to Canada, and imported into Canada and sold by the importer thereof in the condition in which they were imported to a person with whom the importer was not associated at the time of the sale,

---

5   Above note 3, am SOR/2002-349, s 1, SOR/2013-81, s 1 (China); s 2 (Vietnam).

with appropriate adjustments to reflect the differences in terms and conditions of sale, in taxation, and other differences relating to price comparability.

3) However, for the purposes of section 16(1)(b), a "reasonable amount for profits" is
   a) the amount of profit that generally results from sales of like goods by vendors in Canada who are at the same or substantially the same trade level as the importer of the like goods to purchasers in Canada who are not associated with the vendor;
   b) if the amount described in (a) cannot be determined, the amount of profit that generally results from sales of goods of the same general category as the like goods by vendors in Canada, who are at the same or substantially the same trade level as the importer of like goods to purchasers in Canada who are not associated with those vendors; or
   c) where neither (a) nor (b) can be determined, the amount of profit that generally results from sales of goods that are of the group or range of goods that is next largest to the category referred in (b), by vendors in Canada who are at the same or substantially the same trade level as the importer, to purchasers in Canada who are not associated with those vendors.

A country may not be designated by the CBSA under paragraph (2) above if the like goods of that country are also subject to a *SIMA* investigation unless the CBSA is of the opinion that those goods are not dumped, or if the price of the like goods, in the opinion of the CBSA, has been significantly influenced by the designated country.

viii) Goods Sold on Credit

Section 21 provides special rules for adjustment of normal value where (1) like goods are sold on credit terms other than cash discounts, (2) where two or more prescribed purchasers are persons associated with each other, and (3) where an exporter provides benefits to purchasers of like goods for use in the country of export on resale in that country.

ix) Ministerial Prescription of Normal Value

Where sufficient information has not been furnished to the CBSA, or is not available to determine the normal value, or where goods are shipped or are to be shipped to Canada on consignment and there is no known purchaser in Canada, section 29 authorizes the CBSA to determine the normal value in such manner as the Minister specifies.[6]

x) Goods Passing through One or More Countries
For the purposes of determining the normal value, goods shipped to Canada from one country that pass in transit through another country are deemed by section 30 to be shipped directly to Canada, subject to such terms and conditions as to shipment, documentation, warehousing, and transhipment as may be prescribed.

Similarly, where goods shipped to Canada from the country of origin pass through one or more other countries in transit and would, but for section 30, have a normal value that is less than what the normal value would be if the country of export were the country of origin, the normal value of the goods is to be computed as if they were shipped directly to Canada from the country of origin.

xi) Calculation during Start-Up Period
Where the investigation period of normal value includes a start-up of production of the goods, the cost of production and the administrative, selling, and other costs with respect to the goods for that start-up are to be determined as prescribed pursuant to section 23.1.

2) Export Price

a) Primary Method of Determination
Under section 24, the export price of goods sold to an importer in Canada is the lesser of the exporter's sale price for the goods and the price at which the importer has purchased the goods, reduced by any export charges that are included in either or both prices, namely, (1) the costs, charges, and expenses incurred in preparing the goods for shipment to Canada that are additional to the costs generally incurred on sales of like goods for use in the country of export; (2) freight and insurance; and (3) any duty or tax paid in Canada under federal or provincial law by or on behalf of the exporter, or at its request. This export price is determined using the commercial invoice and subtracting any identified export charges, but the invoice or affidavit showing the export price is not conclusive.

---

6   Ministerial prescription with respect to normal value is not a statutory instrument. *Liberty Home Products Corp v Deputy Minister of National Revenue (Customs and Excise)* (1990), 3 TCT 5243 (FCA), rev'g (1987), 12 TBR 42 (Tariff Board).

b) Special Rules Where Price Unreliable

Section 25 contains special rules to determine the export price where that price is not reliable for the following reasons:

1) there is no exporter's sale price or importer's purchase price; and
2) the export price, in the opinion of the CBSA, is unreliable for the reason that the sale of the goods for export to Canada was a sale between associated persons, or by reason of a compensatory arrangement between any two or more of the manufacturer, producer, vendor, exporter, importer in Canada, subsequent purchaser, and any other person that directly or indirectly affects or relates to
   a) the price of the goods;
   b) the sale of the goods;
   c) the net return to the manufacturer, producer, vendor, or exporter of the goods; or
   d) the net cost to the importer of the goods.

In the above situations, the export price of the goods is to be determined in the following manner:

1) If the goods were sold by the importer in the condition in which they were or are to be imported to a person with whom the importer was not associated at the time of the sale, the export price is the price for which the goods were so sold, less the following amounts:
   a) amounts for costs, duties, and taxes incurred after importation but before sale to the person, or resulting from their sale by the importer;
   b) an amount for profit by the importer on the sale;
   c) the costs, charges, and expenses incurred by the exporter, importer, or any other person in preparing the goods for shipment to Canada that are additional to those generally incurred on sales of like goods for use in the country of export; and
   d) all other costs, charges, and expenses incurred by the exporter, importer, or any other person resulting from the exportation of the imported goods, or arising from their shipment, from the place described in section 15(e) or the place substituted therefor in accordance with section 16(1)(a).
2) If the goods are imported for the purpose of assembly, packaging, or other further manufacture in Canada or for incorporation into other goods in the course of such manufacture or producion, the export price is the price of the goods as assembled, packaged, or otherwise further

manufactured, or of the goods into which the imported goods have been incorporated, when sold to a person with whom the vendor is not associated at the time of the sale, less the costs referred to in the previous paragraph, and in addition, the costs attributable to the assembly, packaging, or other further manufacture, or costs incurred on or after the importation of the imported goods and on or before the sale of the goods as assembled, packaged, or otherwise further manufactured or of the goods into which the imported goods have been incorporated.

3) In cases other than (1) and (2), the export price is the price determined as prescribed by the Minister.

c) No Deduction for *SIMA* Duties

Where the export price is determined with respect to goods imported into Canada and sold in the condition in which they were imported, as provided in section 25(1)(c), or where goods are imported for the purpose of assembly, packaging, or further manufacture or for incorporation into other goods, as provided in section 25(1)(d), no deduction is permitted by section 25(2) for duties imposed by the *SIMA* if the CBSA is of the opinion that the export price determined under those paragraphs without making such a deduction is equal to or greater than the normal value of the goods.

d) Undertaking to Pay Anti-dumping Duty

Where a manufacturer, producer, vendor, or exporter undertakes to compensate, indemnify, reimburse, or pay an importer or purchaser in Canada, directly or indirectly, for any anti-dumping duties that are imposed under the *SIMA*, section 26 requires that the compensatory arrangement, indemnity, reimbursement, or payment be deducted in determining the export price.

e) Goods Sold on Credit to Importer in Canada

Specific rules to compute interest, or principal and interest, are provided by section 27 for determining the export price of a unit of goods where goods are sold on credit to an importer in Canada.

f) Exporter Providing Benefits on Resale

In determining the export price, section 28 requires the deduction of all benefits provided by an exporter to an importer or any person buying from the importer subsequently on resale, by way of rebate, service, other goods, or otherwise.

D. LIABILITY FOR ANTI-DUMPING, COUNTERVAILING, AND PROVISIONAL DUTIES

1) Imposition of Duties

Sections 3 to 8 of the *SIMA* authorize the government to levy and collect from an importer

1) an anti-dumping duty in an amount equal to the margin of dumping;
2) a countervailing duty in an amount equal to the amount of subsidy, on imported goods in respect of which the Tribunal has made an order or finding, before their release, that the dumping or subsidizing of goods of the same description has caused injury or retardation, or is threatening to cause injury; and
3) a provisional duty in an amount not exceeding the estimated margin of dumping or amount of subsidy, on imported goods if the goods of the same description previously imported would have caused injury or retardation were it not for the fact that the provisional duty was applied in respect of them.

Section 2(1) defines "injury" to mean "material injury" and "retardation" to mean "material retardation to the establishment of a domestic industry."

The importer is given the option to deposit security in respect of the provisional duty, in an amount not greater than the estimated margin of dumping or the estimated amount of subsidy, as prescribed pursuant to section 8(1)(d).

a) Duties When Massive Importation Causes Injury

Where imported goods have already been released, an anti-dumping or countervailing duty, whichever is applicable in accordance with the Tribunal's order or finding, is payable if (1) there has been considerable importation of like goods, which dumping has caused injury or would have caused injury but for the application of anti-dumping measures, or the importer of the goods was or should have been aware that the exporter was practising dumping and that the dumping would cause injury, and (2) injury has been caused by reason of the massive importation or by reason of the importation being part of a series of importations occurring in a relatively short period, which in the aggregate is massive.

The anti-dumping or countervailing duty, as the case may be, is to be applied on all imported goods that were released during the period of ninety days preceding the day on which the CBSA made a preliminary determination of dumping. Goods released before the initiation of investigation that was commenced pursuant to section 31 are not subject to such duties.

b) Countervailing Duty on Imports from a Specific Country

Section 7 authorizes the Governor in Council, following an investigation by the CBSA, to impose a countervailing duty on goods imported from a specific country, in an amount not exceeding the amount of subsidy determined by the investigation to have been given by the government of that country, by way of an order made on the recommendation of the Minister of Finance, provided that such imposition has been authorized by the Committee on Subsidies and Countervailing Measurers constituted under the *World Trade Organization Agreement*.[7]

c) Provisions in Free Trade Agreements

The *NAFTA* has its own provisions relating to the imposition and application of anti-dumping and countervailing duties. These provisions are found in Part II and Part I.1 of the *SIMA*, which are discussed in Section E(6), below in this chapter.[8] Other free trade agreements (FTAs) may also contain similar provisions. For instance, Article 17 of the *Canada-European Free Trade Agreement (CEFTA)* states that the application of countervailing measures shall be governed by Articles VI and XVI of the *GATT 1994* and the WTO *Agreement on Subsidies and Countervailing Measures*, and Article 18 states that the rights and obligations of the parties in respect of the application of anti-dumping measures shall be governed by Article VI of the *GATT 1994* and the WTO *Agreement on Implementation of Article VI of the General Agreement on Tariffs and Trade 1994*. The Agreement also requires the parties to give advance notice of any action that is proposed to be taken.

2) Liability to Pay

a) When Liability Arises

By section 3(1), the liability to pay the anti-dumping or countervailing duties, or both, arises before the goods are released if there was an order or finding of the Tribunal, but if the goods have already been released, the duties are payable from the day the preliminary determination of dumping or subsidizing was made by the CBSA and ending on the day the Tribunal has made the order or finding. Thereafter, the liability arises by virtue of the Tribunal's order or finding. The amount of duty may not exceed the provisional duty.

---

7   *World Trade Organization Agreement Implementation Act*, SC 1994, c 47 [*WTO Agreement*].
8   *SIMA*, s 77.1 (2) provides that Part II is suspended while Part I.1 is in force.

i) Liability Where Undertaking Accepted

Where an Undertaking has been given by the importer, exporter, or the government of the exporting country pursuant to section 49, and accepted by the CBSA, and it has not been terminated under section 51, and as a result of the Undertaking the preliminary investigation of dumping or subsidizing was suspended, the anti-dumping, countervailing, or provisional duty imposed under sections 3 and 4 is not payable. However, if the Undertaking has been violated or it has been terminated by the CBSA pursuant to section 52, the duty becomes payable on all goods released during the period commencing on the day the Undertaking was violated or terminated and ending on the day the Tribunal makes the order or finding of material injury to or material retardation of domestic industry.[9]

ii) Liability Imposed on Importer

Although the term "importer" is defined by section 2(1) as "the person who in reality is the importer," that definition does not go far enough for the purpose of imposing liability. There have been difficulties in identifying an importer in some cases and, therefore, sections 8 and 11 were amended in 2011, adding the words "in Canada" after the word "importer."[10] Questions such as whether the importer must have a residence or do business in Canada were not answered by the amendment, as the Tribunal pointed out in its rulings on who is the importer, discussed under sections 89 and 90.[11]

iii) Payment during Court and NAFTA Panel Proceedings

The payment of duties is not suspended by reason of the commencement of court proceedings for judicial review under the *Federal Courts Act*,[12] or of a review to set aside an order or finding of the Tribunal or a review of the CBSA in respect of goods of a *NAFTA* country pursuant to Part I.1 by a Binational Panel established under that Part, during the course of those proceedings and until they are finally disposed of. However, the duty ceases to be payable if (1) the Federal Court of Appeal sets aside the order or finding of the Tribunal, or (2) the Federal Court of Appeal sets aside a final determination of the CBSA, pursuant to an application under section 96.1 of the *SIMA*, which was the basis of an order or finding.

---

9   Acceptance of undertakings and of further undertakings, and their termination, are discussed in Section D(2)(b), below in this chapter.
10 SC 2001, c 25, s 92 (amending s 8 of the *SIMA*) and s 93 (amending s 11 of the *SIMA*).
11 See Section F(1), below in this chapter.
12 RSC 1985, c F-7.

The same applies where a review of the Tribunal's order or finding has been requested by Canada or by the government of a *NAFTA* country, or by the importer pursuant to sections 77.011 to 77.013 of Part I.1 in respect of goods imported from a *NAFTA* country.

iv) Duty Reimposed on Referral Back by Binational Panel

If the Binational Panel refers back to the Tribunal an order made by the Tribunal under section 76.01(5) or 76.03(12)(a) of the *SIMA*, by which it rescinded that order or finding made pursuant to any of sections 77.015(3) or (4), 77.019(5), 77.15(3) or (4), or 77.19(4) with respect to the dumping or subsidizing of goods imported from a *NAFTA* country, the duty becomes payable as if the rescinded order or finding had not been rescinded. Payment of the duty during the referral back proceedings does not cease. However, if the Tribunal confirms the rescinding order or finding after the referral back proceedings, the duty ceases to be payable and any duty paid during the course of the proceedings has to be returned to the importer forthwith. If the Tribunal rescinds a rescinding order or finding, and makes a new order or finding, the duty again becomes payable.

v) General Rules Relating to Payment of Duty

a. Where Both or Portion of Duties Payable

Where both an anti-dumping duty on dumped goods and a countervailing duty on subsidized goods are required to be levied, and the CBSA is of the opinion that the whole of the margin of dumping on which the duties are computed is attributable to the export subsidy, then under section 10, no anti-dumping duty, but only a countervailing duty, is payable. However, if only a portion of the margin of dumping is attributable to the export subsidy and the remainder to the dumping, the duty must be apportioned between the two duties in the proportion in which the two are attributable.

b. Duty, Other Than Provisional Duty, Payable by Importer in Canada

Section 11 places the obligation to pay duty, other than the provisional duty, on the importer in Canada notwithstanding that it has deposited a security pursuant to sections 8 or 13.2.

c. Return of Provisional Duty

Section 8(2) requires the CBSA to return the provisional duty, or security deposited in lieu thereof, where the preliminary investigation has been terminated, where all proceedings respecting dumping or subsidizing have been terminated, and where the Tribunal has made an order or finding that the dumping or subsidizing has not caused but is only threatening to cause injury.

d. Return of Duty

Section 12 requires the CBSA to return the duty paid under the *SIMA* on imported goods in the following cases:

1) Where, pursuant to section 96.1 of the *SIMA*, the Federal Court of Appeal following judicial review, or the Panel pursuant to Part I.1 (or II), has set aside or rescinded a Tribunal's order or finding of dumping or subsidizing described in sections 3 to 6, and all proceedings under the *SIMA* are subsequently terminated with respect to all imported goods or to particular goods, any duty paid under the *SIMA* on imported goods that are of the same description as goods with respect to which such proceedings are so terminated, has to be returned to the importer forthwith after the proceedings are terminated. Any security deposited must also be returned to the importer or to the person who deposited it.

2) Any duty, or part of duty, that was paid because of a clerical or arithmetical error must be returned to the importer or to the person on whose behalf it was paid.

3) If the person who paid the duty or deposited security is declared by the Tribunal not to be the importer, the duty or security must be returned to that person forthwith.

e. Duty When Tribunal Makes a New Order or Finding

Where the Tribunal makes a new order or finding in place of a rescinded order or finding, the duty paid under the rescinded order has to be adjusted against that payable under the new order or finding, with surplus, if any, returned to the person who had paid the duty.

f. Request for Review When Exporter or Producer Establishes Not to Be Associated

Under section 13.2, an exporter or producer that establishes that it is not associated with another exporter or producer in respect of whose goods an order or finding of dumping or subsidizing was made, and that was not formally notified of the dumping or subsidizing proceedings, may formally request the CBSA to review the normal value, export price, or the amount of subsidy in relation to the goods exported by that exporter. On receipt of the request, the CBSA must initiate a review and conduct it on an expedited basis, and either confirm or amend the normal value, the export price, or the amount of subsidy.

vi) Expedited Review

The expedited review by the Tribunal is deemed to be a re-determination by a designated officer of the normal value, export price, or amount of subsidy. During the re-determination, an importer of the goods of the same description as the goods to which the review applies must, in respect of those goods imported between the date of initiation of the review and its completion, pay or deposit security to cover any liability for duties that may result from the review.

The decision of the Tribunal in *EMCO Electric International-Electrical Resource International v President, Canada Border Services Agency*,[13] in an appeal against the CBSA's determination, is very useful because it not only identifies the importations that are subject to the Tribunal's finding of injury in respect of the goods and the specific normal value on which the anti-dumping duty was payable, but also identifies who the real exporter is. Both parties relied on the same sources to deduce the meaning of the term "exporter," which appeared in several places in the relevant sections of the *SIMA* but was not defined anywhere in the statute. They referred to the statement of Jackett J in *Canada v Singer Manufacturing Co*,[14] in which he defined an exporter and an importer thus: "the essential feature ... is that the exporter must be the person in the foreign country who sends the goods into Canada and the importer must be the person to whom they are sent in Canada."[15] The CBSA, on its part, relied on its own administrative guidelines for identifying the "exporter" for the *SIMA* purposes, which, in its submission, was the unnamed producer, not Plumbtek Industries, who sold the goods to the appellant. Plumbtek Industries was one of the non-party participants in the reference by the CBSA to the Tribunal, which was invited by the Tribunal to make submissions. The appellant did not take issue with the CBSA's re-determinations but asserted that the CBSA had based those re-determinations on a misinterpretation of the language used in standard contracts such as the one used between Plumbtek Industries and the producer's selling agent. The appellant asserted that the producer of the goods in China (whose name was not disclosed) was not the exporter and that the real exporter was Plumbtek Industries, which sold the goods to it and made arrangements to ship them to Canada.

After examining all the documents and the relevant evidence, the Tribunal concluded that it was Plumbtek, not the unnamed producer, that was the

---

13   AP-2008-010 (2009), 13 TTR (2d) 553.
14   (1967), [1968] 1 Ex CR 129, aff'd [1968] 1 Ex CR viii (SCC) [*Singer*].
15   *Ibid* at 136.

exporter of the goods and it was the price paid by the appellant to Plumbtek that should be considered as the export price on which the anti-dumping duty of 183 percent should be levied by the CBSA. The Tribunal, quoting Jackett J in the *Singer* case, decided that "the words 'exporter' and 'importer' are not words of art in the law; they are words that gain the meaning that they have when used in a context such as that found ... from the business or commercial world."[16] In its view, the CBSA's definition of "exporter" did not represent either the normal meaning of the term or the normal industry usage; consequently, the Tribunal did not accept the definition to the extent that it went beyond the definition adopted in previous cases.

Section 89 provides for a corresponding determination of who among two or more persons is the importer. This issue is discussed in Section F(1), below in this chapter.

b) Undertakings

Section 2(1) of the *SIMA* defines an "undertaking" to mean a document given in writing to the CBSA by one or more exporters individually, or by the government of an exporting country, by which

1) in the case of dumped goods, the exporter or exporters individually undertake either to revise the price at which they sell the goods to importers in Canada, or cease to dump the goods in Canada;
2) in the case of subsidized goods, the exporter or exporters individually, who have the consent of their government to give the undertaking, undertakes to revise, in the manner specified in the undertaking, the price at which the exporter sells the goods to importers in Canada; and
3) in the case of an undertaking given by the government of a country of export, the government undertakes to eliminate the subsidy on goods exported to Canada from that country, to limit the amount of subsidy on goods, to limit the quantity of goods exported to Canada, or to otherwise eliminate the effect of the subsidy on the production of like goods in Canada, in the manner specified in the undertaking.

An undertaking replaces full investigation and Tribunal inquiry into dumping and subsidizing, and if it is offered by the exporter or the government of the country of export, the CBSA may accept it after a preliminary decision favouring the Canadian industry is made by both the CBSA and the

---

16 *Ibid* at 135.

Tribunal. If an undertaking is accepted, it usually suspends both the CBSA's investigation and the Tribunal's inquiry.

i) Acceptance

The CBSA is authorized by section 49 to accept an undertaking or undertakings with respect to dumped or subsidized goods that are subject to investigation if it is of the opinion that the exporter or the government that gives the undertaking will eliminate the margin of dumping or the subsidy, as the case may be, or any injury, retardation, or threat of injury that is being caused by such dumping or subsidy.

An undertaking cannot be accepted if (1) the CBSA is of the opinion that the observance of the undertaking will not cause the price at which the goods are sold to importers in Canada by the exporter to increase by more than the margin of dumping or the estimated amount of subsidy; (2) the CBSA has already made a preliminary determination of dumping or subsidizing pursuant to section 38(2); or (3) the CBSA is of the opinion that it would not be practicable to administer the undertaking or undertakings.

In considering whether to accept an undertaking, the CBSA is required to consider any representations it has received from the importer, the exporter, the government of the country of export, or any other interested person.

ii) Termination of Investigation

Forthwith after acceptance of an undertaking, the CBSA must publish a notice of acceptance of the undertaking, suspend the collection of provisional duties, suspend the investigation of dumping or subsidizing unless a formal request was made when offering the undertaking that the investigation be completed, and notify the Tribunal of the suspension of the investigation or its completion if the latter was requested.

Likewise, the Tribunal must suspend its inquiry unless the request for completion had been made. Upon acceptance of an undertaking, the operation of any period specified pursuant to the *SIMA* for the doing of any thing in relation to the dumping or subsidizing of goods covered by the undertaking is suspended and is only resumed if the undertaking expires or is terminated.

iii) Termination of Undertaking

In accordance with sections 51 and 52, an undertaking must be terminated by the CBSA in the following circumstances:

1) if, within thirty days of the notice of acceptance of the undertaking, a request for termination is received from the importer, the exporter, the complainant, or, in the case of subsidized goods, from the government of the country of export, provided the request is received before the Tribunal has made an order;
2) where the CBSA is satisfied that
   a) the undertaking has been or is being violated;
   b) the undertaking would not have been accepted had the information or circumstances that prevailed at the time of the acceptance of the undertaking, which would have led to its rejection, been available at the time of the acceptance;
   c) its determination has established that there was no dumping or subsidizing, or that the margin of dumping or amount of subsidy was insignificant;
   d) where the Tribunal has made an order or finding to the effect that there has been no injury, retardation, or threat of injury as a result of the dumping or subsidizing;
   or
3) if the Tribunal has rescinded an order or finding, or the order or finding is deemed to be rescinded under section 76.03(1), following
   a) the completion of a review of its order or finding pursuant to section 76.01(5)(a),
   b) a review on referral back pursuant to section 76.02(4),
   c) an expiry review pursuant to section 76.03(12),
   d) a review of order or finding with respect to goods from a *NAFTA* country or of one or more other countries, or
   e) a request by the Minister of Finance resulting from the recommendation or ruling of the Dispute Settlement Body established pursuant to Article 2 of Annex 2 to the *WTO Agreement*.

Upon termination of an undertaking, the CBSA must publish a notice of termination if the Tribunal has rescinded its order or finding of injury or retardation, or threat of injury, and where an investigation was suspended by the CBSA, it must be resumed.

Where the CBSA had accepted several undertakings and only one or a few of those have been terminated, it must not, without good reason, terminate those that have not been violated if they account for substantially all the imported goods.

iv) Further Undertakings

Section 51.1 allows the CBSA to accept a further undertaking from the exporter or the government of a country of export that had not previously offered an undertaking that was accepted under section 49(1), where an investigation has been suspended, if it is of the opinion that observance of the undertaking will not cause the export price to increase by more than the estimated margin of dumping or the estimated amount of subsidy.

v) Expiry, Renewal

Sections 53, 53.1, and 54 contain rules relating to expiry, renewal, and amendment of undertakings. Unless sooner terminated, an undertaking expires at the end of five years but it may be renewed for another period not exceeding five years. Prior to its expiry, or expiry after renewal, the CBSA must review it and renew it only if satisfied that it continues to serve its intended purpose and that there is no reason to terminate it. If the CBSA decides not to renew it, the undertaking expires immediately.

When an undertaking has expired, all proceedings taken under the *SIMA* respecting the dumping or subsidizing terminate, but where two or more undertakings have been accepted with respect to the same goods, the CBSA may for good reason direct otherwise. Notice of renewal or non-renewal must be given to all parties involved in the investigation, published in the *Canada Gazette*, and filed with the Secretary of the Tribunal.

The decision of the CBSA to renew an undertaking or not to renew it may be set aside by the Federal Court or referred back to the CBSA on an application made by the parties under section 96.1, and the CBSA is required to make a new decision, give notice of the action taken and publish it in the *Canada Gazette*, and file its decision with the Secretary of the Tribunal. With respect to the decision not to renew an undertaking, the undertaking is deemed by section 53.2(b) to have been renewed on the day on which the order is made until the CBSA has taken action in response to the court's decision to confirm, rescind, or vary its decision.

An undertaking that has not expired or terminated and that continues to serve its intended purpose may be amended at any time in accordance with its terms.

E. ADMINISTRATIVE PROCEDURES AND APPEALS

1) Introduction

The *SIMA* springs into action when the protection it offers is invoked by a domestic industry that is facing unfair competition from exporters. Unless the CBSA finds evidence establishing that an exporter has been dumping goods or the goods that were exported were subsidized by the government of the exporting country, and further, the Tribunal makes a finding that such dumping or subsidizing has caused material injury or material retardation to domestic industry, or is threatening to cause material injury, a complainant has no chance of success.

As explained at the beginning of this chapter, there is no dumping if the export price is equal to the margin of dumping, or if the margin of dumping is insignificant, or if the volume of goods dumped is negligible, and in the case of subsidized goods, if the amount of subsidy is negligible or if it is a "non-actionable" subsidy. If a country is able to produce goods at low labour costs and has access to enormous resources of capital and natural resources to produce them without having to rely on government subsidies, its exports cannot reasonably be categorized as "unfair" when they are shipped to high labour cost countries.

Similarly, intricate questions arise as to which imported goods can be characterized as "like" goods that are produced by domestic industry. If a sector of Canadian industry is outmoded, inefficient, or saddled with high labour costs, and the imported goods are superior in quality and performance, it does not seem to be likely that the latter can be categorized as comparable to domestically produced goods; otherwise the Canadian producer will be protected by a monopoly to the detriment of consumers who will have to bear high costs and be satisfied with lower-performing goods than the imports. Cases in point, among many others, are in the electronics industry, such as personal devices, and particularly illustrated by the current saga of Research in Motion (now renamed as BlackBerry) facing off with Apple computers and others.

The first step in the *SIMA* process is for a complainant acting on its own behalf or on behalf of itself and one or more firms that together with the complainant account for a minimum of 50 percent of the production of like goods in Canada, to file a properly documented complaint with the CBSA. In some cases, the CBSA itself, on its own initiative, may commence an investigation into the dumping or subsidizing of goods imported into Canada.

A "properly documented" complaint, as defined by section 2 of the *SIMA*, must (1) allege that imported goods have been or are being dumped or subsidized, that such dumping or subsidizing has caused injury or retardation or is threatening to cause injury; (2) state in reasonable detail the facts on which those allegations are based; and (3) make such additional representations that the complainant deems relevant. The complainant must provide the information that is available to it in support of the alleged facts, the information prescribed by section 37 of the Regulations, and such other information as the CBSA may reasonably require.

The complaint triggers a two-step procedure described below: an investigation by the CBSA into the dumping or subsidizing, and almost contemporaneously an inquiry by the Tribunal on the effects of the dumping or subsidizing on domestic industry—whether it has caused injury or retardation or is threatening to cause injury.

2) Investigations and Inquiries

a) Filing a Complaint

i) Acknowledgement and Notice

Within twenty-one days of receiving a properly documented complaint that is supported by the minimum number of domestic producers specified in section 31, the CBSA must notify the complainant of its receipt and, in the case of an alleged subsidizing, it must also notify the government of the country of export. If the complaint was not properly documented, the CBSA must ask the complainant for any further information that is needed to complete the documentation.

ii) Where Subsidy Notified to WTO

Section 31.1 bars an investigation if a subsidy has been notified by the country of export as a "non-actionable" subsidy to the Committee on Subsidies and Countervailing Measures established by the WTO in accordance with Article 8.3 of the *Subsidies Agreement*,[17] unless it is determined that the subsidy is not a non-actionable subsidy either by the Committee after review under Article 8.3 of the *Subsidies Agreement* or by an arbitration body under Article 8.5 of the *Subsidies Agreement*, or it is re-determined by either of those bodies as no longer non-actionable.

---

17 *Agreement on Subsidies and Countervailing Measures*, Marrakesh, 1994 (WTO).

iii) No Investigation without Domestic Producers' Support

Section 31 bars an investigation if a complaint does not have the support of domestic producers whose production represents more than 50 percent of the total production of like goods by those domestic producers who express either support for or opposition to the complaint; and the production of the domestic producers who support the complaint must represents 25 percent or more of the total production.

The "domestic producers" who matter for the purposes of the complaint are those who are not importers of, nor related to, an exporter or importer of the alleged dumped or subsidized goods; similarly, "domestic industry" must comprise domestic producers who are not related to an exporter or importer of alleged dumped or subsidized goods. "Producers related to exporters or importers" and "domestic industry" are defined in sections 2(1), which definitions are repeated to a substantial extent in section 31(4) and (5), and are based on legal or operational control by or of one or more of the other or others.

The terms "domestic producer" and "domestic industry" have not been defined in the *SIMA*, nor in the *CITT Act*, but in a decision rendered under the *Customs Tariff* with respect to safeguard measures where identical terminology has been used. The Tribunal has held that the terms must be construed in the context of the provisions in the legislation and not on the basis of its ordinary sense. In Textile and Apparel Goods Safeguard Inquiry No CS-2005-002,[18] the Tribunal rejected the complaint filed by Unite Here Canada for lack of standing because it did not represent "domestic producers," nor was it acting on behalf of domestic producers, even though it had alleged support from them. The Tribunal did not equate support for a complaint with "acting on behalf of" the producers, as none of the manufacturers had indicated that Unite Here was authorized to act on their behalf. In its view, there was a significant difference between a party expressing support for another person's actions and that party authorizing the person to act on the party's behalf.

b) Initiation and Notice of Investigation by CBSA

Promptly on receiving a properly documented complaint, if there is evidence that dumping or subsidizing has occurred and there is a reasonable indication that it has caused, or is threatening to cause, injury or retardation, and if the conditions in the preceding paragraphs are met, section 31 requires the CBSA within thirty days after notifying the complainant that the complaint

---

18   (2006), 11 TTR (2d) 326.

is properly documented, to initiate an investigation. The thirty-day period may be extended by the CBSA to forty-five days after giving notice, before the expiration of the thirty days, to the complainant and the government of the country of export, that thirty days are not sufficient to verify compliance with the conditions set out in sections 31(2) (support of the minimum number of domestic producers not related to exporters) and 31.1(1) (whether the subsidy has been notified to the Committee on Subsidies and Countervailing Measures of the WTO as being a "non-actionable" subsidy).

The CBSA may also initiate an investigation on its own initiative. It may initiate an investigation on receiving a written notice from the Tribunal, but it must initiate it if the Tribunal, following a reference, advises it that there is evidence disclosing a reasonable indication of dumping or subsidizing.

As soon as the CBSA decides to initiate an investigation, it must notify the Secretary of the Tribunal, the exporter, the importer, the government of the country of export, the complainant, if any, and any other prescribed persons; publish the notice in the *Canada Gazette*; and provide the Tribunal with the information and material that is required by the Tribunal's rules.

c) Preliminary Inquiry by the Tribunal

Without any delay, the Tribunal, on receipt from the CBSA of the notice of investigation and the material required by the Rules of the Tribunal, conduct a preliminary inquiry into whether the evidence discloses a reasonable indication that the dumping or subsidizing of the imported goods has caused injury or retardation, or is threatening to cause injury. An oral hearing is not required at this stage.

i) Termination of Investigation and Preliminary Inquiry

The CBSA must terminate an investigation if, before making a preliminary determination of dumping or subsidizing, it is satisfied that, in respect of some or all of the imported goods, (1) there is insufficient evidence of dumping or subsidizing, (2) the margin of dumping or the amount of subsidy on the goods of the country of export or of any of the countries involved in the export is insignificant, or (3) the actual and potential volume of dumped or subsidized goods is negligible.

The CBSA must notify the Secretary of the Tribunal of the termination and publish the notice of termination in the *Canada Gazette*.

Similarly, the Tribunal must terminate the preliminary inquiry if it comes to the conclusion in respect of some or all of the imported goods that the evidence does not disclose a reasonable indication that the dumping or subsidizing of those goods has caused injury or retardation or threat of injury. It must also notify the CBSA, the exporter, the importer, the government of the country of export, the complainant, and any prescribed persons, and publish the notice of termination in the *Canada Gazette*.

ii) Goods from Chile

In the case of an investigation or preliminary inquiry in respect of goods imported from Chile that were alleged to have been dumped, section 35.1 requires that investigation or preliminary inquiry to be terminated immediately after the goods have been exempted from the application of the *SIMA* by regulations made under section 14 of the Act. Notice of termination must be given to all the concerned parties, including the complainant, if any, and the government of the Republic of Chile, and published in the *Canada Gazette*.

iii) Tribunal Must Advise CBSA on Reference

Under section 33, the CBSA may request the Tribunal for advice by way of a reference on the question whether there is evidence of reasonable indication of material injury or material retardation, or threat of material injury, in respect of some or all the dumped or subsidized goods, indicating its opinion that there is evidence of dumping or subsidization. The Tribunal is required to give its advice to the CBSA on the basis of the information that was before the CBSA, which must be forwarded to the Tribunal without holding any hearings and within thirty days after the date on which the reference is made. The complainant is also given the same right.

d) Determination of Injury, Dumping, or Subsidizing

i) Preliminary Determination of Injury

Within sixty days after the CBSA has initiated an investigation of a complaint with respect to dumping or subsidizing, and if that investigation has not been terminated, the Tribunal must make a preliminary determination that the evidence provided to it discloses a reasonable indication that the dumping or subsidizing has caused injury or retardation, or is threatening to cause injury, to domestic industry. The Tribunal must provide notification of that preliminary determination to the CBSA, the exporter, the importer, the government of the country of export, the complainant, if any, and other prescribed persons, and must also publish it in the *Canada Gazette*.

After the sixtieth day and on or before the ninetieth day after an investigation of a complaint has been initiated, the CBSA must make a preliminary determination of dumping or subsidizing, specify the goods to which the preliminary determination applies, and

1) in the case of dumping, it must estimate in relation to each exporter the margin of dumping and the name of the importer; and
2) in the case of subsidy, if the whole or any part of the subsidy is a prohibited subsidy, it must
   a) specify whether the whole or only a part thereof is a prohibited subsidy,
   b) estimate the amount of that subsidy, and
   c) specify the name of the importer.

A prohibited subsidy is an export subsidy that is inconsistent with the international obligations of the country of export under the *GATT 1994*.

The CBSA must give notice of the preliminary determination to all persons and the governments involved in the investigation, publish it in the *Canada Gazette*, and file it with the Secretary of the Tribunal, together with reasons and such other material as the Tribunal's rules may require.

The ninety-day period for making the preliminary determination is extended to 135 days if before the ninety days expire, the CBSA gives notice to the persons and the government involved that the circumstances involved in the investigation, such as the complexity or novelty of the issues, the variety of goods or the number of persons involved, or the difficulty of obtaining satisfactory evidence, make it unusually difficult to decide within those ninety days whether to terminate the investigation with respect to some or all of the goods, to proceed to make the preliminary determination, or to accept an undertaking or undertakings.

ii) Final Determination

Section 41 requires the CBSA to make a final determination within ninety days after making the preliminary determination, if it is satisfied on the basis of the available evidence that the goods covered by the investigation have been dumped or subsidized, that the margin of dumping or the amount of subsidy is not insignificant, and that the actual or potential volume of dumped or subsidized goods is not negligible. The final determination must be made in relation to goods from each country or all countries in respect of which the investigation was made. It must specify in relation to each exporter the goods to which its final determination applies, (1) in the case of dumped goods, the margin of dumping; and (2) in the case of subsidized goods, the amount of prohibited subsidy.

If there is no exporter to which the final determination can apply, the investigation must be terminated.

The CBSA must give notice of the final determination or of the termination of the investigation, as the case may be, to all persons and governments involved, publish it in the *Canada Gazette*, and file it with the Secretary of the Tribunal.

iii) **Reconsideration**

The CBSA must reconsider a final determination of dumping or subsidizing, or a decision to terminate an investigation with respect thereto, in the following two cases: (1) if the Federal Court of Appeal sets aside the final determination and refers the matter back to the CBSA, and (2) if the Panel established under the *NAFTA* pursuant to section 77.014 or 77.017 refers the final determination back to the CBSA for review under sections 77.015(3) or (4), 77.019(5), 77.15(3) or (4), or 77.19(4).

If the Federal Court refers the matter back, the CBSA must make a new final determination or decision. If the Panel refers it back, the CBSA must rescind, confirm, or vary the final determination, as the case may be. The CBSA must give notice of the action taken to all parties and governments involved, and publish it in the *Canada Gazette*. It must also notify, in writing, the Secretary of the Tribunal or the Canadian Secretary of the Panel, as the case may be, about the action it has taken.

If after the reconsideration ordered by the Federal Court of Appeal, or directed by the Panel following its review, the CBSA rescinds the final determination or makes a new final determination, section 41 again applies in respect of the goods to which the final determination applied, as if that section had not previously applied. The CBSA must take the action required by the court or the Panel within the time specified by them and if no time was specified, within ninety days of the court's or Panel's decision.

Where the CBSA reconsiders a matter involving a decision upon referral back by the court, or reconsiders and rescinds a decision upon referral back by the Panel, the CBSA is deemed to have made a preliminary determination of dumping or subsidizing in respect of the goods that were the subject of investigation that was terminated, on the date of the court's or Panel's order, and thereafter it must resume the investigation.

The provisions of section 41 dealing with the final determination again apply as set out in Section E(2)(d)(ii), above in this chapter, with the time to take action varied as provided. Similarly, the provisions dealing with Tribunal inquiries described in Sections E(2)(d)(i) and (ii), below in this chapter, again apply, but in this case, the time within which the Tribunal is required to take action is extended to 120 days after the date of the referral back.

iv) Subsidies Agreement

In all investigations into subsidizing, the CBSA must take into account Canada's obligations under paragraphs 10 and 11 of Article 27 of the *Subsidies Agreement*[19] to developing country members.

v) Investigations Illustrating Section 20 Process

Two preliminary determinations of dumping have been selected to illustrate how the CBSA conducts its investigations and how it arrives at its conclusions. The first relates to dumping of polysio insulation board by exporters from the United States, a country with a market economy and Canada's *NAFTA* partner, and the second relates to dumping and subsidizing by the People's Republic of China, a country with a non-market economy. The latter is particularly important because many complaints allege dumping or subsidizing by exporters from the People's Republic of China. It is also important because a third country, a "surrogate," was selected to compare the normal values (the United States, which exported substantial quantities of the subject goods to Canada); and, although in that case there were a few other exporting countries, their exports to Canada were negligible.

---

19 Article 27.10 of the Agreement on Subsidies states as follows:

> Any countervailing duty investigation of a product originating in a developing country Member shall be terminated as soon as the authorities concerned determine that:
> (a) the overall level of subsidies granted upon the product in question does not exceed 2 per cent of its value calculated on a per unit basis; or
> (b) the volume of the subsidized imports represents less than 4 per cent of the total imports of the like product in the importing Member, unless imports from developing country Members whose individual shares of total imports represent less than 4 per cent collectively account for more than 9 per cent of the total imports of the like product in the importing Member.

Article 27.11 states:

> For those developing country Members within the scope of paragraph 2(b) which have eliminated export subsidies prior to the expiry of the period of eight years from the date of entry into force of the WTO Agreement, and for those developing country Members referred to in Annex VII, the number in paragraph 10(a) shall be 3 per cent rather than 2 per cent. This provision shall apply from the date that the elimination of export subsidies is notified to the Committee, and for so long as export subsidies are not granted by the notifying developing country Member. This provision shall expire eight years from the date of entry into force of the WTO Agreement.

INVESTIGATION 1: POLYSIO INSULATION BOARD (UNITED STATES)[20]

On 19 August 2009, the CBSA received a written complaint from IKO Sales Ltd (IKO) alleging that imports of polysio insulation board originating in or exported from the United States were being dumped and that the dumping was causing injury to the Canadian industry. The complaint was properly documented. IKO and the Government of the United States were notified of the complaint.

On 8 October 2009, the CBSA initiated an investigation pursuant to section 31(1), as it was of the opinion that there was evidence of dumping and that the evidence disclosed a reasonable indication that the dumping has caused injury or is threatening to cause injury. It also notified the Tribunal, which commenced its own preliminary injury on the same day, pursuant to section 34(2). The Tribunal made a preliminary determination, pursuant to section 37.1(1), that there was evidence that disclosed a reasonable indication that the dumping of the subject goods has caused injury. The results of that determination are contained in Section E(2)(d)(vi)(f), below in this chapter.

The period of investigation covered all subject goods imported into Canada from 1 December 2008 to 30 September 2009.

At the initiation of the investigation, the CBSA identified fifty-seven potential exporters and sent to each of them a Request For Information (RFI); thirty-one indicated that they did not produce or export the subject goods. Of the remaining twenty-six, the CBSA received complete responses from five and incomplete responses from two.

The CBSA also identified eighty-seven potential importers based on information contained in the CBSA's Customs Commercial System database and sent to each of them an RFI. Five importers were subsequently added as a result of the information from the returned RFIs. Of the total of ninety-two, thirty-three indicated that they were not involved in the importation of the subject goods. Of the remaining fifty-nine, only seven provided a response to the RFI with varying degrees of completeness.

In addition to the complainant IKO, there were two producers of the subject goods in Canada: JMC of Cornwall, Ontario, and ARC of Toronto, Ontario. JMC indicated support for IKO's complaint, but ARC declined. The CBSA confirmed that IKO, which was the largest producer, along with JMC, constituted domestic producers whose production represented more than 50 percent of the total production of like goods by those domestic producers

---

20   (2010), 14 TTR (2d) 492 (CBSA).

who expressed their support for or opposition to the complaint, and as they also met the minimum 25 percent of the total production, the standing requirements of section 31(2) were met.

The CBSA estimated the volume of imports of the subject goods for purposes of the preliminary determination from the import documents and other information received from exporters and importers. Roughly 99 percent of total imports originated in or exported from the United States.

At the time of the investigation, the CBSA invited interested persons to file written submissions or make representations. There was no response.

During the investigation, the CBSA collected information on normal values and export prices and calculated the margin of dumping. To estimate the normal value of the subject goods with respect to exporters who provided substantially complete responses to the RFI, the CBSA utilized the company-specific information; for those who did not submit a complete response to the RFI, the normal value was estimated by advancing the export price by the highest amount by which the normal value exceeded the export price on an individual transaction for an exporter that provided a substantially complete response, excluding anomalies.

The CBSA then estimated the margin of dumping. In calculating this, the estimated margin of dumping found in respect of each exporter was weighted according to each exporter's volume of the subject goods exported to Canada during the period of inquiry.

Based on the foregoing, the CBSA determined that 100 percent of the subject goods were dumped by the United States exporters by an estimated 28.3 percent margin of dumping expressed as a percentage of the export price. The margin of dumping for each exporter was then estimated: for those who provided complete responses, it ranged from a low of 6.4 percent to a high of 23.6 percent; for all other exporters it was estimated at 215.0 percent.

As a result of the investigation, the CBSA concluded that the thresholds for "insignificant" dumping (less than 2 percent) and "negligible" for volume of dumping (less than 3 percent) specified in section 2(1) were exceeded. Based on the preliminary results, the CBSA, on 6 January 2010, made a preliminary determination of dumping respecting the subject goods originating in or exported from the United States, pursuant to section 38(1).

Pursuant to section 8(1), a provisional duty was applied, based on the estimated margin of dumping as indicated above, as of 6 January 2010, the date of the preliminary determination. This provisional duty applied to all imports originating or exported from the United States and would terminate on the day the Tribunal renders its final determination of injury pursuant to section 43(1) of the *SIMA*.

The CBSA noted that there were no circumstances that justified retroactive imposition of provisional duty. Such a retroactive duty can be imposed if there were massive importations close to or after the initiation of the investigation over a relatively short period of time which have caused injury to the Canadian industry.

As will be seen in Section E(2)(d)(vi)(f), below in this chapter, the Tribunal reached the opposite conclusion, and the provisional duty was refunded or, where security or an undertaking was given, it was cancelled.[21]

INVESTIGATION 2: OIL COUNTRY TUBULAR GOODS (THE PEOPLE'S REPUBLIC OF CHINA)[22]

On 14 July 2009, the CBSA received a written complaint from three complainants who accounted for almost all production of oil country tubular goods (pipes) in Canada. They were Tenaris Canada of Calgary, Alberta; Evraz Inc NA Canada of Regina, Saskatchewan; and Lakeside Steel Corporation of Welland, Ontario. The complaint was properly documented. The CBSA notified the Government of the People's Republic of China and provided that government with a non-confidential version of the subsidy portion of the complaint.

On 14 August 2009, the CBSA held consultations with the Government of China as required by Article 13.1 of the WTO *Agreement on Subsidies and Countervailing Measures*.

On 24 August 2009, the CBSA initiated an investigation pursuant to section 31(1) respecting the dumping and subsidizing of the subject goods from China.

It also notified the Tribunal, which commenced its own preliminary injury on the same day, pursuant to section 34(2), to determine whether the evidence disclosed a reasonable indication that the alleged dumping and subsidizing of the subject goods have caused injury or retardation, or are threatening to cause injury to the Canadian industry producing the goods. On 23 October 2009, the Tribunal made a preliminary determination, pursuant to section 37.1(1), that there was evidence that disclosed a reasonable indication that the dumping and subsidizing of the subject goods has caused injury.

The period of investigation with respect to dumping covered all subject goods released into Canada from 1 July 2008 to 30 June 2009, and with respect to subsidizing, the period was from 1 January 2008 to 30 June 2009.

---

21   See text referred to in note 31 below.
22   Injury Inquiry NQ-2009-004 (2010), 14 TTR (2d) 335.

At the initiation of the investigation, the CBSA identified 106 potential exporters and sent to each of them an RFI as well as to each identified producer in China.

After the preliminary determination of dumping and subsidy on 23 November 2009, the CBSA conducted on-site verification with three cooperative exporters.

At the initiation of the investigations, the CBSA identified fifty-one potential importers of subject goods based on a review of the CBSA import documentation and sent an importer RFI to all. Nine provided a response before the determination, one after.

The CBSA sent a subsidy RFI to the Government of China, including all levels of government (federal, central, provincial/state, regional, municipal, city, township, village, local, legislative, administrative or judicial, singular, collective, elected or appointed).

As part of the inquiry, an RFI was also sent to thirty-six producers located in seven countries (Spain, Germany, Brazil, Russia, India, Ukraine, and the United States) who were not subject to the current dumping investigation. Only one RFI response was received—from Wheatland Tube Company, a US producer of the subject goods, but the response was incomplete.

With respect to the dumping determination:

1) The CBSA estimated the volume of imports of the subject goods for purposes of the preliminary determination from the import documents and other information received from exporters and importers. It found that 97.4 percent of total imports originated in or were exported from the People's Republic of China, 2.4 percent from the United States, while all other countries accounted for 0.2 percent.

2) The CBSA then determined the margins of dumping for each of the cooperative exporters by comparing the total normal value with the total export price. For non-cooperative exporters, the normal value was determined under a ministerial prescription pursuant to section 29 of the *SIMA*, based on the export price determined under section 24, plus an amount equal to 166 percent of the export price, which represented the highest amount by which the normal value exceeded the export price on an individual transaction for a cooperative exporter.

3) In calculating the margin of dumping for the country, the margins of dumping found in respect of each exporter were weighted according to each exporter's volume of the subject goods exported to Canada during the dumping period of investigation. Based on this calculation, 100

percent was determined to have been dumped by a weighted average margin of dumping of 137.6 percent, expressed as a percentage of the export price.

4) In calculating the volume of dumping, the CBSA took into consideration each exporter's net aggregate dumping results. Where a given exporter was determined to have been dumping on an overall or net basis, the total quantity of exports attributable to that exporter (that is, 100 percent) was considered dumped. Similarly, where a given exporter's net dumping results were zero, the total quantity of exports deemed to be dumped by that exporter was zero.

With respect to the subsidy determination:

1) The CBSA took into account all the incentives, grants, tax breaks, value of primary materials supplied by the Government of China (as defined earlier), and the amount of each incentive, grant, tax breaks and refunds, and so on of which individual producers and exporters availed themselves.
2) It took into account only "actionable subsidies" as defined by section 2 of the *SIMA*.
3) It estimated that 100 percent of China's exports to Canada were subsidized and such imports were 55 percent of Canada's total imports; thus 55 percent of the total imports of the subject goods were subsidized. The amount of subsidy as a percentage of the export price was 25.7 percent.

Therefore, pursuant to section 41(1)(a) of the *SIMA*, the CBSA made a final determination that the subject goods were dumped during the period of the dumping investigation and that the margin of dumping was not insignificant. Similarly, it made a final determination that the subject goods were subsidized during the period of subsidy investigation, and that the subsidy was not negligible.

A written undertaking proposal was filed by one exporter, which accounted for under 4 percent of the total quantity of subject goods exported to Canada, but that undertaking was objected to by the complainants for the reason that it was the only exporter that filed the proposal and it did not account for all, or substantially all, of the exports to Canada. Accordingly, the CBSA rejected the proposal.

The CBSA provided normal values and amounts of subsidy to the cooperating exporters for future shipments to Canada in the event of an injury finding by the Tribunal. These normal values and amounts of subsidy were to come into effect the day after the date of the injury finding, if there was one. Exporters who were not cooperative in the dumping investigation would have normal values established by advancing the export price by 166.9 percent, based on a ministerial specification pursuant to section 29 of the *SIMA*. Similarly, exporters who were not cooperative in the subsidy investigation would be subject to a countervailing duty in the amount of 4,070 Yuan Renminbi per metric tonne, based on a ministerial specification pursuant to section 30.4(2) of the *SIMA*.

vi) Injury Inquiry by the Tribunal

After the CBSA has notified the Secretary of the Tribunal of its preliminary determination, the Tribunal is required to conduct its own inquiry under sections 42 to 47 of the *SIMA*. That inquiry concerns the determination of injury or retardation, or threat of injury, alleged to have been caused by the dumping or subsidizing. As stated in Section E(2)(c), above in this chapter, the Tribunal makes a preliminary inquiry under section 34(2) without oral hearing and a preliminary determination of injury pursuant to section 37.1 on the basis of the evidence before it and provided by the CBSA when it carried out its investigation into dumping or subsidizing.

The CBSA is authorized to collect provisional duties on imports from the date of its preliminary determination. It will continue its investigation until the Tribunal makes a final finding of injury caused or threatened by the dumping or subsidizing.

As in a preliminary inquiry, the Tribunal seeks to make all interested parties aware of its inquiry by publishing a notice of commencement of inquiry in the *Canada Gazette* and forwarding it to all known interested parties. In conducting the final injury inquiry, the Tribunal requests information from interested parties, receives representations, and holds public hearings. Parties participating in the proceedings may be represented by counsel, or appear personally.

A public hearing is held by the Tribunal about ninety days after commencing the inquiry, that is, after the CBSA has made a final determination of dumping or subsidizing. At the public hearing, Canadian producers attempt to persuade the Tribunal that the dumping or subsidizing of goods has caused injury or retardation or is threatening to cause injury to the domestic industry. Importers, foreign producers, and exporters may challenge the Canadian producers' case. The Tribunal may call witnesses who are knowledgeable of the industry and market in question. Parties may also seek the exclusion of certain goods from the scope of a Tribunal finding.

The *SIMA* requires the Tribunal to consider in its determination certain prescribed factors, as appropriate in the circumstances:

1) The Tribunal must, with respect to dumping or subsidizing to which the preliminary determination of the CBSA applies, inquire whether the dumping or subsidizing
   a) has caused injury or retardation, or is threatening to cause injury to a domestic industry, or
   b) would have caused injury or retardation except for the fact that provisional duty was imposed in respect of the goods.
2) With respect to dumped goods to which the CBSA's preliminary determination applies, the Tribunal must inquire whether
   a) (i) there has occurred a considerable importation of like goods that were dumped, which dumping has caused injury or would have caused injury except for the application of anti-dumping measures, or
      (ii) the importer of the goods was aware, or should have been aware, that the exporter was practising dumping and that the dumping would cause injury; and
   b) injury has been caused by reason of the fact that the dumped goods
      (i) constitute a massive importation into Canada, or
      (ii) form part of a series of importations into Canada that in the aggregate are massive and have occurred in a relatively short period of time; and
      (iii) it appears necessary that duty be assessed on the imported goods in order to prevent the recurrence of that injury.
3) With respect to subsidized goods, the Tribunal must further inquire whether
   a) injury has been caused by reason of the fact that the subsidized goods
      (i) constitute a massive importation into Canada, or
      (ii) form part of a series of importations into Canada that in the aggregate are massive and have occurred within a relatively short period of time, and
   b) a countervailing duty should be imposed on the subsidized goods in order to prevent the recurrence of that injury.

a. Where Undertaking Terminated

Where, with respect to dumped or subsidized goods, the CBSA had, pursuant to section 49, accepted an undertaking from the exporter or the government of the country of export, but that undertaking was terminated for the reasons specified in section 52 and no new undertaking was offered or accepted by the CBSA, the Tribunal, if it had terminated its inquiry because of the undertaking, must forthwith make or resume its inquiry and make the finding and decision referred to in Section D(2)(b)(ii), above in this chapter. The procedures specified in sections 49 to 54 in regard to the acceptance and termination of undertakings are described in Section D(2)(b), above in this chapter.

b. Duties of and Guidance to Tribunal

Sections 42(3) to (6) contain the following directions to the Tribunal in making or resuming its inquiry under section 42:

1) It must assess the cumulative effect of the dumping or subsidizing and take into account Canada's obligations under paragraph 12 of Article 27 of the WTO *Subsidies Agreement*.[23]
2) If the volume of dumped or subsidized goods from a country is negligible, it must terminate the inquiry in respect of those goods.
3) Where domestic industry is based on regional markets, as defined in section 2(1.1) of the *SIMA*, it must not make a finding of injury or retardation, or threat of injury, unless there is a concentration of the dumped or subsidized goods into the regional market and the dumping or subsidizing has caused injury or retardation, or is threatening to cause injury, to producers of all or almost all of the production of like goods in that regional market.

c. Tribunal's Order or Finding

Forthwith after receiving the notice of final determination from the CBSA, but not later than 120 days from the date it received its notice of preliminary determination, the Tribunal must make an order or finding, declaring the goods to which, from what supplier, and from which country of export, the order or finding applies.

A copy of the order or finding must be mailed, forthwith after it is made, to the CBSA, the importer, the exporter, and such other persons as may be specified by the Tribunal's rules, and a copy of the reasons for the order or finding must be mailed within fifteen days after the order or finding is made. Notice of each order or finding must also be published in the *Canada Gazette*.

---

23 Above note 17. Article 27.12 states: "The provisions of paragraphs 10 and 11 shall govern any determination of *de minimis* under paragraph 3 of Article 15."

d. Goods of a *NAFTA* Country

Where an order or finding relates to goods of more than one *NAFTA* country, or goods of one or more *NAFTA* countries and goods of one or more other countries, the Tribunal must make a separate order or finding with respect to goods of each *NAFTA* country. The same requirements respecting the mailing of notice of order or finding, and the reasons therefor, and publishing it in the *Canada Gazette*, referred to in Sections E(2)(d)(i) and (ii), above in this chapter, also apply to the order or finding made under this section.

e. Recommencement Following Judicial Review

Where the Federal Court of Appeal, following judicial review of an application under the *Federal Courts Act*[24] or section 96.1 of the *SIMA*, has set aside an order or finding of the Tribunal, or has set aside an order or finding in relation to particular goods, the Tribunal must take the following action:

1) Where the matter is referred back to the Tribunal, it must forthwith recommence the inquiry in respect of the goods or the particular goods, as the case may be.
2) In any other case, the Tribunal must decide within thirty days after the court has finally disposed of the application for judicial review, whether to recommence the inquiry.

The Tribunal must forthwith make a new order or finding compatible with the court's directions, or recommence the inquiry if it decides to do so pursuant to those directions, and in either case, make a new order or finding within 120 days after the court has set aside the Tribunal's order or finding, or within the same time period where it has decided to recommence the inquiry. In the latter case, the Tribunal may hold a hearing or a new hearing and receive additional evidence that it considers necessary.

The Tribunal must give notice of the recommencement of the inquiry to every person to whom a copy of the order or finding was sent.

f. Illustrative Inquiry Decisions

INQUIRY 1: WOOD VENETIAN BLINDS AND SLATS FROM MEXICO AND CHINA[25]

In this injury inquiry, the Tribunal found that there were three classes of wood blinds and slats: stock blinds, custom blinds, and wood slats. It found that domestically produced custom blinds and slats were "like goods" to the imported custom blinds and slats, but stock blinds were not.

24　Above note 12.
25　NQ-2003-003 (2004), 9 TTR (2d) 113.

The Tribunal terminated its inquiry in respect of custom blinds from China and stock blinds from Mexico, since the production in Canada of the complainant, SBM, and its supporters did not account for a major proportion of total domestic production of custom blinds, and therefore, the dumping of custom blinds in Canada had not caused injury and was not threatening to cause injury to the domestic custom blind industry.

The Tribunal, however, found that there was a surge in the volume of imported slats from China and Mexico, they competed with the like goods, and they had taken market share from the domestic producers, reduced their sales, and restrained domestic production. It found (1) price was the main driving factor behind the surge of imports, and (2) the prices of the dumped "direct" imports caused lost sales to the domestic slat industry. With regard to the dumping of "indirect" imports from the United States originating in China, the Tribunal noted that, while the share of the market represented by their sales might, for the most part, be inaccessible to domestic slat producers, since fabricators were reluctant to purchase slats from potential competitors, they were likely to enter Canada at low prices, which allowed domestic fabricators to market custom blinds with good profit margins in competition with SBM.

With respect to the impact of the dumping on the domestic slat industry, the Tribunal concluded that it had underutilized its capacity, lost market share and revenues, experienced low returns on investment, and suffered other negative impacts on inventory and on financial performance. Accordingly, the Tribunal considered that the increasing volumes of imports at dumped prices from China and Mexico had caused injury to the domestic slat industry.

Since there was no stock blind industry in Canada, the Tribunal found that the dumping of stock blinds in Canada had not caused and was not threatening to cause injury and was not causing material retardation to the establishment of a domestic stock blind industry.

INQUIRY 2: STEEL FUEL TANKS EXPORTED FROM CHINA AND TAIPEI[26]

In this injury inquiry, the Canadian industry was represented by Spectra/Premium Industries (SPI), which was the only manufacturer of replacement fuel tanks in Canada. The Tribunal's findings were as follows:

1) SPI's domestic sales had dropped sharply in 2002, coinciding with a sharp decline in the overall market. While it lost market share in 2002

---

26 NQ-2004-002 (2004), 9 TTR (2d) 370.

to the subject goods, the subject goods displaced a relatively small volume of SPI's sales. The bulk of the decline in SPI's sales resulted from the general market contraction in 2002.

2) SPI's prices eroded by only a small amount over the period of the inquiry. When the appreciation of the Canadian dollar from 2002 onwards was taken into account, the sharp decline in importers' purchasing costs of imports observed in 2003 was attributable more to exchange rates than to a deliberate effort by the foreign producers to reduce their selling prices in the Canadian market.

3) Where SPI experienced price suppression, it was minimal.

4) The cause of SPI's worsening performance in 2002 was the general market contraction, with the remainder of the injury attributable to other non-dumping factors. SPI's market behaviour, in particular its strategy of selling at all trade levels in the Canadian replacement fuel tank market and, in effect, competing with its own consumers, was an important factor negatively affecting its performance.

5) The dumped imports were not threatening to cause injury. Imports had maintained a stable market share since 2002, and there had been no aggressive marketing in Canada by the foreign producers. Further, the Chinese producers' market of choice was the United States.

6) Import prices were increasing in the first quarter of 2004.

INQUIRY 3: FRESH TOMATOES EXPORTED FROM THE UNITED STATES[27]

In this injury inquiry, the Tribunal, first of all, found that domestically grown fresh tomatoes were "like goods" to the imported fresh tomatoes, which included tomatoes for fresh consumption that were grown in greenhouses and tomatoes that were field grown. In the unique circumstances of the case (the Canadian Tomato Trade Alliance, the complainant, had withdrawn from the hearings), and on the basis of the written record, the Tribunal found no convincing evidence that the domestic industry had suffered material injury as a result of the dumped subject goods. It noted that greenhouse tomato growers experienced rising sales, market share, and production in Canada at a time when the market share of imported US tomatoes was stable. It also found that there was no clear correlation between the prices of domestic greenhouse tomatoes and the imported US fresh tomatoes.

As to a threat of injury, the Tribunal saw no sign of a change in the circumstances, such as any imminent major increase in US plantings, production, or shipment to Canada. Therefore, it concluded that the subject

---

27   NQ-2001-004 (2002), 6 TTR (2d) 659.

fresh tomatoes had not caused material injury or retardation and were not threatening to cause material injury to the domestic industry.

INQUIRY 4: CERTAIN GRAIN CORN EXPORTED FROM THE UNITED STATES[28]

This final injury inquiry involved dumped and subsidized grain corn into Canada for use or consumption west of the Manitoba-Ontario border. The producers represented by the Manitoba Corn Growers' Association Inc accounted for about 92 percent of the Western Canadian production of grain corn. Several importers and users of grain corn also participated in the inquiry.

The Tribunal noted that the injury standard for a regional market is very stringent. The evidence must disclose that the subject goods have injured the producers of "all or almost all" grain corn production in Western Canada.

The Tribunal found that dumped and subsidized imports from the United States had caused the prices of corn sold in Western Canada to decline, causing financial injury to many domestic producers. However, it also found that there was a certain proportion of commercial production that had not been materially injured. Evidence showed that some producers were able to achieve better than average prices for their corn despite the presence of dumped and subsidized imports from the United States. In addition, certain major corn users paid a higher-than-average price for domestic corn because it had certain qualities or characteristics that they required for their operations. It was apparent that some producers were able to achieve reasonable rates of return, even in the 1999–2000 crop year, when US import prices were at their lowest levels.

In addition, the Tribunal identified another category of corn grower that was not affected by dumped and subsidized imports in the same way as producers that operated in the commercial market. The Tribunal noted that diversified farmers who had livestock operations and who also grew their own corn for feed were able to achieve certain synergies between their animal and grain operations. The evidence showed that their costs of production were much lower than the industry average. On-farm users were also effectively insulated from most market price fluctuations.

Thus, while many domestic producers that sold their corn on the commercial market had been injured by the subject imports, when the non-injured production represented by on-farm use was combined with the portion of commercial sales that had achieved reasonable returns, there was little doubt that the "all or almost all" injury threshold had not been met in this case.

---

28 NQ-2000-005 (2001), 5 TTR (2d) 501.

INQUIRY 5: STEEL GRATING EXPORTED FROM CHINA[29]

In this final injury inquiry, the Tribunal determined that domestically produced steel grating constituted "like goods" in relation to the subject goods and then concluded that there were two classes of goods, namely, carbon and alloy steel bar grating and stainless steel bar grating. In a separate opinion on classes of goods, one Tribunal member concluded that there were three classes: galvanized carbon and alloy steel grating, non-galvanized carbon and alloy steel grating, and stainless steel grating.

The Tribunal terminated its inquiry in respect of stainless steel grating, due to the negligible volume of imports.

The Tribunal determined that Fisher & Ludlow Ltd alone constituted a major proportion of the total domestic production of the "like goods," so it decided to restrict its analysis of injury to the evidence pertaining to that firm's production.

The following were the Tribunal's findings:

1) There was a significant increase in the volume of imports of the subject goods in absolute terms and relative to the production and consumption of the "like goods."
2) The subject goods had significantly undercut, depressed, and suppressed the price of the "like goods."
3) The prevalence of the subject goods in the Canadian market, especially in 2008 and 2009, had a significant negative impact on Fisher & Ludlow's production and capacity utilization rates.
4) In addition, the dumping and subsidizing of the subject goods resulted in lost sales and market share for the domestic industry, negatively impacted the financial performance of the domestic industry in 2009 and interim 2010, caused declines in employment and productivity, and resulted in negative effects on return on investment and other indicators.

With respect to the accumulative losses suffered by the domestic steel grating industry that were attributable to the recession, the Tribunal concluded that the dumping and subsidizing of the subject goods had, in and of themselves, caused material injury.

INQUIRY 6: GREENHOUSE BELL PEPPERS EXPORTED FROM THE NETHERLANDS[30]

In this final injury inquiry, the Tribunal first determined that greenhouse bell peppers produced in Canada were "like goods" in relation to the sub-

---

29 NQ-2010-002 (2011).
30 NQ-2010-001 (2010), 15 TTR (2d) 1.

ject goods and then concluded that field bell peppers produced in Canada were not "like goods" in relation to the subject goods. It determined that the Ontario Greenhouse Vegetable Growers, which accounted for a major proportion of domestic production in and of itself, constituted the domestic industry.

The Tribunal observed that, despite a significant increase in the volume of imports of the subject goods, the domestic industry generally performed well and was able to increase production, capacity, sales volume, net income, gross margin, employment, wages, and productivity, in addition to maintaining its rate of capacity utilization and market share. The only negative results were lower net returns, gross margin, and net income observed in 2009. Accordingly, the Tribunal concluded that the dumping of the subject goods had not caused material injury to the domestic industry.

However, in its analysis, the Tribunal observed that the general trend in respect of increasing volumes of imports of subject goods observed during the period of inquiry was likely to continue in the near to medium term in the absence of anti-dumping duties. As there was no indication that the Dutch propensity to dump would disappear, the Tribunal considered that the renewed presence of dumped subject goods in the Canadian market was likely to transform the insignificant price depression that had occurred during isolated instances of the period of inquiry into significant price depression over the next two growing seasons. In the absence of anti-dumping duties, there would be increased pressure on other marketers to respond to Dutch lead prices, that is, lower their prices or risk losing business. The Tribunal therefore found that the clearly foreseen and imminent circumstances were such that the dumping of the subject goods was threatening to cause injury to the domestic industry.

The Tribunal received one product exclusion request concerning organic greenhouse bell peppers. That request was denied as the Tribunal was of the view that the domestic industry's evidence had demonstrated that it produced, or was capable of producing, organic greenhouse bell peppers.

INQUIRY 7: POLYSIO INSULATION BOARD EXPORTED FROM THE UNITED STATES[31]

On 6 April 2010, the CBSA determined that 97.8 percent of polysio insulation board (the subject goods) was dumped into Canada from 1 October 2008 to 30 September 2009 by an overall weighted average margin of dumping of 21.9 percent when expressed as a percentage of the market price. The CBSA ruled that the margin of dumping was not insignificant. That determination

---

31 NQ-2009-005 (2010), 14 TTR (2d) 492.

was noted in Section E(2)(d)(v), above in this chapter.[32] On the same day as the CBSA initiated its investigation, the Tribunal commenced a preliminary injury inquiry pursuant to section 34(2) of the *SIMA* and on 7 December 2009 it made a preliminary determination that there was evidence that disclosed a reasonable indication that the dumping of the subject goods had caused injury.

On 6 January 6 2010, pursuant to section 42 of the *SIMA*, the Tribunal commenced an inquiry to determine whether the dumping of the subject goods had caused injury or was threatening to cause injury. All of the CBSA's background investigation was before the Tribunal, which formed the dossier for its determination, the usual *modus operandi*.

At the final injury inquiry, IKO (the complainant) made ten specific injury allegations that it had suffered injury in terms of lost sales, price suppression, and price depression. In particular, IKO asked the Tribunal to assess "but for" injury, that is to say, domestic prices could have been higher than they were, in the absence of the dumped imports.

The Tribunal found that the information provided in all ten injury allegations was vague, imprecise, and/or inaccurate, and for the most part it was contradicted by positive evidence of the parties opposing the complaint. It concluded that IKO's injury allegations of lost sales and price depression were not persuasive and, accordingly, did not ascribe any weight to them.

In its conclusions, the Tribunal also found that there was a significant decline in the absolute volume of dumped imports of the subject goods, as well as a significant decrease relative to the production and consumption of "like goods" over the period of investigation.

With regard to price suppression, the Tribunal examined IKO's cost of manufactured goods compared to selling prices for its domestic sales. The evidence, in its opinion, did not indicate price suppression during the period of investigation.

After weighing the evidence on the record, the Tribunal found that the claims of significant price undercutting, price depression, or price suppression by the dumped subject goods were not persuasive. Moreover, the data did not show evidence of a causal link between the prices of the domestic industry and the presence of the dumped subject goods in the Canadian market.

The Tribunal's conclusion on the injury incurred by the domestic industry was that, while the presence of dumped imports during the period of inquiry caused a certain level of competition in the domestic market and that,

---

32 Above note 20.

but for the dumping, IKO could have made some additional sales, the increase in sales would likely have been limited and would not have occurred at significantly higher prices. Therefore, it found that the effect on IKO's market share, prices, and total sales revenue was not material.

With regard to threat of injury, the Tribunal stated that it typically considered a time frame of eighteen to twenty-four months from the date of its finding. However, in the present case, the Tribunal said its focus would be on the period remaining in 2010 and 2011.

The Tribunal examined whether there was a likelihood of a substantial increase of dumped imports in Canada during that period. Taking into account all the factors specified in section 2(1.5), the Tribunal was of the view that a substantial increase of dumped imports in Canada in the 2010–2011 term was not likely to occur, especially as the economic recovery in the United States was beginning to take hold.

The Tribunal acknowledged that the magnitude of the weighted average margin of dumping determined by the CBSA was not insignificant. Nevertheless, the evidence on the record with respect to the normal values of individual companies indicated that a large volume of the imports of the subject goods would continue to enter the Canadian market at competitive prices, and some at non-dumped prices. The Tribunal was convinced that the evidence did not support a conclusion that the dumping of the subject goods posed a clearly foreseen and imminent threat of injury to the domestic industry. It therefore found that the dumping of the subject goods was not threatening to cause injury to the domestic industry.

In view of the foregoing, the Tribunal's decision was that the dumping of the subject goods had not caused injury and was not threatening to cause injury to the domestic industry in the medium term, namely, the period remaining in 2010 after the finding and in 2011.

e) Public Interest Inquiries

Following a finding of injury, the Tribunal may, pursuant to section 45, initiate a public interest hearing if it is of the opinion that there are reasonable grounds to consider that an anti-dumping or countervailing duty imposed under the *SIMA*, or the full amount of it, would not or might not be in the public interest. It may do this on its own initiative or on request of any interested person. It generally invites public interest submissions with its injury findings by way of a letter to interested persons. The Secretary of the Tribunal then notifies all interested parties by publishing a notice in the *Canada Gazette* informing them that any submissions must be filed within forty-five days. Even before the findings are issued, some public interest organizations may indicate to the Tribunal that they would be making submissions if the Tribunal recommends an anti-dumping or countervailing duty.

Section 45(5) clarifies the options for reducing anti-dumping or countervailing duties if the Tribunal makes a report to the Minister of Finance recommending that a reduction in duties would be in the public interest. The *SIMA Regulations* identify the factors that the Tribunal may take into account in its consideration of the public interest. The key elements are (1) the identification of the public interest issue with supporting information, which may include, among other things, the availability of goods from other sources; (2) the effects of the duties on domestic competition, on Canadian downstream producers of the goods, and on access to goods used as inputs by downstream producers of other goods and services or access to technology; (3) the effects on availability or prices of goods for consumers; and (4) the effects on upstream suppliers of the goods. The Tribunal will return requests that do not meet these requirements for completion within the same forty-five-day time frame.

Where, after the finding of injury or threat of injury, the Tribunal is of the opinion, on the basis of submissions, that the imposition of anti-dumping or countervailing duties, or the full amounts of it, may not be in the public interest, it reports to the Minister of Finance with a statement of the facts and the reasons that led to its conclusions.

If the Tribunal reaches a conclusion that a reduction or elimination of the anti-dumping or countervailing duty is warranted, it makes a report to the Minister of Finance, with specific recommendations and supporting reasons, indicating, if relevant, a price or prices that would be adequate to eliminate injury, retardation, or threat of injury to the domestic industry. The Tribunal will publish a notice of its report in the *Canada Gazette*, and a copy of the report will be sent to all parties to the inquiry. The Minister of Finance decides whether to follow the Tribunal's recommendations.

If, on the other hand, on the completion of its inquiry, the Tribunal determines that no reduction or elimination of duties is warranted, it will publish a brief report to that effect with reasons.

Between 1997–98 and 2011–12 there were only about ten requests for public interest inquiries, or less than one a year, and only half of them went forward. The remaining requests were rejected for lack of sufficient evidence to substantiate assertions of the negative effects that the imposition of anti-dumping and countervailing duties had or might have on the public.

Chapter 3: Special Import Measures Act

i) Selected Inquiry Decisions

INQUIRY 1: CERTAIN PREPARED BABY FOODS[33]

In its injury finding the Tribunal had concluded that the dumping of certain prepared baby foods was causing material injury. Several paediatric and health organizations, and the Director of Investigation and Research, *Competition Act*,[34] had indicated that they would make public interest representations if the Tribunal issued a finding of injury or threat of injury. After considering the submissions and the evidence, and the relevant interests, the Tribunal issued a report to the Minister of Finance in which it concluded that the continued imposition of the anti-dumping duties in the full amount was not in the public interest and recommended that the duties be reduced. The Tribunal's specific import pricing recommendations were included in a confidential appendix provided to the Minister.

INQUIRY 2: IODINATED CONTRAST MEDIA[35]

Following an injury finding in May 2000 into the dumping of iodinated contrast media, the Tribunal conducted a public interest inquiry and issued its report to the Minister of Finance in August 2000. As part of its investigation, the Tribunal sent requests for information to Malinckrodt Canada Inc (MCI), the sole domestic producer, and to importers, exporters, purchasers, and potential producers of generic low-osmolality iodinated contrast media (LOCM), as well as to associations of radiologists and medical radiation technologists, the Patented Medicine Prices Review Board (PMPRB), the Therapeutic Products Programme of the Department of Health, and the Canada Customs and Revenue Agency (CCRA). The Tribunal also received written submissions from several persons and associations, as well as from the Commissioner of Competition.

All, except MCI, stated that there was a public interest warranting the elimination or, alternatively, the reduction of the duties. MCI submitted that there was no public interest.

The Tribunal had found that the dumped imports had caused material injury to MCI in the form of eroded prices, and estimated that the price erosion incurred by MCI on its sales of Optiray amounted to $2 million for the

---

33 NQ-97-002 (1998), 3 TTR (2d) 751. The finding was rescinded when the Tribunal concluded in its expiry review, RR-2002-002 (2003), that Heinz Canada was unlikely to suffer material injury in the near- or mid-term and any injury that it does suffer would be due, for the most part, to the effects of entry of renewed competition in the market, not to dumping: (2003), 7 TTR (2d) 875 at 913.
34 RSC 1985, c C-34.
35 (2000), 4 TTR (2d) 530 (CITT), reviewed (2003), 7 TTR (2d) 783 (*NAFTA* Binational Panel), remand to CITT (2003), 8 TTR (2d) 30 (*NAFTA* Binational Panel).

first nine months of 1999 based on 1996 prices, and that its domestic sales of Hexabrix were also affected, resulting in a 50 percent decline in gross margins between fiscal 1997 and 1999 as well as losses in fiscal 1998 and 1999.

The Commissioner of Competition made a written submission that the economic costs associated with the imposition of anti-dumping duties outweighed the economic benefits and would, *inter alia* (1) result in the elimination of competition in the Canadian market by the creation of monopoly; (2) increase prices and raise serious health and safety risks to patients; (3) reduce choice; and (4) produce an overwhelmingly negative effect on the economic welfare. The Commissioner submitted that, in any case, the duties imposed should not be greater than the minimal amount required to avoid material injury to MCI, which could be achieved by setting the duties at a level that was a small percentage increase over the export price determined by the CCRA.

MCI, which opposed the elimination of anti-dumping duties for the reasons given above, pointed out that Canadian prices had been stable and had not escalated since the imposition of the duties, and that a number of market constraints would maintain the Canadian prices at a relatively low level, especially the PMPRB's price monitoring and the availability of high-osmolality contrast media (HOCM). It also suggested that LOCM were also available from alternate sources. It submitted that if the Tribunal was convinced that a reduction of anti-dumping duties was warranted, the reduction should take the form of a minimum price based on the 1996–97 market price.

The Tribunal received a great deal of evidence on the effect that higher prices for LOCM would have on hospital budgets. It also heard from radiologist groups who testified that it was very important for radiologists to be able to choose the appropriate LOCM for their patients from among the products offered by MCI and the exporters (Nycomed and Bracco).

The Tribunal acknowledged that once a finding of material injury was made and the anti-dumping duties were in place, prices typically increase as the domestic industry is relieved of the downward pressure imposed by the competing imports at dumped prices. However, the price increase may be constrained.

The Tribunal also conceded that if the anti-dumping duties were eliminated, Nycomed and Bracco would be able to sell in the Canadian market at any price level. However, with the full amount of the anti-dumping in place, both would generally not be able to compete in the Canadian market and would only be able to supply up to 15 percent of the Canadian market that MCI was unable to fill. In that situation, MCI would be the dominant supplier to the Canadian market.

On the other hand, a reduction of the anti-dumping duties would address the concern that a large increase in domestic prices would lead to pressures on hospital budgets, which would result in a reduction of the number of procedures that could be undertaken on patients. A reduction of the anti-dumping duties would also enable both Nycomed and Bracco to continue to be an alternative to MCI for buyers of LOCM and would address the public interest concern that radiologists require a choice of alternatives in order to provide the greatest safety and comfort for patients. As well, a somewhat higher price for the imported LOCM would provide scope for MCI to increase its revenues.

Taking all the foregoing arguments into account, the Tribunal was of the opinion that there existed a sufficiently compelling public interest rationale to report to the Minister that a reduction rather than the elimination of the anti-dumping duties was the preferred alternative. A reduction would help to maintain alternative sources of supply of LOCM for the Canadian market and would also minimize the adverse effect of higher prices for LOCM on the quality of patient care. At the same time, the domestic industry would benefit from both higher average prices and an opportunity to increase its share of the market. The Tribunal therefore recommended that the anti-dumping duties on LOCM imported from the United States be reduced. It believed that a duty reduction would best be achieved by establishing new lower normal values calculated by applying a company-specific percentage increase to the exporters' final determination of export price. These new normal values should remain fixed for the duration of the injury finding.[36]

INQUIRY 3: CERTAIN REFRIGERATORS, DISHWASHERS, AND DRYERS FROM THE UNITED STATES[37]

Following its injury finding, in this inquiry, the Tribunal, as required by section 45(1), issued a letter indicating that it would accept representations from all "interested persons" on the issue of whether the Tribunal should conduct a public interest investigation. Eight of the ten representations it received were in favour of eliminating anti-dumping duties and supported a public interest investigation. Two parties (Camco Inc (Canada) and Maytag Corporation) filed responses opposing a public interest hearing.

The following were some of the points presented in favour of eliminating the duties:

---

36   *NAFTA* Panel Review reported at (2003), 7 TTR (2d) 783 and (2003), 7 TTR (2d) 800; *NAFTA* dumping remand to Tribunal reported at (2003), 8 TTR (2d) 30, where the Binational Panel held that the determination on remand provided a reasoned and sustainable explanation of CCRA's findings that *SIMA* ss 15 and 19 did not apply.

37   Injury Inquiry NQ-2000-001 (2000); Public Interest Inquiry PB-2000-002 (2000).

1) Canadian distributors and retailers will suffer significant injury; the anti-dumping duties will cause economic damage to distributors and retailers that were not supported by Camco and that were near the Canada–US border, and Canadian distributors and retailers will lose business to cross-border shopping
2) Significant injury will result to competition in Canada.
3) Prices have increased as a result of the anti-dumping duties.
4) Anti-dumping duties decrease affordable appliance choice for Canadian consumers, particularly first-time buyers and lower-income consumers.
5) Consumers will pay significantly higher prices for the performance-enhanced features offered by Whirlpool and WCI (the two leading US exporters).
6) The price of new homes will increase and there will be a depressing effect on the Canadian housing market.
7) There will be environmental impacts and undue burden on energy and water consumption.

352   The Tribunal carefully reviewed all the representations and submissions received in response to its invitation, as well as the evidence and testimony adduced at the injury hearing. It noted that, despite the anti-dumping duties, Whirlpool Corporation and Whirlpool Canada Inc were not discouraged from continuing to compete in terms of the technological and innovative features that they can offer the Canadian consumer, and as a result they will enhance competition and will provide an incentive for all other companies that compete with them.

Based on the foregoing, the Tribunal was of the view that the application of the anti-dumping duties will not limit the supply of competitively priced and energy-efficient refrigerators, dishwashers, and dryers, or curtail effective price competition in the domestic market for these appliances. There is unlikely to be a negative impact on the housing market as a result of the anti-dumping duties.

For all the above reasons, the Tribunal was not convinced that there was a public interest worthy of further investigation. It therefore determined that it will not conduct a public interest investigation and will not report to the Minister of Finance.

f) Tribunal Must Advise CBSA

If during the section 42 inquiry, the Tribunal is of the opinion that there is dumping or subsidizing of the goods to which a preliminary determination under the *SIMA* applies, and that the evidence discloses a reasonable indication of injury or retardation, or threat of injury, it must so advise the CBSA, setting out the goods to which the preliminary determination applies.

g) Termination of Proceedings/Inquiry

Except in respect of proceedings initiated under the dispute settlement provisions related to goods of a *NAFTA* country set out in Part I.1, and except in respect of the review of orders referred back by the Federal Court for rehearing or reconsideration, an order or finding of the Tribunal terminates all proceedings under the *SIMA* respecting the dumping or subsidizing of the goods.

In respect of goods imported from Chile that were exempted pursuant to section 14 of the *SIMA*, the Tribunal must also terminate any inquiry with respect to those goods. A notice of termination must be sent by the Secretary of the Tribunal immediately upon termination of the proceedings, to the CBSA, the importer, the exporter, the government of the Republic of Chile, and any other persons who are specified by the Tribunal's rules, and must also be published in the *Canada Gazette*.

3) CBSA Action on Final Determination, Order, or Finding

After the CBSA has made a final determination of dumping or subsidizing with respect to imported goods in accordance with section 41(1) and has received from the Tribunal an order or finding on injury or retardation, or threat of injury, to which the final determination applies, the procedures set out in sections 56 to 62 become applicable.

a) Determination by Designated Officer

With respect to goods released after a preliminary determination and on or before an undertaking was accepted and ending on or before the day on which the Tribunal made an order or finding, section 55 requires an officer designated by the CBSA, not later than six months after the date of the Tribunal's order or finding, to determine,

1) whether the imported goods are in fact goods of the same description as those described in the order or finding;
2) the normal value and export price of the goods;
3) the amount of subsidy on the goods, if any; and
4) where sections 6 to 10 of the *SIMA* apply, the export subsidy on the goods.

b) Goods Subsequently Imported

By virtue of section 56, goods that are imported subsequent to the Tribunal's order or finding, or subsequent to an Order in Council imposing a countervailing duty in the circumstances set out in section 7, are bound by the determination made by the designated officer within thirty days after they were accounted for in accordance with the *Customs Act*,[38] that they are of the same (1) description, (2) normal value, and (3) export price or amount of export subsidy, as those to which the order or finding applies.

The determination of the designated officer is final and conclusive unless a request for re-determination is made by the importer within ninety days after the determination and after the importer has paid all duties owing on the goods. If a designated officer does not make a determination within thirty days after the imported goods were accounted for, as required by section 56, a determination that the final determination and the order or finding does not apply to the goods accounted for, is deemed to have been made.[39]

If the goods to which the determination applies were imported from a *NAFTA* country, the government of that *NAFTA* country, the producer, the manufacturer, or the exporter may also make a request for re-determination, but they are not required to pay the duties owing on the goods even if they are not paid by the importer.

The request for re-determination must be made in the prescribed form and manner, accompanied by the prescribed information, to a designated officer.

c) Re-determination

i) Re-determination by Designated Officer

A determination may be re-determined under section 57 by a designated officer when the request has been filed in the prescribed form and manner, in accordance with that request, or, where the designated officer deems it advisable, within two years after the determination; provided, however, the

---

38 RSC 1985, c 1 (2d Supp), as am RSC 1985, c 45 (1st Supp), RSC 1985, c 7 (2d Supp), and subsequently.

39 Re-determination under the *SIMA* s 57 is restricted to the nature, value, and export prices of goods subject to anti-dumping duty, and does not extend to re-determination of the identity of the importer. Any change in or alteration of the identity of the importer is a matter exclusively within the jurisdiction of the International Trade Tribunal: *Weldwood of Canada Ltd v Canada (Deputy Minister of National Revenue, Customs and Excise)* (1991), 44 FTR 31 (TD). (The court held that on a re-determination under this provision, there is no authority pursuant to it to deem assignees of the imported goods to be the importers for purposes of the imposition of anti-dumping duty.)

CBSA has not re-determined the determination under section 59 or the determination was not with respect to goods released after the initiation of an expedited review requested under section 13.2(23) by an exporter who claimed that it is not associated with any exporter whose goods are covered by an order or finding of the Tribunal and before a decision was made under that section.

ii) Further Re-determination by the CBSA

A determination or re-determination by a designated officer in accordance with section 55 or 57 is final and conclusive, but the importer may within ninety days of the determination or the re-determination make a written request under section 58 to the President of the CBSA to make a re-determination, after the importer has paid all duties owing on the goods.

If the imported goods in respect of which the re-determination is requested are from a *NAFTA* country, the government of that *NAFTA* country, as well as the producer or manufacturer or exporter of the goods from that country, may within ninety days of determination by a designated officer, request the President of the CBSA in the prescribed form and manner, accompanied by the prescribed information, for a re-determination, whether or not the importer has paid all duties owing on the imported goods.

iii) Permissive Re-determination

The CBSA is authorized by sections 59(1) and 59(1.1) to make a re-determination pursuant to a request made under sections 55, 56, or 57. It is also authorized to make a re-determination at any time in the following further situations:

1) if the importer or exporter has made a misrepresentation or committed fraud in accounting for the goods under the *Customs Act* or in obtaining release of the goods;
2) where the exporter or manufacturer, producer, vendor, or exporter of any goods has agreed to indemnify the importer for any countervailing duties referred to in section 2(6) or for any anti-dumping duty referred to in section 26 or a benefit on re-sale referred to in section 28; and
3) in order to give effect to a decision of the Tribunal, the Federal Court of Appeal, or the Supreme Court of Canada.

The CBSA may also make a re-determination within two years, if it had not made a re-determination referred to in the two sections immediately above.

iv) Permissive Re-determination of Re-determination

For the purpose of giving effect to a decision of the Binational Panel established under Part I.1, the CBSA may at any time re-determine any determination or re-determination referred to in sections 55, 56, 57, or 59(1) with respect to the goods covered by the decision.

v) Mandatory Re-determination

Section 59(3) requires the CBSA to make a re-determination within one year in the case of a request made within the period and manner specified in section 58(1.1) (any goods, including goods imported from a *NAFTA* country) or 56(1.01) (determination made by a designated officer).

d) Notice of Re-determination

A notice of each re-determination made under section 59 must be given to the importer, and in the case of goods imported from a *NAFTA* country, to the government of that *NAFTA* country, and to such other persons as may be prescribed, as well as to the Canadian Secretary of the Panel established under Part I.1 if the re-determination gives effect to a decision of the Panel. It must also be published in the *Canada Gazette*.

e) Effect of Re-determination

Where a redetermination has been made in accordance with the foregoing provisions, the importer is required by sections 60 and 60.1 to pay any additional duties that are required to be paid, and if any duties were paid in excess of what were owed, they must be returned forthwith to the importer. The notice of the re-determination must be given to the importer in Canada without delay.

4) Appeals

a) Appeal to the Tribunal

Subject to the provisions of Part I.1 with respect to trade dispute settlement provisions of sections 77.012 or 77.12, a person that deems itself to be aggrieved by a re-determination by the CBSA may appeal that re-determination to the Tribunal by filing a notice of appeal in writing with the CBSA and with the secretary of the Tribunal within ninety days after the re-determination was made. Notice of the hearing of the appeal must be published by the secretary in the *Canada Gazette* at least twenty-one days prior to the day of the hearing and any person who enters an appearance with the secretary on or before the day of the hearing may be heard on the appeal.

After hearing the appeal, the Tribunal may make such order or finding as the nature of the matter may require, and may declare what duty is payable or that no duty is payable on the goods that are the subject of appeal.

The order or finding of the Tribunal is final and conclusive unless it is appealed to the Federal Court as provided in section 62.

i) Scope of Tribunal's Findings ("Scope Orders")

Typical issues involved in appeals is the scope of the Tribunal's order, that is to say, whether the goods imported by the appellant on which the CBSA had imposed an anti-dumping or countervailing duty pursuant to the Tribunal's order or finding, are the same as those covered by the Tribunal's order or finding. The Tribunal's starting point for determining this issue is the findings themselves. In doing so, it considers a number of factors, such as the physical description, end-use applications, interchangeability, competition in the marketplace, channels of trade in which the product is sold, expectations of the ultimate purchasers, price, advertising, and marketing.

The Tribunal has indicated that it interprets its findings strictly on the basis of their ordinary meaning, and that it looks behind the findings only if they are ambiguous. In interpreting and applying the description of the goods in those findings, the Tribunal takes the view that it has no authority to amend the scope of the findings, whether by narrowing or enlarging such scope.

ii) Illustrative Decisions ("Scope Orders")

CASE 1: FOOTWEAR

In *M & M Footwear Inc v Commissioner of the Canada Customs and Revenue Agency*,[40] the appellant had imported women's waterproof plastic footwear from the People's Republic of China (China). The CCRA applied anti-dumping duties on the basis that the goods in issue did not meet the definition of excluded waterproof plastic footwear as described in the Tribunal's statement of reasons in the relevant finding of injury. The appellant claimed otherwise.

In the injury inquiry the Tribunal had found that the dumping in Canada of women's leather and non-leather boots originating or exported from China had caused, were causing, and were likely to cause material injury to the production in Canada of like goods, but it specifically excluded sandals, slippers, sports footwear, waterproof rubber footwear, waterproof plastic

---

40 AP-2001-070 (2003), 8 TTR (2d) 36 (Injury Inquiry NQ-89-003).

footwear, safety footwear incorporating protective metal toe caps, orthopedic footwear, wooden shoes, disposable footwear, bowling shoes, curling shoes, motocross racing boots, and canvas footwear. The CCRA's re-determination was based on laboratory reports that the nylon used to make the upper was a textile as defined in the Harmonized Commodity Description and Coding System[41] (HCDCS), generally referred to as the Harmonized System (HS). The appellant submitted that the rules of tariff classification were not relevant in the present case as they were intended for a different purpose. The issue was not whether it is a textile but whether nylon is a plastic.

The Tribunal allowed the appeal, concluding that the goods in issue were excluded from the findings; they met the definition of waterproof plastic footwear and were, therefore, not goods of the same description as those to which its findings applied.

CASE 2: ANCHORING KITS (CONTAINING SHIELDS AND LAG BOLTS)

In the appeal in *Cobra Anchors Co Ltd v President of the Canada Border Services Agency*[42] against the decision of the CBSA, the goods in issue were six different sealed clamshell-type retail packages containing two zinc "shields" and two steel "lag bolts" which, when used together, formed a friction-type anchoring system designed for use in base materials, such as concrete, brick, block, and stone, that were not suitable for directly receiving lag bolts. The issue in the appeal was whether the lag bolt components of the goods were of the same description as the goods to which the Tribunal's injury findings applied and were therefore subject to anti-dumping duties. The CBSA had determined that this was so, whereas the appellant argued that, as a component of the goods in issue (which it described as consumer-ready "anchor kits" put up in packages for retail sale), the lag bolts were not goods that came within the description of the goods to which the Tribunal's findings in *Certain Fasteners* applied. In that case, the Tribunal described the subject goods as follows: "[C]arbon steel and stainless steel fasteners, i.e. screws, nuts and bolts of carbon steel or stainless steel that are used to mechanically join two or more elements . . . originating in or exported from the People's Republic of China."[43]

In order to reach its re-determination, the CBSA had disassembled the imported goods (the anchor kits) to show that there were in reality two

---

41 The HS is governed by the *International Convention on the Harmonized Commodity Description and Coding System*, Can TS 1988 No 38.
42 AP-2008-006 (2009), 13 TTR (2d) 530.
43 *Ibid* at para 7.

goods packaged together, and since the steel lag bolt component was not incidental to the anchor kit, it was properly taken to fall within the scope of the definition of subject goods.

On the other hand, the appellant contended that there was no statutory authority that allowed the CBSA to disassemble an imported product for the purpose of applying anti-dumping duties to a specific component of that product; that the goods in reality constituted a single product, specifically, consumer-ready anchor kits put up in packages for retail sale, which were not intended to be opened and disassembled prior to retail sale. In this regard, the appellant asserted that it was well established in customs law that goods are to be classified according to their nature at the time of importation, which, according to the appellant, was not done by the CBSA in this instance.

The Tribunal allowed the appeal. It concluded that the steel lag bolt and zinc shield were both integral to the overall ability of the anchoring system to fulfill its functional purpose in respect of the specialized applications for which it was specifically designed. From this it followed that separating the lag bolt from the anchoring kit and treating it as a separate good for the purpose of applying anti-dumping duties under the SIMA would deprive the anchoring system (which required both the lag bolt and shield) of its functionality. Therefore, neither the steel lag bolt nor the zinc shield could properly be considered separately from the goods in issue, of which each formed an integral part.

CASE 3: HOT-ROLLED STEEL PLATE (CARBON STEEL OR ALLOY STEEL)
The goods in *Toyota Tsusho America Inc v President of the Canada Border Services Agency*[44] were hot-rolled steel plate, not further manufactured than hot-rolled, heat-treated or not, in cut lengths from 6,096 milimetres (240 inches) to 12,192 milimetres (480 inches), in widths from 2,300 milimetres (96 inches) to 3,050 milimetres (120 inches), and thicknesses from 13 milimetres (½ inch) to 58 milimetres (2-¼ inches). They were produced by Tianjin Iron and Steel Company Ltd, Tianjin, China.

The Tribunal had to determine whether the goods in issue, upon which anti-dumping duties were levied by the CBSA, were of the same description as the goods to which the Tribunal's finding of injury applied. The sole issue was whether the goods in issue constituted alloy steel, as claimed by the appellant, or carbon steel, as determined by the CBSA, in particular, whether

---

44 AP-2010-063 (2011), 16 TTR (2d) 138.

the minute quantity of boron in the goods made them alloy steel instead of carbon steel. If the Tribunal found that the goods were alloy steel they were not within the description of "carbon steel plate," which was unambiguously subject to anti-dumping duties.

The Tribunal considered all the technical evidence proffered by the parties and was satisfied that, in terms of the American Society for Testing and Materials (ASTM) and the American Iron and Steel Institute/Society of Automotive Engineers (AISI/SAE) definitions, the goods in issue constituted carbon steel. The Tribunal was left with choosing either a tariff classification that supported a finding that the goods in issue were alloy steel or the steel industry standards that supported a finding that the goods in issue were carbon steel. On the balance of evidence, considering that the subject matter was steel, the Tribunal gave more weight to the steel industry standards than to the Schedule to the *Customs Tariff*.

Therefore, the Tribunal held that the goods in issue constituted carbon steel and, as such, were of the same description as the goods to which its finding of injury applied. The Tribunal was left with a tariff classification that supported a finding that the goods in issue were alloy steel and steel industry standards that supported a finding that the goods in issue were carbon steel.

Therefore, the Tribunal held that the goods in issue constituted carbon steel and, as such, were of the same description as the goods to which its finding of injury applied.

CASE 4: ALUMINUM DOOR FRAME RAILS WITH FITTINGS

There were two issues involved in the *Aluminart Products Limited v President of the Canada Border Services Agency*[45] appeal. The first concerned the applicability of anti-dumping duties to the goods in issue, and the second concerned the legality of zeroing the margin of dumping. The subject goods were aluminum rails that were transformed into door frames with weather stripping, foam stripping, vinyl strip, screen mesh, and other fittings. They were used in the manufacture or sale of storm doors.

The appellant submitted that the aluminum door frame rails with fittings were not covered by the injury findings because the fittings were attached after the extrusion process had occurred. The CBSA argued that small

---

45   AP-2011-027 (2012), 16 TTR (2d) 548, appeal against the CBSA's determination Injury Inquiry NQ-2008-003 (2009).

additions of fittings did not change the nature or physical characteristics of the rails, which remained in the realm of aluminium extrusions covered by the Tribunal's fittings.

In the Tribunal's view, the issue was whether the attachment of the very narrow strip of non-aluminum material to an aluminum extrusion transformed the aluminum extrusion into something else. It was the Tribunal's opinion that it did not and it concluded that the aluminum rails were covered by the findings.

With regard to the zeroing issue, the appellant complained that by failing to use the zeroing when calculating the anti-dumping duties, the CBSA had inflated the amount of duties. In defending the practice, the CBSA asserted that zeroing was abandoned when investigating into the margin of dumping as required by section 30.2(1), but it continued to be legitimate when assessing anti-dumping duties. The Tribunal agreed with the CBSA. It said that the appellant had misunderstood the interaction between section 3, which imposed an anti-dumping duty equal to the margin of dumping, section 2(1), which defined the "margin of dumping" as "... the amount by which the normal value exceeds the export price of the goods," and section 30.2(1), which provided that the margin of dumping in relation to any particular importer is zero or the amount determined by subtracting the weighted average export price of the goods from the weighted average normal value of the goods, whichever was greater.

Thus, the appellant lost on both issues.

b) Appeal to the Federal Court of Appeal

Any of the parties to the appeal before the Tribunal, including the CBSA, and any person who entered an appearance if that person has a substantial interest in the appeal, and if leave is obtained, may appeal the order or finding to the Federal Court of Appeal within ninety days after the Tribunal has made the order or finding, on any question of law. The court may, on the disposition of the appeal, declare what duty is payable, or that no duty is payable, on the goods with respect to which the appeal was taken, or refer the matter back to the Tribunal for re-hearing, or make such other order or finding as the nature of the matter may require.

i) Judicial Review

Except where a dispute settlement procedure is provided in Part I.1 respecting goods imported from a *NAFTA* country, any of the parties before the Tribunal may also apply for a judicial review of the Tribunal's order or finding on any grounds set out in section 18.1(4) of the *Federal Courts Act*.[46] Judicial review is elaborated further in Section F(2), below in this chapter.

5) Review of Orders and Findings of Injury

a) Interim Review

Under the provisions of section 76.01, the Tribunal may review its orders or findings at any time, on its own initiative or at the request of the Minister of Finance, the CBSA, or any other person or government. The Tribunal commences an interim review where one is warranted and it then determines if the finding or order (or any aspect of it) should be rescinded or continued to its expiry date, with or without amendment.

An interim review may be warranted where there is a reasonable indication that new facts have arisen or that there has been a major change in the circumstances that led to the finding or order. For example, since the finding or order, the domestic industry may have ceased production of like goods, or foreign subsidies may have been terminated. An interim review may also be warranted where there are facts that, although in existence, were not put into evidence during the previous review or inquiry and were not discoverable by the exercise of reasonable diligence at the time.

The Tribunal will, however, not expand the scope of its findings of injury or threat of injury, or retardation, because it does not have jurisdiction to do so. Thus, in one interim review,[47] the Tribunal rejected the request of the Garlic Growers of Ontario to extend the coverage of its finding in *Fresh Garlic Originating in or Exported from the People's Republic of China*[48] to a full calendar year, from the period of July 1 to December 31 during which the finding applied.

If the Tribunal decides not to conduct an interim review, it must make an order to that effect and give reasons for it, and the Secretary of the Tribunal must forward a copy of the order and the reasons to the person or government that requested the review as well as publish the order in the *Canada Gazette*.

In conducting an interim review, the Tribunal may re-hear any matter before deciding it.

On completion of the interim review, the Tribunal must make an order rescinding the order or finding that it reviewed, or continuing it with

---

46 Above note 12.
47 RD-99-002 (2000), 4 TTR (2d) 725.
48 NQ-96-002 (2000), 2 TTR (2d) 30.

or without amendment, as the circumstances require, and give reasons for making the order. The Tribunal may exclude the product for which an exclusion was requested as well as any product with equivalent specifications. The Secretary of the Tribunal must, without delay, forward a copy of the order, with reasons to follow within fifteen days after the date of the order, to the CBSA and any other persons or governments that are specified by the Tribunal's rules. The Secretary must also publish the order in the *Canada Gazette*.

If neither an interim review under section 76.01 nor an expiry review under section 76.03 is conducted by the Tribunal, the order or finding it had made pursuant to sections 3 to 6 that the dumping or subsidizing has caused injury or retardation, or threatens to cause injury, is deemed by section 76.03(12) to expire five years after it was made. The interim order expires five years after it was made, but if, before its expiry, an expiry review is initiated by the Tribunal, the interim order expires on the day the expiry review is initiated.

i) Selected Interim Orders

INTERIM REVIEW 1: FRESH ICEBERG (HEAD) LETTUCE ORIGINATING IN OR EXPORTED FROM THE UNITED STATES OF AMERICA (INJURY INQUIRY)[49]

By interim review, the Tribunal rescinded its 1997 order, which continued, without amendment, its finding in *Fresh Iceberg (Head) Lettuce*, following a request from the BC Vegetable Marketing Commission to have the finding rescinded.

INTERIM REVIEW 2: FLAT HOT-ROLLED CARBON AND ALLOY STEEL SHEET PRODUCTS (INJURY INQUIRY)[50]

On the application of Sollac, Mediterranée SA, and Usinor Canada Inc, the Tribunal, conducting an interim review of its finding in an injury inquiry concerning *Certain Flat Hot-rolled Carbon and Alloy Steel Sheet Products Originating in or Exported from France, Romania, the Russian Federation and the Slovak Republic*, amended its finding and excluded certain products for which the exclusion was requested, as well as any products with equivalent specifications.

---

49 Injury Inquiry NQ-92-001 (1992); Interim Review RD-2001-002 (2002).
50 Injury Inquiry NQ-98-004 (1999); Interim Review RD-2002-003 (2003).

INTERIM REVIEW 3: CERTAIN REFRIGERATORS, DISHWASHERS, AND DRYERS FROM THE UNITED STATES (INJURY INQUIRY)[51]

On the request of Whirlpool Corporation and Whirlpool Canada Inc, the Tribunal in its interim review amended its findings in the injury inquiry concerning *Certain Refrigerators, Dishwashers and Dryers*, to exclude certain top-mount refrigerators in sizes greater than 14.5 cubic feet (0.41 cubic metres) and less than 18.5 cubic feet (0.52 cubic metres), retroactive to 1 January 2003.

INTERIM REVIEW 4: WATERPROOF RUBBER FOOTWEAR (EXPIRY REVIEW)[52]

On the request of Trackton Canada Inc, the Tribunal determined that an interim review of its expiry review concerning waterproof rubber footwear was warranted, and amended the order to exclude steel-studded over-the-shoe rubbers.

INTERIM REVIEW 5: LEATHER FOOTWEAR WITH METAL TOE CAPS (EXPIRY REVIEW)[53]

On the request of AM Footwear Inc, by interim review, the Tribunal amended its order made in an expiry review to exclude certain dumped footwear from the People's Republic of China on the basis that it was not likely to cause or threaten to cause injury to the domestic industry.

b) Further Reviews

Where the Tribunal has received a notice of action taken by the CBSA in respect of which another order or finding of the Tribunal applies, it may on its own initiative, or at the request of the Minister of Finance, the CBSA, or any other person or government who satisfies the Tribunal that a review is warranted, review the order or finding.

i) Review on Referral Back under Part I.1

If an order or finding of the Tribunal is referred back to the Tribunal under the dispute settlement provisions of Part I.1 (sections 77.01 to 77.038), the Tribunal must review the order or finding.

In making the review on referral back, the Tribunal may rehear any matter before deciding it, and on completion of the review it must either confirm the order or finding, or rescind it and make another order or finding as the nature of the matter may require, in respect of the goods. It must give

---

51   Injury Inquiry NQ-2000-001 (2000); Interim Review RD-2002-005 (2003).
52   Expiry Review RR-2001-005 (2002); Interim Review RD-2004-008 (2005).
53   Injury Inquiry NQ-2001-003 (2001), 6 TTR (2d) 245; Expiry Review RR-2005 001 (2005); Interim Review Order RD-2009-003 (2010).

reasons for the decision, and if it makes another order or finding it must declare to what goods and, where applicable, to what supplier and from what country of export, the order or finding applies.

After completing the review on referral back, the Secretary of the Tribunal must send a copy of the order or finding without delay, and not later than fifteen days after the completion of the review, a copy of the reasons for the decision, to the CBSA and to such other persons and governments as may be specified by the Tribunal's rules; the Secretary must also publish a notice of the decision in the *Canada Gazette*.

The order or finding expires at the end of five years unless it is continued or rescinded sooner, or an expiry review is initiated before the expiry.

c) Expiry Review

The purpose of an expiry review is to determine whether anti-dumping or countervailing duties remain necessary.

An order or finding that is not the subject of an interim review pursuant to section 76.02 or an expiry review pursuant to sections 76.03 and 76.03(1) is deemed to expire at the end of five years from its date. If it is not so deemed to expire, the Secretary of the Tribunal must publish in the *Canada Gazette* a notice of expiry setting out the information specified in the rules of the Tribunal, not later than ten months before that expiry date.

i) Initiation of Expiry Review

The Tribunal may initiate an expiry review of its order or finding, on its own initiative or at the request of the Minister of Finance, the CBSA, or any other person or of any government that satisfies the Tribunal that the expiry review is warranted.

The request must be made before the period specified in the notice of expiry ends.

The notice invites persons and governments to submit their views on whether the order or finding should be reviewed and gives direction on the issues that should be addressed in the submissions. If the Tribunal determines that an expiry review is not warranted, it issues an order with reasons for its decision. Otherwise, it initiates an expiry review.

There are two phases in an expiry review. The first phase is the investigation by the CBSA to determine whether there is a likelihood of resumed or continued dumping or subsidizing if the finding or order expires. If the CBSA determines that such likelihood exists with respect to any of the goods, the second phase is the Tribunal's inquiry into the likelihood of injury or retardation. If the CBSA determines that there is no likelihood of resumed dumping or subsidizing for any of the goods, the Tribunal does not consider those goods in its subsequent determination of the likelihood of injury and issues an order rescinding the order or finding with respect to those goods.

The Tribunal's procedures in expiry reviews are similar to those in final injury inquiries.

If the Tribunal refuses to initiate the expiry review at the request of a person or government, it must do so by an order to that effect and give reasons for the refusal. The Secretary of the Tribunal must send a copy of the order and the reasons to the person or government and publish it in the *Canada Gazette*.

If the Tribunal decides to hold the expiry review, the Secretary must notify the CBSA and all other persons specified in the Tribunal's rules, provide the CBSA with a copy of the administrative record on the basis of which the decision to initiate the review was made, and publish a notice of initiation of the review in the *Canada Gazette*.

ii) Determination by CBSA

On receipt of the Tribunal's notice that it will initiate an expiry review, the CBSA must, within 120 days from the date of that notice, determine whether the expiry of the order or finding in respect of goods of a country or countries is likely to result in the continuation or resumption of dumping or subsidizing of the goods, and after making the determination provide, without delay, a notice of the determination. If the determination is negative, the Tribunal must not take those goods into account in assessing the cumulative effect of dumping or subsidizing required to be made under section 76.03(11).

iii) Determination by Tribunal

If the CBSA determines that the expiry of the order or finding in respect of any goods is likely to result in a continuation or resumption of dumping or subsidizing, the CBSA must without delay provide the Tribunal with any information and material with respect to the matter that is required by the Tribunal's rules.

Upon receipt of the CBSA's determination of an affirmative finding described above, the Tribunal must determine whether the expiry of the order or finding in respect of any goods is likely, or is unlikely, to result in injury or retardation. Where goods are imported into Canada from more than one country, the Tribunal, when making the determination must, if in its opinion appropriate, assess the cumulative effect of the dumping or subsidizing of goods to which the order or finding applies that are imported into Canada from any other of those countries. The cumulative effect must take account of the conditions of competition between those goods or "like" goods of domestic production.

If the Tribunal's decision is negative, then it must make an order rescinding the order or finding in respect of those goods. It must also rescind its order or finding in respect of goods that the CBSA has determined and notified the Tribunal are unlikely to be dumped or subsidized after the expiry of the order or finding.

If the Tribunal decides in the affirmative, it must make an order continuing the order or finding, with or without amendment, in respect of the goods which it determines that the expiry of the order or finding is likely to result in injury or retardation.

iv) Separate Order or Finding

If the goods involved in the expiry review are with respect to those imported from more than one *NAFTA* country, or one or more *NAFTA* countries and one or more other countries, and the Tribunal makes another order or finding rescinding or continuing the order or finding with or without amendment, as described in the section immediately above, it must make a separate order with respect to the goods of each *NAFTA* country.

v) Review on Request of Minister of Finance

Where the Dispute Settlement Body established pursuant to Article 2 of Annex 2 to the *WTO Agreement* has issued a recommendation or ruling, and the Minister of Finance considers it necessary to revisit any decision, determination, or re-determination, or any portion of it, or an order or finding of the Tribunal, or any portion of such order or finding, and requests the CBSA or the Tribunal, as the case may be, to review the decision, determination, re-determination, order, or finding, the CBSA and the Tribunal must review their decisions or orders, and so on respectively.

On completion of the review, the CBSA or the Tribunal, as the case may be, must either

1) continue the decision, determination, re-determination, order, finding, and so on as they consider necessary to give effect to the Dispute Settlement Body's recommendation or ruling, and they must give reasons for their action, set out to what goods their decision applies, and, if practicable, name the supplier and the country of export; or

2) rescind the decision, determination, re-determination, order, or finding, and make any other decision, order, and so on that they consider necessary to give effect to the Dispute Settlement Body's recommendation or ruling, giving reasons for their action.

The CBSA, or the Tribunal, must notify the Minister of Finance of the action they have taken.

vi) Disputes Resolved by WTO

Among the disputes that Canada took to the WTO Appellate Body were (1) the softwood lumber dispute with the United States, and (2) the beef hormones dispute with the European Union. In turn, a dispute against Canada's dairy products policy was taken by the United States and New Zealand for adjudication. These three disputes are briefly summarized below.

DISPUTE 1: SOFTWOOD LUMBER[54]

The softwood lumber products dispute has been the longest and most significant trade irritant, at times acrimonious, between Canada and the United States, wherein the US lumber industry, obviously envious of the huge share that the Canadian lumber barons were capturing of the US housing market, fought unsuccessfully to get the US government to impose, at first a countervailing duty, and later an anti-dumping duty as well. The dispute first surfaced in 1982.

The heart of the dispute was the perception that the Canadian federal and provincial governments were subsidizing the lumber industry by non-market based "stumping fees" unlike the United States, whose practice was to auction off the forest lots and to charge the best market rates it could get.

Although initially, the US Department of Commerce (DOC) found no evidence of subsidizing or dumping, it eventually yielded to the pressures of the US lumber industry, and during the height of the dispute in early 2000, collected over five billion dollars in duties, which was held in escrow until the final determination and appeals were concluded. The British Columbia lumber industry, the largest exporter to the United States, was severely affected by these duties.

The US DOC had no success even at the Binational Panel hearing held under Chapter 19 of the *NAFTA*, and little success when the dispute was taken to the WTO's Appellate Body. Eventually, the US Government was forced to

---

54 Dispute WT/DS264/AB/RW (2006), 11 TTR (2d) 191 (WTO). Preliminary Report WT/DS236R at (2002), 7 TTR (2d) 301; Final Report at (2003), 8 TTR (2d) 654.

refund all the duties it collected and came to an agreement, known as the *Softwood Lumber Agreement* of 2006,[55] which bought peace for seven years, and, with the renewal of the Agreement for a further two years, until 2015 when the Agreement expires. The United States agreed to withdraw all appeals and never again to allow petitions from the US lumber industry to hold investigations into the dumping and subsidizing of the lumber products listed in the Agreement. The United States was able to extract some concessions from the Canadian government, though, by way of limiting the total exports each year to a specific quota at the current tariff rates, and if that quota was exceeded to additional tariff rates, and to collect export charges from the BC lumber exporters based upon export volumes. Disputes arising from the implementation of the Agreement, including the imposition of export charges and measures by Canada, were to be settled by arbitration by the London Court of International Arbitration. Until 2013, there have been two arbitrations by that court, which held that Canada's implementation failed to honour commitments made under the Agreement.

DISPUTE 2: EUROPEAN UNION BEEF HORMONES BAN (1996)[56]

Canada and the United States disputed the European Community's (EC) ban on the placing on the market and the importation of meat and meat products treated with certain hormones and appealed the legality of the ban to the WTO Dispute Settlement Body in 1996. The hormones were being used in Canadian and US cattle for fattening them. The WTO established a Panel to investigate the dispute in 1996.

The Panel held that the EC ban was not based on a risk assessment pursuant to Article 5.1 of the *Sanitary and Phytosanitary Agreement*, that the ban was inconsistent with the level of sanitary protection adopted with regard to different substances that posed the same health risks to humans; and that the EC allowed hormones to be used in specific cases, such as for pig feed and for treatment of cattle by veterinarians. This differentiated treatment was a restriction on trade and violated Article 5.5 on equivalence. The Panel further found that the studies and research submitted by the EC did not constitute the necessary risk assessment prescribed by Article 5.1.

The EC appealed certain issues of law and legal interpretation in the Panel's report and the Appellate Body issued its report on 16 January 1998.

---

55 *Softwood Lumber Products Export Charge Act, 2006*, SC 2006, c 13, ratifying the *Softwood Lumber Agreement* of 2006 with the United States.
56 (1998), 3 TTR (2d) 657 (Meat and Meat Products Hormones—Complaint by Canada—WTO Arbitration).

The EC's specific claims on appeal were based on its position that scientific evidence regarding the risks of growth hormones in meat production processes is uncertain, and that the controls necessary to ensure safe administration of the hormones are not consistently implemented in the United States.

The Appellate Body reviewed each of these legal issues, heard arguments by the parties, and made specific holdings with respect to each issue. It found that the Panel's interpretation of Article 5.8 of the Sanitary and Phytosanitary (SPS) Agreement, on the burden of proof, was not based on SPS provisions. The Appellate Body found that the burden of proof is on the complaining party, in this case the importer, and the burden of proof only shifts to the responding party, the "imposer of the ban," once the complainant has met its burden of proof.

In its second recourse to the WTO, the Appellate Body concluded that the Panel correctly found that the EC ban on the use of growth hormones in meat production was inconsistent with Article 5.1 requirements and failed to provide a risk assessment that supports such a measure. It recommended that the Dispute Settlement Body request the European Communities to bring the EC Directive into conformity with the obligations of the EC under the SPS Agreement. The EC asserted that the body of evidence that has developed since the dispute was first arbitrated by the WTO supported the conclusion that precautionary measures were required in order to achieve its chosen level of protection. Accepting Canada's counter-argument, the Appellate Body concluded that those measures were not a substitute for rigorous standards demanded by the SPS.[57] With that ruling against it, the EC signed a Memorandum of Understanding with Canada agreeing to provide compensation to Canada for the EC's ban on imports, and as a result, Canada repealed the retaliatory Surtax Order SOR/99-317 by SOR/2011-157, and the twelve year saga thus ended.

DISPUTE 3: DAIRY PRODUCTS[58]

The complaints against Canada were brought by the United States and New Zealand, pursuant to the recourse procedure provided by Article 2.15 of the Dispute Settlement Undertaking. They alleged that, by not bringing its dairy products marketing regime into conformity with its obligations, through

---

57 (2008), 12 TTR (2d) 384 (Canada-Continued Suspension of Obligations in the EC Hormones Dispute). WTO Dispute Settlement Panel Report (2008) WT/DS/231/R. EC was officially renamed European Union in 2009.
58 Disputes WT/DS103/R2 and WT/DS113/RW2 (2002), 6 TTR (2d) 310, 7 TTR (2d) 1, 7 TTR (2d) 559.

the commercial export milk scheme and the special milk class 5(d), Canada acted inconsistently with its obligations under Articles 3.3 and 8 of the *Agreement on Agriculture* by providing export subsidies for cheese and other dairy products. The WTO Appellate Body upheld the complaints, reversing the finding of the WTO Panel that there was not sufficient evidence to hold that Canada acted inconsistently with its obligations, and held that Canada acted inconsistently by providing export subsidies listed in Article 9.1(c) in excess of the quantity commitment levels specified in Canada's Schedule.

d) Goods of Chile

When, in respect of goods of Chile, the Tribunal has made an order or finding resulting in the levying of anti-dumping duties on them, and the goods are subsequently exempted by an order of the Governor in Council pursuant to section 14 of the *SIMA*, the Tribunal is required by section 77 to rescind its order or finding to the extent that it relates to the dumping of those goods.

6) *NAFTA* Dispute Settlement

Part I.1 of the *SIMA* was enacted in 1993 when Canada, the United States, and Mexico concluded the *North American Free Trade Agreement* respecting goods of a *NAFTA* country. While Part I.1 is in force, the *SIMA* suspends the operation of Part II, which was enacted in 1988 when Canada and the United States signed the *Free Trade Agreement* (*FTA*), respecting goods of the United States. For that reason, Part II provisions are not described in this chapter.

The Minister referred to in Part I.1 (as in Part II) is the Minister of International Trade. Pursuant to section 77.035(b), the Governor in Council on the recommendation of the Minister and the Minister of Finance may make regulations authorizing the performance of the duties and functions of the Minister under this Part to be performed by a designated officer, or an officer of a designated class of officers employed in or occupying a position of responsibility in the service of Her Majesty.

The provisions of Part I.1 override any provision of the *Federal Courts Act*[59] if it is inconsistent with Part I.1 to the extent of the inconsistency, by virtue of section 77.1(2).

Two distinct bodies are created under the *NAFTA* to resolve disputes among the free trade partners: the Binational Panel and the extraordinary challenge committee. In addition, any *NAFTA* partner can request the

---

59   Above note 12.

appointment of a Special Committee. The functions, the procedures, and the effect of decisions rendered by each of these three bodies are dealt with in the sections below.

a) Binational Panel Review

i) Establishment of Binational Panel

On a request by the Minister or the government of a *NAFTA* country for review of a definitive decision of the CBSA or of the Tribunal, a Binational Panel must be established pursuant to section 77.013, in accordance with paragraphs 1 to 4 of Annex 1901.2 to Chapter 19 of the *NAFTA* and any regulations made in connection therewith, and the panel must conduct a review of the definitive decision in accordance with Chapter 19.

A "definitive decision" means a final decision or final determination or re-determination of the CBSA, including an undertaking, and an order or finding of the Tribunal under the various provisions of the *SIMA*, that are made in respect of goods imported from a *NAFTA* country. It does not include a decision, order, or finding that is made for the purpose of giving effect to a decision of the Federal Court of Appeal.

Any person who would be entitled but for section 77.012 of Part I.1 referred to below, to apply under the *Federal Courts Act*,[60] or under section 96.1 of the *SIMA*, or to appeal under section 61 of the *SIMA* in respect of a definitive decision, may, in accordance with paragraph 4 of Article 1904 of *NAFTA*, file a request with the Canadian Secretary of the Secretariat established under the *NAFTA*, that the definitive decision be reviewed by a Binational Panel.

A request of the Minister or the government of a *NAFTA* country, or of a person referred to above, may be made only on a ground set forth in section 18.1(4) of the *Federal Courts Act*, and must be filed within thirty days after the definitive decision was published in the *Canada Gazette*, or if it is a request from the government of a country, within thirty days after the CBSA's notice of re-determination was received by the government of that country.

The Canadian Secretary, upon receiving the request for a Binational Panel review from the government of a *NAFTA* country or from a person referred to above, must notify the Minister and the appropriate *NAFTA* country Secretary of the request and the day on which that request was received.

On the appointment of a Binational Panel, the appropriate authority must forward to it a copy of the administrative record in accordance with

---

60 *Ibid.*

the rules made under Chapter 19 of the *NAFTA*. The "appropriate authority" is referred to in Part I.1 as the CBSA, which made the final decision or determination, and the Tribunal, which made the order or finding.

ii) Request Precludes Application to Federal Court

A request for review of the definitive decision by a binational panel under section 77.011(1) or (2) precludes an application for judicial review under the *Federal Courts Act*[61] or section 96.1 of the *SIMA*, or an appeal under section 61 of the *SIMA*.

iii) Limitation Periods

The following limitation periods apply with respect to an application under the *Federal Courts Act*, section 96.1 of the *SIMA*, and to an appeal under section 61 of the *SIMA*: (1) before the expiry of thirty days after the day on which the definitive decision is published in the *Canada Gazette*; or (2) in the case of a re-determination of the CBSA under section 59(1), (1.1); or (3) before the expiry of thirty days on which the notice of the re-determination was received by the government of the *NAFTA* country.

In order to permit an application to be filed with the Federal Court of Appeal after the expiration of the limitation period established in paragraph 4 of Article 1904 of the *NAFTA*, the limitation period referred to in section 18.1(2) of the *Federal Courts Act* and in section 96.1(3) of the *SIMA* is extended by ten days.

Within twenty days after the day on which the above thirty-day limitation period commences, the applicant or the appellant must give notice of intention to make an application or file an appeal, as the case may be.

iv) Binational Panel Decisions

After completing a review required under section 77.015(1), the Binational Panel must, if it determines that the grounds on which the review was requested have been established, make an order confirming the definitive decision or refer the matter back to the appropriate authority for reconsideration within the period specified by the panel.

The Binational Panel may, on its own initiative or in accordance with the rules made pursuant to Chapter 19 of the *NAFTA*, review the action taken by the appropriate authority pursuant to the order in accordance with section 77.016, and make a further order if necessary within ninety days after

---

61   *Ibid.*

the day on which the Canadian Secretary of the Secretariat receives notice of the action.

A decision of the Binational Panel must be given in writing and include the reasons for the decision. If there are dissenting or concurring opinions of members of the panel, they must also be recorded. On receipt of the panel's order, or further order if any, the Canadian Secretary must forward it to the Minister, the government of the *NAFTA* country involved, the appropriate authority, and any other person who was heard in the review, and publish the order in the *Canada Gazette*.

v) Action on Binational Panel's Order

Within the time specified in the Binational Panel's order made under section 77.015(3) or (4), referring the matter back to the appropriate authority for reconsideration, the appropriate authority must take action under the *SIMA* not inconsistent with the decision of the Binational Panel. It must also comply with any action required by the panel to be taken as a result of its order being referred back to the panel, pursuant to section 77.018, by the extraordinary challenge committee appointed pursuant to section 77.019(5). If the appropriate authority has already taken action under section 77.015(3), it is not required to take any further action unless it is required by the panel's order under section 77.015(4) to take a different action from what it took pursuant to the order it received under section 77.015(3).

vi) Illustrative Binational Panel Decisions

Two decisions of the Binational Panel are noted below to illustrate the use of this procedure by United States exporters whose dumping of goods was held by the Tribunal to have caused injury to Canadian producers.

REVIEW 1: IODINATED CONTRAST MEDIA FROM THE UNITED STATES[62]

In this review, the Binational Panel dealt with the challenge to the CCRA's determination on remand by Nycomed and others, pursuant to Rule 73 of the *NAFTA*, alleging that the CCRA's decision violated the principle of "price comparability" embodied in the *SIMA* and the WTO *Anti-dumping Agreement*, by failing to make deductions for certain freight expenses and profit. This determination on remand was filed by the CCRA in response to the Panel's decision and order of 26 May 2003.

---

62 (2000), 4 TTR (2d) 530 (CITT), reviewed (2003), 7 TTR (2d) 783 (*NAFTA* Binational Panel), remand to CITT (2003), 8 TTR (2d) 30 (*NAFTA* Binational Panel). See also above notes 35 and 36.

The Panel in its prior opinion had affirmed the CCRA's resort to a determination of normal value under section 29 of the *SIMA*. Nevertheless, Nycomed asserted that the CCRA's failure to make deductions for purported freight expenses and internal profit resulted in a section 29 calculation that was unfair because the normal value was calculated from a different shipment point than the export price even though the merchandise sold into the continental United States and Canada originated from the same manufacturing facility.

In making its section 29 determination, the CCRA had based its normal value calculations on an arm's-length transaction in the United States. Based on an analysis of confidential data, the CCRA "deemed" Nycomed to be the exporter and determined normal value using an ex–Memphis warehouse price from Nycomed. Once it had made that selection, the CCRA rejected the adjustment of the normal value to reflect transportation costs from the manufacturing facility in Puerto Rico because the transfer to Nycomed from the manufacturing facility was not the transaction used as the basis for the normal value calculations. It also asserted that the same analysis applied to any profit component that might theoretically be appurtenant to the transfer to Nycomed.

In affirming the CCRA's determination on remand, the Panel said it was obliged to accord considerable deference to the exercise of the discretion created by section 29. Given that, whether judged by the standard of unreasonableness or patent unreasonableness, there was no basis for interfering with the CCRA's decision to deem Nycomed to be the exporter and to fix the normal value by reference to Nycomed's ex–Memphis warehouse price charged to domestic consumers. The Panel pointed out that Nycomed did not meet the heavy burden of establishing that the only reasonable or rational way of protecting the principle of price comparability in this instance required an adjustment for freight and profit.

REVIEW 2: REFRIGERATORS AND DISHWASHERS FROM THE UNITED STATES[63]

The request for a panel review of the CITT's finding in an injury inquiry was filed with the *NAFTA* Secretariat—Canadian Section, by Whirlpool Corporation and Inglis Limited in accordance with Part II of the *NAFTA Rules of*

---

63   CITT Injury Inquiry NQ-2000-001 (2000), 6 TTR (2d) 425; Ruling of the *NAFTA* Binational Panel (USA-CDA-2000-1904-03), reported at (2002), 6 TTR (2d) 502.

Procedure for Article 1904. The products in issue were top-mount electric refrigerators, in sizes greater than 14.5 cubic feet (410.59 litres) and less than 22 cubic feet (622.97 litres); electric household dishwashers, built-in or portable, greater than 18 inches (45.72 centimetres) in width; and gas or electric laundry dryers originating in or exported from the United States and produced by, or on behalf of, WCI and Whirlpool and their respective affiliates, successors, and assigns. Whirlpool, WCI, and Camco Inc were the complainants, and Maytag Corporation and the Tribunal were the respondents.

The CCRA had made a final determination that the subject goods had in fact been dumped under section 41(1)(a) of the *SIMA*. As a result of this preliminary determination, the Tribunal had commenced the inquiry. The Tribunal stated in its final determination that

1. the dumping in Canada of the aforementioned refrigerators has caused material injury to the domestic industry, excluding those:
   - with a capacity of 18.5 cubic feet and above; or
   - destined for use in the Habitat for Humanity Program;
2. the dumping in Canada of the aforementioned dishwashers has caused material injury to the domestic industry (Member Close dissenting), excluding those:
   - with stainless steel interiors (tubs); or
   - destined for use in the Habitat for Humanity Program; and
3. the dumping in Canada of the aforementioned dryers has caused material injury to the domestic industry (Member Close dissenting), excluding those:
   - with controls at the front, removable tops and chassis designed to be stacked on top of washers; or
   - destined for use in the Habitat for Humanity Program.

The Tribunal also finds that the requirements of paragraph 42(1)(b) of the *Special Import Measures Act* with respect to massive dumping and of section 46 of the *Special Import Measures Act* with respect to an advice to the Commissioner regarding other allegedly dumped goods from the United States have not been met.[64]

The complainants asked the Binational Panel to determine whether the Tribunal committed reviewable errors in five primary matters:

---

64 Inquiry NQ-2000-001, *ibid* in headnote.

1) in finding that injury had been caused to the domestic industry via dumping;
2) in not considering Camco's export performance in evaluating Camco's alleged injury;
3) in concluding that the *SIMA* section 42(3) makes allowance for a cumulative finding of injury with respect to specific producers;
4) in granting exclusions to certain of the subject refrigerators, dryers, and dishwashers and not others; and
5) in failing to advise the Commissioner of the CCRA to consider undertaking a dumping investigation under the *SIMA* section 46 with respect to the goods of certain non-targeted US exporters of the subject goods.

Underlying the above was the issue of the appropriate standards of review that should be applied by the Panel in determining whether the Tribunal had committed a reviewable error with respect to each of the contested matters.

For the reasons set out below, the Panel decided unanimously not to remand the decision of the CITT.

The statutory authority for panel review is found in the relevant provisions of the *NAFTA* and the *Federal Courts Act*.[65] Article 1904(3) directs Binational Panels to apply the standard of review set out in Annex 1911 and the general legal principles that a court of the importing party otherwise would apply to a review of a determination of the competent investigating authority. In the present case, the Panel is required to apply the general jurisprudence that would be applicable to the Federal Court in its review of a decision made by the Tribunal.

NAFTA Annex 1911 defines the standard of review as the grounds set forth in section 18.1(4) of the *Federal Courts Act*. Section 18.1(4) provides that the Tribunal's decisions will be reviewed on the grounds that it,

1) acted without jurisdiction, acted beyond its jurisdiction, or refused to exercise its jurisdiction;
2) failed to observe a principle of natural justice, procedural fairness, or other procedure that it was required in law to observe;
3) erred in law in making a decision or order, whether or not the error appears on the face of the record;
4) based its decision or order on an erroneous finding of fact that it made in a perverse or capricious manner or without regard for the material before it;
5) acted, or failed to act, by reason of fraud or perjured evidence; or

---

65 Above note 12.

6) acted in any other way that was contrary to law.

The Binational Panel emphasized that these grounds for review need to be read in light of the standard of review developed by the Supreme Court of Canada, especially in its most recent unanimous decision in *Canada (Deputy Minister of National Revenue) v Mattel Canada Inc.*[66] In that decision, the Supreme Court identified the standards of review as points occurring on a spectrum of curial deference that ranges from patent unreasonableness at one end of the continuum (that of greatest deference), through reasonableness simpliciter, to correctness at the other end of the spectrum, where the least deference is accorded the decision of the administrative tribunal.

The Panel undertook an analysis on an issue-by-issue basis and identified the standard of review for each issue raised by the complainants.

1) With respect to injury and causation, the Panel pointed out these issues concern the existence and cause of injury and they were precisely the questions that the Tribunal had been empowered to decide, and were within its specialized competence and expertise. Those issues were also factually driven, and the issues that the complainants raised under this heading were all issues of mixed fact and law. The Panel found that the applicable standard of review for these issues is one of considerable deference; that is, at least reasonableness simpliciter or higher. It acknowledged that the Tribunal was in a much better position than the Panel to determine the most appropriate method of allocating costs between domestic sales and exports. All that Whirlpool and WCI were able to do was to propose another, albeit plausible, method of allocating costs. Neither Whirlpool nor WCI were able to point to sufficient evidence or legal argument to sustain their argument that the Tribunal's reworking of the data was unreasonable.

2) With respect to the issue of giving reasons, while Whirlpool and WCI failed to show any statutory authority for a duty of the Tribunal to give reasons, the Panel suggested that there was such a statutory obligation, which can be deduced from sections 42 and 43, as well as in Article 1907.3 of *NAFTA*. Although applicable in terms only to Mexican cases, it would seem clear that this requirement was not intended to apply alone to Mexico, but rather that it was deemed already to be a part of Canadian and US law.

Without precisely deciding on the extent of this duty in the context of the Tribunal and the *SIMA*, the Panel found that the reasons the Tribunal had given were sufficient.

---

66 2001 SCC 36.

3) With respect to non-dumping factors, Whirlpool and WCI both argued that the Tribunal failed to consider the effect of those factors in its analysis of injury and causation, and that, in fact, much of the injury suffered by Camco was due to non-dumped goods. The Panel found that the Tribunal had in fact discharged its duty under section 37.1(3) of the *SIM Regulations* to consider the possible injurious effect of non-dumping factors. It said that the Tribunal is owed a high level of deference on the issue and held that the Tribunal's finding, which enumerated the non-dumping factors enumerated by Whirlpool and WCI, was reasonable.

4) The Panel agreed with the complainants that the duty to make a separate analysis and finding for each of the subject goods was implicit in section 42(1) of the *SIMA* and in the section 37.1 of the *SIM Regulations*. However, the Panel found that the Tribunal did, in fact, exercise its jurisdiction to make separate analyses and did make separate findings for each of the subject goods, and that its conclusions were reasonable; therefore, it would not disturb the Tribunal's findings.

5) Camco had asserted that the Tribunal erred by failing to accord proper weight to Camco's export performance in its material injury analysis. The Tribunal majority found that "all the evidence points to the conclusion that Camco was profitable and reasonably healthy with respect to its export sales of dishwashers and dryers," and that "Camco's export business has aided its overall operation by helping to pay for plant and product improvements."

   In this matter, the Panel found that the Tribunal majority did, in fact, consider export performance in making its material injury determination in this case and the impact of imports on the total domestic production of like goods, including production for export. How the Tribunal considers the export performance factor and weighs it against other statutory and regulatory injury factors was a question of fact, and would require the Panel to accord to the Tribunal a considerable degree of deference.

6) According to the complainants, the Tribunal failed to consider the entire industry, including the industry's production for export and export performance. In addition, the Tribunal failed to find that injury was predicated on the impact of imports in specific sectors of the domestic market. Furthermore, they alleged that the Tribunal failed to determine that the injury was causally related to dumped imports.

   The Panel pointed out that in the Tribunal's discussion of "State of the Market and Industry," the Tribunal had explained the factors that it considered in determining whether Camco suffered any injury by reason of subject imports. In the Panel's view, there was nothing in the Tribunal's opinion to suggest that the Tribunal majority limited its injury analysis to Camco's production of like goods for sale to domestic customers.

The Panel found that the Tribunal majority properly examined Camco's export performance and that its conclusions associated therewith were sufficiently grounded in law and fact such that the Panel, applying a deferential standard of review, upheld the Tribunal's decision.

7) Whirlpool claimed that the Tribunal committed a reviewable error in making a "cumulative" determination of material injury in respect of appliances exported to Canada by Whirlpool and WCI. According to Whirlpool, "cumulation," as prescribed under section 42(3) of the *SIMA* and Article 3.3 of the WTO *Anti-Dumping Agreement*, was only permitted where the Tribunal is conducting simultaneous investigations of goods from two or more countries. It asserted that the Tribunal was required to make separate findings respecting material injury with respect to each foreign producer subject to the investigation, but was unable to point to any authority for its position.

The Panel found no basis in law for Whirlpool's contention. The concept of "cumulation" as used in section 42(3) of the *SIMA* and Article 3.3 of the WTO *Anti-Dumping Agreement* was only relevant in cases where the Tribunal was conducting simultaneous investigations of dumped goods from more than one country.

8) The complainants Whirlpool and Inglis had requested two additional exclusions, one of which (large refrigerators) essentially overlapped one of Whirlpool's requests. The Tribunal granted exclusion to three products, namely large refrigerators, stainless steel tub dishwashers, and stackable dryers. Complainant Camco, on the other hand, opposed these exclusions, asserting that the Tribunal erred in granting them.

In addition, Whirlpool contended that the Tribunal committed an error in failing to furnish reasons for the denial of its claims for exclusion for KitchenAid brand products, dryers sold to the builder trade, private label dryers, and certain specialty dryers.

The Panel pointed out that the standard of review with respect to these exclusions was the "pragmatic and functional" test examined by it earlier. It was evident that the determinations regarding these exclusions were largely findings of fact, and under the pragmatic and functional test, the standard naturally devolves along the continuum to patent unreasonableness where the issue is a matter of evidence.

In no manner was the discretion of the Tribunal fettered in making proper factual findings to carry out this responsibility. In a matter so fact-specific as this, it must be clear that the Tribunal has wide discretion to analyze the facts developed in order to determine to which goods the injury finding applies. Indeed, the Panel said, the Tribunal was far better able than the courts or a reviewing Binational Panel as in this case to make these determinations, due to its intimacy with the factual record and experience in making decisions in this area. Under the patent unreasonableness standard to be applied here, the Panel refused to substitute its evaluation of the evidence for the Tribunal's.

b) Extraordinary Challenge Proceedings

Sections 77.017 to 77.019 provide for extraordinary challenge proceedings with respect to a Panel's order made pursuant to section 77.015.

i) Notification of Request

A written request that an extraordinary challenge proceeding be commenced with respect to a Binational Panel's order may be made under section 77.017(1) by the Minister or the government of the *NAFTA* country to which the Panel's order relates. The request must be made to the Canadian Secretary and if it is made within the period after the making of the order that is prescribed by Chapter 19 of the *NAFTA* rules, and if it is based on a ground set forth in paragraph 13 of Article 1904 of the *NAFTA*, the Canadian Secretary must notify the appropriate *NAFTA* country Secretary of the request and the day on which it was received. If the request was received from the government of a *NAFTA* country, the Canadian Secretary must similarly notify the Minister of the request and the day on which it was received.

ii) Appointment of Extraordinary Challenge Committee

On receipt of a request pursuant to section 77.017(1), an extraordinary challenge committee must be appointed for conducting an extraordinary challenge proceeding, in accordance with paragraph 1 to Annex 1904.13 to Chapter 19 of the *NAFTA* and any regulations made in connection therewith.

iii) Action by and Decision of the Committee

The extraordinary challenge committee is required by section 77.019 to conduct the extraordinary challenge proceedings and decide in accordance with Annex 1904.13 to Chapter 19 of the *NAFTA* and the rules made under that chapter. If the grounds for the request are not established, the committee must deny the request, in which case the decision of the panel in respect of which the request was made stands affirmed.

If the order of the Binational Panel is referred back by the extraordinary challenge committee to the Panel, the Panel must take action not inconsistent with the decision of the committee. If the order is set aside by the committee, a new Binational Panel must be appointed, and the new panel must conduct a review of the definitive decision that was the subject of the order.

The extraordinary challenge committee must record its decision in writing and include the reasons for the decision and any dissenting or concurring opinions of members of the committee. The Canadian Secretary must then forward a copy of the decision and of the order to the Minister, the government of the *NAFTA* country involved, the appropriate authority, and any other person who was heard in the proceeding, and publish a notice of the decision in the *Canada Gazette*.

c) Orders and Decisions of Panel and Committee

An order or decision of the Binational Panel and of the extraordinary challenge committee is final and binding and is not subject to appeal or reference to the Federal Court of Appeal under section 18.3(1) of the *Federal Courts Act*.[67] It cannot be questioned, reviewed, set aside, removed, prohibited, or restrained, nor made subject of any proceedings in, or any process or order of, any court, whether by nature of injunction, certiorari, prohibition, *quo warranto*, declaration, or otherwise, on any ground, including the ground that the panel or committee acted beyond its jurisdiction or lost jurisdiction.

d) Stay of Proceedings

The Minister must stay all panel reviews initiated under section 77.011 and committee proceedings commenced under section 77.017 if the government of a *NAFTA* country makes a request to the Canadian Secretary for a review by a special committee provided for in Annex 1904.13 to the *NAFTA* and any regulations made in connection therewith.

e) Appointment of Special Committee

i) Request for Appointment

Upon a written request received by the Canadian Secretary from the government of a *NAFTA* country that a special committee be appointed to review an allegation referred to in Article 1905.1 of the *NAFTA*, section 77.023(2) requires the appointment of a special committee in accordance with Article 19.13 of the *NAFTA* and any regulations made in connection therewith.

---

67 Above note 12.

ii) Stay of Panel Reviews and Extraordinary Challenge Committee Proceedings

Where a special committee makes an affirmative finding on an allegation made against a *NAFTA* country, the Minister is required to stay all Binational Panel reviews and extraordinary challenge committee proceedings that were requested by the government of that *NAFTA* country after the date on which consultations were requested on the allegation referred to in Article 1905.1 of *NAFTA*, except the panel review or extraordinary challenge committee proceeding that was requested more than 150 days prior to the affirmative finding by the special committee.

The stay of Binational Panel reviews and extraordinary challenge committee proceedings becomes effective on the day following the date on which the request for stay was made.

iii) Stay When Affirmative Finding against Canada

Similarly, where the special committee has made an affirmative finding against Canada pursuant to a request made by the government of the United States or Mexico, on a request for stay of panel reviews and extraordinary challenge committee proceedings received from the government of that *NAFTA* country, the Minister must stay all such reviews and proceedings.

The stay of panel reviews and extraordinary challenge committee proceedings becomes effective on the day following the date on which the request for stay was made.

iv) Suspension of Time Periods

Where a special committee makes an affirmative finding against the government of a *NAFTA* country, or Canada, the time periods provided for panel reviews or extraordinary challenge committee proceedings, stipulated in sections 77.011(4) and 77.017(2), respectively, as well as those provided under the *Federal Courts Act* and in section 61 of the *SIMA*, cease to run unless and until those reviews or proceedings are resumed pursuant to section 77.033.

v) Suspension of Article 1904 of NAFTA Panel Process

Following receipt of an affirmative finding of the special committee, section 77.028 authorizes the Minister to suspend the operation of Article 1904 of the *NAFTA* with respect to goods of a *NAFTA* country at any time if the finding is against Canada. If the affirmative finding is against another *NAFTA* country, the suspension is to be made after the expiration of sixty days but not later than ninety days after the affirmative finding against the other

NAFTA country. In the latter case, a notice of suspension must be sent to the Canadian Secretary and published in the *Canada Gazette*.

If, however, the operation of Article 1904 is suspended under section 77.028 in respect of a NAFTA country, benefits under Article 1905.2 of the NAFTA, referred to in the next paragraph, may not be suspended in respect of that NAFTA country, and *vice versa*.

vi) Suspension of NAFTA Benefits

On the recommendation of the Minister of Finance and the Minister of Public Safety and Emergency Preparedness, the Governor in Council may, by an order issued under the authority of section 77.029(1), at any time after the expiration of sixty days, but in no case later than ninety days, following an affirmative finding against a NAFTA country, suspend the application to that country of such benefits under the NAFTA as the Governor in Council considers appropriate.

The order will be in effect for the period specified in the order, unless revoked sooner. The order is not considered to be a statutory instrument for the purposes of the *Statutory Instruments Act*.[68]

If, however, benefits under Article 1905.2 of NAFTA are suspended under section 77.029(1) in respect of a NAFTA country, the operation of Article 1904 of NAFTA, referred to in the previous paragraph, may not be suspended under section 77.028 in respect of that NAFTA country, and *vice versa*.

The Governor in Council has also been authorized by section 77.029(2) to

1) suspend rights or privileges granted by Canada to that NAFTA country against which an affirmative finding was made by the special committee, or to goods, service providers, suppliers, investors, or investments of that country under the NAFTA or an Act of Parliament;
2) modify or suspend the application of any federal law to that country or to goods, service providers, and so on of that country;
3) extend the application of any federal law to that country or to goods, service providers, and so on of that country; and
4) take such other action as the Governor in Council considers necessary.

vii) Determination of Special Committee under Paragraph 1905.10(a) of the NAFTA

If after making an affirmative order against a NAFTA country (or Canada), the special committee makes a determination pursuant to paragraph 1905.10(a)

---

68 RSC 1985, c S-22.

of the *NAFTA*, the Governor in Council must take action consistent with that determination.

viii) Review of Definitive Decision by Federal Court of Appeal

Where (1) the Minister suspends the operation of Article 1904 of *NAFTA* and in consequence stays either the panel review or extraordinary challenge committee proceeding under section 77.024(1), or (2) the government of a *NAFTA* country suspends the operation of Article 1904 of the *NAFTA* with respect to goods of Canada under Article 1905.8 and in consequence a panel review or extraordinary challenge committee proceeding is stayed under section 77.025, the Minister, the government of the *NAFTA* country, or any party to the stayed panel review or the stayed extraordinary challenge committee proceeding in the case of (1) above, or the government of the *NAFTA* country or persons in the case of (2), may apply to the Federal Court of Appeal for review of the definitive decision that was the subject of the original panel review, on any grounds specified in section 18.1(4) of the *Federal Courts Act*. The application for review must be made within thirty days after the date of the suspension of the operation of Article 1904 of *NAFTA*.

Judicial review provisions are described in Section F(2), below in this chapter.

ix) Termination of Suspension

The Minister must terminate any suspension of the operation of Article 1904 effected under section 77.028(1), as referred to in Section E(6)(e)(v), above in this chapter, if a special committee, reconvened pursuant to Article 1905.10 of the *NAFTA*, determines that the problems in respect of which the special committee's affirmative finding was based have been corrected. Upon termination of suspension, section 77.033 requires the resumption, within ninety days after the date on which the affirmative finding was made of all panel reviews and extraordinary challenge committee proceedings that were stayed under sections 77.024(1) or 77.025, and the running of all time periods that were suspended under section 77.027, and the benefits suspended under section 77.029, are resumed.

F. GENERAL PROVISIONS

Part III of the *SIMA* contains several sections that deal with a variety of subjects, such as the issue of who the importer is with respect to specific goods, and judicial review. Other matters dealt with in this Part are (1) evidence to be proffered to the CBSA; (2) designation of evidence as confidential; (3) disclosure of information and the designation of information as confidential; (4) gathering of information by the CBSA with respect to goods located abroad prior to their importation if those goods are to imported or may be subsequently imported into Canada, and if they are or may be goods of the same description as the goods to which an order or finding of the Tribunal as to anti-dumping or countervailing duty applies, in order to estimate the margin of dumping or subsidy on such goods; (5) offences; and (6) the authority granted to the Governor in Council to make regulations and orders for the purpose of administering and enforcing the *SIMA*.

Only three of these matters are discussed below.

1) Who Is "Importer in Canada"?

Provisions on the determination as to which of two or more persons is the importer of goods in Canada of goods imported or to be imported, for the purposes of the *SIMA*, are set out in sections 89 to 95. The CBSA may, and at the request of a person interested in the importation, must, ask the Tribunal for a ruling on that question.

If the goods concerned have already been imported and a ruling has been made by a designated officer, and if more than ninety days have elapsed since that determination, the CBSA may not ask for a ruling.

The CBSA is required to provide the Tribunal with such information as it considers will be useful to the Tribunal to make the ruling, and with such other information as the Tribunal may request. The request must state who in the CBSA's opinion is the importer and, if any of the goods concerned are of the same description as those specified in a preliminary determination made in an investigation initiated by the CBSA, which investigation is still continuing, that fact must be stated in the request. Any investigation leading to a final determination is deemed to continue until the Tribunal makes a ruling.

The CBSA must give notice of the request to such persons as the rules of the Tribunal require or as the Tribunal may direct.

a) Tribunal's Ruling

Forthwith after receiving the CBSA's request pursuant to section 89, the Tribunal must give its ruling. However, if a preliminary determination was made by the CBSA and the Secretary of the Tribunal was given notice of that determination, the Tribunal must not give its ruling until after it makes an order or finding in the inquiry commenced by it as a result of the preliminary determination. If the CBSA has terminated the preliminary investigation and has notified the Secretary of the termination, the Tribunal must give its ruling forthwith after receiving the notice of termination.

b) Illustrative Rulings

RULING 1: FRESH GARLIC FROM CHINA[69]

In this leading case, the Deputy Minister of National Revenue, Customs and Excise requested, on behalf of D & L Business Canada Ltd (D & L), a ruling on the question of which of two persons was the importer in Canada of fresh garlic originating in or exported from the People's Republic of China. The fresh garlic was consigned by Shengli in China to D & L. The evidence showed that D & L simply acted as agent for Shengli in Canada.

D & L and the Deputy Minister submitted opposing arguments. D & L submitted that, if the "real" importer is the one that caused the goods to be imported, then, in the present case, the real importer can only be Shengli. It acknowledged that, for purposes of the *Customs Act*, it was the importer of record; however, when reviewing the facts in the present case, it was obvious that the "real" importer of the garlic was Shengli. D & L submitted that, given the circumstances of this case, to determine that it was the importer and to require it to pay $335,571.67 where it only realized a commission of US$2,000 would be a travesty of justice.

The Deputy Minister argued that D & L was the only one that should be considered to be the importer in Canada of the goods for the purposes of the *SIMA*. The argument was based on section 2(1) of the *SIMA*, in which the term "importer" was defined "in relation to any goods" as "the person who is in reality the importer of the goods" and on the following statement of Jackett J in *Canada v Singer Manufacturing Co*: "The essential feature ... is that the exporter must be the person in the foreign country who sends the goods into Canada and the importer must be the person to whom they are sent in Canada."[70]

The majority of the Tribunal acknowledged that the evidence showed that D & L simply acted as an agent for Shengli in Canada and that there was no "real" transaction between these two companies. Other than the US$2,000 commission, D & L did not profit from the resale of the subject garlic to distributors, wholesalers, and restaurants. The evidence also showed that the

---

69 *Fresh Garlic Originating in or Exported from the People's Republic of China*, MP-97-001 (1998).
70 [1968] 1 Ex CR 129 at 136.

importation was arranged by Shengli, and in particular by its employee, Ms Lee. All that D & L had to do was to provide its best assistance and help during the sales process pursuant to the terms of the Agreement.

The Tribunal referred to the ruling in *Graphite Electrodes*[71] given by its predecessor, the Canadian Import Tribunal, which was faced with a similar situation, and had ruled that the third party who placed the actual purchase order for the imported goods in question with the exporter prior to importation, was in reality the importer, not the so-called "importer of record," who was simply a "paper intermediary," that is, an agent for the exporter. The evidence in the case before the Tribunal was different. Although it showed that the subject garlic was eventually sold to retailers, wholesalers, and restaurants in Canada, there was no evidence of any dealings between any of these entities and Shengli prior to importation. There were only two parties before it, namely, D & L (the acknowledged importer of record) and Shengli, one of which must be identified as the "real" importer of the subject garlic.

After hearing and reviewing all of the evidence, including all of the documents that were filed by both parties to this inquiry, and the jurisprudence, the majority of the Tribunal was of the view that, between D & L and Shengli, it had no choice but to find that D & L was the importer in Canada of the subject garlic. In the view of the majority, to rule otherwise and to find that Shengli was the importer in Canada of the subject garlic would be contrary to the object of the *SIMA*. Although certain arrangements may be made between Revenue Canada and non-resident importers with respect to the payment of anti-dumping duties, as occurred in *Machine Tufted Carpeting Originating in or Exported from the United States of America*,[72] unfortunately for D & L, no such arrangement was made in the present case.

The reasons given by the majority are worth noting. The majority said that "in making a ruling under section 90 of the *SIMA* as to which of two persons is the importer in Canada of imported goods, the Tribunal must take into account the object and purpose of the statute,"[73] and quoted the Canadian Import Tribunal's ruling in *Graphite Electrodes*:

> The liability for payment of anti-dumping duties is placed on the importer of dumped goods. That is part of the general scheme to deal with the mischief of dumping, to discourage it. The object of the statute is to pro-

---

71 *Certain Artificial Graphite Electrodes and Connecting Pins Originating in or Exported from the United States of America*, Request No IR-2-86 (1987) (Can Import Trib) [*Graphite Electrodes*].
72 Inquiry NQ-91-006 (1993).
73 Above note 69 at 6.

tect Canadian producers of goods from injurious importations of dumped goods, and that is achieved by imposing the burden of the special duty on the importer. If the exporter, through its agent, pays the duty, the object of the statute is not being achieved.[74]

RULING 2: BICYCLES FROM CHINA[75]

In another important case, the Tribunal was asked by the CCRA for a ruling on the question of which of the two companies proposed by it, Toys "R" Us (TRU) or Kent International Inc, satisfied the meaning of the expression "importer in Canada" of certain bicycles that were the subject of the Tribunal's order issued on 9 December 2002 in an expiry review hearing. The CCRA also asked the Tribunal for a proper interpretation of the phrase "importer in Canada."

Before making a determination as to the identity of the "importer in Canada," the Tribunal decided to determine the proper interpretation of that phrase. The English version of sections 89 and 90 of the *SIMA* used the phrase "importer in Canada," while the French version used only the term "*importateur.*" In addition, the section 2(1) definition of "importer" and "*importateur*" did not contain the additional words "in Canada."

The inconsistency in wording between the English and French versions of sections 89 and 90 had not been raised in previous appeals.

The CCRA indicated that of the two parties, Kent and TRU, it believed that TRU was the importer in Canada of the goods.

TRU and Kent argued that the phrase "importer in Canada" did not impose any residency requirement and that it merely stated that whoever is in reality the importer of the goods is the importer in Canada. Regarding the inconsistency between the French and English texts, TRU and Kent referred to the shared meaning rule, which provided that, where one version is ambiguous, the shared meaning was taken to be the meaning of the unambiguous provision, which, in this case, was the French version. They stated that if one were to accept the CCRA's argument that the phrase "importer in Canada" imposes a residency requirement, this would create incongruous situations where the person who was in reality the importer in accordance with the definition of importer found in section 2 would not be the importer in Canada.

The Tribunal rejected the shared meaning rule as being inappropriate. It regarded the modern principle of the interpretation of statutes, as described by Elmer Driedger in *Construction of Statutes*, and adopted in Canadian law,

---

74 *Graphite Electrodes*, above note 71 at 5.
75 *Bicycles from China*, Expiry Review RR-2002-001 (2002); Importer Ruling MP-2003-001 (2004).

as correctly stating the law, that "there is only one principle or approach, namely, the words of an Act are to be read in their entire context and in their grammatical and ordinary sense harmoniously with the scheme of the Act, the object of the Act, and the intention of Parliament."[76]

In the scheme of the *SIMA*, the purpose of the Tribunal's ruling under section 89 is to identify the party that is liable for the payment of anti-dumping duties and the subject of the associated rights and obligations under the *SIMA*. In this regard, the two fundamental sections of the *SIMA* that impose the liability for provisional duty and duty other than provisional duty are sections 8 and 11 respectively. Each of these sections uses the phrase "importer in Canada" ("*importateur au Canada*") in both English and French versions.

Parliament had added the phrase "in Canada" ("*au Canada*") to both versions by a recent amendment.

Accordingly, the Tribunal concluded that Parliament intended the language in sections 89 and 90 of the *SIMA* to be consistent with the language in sections 8 and 11, so that the Tribunal's ruling should clearly identify the party liable under the latter sections. Therefore, the Tribunal considered that its ruling should identify the "importer in Canada" rather than merely the "importer."

With respect to the question, who was the importer in Canada, on the basis of the evidence, the Tribunal was of the opinion that the evidence clearly demonstrated that Kent was the party that was in reality the importer of the goods. For good business reasons, TRU had decided that it did not want to take the risks inherent in being the importer. Most of the details of those business reasons formed part of the Tribunal's confidential record. TRU and Kent had been doing business that way for a number of years, and the evidence showed that TRU acted in the same manner in respect of other goods that it purchased from other suppliers. The evidence did not indicate that, for any reason, the arrangement between TRU and Kent was structured in a way that was intended to mask the true identity of the importer. Indeed, TRU testified that the way in which it did business with Kent was the way in which it normally operated.

The bicycles that TRU purchased from Kent were purchased in Canadian dollars. TRU only became the owner when the bicycles were delivered to its warehouses in Canada. The evidence also indicated that TRU generally had no control over the country of origin or the manufacturing process of

---

76   Importer Ruling, *ibid* at 6.

the bicycles that it purchased from Kent. Kent also retained its own customs broker that handled the transactions.

The third element that the Tribunal was required to address was whether Kent was the importer "in Canada." The phrase "in Canada" clearly indicates that there is a requirement for a presence in Canada. However, the *SIMA* does not indicate what type of presence is required. For example, there is no provision in the *SIMA* that imposes a residency requirement or another specific type of presence, such as a permanent establishment in Canada.

In the Tribunal's view, had Parliament intended to impose a residency requirement, it would have expressly provided for it, as it did, for example, in the definition of "purchaser in Canada" under the *Customs Act*.

The Tribunal also noted that neither the *Customs Act* nor the *Excise Tax Act* required an importer to be resident in Canada or to have a permanent establishment in Canada. Non-resident importers and importers without permanent establishments in Canada can therefore be liable for duties under those statutes.

Accordingly, the Tribunal considered that, in its ruling, it should apply the plain and ordinary meaning of "in Canada." In the Tribunal's view, this entailed a presence in Canada that does not necessarily amount to residency or a permanent establishment.

The Tribunal noted that, if one were to adopt an interpretation where a non-resident importer or an importer without a permanent establishment could not qualify as the "importer in Canada" for the purposes of the *SIMA*, this would result in situations where, for the same goods, one company could be liable for anti-dumping duties, while a different company would be liable for duties and taxes under the *Customs Act* and the *Excise Tax Act*. It added that it was also worth noting that customs duties, anti-dumping assessment, and excise tax are accounted for under the CCRA's B-3 forms, all of which are to be completed by the same importer.

Accordingly, the Tribunal ruled that the importer in Canada of the subject bicycles was Kent.

c) Action by CBSA

If the Tribunal makes an order or finding that the importer is other than the person specified by the CBSA in the request made pursuant to section 89, the CBSA must reconsider the final determination and either confirm or rescind it or amend it as appropriate in the circumstances, and notify all persons and governments involved as to the action taken, publish a notice in the *Canada Gazette*, and file the notice with the Secretary of the Tribunal.

Where the CBSA rescinds a final determination as a result of the Tribunal's ruling, all the provisions respecting the review of final determinations again apply as if they had not previously applied in respect of those goods, except that the action taken thereunder is to be taken by the CBSA within sixty days after the Tribunal's ruling.

If the CBSA had terminated an investigation after having made a preliminary determination of dumping or subsidizing, the Tribunal is deemed to have directed the CBSA to initiate an investigation, and the CBSA is required to initiate it forthwith.

d) Reconsideration of Order or Finding

On its own initiative or at the request of the CBSA or any person interested who satisfies the Tribunal that reconsideration of its order or finding as to who of two or more persons is the importer of goods into Canada, and the Tribunal considers that a reconsideration is warranted, it may reconsider the order or finding. Such reconsideration must be commenced not later than ninety days after the making of the initial order or finding, and be completed not later than ninety days after the commencement.

The Tribunal must either confirm its earlier order or finding, or rescind it and make a new order or finding. In the latter case, it must declare to what goods and, where applicable, to what supplier and to what country of export the new order or finding applies.

Where a reconsideration involves goods of the United States as well as goods of other countries, and the Tribunal makes another order or finding, it must make a separate order with respect to goods of the United States.

The Secretary of the Tribunal must

1) send, forthwith, a notice of the action taken with respect to the order or finding, by registered mail, to the CBSA, to the exporter, the importer, and to such other persons or governments as the Tribunal's rules may specify, and where another order or finding is made, a copy thereof;
2) send a copy of the reasons for the order or finding to the same persons as in (1) within fifteen days after completion of the reconsideration; and
3) where the Tribunal makes a new order or finding, publish it in the *Canada Gazette*.

e) Determination Deemed Not Made

Where the Tribunal has ruled that the importer is not the same person as the person that was determined to be the importer,

1) the determination made by a designated officer is deemed, by section 92, not to have been made, and for the purposes of determination by a designated officer, the period of six months within which such determination is required to be made is deemed to commence from the date of Tribunal's order or finding or the making of a new order or finding; and
2) by section 93, a determination or re-determination by the CBSA on the basis that the importer of the goods was a person who was subsequently ruled by the Tribunal not to be the importer, is deemed not to have been made, and the goods are deemed to be accounted for on the earlier of the day that is sixty days after the date of the Tribunal's ruling as to who is the importer, and the day on which a new determination is made in respect of the goods.

f) Tribunal's Ruling Binding

A ruling of the Tribunal on the question of who is the importer in Canada of any goods is binding on the CBSA and on every officer of the CBSA with respect to the particular goods in relation to which the ruling was given, unless the Tribunal was fraudulently misled, or where the goods were not then imported but were to be subsequently imported into Canada, material facts that were not available to the CBSA at the time the Tribunal gave its ruling came to the CBSA's attention after it was given.

g) Disclosure of Importer's Name

Section 95 requires the CBSA to disclose the name of the importer to any person interested in the importation, forthwith after receiving a request from that person, except in prescribed circumstances.[77]

2) Judicial Review: Application to Federal Court of Appeal

Subject to section 77.012 or 77.12 (respecting a definitive decision of the CBSA or the Tribunal referred to a Binational Panel described in Section E(4)(a), above in this chapter), any person directly affected by the determination, decision, order, or finding of the CBSA or of the Tribunal under the various sections of the *SIMA* may make an application for review of their

---

77 *Electrohome Ltd v Canada (Deputy Minister of National Revenue, Customs and Excise)*, [1986] 2 FC 344 (TD). The court rejected the plaintiff's application for disclosure, saying in obiter that if such information were disclosed on request, contrary to the Act, the whole legislative process would halt.

decision or order to the Federal Court of Appeal on the ground that the CBSA or the Tribunal,

1) acted without jurisdiction, or acted beyond their jurisdiction, or refused to exercise their jurisdiction;
2) failed to observe a principle of natural justice, procedural fairness, or other procedure that they were required by law to observe;
3) based their decision or order on an erroneous finding of fact or that they made it in a perverse or capricious manner or without regard to the material before them;
4) acted, or failed to act, by reason of fraud or perjured evidence; or
5) acted in any other way that was contrary to law.

The application for review must be made by filing a notice of the application within thirty days after the time the determination, decision, order, or finding was first communicated to that person by the CBSA or the Tribunal, or within such further time as the court or a judge thereof may, before or after the expiration of those thirty days, fix or allow. The application must be heard without delay and in a summary way in accordance with the rules made in respect of applications for judicial review under sections 18.1 and 28 of the *Federal Courts Act*.[78]

Section 18.3(1) of the *Federal Courts Act* (which provides for judicial review by the Trial Division of the Federal Court) does not apply to the CBSA or the Tribunal in respect of proceedings under the *SIMA* relating to goods of a *NAFTA* country.

The court may dismiss the application; set aside the final determination, decision, order, or finding; or set aside and refer it back to the CBSA or the Tribunal,[79] as the case may be, for determination in accordance with such directions as it considers appropriate.[80]

---

78 Above note 12.
79 *Shaw Industries*, above note 4: An application for certiorari filed by two foreign exporters, where the Minister had made a preliminary determination, was dismissed by the court, as it was premature; a preliminary determination of dumping raises no *lis* between the parties; also, certiorari was inappropriate, given that the *SIMA* contains various appeal procedures.
80 The Supreme Court has held in *National Corn Growers Association of Canada v Canada (Import Tribunal)*, [1990] 2 SCR 1324 that the Federal Court was wrong in finding that recourse to international treaty (*GATT*) was available only where a provision of domestic legislation (*SIMA*) was ambiguous on its face; it was reasonable for the Tribunal, at the outset of its inquiry, to make reference to international agreement to determine whether any ambiguity existed, even latent, in domestic legislation.

Where the Federal Court of Appeal has jurisdiction, the Trial Division is deprived of jurisdiction to entertain any proceeding in respect of the CBSA's or Tribunal's determination, decision, order, or finding.

3) Disclosure of Confidential Information

Where information provided to the CBSA or the Tribunal has been designated as confidential, and it is provided to a counsel for a party in the proceedings on a confidential basis, section 82 makes it an offence for counsel to disclose that information to any person other than the party to the proceedings. Similarly, section 83 makes it an offence for any public servant who comes into possession of such information to disclose it to anyone who has no right to that information. Upon conviction for the offence, the offender is subject to a fine of up to $1 million if the offence is tried on indictment, or $100,000 if tried summarily.

CHAPTER 4

The *Export and Import Permits Act*[1]

A. INTRODUCTION

Canada's export and import legislation has trade, political, cultural, and environmental policy objectives. In addition to the *Customs Tariff*[2] and the *Special Import Measures Act (SIMA)*,[3] which were the subject of Chapters 2 and 3, respectively, there are primarily four other statutes that cover these objectives, namely, the *Export and Import Permits Act (EIPA)* (covered in this chapter), the *Export Act*,[4] the *Cultural Property Export and Import Act*,[5] and the *Export and Import of Rough Diamonds Act*[6] (the latter three are covered in Chapter 5). There are several other statutes that incidentally control exports and imports, including the *Wild Animal and Plant Protection and Regulation of International and Interprovincial Trade Act (WAPPRIITA)*[7] (covered in Chapter 5), which gives effect to the *Convention on International Trade in Endangered Species and Wild Fauna and Flora (CITES)*,[8] and the *Health of Animals Act*,[9] along with other statutes (in Chapter 6), that contain provisions on the control of imports and exports that form part of an overall scheme.

---

1 RSC 1985, c E-19.
2 SC 1997, c 36.
3 RSC 1985, c S-15.
4 RSC 1985, c E-18.
5 RSC 1985, c C-51.
6 SC 2002, c 25.
7 SC 1992, c 52.
8 Signed at Washington, DC, on 3 March 1973, amended at Bonn, Germany, on 22 June 1979 and at Gaborone, Botswana, on 30 April 1983.
9 SC 1990, c 21.

The *Export and Import Permits Act* not only furthers trade policy, but is strategically more important. With respect to the international trade objective, it provides the nexus between the *Customs Tariff*, the *Special Import Measures Act*, and the *Canadian International Trade Tribunal Act (CITT Act)*,[10] implementing tariff rate quota decisions of the Tribunal on safeguard measures through an import permit system, and the export charges and quota system on softwood lumber products agreed to with the United States, which terminated a long-running dispute and is enshrined in the *Softwood Lumber Agreement* of 2006.[11]

The *EIPA* comes under the mandate of the Minister for External Affairs, but within that department, a junior Minister—the Minister of International Trade—has responsibility for Canada's international trade obligations under the *Special Import Measures Act*, the subject of Chapter 3, and gives policy direction in most areas involving market access and trade policy.

B. OBJECTIVES OF THE ACT

The *EIPA* was first enacted in 1947 with the following among its major objectives:

1) to regulate trade in military and strategic dual-use goods, and prevent the proliferation of weapons of mass destruction, under Canada's obligations under multilateral agreements;
2) to prevent the supply of military goods to countries that threaten Canada's security, are under UN sanctions, are threatened by internal or external conflicts, and that threaten or abuse the human rights of their citizens;
3) to protect vulnerable Canadian industries, such as clothing manufacturing;
4) to obtain negotiated benefits from international agreements;
5) to implement trade restrictions in support of Canada's supply management programs; and
6) to fulfil other international obligations.

The Trade Controls and Technical Barriers Bureau (TCTBB) within the Department of Foreign Affairs and International Trade (DFAIT) is responsible for administering the *EIPA*. CBSA officers are empowered by section 25 of the Act to enforce its provisions.

---

10   RSC 1985, c 47 (4th Supp).
11   *Softwood Lumber Products Export Charge Act*, SC 2006, c 13, ratifying the *Softwood Lumber Agreement* of 2006 with the United States, Can TS 2006 No 24.

Being primarily an operational statute with specific powers entrusted to the Minister of International Trade either directly or by way of an Order in Council, the Minister is conferred very wide discretion in granting, issuing, cancelling, or refusing to issue import and export permits. Courts have generally deferred to the Minister's decisions, interfering only when the decision was patently wrong, beyond jurisdiction, or exercised in bad faith or on extraneous grounds. The following dictum of McIntyre J of the Supreme Court of Canada in *Maple Lodge Farms Ltd v Canada Food Inspection Agency*[12] has been applied by the Federal Court of Appeal and the Trial Division in several cases:

> It is ... a clearly-established rule that the courts should not interfere with the exercise of a discretion by a statutory authority merely because the court might have exercised the discretion in a different manner had it been charged with that responsibility. Where the statutory discretion has been exercised in good faith and, where required, in accordance with the principles of natural justice, and where reliance has not been placed upon considerations irrelevant or extraneous to the statutory purpose, the courts should not interfere.

On the basis of the above dictum, the Federal Court has rejected applications for judicial review in several cases, for example, *Aliments Dorchester International Inc v Minister, Department of Foreign Affairs and International Trade*, and *Canadian Association of Regulated Importers v Canada (Attorney General)*.[13] In a few cases, however, the court has granted judicial review because the Minister did not observe the principles of natural justice and fairness to the applicants; for instance, in *Island Timberlands LP v Canada (Minister of Foreign Affairs)*,[14] the court referred back the decision of the Min-

---

12   (1982), 137 DLR (3d) 558 at 562 (SCC).
13   *Aliments Dorchester International Inc v Canada (Department of Foreign Affairs and International Trade)* (2001), 199 FTR 288 (TD) (Minister's denial of allocation of a share of the chicken quota upheld); *Canadian Association of Regulated Importers v Canada (Attorney General)*, [1994] 2 FC 247 (CA) (the Court of Appeal set aside the trial judge's decision to allow judicial review; the Minister's appeal was allowed); see also *Teal Cedar Products (1977) Ltd v Canada (Attorney General)* (1988), 92 NR 308 (FCA); *Parker Cedar Products Ltd v Canada* (1988), 92 NR 318 (FCA); *Timberwest Forest Corp v Canada*, 2007 FC 148, aff'd 2007 FCA 389; *Ultima Foods Inc v Canada (Attorney General)*, 2012 FC 799 (where the Minister issued supplemental import permits allowing Agra-Farma Canada Inc to import quantities of its Chobani brand Greek-style yogurt into Canada, application for judicial review dismissed; court held that the Minister's broad discretion to issue permits suggested there was only a minimal duty of fairness).
14   2008 FC 1380.

ister, giving directions on how the applications for permit should be disposed of, for example, to provide reasons for acceptance or denial of permit.

C. ESTABLISHMENT OF LISTS

The objectives of the *EIPA* are sought to be fulfilled by means of four control lists, namely, (1) an *Export Control List (ECL)*, (2) an *Area Control List (ACL)*, (3) an *Automatic Firearms Country Control List (AFCCL)*, and (4) an *Import Control List (ICL)*. The Governor in Council is authorized by the *EIPA* to create these four lists under sections 3, 4, 4.1, and 5, respectively, and to amend, vary, revoke, and re-establish those lists from time to time. The lists are updated on a regular basis, depending on trade policy and international developments.

Most goods that appear under one or more of the above lists require individual permits for import or export. However, some goods may benefit from general permits, which allow for the pre-authorized export or import of specific goods to or from certain eligible countries. The *Export Permits Regulations*[15] (EPR) and the *Import Permits Regulations*[16] (IPR) establish procedures for obtaining permits.

1) *Export Control List*

a) Establishment of the *Export Control List*
The *Export Control List (ECL)*[17] is created under section 3 of the *EIPA*. In that list the Governor in Council may include any goods and technology the export or transfer of which is deemed to be necessary in order to (1) protect the security of Canada, (2) limit unrestricted export of natural resources, (3) ensure that there is an adequate supply and distribution of the goods or technology in Canada for defence or other needs, (4) implement inter-governmental arrangement or commitment, or (5) ensure orderly export marketing.

Seven groups are listed in the *ECL*. Groups 1 to 4, 6, and 7 consist of dual use goods and technology; munitions; nuclear non-proliferation goods and technology; nuclear-related dual use goods and technology; and strategic, missile, chemical, or biological goods of non-proliferation concern. Group 5 includes softwood lumber, unprocessed logs, and certain other forest prod-

---

15 SOR/97-204.
16 SOR/79-5.
17 SOR/89-202.

ucts, and miscellaneous goods, including goods of US-origin, roe herring, and certain items with medical value.

All goods that appear on the *ECL* require an export permit. Most can be exported under a general permit, but some goods require individual permits.

In terms of value, more than one-third of the goods are exported by road, followed by marine, rail, and air in that order.

Goods that are being exported from Canada are required by the *Customs Act*[18] to be reported to the CBSA. Goods exported by highway transport must be reported immediately prior to export; those exported by air or rail, within a minimum of two hours before the cargo is loaded on the aircraft or assembled to form part of the railcar; and those shipped by a vessel, not less than forty-eight hours before cargo is loaded on the vessel.

The CBSA receives those reports and verifies if the goods are compliant with export laws and regulations. If non-compliant, the goods may be detained and/or seized or be subject to ascertained forfeiture. In addition, exporters or service providers may be issued an administrative monetary penalty or prosecuted in accordance with the provisions of the *Customs Act*.

The Strategic Export Control (SEC) Section of the National Security Division of the Intelligence Directorate in the Enforcement Branch, Department of Foreign Affairs, Trade and Development, enforces and is consulted on export policies that meet the Government of Canada's international agreements related to the non-proliferation of nuclear and other weapons. The SEC Section administers, enforces, and monitors the legislation related to the export of strategic or controlled goods to countries that pose a threat to Canada and its allies, that are involved in or under imminent threat of hostilities, that fall under the United Nations Security Council sanctions, or that have a record of serious human rights violations.

b) Export Declarations

Export declarations must be submitted along with export permits, licences, or certificates when the goods are valued at $2,000 or more and the final destination is a country other than the United States, Puerto Rico, or the US Virgin Islands. The export of goods that are controlled, regulated, or prohibited by other government departments and organizations, such as the Canadian Nuclear Safety Commission, Environment Canada, Health Canada, and Transport Canada, must also be reported in writing to the CBSA.

---

18   RSC 1985, c 1 (2nd Supp).

There must be compliance with the *Reporting of Exported Goods Regulations*,[19] prescribed under the *Customs Act*.

c) Method of Declaration

The most common methods of declaring exports, and available from Statistics Canada to companies with a valid business number, are the Canadian Automated Export Declaration, followed by a paper-based Form B13A declaration and the Summary Reporting option for exporters of bulk, low-risk goods that meet specific CBSA requirements and export on a regular basis. Summary Reports must be submitted within five business days after the end of the month in which the goods are exported, even if there were no exports during that month, by email or fax, directly to Statistics Canada. A fourth form of declaration, the G7 Electronic Data Interchange option, which allows electronic filing, is also available, but is not used as much as the other methods.

2) *Area Control List*

In the *Area Control List*[20] (ACL), created under section 4 of the *EIPA*, the Governor in Council may include any country to which the export or transfer of goods or technology is deemed necessary to control. Exports destined for any of the countries listed in the *ACL* require export permits. Currently, three countries, namely, Belarus, North Korea, and Myanmar are on the *ACL*; however, restrictions in respect of certain non-military goods were removed for Myanmar in early 2012.[21]

3) *Automatic Firearms Country Control List*

Only countries with which Canada has an intergovernmental defence, research, development, and production arrangement, and to which it is deemed appropriate to permit the export of prohibited firearms, weapons, or devices, as defined in the *Criminal Code*,[22] may be included in the *Automatic Firearms Country Control List*[23] (AFCCL), created by the Governor in Council under section 4.1.

---

19 SOR/2005-23.
20 SOR/81-543.
21 SOR/2012-86.
22 RSC 1985, c C-46.
23 SOR/91-575, as amended.

4) Import Control List

a) Inclusion of Goods in *ICL* by Order

A wide variety of goods or technology, the import of which is deemed necessary to control, is placed in the *Import Control List (ICL)*[24] created pursuant to section 5. The purposes of the *ICL* are, *inter alia*, to ensure supply management of scarce articles or articles that are subject to governmental controls in the countries of origin, or subject to allocation under an intergovernmental arrangement; to prevent the frustration or circumvention of the *Agreement on Textiles and Clothing* in Annex 1A of the *World Trade Organization Agreement*;[25] to protect Canada's agriculture and food industries under the *Agricultural Marketing Programs Act* or the *Canadian Dairy Commission Act*, which are under a supply management system; or to facilitate the implementation of action taken under the *Customs Tariff*. This is achieved by restricting the importation of any articles that are like those produced or marketed in Canada and regulated under the *Farm Products Marketing Agencies Act*,[26] tariff rate quotas (TRQ), surtaxes, anti-dumping and countervailing measures under other statutes, and so on.[27] Very high tariff rates are imposed on goods in excess of TRQs.

The *ICL* is also used to reinforce decisions of the Tribunal under the *SIMA* by limiting the importation of goods found by it to cause or threaten serious injury to domestic products of like or directly competitive goods, by limiting the importation of such goods to the extent and for the period necessary to prevent or remedy the injury. If the goods were already subject to an order under section 55(1) of the *Customs Tariff* (surtax on free trade partner goods), an order including those goods in the *ICL* may not be made after the expiry of that order and any related orders made under the *EIPA* section 5(3.3) (extension order) or section 5(4.1) (new order with respect to goods imported from a free trade partner), unless there has elapsed either two years or the total period during which the order or orders were in effect, whichever is greater.

---

24 CRC, c 604.
25 *Marrakesh Agreement Establishing the World Trade Organization*, Marrakesh, 15 April 1994.
26 RSC 1985, c F-4. See also *Dairy Products Disputes*, WT/DS103/R2 and WT/DS113/RW2 (2002), 6 TTR (2d) 310 and (2002), 7 TTR (2d) 1 (WTO Panel Report, July 2002) and (2002), 7 TTR (2d) 559 (Recommendations, December 2002).
27 See tribunal's safeguard measures in Chapter 2, Section G.

b) Extension Order

An order extending the period for which goods have been included in the *ICL*, in accordance with the limitation described in the previous paragraph, may be made by the Governor in Council under section 5(3.2) on the recommendation of the Minister that such an extension is necessary to prevent or remedy serious injury to domestic producers of like or directly competitive goods, *and* there is evidence that the domestic producers are adjusting as determined in accordance with regulations made under the *CITT Act*, section 30.07, for the period specified in the order, but the total period during which the extension order and the previous order may be in force must not exceed eight years.

c) Exclusion of Goods from Peru and Colombia

Goods of any kind imported from Peru or Colombia may be excluded from the *ICL* under the authority of section 5(3.4) if it appears to the satisfaction of the Governor in Council, on the basis of a report of the Tribunal, that the quantity of those goods being imported is not a principal cause of serious injury or threat thereof to domestic producers of like or directly competitive goods. The terms "serious injury," "threat of serious injury," and "principal cause" have the same meaning as in the *Customs Tariff*.[28]

d) Limitation on Inclusion in the *ICL*

Goods originating in a free trade partner country or from a *North American Free Trade Agreement (NAFTA)*[29] country may not be included in the *ICL* unless it appears to the Governor in Council, on a report of the Minister pursuant to an inquiry of the Tribunal,

1) in the case of a free trade partner country, that the quantity of those goods represent a substantial share of the quantity of goods of the same kind that are imported into Canada from all countries and contributes importantly to serious injury, or threat thereof, to domestic producers of like or directly competitive goods or significant overall impairment in the position of domestic producers; or
2) in the case of a *NAFTA* country, that the quantity of those goods, alone or, in exceptional circumstances, together with the quantity imported

---

28 Above note 2, s 54 (definitions of "serious injury" and "threat of serious injury") and s 2(1) (definition of "principal cause").
29 Can TS 1994 No 2.

from each other *NAFTA* country, contributes importantly to the serious injury or threat thereof.

Where an order made by the Governor in Council including goods in the *ICL* does not specifically include goods imported from a free trade partner country, goods from that country or countries may subsequently be included in the *ICL* for the purpose of limiting the quantities, if there is a surge of imports of like goods from that or those countries after the making of the order, for the purpose of preventing the frustration of the order. The term "surge" is defined in the *NAFTA* and the *Canada-Chile Free Trade Agreement (CCFTA)*.[30]

e) Inclusion in *ICL* to Facilitate Information Collection

In addition to the above, the following goods may be included in the *ICL* only for the purpose of collecting information:

- goods subject to an inquiry of the Tribunal, to ascertain whether the importation of those goods is causing or threatening to cause injury to the production of like or directly competitive goods in Canada;
- steel and steel products, if the Minister is of the opinion that a certain type of steel or steel product is being traded in world markets in circumstances of surplus supply and depressed prices and that a significant proportion of world trade in that type of steel or steel product is subject to control through non-tariff barriers;
- goods subject to any action that is taken under prescribed sections of the *Customs Tariff*, for the purpose of implementing such action;
- goods specified in the *Agreement on Agriculture* in Annex 1A of the *WTO Agreement*, for the purpose of implementing that Agreement; and
- goods imported from a free trade partner to which an order under the *EIPA* or the *Customs Tariff* does not apply because the quantity of those goods does not represent a substantial share of the quantity of goods of the same kind imported from all countries and does not contribute importantly to the serious injury or threat thereof to Canadian producers of like or directly competitive goods.

Similarly, any goods exported to or imported from a free trade partner country may be included in the *ECL* or *ICL* (1) if under the free trade agreement there is a specified quantity eligible each year for the rate of duty pro-

---

30 Definition of "surge" in *CCFTA*, July 1997, art F-05; *NAFTA*, *ibid*, art 800.

vided in them, without reference to the quantity in the List; or (2) for the purpose of implementing a free trade agreement.

f) Removal of Goods from *ICL*

Goods included in the *ICL* are deemed to be removed therefrom at the expiration of four years after the day on which they were included, or earlier if the order to include them specifies an earlier date.

g) Goods Originating in the People's Republic of China

Section 5.4 makes special provisions with respect to goods imported from the People's Republic of China, giving effect to the agreements China concluded as a condition of being admitted to membership in the World Trade Organization and adhering to the *WTO Agreement*. The section, which ceased to have effect on 11 December 2013, provided as follows:

i) Imports Causing Market Disruption or Trade Diversion

If at any time it appears to the Governor in Council on a report of the Minister pursuant to an inquiry by the Tribunal under the *CITT Act* that goods originating in the People's Republic of China are being imported into Canada in such increased quantities or under such conditions as to cause or threaten to cause market disruption, the Governor in Council may include those goods in the *ICL*. Similarly, goods may be included in the *ICL* and their importation limited to the extent necessary to prevent or remedy trade diversion, if the Governor in Council is satisfied on a report of the Minister as a result of an inquiry made by the Tribunal, that an action taken by the People's Republic of China causes or threatens to cause a significant diversion of trade in the domestic market in Canada.[31]

Orders including the goods in the *ICL* as above, or orders made under the corresponding provisions of the *Customs Tariff* (sections 77.1 and 77.3) may be extended before they expire if, in the opinion of the Governor in Council, as a result of the Tribunal's inquiry, they continue to be necessary to prevent or remedy market disruption.

ii) Inclusion of Goods for Information Collection

In addition to the above, the goods being imported from the People's Republic of China may be included in the ICL for the following purposes: (1) in order

---

31   Certain Outdoor Barbeques, Safeguard Inquiry No. CS-2005-001 (2005), 10 TTR (2d) 463 (outdoor barbeques).

to ascertain whether goods are being imported or are likely to be imported into Canada at such prices, in such quantities, or under such conditions that such importation is causing or threatening to cause market disruption, and it is advisable to collect information with respect to such importation; and (2) in order to facilitate the implementation of an order made under the *Customs Tariff* (sections 77.1, 77.3, or 77.6), if the Governor in Council considers it necessary.

h) Bilateral Emergency Measures: Textiles and Apparel Goods *Not* Originating in a Free Trade Partner Country

The Minister may, pursuant to section 6.1, take the bilateral emergency measures specified in the prescribed annexes to the free trade agreements in respect of goods listed in the specified appendices thereto, that are imported from a free trade partner country but did not originate in that country and for that reason are not entitled to the US Tariff, Mexico Tariff, Mexico-US Tariff, Chile Tariff, or Costa Rica Tariff, as the case may be, if the Minister is satisfied that such goods are being imported in such increased quantities, measured in absolute terms or relative to the domestic market, and under such conditions as to cause serious damage or actual threat thereof to domestic producers of like or directly competitive goods.

In determining whether the above conditions exist, the Minister is required to have regard to the provisions of the relevant Annex.

i) Import Access

Where any goods have been included on the *ICL* for the purpose of implementing an intergovernmental arrangement or commitment, the Minister is authorized by section 6.2 to (1) determine import access quantities or the basis for calculating them; (2) establish a method for allocating the quantity to residents of Canada who apply for an allocation; and (3) issue an allocation to the applicant subject to such terms and conditions as the Minister may specify.

The Minister may consent to the transfer of an import allocation from one resident of Canada to another.

ii) Export Access

a. Softwood Lumber Products Export Access

The *Softwood Lumber Agreement* was concluded when Canada and the United States temporarily resolved an ongoing trade dispute, and Parliament enacted the *Softwood Lumber Products Export Charge Act, 2006 (SLPECA)*[32] to give effect to that agreement. Under the *SLPECA*, if any softwood lumber products have been included on the *ECL* pursuant to section 6.3, the Minister may determine the quantity of those products that may be exported from a Western province or from Ontario and Quebec, during a month, or the basis for calculating such quantities for the purposes of section 6.3(3) or section 8.4.

For the purpose of determining the quantities, the Minister may by order establish a method for allocating the quantity to persons registered under section 23 of the *SLPECA* who make an application, and issue them an export allocation for a month, subject to regulations and any terms and conditions that the Minister may specify in the export allocation. An export allocation may be transferred from one registered person to another registered person with the Minister's consent.

An exported softwood lumber product is deemed to have originated in a Western province, Ontario, or Quebec if it was first processed in any of those provinces, and it is deemed to be exported from that province, even if it was processed in the Atlantic provinces or in the Territories, provided that it was processed from softwood sawlogs originating in a Western province, Ontario, or Quebec.

D. EXPORT AND IMPORT PERMITS AND CERTIFICATES

1) Permits That Are Required

Exports and imports may require permits. The requirements are set out in sections 7, 8, and 8.1 to 8.5. The *ECL* in the *Export Permits Regulations*[33] prescribed under the *EIPA* includes items controlled for the reasons referred to in Section C(1)(a), above in this chapter. Similarly, the *ICL* includes several items that require an individual or general permit for importation.

2) Export Permits

Some of the important individual export regulations are the *Export Permits Regulations (Softwood Lumber Products 2006)*,[34] *Export of Logs Permit*,[35] *Export*

---

32 SC 2006, c 13.
33 Above note 15.
34 SOR/2007-15.
35 CRC, c 612.

of *Sugar Permit*,[36] *Export of Specimens Permit*,[37] and *Export of One Cent Bronze Coins Permit*.[38] Exports of such items must be authorized in advance by an export permit issued by the Export and Import Controls Bureau of the Export Controls Division at Foreign Affairs and International Trade Canada (DFAIT). Many exports are permitted under a General Export Permit (GEP). The Bureau is responsible for administering export permits for controlled goods or goods destined for controlled areas, in accordance with the *EIPA*. Exports that do not fall under the *ECL* may require a licence, permit, or certificate from other government departments. Permits must be presented to the CBSA with the corresponding export declaration.

3) Import Permits

Where an *ICL* has been created, the Minister may issue to any resident of Canada applying therefor, an import permit specifying the quantity and quality of goods that may be imported, and the persons by whom, the places from which, and the persons from whom they may be imported, and the terms and conditions under which they may be imported.

4) General Import or Export Permits

The Minister must also issue a general permit, generally to all residents of Canada,

1) to import any goods included in the *ICL*, other than goods subject to access allotment, that are specified in the permit, subject to such terms and conditions as are described in the permit; and
2) to import or export goods included in the *ICL* or *ECL* solely for the purpose of collecting information from a free trade partner country subject only to compliance with and the application of any regulations made under section 12 that it is reasonably necessary to comply with or apply in order to achieve that purpose.

The Minister is also authorized to issue an individual permit, or general permits, to import supplemental quantities.

---

36   SOR/83-722.
37   CRC, c 616.
38   CRC, c 613.

5) Permit to Import Access Quantity

Where goods have been included in the *ICL* for the purpose of implementing an intergovernmental arrangement or commitment, and the Minister has determined an import access quantity for those goods, the Minister must issue an import permit to any resident of Canada who applies, whether or not that person has been issued an import allocation, subject to compliance with and application of such regulations as are reasonably required to achieve that purpose.

In addition, export permits are required for any and all exports to countries on the *ACL*. Listed items that are only transiting the United States for export to other destinations may also require a Canadian export permit, depending on the country of final destination. Exporters or their agents may apply for an individual permit electronically through Export Controls On-Line (EXCOL) or submit a paper application to DFAIT.

6) Prohibited Firearms and Weapons

The Minister may not issue a permit in respect of a prohibited firearm, weapon, or device, or a component or part thereof, that is included in an *ECL*, unless the export is to a country included in the *AFCCL*, established under section 4.1, and the export is to the government of, or a consignee authorized by the government of, that country.

7) Import and Export Certificates

In order to facilitate the importation of goods into Canada and comply with the laws of the export country, the Minister is authorized by sections 9, 9.1, 9.2, 10, and 11 to issue to any Canadian resident applying therefor, an import certificate stating that the applicant has undertaken to import the goods described in the certificate within the time specified therein, and containing such other information as the regulations require. The *Issuance of Certificates Regulations*[39] provide for the issuance of such a certificate.

Where an importation is from a *NAFTA* country, Chile, or Costa Rica, the Minister may, for the purpose of implementing an intergovernmental arrangement with that country under the relevant free trade agreement, state in the certificate the specific quantity of those goods that is eligible under the free trade agreement.

---

39 SOR/93-587.

Export certificates may be issued to a Canadian resident for exporting goods to any country, stating the quantity of goods in a shipment that may be eligible for benefits that are provided by a country or customs territory, under a quantitative limitation the export certificates have imposed with respect to the exportation of the goods, in order to implement an intergovernmental agreement with that country or customs territory.

Section 11 makes it abundantly clear that the issue or granting of a permit, certificate, or other authorization under the *EIPA* does not affect the obligation of any person to obtain any licence, permit, or certificate to export or import under any law or to pay any duties, taxes, or other amounts required by any law to be paid in respect of the exportation or importation of the goods.

8) Amendment, Suspension, Cancellation, and Reinstatement

Any permit or certificate issued under the *EIPA* may be amended, suspended, cancelled, or reinstated by the Minister. However, where a person had given false or misleading information in the permit application, or another certificate was issued for the same goods, or the goods have been subsequently included in the *ECL*, the Minister may cancel the certificate. Errors may also be corrected by the Minister. Principles of natural justice and fairness must be observed by the Minister.

9) International Import Certificates

An International Import Certificate is designed to facilitate a foreign supplier to obtain the approvals it needs from its own government to allow the export of goods or technology to Canada. It is a document that formally recognizes that the Government of Canada is aware of, and has no immediate objections to, the proposed import of specific goods into Canada by the stated importer, for the stated end-use and end-user. It does not authorize the import of goods into Canada.

E. OFFENCES AND PENALTIES

Section 19 of the *EIPA* makes it an offence, punishable on indictment or by summary procedure, to contravene any provision of the Act or the regulations prescribed pursuant to it. If the offence is prosecuted by indictment, the fine is at the discretion of the court, and the prison term is a maximum of ten years, or both the fine and the prison term. A summary conviction offence is punishable with a maximum fine of $25,000, or a prison term of twelve months, or both. In imposing a sentence, the court is required to consider, among other factors, the nature and value of the exported or transferred goods or technology, or the imported goods that are the subject matter of the offence.

Section 25 of the Act empowers CBSA officers to exercise all the powers given them by the *Customs Act* relating to the importation and exportation of the goods that are the subject of a proceeding under the *EIPA*.

In *R v Wulff*,[40] the British Columbia Court of Appeal upheld the conviction of an accused who attempted to export silver coins without permit contrary to section 13. It held that proof of intent to take the coins out of the country was sufficient. It was not necessary to show that the accused intended to leave or dispose of the goods out of the country or bring them back to Canada. The court approved the *Shorter Oxford Dictionary* definition of "export," which, in secondary commercial sense, meant "to send out (commodities) from one country to another."

Jurisprudence on an accused's rights under the *Canadian Charter of Rights and Freedoms*[41] applies. In *R v Marstar Trading International Inc*,[42] the Ontario Court of Appeal upheld the acquittal of the individuals accused of the offences charged because there was an undue delay in proceeding to prosecution after the charges were laid. The court, following *R v Oakes*,[43] held that a total delay of two years and two months from the time charges were laid resulted in a violation of the rights of the accused to be tried within a reasonable time. The corporation was however denied the same right.

The Supreme Court of Canada reaffirmed that an offence under the Act that is punishable by imprisonment requires, at a minimum, a showing of negligence and that the defence of due diligence was available. In *R v Martin*,[44] the Court held that its decision in *R v Wholesale Travel Group Inc*[45] governed this prosecution.

---

40 (1970), 74 WWR 549 (BCCA). See also *R v Mauder* (1965), 47 CR 101 (Ont Magis Ct), a decision in which the provincial magistrate held that an embassy is not part of the soil of the country of its occupant; therefore, as the sale to the Soviet embassy was not an export to the USSR, the accused was acquitted of the charge but was convicted on another charge.
41 *Constitution Act, 1982*, being Schedule B to the *Canada Act 1982* (UK), 1982, c 11.
42 (1999), 138 CCC (3d) 87 (Ont CA).
43 [1986] 1 SCR 103.
44 (1991), 63 CCC (3d) 71 (Ont CA), aff'd [1992] 1 SCR 838.
45 [1991] 3 SCR 154.

CHAPTER 5

Other Statutes Relating to Import and Export

This chapter deals with four principal statutes that contain provisions exclusively on exports from Canada, under the *Export Act*, and on both imports into and exports from Canada, under the *Wild Animals and Plant Protection Regulation of International and Interprovincial Trade Act*, the *Cultural Property Export and Import Act*, and the *Export and Import of Rough Diamonds Act*. Statutes that have import and export control provisions but whose primary concern is to regulate other aspects of the commodities are the subject of the final chapter. Those statutes include the *Canada Consumer Product Safety Act*, the *Controlled Drugs and Substances Act*, the *Canadian Environmental Protection Act*, the *Health of Animals Act*, the *Plant Protection Act*, the *Precious Metals Marking Act*, and the *Textile Labelling Act*.

A. THE *EXPORT ACT*[1]

1) Introduction

The *Export Act* was first enacted in 1896–97,[2] and the duties on certain logs and pulpwood and on certain ores, enumerated below, have been maintained throughout its revisions to the present time.

The main purpose of the *Export Act* is to impose export duties on timber logs and lumber, nickel, copper, lead, silver, and other ores, making Can-

---

1 RSC 1985, c E-18.
2 *An Act Respecting Export Duties*, SC 1896–97, c 17.

adian exports of those commodities more expensive. By a proclamation of the Governor in Council, the following duties are imposed:

- Under section 2—On pine, Douglas fir, spruce, fir balsam, cedar and hemlock logs, and pulpwood exported from Canada to any country that imposes a duty on any of the timber or lumber or wood products listed in the Schedule to the Act, the maximum rate of duty must not exceed three dollars per thousand feet, board measure, but if the logs or pulpwood are shorter than nine feet in length, the export duty is chargeable at a rate per cord that is not greater than the equivalent of three dollars per thousand feet, board measure.
- Under section 3—On nickel ore at a rate not exceeding ten cents per pound; on copper ore at a rate not exceeding two cents per pound; on any ores that contain copper or any metal other than nickel or lead, at a rate not exceeding fifteen percent of the value of the ores; and on lead ores, lead, and silver ores, if the country of import imposes a duty on Canadian imports in excess of the import duty on goods from other countries, the rate of export duty is equivalent to the excess.

The export duties are chargeable after the publication of the proclamation by which they are imposed, presumably in the *Canada Gazette*. They may be removed and reimposed by another proclamation.

2) Prohibition of Export

In addition to the power to impose duties under sections 2 and 3, section 5 authorizes the Governor in Council to prohibit, by regulation, the export of petroleum in crude or partly manufactured state, and of pulpwood of the variety, kind, place of origin, or having the particulars of identification or ownership or production described in the regulation. The said regulation must be tabled in Parliament and ceases to be in force at the end of the Parliamentary session unless it is approved by a resolution of both Houses of Parliament.

3) Export of Intoxicating Liquor

Where a country prohibits the importation of intoxicating liquor by law, the export of such liquor to that country is made unlawful by section 6. Intoxicating liquor includes any spirituous or malt liquor, wine, and any and every combination of liquors or drinks that is intoxicating, and any mixed liquor beverage that is intoxicating.

4) General Note

Although the *Export Act* has been on the statute books for over a century, no export duties seem to have been levied, nor has a prohibition against the export of petroleum or certain wood varieties under section 5 been declared—no proclamation or regulation, which is necessary for such action, has been found in the statute book. Perhaps the condition precedent to the imposition of duties has not existed, namely, that they are imposable only when a country to which Canadian lumber or timber or wood products listed in the Schedule, or nickel or iron or other ores referred to in section 3, are imported, charges import duties on the Canadian products. Negotiated agreements, such as the *Softwood Lumber Agreement* concluded by Canada with the United States temporarily resolving an ongoing trade dispute and ratified by the *Softwood Lumber Products Export Charge Act, 2006*[3] may also make it unnecessary to resort to the *Export Act* mechanism.

B. THE *WILD ANIMALS AND PLANT PROTECTION REGULATION OF INTERNATIONAL AND INTERPROVINCIAL TRADE ACT*[4]

1) *Convention on International Trade in Endangered Species of Wild Fauna and Flora*

The *Wild Animals and Plant Protection Regulation of International and Interprovincial Trade Act* (WAPPRIITA) provides the legislative base for the *Convention on International Trade in Endangered Species of Wild Fauna and Flora* (CITES), an intergovernmental treaty signed in Washington, DC, in 1973,[5] and ratified by Canada in April 1975. CITES applies to any (1) specimen, whether living or dead, of any species of animal that is listed as "fauna" in an appendix to the CITES, and includes any egg, sperm, tissue culture, or embryo of any such animal; and (2) "plant" or any specimen, whether living or dead, of any

---

3   SC 2006, c 13.
4   SC 1992, c 52; *Wild Animal and Plant Trade Regulations*, SOR/96-263.
5   The *Convention* was amended at Bonn, Germany, on 22 June 1979 and at Gaborone, Botswana, on 30 April 1983.

species of plant that is listed as "flora" in an appendix to the *CITES*, and includes any seed, spore, pollen, or tissue culture of any such plant.

2) Classification of Wild Fauna and Flora

For the purposes of *CITES* classification, wild fauna and flora are placed into one of three categories, their placement made on the basis of the degree to which the species is considered endangered. These categories appear as appendices to the *CITES* as follows:

- Appendix I—Species threatened with extinction worldwide that are or may be affected by trade. Trade in specimens of these species is subject to particularly strict regulation in order not to endanger further their survival and may only be authorized in exceptional circumstances.
- Appendix II—Species although not necessarily now threatened with extinction but may become so unless trade in specimens of such species is subject to strict regulation in order to avoid utilization incompatible with their survival.
- Appendix III—Species which any Party identifies as being subject to regulation within its jurisdiction for the purpose of preventing or restricting exploitation, and as needing the co-operation of other Parties in the control of trade.

3) Import and Export

With some exceptions noted below, section 6(2) of *WAPPRIITA* requires every person who imports into or exports from Canada any animal or plant, or any part or derivative of animal or plant, to have a permit issued pursuant to section 10(1) of the Act.

The importation of all species listed in Appendix I of the *CITES* requires an import permit issued by the office of *CITES* Administrator, Canadian Wild Life Service, Ottawa. Those in Appendix II or III of the *CITES* are exempt if they are not listed in Schedule II of the *WAPPRIITA Regulations*[6] and if the importer has obtained, before import, a permit, certificate, or written authorization from a competent authority of the country of export, that satisfies the requirement of the *CITES*.

---

6   Above note 4.

4) Interprovincial Transport

A permit is also required by section 7 for the interprovincial transport of a wild animal or plant, or any part or derivative of an animal or plant, unless one holds a permit issued by a competent authority in the province in which it was captured or taken, and transports them in accordance with such permit, as specified in sections 10 to 12 of the Regulations.

5) Possession

Unless authorized by section 13 of the Regulations, section 8 makes it an offence to knowingly possess an animal or plant, or any part or derivative of an animal or plant, (1) that has been imported or transported in contravention of the Act; (2) for the purpose of transporting it from one province to another province in contravention of the Act or exporting it from Canada in contravention of the Act; or (3) for the purpose of distributing or offering to distribute it if the animal or plant, or the animal or plant from which the part or derivative comes, is listed in Appendix I to the *CITES*.

6) Exemptions

Sections 15 to 17 of the Regulations provide exemption from holding a *CITES* permit in the following cases:

1) *Canadian Residents and Visitors to Canada*
   Examples include a Canadian resident returning home from travelling with an elephant ivory bracelet; a person from an African country visiting Canada with a traditional leopard fur hat (Appendix I); a US resident crossing the border with a pair of python skin boots (Appendix II); a European citizen visiting Canada wearing a lynx fur coat (Appendix II).

2) *Tourist Souvenirs*
   This applies to Canadian residents returning from a trip outside the country with souvenirs of CITES Appendix II or III species, if imported in their accompanying baggage or as part of their clothing or accessories.

3) *Household Effects*
   Individuals moving to or from Canada can bring or take out goods listed on the *CITES* control list that they had owned and possessed in their ordinary country of residence and that form part of their household belongings, which are being shipped to or from Canada to their new resi-

dence, and includes goods from an inheritance that are being imported into or exported from Canada.

4) *US and Canadian Hunters in Canada*
Such goods as a black bear or sandhill crane hunting trophy may be exempted from the need to obtain a Canadian *CITES* export permit when exported from Canada to the United States by a US resident, or exported and re-imported into Canada by a Canadian resident, if (a) the trophy is in a fresh, frozen, or salted condition, (b) it is part of the individual's accompanying baggage, and (c) it was acquired and possessed through legal hunting in Canada or the United States. This exemption is not available for taxidermy trophies. All other permits, certificates, or licences that may be required by other government departments (OGDs) continue to apply and must be presented to customs at the border as required.

5) *Diplomats*
All importations of *CITES* controlled species (including live animals) are subject to the requirements outlined above, regardless of any diplomatic immunity or privilege extended to the person importing the goods.

7) Limitations and Restrictions

The exemption does not apply to items imported or exported for commercial purposes; live animals (other than pets that are to be re-exported in accordance with section 17 of the Regulations); *CITES* species that are listed as endangered or threatened in Canada (Schedule III); tourist souvenirs consisting of live animals or live plants (definition of "tourist souvenirs" in section 14 of the Regulations); or items made from any species listed in Appendix I of the *CITES* control list (species threatened with extinction).

Furthermore, by section 18 of the Regulations, an individual may not sell or dispose of the exempted goods within ninety days after the date on which the exemption is claimed.

8) Issue of Permits

Pursuant to section 10(1), on application and on such terms and conditions as the Minister of the Environment thinks fit, and on payment of the prescribed fees, the Minister of the Environment may issue a permit authorizing the importation, exportation, or interprovincial transportation of an animal or plant, or any part or derivative of an animal or plant, covered by the *CITES*.

A special import permit may be issued by the *CITES* Administrator under special circumstances where it would be considered unreasonable to refuse importation of the item.

C. THE *CULTURAL PROPERTY EXPORT AND IMPORT ACT*[7]

The *Cultural Property Export and Import Act* (*CPEIA*) is designed to protect Canada's national heritage through the establishment of export controls for objects of historical, scientific, and cultural significance. It was enacted in fulfilment of Canada's obligations under the UNESCO-sponsored 1970 *Convention on the Means of Prohibiting and Preventing the Illicit Import, Export and Transfer of Ownership of Cultural Property*.[8] The *CPEIA* was amended in 2005[9] to give effect to the 1954 *Convention for the Protection of Cultural Property in the Event of Armed Conflicts*[10] and its Protocols.[11] The *Criminal Code*[12] was also amended in 2005[13] to create the offence of mischief in relation to cultural property defined in the second-mentioned Convention.

1) Export of Canadian Cultural Property

a) Export Control List

The export of Canadian cultural property is accomplished through the Canadian *Cultural Property Export Control List* (Export Control List), created pursuant to section 4. The section defines categories of cultural property according to age, weight, and dollar value limits. The broad categories include mineralogy, palaeontology, and archaeology; ethnographic material culture; military objects; objects of applied and decorative art; objects of fine art; scientific or technological objects; textual records, graphic records, and sound recordings; and musical instruments. An object within a class of objects included in the

---

7   RSC 1985, c C-51 [*CPEIA*].
8   Can TS 1978 No 33, adopted in Paris in 1970 and ratified by 122 members.
9   *An Act to Amend the Criminal Code and the Cultural Property Export and Import Act*, SC 2005, c 40, adding ss 7(2.01) to the *Criminal Code* (allowing prosecution of Canadians for offences committed outside Canada); and ss 430(4.2) (creating the offence of mischief in relation to cultural property).
10 Done at The Hague, 14 May 1954. Section 36.1 and a Schedule was added to the *CPEIA* by SC 2005, c 40.
11 *First Protocol*, done at The Hague, 14 May 1954; *Second Protocol*, done at The Hague, 26 March 1999.
12 RSC 1985, c C-46.
13 Above note 9.

Export Control List is deemed by section 4(4) to be an object included in that list.

The Export Control List corresponds to and is in conformity with the definition of "cultural property" in Article 1 of the 1970 Convention. For the purposes of Article 1 of the Convention, section 38 designates an object included in the Export Control List as being of importance for archaeology, prehistory, history, literature, art, or science.

Section 4(3) excludes from the Export Control List any object that is less than fifty years old or made by a person still living.

The export of controlled cultural property is subject to a permit procedure that is administered by permit-issuing officers of the CBSA designated by the Minister of Public Safety and Emergency Preparedness under the authority of section 5.[14] These officers are located in the CBSA offices across Canada. Section 40 expressly points out that an export permit or other permit to export issued under the Act does not affect the obligation of any person to obtain any licence, permit, or certificate to export that may be required under any other law or to pay any tax, duty, toll, or other sum required by any law to be paid in respect of the export of any goods.

b) Export Permits

Application for an export permit, the issuing of such a permit, and the terms and conditions of issue are set out in sections 3 to 12 of the Regulations. Upon completion of an application form by a person who wishes to export cultural property, the permit-issuing officers will verify the application for completeness. They will then either issue the export permit or refer the application to an expert examiner for a decision. Expert examiners are affiliated with Canadian institutions designated by the Minister of Canadian Heritage pursuant to section 6.

Section 7 requires a permit officer to issue forthwith a permit if the applicant satisfies the officer that the cultural object was

1) imported into Canada within the thirty-five years immediately preceding the date of application for the permit and was not exported from Canada under a permit issued before the application was made;
2) borrowed by an institution or public authority of Canada from a person who was not a resident of Canada at the time the loan was made; and
3) to be removed from Canada for a temporary period, not exceeding the period prescribed by the Regulations.

---

14   *Cultural Property Export Regulations*, CRC c 449.

Where an object is not included in the Export Control List, section 8 requires a permit officer to issue a permit forthwith. If the officer is unsure whether the object comes within that list, the officer must refer the matter for advice to an expert examiner for consideration, and only upon receipt of the examiner's advice can the officer issue an export permit.

i) General Permits and Open General Permits

Section 17 authorizes the Minister of Heritage to issue a general permit to any resident of Canada to export any object included in the Export Control List on such terms and subject to such conditions as the Minister specifies, and to amend, suspend, cancel, or reinstate the permit. The Minister may also issue an open general permit to all persons to export an object included in that list and that is specified in the permit, but such a permit needs the concurrence of the Minister of Foreign Affairs. The permit application procedure is set out in sections 17 to 20 of the Regulations.

ii) Copy of Object to Be Deposited in Public Institution

A copy of an object that is a manuscript, original document, archive, photographic positive and negative, and film and sound recording, and is prescribed under regulations made pursuant to section 39(d) of the Act, must be deposited with "an institution that is publicly owned and operated solely for the benefit of the public, that is established for educational or cultural purposes, and that conserves objects and exhibits them or otherwise makes them available to the public" (section 2 definition of "institution"). There is no such requirement where an export permit is issued under section 7 or 8.

iii) Objects of Outstanding Significance or National Importance

If an expert examiner determines that an object referred by the CBSA permit officer is included in the Export Control List, the expert examiner must further determine (1) whether the object is of outstanding significance by reason of its close association with Canadian history or national life, its aesthetic qualities, or its value in the study of the arts or sciences; and (2) whether the object is of such a degree of national importance that its loss to Canada would significantly diminish the national heritage.

If these considerations are not present, the expert examiner must forthwith advise the permit officer who, thereupon, must issue an export permit. If the considerations are present, the expert examiner must so advise the permit officer and the latter must send a notice to the applicant stating that the application for an expor t permit is denied. In the latter case, an export permit may not be issued for a period of two years after the notice of refusal was sent to the applicant, unless the Review Board established under section 18 directs otherwise pursuant to section 29 or 30.

iv) Review of Permit Decisions

a. Request for Review

Any person who has been denied an export permit or whose permit has been cancelled, suspended, amended, or otherwise altered by the Minister may, in accordance with section 29, request the Canadian Cultural Property Export Review Board (Review Board) to review the refusal or alteration of the permit, provided the request is made in writing and is sent to the Review Board within thirty days after the date on which the refusal was sent or the Minister sent a notice of alteration of the permit.

The Review Board must review the request and make a determination within four months from the date of the request, unless the circumstances of the case require otherwise. If the Review Board determines that the object under review meets all three conditions specified in section 29(3), namely, (1) it is included in the Export Control List, (2) it is of outstanding significance for one or more reasons set out in section 11(1)(a) of the Act, and (3) it meets the degree of national importance referred to in section 11(1)(b), it must decide in one of the following two ways:

1) If it is of the opinion that a fair offer to purchase the object might be made by an institution or public authority of Canada within six months after the date of its determination, and establishes a delay period of not less than two months and not more than six months, it will not direct the issuance of an export permit;
2) In any other case, it will direct a permit officer to issue an export permit forthwith in respect of the object.

b. Determination of Fair Offer

If a fair offer to purchase is made by an institution or a public authority referred to in section 29 within the delay period and is refused by the person who applied for an export permit, either of the parties may request the Review Board to determine the amount of fair cash offer to purchase. Such request must be made in no less than thirty days before the end of the delay period. The Review Board must make a determination of the fair cash offer to purchase and advise the parties of its determination.

If the Review Board does not receive a request from either party for determination of a fair offer to purchase within the delay period, it must forthwith, after the expiration of the delay period and on the request of the person who requested the review under section 29(1), direct the permit officer to issue an export permit in respect of the object. However, if the Review Board is satisfied that an amount equal to or greater than the fair cash offer to purchase was made by the institution or public authority, it must not direct the issue of an export permit.

Section 31 prohibits the Review Board from directing the issue of an export permit except in conformity with section 29 or 30.

2) Protection of Foreign Cultural Property

a) Designation

Section 37 defines a foreign cultural property as any property that is designated by a foreign State that is a party to an agreement with Canada, or to an international agreement to which Canada and the foreign State are both parties ("reciprocating State"), as being an object of importance for archaeology, prehistory, history, literature, art, or science.

Section 37(2) makes it illegal to import into Canada any foreign cultural property that has been illegally exported from a reciprocating foreign State, from and after the coming into force of a cultural property agreement between Canada and that State or of an international agreement to which both Canada and the foreign State are parties.

b) Action to Recover Cultural Property

Sections 37(3) to (9) contain provisions for the recovery of cultural property.

The Attorney General of Canada may, where the Minister receives a request from a reciprocating State for the recovery of any foreign cultural property, institute an action in the Federal Court or in a superior court of a province for the recovery of the cultural property that is in the possession of or under the control of any person, institution, or public authority, at the request of a State that is a party to the *Second Protocol*.[15]

Compensation that is deemed to be just in the circumstances must be paid by the State Party to a person from whom the property is recovered, if the court is satisfied that the person was a *bona fide* purchaser of the property and was unaware at the time of purchase that the property had been export-

---

15 Above note 11.

ed in contravention of the applicable laws of the State Party, or that it had been imported into Canada for the purpose of its protection or preservation.

The limitation period for taking action specified in section 39 of the *Federal Courts Act*[16] does not apply to the recovery action taken under section 37(3).

On receipt of a court order directing the return of the property, an export permit must be issued by the Minister to the person authorized by the State Party on behalf of which the action was taken.

3) *Convention for the Protection of Cultural Property in the Event of Armed Conflict* and Its Protocols

The *Convention for the Protection of Cultural Property in the Event of Armed Conflict*[17] (*Second Convention*) and its Protocols are implemented through section 36.1 and amendments to the *Criminal Code*.[18] Article 1 of the *Second Convention*, which defines cultural property, is set out in the Schedule to the Act.

a) Definition

Section 36.1 applies to cultural property as defined in Article 1 of the Schedule. Cultural property, irrespective of origin or ownership, covers the following:

> (a) movable or immovable property of great importance to the cultural heritage of every people, such as monuments of architecture, art or history, whether religious or secular; archaeological sites; groups of buildings which, as a whole, are of historical or artistic interest; works of art; manuscripts, books and other objects of artistic, historical or archaeological interest; as well as scientific collections and important collections of books or archives or of reproductions of the property defined above.
>
> (b) buildings whose main and effective purpose is to preserve or exhibit the movable cultural property defined in paragraph (a), such as museums, large libraries and depositories of archives and refuges intended to shelter, in the event of armed conflict; and
>
> (c) centres containing a large amount of cultural property to be known as "centres containing monuments".

---

16   RSC 1985, c F-7.
17   Above note 10.
18   Above note 12.

b) Offence to Export or Remove Cultural Property

Section 36.1(2) prohibits a person from knowingly exporting or otherwise removing cultural property from an occupied territory of a State that is a party to the *Second Protocol*, unless the export or removal conforms with the applicable laws of that territory or is necessary for the protection or preservation of the property. Notwithstanding any Canadian statute, an offence committed under section 36.1(2) outside Canada is deemed by section 36.1(3) to have been committed in Canada, despite anything in the Act or any other Act, if the offender is (a) a Canadian citizen; (b) is not a citizen of any state and ordinarily resides in Canada; or (c) is a permanent resident of, and is present in, Canada after the commission of the offence.[19]

c) Recovery Action

Sections 36.1(4) to (10) contain provisions for the recovery of and the payment of compensation for cultural property illegally removed or exported, limitation of actions, and the issue of export permits. They are very similar to the provisions set out in section 37 for the recovery of foreign cultural property discussed in Section C(2)(i), above in this chapter.

4) Offences and Punishment

a) Offences

The following offences are created by sections 40 to 44:

1) exporting or attempting to export from Canada any object included in the Export Control List without a permit issued under the Act and in accordance with that permit (section 40);
2) transferring a permit to another person or allowing it to be used by a person who is not authorized (section 41);
3) giving false information to secure a permit or in connection with its use or in the disposition of an object to which the permit relates (section 42);
4) importing or attempting to import foreign cultural property that is illegal to import into Canada (section 43);
5) exporting or attempting to export from Canada during the pendency of an action that has been instituted in relation thereto, while the action is being considered, or where an order for recovery of foreign cultural property has been made, unless the object is exported under the author-

---

19   CPEIA, above note 7, ss 36.1(3) and *Criminal Code*, above note 12, s 7(2.01).

ity of, and in accordance with, the permit that is issued pursuant to the court order (section 44).

b) Punishment under the Act

The offender is liable under section 45 for the following punishment: (1) on summary conviction, to a fine not exceeding five thousand dollars, or to imprisonment not exceeding twelve months, or to both, with a three year limitation period for instituting the prosecution; or (2) on conviction on indictment, to a fine not exceeding $25,000, or to imprisonment not exceeding five years, or to both.

c) Punishment under the *Criminal Code*

The *Criminal Code* was amended in 2005 by adding an offence of mischief in relation to cultural property as defined in Article 1 of the 1954 Convention. The offender is liable to punishment on indictment by imprisonment for a term not exceeding ten years, or on summary conviction. The punishment on summary conviction, under the "general penalty" section 787(1) of the *Criminal Code* is a fine not exceeding $5,000 or six months imprisonment, or both. Section 7 of the *Criminal Code* was also amended by adding subsection (2.01) whereby a person who has committed an offence of mischief in relation to cultural property, or a conspiracy or an attempt to commit such an offence, or being an accessory after the fact or counselling in relation to such an offence, is deemed to have committed that act or omission in Canada if the person (a) is a Canadian citizen, (b) is not a citizen of any state and ordinarily resides in Canada, or (c) is a permanent resident within the meaning of section 2(1) of the *Immigration and Refugee Protection Act*, and is, after the commission of the act or omission, present in Canada.

D. THE *EXPORT AND IMPORT OF ROUGH DIAMONDS ACT*[20]

The *Export and Import of Rough Diamonds Act* (*EIRDA*) was passed by Parliament in 2002 to give effect to the commitments internationally agreed upon by governments, the international diamond industry, and non-governmental organizations that participated in what was called the Kimberley Process Certification Scheme, to prevent the international movement of, and thus international trade in, the so-called "blood" or conflict diamonds that were being used to fund rebel activities in various African countries. All members

---

20   SC 2002, c 25, am SC 2005, c 51.

of the United Nations General Assembly, including Canada, supported the Kimberley Process by General Assembly Resolution 55/66 on 1 December 2000.

States, international organization of states, dependent territories of a state, and customs territories named in the schedule to the *EIRDA*, are called "participants." There are seventy-four participants, including Canada and the European Community. The Minister of Natural Resources administers the statute.

1) Definition of Rough Diamond

Section 2 of the *EIRDA* defines a rough diamond as "a diamond that is unsorted, unworked, or simply sawn, cleaved, or bruted, and that falls under subheading 7102.10, 7102.21 or 7102.31 in the List of Tariff Provisions in the Schedule to the *Customs Tariff*."[21] Diamonds that are cut and polished and ready to be mounted, set, or fitted do not fall under the provisions of the *EIRDA* and they do not require a Kimberley Process Certification.

2) Trade Regulation

a) Export Control

Section 9 of the Act requires an exporter to have a Canadian Kimberley Certificate issued pursuant to sections 2 to 5 of the Regulations.[22] The Certificate must accompany each export. Section 13 requires every person who exports rough diamonds to report the export to the Minister in accordance with the regulations and to export them at a point of exit designated under the Regulations, if any. Section 7 of the Regulations specifies the information that must be reported.

b) Import Control

Section 14 requires every person who imports rough diamonds to ensure that, on import, the diamonds are in a container that meets the requirements of section 9 of the regulations and are accompanied by a Kimberley Process Certificate issued by a participant, that has not been invalidated by the participant, and that contains accurate information; and, further, to ensure that the rough diamonds in the container were not parcelled with

---

21   SC 1997, c 36.
22   *Export and Import of Rough Diamonds Regulations*, SOR/2003-15, am SOR/2007-80.

diamonds excluded from the definition of "rough diamond" or with anything else. If it is found that on opening the container, diamonds meeting the requirement of section 14 were parcelled with the "rough diamonds" as defined, or something else, the Minister may order the rough diamonds to be returned to the participant who issued the certificate; if they are ordered to be returned, they may not be seized.

Section 16 requires every person who imports rough diamonds to import them at a point of entry designated under the regulations, if any, and to report them to the Minister in accordance with the regulations. The reporting requirements are set out in section 8 of the Regulations.

c) In-Transit Shipment

An investigator appointed by the Minister is empowered by section 17 to seize rough diamonds in transit that are not accompanied by a Kimberley Process Certificate or if they are found in a container that had been opened. The Minister may order the return of rough diamonds that are accompanied by a Kimberley Process Certificate that were found in an opened container. In that case, the rough diamonds may not be seized.

d) Regulations

Section 9 of the Regulations requires containers that are used to export or import rough diamonds to be so constructed that they cannot be opened when sealed without showing evidence of having been opened. In addition, containers in which rough diamonds are exported must be secured with a seal that bears a seal number listed on the accompanying Canadian Kimberley Process Certificate and bears the serial number of the Canadian Certificate.

3) Offences

Sections 36 to 40 create the following offences:

1) wilfully furnishing false or misleading information or knowingly making a misleading representation in an application for a Canadian Certificate or in connection with the subsequent use of the certificate or the export or disposition of the rough diamonds to which it relates (section 36);
2) forging or altering a Canadian Certificate (section 37);
3) transferring or selling a Canadian Certificate with knowledge or deemed knowledge that the certificate will be used to export rough diamonds other than those in respect of which it was issued (section 38);

4) failing to maintain or falsifying records in order to avoid compliance with the Act (section 39);
5) obstructing an inspector who is performing duties under the Act (section 40); and
6) contravening sections 13(1) or (2), 16(1) or (2), 22, and 40. The offences enumerated in these provisions are summary conviction offences (section 40(1)).

The contravention of sections 8 and 14 is also an offence (container requirements).

4) Punishment

Section 41 provides that for offences against sections 8, 14, and 36 to 39, if prosecuted by indictment, the offender is liable to a fine in an amount that is in the discretion of the court, or to imprisonment for a term not exceeding ten years, or to both; or by summary conviction procedure, the offender is liable to a fine not exceeding $25,000, or to imprisonment for a term not exceeding twelve months, or to both. A three-year limitation period applies for prosecuting under the summary conviction procedure.

However, where the Minister had ordered the return of imported diamonds pursuant to section 14, a person cannot be convicted of the offence under that section.

Sections 41(4) and (5) set out guidelines when imposing a sentence and the imposition of an additional fine to recoup the monetary benefits derived from the commission of the offences.

CHAPTER 6

Miscellaneous Federal Statutes

This chapter covers nine from among a number of Federal statutes that primarily regulate domestic trade; commerce; and human, animal and plant health, but for the purpose of a seamless regulatory system, they also cover exports and imports. The regulatory system is touched upon incidentally since it would be straying beyond the scope of this book, which is to give a broad picture of export and import control regulation.

The nine statutes, in alphabetical order, are the *Canada Consumer Product Safety Act*, the *Canadian Environmental Protection Act*, the *Consumer Packaging and Labelling Act*, the *Controlled Drugs and Substances Act*, the *Health of Animals Act*, the *Pest Control Products Act,* the *Plant Protection Act*, the *Precious Metals Marking Act*, and the *Textile Labelling Act*.

A. THE *CANADA CONSUMER PRODUCT SAFETY ACT*[1]

1) Introduction

The *Canada Consumer Product Safety Act* (*CCPS Act*) was enacted in 2010. It amends the *Hazardous Products Act*,[2] which is now limited in its applicaton to controlled products or hazardous products listed in Schedule II and the Regulations that prescribe the goods set out in that Schedule. Those goods fall into six categories, namely compressed gas, flammable and combustible material, oxidizing material, poisonous or infectious material, corrosive

---

1   SC 2010, c 21.
2   RSC 1985, c H-3.

material, and dangerously reactive material. Importation of those goods must be accompanied by the prescribed hazardous material safety information data. The *Hazardous Products Act* ceases to apply to consumer products as defined in the *CCPS Act*, but the regulatory structure, including the prohibitions against importations without the appropriate material safety data sheets, and the enforcement and offence sections, are generally the same in the two statutes.

The *CCPS Act* applies to all consumer products except those listed in Schedule 1 to the Act. Tobacco products are included only in respect of their ignition propensity. The items listed in Schedule 1 are also controlled by other legislation, such as the *Criminal Code*, the *Controlled Drugs and Substances Act*, the *Canada Shipping Act*, the *Explosives Act*, the *Feeds Act*, the *Fertilizers Act*, the *Food and Drugs Act*, the *Health of Animals Act*, the *Pest Control Products Act*, the *Plant Protection Act*, and the *Motor Vehicle Safety Act*, some of which are covered below in this chapter.

2) Purpose, Definitions, and Application

The stated purpose of the *CCPS Act* is to protect the public by addressing or preventing dangers to human health or safety that are posed by consumer products in Canada, including those that circulate within Canada and those that are imported.

The expression "danger to human health or safety" is defined by section 2 of the Act as

> any unreasonable hazard—existing or potential—that is posed by a consumer product during or as a result of its normal or foreseeable use and that may reasonably be expected to cause the death of an individual exposed to it or have an adverse effect on that individual's health—including an injury—whether or not the death or adverse effect occurs immediately after the exposure to the hazard, and includes any exposure to a consumer product that may reasonably be expected to have a chronic adverse effect on human health.

Section 2 defines a "consumer product" as

> a product, including its components, parts or accessories, that may reasonably be expected to be obtained by an individual to be used for non-commercial purposes, including for domestic, recreational and sports purposes, and includes its packaging.

The Act and the Regulations prescribed under its authority apply to any article that is

1) a consumer product;
2) anything used in the manufacturing, importation, packaging, storing, advertising, selling, labelling, testing, or transportation of a consumer product; or
3) a document that is related to any of the above activities or a consumer product.

Many of the Regulations enacted under the *Hazardous Products Act* were repealed when the *CCPS Act* was enacted, but others, namely, those relating to carpets, cellulose insulation, charcoal, expansion gates and expandable enclosures, infant feeding bottle nipples, matches, mattresses, and tents were re-enacted under the new Act.

3) Prohibitions

Sections 5 to 9 enumerate the prohibitions. It is an offence against sections 5 and 6 to manufacture, import, advertise, or sell a consumer product listed in Schedule 2 to the Act, or to do these things with respect to consumer products that do not meet the requirements set out in the Regulations.

Schedule 2 contains a list of fifteen items, from Jequirity beans, certain types of baby walkers, baby bottles, baby bottle nipples, pacifiers, and kites, to sneezing powders and textile fibre products that contain trisphosphate.

Section 7 prohibits the manufacturing, importing, advertising, or selling of a consumer product that is

1) a danger to human health or safety;
2) the subject of a recall order under section 31 or of a voluntary recall in Canada because the product is a danger to human health or safety; or
3) the subject of a measure that the manufacturer or importer has not carried out as required by an order issued under section 32 by Industry Canada, or such an order that is reviewed under section 35.

The advertising or sale of a consumer product that is a danger to human health or safety or that is subject to a recall order is prohibited by section 8. Packaging or labelling a consumer product in a manner that is false, misleading, or deceptive is prohibited by section 9.

4) Duties and Obligations

a) Incident Reports

A manufacturer, importer, or seller of a consumer product is required by section 14 to provide the Minister of Industry and, if applicable, the person from whom the consumer product is received, with all the information in their possession or control concerning any "incident" related to the product within two days after the day on which they become aware of the incident.

An "incident" is

1) an occurrence in Canada or elsewhere that results or may reasonably have been expected to result in an individual's death or in serious adverse effects on their health, including serious injury;
2) a defect or characteristic that may reasonably be expected to result in such death or injury;
3) incorrect or insufficient information on a label or in instructions, or the lack thereof, that may result in such death or injury; or
4) a recall that is initiated for human health or safety reasons by a foreign entity or a provincial or Aboriginal government in Canada.

The manufacturer of the consumer product or, if the manufacturer carries on business outside Canada, the importer must provide a written report containing information about the incident, the product involved in the incident, and any products that they manufacture or import, as the case may be, that to their knowledge could be involved in a similar incident, and any measure they propose be taken with respect to other products, within ten days after the day on which they became aware of the incident, or within the period that the Minister specifies by written notice.

b) Recalls

The Minister of Industry may issue a recall order under section 31 if the Minister believes on reasonable grounds that a danger is posed to human health or safety by a consumer product. Section 32 requires every person to whom the order is issued or addressed to comply with the order. If the person does not comply, the Minister may direct the person to take measures to stop manufacturing, importing, packaging, storing, advertising, or selling the product, and may order any other measure considered necessary to rectify a non-compliance with the Act or the Regulations or to prevent a danger to human health or safety that is posed by the product.

c) Regulations

Section 37 gives the Governor in Council the power to make regulations respecting the manufacture, importation, advertisement, sale, and so on, and to prohibit the manufacture, importation, advertisement, or sale of any consumer product that poses or may pose a hazard to human health or safety. As well, regulations can be made to exempt with or without conditions a consumer product or class of consumer products from the application of the *CCPS Act* or the Regulations, or a provision thereof, including exempting a consumer product manufactured in Canada for the purpose of export, or imported solely for the purpose of export.

5) Criminal Penalties

Severe punishment is provided in the *CCPS Act* for offences against it or against the Regulations. For some offences, for example, against section 8, the penalty can be up to $5 million in fine and/or a two-year prison term, or both, if a conviction is on indictment; on summary conviction, for the first offence the fine can be up to $250,000 and/or a six-month prison term; and for a second and subsequent offences, the penalty is a fine of up to $500,000 and/or an eighteen-month prison term. The defence of due diligence is allowed. If the offence is committed knowingly, the Act provides for a maximum of a five-year prison term and/or a fine in the discretion of the court, if the conviction is on indictment; if it is on summary conviction, to a maximum of $500,000 and/or eighteen months for a first offence, and $1 million and/or two years for a second and subsequent offences.

6) Administrative Monetary Penalties

In lieu of prosecution, the *CCPS Act* also provides for the imposition of administrative monetary penalties (AMPs), which, with the exception of review and appeal provisions, are patterned after the groundbreaking *Agriculture and Agri-Food Administrative Monetary Penalties Act* (*AAAMP Act*).[3] Like the *AAAMP Act*, the defence of due diligence is not permitted. Compliance agreements are also provided for. The penalties are reviewed by the Minister and there is no further appeal, but judicial review is available. The AMPs provisions are contained in sections 49 to 65.

---

3   SC 1995, c 40.

B. THE *CANADIAN ENVIRONMENTAL PROTECTION ACT, 1999*[4]

The *Canadian Environmental Protection Act, 1999* (CEPA) regulates, controls, or prohibits, *inter alia*, the import of ozone-depleting substances (ODS) specified in the schedules to the *Ozone-Depleting Substances Regulations, 1998* (ODSR)[5] and the export of substances on the Export Control List created by the *Export of Substances on the Export Control List Regulations*.[6]

1) Controlled Ozone-Depleting Substances

Controlled ozone-depleting substances (ODS) include chlorofluorocarbons (CFCs), hydrochlorofluorocarbons (HCFCs), hydrobromofluorocarbons (HBFCs), methyl chloroform (MCF), carbon tetrachloride (CTC), bromofluorocarbons and bromochlorofluorocarbons (Halons), methyl bromide, and bromochloromethane (BCM). Appendix A to the *ODSR* contains a complete listing of controlled substances and Appendix B gives their common/trade names. These substances may exist alone or in a mixture.

a) Report of Import or Export

Every person who imports or exports a controlled substance during any year is required by section 17(3) of the *ODSR* to provide to the customs office where the substance is required to be reported under section 12 or 95 of the *Customs Act* a copy of their permit, the Minister's written confirmation of their consumption allowance, or an acknowledgement of their notice of shipment in transit.

Generally, the import and export of ODS is prohibited except in controlled and exempted cases.

b) Importation

i) Written Authorization

Importation is permitted only if a valid permit or written confirmation of allowance from Environment Canada has been presented to the CBSA. A written authorization is required to import the following:

1) ODS that are to be used for a purpose set out in Schedule 3(i). In the case of a CFC or a product containing CFCs, it must be supplied in a container

---

4   SC 1999, c 33.
5   SOR/99-7, am SOR/2000-102, SOR/2001-2, SOR/2002-100, SOR/2004-315, SOR/2007-129.
6   SOR/2013-88.

of three litres or less and be used for an essential use that is a laboratory or analytical use (*ODSR*, section 20(5));
2) recovered, recycled, reclaimed, or used controlled substances; and
3) HCFCs, by way of an allowance or a transfer of allowance. HCFC-22, HCFC-141b, and HCFC-142b can only be imported under an allowance if they are intended to be exported or to be used as a refrigerant.

ii) Exemptions

Importation of the following ODS and products containing ODS is exempted under the *ODSR*:

1) non-commercial importation of CFC, bromofluorocarbon, bromochlorodifluoromethane, tetrachloromethane, or 1,1,1-trichloroethane, or products containing these ODS, for the personal use and consumption of the importer and transported in a consignment of personal or household effects;
2) aircraft, ships, or any vehicle manufactured before 1 January 1999 and that contain or are designed to contain any CFC, bromofluorocarbon, bromochlorodifluoromethane, tetrachloromethane, or 1,1,1-trichloroethane;
3) fire extinguishers containing or designed to contain any bromofluorocarbon or bromochlorodifluoromethane to be used in aircraft or military ships or military vehicles, if the equipment is imported from a Party;[7]
4) products containing or designed to contain HCFCs other than HCFC-22, HCFC-141b, and HCFC-142b, for example, air-conditioning systems, refrigerators, chillers, and vending machines are exempted. (They are not included in the *ODSR*, but section 22 prohibition, and products that contain or are designed to contain HCFC-22, HCFC-141b, and HCFC-142b, are controlled under section 28.);
5) a product containing HCFCs in a pressurized container that is
    i) a mold release agent used in the production of plastic and elastomeric materials,
    ii) a spinnerette lubricant or cleaning spray used in the production of synthetic fibres,
    iii) a document preservation spray,
    iv) fire extinguishing equipment used for non-residential applications,
    v) a wasp and hornet spray,
    vi) a rigid foam product,
    vii) refrigerant R-412A, or

---

7   Above note 5, s 1.

viii) refrigerant R-509A;
6) a product containing HCFC that is used as an animal or human health care product; and
7) a rigid foam product in which any HCFC has been used as a foaming agent.

c) Exportation

There are fewer restrictions on the exportation of ODS under the *ODSR* as compared to importation. The country receiving a shipment of ODS can prescribe its own restrictions through its domestic legislation, as Canada does under the *ODSR*. As a consequence, products for export that contain or are designed to contain ODS are not controlled in Canada, except those subject to section 21 of the *ODSR*.

i) Written Authorization

Exportation is permitted only on the condition that a valid permit from Environment Canada is presented to the CBSA. The exportation of the following ODS and products containing ODS are controlled:

1) recovered, recycled, reclaimed, or used (RRRU) ODS, or for destruction (*ODSR* 1998, section 7(2)(a));
2) ODS exported for a purpose set out in Schedule 3 that was previously imported or manufactured for a purpose set out in Schedule 3 (*ODSR* 1998, section 7(2)(d));
3) ODS exported because it was imported by mistake or without consent to its importation (*ODSR* 1998, section 7(2)(e)); and
4) a product that contains or is designed to contain any CFCs, bromofluorocarbons, bromochlorodifluoromethane, tetrachloromethane, or 1,1,1-trichloroethane exported to developing countries (Article 5 of the *Montreal Protocol on Substances that Deplete the Ozone Layer*[8]) (section 21).

ii) Exemptions

Written authorization is not required for the export of the following ODS and products containing ODS:

1) ODS that are a heel (section 6(2));
2) ODS that are sold in Canada to a foreign ship for the refilling or servicing of its refrigeration, air conditioning, or fire extinguishing equipment, in

---

8 Defined by s 2 of the *ODSR* as the "*Montreal Protocol on Substances that Deplete the Ozone Layer*, as amended from time to time," Can TS 1989 No 42, signed by Canada 16 September 1987.

a quantity that does not exceed the total capacity of the equipment (section 6(3)); and
3) any products that contain or are designed to contain any ODS other than those specified in section 21.

d) Maintenance of Records

Every importer and exporter of controlled substances is required to keep records and to report to the Minister of the Environment as specified in the *ODSR*.

e) Penalties

Any person who contravenes or fails to comply with the Regulations made under the Act is guilty of an offence and is liable on summary conviction, to a fine not exceeding $300,000, or to imprisonment for a term not exceeding six months, or to both; or on indictment, to a fine not exceeding $1 million, or to imprisonment for a term not exceeding three years, or to both.

2) Export of Other Controlled Substances

a) Export Control List

Pursuant to sections 100 to 103 of the *CEPA*, a list of substances is created in the Export Control List in Schedule 3 to the Act under three parts:

- Part 1: sixteen substances the use of which are prohibited in Canada, including PBBs, PCTs, endrin, and toxaphene;
- Part 2: thirty-four substances that are subject to an international agreement that requires notification or consent of the country of destination before export from Canada, including dieldrin, chlordane, DDT, hexachlorobenzene, polychlorinated biphenyls (PCBs), and endosulfan; and
- Part 3: nineteen substances the use of which is restricted in Canada, including CFCs, carbon tetradioxide, benzidine, and tetrachlorobenzenes.

b) Prohibition

Section 101 sets out the following restrictions on the export of substances specified in the Export Control List in Schedule 3:

1) By section 101(1), an exporter must give prior notice of the proposed export to the Minister of the Environment in accordance with regulations made under section 102(1); and
2) By section 101(2), the export of a substance specified in the Export Control List is prohibited

a) if the export of the substance is prohibited by a regulation made under section 102(2); if not prohibited, the export must be done in accordance with any regulations made under section 102(1);
b) if the substance is listed in Part 2 of the Export Control List, the export must be done in accordance with any regulation made under section 102(1);
c) if the substance is listed in Part 1, the export must be done
    i) for the purpose of destroying the substance or complying with a direction under section 99(b)(iii), and
    ii) is done in accordance with any regulations made under section 101(2).

c) Regulations

The *Export of Substances on the Export Control List Regulations*[9] set out the content of the notice of proposed export that is required under section 101(1) of the *CEPA* for Schedule 3 substances, and the period within which and the manner in which the notice must be provided. The *ODSR* also set out the conditions applicable to the export of a substance that is specified in Part 2 or 3 of Schedule 3 to the Act and that is also targeted by the *Stockholm Convention on Persistent Organic Pollutants*,[10] as well as the permit, liability insurance, and labelling requirements.

The notice of proposed export must contain the information set out in Schedule 1, accompanied by a certification, dated and signed by the person proposing the export, or by their duly authorized representative, stating that the information provided in the notice is accurate and complete. It must be provided to the Minister of the Environment at least thirty days before the export. The Minister must also be notified of any changes in the information provided in the notice of the proposed export within thirty days after learning of it. Electronic submission is optional.

C. THE *CONSUMER PACKAGING AND LABELLING ACT*[11]

The *Consumer Packaging and Labelling Act* is a consumer protection law that regulates the packaging and labelling of prepackaged consumer products.

---

9   Above note 6.
10 Stockholm, Sweden (22 May 2001, entered into force 17 May 2004 (Registration #40214)). Canada became a Party on 23 May 2001. Convention amended in 2009 and 2011.
11 RSC 1985, c C-38.

1) Statutory Requirements

Sections 4 to 7 and 9 require the sale, import, or advertising of any prepackaged consumer product to have a label applied to the product that contains a declaration of net quantity of the product in a form and manner required by the Act or the Regulations in terms of either a numerical count or a unit of measurement that conforms to the *Weights and Measures Act*.[12] The advertising on the label must not contain any false or misleading representation relating to the product by way of any expression, word, figure, depiction, or symbol that implies the product contains any matter not contained in it or does not contain any matter that is in fact contained in it, or any description or illustration of the type, quality, performance, function, origin, or method of manufacture or production that may reasonably be regarded as deceptive to consumers. Section 6 requires the prepackaged product to comply with the regulations made pursuant to section 11(1) of the Act.

Certain tolerances in the declared net quantity are permitted by section 7(3), provided it is not less than the declared amount, and section 9(2) relieves a vendor or importer from criminal liability if recognized and accepted production practice that is reasonably necessary for packaging the product is followed.

Section 10 requires additional information on the product label, such as the identity and principal place of business of the person by or for whom the prepackaged product was manufactured or produced for sale; the identity of the product in terms of its common or generic name or in terms of its function; and such information respecting the nature, quality, age, size, material content, composition, geographic origin, performance use, or method of manufacture or production, as may be prescribed by the *Consumer Packaging and Labelling Regulations*.[13]

The Regulations exempt certain products from the packaging, labelling, and marking requirements. These are prepackaged products regulated by the *Feeds Act*,[14] the *Fertilizers Act*,[15] the *Pest Control Products Act*,[16] and the *Seeds Act*[17]; and soft drink containers that are reused by a dealer and are permanently labelled as required by the *Food and Drugs Act*, and that are manufactured during a period of twelve months after 1 March 1974. Prepackaged "one-bite"

---

12 RSC 1985, c W-6.
13 CRC, c 417.
14 RSC 1985, c F-9.
15 RSC 1985, c F-10.
16 SC 2002, c 28.
17 RSC 1985, c S-8.

confections that are usually sold individually to a consumer, prepackaged fresh fruits and vegetables that are packaged in a wrapper or confining band of less than one-half inch in width, and raspberries and strawberries prepackaged in the field in a container of less than 1.4-litre capacity are also exempt by the Regulations.

Additional exemptions are provided by section 4 of the Regulations and section 10(b) of the Act for prepackaged products that are not food (1) if they are usually sold by numerical count of seven articles in a package, or more than seven but less than thirteen if the number can be readily ascertained by a visual examination of the container; and (2) if they are single articles or consist of more than one article if a pictorial representation on the principal display panel adequately indicates the identity and quantity of the product contents.

2) Offences and Criminal Penalties

Section 20 contains criminal penalties. For offences against sections 4 to 9, the maximum fine is $5,000 on summary conviction or $10,000 on conviction on indictment. For offences against other sections, the maximum fine on summary conviction is $1,000, or imprisonment for a term not exceeding six months, or both; and on conviction on indictment, the maximum fine is $3,000, or imprisonment for a term not exceeding one year, or both. However, if the offence relates to a prepackaged food as defined in section 2 of the *Food and Drugs Act*,[18] the criminal penalty is far higher: on summary conviction, the maximum fine is $50,000 and/or six months imprisonment, and on conviction on indictment, the maximum fine is $250,000 and/or two years imprisonment.

D. THE *CONTROLLED DRUGS AND SUBSTANCES ACT*[19]

In 1996, the *Controlled Drugs and Substances Act* (*CDS Act*) replaced the *Narcotic Control Act*,[20] which had been in place since 1961. The new Act continued but modified the regulatory controls of the old Act.[21] A controlled substance is defined as any type of drug that the federal government has designated as having a higher-than-average potential for abuse or addiction. Controlled substances range from illegal street drugs to prescription medi-

---

18   RSC 1985, c F-27.
19   SC 1996, c 19.
20   RSC 1985, c N-1 (repealed by SC 1996, c 19, s 94).
21   *Narcotic Control Regulations*, CRC c 1041.

cations. A substance included in any of the Schedules I to V to the Act is defined by section 2 of the Act to be a "controlled substance."

Three principal regulations have been enacted pursuant to the Act, namely the *Industrial Hemp Regulations*,[22] the *Narcotic Control Regulations*,[23] and the *Precursor Control Regulations*.[24] These regulations are briefly summarized below.

1) Possession and Trafficking

Sections 4 to 7 of the *CDS Act* prohibit the possession, trafficking, importing, and exporting of controlled substances included in the Schedules to the Act unless authorized under the Regulations: in the case of possession, those in Schedules I, II, or III; in the case of trafficking, in addition to those included in these three schedules, any substance that is specified in Schedule IV or any substance that is represented or held out by the person trafficking to be such a substance; and in the case of importing into Canada or exporting from Canada, those included in all four schedules plus Schedule V and precursor substances included in Schedule VI.

Section 7.1 was added to the *CDS Act* in 2011[25] to prohibit the possession, production, sale, or importation of anything that the person knows will be used to produce or traffic in a substance referred to in item 18 of Schedule I (methamphetamine) or in item 19 (sub-item 8) (N-methyl-3,4-methylenedioxy-amphetamine (N,α-dimethyl-1,3-benzodioxole-5-ethanamine) (or ecstasy).

Each of the four sections referred to above contain provisions for the punishment of the offence created by it. Persons convicted of the offences are liable to fines and imprisonment that can range from $1,000 and six months to up to a maximum of life sentence, the severest punishment being reserved for possession for the purpose of trafficking (up to ten years if it is a Schedule III substance, up to life if it is a Schedule I or II substance). For the offence of possession for the purpose of exporting or importing any substance included in Schedule I or II, the punishment is life imprisonment; if the substance is listed in Schedules III or VI, the punishment is imprisonment for a period of up to ten years. Lighter sentences are prescribed in respect of substances listed in Schedules V and VI.

Where an offence under the Act is not specifically punished, or the offence is against a regulation other than a designated regulation within the

---

22 SOR/98-156.
23 Above note 21.
24 SOR/2002-359.
25 SC 2011, c 14.

meaning of Part V of the Act, the penalty on conviction on indictment is a maximum fine of $5,000, or imprisonment for a term not exceeding three years, or both; on summary conviction, the maximum fine is $1,000 and/or a prison term of six months.

2) Forfeiture of Offence-Related Property

On conviction of any "designated substance offences," in addition to fines and imprisonment, on the application of the Attorney General of Canada or of a province, whoever initiated the prosecution, the sentencing court is required by section 16 to order the forfeiture of any offence-related property to Her Majesty in right of Canada or the province as the case may be. The prosecution of an offence of exporting or importing a Schedule VI substance is initiated by the Attorney General of Canada, and the substance will be ordered forfeited to Her Majesty in right of Canada.

"Designated substance offences" are (1) offences under Part 1 of the Act, except simple possession of Schedule I, II, or III substances; and (2) a conspiracy or an attempt to commit, being an accessory after the fact in relation to, or any counselling in relation to an offence referred to in (1).

Section 2 of the Act defines an "offence-related property" as any property, other than a controlled substance, whether situate within or outside Canada, (1) by means of or in respect of which a designated substance offence is committed, (2) that is used in any manner in connection with the commission of a designated substance offence, or (3) that is intended for use for the purpose of committing a designated substance offence.

The forfeited substance or other offence-related property is to be disposed of in accordance with the law.

3) Industrial Hemp Regulations[26]

a) Definition

Section 1 of the *Industrial Hemp Regulations* defines "industrial hemp" to mean

> ... the plants and plant parts of the genera Cannabis, the leaves and flowering heads of which do not contain more than 0.3% THC w/w, and includes the derivatives of such plants and plant parts. It also in-

---

26 Above note 22.

cludes the derivatives of non-viable cannabis seed. It does not include plant parts of the genera Cannabis that consist of non-viable cannabis seed, other than its derivatives, or of mature cannabis stalks that do not include leaves, flowers, seeds or branches, or of fibre derived from those stalks (*chanvre industriel*).

Section 2 states that the *Industrial Hemp Regulations* apply, *inter alia*, to the importation, exportation, and possession of industrial hemp, as well as to an offer to do any of those things, but they do not apply to whole industrial hemp plants, their sprouts, leaves, flowers, or bracts, or to derivative or products made from them. They also apply to the production, sale, provision, transport, sending, or delivering of industrial hemp and for offering to do any of those things.

Section 3 excludes from the application of the Act and the Regulations the importation, exportation, or wholesale sale of a derivative of seed, viable grain, or non-viable cannabis seed, or a product made from that derivative, if the following conditions are met:

1) the derivative or product was not made from whole industrial hemp plants, including sprouts, or the leaves, flowers, or bracts of those plants;
2) a representative sample from each lot or batch has been found when laboratory tested to contain 10 µg/g THC or less;
3) in the case of importation or exportation, the shipment is accompanied by a certificate from a competent laboratory in the country of origin of the derivative or product that sets out the concentration of THC in the samples; and
4) in the case of the wholesale sale of a derivative, the package containing the derivative is labelled, "Contains 10 µg/g THC or less—Contient au plus 10 µg/g THC."

Section 3 further provides that if the importation, exportation, or wholesale sale has met the above conditions, and the product has not changed in any way that results in its containing more than 10 µg/g THC, the Act and the Regulations do not apply to the retail sale, provision, possession, transport, sending, or delivering of a derivative of seed, viable grain, or non-viable cannabis seed, or a product made from that derivative.

b) **Importation of Seed, Grain, or Hemp**

Sections 18 and 19 require a seed import licensee to import only seed that is of an approved cultivar or, in the case of a plant breeder, seed of a variety of industrial hemp specified in the licence, accompanied by a country of origin certificate issued by a competent authority of a country set out in the *List of Countries Approved for the Importation of Viable Grain*.[27]

An "approved cultivar" is any variety of industrial hemp designated by the Minister of Health in accordance with section 39 and specified in the above referred *List of Countries*.

Sections 21 to 25 sets out the procedure for obtaining a permit to import industrial hemp and the information to be provided in the application, the grounds for refusing to issue a permit, and the authority to revoke it. The import permit must be attached to the shipment of the industrial hemp, which is valid for a maximum of three months or shorter if the permit holder's import licence expires earlier.

Section 20 prohibits the importation of seed or viable grain solely for the purpose of conditioning, unless it is of an approved cultivar that will be exported once it has been conditioned. Conditioning is a process that renders viable grain into non-viable, that is, incapable of germination.

c) Exportation of Industrial Hemp

Sections 27 to 30 set out the procedure for obtaining a permit to export industrial hemp and the information to be provided in the application, the grounds for refusing to issue a permit, and the authority to revoke it. The export permit must be attached to the shipment of the industrial hemp, which is valid for a maximum period of three months or shorter if the permit holder's licence expires earlier.

4) *Narcotic Control Regulations*[28]

The *Narcotic Control Regulations* contain a comprehensive scheme for the control and regulation of narcotics through licensing and permits. They impose duties on dealers, pharmacists, practitioners, hospitals, and institutions, as well as law enforcement officials, with respect to possession, sale, export, import, handling, provision, delivery, transport, and all other activities involved to ensure that the rigid procedures set out in the Regulations are complied with. A "narcotic" is defined by the Regulations as "any substance set out in the Schedule or anything that contains a substance set out in the Schedule."

---

27 Published by Health Canada.
28 Above note 21.

This section is only concerned with the export and import aspects of the regulation and control and to activities necessarily incidental thereto.

a) Import and Export

Under the Regulations, and subject thereto, section 8 allows only a licensed dealer to produce, import, export, sell, send, deliver, or transport a narcotic. Eligibility rules to obtain a dealer's licence are set out in section 8.2. These are as follows:

1) the applicant must ordinarily reside in Canada and, if a corporation, must have its head office or an operating branch in Canada;
2) the applicant must appoint a senior qualified person (who can be the dealer himself or herself) with knowledge of and responsibility for compliance with the Act and the Regulations; and
3) the applicant must not have been convicted in the ten years preceding the date of the application for a licence, of any of the designated *Criminal Code* offences, or those specified in the *Food and Drugs Act*, the *Narcotic Control Act* (now repealed), and Part I of the *Controlled Drugs and Substances Act* other than section 4(1).

The person in charge appointed by the licensed dealer (or the licensed dealer himself or herself if in charge) must

1) have a knowledge of chemistry and pharmacology, and experience in those fields to properly carry out their responsibilities under the Regulations, and
2) be a pharmacist or practitioner registered by a professional licensing authority or possess a degree in applicable science—such as pharmacy, medicine, dentistry, veterinary medicine, pharmacology, organic chemistry, or chemical engineering—from a Canadian university or a university recognized by a Canadian university, or a professional body in Canada.

The qualified person in charge must work at the premises specified in the licence.

A licensed dealer may designate an alternate qualified person who has the same qualifications and knowledge and experience as the qualified person in charge.

The application procedure and requirements for the issuance of licence, and the grounds for refusal, suspension, and revocation of a licence are set out in sections 9, 9.1, and subsequent sections.

Holders of a position of responsibility for a narcotic on behalf of the Government of Canada or of a province, police force, hospital, or university in Canada may also apply for a dealer's licence.

b) Permit Required

A licensed dealer may only import into or export out of Canada a narcotic at the place specified in, and subject to the terms and conditions of, the permit issued under section 10.

c) Narcotics Schedule

The Schedule to the Regulations lists seventeen types of narcotics and their preparations, derivatives, alkaloids, salts, and so on, and include opium poppy, coca, methadone, heroin, and cannabis.

d) Prohibitions

A licenced dealer may, subject to the terms and conditions of the licence, produce, make, assemble, sell, provide, transport, send, or deliver only narcotics specified in the licence, but may not sell or provide them to any person except to another licensed dealer, a pharmacist, a practitioner, or an employee of or a practitioner in a hospital.

e) Duties of Licensed Dealer

Sections 15 to 29 set out the duties of the licensed dealer, which include the keeping of prescribed books and records, making them available for inspection and audit, furnishing information to Health Canada as required, securing of premises, and protecting against loss.

5) *Precursor Control Regulations*[29]

Section 2 of the *Controlled Drugs and Substances Act*[30] defines a "precursor" as a substance included in Schedule VI. Precursors are essential to the production of a controlled substance. They have a wide legitimate use in the production of consumer goods such as pharmaceuticals, fragrances, flavouring agents, petroleum products, fertilizers, and paints. For example, ephedrine and pseudoephedrine, commonly used in cold and decongestant medicine, are precursor chemicals that are used to produce methamphetamine.

---

29 Above note 24.
30 Above note 19.

Two classes of precursor are specified in the *Precursor Control Regulations*: Class A (substances listed in Part 1 of Schedule VI to the *CDS Act*) and Class B (substances listed in Part 2, or a mixture or preparation referred to in Part 3, of Schedule VI to the *CDS Act*). Any item or portion of item may be deleted and a new item or items added by a Governor in Council order if deemed necessary in the public interest.

This section is concerned only with the import and export of precursors.

a) Import and Export of Class A Precursors

Class A precursors are listed in Part 1 of Schedule VI, which contains twenty-three items, ranging from acetic anydride, ephedrine, and pseudoephedrine, to potassium permanganate and hydrochloric acid, and their salts. A preparation or mixture that contains any of these is placed in Part 3.

i) Permit

A licensed dealer may import or export a Class A precursor, or possess a Class A precursor for the purpose of export, only if the dealer holds a Class A permit for the import or export of the precursor named in the permit and complies with the conditions set out in the permit.

Section 10 prohibits the transportation or transhipment of a Class A precursor in transit through Canada to another country unless the person is authorized to do so by a permit issued under section 40.

ii) Authorization

The above prohibitions relating to import, export, transhipment in or transit through Canada to another country, sale, delivery, provision, possession, and so on do not apply to preparations and mixtures (Part 3, Schedule VI of *CDS Act*) if the person has a valid, unrevoked authorization certificate issued by Health Canada under section 49.

iii) Dealer Licensing

Sections 12 to 24 set out the licensing provisions for a dealer to import and export Class A precursors, including the eligibility criteria, procedure for issuance of a licence, grounds for refusal to issue a licence, amendment and surrender of a licence, suspension and revocation, and the expiration of the term. These provisions are almost identical to those for a licence under the *Narcotic Control Regulations*, described in Section D(4)(a), above in this chapter.

iv) Importation

As noted earlier, a licensed dealer must obtain a permit to import Class A precursors. The conditions for the issuance of a permit, eligibility, grounds for refusal, amendment, suspension, revocation, and so on are set out in sections 25 to 31, which, again, are similar to those in the *Narcotic Control Regulations*.

In addition, section 28.1 requires the licensed dealer, on the importation of a Class A precursor, to notify the Minister of Health, within fifteen days after a shipment has been released by customs, declaring the information specified in paragraphs (a) to (e) of that section, such as the name of the holder and the permit number for the shipment, the port of entry in Canada for the shipment, the name of the precursor being shipped, and if it is a preparation or mixture, the quantity of the precursor set out in Part 1 of Schedule VI with its contents.

b) Exportation

Sections 32 to 38 govern the application for an export permit, issuance of the permit, grounds for refusal, and so on, along the same lines as the application procedure for an import permit referred to in the previous sections. The licensed dealer must write his or her name and address and the principal place of business, the business number assigned by the Minister of National Revenue, the name or description of the chemical composition of the Class A precursor as stated in the licence and the Harmonized System Code (if it is a salt, the name of salt; if a preparation or mixture, its brand name and names of all precursors set out in Part 1 of Schedule VI with its contents; and, if a raw material, its purity). In addition, the applicant must give the name of the importer and its address in the country of final destination, the proposed means of transportation, the name of any proposed country of transit or transhipment, the proposed port of exit fom Canada, and the proposed date of export. If a broker is employed, the name of the broker must also be given.

i) Declaration

Within fifteen days after shipping a Class A precursor, the licensed dealer must provide the Minister of Health with a declaration containing the following information: the name of the licensed holder and permit number for the shipment', the port of exit from Canada; the date of export; the name of the precursor or description of its chemical composition; the quantity of the precursor being shipped; if it is a preparation or mixture, the quantity of all precursors set out in Part 1 of Schedule VI; and so on.

ii) In-Transit and Transhipment Permits

Section 39 sets out the procedure for the application of a permit for transit or transhipment of a Class A precursor if it is to be shipped from one country to another country by a route that requires it to pass through Canada. The exporter in the country of export or an agent of the exporter in Canada of that exporter must apply for the permit, which must contain the following information: name of the exporter, the address, and the telephone number in the country of export; the name of the importer, the address, and the telephone number in the country of final destination; the name, address, and telephone number of the person who will be responsible for the precursor while it is in Canada; the name, quantity, and so on of the precursor and, if it is a raw material, its purity; the expected date or dates of transit or transhipment in Canada and ports of entry in and exit from Canada; each proposed means of transport that is to be used whilst in Canada; if there is transhipment, and if applicable, every place in Canada at which the precursor will be stored during transhipment and the expected duration of each storage; and so on.

Sections 40 to 46 set out the rules relating to the issuance of the transit/transhipment permit, grounds for refusal, surrender of permit at the ports of entry set out in the permit, revocation or suspension of permit, and so on.

Section 43 requires the holder of a permit for transit or transhipment to notify the Minister of Health in writing of the departure date of the shipment within fifteen days after it leaves Canada.

iii) Authorization Certificate

Sections 48 to 57 set out regulations relating to the issuing of an authorization certificate for preparations and mixtures of Class A precursors. A person who produces or imports a Class A precursor that is a preparation or mixture, or desires to produce or import, must appy for an authorization certificate containing all the particulars set out in the section, such as the name and licence number and so on, and information about the preparation or mixture. Sections 49 to 65 set out the application procedure, eligibility criteria, rules relating to the issuance of a certificate, grounds for refusal, suspension, and so on. These rules are almost identical to those for the issuing of a permit to import the precursor itself.

Section 51 requires every person who imports or exports a Class A precursor that is a preparation or mixture mentioned in the authorization certificate to ensure that the shipment is accompanied by a document containing the statement that the preparation or mixture, as the case may be, is subject to an authorization issued under section 49. The authorization certificate number must be quoted.

c) Class B Precursors

Class B precursors are listed in Part 2 of Schedule VI, which has only six items: acetone, ethyl ether, hydrochloric acid (also a Class A precursor), methyl ethyl ketone, sulphuric acid, and toluene. Each of these includes synthetic forms, and a preparation or mixture that contains any of these comes under Part 3 of the same Schedule.

i) Limitation on Activities and Exemption

Under section 57, no person other than a registered dealer may produce for the purpose of sale or provision, possess for the purpose of export except under conditions set out in the section, or import a Class B precursor.

A person who conducts the activities referred to in section 57 above is exempted by section 55 from the requirements of the Regulations except those who apply to produce for the purpose of sale or provision, if the preparation or mixture contains a precursor set out in Part 2 of Schedule VI of the *CDS Act* and the contained precursor either alone or with any other precursor of the same type does not constitute more than 30 percent of the preparation or mixture by weight or volume, and in the case of a solid or liquid, by volume.

Despite section 57, a person may import, export, or possess a Class B precursor that is a preparation or mixture, or possess it for those purposes, if the preparation or mixture is subject to a valid and unrevoked authorization certificate issued under section 77.

ii) Dealer Registration

Sections 58 to 68 set out requirements for registration as a dealer of a Class B precursor, which are identical to those for a registered dealer of Class A precursors, and include eligibility, the appointment of a senior qualified person in charge and an alternate person at the place where the activities of the dealer are conducted, application procedure, issuance of registration, and grounds for refusal and suspension.

iii) Export Permit

Rules relating to the requirement of a permit to export a Class B precursor, such as the application procedure, issuance of a permit, grounds for refusal of a permit, suspension and revocation, and so on, are set out in sections 69 to 75. Again, these are identical to the rules for an import permit described in Section D(5)(a)(iv), above in this chapter.

iv) Authorization Certificate

A registered dealer who produces for the purpose of sale or provision, or imports, or desires to do either, a Class B precursor that is a preparation or mixture, requires an authorization certificate issued under section 77. These rules are identical to those for a Class A precursor that is a preparation or mixture described in Section D(5)(b)(iii), above in this chapter.

E. THE *HEALTH OF ANIMALS ACT*[31]

The *Health of Animals Act* was enacted by Parliament in 1990, repealing two older statutes, the *Animal Disease and Protection Act*[32] and the *Livestock and Livestock Products Act*.[33]

The purpose of the Act is to protect food-producing animals from disease and toxic substances introduced both within and from outside Canada, as well as to protect domestic animals generally from such diseases. This section is concerned only with the regulation and control of imports and exports of livestock and birds, including their products and by-products, and to a limited extent pet animals and birds. The *Health of Animals Regulations*[34] contain the detailed regulatory regime for the control of diseases and toxic substances, including the importation and exportation and humane transport, licensing, and permitting, and other operations incidental thereto. The Minister of Agriculture and Agri-Food, and in some cases, the Governor in Council, is authorized to prescribe regulations. Enforcement is the responsibility of the Canadian Food Inspection Agency (CFIA).

1) Importation

a) Statutory Prohibitions

Sections 14 to 18 of the Act contain prohibitions and requirements relating to importations, which are elaborated in the Regulations under Parts II to VII.

Section 14 empowers the Minister of Agriculture and Agri-Food ("the Minister") to make regulations prohibiting the importation of any animal or

---

[31] SC 1990, c 21.
[32] RSC 1970, c A-13 (repealed).
[33] RSC 1985, c L-9, repealed by SC 1990, c 21.
[34] CRC, c 296.

other thing into Canada, any part of Canada, or any Canadian port, either generally or from any place named in the Regulations, for such period as the Minister considers necessary for the purpose of preventing a disease or toxic substance from being introduced into or spreading within Canada. Section 15 prohibits a person from possessing or disposing of any animal that the person knows was imported in contravention of the Act or the Regulations.

Section 16 requires every person who imports into Canada an animal, any product or by-product or food, or a veterinary biologic, or any other thing used in respect of animals, or contaminated by a disease or toxic substance, to present the animal and the other things herein referred, to an inspector or officer of the CFIA, or to an officer of the CBSA, before or at the time of importation, for inspection. The inspector or officer may, if necessary, detain the animal or other thing until it is inspected or otherwise dealt with as authorized by the Act or the Regulations. The Minister is authorized to make regulations exempting animals or things from the obligations of the section and respecting the manner of presenting the animals or things for inspection.

Section 17 authorizes the seizure and forfeiture of an animal or thing that is imported in contravention of the provisions of the Act or the Regulations, and empowers the CFIA to order the disposal of the same as it directs. Instead of seizing as forfeit, the CFIA may, under section 18, permit the importer, owner, or person in possession or control of the animal or thing to remove the same from Canada, but if that person fails to do so, the animal or thing may be forfeited.

In respect of importation and exportation, section 64 of the Act gives the Governor in Council wide authority to make regulations,

- prohibiting or regulating the importation, exportation, and possession of animals and things in order to prevent the introduction of any vector, disease, or toxic substance into Canada, or into another country from Canada;
- subjecting animals and things that may transmit a disease or toxic substance to quarantine or requiring their destruction on importation into Canada, and requiring the disposal on importation into Canada of things that may transmit a disease or toxic substance;
- requiring proof of the fact that animals imported into or passing through Canada have not been brought from any place where there was at the time of their embarkation a disease or toxic substance;
- prescribing or regulating the importation of garbage into Canada and requiring the handling and disposal of garbage imported into Canada;

- prohibiting or regulating the importation, preparation, manufacturing, preserving, packing, labelling, storage, sale, use, disposal, and so on of products of animal deadyards, rendering plants, and animal food factories, and regulating their purity, potency, efficacy, and safety; and
- governing the issue, renewal, suspension, or revocation of licences, permits, approvals, certificates, or other documents on such terms and conditions as may be required for the purposes of the Act.

b) Regulatory Regime

The regulatory regime for importation is contained in Parts II to VII of the *Health of Animals Regulations*, sections 7 to 62.

i) Part II: General Provisions, Germplasm, and Regulated Animal

Sections 7 to 9 of Part II contain general provisions relating to Part II. In accordance with section 7, the Minister may designate a country or part of a country as being free of a disease or as posing a negligible risk for a disease. Where a certificate is required to accompany an importation, the importer is permitted by section 8 to file it electronically, but the Minister may require the original of the certificate to be produced. For the purpose of preventing the introduction of a communicable disease, section 9 gives an inspector the power to order the quarantine of an animal or thing imported into Canada if the inspector finds or suspects that a thing is a disease agent, or an animal or thing is affected by or contaminated with a communicable disease, or information or documentation required by or under the Act or the Regulations to be presented has not been presented to an inspector.

a. Definitions

A "germplasm" is defined by section 10 as the semen of a male animal, germ cells, or genetic material taken from a male or female germ cell, but not a hatching egg.

A "regulated animal" is defined by section 10 to mean a hatching egg, turtle, tortoise, bird, honeybee, or mammal but does not include (1) a germplasm defined above; (2) members of the orders *Catacea*, *Pinnipedia*, *and Sirenia*; or (3) members of the order *Rodentia* other than the following: (a) prairie dogs, African giant pouched rats, and squirrels of the family *Sciuridae* from any country; and (b) any other members of the order from Africa.

b. Prohibition

Section 11 prohibits the importation of any germplasm of any regulated animal except in accordance with a permit issued by the CFIA under section

160 or in accordance with all applicable provisions of the Import Reference Document. An Import Reference Document is a document prepared by the CFIA entitled "Import Reference Document dated January 25, 2007 and Policy AHPD-DSAE-IE-20020304" ("IRD").

Section 11 also prohibits the importation of a regulated animal unless it is authorized by a permit issued under section 160 and the provisions of section 51 are complied with. However, a permit is not required for the import of a regulated animal from an area that is designated by the IRD as an area of "equivalent risk" for an animal of that species, or as being from a "low risk area," from an "undesignated area," or for the transportation of the regulated animal (other than porcine) between Rainy River, Ontario, and Sprague, Manitoba, but passing through the US state of Minnesota, provided the following requirements are met:

- The animal, in the case of "equivalent risk area," must be accompanied by a certificate of an official veterinarian from that area that (1) clearly identifies the animal and its area of origin; and (2) verifies that a veterinarian has inspected the animal within five days before it was exported to Canada and found it to be clinically healthy and fit to travel without undue suffering.
- In the case of a "low risk area," the importer must meet any applicable post-entry conditions set out in the IRD and the animal must be accompanied by an official veterinarian's certificate as described above for the import of an animal from an "equivalent risk area," certifying that the animal conforms with all applicable conditions other than post-entry conditions that are set out in the IRD.
- In the case of an import from an area that is an undesignated area for an animal of that species, all provisions in the IRD that relate to the importation of that species, if any, must be complied with.
- A regulated animal that is imported for slaughter or for confinement in a restricted premises, such as a zoo or laboratory facility, must comply with all applicable provisions of the IRD and the following conditions must be met:
  » the animal must be transported directly from its port of entry to its destination in accordance with a licence issued by the CFIA under section 160;
  » the animal must be transported by means of a conveyance that has had all exits by which the animal could leave the conveyance sealed by an official of the government of the country from which it is imported; and

> the animal must not come into contact with a national herd in Canada.
- If a regulated animal is not a porcine, it must be transported directly between Rainy River, Ontario, and Sprague, Manitoba, via the state of Minnesota, by means of a conveyance that had all exits by which the animal could leave the conveyance sealed by an official of the Government of Canada or of the United States.

c. False or Misleading Information

Section 13 prohibits the importation of a regulated animal if a certificate or an import permit, as the case may be, required by Part II, contains any false or misleading information.

d. Animal in Contact with Diseased Animals or Things

Section 14 prohibits the importation of a regulated animal that has on or after the day described in section 14(2) been in contact with another animal or with a thing used in respect of another animal, if that other animal poses a greater risk for the transmission or spreading of a disease than does the regulated animal. The day referred to is specified by section 14(2) as the earliest of the day on which begins any period of isolation, any testing, or the performance of any other procedure required in respect of the importation by the IRD or by a permit issued under section 160.

e. Identification and Record Keeping

Sections 15 and 16 require every person who imports a regulated animal to clearly identify it at the time of importation, and keep records that clearly indicate its original source and date and place of importation.[35]

ii) Part III: Animal Products

Part III of the Regulations has two sections (sections 34 and 34.1) that contain provisions with respect to the importation of milk and milk products and unfertilized bird eggs and egg products.

a. Milk and Milk Products from a Country Other than the United States

Section 34(1) prohibits the importation of milk or milk products into Canada from any country or part of country, other than the United States, unless the country or part of the country is designated, pursuant to section 7, as free of foot-and-mouth disease and the person produces a certificate of origin signed by an official of the government of the country of origin that

---

35 Detailed requirements relating to the transportation are set out in Part XII of the Regulations, discussed in Section E(1)(b)(x), below in this chapter.

shows that the country or part of the country of origin is the designated country or part thereof that is free of foot-and-mouth disease.

b. Bird Eggs or Egg Products from a Country Other than the United States
Section 34(2) contains the same prohibition with respect to the import of unfertilized bird eggs or egg products into Canada from a country or part of country other than the United States as in section 34(1). The diseases referred to in this section are Newcastle disease (avian pneumopencephalitis) and fowl plague. There is, however, a further requirement: the eggs must be packed in containers that are clean and free from dirt and residue of eggs. The prohibition against import of unfertilized eggs referred to herein does not apply to eggs that are transported under seal of an inspector direct from the place of entry to a registered processed egg station approved by the CFIA.

c. Exemption
Section 34.1 allows the importation of animal products referred to in section 34 if the importer produces a document that shows the details of the treatment of the animal product and the inspector is satisfied, based on the source of the document, the information contained in the document, and any other relevant information available to the inspector and, where necessary, on the inspection of the animal product, that the importation of the animal product into Canada would not, or would not be likely to, result in the introduction into Canada, or the spread into Canada, of a vector, disease, or toxic substance.

iii) Part IV: Animal By-products and Animal Pathogens
Part IV has 14 sections, from 40 to 53. They deal with the importation of a variety of articles, including animal by-products (raw wool, hair, bristles, hides or skin that originate from a bird or from any mammal, except a member of the order *Rodentia, Cetacea, Pinnipedia, and Sirenia*); animal glands and organs; boneless beef; gluestock; meats and bone meal; rendering plant products; aircraft garbage and ship's refuse and stores; carcasses of game animals; animal pathogens, animal or other organisms, animal blood and serum; as well as animal food.

a. Prohibition
Unless authorized by Part IV, and the import is in accordance with that Part, section 40 prohibits the importation into Canada of an animal by-product, manure, or thing containing animal by-product. An animal by-product is defined by section 2 as an animal by-product that originated from a bird or

from any mammal, except a member of the orders *Rodentia, Cetacea, Pinnipedia,* and *Sirenia.*

b. Exemption

Section 41 allows the importation of animal by-products, manure, or things containing animal by-products, except those described in the following sections,

- section 45—gluestock;
- section 46—rendering plant products;
- sections 47—garbage, and 47.1—aircraft garbage;
- section 49—carcasses of game animals;
- section 50—matted or blood-stained wool, hair, and so on;
- sections 51 and 51.2—animal pathogens, animals or other organisms, animal blood and serum; and
- section 53—animal food.

The importation will be allowed under two circumstances. The country of origin must be either

1) the United States—but it must not be derived from an animal of the species *Bovinae* or *Caprinae*, or
2) a country or a part of the country that is designated under section 7 as being free of, or as posing a negligible risk for, any reportable disease, any disease referred in Schedule VI, and any serious epizootic disease to which the species from which the by-product, manure, or thing was derived is susceptible and that can be transmitted by the by-product, manure, or thing. The importation is allowed only if
    a) the importer produces a certificate of origin signed by an official of the government of that country attesting to that origin; or
    b) the by-product, manure, or thing has been collected, treated, prepared, processed, stored, and handled in a manner that would prevent the introduction into Canada of a reportable disease or disease referred to in Schedule VII, and any serious epizootic disease to which the species from which the animal by-product, manure, or thing is susceptible and that can be transmitted by it, and the person produces a certificate signed by an official of the government of the country of origin attesting that the by-product, manure, or thing was collected, treated, prepared, processed, stored, and handled in the manner referred to above and the certificate shows the details of how it was collected, treated, prepared, processed, stored, and handled.

The exemption in section 41(1) does not apply in respect of manure found in or on a vehicle that is entering Canada from the United States if the manure was produced by animals other than swine that are being transported by the vehicle.

c. By-products Not Intended as Animal Food

Despite section 41, a person may import into Canada an animal by-product or thing containing an animal by-product, other than that described in sections 45 (gluestock), 46 (rendering plant products), 47 (garbage) and 47.1 (aircraft garbage), 49 (carcasses of game animals), 50 (matted or bloodstained wool, hair, bristles, and so on), 51 and 51.2 (animal pathogens, animals or other organisms, animal blood and serum), and 53 (animal food), if an inspector has reasonable grounds to believe that the importation of the by-product or thing, by its nature, end use, or the manner in which it has been processed, would not or would not be likely to result in the introduction into Canada of a reportable disease or disease listed in Schedule VII, and any serious epizootic disease of which the species from which the by-product or thing was derived is susceptible, and that can be transmitted by the by-product or thing, and the by-product or thing is not intended for use as animal food or as an ingredient in animal food.

Section 41.1(2) prohibits the use of the exempted animal by-product or thing as animal food or as an ingredient in animal food.

d. Raw Wool, Hair, or Bristles, and Hide or Skin

Section 42 allows a person to import raw wool, hair, and bristles, and untanned hide or skins ("animal by-product") from a country referred to in section 41 only if one of the following conditions is met:

1) the animal by-product is transported under seal of an inspector directly from the place of entry to an approved disinfection establishment for disinfection in accordance with the Regulations, or
2) in the case of untanned hide or skin, an inspector is satisfied that the article
   a) is a hard dried hide or skin of an animal;
   b) has been pickled in a solution of salt containing mineral acid and was packed in a leak-proof container while still wet with such solution; or
   c) is the hide or skin of an animal that has been treated with lime so as to become de-haired.

e. Animal Glands and Organs

Section 42.1 allows a person to import raw animal glands and organs into Canada from a country not referred to in section 41, only if the glands and organs are transported under the seal of an inspector directly from the place of entry to an establishment approved by the CFIA for purposes of processing, if the establishment processes the raw glands and organs in a manner that would prevent the introduction of a reportable disease, any disease referred to in Schedule VII, and any serious epizootic disease from which the raw glands and organs were taken is susceptible and that may be transmitted by the glands and organs. Section 2 defines "animal glands and organs" as including oxtail or bile, rennet, and similar substances taken from a domestic animal.

Section 42.1(3) prohibits the importer of the raw animal glands and organs to transport it to any place other than the approved processing establishment.

f. Cooked Boneless Beef

Section 43 allows a person to import into Canada cooked boneless beef from a country not referred to in section 41 only if (1) it was processed in a place and in a manner approved by the CFIA; (2) it is accompanied by a meat inspection certificate of an official veterinarian of the exporting country in a form and manner approved by the CFIA; and (3) on examination, the inspector is satisfied that it is thoroughly cooked.

g. Importation of Gluestock

"Gluestock" is defined by section 2 to mean hair, bones, hoofs, horns, fleshings, hide, and tags or parings of an animal or any other product of an animal that may be used in the manufacture of glue.

Section 45 allows the importation of gluestock only if all the following conditions are met:

1) The conditions referred to in section 41 are met.
2) The importer of the gluestock transports it directly from the place of entry to an establishment approved by the CFIA for purposes of processing the gluestock in a manner that would prevent the introduction of any reportable disease, any disease referred to in Schedule VII, and any serious epizootic disease from which the gluestock was taken is susceptible and that may be transmitted by the gluestock; and the person produces a certificate signed by an official of the government of the country of origin attesting that the gluestock was so collected, treated, prepared,

processed, stored, and handled, and the certificate shows the details of how it was collected, treated, prepared, processed, stored, and handled.
3) The gluestock is transported only to the approved establishment.

h. Rendering Plant Products

Section 46 prohibits the importation of meat and bone meal, bone meal, blood meal, and other rendering plant products unless, in addition to the requirements of sections 166 to 171, the country of origin, or a part of that country, is designated under section 7 as being free of, or as posing negligible risk for, any reportable disease, any disease referred to in Schedule VII, or any epizootic disease to which the product from which it is derived is susceptible; the person produces a certificate signed by an official of the government of the country of origin attesting to that origin; and an inspector has reasonable grounds to believe that the product has been processed in a manner that would prevent the introduction of the above diseases.

Sections 166 to 171 regulate the importation of products of rendering plants and are found in Part XIV of the Regulations, as discussed in Section E(1)(b)(vii), below in this chapter.

i. Garbage, Refuse, and Animal Manure

Sections 46, 47, and 47.1 contain strict rules in relation to the importation into or discharge in Canada of ship's refuse, aircraft garbage (for example, food wastes, animal and human wastes, and animal manure), with a view to preventing the introduction of any reportable disease, any disease referred to in Schedule VII, or any epizootic disease, and so on. Although specific rules apply to refuse, garbage, or animal manure carried on board or emanating from the United States and from other countries, they are not very different nor less stringent.

j. Ships' Stores

Section 48 prohibits the importation of meat or meat products into Canada from a country or part of a country not referred to in section 41, if the meat or meat by-product is kept on a ship as ships' stores.

k. Carcasses of Game Birds

Section 49 prohibits the importation of a carcass of a game bird unless the CBSA has determined under the *Customs Tariff* that the carcass originated in the United States and the importer holds a permit for that game animal issued by the United States or a US state under its applicable legislation. The number of carcasses that can be imported cannot exceed the number established by the legislation of the United States or US state.

l. Matted or Blood-Stained Wool, Hair, or Bristles

Section 50 prohibits the importation into Canada of matted or blood-stained wool, hair, or bristles; or any animal by-product or manure that was derived from an animal affected by anthrax, foot-and-mouth disease, rinderpest, Bovine Spongiform Encephalopathy (BSE), or any reportable disease, any disease referred to in Schedule VII, and any serious epizootic disease to which the species from which the by-product or manure was derived is susceptible and that can be transmitted by the by-product or manure.

m. Animal Pathogens and By-products

Animal pathogens, animal products and by-products, other organisms carrying animal pathogens or part of one, and animal blood or serum, other than a veterinary biologic, from a bird or mammal (except a member of the orders *Rodentia*, *Cetacea*, *Pinnipedia*, and *Serinea*) that are to be used in animals, are prohibited from importation into Canada by section 51 unless by a permit issued under section 160 by the CFIA. When they are imported under the permit, the importer must strictly adhere to the conditions specified in the permit regarding the movement of the imported pathogens, and so on, as required by section 51.1.

Section 51.2, however, allows the importation from the United States of animal blood or animal serum, other than a veterinary biologic, if it does not contain an animal pathogen or part of one, if the blood or serum is not derived from an animal of the subfamily *Bovinae* or *Caprinae*. The section also allows the importation of the blood or serum from a country of origin, or part of the country, that is designated under section 7 as being free of, or as posing a negligible risk for, any reportable disease, any disease referred to in Schedule VII, and any serious epizootic disease to which the species from which the blood or serum is derived is susceptible, and the person produces a certificate of origin signed by an official of the government of the country of origin attesting that the blood or semen has been collected, treated, prepared, processed, stored, and handled in the manner referred to above and the certificate shows the details of how it was collected, treated, prepared, processed, stored, and handled.

n. Animal Food with Animal Products or By-products

Section 53(1) prohibits the importation of animal food that contains an animal product or by-product, except in the following cases:

1) If the country of origin of the animal food is the United States and the animal food is not from an animal of the subfamily *Bovinae* or *Caprinae*;

or if the animal food, and each animal product and by-product contained in that food, originated from a part of the country that is designated under section 7 as being free of, or as posing a negligible risk for, any reportable disease, any disease referred to in Schedule VII, and any serious epizootic disease to which the species from which the animal food, or animal product or by-product is derived, is susceptible, and the person produces a certificate of origin signed by an official of the government of the country of origin attesting to that origin.

2) In the case of animal food that is carried on board a vessel, unless the master of the vessel certifies that no ruminant or swine, other than those imported in accordance with a permit issued under section 160 was taken on board the vessel.

The same prohibition against importation, and the same exemption as in section 53(1)(a), applies under section 53(2) to animal products and by-products imported into Canada that are to be used as animal food or as an ingredient in animal food.

iv) Part V: Fodder

Part V consists of a single section (section 54), which prohibits the importation of fodder, other than grains, cereals, and seeds, to be used to feed ruminants, swine, or horses. The United States is exempt from this prohibition.

v) Part VI: Packing Material, Beehives, and Beeswax

Part VI has two sections: sections 55 and 57. Section 55 concerns the importation of packing material, and section 55 concerns the importation of beehives and beeswax.

a. Packing Material

Section 55(1) prohibits the importation into Canada of hay, straw, or grasses in which merchandise, goods, or articles are packed unless (1) the shipment is accompanied by a certificate of an official veterinary of the exporting country showing that the hay, straw, or grass were disinfected in a manner approved by the CFIA, or (2) in the absence of the certificate, the hay, straw, or grass is disinfected on arrival under the supervision of an inspector at a fumigation station approved by the CFIA or is incinerated. However, an exemption is given by section 55(2) for packing material from a country designated by the CFIA as free of foot-and-mouth disease, pursuant to section 7.

b. Beehives and Beeswax

Used beehives and used beehive equipment are prohibited from importation into Canada by section 57. Bee products for bee feeding are also prohibited by the same section, unless they are accompanied by a certificate stating that they have been treated in a manner approved by the CFIA to prevent the introduction or spread of any disease; or they are transported under the seal of an inspector directly from the point of importation to an establishment approved by the CFIA for treatment.

vi) Part XI: Veterinary Biologics

A "veterinary biologic" is defined by section 2 of the Act as a "helminth, protozoa or microorganism, a substance or mixture of substances derived from animals, or a substance of synthetic origin." Section 2 of the Regulations extends the definition to include any veterinary biologic derived through biotechnology.

Section 121 requires a CFIA permit to import a veterinary biologic. The veterinary biologic must be imported in accordance with the permit conditions and must be directly shipped to Canada from the manufacturer's premises under the applicable foreign laws, as designated in the permit. Details required to be furnished in the application, the submission of samples, and so on are specified in section 122.

Unless the veterinary biologic is packed and labelled in accordance with the Regulations, and all information required by section 134 is clearly and prominently displayed and readily visible to a purchaser, it cannot be imported, sold, offered for sale, or advertised. Section 133 exempts one-shot killed veterinary biologic that is packed in ready-to-use syringes and in sealed pouches that carry the label.

vii) Part XIV: Products of Rendering Plants

a. Definition

Section 2 of the Act defines a rendering plant to mean a place where

- animal by-products are prepared or treated for use in or converted into fertilizers, animal food, fats, or oils, other than fats or oils used for human consumption;
- a substance resulting from a process of preparation or treatment of animal by-products is stored, packed, or marked; or
- a substance resulting from that process is shipped.

b. Offence

Section 167 of the Regulations makes it an offence, punishable under the Act, for any person to import, or be in possession, care, or control of a product of a rendering plant, or to sell or distribute the product, without the documentation required by the Regulations in relation to the product, or without marking the product conspicuously, legibly, and indelibly on any label or any packaging or container containing the product with the following statement (in both English and French) required by section 168(4): "Feeding this product to cattle, sheep, deer or other ruminants is illegal and is subject to fines or other punishment under the *Health of Animals Act*."

c. Requirements to Facilitate Recall

Section 170.1 requires an importer, a manufacturer, or a person who packages, labels, stores, distributes, sells, or advertises for sale any animal food for ruminants, equines, porcines, chickens, turkeys, ducks, geese, ratites, or game birds, to establish and maintain written procedures to facilitate effective recall of the animal food.

Section 171.2 requires every importer or other persons referred to above who imports a fertilizer or fertilizer supplement containing a prohibited product other than a rendered fat to keep for ten years records that are sufficient to facilitate effective recall of the fertilizer or fertilizer supplement, including the name, lot number, and other information used to identify the product, the name and address of any person to whom the product is sold or distributed, and a description of the product, including the name and quantity.

Section 162 defines a "prohibited product" to mean anything that is or that contains any protein that originated from a mammal other than (1) porcine or equine; (2) milk or milk products; (3) gelatin derived exclusively from hides or skins, or products of gelatin derived therefrom; (4) blood or blood products; or (5) rendered fats derived from ruminants that contain no more than 0.15 percent insoluble impurities from products.

viii) Part XVI: Aquatic Animals

a. Prohibition

An "aquatic animal" is defined by section 190 as any finfish, mollusc, or crustacean, or these at any stage, as well as any germplasm of these animals. Section 191 prohibits the importation of aquatic animals without a CFIA permit issued under section 160. However, certain pet aquatic animals listed in Schedule III[36] can be imported without a permit by its owner if the owner presents proof of ownership and identity of the aquatic animals to the inspector, and the owner had not in the previous ninety days imported an aquatic animal. The section requires the owner who imports the aquatic animal to keep the records of the importation, to keep the aquatic animal in an aquarium in the owner's household, and, for a year following the importation, to not expose it to any other aquatic animal except those kept in the household.

Despite section 191, an aquatic animal listed in Schedule III may be imported without a permit under section 192 by an owner, or picked up by the owner at the point of entry into Canada, if (1) the aquatic animal is for personal use, (2) the person proves his or her identity and the manner in which the aquatic animal was acquired, and (3) the aquatic animal does not exceed the quantitative limits imposed by the section, namely four crustaceans, three kilograms of molluscs, and ten finfish that are not eviscerated (that is, where the internal organs, excluding the brain and gills, have been removed).

b. Aquatic Animals Not in Schedule III

Section 194 prohibits the importation of an aquatic animal that is not listed in Schedule III, unless it is accompanied by a document that is satisfactory to an inspector that includes (1) the name and address of the exporter and the importer; (2) the taxonomic name of the aquatic animal, the life stage, and the number being imported, if more than one; and (3) the country in which the aquatic animal was born or from which the germplasm came from, and whether the aquatic animal was born in captivity or in the wild.

c. Carcasses and Offal

An "offal" is defined by section 190 to mean the waste portions, including the visceral and non-visceral organs, cut-offs, and raw material of an aquatic animal.

Section 195 prohibits the importation of a carcass or offal of a finfish, mollusc, or crustacean listed in Schedule III without a CFIA permit issued under section 160 and in accordance with the permit conditions, which are

1) in the case of a finfish, its carcass or part of its carcass is for use as bait; for use in feeding to, or manufacturing feed for, aquatic animals; for research or diagnosis; or, if the finfish is eviscerated, for any purpose that will produce offal or effluent containing anything from finfish;

---

36 Schedule III lists 235 types of finfish, 54 types of molluscs, and 116 types of crustaceans.

2) in the case of a mollusc or a crustacean, its carcass or part of its carcass is for use as bait; for use in feeding to, or manufacturing feed for, aquatic animals; for research or diagnosis; or, if the mollusc or crustacean is eviscerated, for any purpose that will produce offal or effluent containing anything from the mollusc or crustacean.

The same conditions apply to the offal as for a finfish, mollusc and crustacean.

Where a permit, certificate, or other document is required for the removal or transportation of an aquatic animal, section 202 requires the person having the possession, care, or control of the aquatic animal to produce that document when requested, to an inspector or a peace officer appointed under the Act.

ix) Part VII: Quarantine of Imported Animals

Sections 58 to 62 of Part VII set out rules concerning the quarantine of imported animals. Unless exempted by the Regulations, an imported animal is subject to inspection, testing, and treatment. For that reason, animals may only be admitted at a quarantine port, an inspection port, or other place approved by the CFIA.

If an animal is imported by air and comes from any country other than the United States, it may be admitted only at one of eight airports: Gander, Halifax, Montreal, Toronto, Winnipeg, Calgary, Edmonton, and Vancouver. On importation, the CFIA may require the animal to be quarantined and tested at a quarantine port or other place approved by the CFIA for quarantine purposes. The reason for quarantine is to prevent the introduction of a communicable disease into Canada or into any other country from Canada. If the animal fails to prove negative to any test for a disease, the CFIA may order the importer, or the person in possession, care, or control, to remove the animal from Canada or to destroy it.

x) Part XII: Transportation of Animals

Part XII (sections 136 to 159) contains a comprehensive code on the transportation of animals that enter or leave Canada, or are transported within Canada.

a. Prevention of Injury or Undue Suffering

In order to ensure safety and prevent injury and undue suffering, in accordance with sections 138 to 159, every animal is subject to inspection at all times by an inspector to ensure that they are loaded, unloaded, transported, and provided with proper ventilation in the conveyance, and, if in a cage, that they are fed, watered, cleaned when necessary, and cared for and treated if injured or sick while they are being transported to their destination. Containers and crates, loading and unloading equipment, ramps, gangways, and the conveyance itself must meet the requirements of Part XII. The following are some of the most important provisions that apply to railway cars, motor vehicles, aircraft, and vessels, and to containers and crates:

- Section 138—Sick, pregnant, and unfit animals must not be transported. This section prohibits the carriage for exportation out of Canada of any animal that is affected with or suffering from a communicable disease; and the loading, unloading, or transport of any animal that by reason of infirmity, illness, fatigue, or any other cause cannot be transported without undue suffering during the expected journey, or an animal that is expected to give birth during the journey, and, subject to exception, an animal that has not been fed and watered within five days before being loaded, if the expected duration of the animal's confinement is longer than twenty-four hours from the time of loading. Some exceptions apply.
- Section 139—Loading and unloading equipment must meet the requirements specified in Part XII. The section prohibits the beating of an animal that is being loaded or unloaded, or to load or unload it in a way that is likely to cause injury or undue suffering to the animal. The ramp, gangway, chute, box, or other apparatus used by a carrier must be maintained and used in a way so as not to cause injury or undue suffering; the slope of the ramp that loads or unloads livestock must not be greater than 45 degrees; ramps and gangways must have sides of sufficient strength and height to prevent animals from falling off, and so on.
- Section 140—Overcrowding the conveyance (loading to such an extent as to cause injury or undue suffering) is prohibited.
- Section 141—Animals must be segregated, based upon their species, weight, age, and propensity to charge at and injure other animals; female animals and their suckling offspring should be kept together; cows, sows, and mares with their suckling to be segregated from all other animals during transit; groups of bulls, de-tusked boars, rams, and goat buds, if mature, must be segregated from all other animals during transport.
- Section 142—Animals must not be transported unless each animal is able to stand in its natural position without coming into contact

with a deck or roof; provision must be made for the draining of urine from all decks or levels.
- Section 143—Animals must be protected from injury or sickness. It is prohibited to transport an animal in a conveyance, crate, or container if injury or undue suffering is likely to be caused to the animal by reason of inadequate construction of the conveyance, unsecured fittings, presence of bolt-heads, angles, and other projections; if there is undue exposure to the weather; and if there is inadequate ventilation.
- Sections 146 and 147—Regarding ventilation of aircraft and vessels, there must be provided ventilation that provides change of air every five minutes (four minutes on a flight, five minutes on a vessel on lower decks). Natural ventilation on main deck and superstructure is sufficient.
- Section 148—An adequate supply of food and potable water in transit must be provided.
- Section 149—Special food for calves must be provided.
- Section 152—There must be attendants and inspectors in the conveyance.
- Section 153—There must be adequate protection on board vessels.
- Section 154—Animals must be fully secured: bovine, if not in a pen, must be securely tied by the head or neck to a securing rail with a halter or rope; equines must be tied by rope in such a manner as to prevent them from biting other animals or striking their heads on the deck above; sheep, goat, and swine must be secured in pens or enclosed containers.
- Sections 156 and 157—Proper lighting and insulation of the vessel must be provided: there must be adequate lighting to permit animals to be fed, watered, and properly cared for; animals must not be housed near the engine or boiler room unless there are adequate casings separating them.
- Section 159—Veterinary drugs must be carried on board a vessel.

b. Report of Death or Injury of Animal

Section 158 requires a sea carrier to provide suitable humane killing devices that are in working order, and an adequate supply of ammunition for the device, for destroying an animal if the animal cannot be kept alive without undue suffering. On the completion of a voyage or flight, section 159 requires a sea or air carrier to report to the veterinary inspector at the port of embarkation respecting any animal that died or was killed or seriously injured during the voyage or flight, stating in each case the cause of the death or injury.

2) Exportation

a) Statutory Provision: Veterinarian's Certificate

Section 19 of the Act requires prior notice of export of an animal by vessel or aircraft to be given to a customs officer in charge of the place from where the animal is to board the vessel or aircraft, and the presentation of a certificate of a veterinary inspector to the officer certifying that the prescribed requirements respecting the health, protection, and transportation of the animal have been complied with. A copy of the certificate must be delivered by the master or agent of the vessel or the pilot in command of the aircraft to the chief officer of customs at the port or airport from which the vessel or aircraft is to depart. Unless this is done, the vessel or aircraft cannot depart from the port or airport with an animal on board, and the chief officer of customs is empowered to detain the vessel or aircraft.

An exemption may be granted by the Minister from the application of this section.

b) Regulatory Provisions

The regulatory provisions governing the export of animals are contained in sections 69 to 71 of Part VIII and section 188 of Part XVI.

i) Livestock, Poultry, Animal Embryo, or Animal Semen

Section 69 prohibits the export out of Canada of any livestock, poultry, animal embryo, or animal semen unless the following requirements are complied with:

1) The exporter must obtain a certificate of a veterinary inspector or from an accredited veterinarian endorsed by a veterinary inspector, issued before the shipment, that clearly identifies the livestock, poultry, animal embryo, or animal semen, and shows
   a) that the veterinary inspector or accredited veterinarian has inspected the livestock, poultry, animal embryo, or animal semen, and found it to be free from any communicable diseases;
   b) the date and place of inspection;
   c) where tests have been performed, the nature of each test and that the livestock, poultry, animal embryo, or animal semen proved negative to such tests; and

d) the certificate bears the mark containing the following words (in both English and French), of the official export stamp, applied only by a veterinary inspector: "Government of Canada—Canadian Food Inspection Agency."

"Animal embryo" for the purposes of section 69 means the fertilized ovum of a mammal before it is implanted into a mammal.

The above requirement does not apply in respect of swine or ruminants exported to the United States for immediate slaughter or to a regulated animal, other than a porcine, if it is transported directly between Rainy River, Ontario, and Sprague, Manitoba, via the state of Minnesota, by means of a conveyance that has all its exits by which the animal could leave the conveyance sealed by an official of the Government of Canada or of the United States.

2) The exporter must comply with the importation requirements of the country to which the livestock, poultry, animal embryo, or animal semen are exported. This requirement does not apply in respect of a regulated animal, other than a porcine, if it is transported directly between Rainy River, Ontario, and Sprague, Manitoba, via the state of Minnesota by means of a conveyance that has all its exits by which the animal could leave the conveyance sealed by an official of the Government of Canada or of the United States.

3) The number of the approved tag of a bison or bovine must be reported to the Administrator of the Livestock Identification Program within thirty days after the animal is exported, as required by section 188.

With respect to the export of animal semen, section 69(2) prohibits its export unless the semen, from the time it was collected, was stored in an animal semen production centre or other place approved by the CFIA.

ii) Product of Rendering Plant

Section 70 prohibits the export from Canada of a product of a rendering plant, fertilizer, fertilizer equipment, or animal food that contains a product of a rendering plant, without the certificate of an inspector, a veterinary inspector, or a person authorized by either of them. The certificate must comply with the same requirements as aforementioned for the export of livestock, poultry, animal embryo, or animal semen, and with the importation requirements of the country to which the product of the rendering plant, fertilizer, fertilizer equipment, or animal food containing the product of a rendering plant is exported.

iii) Rest Period for Animals

Section 71 prohibits a person from exporting any animal out of Canada to any country other than the United States if the animal has not been at the place of embarkation for at least twelve hours, without the consent of an inspector. This requirement does not apply to the export of animals out of Canada from an airport.

3) Permits and Licences

Part XIII contains provisions relating to the issue of permits and licences. Section 160 authorizes the CFIA to issue a permit or licence required under the Act or the Regulations, subject to section 37(1)(a) of the *Canadian Environmental Assessment Act*, 2012, and subject to such terms and conditions as the Minister determines, if the CFIA is satisfied to the best of its knowledge and belief that the activity for which the permit or licence is issued would not, or would not likely, result in the introduction into Canada or introduction into another country from Canada, or spread within Canada, a vector, disease, or toxic substance. The section also contains provisions respecting the cancellation, suspension, and revocation of the permit or licence. Section 161 requires the permittee or the licensee to comply with the terms and conditions of the permit or the licence, as the case may be.

4) Offences, Violations, and Penalties

a) Criminal Offences

Sections 65 to 68 of the Act provide for the punishment of offences under the Act or the Regulations. With the exception of an offence against section 15 (possession and disposal of an animal or thing illegally imported), on summary conviction, the offender is liable to a fine not exceeding $50,000, or a term of imprisonment not exceeding six months, or to both; or on conviction on indictment, to a fine not exceeding $250,000, or a term of imprisonment not exceeding two years, or both. The same punishment is applicable for failure to comply with a notice issued under sections 18, 25, 27, 37, 43, and 48 of the Act or a notice issued under the Regulations. If an offence is committed on a vessel, the fine provided by section 67 is an amount not exceeding $50,000. Section 68 limits the period applicable to a prosecution, if an offence is proceeded with summarily, to two years.

The offence of possession and disposal of an animal, animal product or by-product, or thing contrary to section 15 of the Act, is punishable under sections 65(2) and (3) only on summary conviction with a maximum fine of $50,000, and there is no term of imprisonment.

b) Administrative Monetary Penalties

Instead of prosecuting, an offence under the Act or the Regulations designated pursuant to the *Agriculture and Agri-Food Administrative Monetary Penalties Act*[37] as a violation may be penalized under that Act by way of an administrative penalty ranging from a minimum of $500 for a minor violation to a maximum of $15,000 for a very serious violation. A violation is not a criminal offence. The defence of due diligence or a reasonable mistake of fact is not permitted. If this option is chosen by the Minister, criminal prosecution of the offence is barred.

F. THE *PEST CONTROL PRODUCTS ACT*[38]

1) Introduction

472 The *Pest Control Products Act* (*PCP Act*) is the successor to the *Agricultural Pests' Control Act, 1927*,[39] first enacted in 1926–27 and re-enacted in 1939 and 1968–69.

Prior to 1996, the PCP Act was administered by the Minister of Agriculture and Agri-Food, but when the Pest Management Regulatory Agency (PMRA) was created within the Department of Health, its administration and enforcement were transferred to the new agency, while the *Plant Protection Act*,[40] with which it has a lot in common, continued to be administered and enforced by Agriculture Canada through the CFIA. The reasons for this transfer of enforcement are not entirely clear, especially when some of the provisions of the *Food and Drugs Act*[41] as they relate to food, which is under Health Canada's mandate, are enforced by the CFIA.

The Act sets up a comprehensive regulatory system to ensure that pest control products do not pose unacceptable risks to human health and safety and to the environment. This is accomplished through registration and control of production, distribution, sale, advertising, import, and export of those products. Only the import and export aspects of the Act are described in this section.

---

37 Above note 3.
38 Above note 16.
39 SC 1926–27, c 40, re-en as *Pest Control Product Act, 1939* SC 1939, c 21, re-en SC 1968–69, c 50.
40 SC 1990, c.22.
41 Above note 18.

Section 2 of the Act defines a "pest" as "an animal, a plant or other organism that is injurious, noxious or troublesome, whether directly or indirectly, and an injurious, noxious or troublesome condition or organic function of an animal, a plant or other organism." The section defines a "pest control product" as

1) a product, an organism, or a substance, including a product, an organism, or a substance derived through biotechnology, that consists of its active ingredient, formulants, and contaminants, and that is manufactured, represented, distributed, or used as a means for directly or indirectly controlling, destroying, attracting, or repelling a pest or for mitigating or preventing its injurious, noxious, or troublesome effects;
2) an active ingredient that is used to manufacture anything described in (1); or
3) any other thing that is prescribed to be a pest control product.

2) Import Control

a) Prohibition

Sections 6(1) and (2) of the Act prohibit the manufacture, possession, handling, storage, transport, importation, distribution, or use of a pest control product that is not registered under the Act, unless authorized under the Act, and under the *Pest Control Products Regulations*,[42] or unless the manufacture, import, export, or distribution of a registered pest control product conforms to the conditions of registration respecting its composition and the other conditions of registration are complied with.

In addition, section 6(3) requires a pest control product to be packaged in accordance with the regulations and the conditions of registration, and prohibits the storage, import, export, or distribution of that product if not so packaged. Similar rules apply to the labelling of pest control products.

Contravention of the provisions of section 6 is an offence under section 6(9) and is punishable under that section (see Section F(4)(a), below in this chapter).

b) Registration

Section 7 provides for the registration of a pest control product by an applicant and the information that must be provided with respect to the product, which must conform to the standards of composition, safety, and efficacy set out in the regulations. If the application is accepted, the Minister of Health

---

42 SOR/2006-124.

may specify the conditions relating to its manufacture, handling, storing, transport, import, export, packaging and labelling, distribution, and use, including the conditions relating to its composition, and subject further to the condition that the registrant must record, retain, and report to the Minister information on sales of the product in the form and manner as directed by and in accordance with the regulations prescribed pursuant to section 67(1)(b) of the Act. This requirement to report sales continues even after the product ceases to be registered.

3) Export Control

a) Pest Control Product Export Control List

Section 33 authorizes the Governor in Council to establish a Pest Control Product Export Control List (PCP EC List) consisting of pest control products that meet the prescribed criteria.

It is an offence to export a pest control product that is on the PCP EC List except as authorized under the *PCP Act*. A person who proposes to export must obtain an authorization by submitting an application to the PMRA to export in the form and manner directed by the Minister. The PMRA may issue an authorization to export a pest control product to a specified country if the applicant satisfies the PMRA that the prescribed requirements for the authorization are met and the proposed export is not prohibited under any other Act of Parliament.

Contravention of the above rules is an offence under section 33(2). The criminal penalties for contravention prescribed by section 33(7) are the same as those under section 6(9) (see Section F(4)(a), below in this chapter).

b) Regulations

Parliament has given extensive regulation-making authority to the Governor in Council by section 67, with respect to, among others, the following:

- establishment of the Pest Control Product Export Control List, authorization to export a pest control product, and the amendment, suspension, and cancellation of that authorization;
- manufacture, possession, handling, storage, transport, import, export, distribution, use, or disposal of pest control products;
- packaging and advertising of pest control products; and
- keeping of records by registrants, manufacturers, importers, exporters, and so on of pest control products.

The Governor in Council is also authorized to make regulations deemed necessary for the purpose of implementing, in relation to pest control products, Article 1711 of the *NAFTA* or Article 39(3) of the *Agreement on Trade-related Aspects of Intellectual Property Rights* set out in Annex C to the *World Trade Agreement*.[43]

4) Penalties and Punishment

a) Criminal Penalties

Contravention of section 6 is punishable under section 6(9) on summary conviction, by a fine not exceeding $200,000, or a term of imprisonment not exceeding six months, or both; or on conviction on indictment, by a fine not exceeding $500,000, or a term of imprisonment not exceeding three years, or both. There are a few exclusions from criminal liability with respect to labelling, if the directions on the label accompanying the pest control product comply with the regulations. The same penalties are prescribed by section 33(7) for an offence against section 33(2).

Section 68 prescribes additional criminal penalties. If in contravening the *PCP Act* or the Regulations a risk of imminent death or serious bodily harm to person, or a risk of substantial harm, or harm to the environment is caused, the offender is liable to a fine not exceeding $200,000, or imprisonment for a term not exceeding six months, or both, on summary conviction; or a fine not exceeding $500,000, or imprisonment for a term not exceeding three years, or both, on conviction on indictment.

A more severe punishment is provided by section 68(3) if the effects referred to above were caused by wilful or reckless contravention of the Act or the Regulations. In that event, the fine levels are higher: $300,000 on summary conviction or $1 million on indictment; the prison term is the same (three years).

Contravention of the Regulations is also made an offence by section 69, with the same penalties as those for contravening the Act.

b) Administrative Monetary Penalties

Instead of prosecuting, an offence under the Act that is designated pursuant to the *Agriculture and Agri-Food Administrative Monetary Penalties Act* as a violation may be penalized under the that Act by way of an administrative monetary penalty. The penalty levels range from a minimum of $500 for a

---

43   1869 UNTS 299, 33 ILM 1197 (1994).

minor violation to a maximum of $15,000 for a very serious violation. Violations are not criminal offences. The defence of due diligence or a reasonable mistake of fact is not permitted. If this option is chosen by the Minister, criminal prosecution of the offence is barred.

The PMRA may, pursuant to section 79 of the Act, publish information about any contravention of the *PCP Act* and the *PCP Regulations*, including a contravention designated as a violation, for the purpose of encouraging compliance.

G. THE *PLANT PROTECTION ACT*[44]

The *Plant Protection Act* (PPA) was enacted in 1990, repealing its predecessor, the *Plant Quarantine Act*.[45]

The purpose of the Act is described by section 2 as the protection of plant life and the agricultural and forestry sectors of the Canadian economy by preventing the importation, exportation, and spread of pests and by controlling and eradicating pests in Canada.

1) Import and Export Control

a) Statutory Provisions

i) Permit

Section 7 of the Act requires a permit to import into Canada or export from Canada any thing that is a pest, that is or may be infested with a pest, or that constitutes or could constitute a biological obstacle to the control of pests. Section 3 defines a "pest" as "anything that is injurious or potentially injurious, whether directly or indirectly, to plants or to products or by-products of plants and includes any plant prescribed as a pest." It also defines a "thing" to include a "plant and a pest."

A person who imports or exports a thing, as so defined, must (1) present the thing to an inspector in the manner and under such conditions as the inspector considers necessary to carry out the inspection, at a place designated by the *Plant Protection Regulations*[46] or by the inspector; (2) produce all permits, certificates, or other documentation required by the Regulations; and (3) comply with all the requirements set out in the Regulations.

---

44 Above note 40.
45 RSC 1985, c P-15, repealed by SC 1990, c 22, s 59.
46 SOR/95-212.

ii) Removal of Imports and Disposal

An inspector is authorized by section 8 to order the owner or person having possession, care, or control of a thing (that is, a plant or pest) to remove the thing from Canada, whether or not it is seized, if the inspector believes on reasonable grounds that the thing was imported in contravention of the Act or the Regulations, or is a pest, or is or could be infested with a pest, or constitutes or could constitute a biological obstacle to the control of pests. If the thing is not removed, it is deemed forfeited and may be disposed of by the CFIA.

Section 9 prohibits the possession or disposal of any thing that the person knows was imported in contravention of the Act or the Regulations.

b) Regulatory Provisions

Section 47 of the Act confers authority on the Governor in Council to make regulations, among others,

1) to prohibit or regulate the importation and admission into Canada, the exportation from Canada, and the processing, handling, packaging, distributing, and transporting within Canada, of pests and other things that are or could be infested with pests or that constitute or could constitute a biological obstacle to the control of pests;
2) to issue, renew, amend, suspend, and revoke permits, certificates, or other documents on such terms and conditions as may be required for the purposes of the Act; and
3) to prohibit or regulate the importation of food or garbage into Canada.

Part II of the Regulations sets out the importation requirements and Part IV, the exportation requirements. Part III contains regulations on the movement of the thing within Canada. The reference to sections in the following sections is a reference to the sections of the Regulations except where otherwise expressly noted.

2) Importation

a) Permits and Phytosanitary Certificates

Section 29 requires every person who imports a thing to furnish a permit and, if applicable, a foreign phytosanitary certificate attesting to the phytosanitary status of the thing, issued by the government of the country of origin of the thing and containing the information required by the Model Phytosanitary Certificate set out in the Annex to the 1997 revised *International Plant*

Protection Convention[47] approved by the United Nations Food and Agriculture Organization. The certificate must have been issued within fourteen days before the thing is shipped to Canada and must be signed by an official of the country of origin who has been authorized by the government of that country to sign such a certificate.

If the thing was re-exported to Canada from another country, the importer must furnish a foreign phytosanitary certificate for re-export, which is a document issued by the government of the foreign country from which the thing was re-exported, that indicates that the thing is considered to conform with Canadian phytosanitary import requirements and that contains the information specified in the preceding paragraph.

A valid phytosanitary certificate number can be provided by the importer in electronic form where the country has an agreement with Canada to furnish the certificate directly.

i) Exemptions

Section 29(2) provides an exemption from the permit requirements if the CFIA determines on the basis of a pest risk assessment that the thing is not a pest, not infested with a pest, or does not constitute a biological obstacle to the control of pests, and the thing originates from an area listed in the List of Pests Regulated in Canada[48] published by the CFIA to be free of pests.

Alternatively, if the thing has been subjected to a treatment or process in the country or place of origin, or to re-shipment that results in the elimination of the pest or that renders it non-viable, and the importer demonstrates before importation that the treatment or process has been successful, the thing can be imported without the applicable certificates. The importer in either case must have the thing packaged, moved, handled, controlled, and used in a manner that ensures that the thing does not become a pest, infested, or a biological obstacle to the control of pests.

No foreign phytosanitary certificate is required where the CFIA determines on the basis of a pest risk assessment that the thing is not a pest, is not infested with a pest, and does not constitute a biological obstacle to the control of pests.

The importer must, however, furnish a document to the inspector that attests to the origin of the thing.

---

47 Rome, 17 November 1997, acceptance by Canada 22 October 2001.
48 See online: www.inspection.gc.ca/plants/plant-protection/pests/regulated-pests/eng/1363317115207/1363317187811.

ii) Issue of Permit

Sections 30 to 37 set out the application process, including the requirement of the applicant's residency in Canada for obtaining a permit and the requirements for the issue, amendment, and revocation of the permit. Importers required to keep a record respecting activities undertaken in respect of the thing for the period specified in the permit and to furnish the record to an inspector on request.

If any condition of the permit has not been complied with, or where the CFIA believes that there is an infestation in the country of origin or the country from which the thing was re-shipped, an inspector may detain or prohibit admission into Canada of the thing in respect of which the permit was issued, or may order the thing to be disposed of.

b) Treatment or Processing

Section 38 prohibits the importation into Canada of any thing that is a pest, or is or could be infested with a pest, or constitutes or could constitute a biological obstacle to the control of pests, unless the thing is treated or processed at origin in a manner that eliminates any pest or biological obstacle to the control of pests, or results in the pest or biological obstacle being rendered non-viable, in a manner and at the place specified in the permit.

c) Declaration

In accordance with section 39, an importer at the time of importation must declare that the thing that is being imported is not a pest, nor infested with a pest, nor a biological obstacle to the control of pests, to an inspector or customs officer at the place of admission of the thing set out in section 40. Places of admission have been identified for each province.

d) Packaging and Labelling

Section 41 requires a thing that is a pest, or is or could be infested with a pest, or constitutes or could constitute a biological obstacle to the control of pests, to be packaged and labelled, and its container or accompanying invoice to show such marks as will identify the person importing the thing, the foreign exporter, the thing, and, if applicable, the permit number. The packaging must be done in such a manner as to prevent the thing from becoming infested or spreading the pest or becoming a biological obstacle to the control of pests.

e) Import for Special Purposes

Where a person applies for a permit to import a thing for the purpose of scientific research, educational, processing, industrial, or exhibition purposes, section 43 requires the CFIA to issue a permit if the person is willing and able to comply with the conditions to be set out in the permit and will take every precaution to prevent the spread of any pest or biological obstacle to the control of pests. The thing must be packaged, transported, handled, controlled, and used in a manner that ensures a pest or biological obstacle to the control of pests is not introduced into Canada or spread within Canada.

f) Prohibiting Entry

The CFIA is authorized by section 42 to prohibit the entry of a thing into Canada where it determines on the basis of the type of the thing or of a known or suspected infestation at the place of propagation or production, or place from which the thing was shipped, that (1) the thing is a pest, or is or could be infested with a pest, or constitutes or could constitute a biological obstacle to the control of pests, and that it could not be treated or processed to the extent necessary to eliminate those risks; (2) a foreign phytosanitary certificate cannot be obtained from the country of origin or a foreign phytosanitary certificate for re-export cannot be obtained from the country of re-export of the thing; and (3) the failure to do so would or could result in the introduction into Canada or spread within Canada of a pest or a biological obstacle to the control of a pest. The CFIA is also authorized by section 44 to prohibit the entry into Canada or into Canadian territorial waters of any thing or conveyance if they pose the same risks as above, or on entering Canada would contravene the Act or any regulation.

3) Exportation

The exportation requirements are set out in sections 55 to 60 of Part IV of the Regulations.

a) Certificates

In order to export any thing (that is, a plant or pest as defined above), a Canadian Phytosanitary Certificate (CPC), or a Canadian Phytosanitary Certificate for Re-export (CPC-R), or any other document required by the phytosanitary certification authorities in the country of final destination may be required by section 55. This certificate is issued by the CFIA and it may be issued only if it believes on reasonable grounds that the thing to be exported conforms with the laws of the importing country respecting the phytosanitary requirements.

Section 57 prohibits the export or re-export of any thing from Canada unless it meets the laws of the importing country respecting phytosanitary import requirements.

b) Export Permit

In addition to a CPC or CPC-R, section 56 requires a Canadian export permit issued under the *Export and Import Permits Act*[49] if the thing is referred to in section 7000 of the Schedule to the Export Control List prescribed under that Act, or any thing that is infested with a thing referred to in section 56. A thing in respect of which the export is issued must be packed, contained, and moved in such manner as to prevent the thing from spreading a pest or a biological obstacle to the control of a pest. If exported in this manner, a movement certificate issued under Part III of the Regulations is not required.

c) Export of Grain by Vessel

If grain or grain product is being exported from Canada by a vessel ("ship, boat or water transport"), section 58 requires that, prior to loading or completing the loading of the grain or grain product aboard the vessel, the vessel be inspected before and during the loading, and the loading be approved. The loading can be halted at any time by an inspector. The inspection requirement may be waived by the CFIA if it believes on reasonable grounds that the vessel is not infested or does not or could not constitute a biological obstacle to the control of a pest. If otherwise, the CFIA may require the owner or person having the possession, care, or control of the vessel to treat or clean the vessel and to treat, move, or dispose of any thing found on or in the vessel.

Where a CPC or a CPC-R is required by the phytosanitary authorities of a foreign country with respect to any thing that is to be exported to that country, section 60 authorizes the CFIA to inspect the conveyance prior to its being loaded and at any time during the loading. If the CFIA is of the opinion that the conveyance is or could be infested or constitutes or could constitute a biological obstacle to the control of a pest, it may order the owner of the conveyance, or the person in possession, care, or control of it, to treat or clean the conveyance and to treat, move, or dispose of any thing found on or in the conveyance. The same section authorizes the inspection

---

49   RSC 1985, c E-19.

of a facility used for any activity undertaken in respect of that thing being exported, and authorizes an inspector to order the owner or person in possession, care, or control to treat or clean it.

4) Offences and Violations

a) Offences

Sections 48 to 51 of the Act provide for the punishment of offences against the Act or the Regulations. With the exception of an offence against section 9(1) (possession and disposal of things while knowing they were illegally imported), on summary conviction, the offender is liable to a fine not exceeding $50,000, or a term of imprisonment not exceeding six months, or to both; or on conviction on indictment, to a fine not exceeding $250,000, or a term of imprisonment not exceeding two years, or both. The same punishment is applicable for failure to comply with a notice issued under other sections of the Act or the Regulations. Section 51(1) limits the period applicable to a prosecution to two years if an offence is proceeded with summarily.

The offence against section 9(1) of the Act, namely, possession and disposal of a thing that the person knows was imported in contravention of the Act or the Regulations, is a summary conviction offence and punishable under section 48(2) and (3) with a maximum fine of $50,000, and the person may not be given a prison term for failure to pay the fine.

b) Administrative Monetary Penalties

Instead of prosecuting, an offence under the Act or the Regulations that is designated as a violation pursuant to the *Agriculture and Agri-Food Administrative Monetary Penalties Act*[50] may be penalized under that Act by way of an administrative monetary penalty, which ranges from a minimum of $500 for a minor violation to a maximum of $15,000 for a very serious violation. The defence of due diligence or a reasonable mistake of fact is not permitted. If this option is chosen by the CFIA, criminal prosecution of the offence is barred.

---

50   Above note 3.

H. THE *PRECIOUS METALS MARKING ACT*[51]

The *Precious Metals Marking Act* was enacted in 1906 as the *Gold and Silver Marking Act*,[52] which covered gold and silver only, as the title indicated. To cover platinum, the Act was renamed to its current title in 1928.

The purpose of the Act is to protect consumers against deceptive or fraudulent application of quality marks on gold, palladium, platinum, and silver (each defined as a "precious metal" by section 2), on alloys of the precious metal, and on articles on the surface of which a layer or plating of the precious metal is deposited by any chemical, electrical, mechanical, or metallurgical process, as well as on an article made of an inferior metal on which a covering or sheeting of a precious metal is fixed by brazing, soldering, or other mechanical process ("plated article"). Any metal or alloy may be designated as a "precious metal" by regulations.

1) Application of Marks

Section 3 of the Act prohibits the importation of an article that has applied to it a mark that suggests or indicates that it is a precious metal. Section 4 authorizes the application of a "quality mark" that (1) truly and correctly indicates the quality of the precious metal of which the article is in whole or in part, and that it meets the standards provided in the *Precious Metals Marking Regulations*[53] with respect to that precious metal; and (2) the mark is applied in a manner authorized by the Regulations.

If, however, a trademark is registered for a precious metal, or an application for the registration of the trademark has been made, that trademark must be applied to the precious metal in the manner authorized by the Regulations. This provision does not apply to a precious metal hallmarked in accordance with the laws of the United Kingdom, or has applied to it a mark authorized under the laws of a foreign country that truly and correctly indicates the quality of the precious metal of which the article is in whole or in part composed.

---

51 RSC 1985, c P-19.
52 RSC 1906, c 90, re-en SC 1908, c 30 and SC 1913, c 19, renamed *Precious Metals Marking Act*, SC 1928, c 40.
53 CRC, c 1303.

2) Other Marks

If a quality mark has been applied to a precious metal, other marks, namely, numerals intended to identify the article or pattern and the name or initials of a dealer, or any other mark, may be applied to it so long as it is applied in a manner not calculated to mislead or deceive.

Section 3 of the Regulations exempts the application of a quality mark to an article sold to a dealer who is outside Canada, and section 4 exempts from assay the parts of an article that are any mechanism, movement, or works, where the article consists of a case or cover containing or incorporating the mechanism, movement, or works; brooch pins, joints, and catches; and small articles such as springs, winding bars, hat pins, scarf pins, bracelet tongues, locket bezels, knife skeletons and blades, lapel buttons, earring setting posts, and so on.

The Regulations specify the marks and the manner of marking the quality marks. Section 5 applies to precious metals that are not plated articles, plated articles other than watch cases, spectacle frames, flatware, and hollow ware.

3) Offences and Criminal Penalties

Under section 10, an offence against the quality mark provisions, or any other provisions of the Act, is punishable on summary conviction by a fine not exceeding $500. If convicted, section 11 provides for forfeiture of the articles other than precious or semi-precious stones, watch movements, and any other part designated by the Regulations; such forfeited articles are to be disposed of in accordance with the procedures set out in sections 74 to 76 of the *Fisheries Act*.[54]

I. THE *TEXTILE LABELLING ACT*[55]

The *Textile Labelling Act* was first enacted in 1969–70 for the purpose of protecting consumers by ensuring that they are not misled by manufacturers, sellers, and importers by false indication of the type of textile article purchased. This purpose is sought to be achieved by requiring consumer textile articles to have an approved label that complies with all applicable provisions of the Act.

---

54   RSC 1985, c F-14.
55   RSC 1985, c T-10, previously SC 1969–70, c 34

Section 2 defines a "consumer textile article" as any textile fibre, yarn, or fabric, or any product made in whole or in part from a textile fibre, yarn, or fabric; and defines "textile fibre" as any natural or manufactured matter that is capable of being made into yarn or fabric. It includes human hair, kapok, feathers, and down as well as animal hair and fur that have been removed from an animal skin. A "label" means any label, mark, sign, device, imprint, stamp, brand, or ticket.

1) Prohibition

Section 3 of the Act prohibits a dealer from importing or advertising (1) a prescribed consumer textile article unless that article has applied to it a label containing a representation with respect to the textile fibre content of the article; or (2) any consumer textile article that has applied to it a label containing a representation with respect to the textile fibre content of the article unless the label is applied to it in accordance with and complies with all applicable provisions of the Act.

A label applied to a consumer textile fabric must not contain any false or misleading representation that relates to or may reasonably be regarded as relating to the article. A "false or misleading representation" is widely defined by section 5(3)(c).

2) Regulatory Requirements

Section 5 of the *Textile Labelling and Advertising Regulations*[56] requires every representation label, that is, a label that contains any representation as to the textile fibre content of the article to which it is applied, to meet the requirements for a disclosure label in accordance with the Act and the Regulations as to its form, the information shown on the article, and the manner in which it is shown. Where the information is required to be shown on two labels, it must be shown on both labels. The representation label must not contain any representation that detracts from, qualifies, or contradicts any representation in the disclosure label, or contravenes section 5 of the Act.

Section 11 of the Regulations specifies the information that must be shown on a disclosure label, which includes (1) the textile fibre content of the article (in the manner prescribed in Part III); (2) the name and postal address of the dealer; and (3) where the article is imported and the name of the coun-

---

56   CRC, c 1551 as amended.

try of origin. If a dealer is a resident of Canada, manufactures or processes the article in Canada, imports it into Canada or distributes it in Canada, and obtains an identification number from the Minister of Industry, the identification number can be applied in place of the dealer's name and postal address.

Sections 13 to 20 specify the manner in which the prescribed information must be shown on label, the form of label, and the manner of application, and so on.

Part III specifies, among other things, the manner in which the textile fibre content must be shown and the amount and content of the textile fibre.

3) Exemptions

The disclosure or representation labelling requirements of section 3 of the Act are exempted with respect to a consumer textile article that is not prescribed in Schedule I or is not included in Schedule II to the Regulations, or that is sold to a dealer outside Canada or sold to a duty-free shop in Canada.

Schedule I prescribes thirteen different categories of consumer textile articles, ranging from floor coverings, outer coverings of upholstered furniture, draperies, towels, afghans and sleeping bags, piece goods, umbrellas, tents, to bed canopies.

Schedule II exempts a large number of consumer textile articles or articles that have incorporated in them a textile fibre, including toys, ornaments, lampshades, lawn and beach furniture, belts and suspenders, carpet underpadding, non-fibrous materials that do not have a fabric support, and household twine, string, craft ribbons, and so on.

Also exempt from the requirements are imported textile articles

1) if they are labelled before resale in accordance with section 8 of the Regulations; or
2) if the articles are made up for or sold to
   a) a commercial or industrial enterprise;
   b) a federal, provincial, or municipal department or agency;
   c) a public utility;
   d) an educational institution;
   e) a religious order or organization; or
   f) a health care facility, for use by any of these entities or for sale to its employees or students or, in the case of a religious order or organization, for use by or sale to members of the order or organization; or
3) if they are sold by the manufacturer to an employee.

Furthermore, by virtue of section 7, if a consumer textile article is made up for the use of an individual or, in the case of a floor covering, cut for the use of the individual, the dealer is exempt from the labelling requirements if the individual has the opportunity to examine the textile fibre product or a sample or swatch thereof from which the article is to be made up or cut, and the textile fibre, product, sample, or swatch is labelled as required by the Act or the Regulations.

4) Prescribed Consumer Textile Article

A dealer will be allowed to import a prescribed consumer textile article without a disclosure label applied to it if the dealer complies with the following requirements set out in section 8 of the Regulations:

1) The dealer must inform an inspector designated by Industry Canada of the intention to import or, if the dealer has already imported the article, the dealer must inform the inspector before its entry, the date and place or the proposed date and place of such importation; the nature and quantity of the article imported or to be imported; and the address of the premises where the article will be labelled in accordance with the statutory requirements.

2) Prior to the resale of the article, the dealer must apply a disclosure label to the article in the prescribed manner, notify the inspector that this has been done, and afford the inspector a reasonable opportunity to inspect the article so labelled.

5) Offences and Penalties

Contraventions of sections 3, 4, or 5 of the Act are offences under sections 12 and 13 and are punishable on summary conviction by a fine not exceeding $5,000, or on conviction on indictment, by a fine not exceeding $10,000. Contraventions of provisions other than of sections 3, 4, or 5 are punishable on summary conviction by a fine not exceeding $1,000, or by imprisonment for a term not exceeding six months, or both, or on conviction on indictment, by a fine not exceeding $3,000, or imprisonment for a term not exceeding one year, or both. Section 13 provides a defence of due diligence.

Table of Cases

6572243 Canada Ltd o/a Kwality Imports v President of the Canada Border Services Agency, AP-2010-068 (2012), 17 TTR (2d) 1 (CITT).....................155

A & R Dress Co Inc v Canada (Minister of National Revenue), 2006 FCA 298.........282

AAi.FosterGrant of Canada Co v Canada (Customs and Revenue Agency) (2003), 8 TTR (2d) 51, [2003] CITT No 51, rev'd 2004 FCA 259........................ 21, 22

Abbott Laboratories, Ltd v Canada (Minister of National Revenue), 2004 FC 140...44

Accessories Machinery Ltd v Canada (Deputy Minister of National Revenue, Customs and Excise), [1957] SCR 358 182

Accessories Sportracks Inc de Thule Canada Inc v President of the Canada Border Services Agency, AP-2010-036 (2012), 16 TTR (2d) 320 (CITT)................198

Active Marble & Tile Ltd v Commissioner of the Canada Customs and Revenue Agency, AP-2001-017 (2002), 6 TTR (2d) 631 (CITT) 125

Aliments Dorchester International Inc v Canada (Department of Foreign Affairs and International Trade) (2001), 199 FTR 288, [2001] FCJ No 102 (TD)... 398

Allen Zerr v President of the Canada Border Services Agency, AP-2006-057 (2008), 12 TTR (2d) 272 (CITT) 290

Alliance Ro-Na Home Inc v Commissioner of the Canada Customs and Revenue Agency, AP-2001-065 (2002), 6 TTR (2d) 794 (CITT)............................ 157

Aluminart Products Limited v President of the Canada Border Services Agency, AP-2011-027 (2012), 16 TTR (2d) 548, appeal against the CBSA's determination Injury Inquiry NQ-2008-003 (2009) (CITT).................................. 360

AMA Plastics Ltd v President of the Canada Border Services Agency, AP-2009-052 (2010), 15 TTR (2d) 149 (CITT) 208

Arctic Cat Sales Inc v Deputy Minister of National Revenue, AP-2005-005,
  A9-2005-010, AP-2005, 011, and AP-2005-020 (2006),
  10 TTR (2d) 693 (CITT), aff'd 2007 FCA 277 152
Asea Brown Boveri Inc v Commissioner of the Canada Customs and
  Revenue Agency, AP-98-001 (2000) (CITT) 189, 205
Avon Canada Inc v Commissioner of the Canada Customs and
  Revenue Agency, AP-99-074 (2000), 5 TTR (2d) 11 (CITT) 154

Bauer Hockey Corporation v President of the Canada Border Services
  Agency, AP-2011-011 (2012), 16 TTR (2d) 611 (CITT) 116
Beach v Deputy Minister of National Revenue (Customs and Excise) (1992),
  8 TTR 55, [1992] OJ No 322 (Gen Div), rev'd in part on costs (1992),
  11 TTR 38, 10 OR (3d) 572 (CA) 66
Beckman Coulter Canada Inc v President of the Canada Border
  Services Agency, AP-2010-065 (2012), 16 TTR (2d) 365 (CITT) 217
Bernard Chaus Inc (Re), [2003] CITT No 99 47
Bicycles from China, Expiry Review RR-2002-001 (2002); Importer
  Ruling MP-2003-001 (2004) (CITT) 389
Black & Decker Canada Inc v Deputy Minister of National Revenue for
  Customs and Excise, AP-2003-007 (2004) (CITT) 161, 162
BMC Coaters Inc v President of the, Canada Border Services Agency,
  AP-2009-071 (2010), 15 TTR (2d) 171 (CITT) 114
Brown's Shoe Shops Inc v Canada (Customs and Revenue Agency)
  (2004), 8 TTR (2d) 574, [2004] CITT No 14 26
Brunswick International (Canada) Ltd v Canada (Deputy Minister of
  National Revenue) (1999), 4 TTR (2d) 279, [1999] CITT No 95 21
Buffalo Inc v Commissioner of the Canada Customs and Revenue Agency,
  AP-2002-023 (2004), 8 TTR (2d) 787 (CITT) 226

Calego International Inc v Deputy Minister of National Revenue,
  AP-98-102 (2000), 4 TTR (2d) 672 (CITT) 87, 167
Canada (Attorney General) v Consolidated Canadian Contractors Inc
  (1998), 165 DLR (4th) 433, [1999] 1 FC 209, [1998] FCJ No 1394 (CA) 69
Canada (Attorney-General) v JC Ayer Co, (1887), 1 Ex CR 232 73
Canada (Attorney-General) v Racicot (1913), 14 Ex CR 214, 11 DLR 149 73
Canada (Customs and Revenue Agency) v Suzuki Canada Inc,
  2004 FCA 131 .... 83, 151, 152, 153
Canada (Deputy Minister of National Revenue) v Mattel Canada Inc,
  2001 SCC 36 .... 19, 31–33, 34, 52, 378
Canada (Deputy Minister of National Revenue) v Toyota Canada Inc
  (1999), 247 NR 223, 4 TTR (2d) 108, [1999] FCJ No 1035 (CA),
  rev'g (1996), 1 TTR (2d) 385, [1996] CITT No 50 .... 19–20, 36

Table of Cases

Canada (Minister of Human Resources Development) v Hogervest,
    2007 FCA 41 48
Canada v Bureau, [1949] SCR 367, 95 CCC 1, [1949] SCJ No 14 72
Canada v Kay Silver Inc (1980), [1981] 2 FC 436, 2 CER 307, [1980]
    FCJ No 285 (TD) 26
Canada v Mondev Corp Ltd (1974), 33 CPR (2d) 193, [1974] FCJ No 213 (TD) 31, 32
Canada v Singer Manufacturing Co (1967), [1968] 1 Ex CR 129,
    aff'd [1968] 1 Ex CR viii (SCC) 319–20, 387
Canada v Sun Parlor Advertising Company, [1973] FC 1055, [1973]
    FCJ No 130 (CA) 73
Canada-Continued Suspension of Obligations in the EC-Hormones
    Dispute (2008), 12 TTR (2d) 384 (WTO Dispute Settlement Panel—
    Panel Report) 370
Canadian Admiral Corporation v Deputy Minister of National Revenue
    (Customs and Excise), [1959] SCR 832, 20 DLR (2d) 689 18
Canadian Association of Regulated Importers v Canada (Attorney General),
    [1994] 2 FC 247, 164 NR 342, [1994] FCJ No 1 (CA) 398
Canadian Tire Corporation Limited v President of the Canada Border
    Services Agency, AP-2011-020 (2012), 16 TTR (2d) 511 (CITT) 176
Canadian Tire Corporation Ltd v President of the Canada Border
    Services Agency, AP-2011-024 (2012), 16 TTR (2d) 675 (CITT) 130
Canadian Tire Corporation Ltd v President of the Canada Border Services
    Agency, AP-2009-019 (2010), 14 TTR (2d) 631, aff'd 2011 FCA 242 115
Canadian Tire Corporation Ltd v President of the Canada Border Services
    Agency, AP-2006-041 (2007), 12 TTR (2d) 135 (CITT) 126
Canadian Tire Corporation Ltd v President of the Canada Border
    Services Agency, AP-2006-038 (2007), 12 TTR (2d) 39 (CITT) 136, 139
Canadisc Inc v Commissioner of the Canada Customs and Revenue
    Agency, AP-99-086 (2000), 5 TTR (2d) 111 (CITT) 148
Canmade Furniture Products Inc v Commissioner of the Canada Customs
    and Revenue Agency, AP-2003-025 (2004), 8 TTR (2d) 10 (CITT) 131, 138, 199
Capital Garment Co v Canada (Deputy Minister of National Revenue)
    (1997), 2 TTR (2d) 466, [1997] CITT No 54 30
Carter, Macy & Co v Canada (1890), 2 Ex CR 126, aff'd (1890), 18 SCR 706 228
CB Powell Ltd v Canada (Border Services Agency), 2010 FCA 61,
    rev'g 2009 FC 528 45
Certain Artificial Graphite Electrodes and Connecting Pins Originating
    in or Exported from the United States of America, Request
    No IR-2-86 (1987) (Can Import Trib) 388, 389
Certain Grain Corn Originating in or Exported from the United States of
    America and Imported into Canada for Use or Consumption West of the
    Manitoba-Ontario Border NQ-2000-005 (2001), 5 TTR (2d) 501 (CITT) 343

Certain Iodinated Contrast Media (2000), 4 TTR (2d) 530 (CITT), reviewed
(2003), 7 TTR (2d) 783 (NAFTA Binational Panel), remand to
CITT (2003), 8 TTR (2d) 30 (NAFTA Binational Panel) 349, 374
Certain Outdoor Barbeques Safeguard Inquiry No CS-2005-001
(2005), 10 TTR (2d) 463 (CITT) 270, 405
Certain Prepared Baby Foods Originating in or Exported from the
United States of America NQ-97-002 (1999), 3 TTR (2d) 751
(CITT), reviewed RR-2002-002 (2003), 7 TTR (2d) 875 (CITT) 349
Certain Refrigerators and Dishwashers from the United States Inquiry,
NQ-2000-001 (2000), 6 TTR (2d) 425; USA-CDA-2000-1904-03 (2002),
6 TTR (2d) 502 (CITT) 375
Certain Refrigerators, Dishwashers and Dryers Injury Inquiry NQ-2000-001 (2000);
Interim Review RD-2002-005 (2003) (CITT).. 364
Certain Refrigerators, Dishwashers, and Dryers Injury Inquiry NQ-2000-001 (2000);
Public Interest Inquiry PB-2000-002 (2003) (CITT).. 351
Certain Steel Fuel Tanks NQ-2004-002 (2004), 9 TTR (2d) 370 (CITT) 341
Certain Waterproof Rubber Footwear Originating in or Exported
from the People's Republic of China Expiry Review RR-2001-005
(2002); Interim Review RD-2004-008 (2005) (CITT) 364
Chaps Ralph Lauren, a Division of 131384 Canada Inc v Canada
(Deputy Minister of National Revenue) (1997), 1 TTR (2d) 781,
[1997] CITT No 136... 26
Charley Originals Ltd, division of Algo Group Inc v Canada (Deputy
Minister of National Revenue) (1997), 2 TTR (2d) 106, [1997]
CITT No 42, aff'd (2000), 257 NR 104, 4 TTD (2d) 735,
[2000] FCJ No 699 (CA)... 31
Cherry Stix Ltd v President of the Canada Border Services Agency
(2005), 14 TTR (2d) 435 (CITT)... 19
Clothes Line Apparel, division of 2810221 Canada Inc v Canada
(Border Services Agency) (2008), 12 TTR (2d) 967, [2008]
CITT No 36, aff'd 2009 FCA 366 .... 28, 34
Cobra Anchors Co Ltd v President of the Canada Border Services
Agency, AP-2008-006 (2009), 13 TTR (2d) 530 (CITT) 358
Coloridé Inc v Deputy Minister of National Revenue (Customs and
Excise), AP-99-037 (2000) (CITT)... 88, 110
Comité Paritaire de l'Industrie de la Chemise v Potash, [1994] 2 SCR 406,
115 DLR (4th) 702, [1994] SCJ No 7 58
Commonwealth Wholesale Corp v President of the Canada Border
Services Agency, AP-2011-010 and AP-2011-019 (2012),
16 TTR (2d) 402 (CITT) 185
Contech Holdings Canada Inc v President of the Canada Border Services
Agency, AP-2010-033 and AP-2010-042 (2012) (CITT) 209

Table of Cases

Convoy Supply Ltd v Commissioner of the Canada Customs and Revenue Agency, AP-99-015 to AP-99-025 (2000), 4 TTR (2d) 423 (CITT) 125
Coombs v Canada (Deputy Minister of National Revenue, Customs and Excise) (1992), 102 Nfld & PEIR 23, 10 TTR 235, [1992] NJ No 287 (SCTD) 67
Costco Canada Inc v Commissioner of the Canada Customs and Revenue Agency, AP-2000-050 (2001) (CITT) 161
Costco Wholesale Canada Ltd v President of the Canada Border Services Agency, AP-2011-009 (2012), 16 TTR (2d) 380 (CITT) 138
Costco Wholesale Canada v President of the Canada Border Services Agency, AP-2008-031 (2010), 14 TTR (2d) 215 (CITT) 157
Criterion Catalysts & Technologies Canada Inc v President of the Canada Border Services Agency, AP-2009-061 (2010), 15 TTR (2d) 165 (CITT) 98
Curve Distribution Services Inc v President of the Canada Border Services Agency, AP-2011-023 (2012), 16 TTR (2d) 742 (CITT) 106, 212

Dairy Farmers of Canada v Canada (Deputy Minister of National Revenue), 2001 FCA 77 53
Dairy Products Disputes, WT/DS103/R2 and WT/DS113/RW2 (2002), 6 TTR (2d) 310 and (2002), 7 TTR (2d) 1 and (2002), 7 TTR (2d) 559 (WTO) 402
Danson Décor Inc v President of the Canada Border Services Agency, AP-2009-066 (2011), 15 TTR (2d) 646 (CITT) 173
Deputy Minister of National Revenue (Customs and Excise) v Ferguson Industries Ltd, [1973] SCR 21, 28 DLR (3d) 352, [1972] SCJ No 71 .... 52, 82, 181
Deputy Minister of National Revenue (Customs and Excise) v Macmillan & Bloedel (Alberni) Ltd, [1965] SCR 366, 50 DLR (2d) 1, [1965] SCJ No 10 82
Deputy Minister of National Revenue for Customs and Excise v Androck Inc (1987), 74 NR 255, [1987] FCJ No 45 (CA) 108
DMG Trading Company v Canada (Deputy Minister of National Revenue) (1997), 1 TTR (2d) 104, [1997] CITT No 85 29
Dominion Engineering Works Ltd v A B Wing Ltd, [1956] Ex CR 379 51
Dominion Sample Limited v Canada (Customs and Revenue Agency), 2003 FC 1244 285
Down East Toyota v Canada (Minister of National Revenue, Customs and Excise) (1994), 145 NBR (2d) 116, 372 APR 116, [1994] NBJ No 97 (CA) 67
Doyon v Canada (Attorney General), 2009 FCA 152 70
DSM Nutritional Products Canada Ltd v President of the Canada Border Services Agency, AP-2007-012 (2007) (CITT) 98
Duhamel & Dewar Inc v President of the Canada Border Services Agency, AP-2005-046 (2007), 11 TTR (2d) 372 (CITT) 226
Dumping and Subsidizing of Steel Grating Originating in or Exported from the People's Republic of China NQ-2010-002 (2011) (CITT) 344

Dynamo Industries, Inc v President of the Canada Border Services Agency,
AP-2008-007 (2009), 13 TTR (2d) 500 (CITT) 178

Éditions Panini du Canada Ltée v Deputy Minister of National Revenue
for Customs and Excise, AP-92-018 (1993) (CITT) 109
El Khoury v Canada (Minister of National Revenue, Customs and Excise)
(1996), 207 NR 311, [1996] FCJ No 1339 (CA) 67
Electrohome Ltd v Canada (Deputy Minister of National Revenue,
Customs and Excise), [1986] 2 FC 344 (TD) 393
Elfe Juvenile Products v President of the Canada Border Services Agency,
AP-2011-029 (2012), 16 TTR (2) 830 (CITT) 164
EM Plastic & Electric Products Ltd v Deputy Minister of National
Revenue, AP-98-012 (2000) (CITT) 206
EMCO Electric International-Electrical Resource International v President
of the Canada Border Services Agency, AP-2008-010 (2009),
13 TTR (2d) 553 (CITT) 319
Entrelec Inc v Canada (Minister of National Revenue), 2004 FCA 159 209
European Union Beef Hormones Ban (1998), 12 TTR (2d) 384
(WTO Dispute Settlement Panel—Panel Report) 369, 370
Eurotrade Import-Export Inc v Commissioner of the Canada Border
Services Agency, AP-2001-090 (2003), 7 TTR (2d) 645 (CITT) 96
Evan's Sales & Service Ltd v Canada (Minister of National Revenue,
Customs and Excise) (1990), 85 Nfld & PEIR 343, 3 TTR 270,
[1990] NJ No 258 (SCTD) 67
Evenflo Canada Inc v President of the Canada Border Services Agency,
AP-2009-049 (2010), 14 TTR (2d) 470 (CITT) 139, 158
Excelsior Foods Inc v Commissioner of the Canada Customs and
Revenue Agency, AP-2002-113 (2004), 9 TTR (2d) 295 (CITT) 93, 95

Fenwick Automotive Products Limited v President of the Canada Border Services
Agency, AP-2006-063 (2009), 13 TTR (2d) 316 (CITT) 217
Flat Hot-rolled Carbon and Alloy Steel Sheet Products Injury Inquiry
NQ-98-004 (1999); Interim Review RD-2002-003 (2003) (CITT) 363
Flora Manufacturing & Distributing Ltd v Deputy Minister of National
Revenue, AP-97-002 (1998) (CITT), rev'd A-720-98 (2000),
258 NR 134, 4 TTR (2d) 791, [2000] FCJ No 1196 (CA) 98
Formica Canada Inc v Commissioner of Canada Customs and
Revenue Agency, AP-2000-041 (2002), 6 TTR (2d) 417 (CITT) 104
Formica Canada Inc v Deputy Minister of National Revenue,
AP-96-205 (1998) (CITT) 207
Franklin Mint Inc v Commissioner of the Canada Customs and
Revenue Agency, AP-2003-013 (2004), 8 TTR (2d) 766 (CITT) 102, 103

Table of Cases

"Frederick Gerring Jr" (The) v Canada (1897), 27 SCR 271..................................62, 63
Fresh Garlic Originating in or Exported from the People's Republic
 of China, MP-97-001 (1998) (CITT) 387
Fresh Garlic Originating in or Exported from the People's Republic
 of China RD-99-002 (2000), 4 TTR (2d) 725 (CITT).......................................362
Fresh Garlic Originating in or Exported from the People's Republic
 of China NQ-96-002 (2000), 2 TTR (2d) 30 (CITT)...362
Fresh Iceberg (Head) Lettuce Originating in or Exported from the
 United States of America Injury Inquiry NQ-92-001 (1992);
 Interim Review RD-2001-002 (2002) (CITT)..363
Fresh Tomatoes, Originating in or Exported from the United States
 of America, Excluding Tomatoes for Processing NQ-2001-004 (2002),
 6 TTR (2d) 659 (CITT) 342–43
Fritz Marketing Inc v Canada (Border Services Agency) (2006),
 1 TTR (2d) 954, [2006] CITT No 122, aff'd (sub nom Fritz
 Marketing Inc v Canada (Border Services Agency, President))
 (2010), 14 TTR 447, [2010] CITT No 56...30, 36
Future Product Sales Inc v President of the Canada Border Services
 Agency, AP-2009-056 (2010), 14 TTR (2d) 561 (CITT) 108

GCP Elastomeric Ltd v President of the Canada Border
 Services Agency, AP-2010-011 (2011), 15 TTR (2d) 553 (CITT)....................105
General Supply Co of Canada v Deputy Minister of National Revenue
 (Customs and Excise) (1952), [1953] Ex CR 185, [1953] 2 DLR 556...............51
GFT Mode Canada v Canada (Deputy Minister of National Revenue),
 [2000] CITT No 35..50
GL&V/Black Clawson-Kennedy v Deputy Minister of National Revenue,
 AP-99-063 (2000), 5 TTR (2d) 59 (CITT), aff'd 2002 FCA 43 188
Global Safeguard Inquiry into the Importation of Bicycles and
 Finished Painted Bicycle Frames, GS-2004-001 and
 GS-2004-002 (2005), 10 TTR (2d) 1 (CITT)...246–47
Global Safeguard Inquiry on Certain Steel Goods, GC-2001-001
 (4 July 2002) (CITT) 245
Globe Electric Company Inc v President of the Canada Border
 Services Agency, AP-2008-022 (2010), 14 TTR (2d) 394 (CITT) 162
Gordon Schebek v President of the Canada Border Services Agency,
 AP-2005-009 (2006), 10 TTR (2d) 877 (CITT) 290, 291
Gosselin v Canada, [1954] Ex CR 658..61
Granovsky v Canada (Minister of Employment and Immigration),
 2000 SCC 28 219
Great West Van Conversions Inc v President of the Canada Border
 Services Agency, AP-2010-037 (2011) (CITT) 215, 216

Greenhouse Bell Peppers Exported from the Netherlands NQ-2010-001
(2010), 15 TTR (2d) 1 (CITT) 344
Grodan Inc v President of the Canada Border Services Agency,
AP-2011-030 (20 June 2012) (CITT) 56
Groupe Cabico Inc v President of the Canada Border Services Agency,
AP-2006-004 (2007), 12 TTR (2d) 51 (CITT) 133, 137

Havi Global Solutions (Canada) Limited Partnership v President of the
Canada Border Services Agency, AP-2007-014 (2008),
13 TTR (2d) 23 (CITT) 168
HBC Imports c/o Zellers Inc v President of the Canada Border Services
Agency, AP-2011-018 (2012), 16 TTR (2d) 530 (CITT) 178
Helly Hansen Leisure Canada v President of the Canada Border
Services Agency, AP-2006-054 (2008), 14 TTR (2d) 53 (CITT),
aff'd 2009 FCA 345 .... 14, 111
Hilary's Distribution Ltd v Deputy Minister of National Revenue,
AP-97-010 (1998) (CITT) 221
Hoang v Canada (Minister of National Revenue), 2006 FC 182 4
Holland Hitch of Canada Limited v President of the Canada Border
Services Agency, AP-2012-004 (2013), 17 TTR (2d) 349 (CITT) 215

Imation Canada Inc v Commissioner of the Canada Customs and
Revenue Agency, AP-2000-047 (2001), 6 TTR (2d) 239 (CITT) 206, 209
Industrial Acceptance Corp v Canada, [1953] 2 SCR 273, [1953]
4 DLR 369, [1953] SCJ No 47 62
Ingram Micro Inc v President of the Canada Border Services Agency,
AP-2009-073 (2011), 15 TTR (2d) 323 (CITT) 144
Ingredia SA v Canada, 2009 FC 389, aff'd 2010 FCA 176 75
Innovak DIY Products Inc v President of the Canada Border Services
Agency, AP-2006-009 (2006), 10 TTR (2d) 674 (CITT) 110
Intersave West Buying and Merchandising Service v Commissioner
of the Canada Customs and Revenue Agency, AP-2000-057 (2002),
6 TTR (2d) 357 (CITT) 95–96
Intersave West Buying and Merchandising Service v Commissioner
of the Canada Customs and Revenue Service Agency,
AP-2000-017 (2001), 5 TTR (2d) 386 (CITT) 163
IPSCO Inc (Re), [2005] CITT No 10 47
IPSCO Inc v President of the Canada Border Services Age,
AP-2005-041 (2007), 11 TTR (2d) 676 (CITT) 190
Island Timberlands LP v Canada (Minister of Foreign Affairs), 2008 FC 1380 398
Ivan Hoza v President of the Canada Border Services Agency,
AP-2009-002 (2010), 14 TTR (2d) 435 (CITT) 289

Table of Cases

Jam Industries Ltd v President of the Canada Border Services Agency, AP-2005-006 (2006), 10 TTR (2d) 748 (CITT), aff'd 207 FCA 20 213
Jan K Overweel Limited v President of the Canada Border Services Agency, AP-2011-075 (2013), 17 TTR (2d) 406 (CITT) 225
JIT Industrial Supply & Distribution Ltd v President of the Canada Border Services Agency, AP-2008-015 (2010), 14 TTR (2d) 244 (CITT) 199
Jockey Canada Co v Canada (Minister of Public Safety and Emergency Preparedness), 2010 FC 396 50
Jonathan Bell v President of the Canada Border Services Agency, AP-2007-021 (2008) (CITT) 290–91

Kearns & McMurchy Inc v Canada, 2003 FCT 814 75
Kelly v Palazzo, 2008 ONCA 82, leave to appeal to SCC refused, [2008] SCCA No 152 59
Kinedyne Canada Limited v President of the Canada Border Services Agency, AP-2010-027 (2011), 15 TTR (2d) 790 (CITT) 120
Komatsu International (Canada) Inc v President of the Canada Border Services Agency, AP-2010-006 (2012), 16 TTR (2d) 479 (CITT) 182
Kong v Canada (1984), 10 DLR (4th) 226, [1984] FCJ No 412 (TD) 2, 4
Korhani Canada Inc v President of the Canada Border Services Agency, AP-2007-008 (2008), 13 TTR (2d) 63 (CITT) 170
Kverneland Group North America Inc v President of the Canada Border Services Agency, AP-2009-013 (2010), 14 TTR (2d) 422 (CITT) 210

Laxus Products Ltd v Commissioner of the Canada Customs and Revenue Agency, AP-99-117 (2001), 5 TTR (2d) 372 (CITT) 124
Leather Footwear with Metal Toe Caps Injury Inquiry NQ-2001-003 (2001), 6 TTR (2d) 245; Expiry Review RR-2005 001 (2005); Interim Review Order RD-2009-003 (2010) (CITT) 364
Liberty Home Products Corp v Deputy Minister of National Revenue (Customs and Excise) (1990), 3 TCT 5243 (FCA), rev'g (1987), 12 TBR 42 (Tariff Board) 311
Little Sisters Book and Art Emporium v Canada (Minister of Justice) (1996), 131 DLR (4th) 486, 18 BCLR (3d) 241, [1996] BCJ No 71 (SC), aff'd (1998), 160 DLR (4th) 385, 109 BCAC 49, [1998] BCJ No 1507, rev'd 2000 SCC 69 .... 54, 293
Loblaws Companies Limited v President of the Canada Border Services Agency, AP-2010-022 (2011), 15 TTR (2d) 853 (CITT) 174

M & M Footwear Inc v The Commissioner of the Canada Customs and Revenue Agency, AP-2001-070 (2003), 8 TTR (2d) 36 (Injury Inquiry NQ-89-0030) (CITT) 357

M Miner v President of the Canada Border Services Agency, AP-2009-080
  (2011) (CITT), rev'd 2012 FCA 81, remand to CITT AP-2009-080R (2012),
  15 TTR (2d) 310 (CITT).. 289
Machine Tufted Carpeting Originating in or Exported from the
  United States of America Inquiry NQ-91-006 (1993) (CITT)................... 388
Maple Lodge Farms Ltd v Canada Food Inspection Agency [1982]
  2 SCR 2, 44 NR 354, 137 DLR (3d) 558 398
Marun v Canada, [1965] 1 Ex CR 28, [1964] CTC 444, 64 DTC 5238............................ 71
Masai Canada v President of the Canada Border Services Agency,
  AP-2010-025 (2011) (CITT) 223
McGregor v Canada (Minister of National Revenue, Customs and Excise)
  (1994), 93 FTR 247, [1994] FCJ No 1344 (TD)... 67
Meat and Meat Products (Hormones)—Complaint by Canada—
  Arbitration (1998), 3 TTR (2d) 657 (WTO)..369, 370
Monterra Lumber Mills Ltd v President of the Canada Border Services
  Agency, AP-2011-055 (2012), 17 TTR (2d) 57 (CITT) 99
Mon-Tex Mills Ltd v Commissioner of the Canada Customs and Revenue
  Agency, AP-2002-103 (2003), 8 TTR (2d) 419 (CITT),
  rev'd 2004 FCA 346..160
Morris National Inc v President of the Canada Border Services
  Agency, AP-2005-039 (2007) (CITT) 91
MRP Retail Inc v President of the Canada Border Services Agency,
  AP-2006-005 (2007), 12 TTR (2d) 1 (CITT) 226

National Corn Growers Association of Canada v Canada (Import
  Tribunal), [1990] 2 SCR 1324, 4 TTR 267; 1990 CanLII 49 394
NC Cameron & Sons Ltd v President of the Canada Border Services
  Agency, AP-2006-022 (2007), 11 TTR (2d) 634 (CITT)............................. 101
New Asia (Brampton) Food Centre v President of the Canada Border
  Services Agency, AP-2006-042 (2007), 11 TTR (2d) 709 (CITT)............ 92
Newtech Beverage Systems Ltd v Commissioner of the Canada Customs
  and Revenue Agency, AP-2003-029 (2004), 9 TTR (2d) 62 (CITT) 203
Nike Canada Ltd v Canada (Deputy Minister of National Revenue)
  (1999), 85 ACWS (3d) 820, [1999] FCJ No 53 (CA)....................................32
Nokia Products Limited & Primecell Communications Inc v Commissioner
  of the Canada Customs and Revenue Agency, AP-2001-073,
  AP-2001-074, AP-2001-084 (2003), 9 TTR (2d) 314 (CITT) 107, 183
Nokia Products Limited v Deputy Minister of National Revenue,
  AP-99-082 (2000), 4 TTR (2d) 797 (CITT)..188
Nordic Laboratories Inc v Canada (Deputy Minister of National
  Revenue, Customs and Excise) (1992), 10 TTR 13, [1992]
  CITT No 87, rev'd (1996), 113 FTR 1, [1996] FCJ No 1067 (TD)...................36

Table of Cases

Nu Skin Canada Inc v Canada (Deputy Minister of National Revenue)
(1997), 3 TTR (2d) 95, [1997] CITT No 84.. 24
Nutricia North America v President of the Canada Border Services
Agency, AP-2009-017 (2011) (CITT) 220

Oil Country Tubular Goods (the People's Republic of China) Injury
Inquiry NQ-2009-004 (2010), 14 TTR (2d) 335 (CITT).. 334
Oriental Trading (MTL) Ltd v Deputy Minister of National Revenue,
AP-91-081 and AP-91-223 (1992), 10 TTR 347 (CITT) 160
Outdoor Gear Canada v President of the Canada Border Services
Agency, AP-2010-060 (2011), 16 TTR (2d) 155 (CITT) 199
Outils Gladu Inc v President of the Canada Border Services Agency,
AP-2004-018 (2005), rev'd 2007 FCA 213, remand to
CITT AP-2004-18R (2008) 129

Pacific Shower Doors (1995) Ltd v Canada (Canadian International
Trade Tribunal), 2009 FCA 317... 48
Parker Cedar Products Ltd v Canada (1988), 92 NR 318, [1988]
FCJ No 1111 (CA) 398
Patagonia International, Inc v Canada (Deputy Minister of National
Revenue) (2000), 5 TTR (2d) 74, [2000] CITT No 87.. 40
Pelco Worldwide Headquarters v President of the Canada Border
Services Agency, AP-2006-016 and AP-2006-018 (2007),
12 TTR (2d) 15 (CITT).. 146
Pfizer Canada Inc v Commissioner of the Canada Customs and
Revenue Agency, AP-2002-038 to AP-2002-090 (2003) (CITT)........................... 221
PHD Canada Distributing Ltd v Commissioner of the Canada Customs
and Revenue Agency, AP-99-116 (2002), 7 TTR (2d) 254 (CITT).................. 194, 214
Philips Electronics Ltd v President of the Canada Border Services
Agency, AP-2011-042 (2012), 16 TTR (2d) 722 (CITT) 104
PL Light Systems Canada Inc v President of the Canada Border Services
Agency, AP-2008-012 (2009), 13 TTR (2d) 739, remand to
Tribunal by FCA, AP-2008-012R (2011), 16 TTR (2d) 127 210
Polysio Insulation Board Imported from the United States (2010),
14 TTR (2d) 492 (CBSA) 332, 345
Prins Greenhouses Ltd v Deputy Minister of National Revenue,
AP-99-045 (2001), 5 TTR (2d) 553 (CITT) 187, 205

R & H Products Ltd v Deputy Minister of National Revenue
(Customs and Excise) (1978), 6 TBR 257 (Tariff Bd).. 37
R Joschko v President of the Canada Border Services Agency,
AP-2011-012 (2011), 16 TTR (2d) 155 (CITT).. 292

R v Cook (1992), 70 CCC (3d) 239, 54 OAC 325, [1992] OJ No 171 (CA) 4
R v Hasselwander, [1993] 2 SCR 398, 1993 CanLII 90 288
R v Jarvis, 2002 SCC 73 58
R v Krakowec, [1932] SCR 134, 57 CCC 96, [1932] 1 DLR 316 63–64
R v Ling, 2002 SCC 74..58
R v Marstar Trading International Inc (1999), 122 OAC 373,
　138 CCC (3d) 87, [1999] OJ No 2644 (CA).. 411
R v Martin (1991), 2 OR (3d) 16, 63 CCC (3d) 71, [1991] OJ No 161 (CA),
　aff'd [1992] 1 SCR 838, 71 CCC (3d) 572, [1992] SCJ No 32 411
R v Mason, [1935] SCR 513, [1935] 4 DLR 313, [1935] SCJ No 21...............................63
R v Mauder (1965), 47 CR 101, [1966] 1 CCC 328 (Ont Magis Ct) 411
R v Monney (1997), 153 DLR (4th) 617, 120 CCC (3d) 97, [1997]
　OJ No 4806 (CA), rev'd [1999] 1 SCR 652, 171 DLR (4th) 1,
　[1999] SCJ No 18 60
R v Oakes, [1986] 1 SCR 103, 24 CCC (3d) 321, 26 DLR (4th) 200 .... 74, 411
R v Simmons (1984), 45 OR (2d) 609, 7 DLR (4th) 719, [1984] OJ No 3147
　(CA), aff'd [1988] 2 SCR 495, 55 DLR (4th) 673, [1988] SCJ No 86........................59
R v Taafe, [1984] 1 All ER 747, [1984] AC 539 (HL) 73
R v Therriens, [1985] 1 SCR 613, 18 DLR (4th) 655, [1985] SCJ No 30 60
R v Vaughan, [1991] 3 SCR 691, 69 CCC (3d) 576, [1991] SCJ No 103 289
R v Wholesale Travel Group Inc, [1991] 3 SCR 154, 67 CCC (3d) 193,
　1991 CanLII 3 411
R v Wulff (1970), 74 WWR 549, 1 CCC (2d) 281, [1970] BCJ No 603 (CA)................ 411
Rebecca Wigod v Commissioner of the Canada Customs and
　Revenue Agency, AP-2000-013 (2002), 6 TTR (2d) 366 (CITT)............................292
Reebok Canada, a division of Avrecan International Inc v Canada
　(Deputy Minister of National Revenue, Customs and Excise),
　2002 FCA 133 .... 34, 35
Reference by the Deputy Minister of National Revenue under section 70
　of the Customs Act, RSC 1985, c 1 (2nd Supp), regarding the tariff
　classification of certain Reebok Canada blends, AP-98-055 (CITT) 53
Reference Re Section 94(2) of the Motor Vehicle Act (BC) (1983),
　4 CCC (3d) 243, 147 DLR (3d) 539, [1983] BCJ No 2259 (CA),
　aff'd [1985] 2 SCR 486, 23 CCC (3d) 289, 24 DLR (4th) 536 73
Regal Confections Inc v Deputy Minister of National Revenue,
　AP-98-043, AP-98-044 and AP-98-051 (1999) (CITT).............................. 92, 103, 169
Renelle Furniture Inc v President of the Canada Border Services
　Agency, AP-2005-028 (2007), 11 TTR (2d) 531 (CITT) 86–87
Richards Packaging Inc v Deputy Minister of National Revenue
　(2000), 266 NR 352, [2000] FCJ No 2027 (CA) 52
Rlogistics Limited Partnership v President of the Canada Border
　Services Agency, AP-2010-057 (2011), 16 TTR (2d) 94 (CITT) 148

Table of Cases

Robert Gustas v Deputy Minister of National Revenue,
 AP-96-006 (1997), 1 TTR (2d) 904 (CITT)..292
Rollins Machinery Ltd v Deputy Minister of National Revenue,
 AP-99-073 (2000), 2 TTR (2d) 348, appeal allowed and remand
 to Tribunal (sub nom Deputy Minister of National Revenue v
 Rollins Machinery Limited), A-3-98 (1999), 4 TTR (2d) 177 (FCA)....................... 106
Romain L Klaasen v Commissioner of the Canada Customs and
 Revenue Agency, AP-2004-007 (2005), 10 TTR (2d) 542 (CITT)....................289–90
Rona Corporation Inc v President of the Canada Border Services
 Agency, AP-2006-033 (2008), 12 TTR (2d) 295 (CITT)..128
Rona Corporation Inc v President of the Canada Border
 Services Agency, AP-2009-072 (2011) (CITT)..137, 139
Rui Royal International Corp v President of the Canada Border Services
 Agency, AP-2010-003 (2011), 15 TTR (2d) 485, appeal dismissed,
 A-229-11 (28 October 2011) (FCA) 121, 184

Sable Offshore Energy Inc v Canada (Customs and Revenue Agency)
 (2002), 6 TTR (2d) 567, [2002] CITT No 21, rev'd 2003 FCA 220...............53, 89, 191
Sandness v Canada, [1933] Ex CR 78, [1933] 4 DLR 662, 60 CCC 220 61
Sandvik Tamrock Canada Inc v Commissioner of the Canada Customs
 and Revenue Agency, AP-99-083 (2000), 4 TTR (2d) 759 (CITT),
 rev'd 2001 FCA 340 211
Sanyo Canada Inc v Deputy Minister of National Revenue,
 AP-99-029 and AP-99-046 (2000), 4 TTR (2d) 770 (CITT)....................................143
Sarstedt Canada Inc v President of the Canada Border Services Agency,
 AP-2008-011 (2010), 14 TTR (2d) 401 (CITT)..133
SC Johnson & Son, Limited v President of the Canada Border Services
 Agency, AP-2005-015 (2006), 11 TTR (2d) 77 (CITT).. 140
Serge Poirier v President of the Canada Border Services Agency,
 AP-2006-012 (2007), 11 TTR (2d) 439 (CITT)..292
Shaw Industries v Deputy Minister of National Revenue (Customs
 and Excise) (1992), 53 FTR 15, 8 TTR 141, [1992] FCJ No 22 (TD)................. 306, 394
Shell Canada Ltd v Canada, [1999] 3 SCR 622, 1999 CanLII 647 21
Sherson Marketing Corporation v Canada (Deputy Minister of National
 Revenue) (Sherson No 3) (2000), 4 TTR (2d) 832, [2000] CITT No 60..................27
Sherson Marketing Corporation v Canada (Deputy Minister of National
 Revenue) (Sherson No 4) (2000), 4 TTR (2d) 842, [2000] CITT No 61 27
Sherson Marketing Corporation v Canada (Deputy Minister of National
 Revenue) (Sherson No 2) (2000), 4 TTR (2d) 821, [2000] CITT No 59 27
Sher-Wood Hockey Inc v President of the Canada Border Services
 Agency, AP-2009-045 (2011), 15 TTR (2d) 336, appeal to
 Federal Court of Appeal discontinued A-167-11..112

Signature Plaza Sport Inc v Minister of National Revenue (Customs & Excise) (1990), 32 FTR 287, 1 TTR 318, [1990] FCJ No 187 (TD) 26
Sigvaris Corporation v President of the Canada Border Services Agency, AP-2007-009 (2009), 13 TTR (2d) 291 (CITT) 218, 223
Simms Sigal & Co Ltd v Canada (Customs and Revenue Agency) (2003), 8 TTR (2d) 20, [2003] CITT No 44 26
Softwood Lumber Dispute Dispute WT/DS264/AB/RW (2006), 11 TTR (2d) 191 (WTO) Preliminary Report WT/DS236R at (2002), 7 TTR (2d) 301; Final Report at (2003), 8 TTR (2d) 654 (WTO) 368
Sony of Canada Ltd v Commissioner of the Canada Customs and Revenue Agency, AP-2001-097 (2004), 8 TTR (2d) 554 (CITT) 145, 192, 194, 214
Spectra/Premium Industries Inc v President of the Canada Border Services Agency, AP-2006-053 (2008), 12 TTR (2d) 912 (CITT) 134
Sport Dinaco Inc v Deputy Minister of National Revenue, AP-99-061 (2000), 4 TTR (2d) 524 (CITT) 153
Supertek Canada Inc v Commissioner of the Canada Customs and Revenue Agency, AP-2001-095 (2003), 7 TTR (2d) 931 (CITT) 162
Suzuki Canada Inc and Canadian Kawasaki Motors Inc v Commissioner of the Canada Customs and Revenue Agency, AP-99-114, AP-99-115, and AP-2000-008 (2003), 8 TTR (2d) 1 (CITT), rev'd (sub nom Suzuki Canada Inc v Canada (Customs and Revenue Agency)), 2004 FCA 131 .... 83, 151, 152, 153
Sy Marketing Inc v President of the Canada Border Services Agency, AP-2006-040 (2008), 12 TTR (2d) 1024 (CITT) 95

Tai Lung (Canada) Ltd v President of the Canada Border Services Agency, AP-2006-034 (2007), 11 TTR (2d) 684 (CITT) 87, 122
Tara Materials Inc v President of the Canada Border Services Agency, AP-2009-016 (2010), 14 TTR (2d) 609 (CITT) 227
Teal Cedar Products (1977) Ltd v Canada (Attorney General) (1988), [1989] 2 FC 15, 92 NR 308, [1988] FCJ No 1109 (CA) 398
Textile and Apparel Goods Safeguard Inquiry No CS-2005-002 (2006), 11 TTR (2d) 326 (CITT) 266, 326
The Pampered Chef, Canada Corporation v President of the Canada Border Services Agency (2008), 12 TTR (2d) 284, [2008] CITT No 6 .... 21, 22, 28
Tiffany Woodworth v President of the Canada Border Services Agency, AP-2006-035 (2007), 11 TTR (2) 718 (CITT) 82, 292
Timberwest Forest Corp v Canada, 2007 FC 148, aff'd 2007 FCA 389 398
Time Data Recorder International Ltd v Canada (Minister of National Revenue) (1993), 66 FTR 253, 13 TTR 332, [1993] FCJ No 768 (TD), aff'd (1997), 211 NR 229, 2 TTR (2d) 122, [1997] FCJ No 475 (CA) 4

Table of Cases

Tourki v Canada (Minister of Public Safety and Emergency Preparedness), 2006 FC 50, aff'd 2007 FCA 186 5
Toyota Tsusho America Inc v President of the Canada Border Services Agency, AP-2010-063 (2011), 16 TTR (2d) 138 (CITT) 359
Toys "R" Us (Canada) Ltd v Deputy Minister of National Revenue, AP-99-067 (2001) (CITT) 173
Transilwrap of Canada Ltd v Commissioner of the Canada Customs and Revenue Agency, AP-2000-018 (2001), 6 TTR (2d) 220 (CITT) 207
Triple-A Specialty Co v Deputy Minister of National Revenue (Customs and Excise) (1978), 6 TBR 701 (Tariff Bd) 37
Triton Industries Ltd v Canada (Deputy Minister of National Revenue for Customs and Excise) (1980), 2 CER 34, 7 TBR 33 (Tariff Bd) 32
Tyco Safety Products Canada Ltd v President of the Canada Border Services Agency, AP-2010-055 (2011), 16 TTR (2d) 29 (CITT) 194

Ulextra Inc v President of the Canada Border Services Agency, AP-2010-024 (2011), 15 TTR (2d) 765 (CITT) 201
Ultima Foods Inc v Canada (Attorney General), 2012 FC 799 398
United Parcel Service Canada Ltd v Canada (Minister of Public Safety and Emergency Preparedness), 2011 FC 204 69
Utex Corporation v Canada (Deputy Minister of National Revenue), 2001 FCA 54 .... 26, 52
Uvex Toko Canada Ltd v Deputy Minister of National Revenue, AP-95-269 and AP-95-285 (1996) (CITT) 196, 198

VGI Village Green Imports v President of the Canada Border Services Agency, AP-2010-046 (2012), 16 TTR (2d) 333 (CITT) 117
Volpak Inc v Canada (Border Services Agency) (2010), 15 TTR (2d) 52 (CITT) 48

Wal-Mart Canada Corporation v President of the Canada Border Services Agency, AP-2010-035 (2011), 15 TTR (2d) 726 (CITT) 156
Wayne Ericksen v Commissioner of the Canada Customs and Revenue Agency, AP-2000-059 (2002) (CITT) 289
Weldwood of Canada Ltd v Canada (Deputy Minister of National Revenue, Customs and Excise) (1991), 44 FTR 31, 5 TTR 258, [1991] FCJ No 100 (TD) 354
Western RV Coach v President of the Canada Border Services Agency, AP-2006-002 (2007), 11 TTR (2d) 576 (CITT) 226
Wilton Industries Canada Ltd v Commissioner of the Canada Customs and Revenue Agency, AP-2001-088 (2002), 6 TTR (2d) 802 (CITT) 127
Windsor Wafers, Division of Beatrice Foods v Deputy Minister of National Revenue, AP-89-281 (1991) (CITT) 191–92

Wirth v Deputy Minister of National Revenue (Customs & Excise) (1990), 3 TCT 2012, 1 TST 1385, [1990] CITT No 1 6

Wood Venetian Blinds and Slats from Mexico and China NQ-2003-003 (2004), 9 TTR (2d) 113 (CITT) 340

Woodward Stores Ltd v Deputy Minister of National Revenue (Customs and Excise) (1974), 6 TBR 184 (Tariff Bd) 26

Yamaha Motor Canada Ltd v Commissioner of the Canada Customs and Revenue Agency, AP-99-105 (2000), 4 TTR (2d) 108 (CITT), aff'd 2002 FCA 34 .... 149, 152

Yves Ponroy Canada v Deputy Minister of National Revenue, AP-96-117 (1997), 4 TTR (2d) 779 (CITT) 97

Zellers Inc v Deputy Minister of National Revenue, AP-97-057 (1998) (CITT) 103, 124, 169

Table of Conventions and Agreements

NOTE: *Pinpoints refer to chapter and section numbers.*

Agreement Establishing the World Trade Organization. See WTO Agreement
Agreement Establishing the WTO. See WTO Agreement
Agreement on Agriculture. See WTO Agreement on Agriculture
Agreement on Antidumping. See WTO Antidumping Agreement
Agreement on Safeguards. See WTO Agreement on Safeguards
Agreement on Sanitary and Phytosanitary Measures. See WTO Agreement on Sanitary and Phytosanitary Measures
Agreement on Subsidies and Countervailing Measures. See WTO Agreement on Subsidies and Countervailing Measures
Agreement on Textiles and Clothing. See WTO Agreement on Textiles and Clothing
Agreement on Trade-Related Aspects of Intellectual Property. See WTO Agreement on Trade-Related Aspects of Intellectual Property
Agriculture Agreement. See WTO Agreement on Agriculture
Antidumping Agreement. See WTO Antidumping Agreement

Canada-Chile Free Trade Agreement (CCFTA), 1997 .... 1D, 2F, 4C
    Article F-02 .... 2G
    Article F-05 .... 2G
    Annex C-00-B, Appendix 5.1 .... 2F
Canada-Columbia Free Trade Agreement (CCOFTA), 2011 .... 2F
    Article 317 .... 2F
Canada-Costa Rica Free Trade Agreement (CCRFTA), 2002 .... 1D, 2F
    Annex III.1, Appendix III.1.1.1 .... 2G
    Annex III.1, Appendix III.1.6.1 .... 2F
    Annex III.3.1 .... 2G
Canada-European Free Trade Agreement (CEFTA), 2009 .... 2F

Article 17 .... 3D
Article 18 .... 3D
Canada-Israel Free Trade Agreement (CIFTA), 1997 .... 1D, 1H, 2F, 2H
Article 4.6 .... 2G
Canada-Peru Free Trade Agreement (CPFTA), 2008 .... 2F
Canada-US Free Trade Agreement (CUSFTA), 1987 (superseded by NAFTA,
  which includes Mexico) 2F, 3E
Convention for the Protection of Cultural Property in the Event of Armed
  Conflicts, 1954 .... 5C
  First Protocol, 1954 .... 5C
  Second Protocol, 1999 .... 5C
  Article I 5C
Convention on International Trade in Endangered Species of Wild Fauna
  and Flora (CITES), 1973 .... 1C, 4A, 5B
  Appendix I 5B
  Appendix II 5B
  Appendix III 5B
Convention on the Means of Prohibiting and Preventing the Illicit Import,
  Export and Transfer of Ownership of Cultural Property, 1978 .... 5C
  Article I 5C
Customs Valuation Agreement. See WTO Agreement on Implementation of Article VII of
  the General Agreement on Tariffs and Trade 1994. See Customs Valuation Agreement

Free Trade Agreements (FTAs) 2E, 2F, 2H, 3D, 4C

GATT. See WTO General Agreement on Tariffs and Trade
General Agreement on Tariffs and Trade. See WTO General Agreement on Tariffs and Trade

International Convention on the Harmonized Commodity Description
  and Coding System (HS Convention), 1988 .... 2D, 3E
  General Interpretive Rules 2D
  Chapter 98 .... 2D
  Chapter 99 .... 2D
International Plant Protection Convention, 1997
  Annex 6G

Marrakesh Agreement Establishing the World Trade Organization. See WTO Agreement
Montreal Protocol on Substances that Deplete the Ozone Layer, 1989 .... 6B

North American Free Trade Agreement (NAFTA), 1994 .... 1D, 1F, 1H, 2E, 2F, 2G,
  2H, 3A, 3D, 3E, 3F, 4C, 4D
  Article 802 .... 2G

Table of Conventions and Agreements

Article 805 .... 2G
Chapter 3, Annex 300-B, Appendix 6 .... 2F
Article 1711 .... 6F
Chapter 19 .... 3E
Article 19.13 .... 3E
Annex 1901.2 .... 3E
Article 1904 .... 3E
Annex 1904.13 .... 3E
Article 1905.1 .... 3E
Article 1905.2 .... 3E
Article 1905.8 .... 3E
Article 1905.10 .... 3E
Article 1907.3 .... 3E
Annex 1911 .... 3E

Protocol on the Accession of the People's Republic of China to the WTO, 2001 ..... 2G

Safeguards Agreement. See WTO Agreement on Safeguards
Sanitary and Phytosanitary Agreement. See WTO Agreement on Sanitary and Phytosanitary Measures
Softwood Lumber Agreement, 2006 .... 4A, 4C, 5A
Stockholm Convention on Persistent Organic Pollutants, 2004 .... 6B
Subsidies Agreement. See WTO Agreement on Subsidies and Countervailing Measures

Textiles and Clothing Agreement. See WTO Agreement on Textiles and Clothing

Universal Postal Convention, 1994 .... 1I
  Letter Post Regulations 1I

World Trade Organization Agreement. See WTO Agreement, 1994
WTO Agreement, 1994 .... 2A, 2F, 2G, 3D, 4C
  (also referred to as Agreement Establishing the World Trade Organization; Agreement Establishing the WTO; Marrakesh Agreement Establishing the World Trade Organization; World Trade Organization Agreement)
  Annex 2 .... 3B
  Annex 2, Article 2 .... 3D
  Annex 2, Article 2.15 .... 3E
WTO Agreement on Agriculture, 1994 .... 3B, 4C
  Article 3.3 .... 3E
  Article 5 .... 2G
  Article 8 .... 3E
  Annex 1 .... 3B

　　　　Annex 2 .... 3B
WTO Agreement on Implementation of Article VII of the General Agreement
　　on Tariffs and Trade, 1994 .... 1E, 3D
WTO Agreement on Safeguards, 1994 .... 2G
　　Article 3 .... 2G
　　Article 4 .... 2G
　　Article 6 .... 2G
WTO Agreement on Sanitary and Phytosanitary Measures, 1994 .... 3E
　　Article 5.1 .... 3E
　　Article 5.5 .... 3E
　　Article 5.8 .... 3E
　　Article 9.1 .... 3E
WTO Agreement on Subsidies and Countervailing Measures, 1994 .... 3A, 3D
　　Article 8.3 .... 3E
　　Article 8.5 .... 3E
　　Article 13.1 .... 3E
　　Article 27 .... 3E
WTO Agreement on Textiles and Clothing, 1994 .... 4C
WTO Agreement on Trade-Related Aspects of Intellectual Property, 1994
　　Article 39(3) 6F
WTO Anti-dumping Agreement, 1994 .... 3E
　　Article 3.3 .... 3E
WTO General Agreement on Tariffs and Trade (GATT 1994) 2G, 3A, 3E
　　Article VI 3A, 3B, 3D
　　Article XVI 3D
　　Article XIX 2G

Table of Customs Memoranda

NOTE: *Pinpoints refer to chapter and section numbers.*

Customs D Memorandum D7-4-3, "NAFTA Requirements for Drawback
and Duty Deferral" (12 April 1996) 2H
Customs D Memorandum D8-1-1, "Temporary Importation" (22 January 2010) 2H
Customs D Memorandum D8-1-4 "Form E29B, Temporary admission permit"
(7 November 2005) 2H
Customs D Memorandum D8-1-7, "Use of ATA Carnets and
Canada-China-Taiwan Carnets for the Temporary Admission
of Goods" (8 June 2007) 2H
Customs D Memorandum D8-2-1, "Canadian Goods Abroad Program"
(22 June 2009) 2H
Customs D Memorandum D8-2-4, "Canadian Goods Abroad Program—
Emergency Repairs" (22 June 2009) 2H
Customs D Memorandum D10-0-1, "Classification of Parts and Accessories
in the Customs Tariff" (24 January 1994) 2D
Customs D Memorandum D10-14-30, "Tariff Classification of Medicaments
including Natural Health Products" (20 August 2004) 2D
Customs D Memorandum D11-3-3, "NAFTA Country of Origin Marking
Rules" (23 March 2007) 2E
Customs D Memorandum D13-3-2 "Related Persons" (9 August 2013) 1E
Customs D Memorandum D13-4-12 "Commissions and Brokerage
(Customs Act, Section 48)" (13 June 2008) 1E
Customs D Memorandum D13-8-1 "Computed Value Method"
(4 February 2014) 1E
Customs D Memorandum D13-9-1 "Residual Basis of Appraisal Method"
(19 November 2013) 1E, 1F
Customs D Memorandum D17-1-7 "Customs Self Assessment Program
for Importers" (17 December 2010) 1D, 1I

Table of Regulations

NOTE: Pinpoints refer to chapter and section numbers.

Canadian Environmental Protection Act, 1999, SC 1999, c 33
Export of Substances on the Export Control List Regulations, SOR/2013-88 .... 6B
    Schedule I 6C
Ozone-Depleting Substances Regulations, 1998, SOR/99-7 .... 6B
    s 2 .... 6B
    s 6 .... 6B
    s 7 .... 6B
    s 17 .... 6B
    s 20 .... 6B
    s 21 .... 6B
    s 22 .... 6B
    s 28 .... 6B

Canadian International Trade Tribunal Act, RSC 1985, c 47 (4th Supp)
Canadian International Trade Tribunal Regulations, SOR/89-35 .... 2G, 4C

Consumer Packaging and Labelling Act, RSC 1985, c C-38
Consumer Packaging and Labelling Regulations, CRC, c 417 .... 6C
    s 4 .... 6C

Controlled Drugs and Substances Act, SC 1996, c 19
Industrial Hemp Regulations, SOR/98-156 .... 6D
    s 1 .... 6D
    s 2 .... 6D
    s 3 .... 6D
    s 18 .... 6D

    s 19 .... 6D
    s 20 .... 6D
    ss 21 to 25 .... 6D
    ss 27 to 30 .... 6D
    s 39 .... 6D
  Narcotic Control Regulations, CRC c 1041 .... 6D
    s 8 .... 6D
    s 8.2 .... 6D
    s 9 .... 6D
    s 9.1 .... 6D
    s 10 .... 6D
    ss 15 to 29 .... 6D
    Schedule 6D
  Precursor Control Regulations, SOR/2002-359 .... 6D
    s 10 .... 6D
    ss 12 to 24 .... 6D
    ss 25 to 31 .... 6D
    s 28.1 .... 6D
    ss 32 to 38 .... 6D
    s 39 .... 6D
    s 40 .... 6D
    ss 40 to 46 .... 6D
    s 43 .... 6D
    ss 48 to 57 .... 6D
    s 49 .... 6D
    ss 49 to 65 .... 6D
    s 51 .... 6D
    s 57 .... 6D
    ss 58 to 68 .... 6D
    ss 69 to 75 .... 6D
    s 77 .... 6D

Criminal Code, RSC 1985, c C-46
  Regulations Prescribing Antique Firearms, SOR/98-464 .... 2I
  Regulations Prescribing Certain Firearms and Other Weapons, Components and Parts of Weapons, Accessories, Cartridges, Magazines, Ammunitions and Projectiles as Prohibited Weapons, SOR/98-462 .... 2I
  Schedule, Part 3, Item 12 .... 2I

Cultural Property Export and Import Act, RSC 1985, c C-51
  Canadian Cultural Property Export Control List, CRC, c 448 .... 5C
  Cultural Property Export Regulations, CRC, c 449 .... 5C

Table of Regulations

ss 3 to 12 .... 5C
ss 17 to 20 .... 5C

Customs Act, RSC 1985, c 1 (2d Supp)
Abatement of Duties Payable Regulations, SOR/86-946 .... 1H, 2H
Accounting for Imported Goods and Payment of Duties Regulations,
   SOR/86-1062 .... 1B
   s 41 .... 1J
CCFTA Rules of Origin Regulations, SOR/97-340 .... 1D
Customs Brokers Licensing Regulations, SOR/86-1067 .... 1C
Customs Sufferance Warehouses Regulations, SOR/86-1065 .... 1C
   s 12 .... 1J
   s 17 .... 1J
Designated Provisions (Customs) Regulations, SOR/2002-336 .... 1I, 1J
Direct Shipment of Goods Regulations, SOR/86-876 .... 2E
Free Trade Agreement Advance Rulings Regulations, SOR/97-72 .... 1D
   s 7 .... 1D
NAFTA Rules of Origin Regulations, SOR/94-14 .... 1D
Persons Authorized to Account for Casual Goods Regulations, SOR/95-418 .... 1B
Presentation of Persons (2003) Regulations, SOR/2003-323 .... 1I
Proof of Origin of Imported Goods Regulations, SOR/98-52 .... 1D, 2E
   s 4 .... 2E
   s 5 .... 2E
   ss 6 to 9 .... 2E
   s 10 .... 2E
Refund of Duties Regulations, SOR/98-48 .... 1H, 2H
Reporting of Exported Goods Regulations, SOR/2005-23 .... 4C
   s 5 .... 1J
Reporting of Imported Goods Regulations, SOR/86-873 .... 1B
Tariff Classification Advance Rulings Regulations, SOR/2005-256 .... 1D
   s 6 .... 1D
Tariff Items 9971.00.00 and 9992.00.00 Accounting Regulations,
   SOR/98-47 .... 2H
Valuation for Duty Regulations, SOR/86-792 .... 1E
   s 2.1 .... 1E
   s 3 .... 1E

Customs Tariff, SC 1997, c 36
Australia Tariff and New Zealand Tariff Rules of Origin Regulations,
   SOR/98-35 .... 1D
CCFTA Tariff Preference Regulations, SOR/97-322 .... 2E
CCOFTA Rules of Origin Regulations, SOR/2011-131 .... 1D, 2E

CCRFTA Rules of Origin Regulations, SOR/2002-395 ...... 1D
CEFTA Rules of Origin Regulations, SOR/2009-198 ...... 1D, 2E
CEFTA Tariff Preference Regulations, SOR/2009-200 ...... 2E
CIFTA Rules of Origin Regulations, SOR/97-63 ...... 1D
CIFTA Tariff Preference Regulations, SOR/97-64 ...... 2D
CJFTA Rules of Origin Regulations, SOR/2012-179 ...... 1D, 2E
CJFTA Tariff Preference Regulations, SOR/2012-181 ...... 2E
Commonwealth Caribbean Countries Tariff Rules of Origin
    Regulations, SOR/98-36 ...... 1D
CPAFTA Rules of Origin Regulations, SOR/2013-50 ...... 1D, 2E
CPAFTA Tariff Preference Regulations, SOR/2013-52 ...... 2E
Customs Bonded Warehouses Regulations, SOR/96-46 ...... 1C, 2H
    s 12 ...... 1J
Determination of the Country of Origin for the Purposes of Marking
    of Goods (NAFTA Countries) Regulations, SOR/94-23 ...... 2F
European Union Surtax Order SOR/99-317 [repealed] 2E, 3E
    Preamble 2E
General Preferential Tariff and Least Developed Country Tariff Rules of
    Origin Regulations, SOR/98-34 ...... 1D
Haiti Deemed Direct Shipment (General Preferential Tariff and Least
    Developed Country Tariff) Regulations, SOR/2010-58 ...... 2E
Marking of Imported Goods Regulations, SOR/94-10 ...... 2E
Most-Favoured-Nation Tariff Rules of Origin Regulations, SOR/98-33 ...... 1D, 2E
NAFTA Rules of Origin Regulations, SOR/94-14 ...... 2E
    s 15 ...... 2E
Temporary Importation (Excise Levies and Additional Duties) Regulations,
    SOR/89-427 ...... 2H
Temporary Importation Tariff Item 9993.00.00 Regulations, SOR/98-58 ...... 2H

Excise Tax Act, RSC 1985, c E-15
    Value of Imported Goods (GST/HST) Regulations, SOR/91-30 ...... 2H

Export and Import Permits Act, RSC 1985, c E-19
    Area Control List, SOR/81-543 ...... 4C, 4D
    Automatic Firearms Country Control List, SOR/91-575 ...... 4C, 4D
    Import Permits Regulations, SOR/79-95 ...... 4C
    Export Control List, SOR/89-202 ...... 4C, 4D
    Export of Logs Permit, CRC, c 612 ...... 4D
    Export of One Cent Bronze Coins Permit, CRC, c 613 ...... 4D
    Export of Specimens Permit, CRC, c 616 ...... 4D
    Export Permits Regulations, SOR/97-204 ...... 4C, 4D
    Export Permits Regulations (Softwood Lumber Products 2006),
        SOR/2007-15 ...... 4D

Table of Regulations

General Export Permits 4D
Import Control List, CRC, c 604 .... 4C, 4D
Issuance of Certificates Regulations, SOR/93-587 .... 4D

Export and Import of Rough Diamonds Act, SC 2002, c 25
Export and Import of Rough Diamonds Regulations, SOR/2003-15 .... 5D
    ss 2 to 5 .... 5D
    s 7 .... 5D
    s 8 .... 5D
    s 9 .... 5D

Hazardous Products Act, RSC 1985, c H-3
Controlled Products Regulations, SOR/88-66 .... 6A

Health of Animals Act, SC 1990, c 21
Health of Animals Regulations, CRC, c 296 .... 6E
    s 2 .... 6E
    Part II 6E
    Parts II to VII 6E
    s 7 .... 6E
    ss 7 to 9 .... 6E
    ss 7 to 62 .... 6E
    s 8 .... 6E
    s 9 .... 6E
    s 10 .... 6E
    s 11 .... 6E
    s 13 .... 6E
    s 14 .... 6E
    s 15 .... 6E
    s 16 .... 6E
    Part III 6E
    s 34 .... 6E
    s 34.1 .... 6E
    Part IV 6E
    s 40 .... 6E
    ss 40 to 53 .... 6E
    s 41 .... 6E
    s 41.1 .... 6E
    s 42 .... 6E
    s 42.1 .... 6E
    s 43 .... 6E
    s 45 .... 6E
    s 46 .... 6E

s 47	6E
s 47.1	6E
s 48	6E
s 49	6E
s 50	6E
s 51	6E
s 51.1	6E
s 51.2	6E
s 53	6E
Part V	6E
s 54	6E
Part VI	6E
s 55	6E
s 57	6E
Part VII	6E
ss 58 to 62	6E
Part VIII	6E
s 69	6E
ss 69 to 71	6E
s 70	6E
s 71	6E
Part XI	6E
s 121	6E
s 122	6E
s 133	6E
s 134	6E
Part XII	6E
ss 136 to 159	6E
s 138	6E
ss 138 to 159	6E
s 139	6E
s 140	6E
s 141	6E
s 142	6E
s 143	6E
s 146	6E
s 147	6E
s 148	6E
s 149	6E
s 152	6E
s 153	6E
s 154	6E
s 156	6E

Table of Regulations

s 157	6E
s 158	6E
s 159	6E
Part XIII	6E
s 160	6E
s 161	6E
Part XIV	6E
s 162	6E
ss 166 to 171	6E
s 167	6E
s 168	6E
s 170.1	6E
s 171.2	6E
Part XVI	6E
s 188	6E
s 190	6E
s 191	6E
s 192	6E
s 194	6E
s 195	6E
s 202	6E
Schedule III	6E
Schedule VI	6E
Schedule VII	6E

Pest Control Products Act, SC 2002, c 28
Pest Control Products Regulations, SOR/2006-124 .... 6F

Plant Protection Act, SC 1990, c 22
Plant Protection Regulations, SOR/95-212 .... 6G
    Part II 6G
    Part III 6G
    Part IV 6G

Precious Metals Marking Act, RSC 1985, c P-19
Precious Metals Marking Regulations, CRC, c 1303 .... 6H
    s 3 .... 6H
    s 4 .... 6H
    s 5 .... 6H

Proceeds of Crime (Money Laundering) and Terrorist Financing Act, SC 2000, c 17
Cross-Border Currency and Monetary Instruments Reporting Regulations, SOR/2002-412 .... 1B

Softwood Lumber Products Export Charge Act, 2006, SC 2006, c 13
Export Permits Regulations (Softwood Lumber Products 2006),
SOR/2007-15 .... 4D

Special Import Measures Act, RSC 1985, c S-15
Special Import Measures Regulations, SOR/84-927 .... 3E
    s 16 .... 3C
    s 17.1 .... 3C
    s 17.2 .... 3C
    Part II 3B
    s 27 .... 3B
    s 27.1 .... 3B
    ss 28 to 31 .... 3B
    s 31.1 .... 3B
    s 32 .... 3B
    s 33 .... 3B
    s 34 .... 3B
    s 35 .... 3B
    s 35.01 .... 3B
    s 35.1 .... 3B
    s 35.2 .... 3B
    s 36 .... 3B
    s 36.001 .... 3B
    Part III 3B
    s 37 .... 3E
    s 37.1 .... 3E

Textile Labelling Act, RSC 1985, c T-10
Textile Labelling and Advertising Regulations, CRC, c 1551 .... 6I
    s 5 .... 6I
    s 8 .... 6I
    s 11 .... 6I
    ss 13 to 20 .... 6I
    Part III 6I
    Schedule I 6I
    Schedule II 6I

Wild Animals and Plant Protection Regulation of International and Interprovincial Trade Act, SC 1992, c 52
Wild Animal and Plant Trade Regulations, SOR/96-263 .... 5B
    ss 10 to 12 .... 5B
    s 13 .... 5B

Table of Regulations

ss 15 to 17 .... 5B
s 14 .... 5B
s 17 .... 5B
s 18 .... 5B
Schedule II 5B

Table of Statutes

NOTE: *Pinpoints refer to chapter and section numbers.*

Agricultural Marketing Programs
    Act, SC 1997, c 20 .... 4C
Agricultural Pests' Control Act,
    1927, SC 1926–27, c 40 .... 6F
Agriculture and Agri-Food
    Administrative Monetary
    Penalties Act, SC 1995,
    c 40 .... 1I, 1J, 6A, 6E, 6F, 6G
An Act respecting Export Duties,
    SC 1896–97, c 17 .... 5A
An Act to Amend the Criminal Code
    and the Cultural Property Export
    and Import Act, SC 2005, c 40 .... 5C
Animal Disease and Protection Act,
    RSC 1970, c A-13 [repealed] 6E

Canada Border Services Agency Act,
    SC 2005, c 38 .... 1C
Canada Consumer Product Safety
    Act, SC 2010, c 21 .... 5A, 6A
    s 2 .... 6A
    s 5 .... 6A
    ss 5 to 9 .... 6A
    s 6 .... 6A
    s 7 .... 6A
    s 8 .... 6A
    s 9 .... 6A

    s 14 .... 6A
    s 31 .... 6A
    s 32 .... 6A
    s 35 .... 6A
    s 37 .... 6A
    ss 49 to 65 .... 6A
    Schedule 1 .... 6A
    Schedule 2 .... 6A
Canada-Jordan Economic Growth
    and Prosperity Act, SC 2012,
    c 18 .... 2F
    Schedule 3 .... 2F
Canada-Panama Economic Growth
    and Prosperity Act, SC 2012, c 26 ... 2F
    Schedule 4 .... 2F
    Schedule 5 .... 2F
Canada Shipping Act, SC 2001, c 26 ... 6A
Canadian Charter of Rights and
    Freedoms, 1982, being Schedule B
    to the Canada Act 1982
    (UK), c 11 .... 1G, 1I, 2I, 4E
    s 1 .... 1I
    s 10 .... 1I
    s 11 .... 1I, 1K
    s 24 .... 1I
Canadian Dairy Commission Act,
    RSC 1985, c C-15 .... 4C

Canadian Environmental Assessment
Act, 2012, SC 2012, c 19, s 52
    s 37 .... 6E
Canadian Environmental Protection
Act, 1999, SC 1999, c 33 ...... 5A, 6A, 6B
    s 99 .... 6B
    s 101 .... 6B
    ss 101 to 103 .... 6B
    s 102 .... 6B
    Schedule 3 .... 6B
Canadian International Trade
Tribunal Act, RSC 1985, c 47
(4th Supp) 2G, 3E, 4A, 4C
    s 19.01 .... 2G
    s 19.012 .... 2G
    s 19.013 .... 2G
    s 19.0131 .... 2G
    ss 19.014 to 19.016 .... 2G
    s 19.017 .... 2G
    s 19.018 .... 2G
    s 19.02 .... 2G
    s 19.1 .... 2G
    s 20 .... 2G
    s 23 .... 2G
    s 26 .... 2G
    s 29 .... 2G
    s 30.07 .... 2G, 4C
    ss 30.2 to 30.26 .... 2G
    s 30.21 .... 2G
    s 30.22 .... 2G
    s 30.23 .... 2G
    s 30.25 .... 2G
    s 40 .... 2G
Competition Act, RSC 1985, c C-34 ..... 3E
Consumer Packaging and Labelling
Act, RSC 1985, c C-38 .... 6A, 6C
    ss 4 to 7 .... 6C
    ss 4 to 9 .... 6C
    s 6 .... 6C
    s 7 .... 6C
    s 9 .... 6C
    s 10 .... 6C

    s 11 .... 6C
    s 20 .... 6C
Controlled Drugs and Substances
Act, SC 1996, c 19 .... 5A, 6A, 6D
    s 2 .... 6D
    Part I 6D
    s 4 .... 6D
    ss 4 to 7 .... 6D
    s 7.1 .... 6D
    s 16 .... 6D
    Schedule I 6D
    Schedules I to V 6D
    Schedule II 6D
    Schedule III 6D
    Schedule IV 6D
    Schedule V 6D
    Schedule VI 6D
Copyright Act, RSC 1985, c C-42 .... 2I
Criminal Code, RSC 1985,
c C-46 .... 2I, 4C, 6A, 6D
    s 2 .... 2I
    s 7 .... 5C
    s 46 .... 2I
    s 59 .... 2I
    s 60 .... 2I
    s 84 .... 2I
    s 117.07 .... 2I
    s 117.15 .... 2I
    s 163 .... 1G, 2I
    s 163.1 .... 1G, 2I
    s 320 .... 2I
    s 430 .... 5C
    s 787 .... 5C
Cultural Property Export and Import
Act, RSC 1985, c C-51 .... 4A, 5A, 5C
    s 2 .... 5C
    s 4 .... 5C
    s 5 .... 5C
    s 6 .... 5C
    s 7 .... 5C
    s 8 .... 5C
    s 11 .... 5C

Table of Statutes

s 17	5C
s 18	5C
s 29	5C
s 30	5C
s 31	5C
s 36.1	5C
s 37	5C
s 38	5C
s 39	5C
s 40	5C
ss 40 to 44	5C
s 41	5C
s 42	5C
s 43	5C
s 44	5C
s 45	5C
Schedule	5C

Customs Act, RSC 1927, c 44
s 2	1G

Customs Act, RSC 1985, c 1 (2d Supp) ... 1A, 1C, 1E, 1F, 1G, 1I, 1J, 1K, 2A, 2B, 2C, 2D, 2E, 2F, 2H, 3E, 3F, 4C

s 2	1A, 1B, 1E
s 7.1	1J
s 11	1B, 1I, 1J, 1K
s 12	1B, 1J, 1K, 6B
ss 12 to 16	1B
s 13	1J, 1K
s 15	1K
s 19	1B
s 20	1K
s 29	2F
s 31	1J, 1K
s 32	1B, 1D, 1G, 1J, 2D
s 32.2	1J, 2D
s 33	1J
s 35.01	1G, 1J, 2E
s 35.02	2E
s 35.1	1D
s 36	1B
s 37	1B
s 40	1K
s 43	1K
s 43.1	1D
s 44	1E
s 45	1E
ss 45 to 55	1E, 2C
s 46	2H
s 47	1E
ss 47 to 55	1G
s 48	1E
ss 48 to 50	1E
s 49	1E
s 51	1E
s 52	1E
s 54	2E
s 57.01	1G
s 58	1G, 2D
s 59	1G, 1H, 2D
s 60	1G
s 60.1	1G
s 60.2	1G
s 61	1G
s 67	1G, 1L
s 67.1	1G
s 68	1G, 1L
s 70	1G
s 71	1G, 2I
s 73	1H
ss 73 to 81	1H
s 74	1H, 2H
s 75	2H
ss 76.78 to 79.1	2H
s 80	2H
s 80.1	2H
s 80.2	2H
s 81	1H, 2H
s 95	1J, 1K, 6B
s 98	1I
ss 98 to 105	1I
s 99	1I
s 99.1	1I
ss 99.2 to 99.4	1I
s 101	1I

s 102	1I
s 103	1K
s 104	1I
s 106	1L
s 107	1K
s 107.1	1J
s 109.1	1J
s 113	1I
s 122	1I
s 124	1I
s 127.1	1J
s 129	1I
ss 129 to 133	1J
s 130	1I
s 131	1I, 1J
s 135	1I
s 138	1I
ss 138 to 141	1I
s 139	1I
s 139.1	1I
s 141	1I
s 151	1K
s 152	1K, 2I
s 153	1K
ss 153 to 157	1K
ss 153 to 163	2B
s 153.1	1K
s 154	1K
s 155	1K
s 156	1K
s 157	1K
s 158	1K
s 159	1K
s 159.1	1K
s 160	1B, 1K
s 160.1	1K
s 161	1K
s 163	1K

Customs Tariff, RSC 1985 (3d Supp), c 41

s 4	2D
s 10	2D

Schedule II	2D
General Rules	2D
Rule 3	2D
Code 2000	2D
Code 2101	2D
Code 2546	2D
Code 7934	2D

Customs Tariff, SC 1997, c 36 .... 1A, 1C, 1E, 1F, 1H, 1K, 2A, 2B, 2D, 2E, 2F, 2G, 2H, 2I, 3A, 3E, 4A, 4C, 5D, 6E

s 2	2D
s 10	1G, 2D
s 11	1G, 2D
s 13	2D
s 14	2D
s 15	2D
s 16	1G, 2E, 2F
s 17	2E
s 19	1F, 2E
s 20	1E, 2C
s 21	2C
s 22	2C
s 24	2E, 2F
s 25	2F
s 26	2E, 2F
s 29	2C, 2F
s 30	2F
s 31	2E, 2F
s 33	2F
s 34	2F
s 35	2F
s 36	2F
s 37	2F
s 38	2E, 2F
s 39	2F
s 40	2F
s 41	2F
s 42	2E, 2F
s 43	2F
s 44	2F
s 45	2F
s 48	2F

Table of Statutes

s 49	2F	s 71.41	2G
s 49.01	2F, 2G	s 71.5	2G
s 49.08	2F	s 71.6	2G
s 49.1	2F, 2G	s 77.1	2G, 4C
s 49.2	2F	ss 77.1 to 77.8	2G
s 49.4	2F	s 77.3	2G, 4C
s 49.41	2F, 2G	s 77.4	2G
s 49.5	2F, 2G	s 77.6	2G, 4C
s 50	2F	s 78	2G
s 51	2F	s 79	2G
s 52	2F	s 81	2H
s 52.1	2F, 2G	s 82	2H
ss 52.1 to 52.4	2F	s 83	1E
s 52.2	2F, 2G	s 84	1E
s 52.3	2F, 2G	s 87	1E, 1G
s 52.4	2G	s 88	1E, 2H
s 53	2G	s 89	2H
s 54	2G	ss 89 to 101	2H
s 54.5	2F	s 90	2H
s 55	2G, 4C	s 91	2H
ss 55 to 65	2G	s 92	2H
ss 55 to 66	2G	s 95	2H
s 57	2G	s 98	2H
s 59	2G	s 101	2H
s 59.1	2G	s 102	2H
s 60	2G	s 105	1E, 2H
s 61	2G	s 106	2H
s 62	2G	ss 109 to 111	2H
s 63	2G	s 110	2H
s 64	2G	s 113	2H
s 66	2G	s 114	2H
s 67	2G	s 115	2H
s 68	2G	s 116	2H
s 69	2G	ss 116 to 127	2H
s 70	2G	s 118	1J, 2H
s 71	2G	s 119	2H
s 71.01	2G	s 121	2H
s 71.1	2G	s 122	2H
s 71.2	2G	s 136	2I
ss 71.2 to 71.4	2G	Schedule	2A, 2D, 2F, 2H, 2I, 3E, 5A, 5D
s 71.3	2G		
s 71.4	2G		

General Rules for the Interpretation of the Harmonized System .... 2D, 2I, 2 Addendum
    General Rule 1 .... 2D
    General Rule 2 .... 2D
    General Rule 3 .... 2D
    General Rule 4 .... 2D
    General Rule 5 .... 2D
    General Rule 6 .... 2D
Canadian Rules .... 2D, 2I, 2 Addendum
    Canadian Rule 1 .... 2D
    Canadian Rule 6 .... 2D
Table of Sections and Chapters of the Harmonized System .... 2D, 2 Table 1
List of Countries 2D, 2F
List of Tariff Provisions 2C, 2D, 2F, 2H, 5D
Chapter 7 .... 2G
Chapter 8 .... 2G
Section IV: Chapters 16 to 24 ..... 2D
Chapter 21 .... 2D
Section VI: Chapters 28 to 38 .... 2D
Chapter 30 .... 2D
Section VII: Chapters 39 and 40 .... 2D
Chapter 39 .... 2D
Chapter 40 .... 2D
Section VIII: Chapters 41 to 43 .... 2D
Chapter X: Chapters 47 to 49 ... 2D
Chapter 49 .... 2D
Section XI: Chapters 50 to 63 .... 2D
Chapter 57 .... 2D
Chapter 59 .... 2D
Chapter 61 .... 2D
Chapter 62 .... 2D
Chapter 63 .... 2D
Section XII: Chapters 64 to 67 .... 2D

Section XIII: Chapters 68 to 70 .... 2D
Section XV: Chapters 72 to 83 ... 2D
Chapters 72 to 76 .... 2D
Chapter 73 .... 2D
Chapters 73 to 76 .... 2D
Chapters 78 to 81 .... 2D
Chapters 78 to 82 .... 2D
Chapter 82 .... 2D
Chapter 83 .... 2D
Section XVI: Chapters 84 and 85 .... 2D
Chapter 84 .... 2D
Chapter 85 .... 2D
Section XVII: Chapters 86 to 89 .... 2D
Chapters 86 to 88 .... 2D
Chapter 87 .... 2D
Chapter 89 .... 2G
Section XVIII: Chapters 90 to 92 .... 2D
Chapter 90 .... 2D
Chapter 91 .... 2D
Chapter 92 .... 2D
Chapter 93 .... 2D
Section XX: Chapters 94 to 96 ... 2D
Chapter 94 .... 2D
Chapter 95 .... 2D
Chapter 96 .... 2D
Chapter 98 .... 2A, 2C, 2D
Chapter 99 .... 2C, 2D, 2F
"F" Staging List 2C, 2D, 2F, 2H

Customs Tariff—Specific Tariff Headings/Items (*Note: from both current and previous versions of the Schedule to the Customs Tariff*)
    0603.10.11 .... 2F
    1701.91.10 .... 2F
    1701.99.10 .... 2F
    1702.90.21 .... 2F
    1702.90.61 .... 2F

Table of Statutes

1702.90.70	2F
1702.90.81	2F
18.06	2D
1806.90.90	2D
19.02	2D
1902.19.29	2D
1902.30.40	2D
20.08	2D
2008.80.19	2D
2008.99.30	2D
20.09	2D
2009.80.19	2D
2103.90.20	2D
21.04	2D
2104.10.00	2D
21.06	2D
2106.90	2D
2106.90.99	2D
22.02	2D
2202.90.90	2D
2309.90.99	2D
25.03	2D
28.02	2D
28.43 to 28.46	2D
30.02	2D
30.03	2D
3003.90.00	2D
30.04	2D
3004.50.00	2D
30.05	2D
30.06	2D
32.12	2D
33.03	2D
33.04	2D
33.05	2D
33.06	2D
33.07	2D
3307.49.00	2D
35.05	2D
35.06	2D
37.07	2D
38.08	2D
38.15	2D
3815.90.90	2D
38.24	2D
3824.90	2D
3824.90.10	2D
39.01 to 39.14	2D
39.16	2D
3916.10.00	2D
3920.10	2D
3920.62	2D
3921.90.90	2D
3921.90.91	2D
3921.90.99	2D
39.23	2D
39.24	2D
3924.90.00	2D
39.26	2D
3926.20.92	2D
3926.20.95	2D
3926.40	2D
3926.40.10	2D
3926.90	2D
3926.90.90	2D
3926.90.90.94	2D
40.03	2D
4003.00.00	2D
40.08	2D
4008.21.90	2D
40.09	2D
40.10	2D
4010.19.90	2D
40.15	2D
4015.90.10	2D
4015.90.20	2D
40.16	2D
4016.10.00	2D
4016.99.90	2D
42.02	2D
4202.12.90	2D
4202.32	2D
4202.32.90	2D
4202.91.90	2D

4202.92	2D	6307.10	2D
4202.92.11	2D	6307.20	2D
4202.92.90	2D	6307.20.00	2D
4202.99.90	2D	6307.90	2D
427	1G	6307.90.99	2D
431	1G	63.09	2D
438	1G	63.10	2D
44022-1	1G	64.01 to 64.05	2D
44.10	2D	64.03	2D
4410.11.90	2D	6404.11.99	2D
4410.19.90	2D	64.05	2D
44516-1	1G	6405.20.90	2D
49.11	2D	64.06	2D
4911.99.90	2D	65.05	2D
55.03	2D	6505.90	2D
56.04	2D	6505.90.90	2D
56.07	2D	67.03	2D
56.08	2D	6802.21.00	2D
5608.19.90	2D	6802.23.00	2D
56.09	2D	6802.91.00	2D
5609.00.00	2D	6802.93.00	2D
57.03	2D	68.06	2D
5703.20.10	2D	68.07	2D
59.06	2D	6807.10.00	2D
6104.43.00	2D	70.19	2D
61.10	2D	7019.32	2D
61.14	2D	7019.32.10	2D
6114.30.00	2D	7102.10	5D
6115.12.00	2D	7102.21	5D
6115.93.00	2D	7102.31	5D
61.16	2D	73.07	2D
6116.93.00	2D	73.08	2D
6204.43.00	2D	7308.90.90	2D
6210.30.00	2D	73.12	2D
6211.33.90	2D	73.15	2D
62.16	2D	73.17	2D
6216.00.00	2D	73.18	2D
63.05	2D	7323.93.00	2D
6305.33.00	2D	73.26	2D
63.06	2D	7610.90.00	2D
6306.22.00	2D	76.15	2D
63.07	2D	7615.19.00	2D

Table of Statutes

82.05	2D
8205.70.90	2D
82.07	2D
82.08	2D
8208.20.00	2D
82.09	2D
8209.00	2D
8209.00.91	2D
82.10	2D
8212.10.00	2D
8212.20.00	2D
8212.90.00	2D
83.01	2D
83.02	2D
8302.42.00	2D
83.06	2D
83.08	2D
83.10	2D
8403.10.10	2D
8403.90.00	2D
84.12	2D
84.13	2D
8413.19.90	2D
8413.20.00	2D
8413.91.30	2D
84.14	2D
8414.10	2D
8414.90.90	2D
84.15	2D
8415.20	2D
8415.20.10	2D
8415.20.90	2D
8415.90	2D
8415.90.29	2D
84.19	2D
8419.60.00	2D
8419.81	2D
8419.81.10	2D
8419.81.90	2D
8419.89.90	2D
8419.90	2D
8419.90.00	2D
8421.31.90	2D
84.25 to 84.30	2D
84.29	2D
84.31	2D
8431.10.00	2D
8431.49.00	2D
84.36	2D
8436.80.10	2D
84.39	2D
8439.99.90	2D
84.55	2D
8455.10.00	2D
8455.90.90	2D
84.65	2D
8465.99.90	2D
84.67	2D
8467.29	2D
8467.29.10	2D
8467.29.90	2D
84.71	2D
8471.10.00	2D
8471.49.00	2D
8471.70	2D
8471.70.00	2D
84.79	2D
8479.89.99	2D
8479.90	2D
8479.90.90	2D
84.81	2D
8481.80	2D
8481.80.00	2D
8481.30.00	2D
84.82	2D
8482.80.90	2D
85.04	2D
8504.40	2D
8504.40.90	2D
8504.40.99	2D
8504.90.91	2D
85.07	2D
8507.20.90	2D
8507.30.90	2D

85.08	2D	8528.22.00	2D
85.13	2D	85.29	2D
8513.10.10	2D	8529.90.90	2D
8513.99.91	2D	8529.90.99	2D
85.14	2D	85.36	2D
8514.40	2D	85.37	2D
8514.40.90	2D	85.44	2D
85.15	2D	8544.41.10	2D
8515.21	2D	8544.60.00	2D
8515.21.10	2D	86.09	2D
85.16	2D	87.01	2D
8516.79	2D	87.01 to 87.08	2D
8516.79.10	2D	8701.90	2D
8516.79.90	2D	87.03	2D
85.17	2D	8703.21	2D
8517.11.00	2D	8703.21.90	2D
85.18	2D	87.08	2D
8518.30.91	2D	8708.29.99	2D
8518.30.99	2D	8708.39.90	2D
8519.99.10	2D	8708.99.90	2D
85.20	2D	8708.99.99	2D
8520.90.90	2D	87.11	2D
85.21	2D	87.12 to 87.13	2D
8521.90	2D	87.14	2D
8521.90.10	2D	8714.99.10	2D
8521.90.90	2D	8714.99.90	2D
85.22	2D	87.15	2D
8522.90.90	2D	8715.00.00	2D
85.23	2D	8716.80.10	2D
8523.11.00	2D	8901.10.90	2G
85.24	2D	8901.20.90	2G
8524.22.90	2D	8901.90.99	2G
8524.32.00	2D	8902.00.10	2G
8524.32.90	2D	8904.00.00	2G
8524.51.90	2D	8905.10.00	2G
8524.99.91	2D	8905.20.10	2G
85.25	2D	8905.20.20	2G
8525.10.00	2D	8905.90.10	2G
8525.20.90	2D	8905.90.90	2G
8525.50.00	2D	8906.90.99	2G
85.25	2D	90.18	2D
8528.21.82	2D	90.22	2D

Table of Statutes

90.29	2D
9029.20.91	2D
9029.90.92	2D
9032.89.20	2D
9102.12.00	2D
9105.99.90	2D
91.14	2D
9207.10.00	2D
9209.94.90	2D
94.01	2D
9401.40.00	2D
9401.61	2D
9401.61.00	2D
9401.61.10	2D
9401.61.90	2D
9401.71	2D
9401.71.10	2D
9401.71.90	2D
9401.80	2D
9401.80.10	2D
9401.80.90	2D
9401.90	2D
94.03	2D
9403.20.00	2D
9403.90	2D
9403.90.00	2D
9403.00.00	2D
94.05	2D
9405.10.00	2D
9405.40.90	2D
9405.99.00	2D
95.02	2D
9502.10.00	2D
95.03	2D
9503.00	2D
9503.00.90	2D
9503.41.00	2D
9503.49.00	2D
9503.70	2D
9503.70.10	2D
9503.90.00	2D
95.04	2D
9504.10.00	2D
95.05	2D
9505.10.00	2D
9505.10.00.10	2D
9505.90.00	2D
95.06	2D
9506.91	2D
9506.91.10	2D
9506.91.90	2D
9506.99	2D
9506.99.10	2D
9506.99.90	2D
9603.40.10	2D
9617.00.00	2D
98.04	2H
9804.10.00	1E, 2H
9804.20.00	1E, 2H
9804.30.00	1E, 2H
9804.40.00	2H
98.05	2H
9805.00	1E
9805.00.00	2H
98.06	2H
9806.00.00	2H
98.07	2H
9807.00.00	2H
9810.00.00	2I
9811.00.00	2I
9813.00.00	1B, 2H
9814.00.00	1B, 2H
9897.00.00	1G, 2A, 2I
9898.00.00	1G, 2A, 2D, 2I
9899.00.00	1G, 2A, 2D, 2I
9903.00.00	2D
9908.00.00	2D
99.37	2H
9937.00	1E
9937.00.00	2H
9948.00.00	2D
9958.00.00	2D
9959.00.00	2D
9961.00.00	2D

9962.00.00	2D
9971.00.00	1E,
9977.00.00	2D
9979.00.00	2D, 2F

Excise Act, RSC 1985, c E-14 .... 2A
Excise Act, 2001, SC 2002,
    c 22 .... 1E, 1H, 2A, 2H
    ss 21.1 to 21.3 .... 2H
Excise Tax Act, RSC 1985,
    c E-15 .... 1E, 1H, 2C, 2H, 3F
    Part IX 2A
    s 181 .... 1I
    s 280 .... 1J
Explosives Act, RSC 1985, c E-17 .... 6A
Export Act, RSC 1985, c E-18 ... 1C, 4A, 5A
    s 2 .... 5A
    s 3 .... 5A
    s 5 .... 5A
Export and Import of Rough
    Diamonds Act, SC 2002,
    c 25 .... 4A, 5A, 5D
    s 2 .... 5D
    s 8 .... 5D
    s 9 .... 5D
    s 13 .... 5D
    s 14 .... 5D
    s 16 .... 5D
    s 17 .... 5D
    s 22 .... 5D
    s 36 .... 5D
    ss 36 to 39 .... 5D
    ss 36 to 40 .... 5D
    s 37 .... 5D
    s 38 .... 5D
    s 39 .... 5D
    s 40 .... 5D
    s 41 .... 5D
Export and Import Permits Act,
    RSC 1985, c E-19 .... 1C, 2D, 2F, 2G, 4A,
    4B, 4C, 4D, 4E, 6G
    s 3 .... 4C

s 4 .... 4C
s 4.1 .... 4C, 4D
s 5 .... 2G, 4C
s 5.4 .... 2G, 4C
s 6.1 .... 4C
s 6.2 .... 4C
s 6.3 .... 4C
s 7 .... 4D
s 8 .... 2I, 4D
ss 8.1 to 8.5 .... 4D
s 8.4 .... 4C
s 9 .... 4D
s 9.1 .... 4D
s 9.2 .... 4D
s 10 .... 4D
s 11 .... 4D
s 13 .... 4E
s 19 .... 4E
s 25 .... 4B, 4E

Farm Products Marketing Agencies
    Act, RSC 1985, c F-4 .... 4C
Federal Courts Act, RSC 1985,
    c F-7 .... 1G, 1J, 1L, 3D, 3E
    s 18.1 .... 3E, 3F
    s 18.3 .... 3E, 3F
    s 18.5 .... 1G
    s 28 .... 3F
    s 39 .... 5C
Feeds Act, RSC 1985, c F-9 .... 6A, 6C
Fertilizers Act, RSC 1985, c F-10 .... 6A, 6C
Financial Administration Act,
    RSC 1985, c F-11 .... 2H
Firearms Act, SC 1995, c 39
    s 2 .... 2I
    s 35 .... 2I
    s 139 .... 2I
Fisheries Act, RSC 1985, c F-14
    ss 74 to 76 .... 6H
Food and Drugs Act, RSC 1985,
    c F-27 .... 6A, 6C, 6D, 6F
    s 2 .... 6C

Table of Statutes

Gold and Silver Marking Act,
RSC 1906, c 90 .... 6H

Hazardous Products Act, RSC 1985,
c H-3 .... 6A
    Schedule II 6A

Health of Animals Act, SC 1990,
c 21 .... 1C, 4A, 5A, 6A, 6E
    s 2 .... 6E
    s 14 .... 6E
    ss 14 to 18 .... 6E
    s 15 .... 6E
    s 16 .... 6E
    s 17 .... 6E
    s 18 .... 6E
    s 19 .... 6E
    s 25 .... 6E
    s 27 .... 6E
    s 37 .... 6E
    s 43 .... 6E
    s 48 .... 6E
    s 64 .... 6E
    s 65 .... 6E
    ss 65 to 68 .... 6E
    s 67 .... 6E
    s 68 .... 6E

Imperial Customs Act, 1825 (UK),
6 Geo IV, c 105 .... 1A

Immigration and Refugee Protection
Act, SC 2001, c 27
    s 2 .... 5C

Livestock and Livestock Products Act,
RSC 1985, c L-9 [repealed] 6E

Motor Vehicle Safety Act, SC 1993,
c 16 .... 6A

Narcotic Control Act, RSC 1985, c N-1
[repealed] 6D

Pest Control Product Act, 1939,
SC 1939, c 21 .... 6F

Pest Control Products Act,
SC 2002, c 28 .... 6A, 6C, 6F
    s 2 .... 6F
    s 6 .... 6F
    s 7 .... 6F
    s 33 .... 6F
    s 67 .... 6F
    s 68 .... 6F
    s 69 .... 6F
    s 79 .... 6F

Plant Protection Act, SC 1990,
c 22 .... 5A, 6A, 6F, 6G
    s 2 .... 6G
    s 3 .... 6G
    s 7 .... 6G
    s 8 .... 6G
    s 9 .... 6G
    s 29 .... 6G
    ss 30 to 37 .... 6G
    s 38 .... 6G
    s 39 .... 6G
    s 41 .... 6G
    s 42 .... 6G
    s 43 .... 6G
    s 44 .... 6G
    s 47 .... 6G
    s 48 .... 6G
    ss 48 to 51 .... 6G
    s 51 .... 6G
    Part IV 6G
    s 55 .... 6G
    ss 55 to 60 .... 6G
    s 56 .... 6G
    s 57 .... 6G
    s 58 .... 6G
    s 60 .... 6G

Plant Quarantine Act, RSC 1985,
c P-15 [repealed] 6G

Precious Metals Marking Act,
SC 1928, c 40 .... 6H

Precious Metals Marking Act,
    RSC 1985, c P-19 .... 1F, 5A, 6A, 6H
    s 2 .... 6H
    s 3 .... 6H
    s 4 .... 6H
    s 10 .... 6H
    s 11 .... 6H
Proceeds of Crime (Money
    Laundering) and Terrorism
    Financing Act, SC 2000, c 17 .... 1B
    s 12 .... 1B

Sale of Goods Acts 1E
Seeds Act, RSC 1985, c S-8 .... 6C
Softwood Lumber Products
    Export Charge Act, 2006,
    SC 2006, c 13 .... 4A, 4C, 5A
    s 23 .... 4C
Special Import Measures Act,
    RSC 1985, c S-15 .... 1E, 1G, 1H, 2A,
    2C, 2G, 3A, 3B, 3C, 3D, 3E, 3F, 4A, 4C
    s 2 .... 3B, 3C, 3D, 3E, 3F
    s 3 .... 3D, 3E
    ss 3 to 6 .... 3D, 3E
    ss 3 to 8 .... 3D
    s 4 .... 3D
    ss 6 to 10 .... 3E
    s 7 .... 3D, 3E
    s 8 .... 3D, 3E, 3F
    s 10 .... 3D
    s 11 .... 3D, 3F
    s 12 .... 3D
    s 13.2 .... 3D, 3E
    s 14 .... 3A, 3E
    s 15 .... 3C
    ss 15 to 23 .... 3C
    s 16 .... 3C
    s 19 .... 3C
    s 20 .... 3C, 3E
    s 21 .... 3C
    s 23.1 .... 3C
    s 24 .... 3C, 3E

s 25 .... 3C
s 26 .... 3C, 3E
s 27 .... 3C
s 28 .... 3C, 3E
s 29 .... 3C, 3E
s 30 .... 3C
s 30.1 .... 3B
s 30.2 .... 3B, 3E
s 30.4 .... 3B, 3E
s 31 .... 3D, 3E
s 31.1 .... 3E
s 33 .... 3E
s 34 .... 3E
s 35.1 .... 3E
s 37.1 .... 3E
s 38 .... 3D, 3E
s 41 .... 3E
s 42 .... 3E
ss 42 to 47 .... 3E
s 43 .... 3E
s 45 .... 3E
s 46 .... 3E
s 49 .... 3D, 3E
ss 49 to 54 .... 3E
s 51 .... 3D
s 51.1 .... 3D
s 52 .... 3D, 3E
s 53 .... 3D
s 53.1 .... 3D
s 53.2 .... 3D
s 54 .... 3D
s 55 .... 3E
s 56 .... 3E
ss 56 to 62 .... 3E
s 57 .... 3E
s 58 .... 3E
s 59 .... 3E
s 60 .... 3E
s 60.1 .... 3E
s 61 .... 3E
s 62 .... 3E
s 76.01 .... 3D, 3E

Table of Statutes

s 76.02 .... 3D, 3E
s 76.03 .... 3D, 3E
s 77 .... 3E
Part I.1 .... 3A, 3D, 3E
ss 77.01 to 77.038 .... 3E
s 77.011 .... 3E
ss 77.011 to 77.013 .... 3D
s 77.012 .... 3E, 3F
s 77.013 .... 3E
s 77.014 .... 3E
s 77.015 .... 3D, 3E
s 77.016 .... 3E
s 77.017 .... 3E
ss 77.017 to 77.019 .... 3E
s 77.018 .... 3E
s 77.019 .... 3D, 3E
s 77.023 .... 3E
s 77.024 .... 3E
s 77.025 .... 3E
s 77.027 .... 3E
s 77.028 .... 3E
s 77.029 .... 3E
s 77.033 .... 3E
s 77.035 .... 3E
Part II 3A, 3D, 3E
s 77.1 .... 3A, 3D, 3E
s 77.12 .... 3E, 3F
s 77.15 .... 3D, 3E
s 77.19 .... 3D, 3E
Part III 3F
s 82 .... 3F
s 83 .... 3F
s 89 .... 3D, 3F
ss 89 to 95 .... 3F
s 90 .... 3D, 3F
s 96.1 .... 3D, 3E
s 93 .... 3F
s 95 .... 3F
s 98 .... 3A
Statistics Act, RSC 1985, c S-19 .... 2D
Statutory Instruments Act,
   RSC 1985, c S-22 .... 2G, 3E

Supreme Court Act, RSC 1985, c S-26.1G

Textile Labelling Act, RSC 1985,
   c T-10 .... 1F, 5A, 6A, 6I
   s 2 .... 6I
   s 3 .... 6I
   s 4 .... 6I
   s 5 .... 6I
   s 7 .... 6I
   s 12 .... 6I
   s 13 .... 6I
Trade-marks Act, RSC 1985, c T-13 .... 2I

Visiting Forces Act, RSC 1985, c V-2
   s 2 .... 2I

Weights and Measures Act,
   RSC 1985, c W-6 .... 6C
Wild Animals and Plant Protection
   Regulation of International and
   Interprovincial Trade Act,
   SC 1992, c 52 .... 1C, 4A, 5A, 5B
   s 6 .... 5B
   s 7 .... 5B
   s 8 .... 5B
   s 10 .... 5B

World Trade Organization
   Agreement Implementation
   Act, SC 1994, c 47 .... 2A, 3D

Table of Tariffs

NOTE: *Pinpoints refer to chapter and section numbers.*

Australia Tariff (AUT)	2E, 2F
British Preferential Tariff (BPT)	2F
Canada-Israel Agreement Tariff (CIAT)	2F
Chili Tariff (CT)	2F, 2G, 4C
Colombia Tariff (COLT)	2F, 2G
Commonwealth Caribbean Countries Tariff (CCCT)	2E, 2F
Costa Rica Tariff (CRT)	2F, 2G, 4C
General Preferential Tariff (GPT)	2E, 2F
General Tariff (GT)	2F
Iceland Tariff (IT)	2F, 2G
Jordan Tariff (JT)	2F, 2G
Least Developed Country Tariff (LDCT)	2E, 2F
Mexico Tariff (MT)	2F, 2I, 4C
Mexico-US Tariff (MUST)	2F, 2G, 2I, 4C
Most-Favoured-Nation Tariff (MFNT)	2E, 2F, 2G
New Zealand Tariff (NZT)	2E, 2F
Norway Tariff (NT)	2F, 2G
Panama Tariff (PAT)	2F, 2G
Peru Tariff (PT)	2F, 2G
Switzerland-Liechtenstein Tariff (SLT)	2F, 2G
US Tariff (UST)	2F, 2I, 4C

Index

Administrative determinations and appeals
  abatement and refund of duties, 54–55
  appeals to provincial courts, 54
  appeals to the Tribunal, 49–53
  determination of value of duty, tariff classification, and origin, 44
  enforcement
    administrative and investigative powers, 57–58
    appeals, 65
    ascertained forfeiture, 64
    criminal offences and punishment, 70–75
    Detailed Adjustment Statements (DAS), 57
    examination of goods, 60–61
    forfeiture, 61–64
    penalty for violations, 68–70
    search of the person, 59–60
    seizure of goods and conveyances, 61
    third party claims, 65–68
  marking determination, 44
  payment of duties and taxes before appeal, 45–49
  references to Tribunal, 53

Administrative Monetary Penalty System (AMPS), 13, 68–69, 72. *See also* Administrative determinations and appeals, enforcement
Agricultural Marketing Programs Act, 402. *See also* Export and Import Permits Act, establishment of lists, *Import Control List (ICL)*
Agricultural Pests' Control Act, 1927. *See* Pest Control Products Act
Agriculture and Agri-Food Administrative Monetary Penalties Act (AAAMP), 65, 69–70, 433, 472, 475–76, 482. *See also* Administrative determinations and appeals, enforcement; Canada Consumer Product Safety Act (CCPS Act), administrative monetary penalties
Agriculture Review Tribunal, 65
Animal Disease and Protection Act. *See* Health of Animals Act
ATA Carnet, 279

Canada Border Services Agency (CBSA)
  accounting and payment of duties, required documentation, 10–13

cargo control document (CCD), 10
cargo control number (CCN), 10
final accounting package, 13
release on minimum documentation (RMD), 10–11, 13
Administrative Monetary Penalty System (AMPs), 68–69. *See also* Administrative Monetary Penalty System (AMPs)
advance ruling regulations, 14
advance rulings, qualifications for, 14. *See also* Canadian International Trade Tribunal
appeals to, 50
complaint
 filing, 325
 investigation initiated by, 326–27
Customs D Memorandum D10-0-1, 181
Customs D Memorandum D13-3-2, 23–24
Customs D Memorandum D13-4-12, 29–30. *See also* Goods, methods of valuation
Customs D Memorandum D13-8-1, 42–43. *See also* Goods, methods of valuation
Customs D Memorandum D13-9-1, 43. *See also* Goods, methods of valuation
Customs D Memorandum D17-1-7, 13, 14
Customs Self-Assessment (CSA) Program for Importers, 13
Customs Tariff, administration and enforcement of, 77–78
dumping and subsidies, investigations into, 299–300, 302, 304, 306, 353. *See also* Special Import Measures Act (SIMA)
 countervailing duty on imports from a specific country, 315
 duties, liability to pay, 315–23
 duties when massive importation causes injury, 314
 Federal Court of Appeal, appeals to, 361
 final determination, order, or finding, action on, 329–30, 353–56
 initiated, 327
 NAFTA dispute settlement, 372–73
 orders, review of, and injury, findings of, 362–68
 preliminary determination of injury, 328–29
 reconsideration, 330
 Reference, request to Tribunal for, 328
 termination of investigation before preliminary determination, 327–28
 Tribunal, appeals to, 356–60. *See also* Canadian International Trade Tribunal, appeals to
duties for emergency repairs, application for relief from, 280, 282
Export Control List (ECL)
 cultural property, 419–20
 establishment of, 399–401
 exports, determination of values for. *See Special Import Measures Act (SIMA)*, export price; *Special Import Measures Act (SIMA)*, normal value
 general provisions, 391–92. *See also Special Import Measures Act (SIMA)*, general provisions
 goods, marking requirement for. *See* Goods, marking of
Grodan Inc v President of the Canada Border Services Agency, 56. *See also* Administrative determinations and appeals, abatement and refund of duties
imported goods, disposal of unclaimed or abandoned, 7

licences, registering for, 7–8
licences, warehouse
  customs bonded, 8, 9
  highway frontier, 8, 9
  Queen's, 9, 10
  sufferance, 8, 9
NAFTA, allowance of benefit, 227
officers (officials), powers of, 44, 56–57, 58–59, 60–61, 64, 229. See also Administrative determinations and appeals, enforcement
ozone-depleting substances, import of controlled, 434–36
penalties and enforcement tools, 61–62
Presentation of Persons (2003) Regulations, 56–57. See also Administrative determinations and appeals, enforcement
President's duties and powers, 46, 48–49, 51, 53
prohibited goods, 289–91, 293
public interest inquiry, Polysio insulation board exported from the United States, 345–47
remissions, administering of, 284
Renelle Furniture Inc v President of the Canada Border Services Agency. See Canadian International Trade Tribunal cases, *Renelle Furniture Inc v President of the Canada Border Services Agency*
section 20 process, 331–34. See also *Special Import Measures Act (SIMA)*, section 20 process investigations
surtax, power to relieve from payment of, 254
tariff classification appeals, 81–82
tariff classifications, competing. See *Customs Tariff*, Competing Tariff Classification
Tribunal, injury inquiry by, 337–40.

values for duty, determination of, 44, 45, 46, 56. See also Goods, methods of valuation
  first trade level, 39
  purchaser and vendor not related, 23–24
  selling commissions, 35
Volpak Inc v Canada (Border Services Agency), 48. See also Canadian International Trade Tribunal cases, *Volpak Inc v Canada (Border Services Agency)*
warehouses, regulation of customs bonded, 275–76, 277
Canada Consumer Product Safety Act (CCPS Act)
  administrative monetary penalties (AMPs) (sections 49–65), 433
  criminal penalties (section 8), 433
  duties and obligations, 432–33
  incident reports (section 14), 432
  recalls (sections 31, 32), 432
  regulations (section 37), 433
  Hazardous Products Act, CCPS as amendment to, 429–30
  prohibitions (sections 2, 5–9), 431
  purpose, definitions, and application of, 430–31
Canada Customs Coding Form (Form B3), 11. See also Canada Border Services Agency (CBSA), accounting and payment of duties, required documentation
Canada Customs and Revenue Agency (CCRA), 349–50, 389
Bernard Chaus Inc (Re), 47–48
binational panel decisions
  iodinated contrast media from the United States, 374–75
  refrigerators and dishwashers from the United States, 375–77

Canada Border Services Agency
(CBSA) as successor to, 81
M & M Footwear Inc v Commissioner of
the Canada Customs and Revenue
Agency, 357–58
Simms Sigal & Co Ltd v Canada (Customs and Revenue Agency), 26–27
tariff classifications, competing. See
Customs Tariff, Competing Tariff
Classification
Tribunal rulings, bicycles from China,
389
Canadian Charter of Rights and Freedoms.
See also Administrative determinations and appeals, enforcement
accused's rights in export cases, 411
administrative and investigative powers of CBSA officials, 57–58
Little Sisters Book and Art Emporium v
Canada (Minister of Justice), intrusion into citizen's rights, 54, 293
R v Oakes, conviction with existence
of reasonable doubt, 74–75
R v Simmons, claims that Charter
rights were violated and admittance of evidence, 59–60
Canadian Dairy Commission Act, 402.
See also Export and Import Permits
Act, establishment of lists, Import
Control List (ICL)
Canadian Environmental Assessment Act.
See Health of Animals Act, permits
and licences (section 160)
Canadian Environmental Protection Act
(CEPA), 1999
export of other controlled substances,
437–38
Export Control List (sections 100–3),
437
prohibition (section 101), 437–38
regulations (section 101), 438

ozone-depleting substances, controlled, 434–36
exportation, 436–37
importation, 434
maintenance of records, 437
Ozone-Depleting Substances Regulations, 1998 (ODSR), 434–36
penalties, 437
report of import or export (section
17), 434
Canadian Food Inspection Agency, 11. See
also Canada Border Services Agency
(CBSA), accounting and payment of
duties, required documentation
Canadian Goods Abroad Program, 279–
80. See also Customs Tariff, Duties
Relief Programs, other duties relief
programs
Canadian International Trade Tribunal
appeals to, 49–53
references to, 53
tariff classification appeals, 81
tariff classification disputes, competing. See Customs Tariff, Competing Tariff Classification
valuation, disputes about between
government and importers, 15. See
also Goods, valuation of imported
Canadian International Trade Tribunal Act
(CITT)
2002 amendment, addition of sections 30.2 to 30.26 ("Safeguard
Measures in Respect of China"),
266–67, 405
China, safeguard measures in respect
of, 165–70
"domestic producer" and "domestic industry," lack of definition for, 326.
See also Customs Tariff, "domestic
producers," meaning of
"market disruption" and "significant
cause," meaning of, 267–68

Regulations, 267
  section 19, 250–51
  section 20 or 26, 248–50
  section 20 or 29, 248–250
  section 30, 165–70, 252, 268–69
  section 40, 252–53
  sections 19 and 23, 255, 256, 264–65
Canadian International Trade Tribunal
  cases, 14
  A & R Dress Co Inc v Canada (Minister of National Revenue), 282. See also Customs Tariff, Duties Relief Programs, other duties relief programs
  AAi.FosterGrant of Canada Co v Canada (Customs and Revenue Agency), 20–21, 22. See also Goods, methods of valuation, purchaser in Canada
  Bernard Chaus Inc (Re), 47. See also Administrative determinations and appeals, payment of duties and taxes before appeal
  Brown's Shoe Shops Inc v Canada (Customs and Revenue Agency), 26
  Brunswick International (Canada) Ltd v Canada (Deputy Minister of National Revenue), 21–22. See also Goods, methods of valuation, purchaser in Canada
  Buffalo Inc v Commissioner of the Canada Customs and Revenue Agency, 226. See also Customs Tariff, Origin of Goods and Marking
  Canada v Kay Silver Inc, 26. See also Goods, methods of valuation, adjustments to transaction value of goods
  Canada (Minister of Human Resources Development) v Hogervest, 48. See also Administrative determinations and appeals, payment of duties and taxes before appeal
  Chaps Ralph Lauren, a Division of 131384 Canada Inc v Canada (Deputy Minister of National Revenue), 26
  Coloridé Inc v Deputy Minister of National Revenue (Customs and Excise), 88
  DMG Trading Company v Canada (Deputy Minister of National Revenue), 29. See also Goods, methods of valuation, adjustments to transaction value of goods
  DSM Nutritional Products Canada Ltd v President of the Canada Border Services Agency, 98
  Duhamel & Dewar Inc v President of the Canada Border Services Agency, 226. See also Customs Tariff, Origin of Goods and Marking
  Flora Manufacturing & Distributing Ltd v Deputy Minister of National Revenue, 98
  Franklin Mint Inc v Commissioner of the Canada Customs and Revenue Agency, 102–3
  Fritz Marketing Inc v Canada (Border Services Agency), 30–32. See also Goods, methods of valuation, adjustments to transaction value of goods
  GFT Mode Canada v Canada (Deputy Minister of National Revenue), 49–50. See also Canadian International Trade Tribunal, appeals to
  Helly Hansen Leisure Canada v Canada (Border Services Agency), 14.
  IPSCO Inc (Re), 47. See also Administrative determinations and appeals, payment of duties and taxes before appeal
  Jan K Overweel Limited v President of the Canada Border Services Agency, 225

MRP Retail Inc v President of the Canada Border Services Agency, 226. See also Customs Tariff, Origin of Goods and Marking
Oriental Trading (MTL) Ltd v Deputy Minister of National Revenue, 160
Pampered Chef, Canada Corporation, The v President of the Canada Border Services Agency, 22, 28–29. See also Goods, methods of valuation
Patagonia International, Inc v Canada (Deputy Minister of National Revenue), 41. See also Goods, methods of valuation, adjustments to transaction value of goods
PHD Canada Distributing Ltd v Commissioner of the Canada Customs and Revenue Agency, 194
Regal Confections Inc v Deputy Minister of National Revenue, 92, 103
Renelle Furniture Inc v President of the Canada, 86–87. See also General Rules for the Interpretation of the Harmonized System, application of
Sable Offshore Energy Inc v Commissioner of the Canada Customs and Revenue Agency, 191–92
Sherson Marketing Corporation v Canada (Deputy Minister of National Revenue) (Sherson No 3), 27. See also Goods, methods of valuation, adjustments to transaction value of goods
Signature Plaza Sport Inc v Minister of National Revenue (Customs & Excise), 26. See also Goods, methods of valuation, adjustments to transaction value of goods
Simms Sigal & Co Ltd v Canada (Customs and Revenue Agency), 26–27. See also Goods, methods of valuation, adjustments to transaction value of goods

Tai Lung (Canada) Ltd v President of the Canada Border Services Agency, 87
Tara Materials Inc v President of the Canada Border Services Agency, 226–27
Triple-A Specialty Co v Deputy Minister of National Revenue (Customs and Excise), 36–37
Volpak Inc v Canada (Border Services Agency), 48. See also Administrative determinations and appeals, payment of duties and taxes before appeal
Western RV Coach v President of the Canada Border Services Agency, 226. See also Customs Tariff, Origin of Goods and Marking
Windsor Wafers, Division of Beatrice Foods v Deputy Minister of National Revenue, 191–92
Certificate of Origin. See Form A—Certificate of Origin
Compendium of Classification Opinions. See General Rules for the Interpretation of the Harmonized System
Construction of Statutes, 389–90. See also Special Imports Measures Act (SIMA), general provisions, rulings
Consumer Packaging and Labelling Act
Consumer Packaging and Labelling Regulations, 439
offences and criminal penalties (section 20), 440
statutory requirements (sections 4–7, 9, 10), 439–40
Controlled Drugs and Substances Act (CDS Act)
Industrial Hemp Regulations, 442–44
Narcotic Control Act, 440
Narcotic Control Regulations, 444–46
offence-related property, forfeiture of, 442 (sections 2, 16)
Precursor Control Regulations, 446–48

Class A precursors, import and
 export of, 447–48
Class B precursors, 450–51
 exportation (sections 32–38), 448–49
 possession and trafficking (sections
  4–7), 441–42
Convention for the Protection of Cultural
 Property in the Event of Armed Con-
 flicts, 418. See also Cultural Property
 Export and Import Act (CPEIA)
Convention on the Means of Prohibiting
 and Preventing the Illicit Import,
 Export and Transfer of Ownership
 of Cultural Property, 418. See also
 Cultural Property Export and Import
 Act (CPEIA)
Copyright Act, 286. See also Customs
 Tariff, Prohibited Goods
Cost, Insurance, and Freight (CIF), 35–36.
 See also Goods, methods of valuation, adjustments to transaction
 value of goods
Criminal Code of Canada
 firearms and prohibited weapons,
  287, 401. See also Customs Tariff,
  Prohibited Goods, firearms and
  prohibited weapons and devices
 prohibited goods, 285–86, 293, 424–25,
  445. See also Customs Tariff, Prohibited Goods
 section 2, 287, 291. See also Customs Tariff, Prohibited Goods, firearms, and
  prohibited weapons and devices
 section 84, 287–91. See also Customs
  Tariff, Prohibited Goods, firearms,
  and prohibited weapons and
  devices
 section 117.07(2), 287. See also Customs Tariff, Prohibited Goods,
  firearms, and prohibited weapons
  and devices
 section 163.1, 54

Cross-Border Currency and Monetary Instruments Reporting Regulations, 3–4.
 See also Goods, failure to report
Cultural Property Export and Import Act
 (CPEIA)
 Canadian cultural property, export
  of, 418
 Convention for the Protection of
  Cultural Property in the Event of
  Armed Conflict (Second Convention) (section 36), 423–24
 export permits (sections 3–12 of Regulations), 419–21
 Export Control List (ECL) (section 4),
  418–19, 421, 424
 offences and punishments (sections
  40–44), 424–25
 protection of foreign cultural property
  (section 37), 422–23
Customs Act
 administrative determinations and
  appeals. See Administrative determinations and appeals
 enactment (1985), 1
 enforcement of. See Canada Border
  Services Agency (CBSA)
 function of, 2
 goods
 marking of. See Goods, marking of
 methods of valuation. See Goods,
  methods of valuation
 reporting, 2–3
 valuation of imported. See Goods,
  valuation of imported
 issuance of warehouse licences, 8. See
  also Canada Border Services Agency
  (CBSA), licences, warehouse
  licences. See Licences
Proceeds of Crime Act, section 12, 5
"purchaser in Canada," 391. See also
 Goods, methods of valuation,
 purchaser in Canada

545

Reporting of Exported Goods Regulations, 400

section 2, definition of "goods," 1–2, 83. *See also* Goods, classification of

section 19(3). *See* Goods, movement of

section 32. *See* Administrative determinations and appeals, marking determinations; Canadian Border Services Agency, Customs Self-Assessment (CSA) Program for Importers; Goods, release of, prior to accounting and payment of duties

section 35. *See* Administrative determinations and appeals, marking determination; *Customs Tariff*, Origin of Goods and Marking, marking of goods; Form A—Certificate of Origin

section 36. *See* Goods, abandoned and unclaimed

section 37(4). *See* Goods, abandoned and unclaimed, designated place of safekeeping for

section 43.1. *See* Canada Border Services Agency (CBSA), advance rulings, qualifications for

section 45. *See* Goods, valuation of imported

section 48. *See* Goods, valuation of imported

section 67. *See* Administrative determinations and appeals; Canadian Border Services Agency, President's duties and powers; Canadian International Trade Tribunal, appeals to

section 68. *See* Administrative determinations and appeals, enforcement, criminal offences and punishment; Canadian International Trade Tribunal, appeals to

section 70. *See* Canadian International Trade Tribunal, references to

section 71. *See* Administrative determinations and appeals, appeals to provincial courts

section 87. *See* Administrative determinations and appeals, determination of value of duty, tariff classification, and origin

section 106. *See* Administrative determinations and appeals, enforcement, criminal offences and punishment

sections 10–11, 4

sections 12–16. *See* Administrative determinations and appeals, determination of value of duty, tariff classification, and origin; Goods, failure to report; Goods, obligation to report

sections 45–55. *See* Administrative determinations and appeals, determination of value for duty, tariff classification, and origin; *Customs Tariff*, rate of duty; Goods, valuation of imported

sections 57–61. *See* Administrative determinations and appeals, marking determination

sections 73–81. *See* Administrative determinations and appeals, abatement and refund of duties

sections 98–105, 109, 122, 124–35, 138–41. *See* Administrative determinations and appeals, enforcement

sections 151 and 152. *See* Administrative determinations and appeals, enforcement, criminal offences and punishment

sections 153 and 163. *See Customs Tariff*, administration and enforcement of

sections 160, 161, and 163. *See* Administrative determinations and appeals, enforcement, criminal offences and punishment
Customs brokers, use of by importers and exporters of business items, 7
Customs Brokers Licensing Regulations. *See* Licences, Brokers, requirements for obtaining
Customs Tariff
  "action," meaning of, 269–70
  administration and enforcement of, 77–78
  commodity nomenclature and description, 82
  "domestic producers," meaning of, 266–67
  duties and taxes levied on goods, 35
  duties and taxes paid and payable, 40
  enactment (1996), 1, 82
  "F" Staging List. *See also* Tariff agreements and accords
    Australia (AUT) and New Zealand (NZT) Tariff rates, 236
    Canada-Israel Agreement Tariff (CIAT) rate, 241
    Columbia Tariff (COLT) rate, 238
    Commonwealth Caribbean Countries Tariff (CCCT) rate, 235
    Costa Rica Tariff (CRT) rate, 239
    custom duties rate, 78, 81, 272
    General Preferential Tariff (GPT) rate, 233–34
    Iceland Tariff (IT) rate, 241
    Least-Developed Country Tariff (LDCT) rate, 235
    Most-Favoured-Nation Tariff (MFNT) rate, 232
    Norway Tariff (NT) rate, 241–42
    Peru Tariff rate, 240
    Switzerland-Liechtenstein Tariffs (SLT) rates, 242
  "import," lack of definition for, 2
  imported goods, refund of duties on, 55
  imports, primary regulator of, 2
  "market disruption" and "significant cause," meaning of, 267–68
  "principal cause," definition of, 403. *See also* Tariff agreements and accords
    Columbia, in respect to goods from, 257
    EFTA countries, in respect to goods from, 261
    Jordan, in respect to goods from, 264
    Mexican and MUST, in respect to goods from, 255
    Panama, in respect to goods from, 265
    Peru, in respect to goods from, 250, 262
    Republic of Chile, in respect to goods from, 256
    US, in respect to goods from, 255
  rate of duty, 15–16. *See also* Goods, valuation of imported
  prohibited goods, 15
  Schedule to
    amendment to the, 81. *See also* Tariff items, 9898.00.00
    Canadian Rules. *See General Rules for the Interpretation of the Harmonized System, Canadian Rules*
    Chapter 99, 204
    free trade agreements, 230. *See also* Free trade agreements (FTAs); Tariff agreements and accords
    General Tariff (GT) rate, 232. *See also* Tariff agreements and accords, General Tariff (GT)
    goods being imported into Canada, purposes for, 279
    List of Countries, 233

List of Tariff Provisions, 2, 78, 179–80, 181, 205, 243, 260, 272, 426
Most-Favoured Nation Tariff (MFNT) rate, 232. *See also* Tariff agreements and accords, Most-Favoured Nation Tariff (MFNT)
organization of, 80–82
parts and accessories, 179
rough diamond, definition of, 426
Toyota Tsusho America Inc v President of the Canada Border Services Agency, 359–60
section 10. *See Customs Tariff*, Schedule to section 16. *See Customs Tariff*, Origin of Goods and Marking, origin of goods
section 18. *See Customs Tariff*, Origin of Goods and Marking, origin of goods
section 19. *See* Goods, marking of, regulations
section 20(2). *See* Goods, valuation of imported
section 34. *See Customs Tariff*, Tariff treatment, General Preferential Tariff (GPT)
section 36. *See Customs Tariff*, Tariff treatment, General Preferential Tariff (GPT)
section 39. *See* Governor in Council, powers concerning TRQ
section 40. *See* Governor in Council, powers concerning LDCT
section 42. *See* Governor in Council, powers concerning CCCT
section 43. *See* Governor in Council, powers concerning TRQ
section 44. *See* Goods, valuation of imported, ad valorem; Tariff agreements and accords, Australia Tariff (AUT); Tariff agreements and accords, New Zealand Tariff (NZT)
section 45. *See* Tariff agreements and accords, *NAFTA*, Mexico Tariff; Tariff agreements and accords, *NAFTA*, US Tariff (UST)
section 47. *See* Goods, methods of valuation
section 48. *See* Goods, methods of valuation; Minister of Finance, power to extend tariff entitlement
section 49. *See* Governor in Council, powers concerning TRQ; Minister of Finance; Tariff agreements and accords
section 51. *See* Governor in Council, powers concerning TRQ
section 54. *See* Tariff agreements and accords, *Canada-Jordan Economic Growth and Prosperity Act*
section 83. *See* Goods, methods of valuation
section 87. *See* Goods, methods of valuation, goods in Iceland, Norway, Switzerland, or Liechtenstein, repairs or alterations made to
section 88. *See Customs Tariff*, Duties Relief Programs, traveller's exemption; Goods, valuation of imported, ethno-cultural exemption
section 101. *See* Canadian Goods Abroad Program; *Customs Tariff*, Duties Relief Programs, other duties relief programs
section 105. *See* Goods, methods of valuation, goods abroad, value for duty of work on the
section 106. *See Customs Tariff*, Duties Relief Programs, other duties relief programs; *Temporary Importation (Excise Levies and Additional Duties) Regulations*

section 113. *See Customs Tariff*, Duties Relief Programs, other duties relief programs

section 115. *See Customs Tariff*, Duties Relief Programs, other duties relief programs

sections 13 and 15. *See* Tariff items, renumbering

sections 17 and 18. *See Customs Tariff*, Origin of Goods and Marking, origin of goods

sections 81 and 82. *See Customs Tariff*, Duties Relief Programs

sections 109–11. *See Customs Tariff*, Duties Relief Programs, other duties relief programs

tariff classification appeals, dispute process for, 81

Customs Tariff, Competing Tariff Classification

base metals (Chapters 72–83), 127–31
  Canadian Tire Corporation Ltd v President of the Canada Border Services Agency, 130–31
  Canmade Furniture Products Inc v Commissioner of the Canada Customs and Revenue Agency, 131–32
  Outils Gladu Inc v President of the Canada Border Services Agency, 129–30
  Rona Corporation Inc v President of the Canada Border Services Agency, 128–29
  Wilton Industries Canada Ltd v Commissioner of the Canada Customs and Revenue Agency, 127–28

foodstuffs, beverages, tobacco (Chapters 16–24), 91–96
  Eurotrade Import-Export Inc v Commissioner of the Canada Border Services Agency, 96
  Excelsior Foods Inc v Commissioner of the Canada Customs and Revenue Agency, 93. *See also* Tariff items, 2202.90.90
  Intersave West Buying and Merchandising Service v Commissioner of the Canada Customs and Revenue Agency, 95–96
  Morris National Inc v President of the Canada Border Services Agency, 91
  New Asia (Brampton) Food Centre v President of the Canada Border Services Agency, 92–93
  Sy Marketing Inc v President of the Canada Border Services Agency, 94–95

footwear, headgear, others (Chapters 64–67), 122–24
  Laxus Products Ltd v Commissioner of the Canada Customs and Revenue Agency, 124
  Tai Lung (Canada) Ltd v President of the Canada Border Services Agency, 122–24

machinery, mechanical appliances, electrical equipment, television image and sound recorders (Chapters 84–85), 133–48
  Asea Brown Boveri Inc v Commissioner of the Canada Customs and Revenue Agency, 189–90
  Canadian Tire Corporation Ltd v President of the Canada Border Services Agency, 136–37
  Canadisc Inc v Commissioner of the Canada Customs and Revenue Agency, 148–49
  Costco Wholesale Canada Ltd v President of the Canada Border Services Agency, 138–39

549

Groupe Cabico Inc v President of the Canada Border Services Agency, 133
Ingram Micro Inc v President of the Canada Border Services Agency, 144–45
Pelco Worldwide Headquarters v President of the Canada Border Services Agency, 146–48
Rona Corporation Inc v President of the Canada Border Services Agency, 139–40
Sanyo Canada Inc v Deputy Minister of National Revenue, 143–44
Sarstedt Canada Inc v President of the Canada Border Services Agency, 133–34
SC Johnson & Son, Limited v President of the Canada Border Services Agency, 140–43
Sony of Canada Ltd v Commissioner of the Canada Customs and Revenue Agency, 145–46. See also Tariff items, 8520.90.90
Spectra/Premium Industries Inc v President of the Canada Border Services Agency, 134–36
miscellaneous manufactured articles (Chapters 94–96), 155–78
Alliance Ro-Na Home Inc v Commissioner of the Canada Customs and Revenue Agency, 157
Calego International Inc v Deputy Minister of National Revenue, 167–68
Canadian Tire Corporation Ltd v President of the Canada Border Services Agency, 176–78
Costco Wholesale Canada Ltd v President of the Canada Border Services Agency, 157–58
Danson Décor Inc v President of the Canada Border Services Agency, 173–74
Dynamo Industries, Inc v President of the Canada Border Services Agency, 178
Elfe Juvenile Products v President of the Canada Border Services Agency, 164–67. See also Tariff items, 9503.00.90
Evenflo Canada Inc v President of the Canada Border Services Agency, 158–62
Globe Electric Company Inc v President of the Canada Border Services Agency, 162–63
Havi Global Solutions (Canada) Limited Partnership v President of the Canada Border Services Agency, 168–70
HBC Imports c/o Zellers Inc v President of the Canada Border Services Agency, 178–79
Intersave West Buying and Merchandising Service v Commissioner of the Canada Customs and Revenue Agency, 163–64
Korhani Canada Inc v President of the Canada Border Services Agency, 170–73
Loblaws Companies Limited v President of the Canada Border Services Agency, 174–76
Toys "R" Us (Canada) Ltd v Deputy Minister of National Revenue, 173
Wal-Mart Canada Corporation v President of the Canada Border Services Agency, 156–57
optical, photographic, cinematographic, measuring, medical instruments; clocks and watches; musical instruments (Chapters 90–92), 153–54
Avon Canada Inc v Commissioner of the Canada Customs and Revenue Agency, 154–55

Index

Sport Dinaco Inc v Deputy Minister of National Revenue, 153–54
plastics and rubber (Chapters 39–40), 99–106
  Formica Canada Inc v Commissioner of Canada Customs and Revenue Agency, 104
  GCP Elastomeric Ltd v President of the Canada Border Services Agency, 105–6
  Monterra Lumber Mills Ltd v President of the Canada Border Services Agency, 99–100
  NC Cameron & Sons Ltd v President of the Canada Border Services Agency, 100
  Philips Electronics Ltd v President of the Canada Border Services Agency, 104–5
  Rollins Machinery Ltd v Deputy Minister of National Revenue, 106
products of chemical or allied industries (Chapters 28–35), 97–98
  Criterion Catalysts & Technologies Canada Inc v President of the Canada Border Services Agency, 98–99
  Yves Ponroy Canada v Deputy Minister of National Revenue, 97
raw hides, travel goods, handbags (Chapters 41–43), 106–7
  Curve Distribution Services Inc v President of the Canada Border Services Agency, 106–7
  Future Product Sales Inc v President of the Canada Border Services Agency, 108–9
  Nokia Products Limited & Primecell Communications Inc v Commissioner of the Canada Customs and Revenue Agency, 107
stone, plaster, cement, asbestos, ceramic, glass (Chapters 68–70), 125–26

Active Marble & Tile Ltd v Commissioner of the Canada Customs and Revenue Agency, 125–26
  Canadian Tire Corporation Ltd v President of the Canada Border Services Agency, 126–27
  Convoy Supply Ltd v Commissioner of the Canada Customs and Revenue Agency, 125–26
textiles (Chapters 50–63), 110–21
  Agri-Pack v Commissioner of the Canada Customs and Revenue Agency, 115
  Bauer Hockey Corporation v President of the Canada Border Services Agency, 116
  BMC Coaters Inc v President of the Canada Border Services Agency, 114
  Canadian Tire Corporation Ltd v President of the Canada Border Services Agency, 115
  Coloridé Inc v Deputy Minister of National Revenue (Customs and Excise), 110
  Helly Hansen Leisure Canada v President of the Canada Border Services Agency, 111–12
  Innovak DIY Products Inc v President of the Canada Border Services Agency, 110. See also Tariff items, 40.16
  Kinedyne Canada Limited v President of the Canada Border Services Agency, 120–22
  Rui Royal International Corp v President of the Canada Border Services Agency, 121–22. See also Tariff items, 63.07
  Sher-Wood Hockey Inc v President of the Canada Border Services Agency, 112–13

VGI Village Green Imports v President of the Canada Border Services Agency, 117–18
vehicles, aircraft, vessels, and associated transport equipment (Chapters 86–89), 149–50
Suzuki Canada Inc and Canadian Kawasaki Motors Inc v Commissioner of the Canada Customs and Revenue Agency, 151–52
Yamaha Motor Canada Ltd v Commissioner of the Canada Customs and Revenue Agency, 149–51
Customs Tariff, Duties Relief Programs
free trade zones, compared to, 271–72
drawback program, 278
duties relief option: manufacturing, 277
duty deferral, 274–77
drawback program, 274
duties relief program, 274
other duties relief programs, 278–82
refunds for other reasons, 282–84
traveller's exemption, 272–73
warehouse program, customs bonded, 274, 276, 277
Customs Tariff, Duty-Free Treatment (Chapter 99)
Code 2000 (Article "for use in" goods of tariff item 8436.80.10—agricultural, horticultural, poultry farming and other machinery), 205
Code 2101 (Article "for use in" goods of tariff item 9032.89.20—process control equipment), 205–6
Code 2546 (Article for 'use in" goods of tariff headings 90.18 or 90.22—laser imagers), 206
Code 7934 (Article for 'use in" goods of tariff item 3921.90.90—composite goods of plastic sheets), 206–7

"for use in," definition of, 204
Notes to Chapter 99, 204–5
tariff item 9903.00.00 (agricultural and horticultural machinery), 207–11
tariff item 9908.00.00 (utility vehicles for use in mining), 211
tariff item 9948.00.00 (data processing machines), 212–15
tariff item 9958.00.00 (passenger vehicles), 215–16
tariff item 9961.00.00 (repair of road tractors), 217
tariff item 9977.00.00 (medical goods), 217–18
tariff item 9979.00.00 (assists for persons with disabilities), 218–23
Customs Tariff, Origin of Goods and Marking
marking of goods, 229. See also Administrative determinations and appeals, marking determination; Goods, marking of
origin of goods, 224
country of origin, wholly produced in, 226. See also Tariff agreements and accords, Least Developed Country Tariff (LDCT)
direct shipment and transhipment, 228
goods in transit. 228–29
substantially manufactured or processed, 227. See also Tariff agreement and accords, Least Developed Country Tariff (LDCT)
preferential tariff treatment under tariff agreements, free trade agreements, and NAFTA, 225. See also Tariff agreements and accords, NAFTA, preferential tariff treatment

Customs Tariff, Parts and Accessories
  base metals (Chapters 82–83), 185–86
    Commonwealth Wholesale Corp v
      President of the Canada Border
      Services Agency, 185–86
  machinery, mechanical appliances,
    electrical equipment, television
    image and sound recorders
    (Chapters 84–85), 187–94
    Asea Brown Boveri Inc v Commissioner of the Canada Customs
      and Revenue Agency, 189–90.
      See also Tariff items, 85.04
    GL&V/Black Clawson-Kennedy v
      Deputy Minister of National
      Revenue, 188
    IPSCO Inc v President of the Canada
      Border Services Agency, 190–92
    Nokia Products Limited v Deputy Minister of National Revenue, 188–89
    Prins Greenhouses Ltd v Deputy Minister of National Revenue, 187
  miscellaneous manufactured articles
    (Chapters 94–96), 199–203
    JIT Industrial Supply & Distribution
      Ltd v President of the Canada
      Border Services Agency, 199–201
    Newtech Beverage Systems Ltd v Commissioner of the Canada Customs
      and Revenue Agency, 203–4
    Ulextra Inc v President of the Canada
      Border Services Agency, 201–3
  plastics and rubber (Chapters 39–40), 182
    Komatsu International (Canada) Inc v
      President of the Canada Border
      Services Agency, 182–83
  raw hides, travel goods, handbags
    (Chapters 41–43), 183–84
    Nokia Products Limited & Primecell
      Communications Inc v Commissioner of the Canada Customs
      and Revenue Agency, 183–84
    Sony of Canada Ltd v Commissioner
      of the Canada Customs and
      Revenue Agency, 192–94. See
      also Tariff items, 8520.90.90
    Tyco Safety Products Canada Ltd v
      President of the Canada Border
      Services Agency, 194–96
  textiles (Chapters 50–63), 184–85
    Rui Royal International Corp v
      President of the Canada Border
      Services Agency, 184–85. See
      also Tariff items, 63.07
  vehicles, aircraft, vessels, and associated transport equipment
    (Chapters 86–89), 196–98
    Accessories Sportracks Inc de Thule
      Canada Inc v President of the
      Canada Border Services Agency,
      198
    Outdoor Gear Canada v President
      of the Canada Border Services
      Agency, 199
    Uvex Toko Canada Ltd v Deputy Minister of National Revenue, 196–98
Customs Tariff, Prohibited Goods
  books and depictions of obscenity,
    sedition, violence, child pornography, and others, 293
    Little Sisters Book and Art Emporium
      v Canada (Minister of Justice),
      54, 293
  certain wildlife and plumage, copyright, second-hand motor vehicles, and others, 286
  firearms, and prohibited weapons and
    devices, 287
    Gordon Schebek v President of the
      Canada Border Services Agency,
      290–91
    Jonathan Bell v President of the
      Canada Border Services Agency,
      290–91

M Miner v President of the Canada Border Services Agency, 289
R v Hasselwander, 288
R v Vaughan, 289
Rebecca Wigod v Commissioner of the Canada Customs and Revenue Agency, 292
Robert Gustas v Deputy Minister of National Revenue, 292
Romain L Klaasen v Commissioner of the Canada Customs and Revenue Agency, 289–90
Walter Seaton v Commissioner of the Canada Customs and Revenue Agency, 291
Wayne Ericksen v Commissioner of the Canada Customs and Revenue Agency, 289–90
Customs Tariff, Special Measures, Emergency Measures, and Safeguards, 243–44
 bilateral emergency measures, 254–65. *See also* Tariff agreements and accords
 Canada's external financial position in jeopardy, surtax when, 271
 China, safeguard measures in respect of, 165–70
 Columbia, 256–57
 Costa Rica, 257–58
 EFTA countries, goods from, 258–61
 Jordan, 263–64
 Mexican and MUST goods, 255–56
 Panama, goods from, 264–65
 Peru, goods from, 261–63
 Republic of Chile goods, 256
 US goods, 254–55
 agricultural goods, safeguard measures for, 253–54
 agricultural goods, surtax order on, 253–54
 duties relief programs, 271–84
 global emergency measures, 244–46
 goods from a free trade partner, surtaxes on, 248–50
  extension order, 252–53
  goods in transit, 253
  NAFTA partner, Chile, or Peru, 248–50
  regulations, 253
  surge of goods, 250–51
Customs Tariff, Tariff treatment. *See also* Tariff agreements and accords
 duty-free or preferential treatment, claiming, 231
 free trade agreements, 230. *See also* Free trade agreements (FTAs)
 General Preferential Tariff (GPT), 233–34. *See also* Governor in Council, powers concerning GPT; Tariff agreements and accords, General Preferential Tariff (GPT)
 General Tariff (GT), 231–32. *See also* Tariff agreement and accords, General Tariff (GT)
 Least-Developed-Country Tariff (LDCT), 234–35. *See also* Tariff agreements and accords, Least-Developed-Country Tariff (LDCT)
 Most-Favoured Nation Tariff qualification, 231–32. *See also* Tariff agreements and accords, Most-Favoured Nation Tariff (MFNT)

Department of Foreign Affairs and International Trade. *See also* Canada Border Services Agency (CBSA), accounting and payment of duties, required documentation
 Aliments Dorchester International Inc v Minister, Department of Foreign Affairs and International Trade and *Canadian Association of Regulated Importers v Canada (Attorney General)*, 398

Index

Export and Import Permits Act, 234, 252–53. *See also* Customs Tariff, Tariff treatment, General Preferential Tariff (GPT)
    requirement of import permits for certain goods, 11
    tariff rate quotas (TRQs), establishment of, 80, 234
    Trade Controls and Technical Barriers Bureau (TCTBB), 397–99
Deputy Minister of National Revenue, Customs and Excise
    adjustments, no
        Nordic Laboratories Inc v Canada (Deputy Minister of National Revenue, Customs and Excise), 36
    commissions, buying
        Chaps Ralph Lauren, a Division of 131384 Canada Inc v Canada (Deputy Minister of National Revenue), 26
        Sherson Marketing Corporation v Canada (Deputy Minister of National Revenue) (Sherson No 3), 26–27
        Utex Corporation v Canada (Deputy Minister of National Revenue), 26, 52
        Woodward Stores Ltd v Deputy Minister of National Revenue (Customs and Excise), 26
    commissions, selling
        DMG Trading Company v Canada (Deputy Minister of National Revenue), 29
    design costs
        Capital Garment Co v Canada (Deputy Minister of National Revenue), 30
    dutiable if condition of sale
        Avrecan International Inc v Canada (Deputy Minister of National Revenue, Customs and Excise), 34

Federal Court of Appeal, appeals to
    General Supply Co of Canada v Deputy Minister of National Revenue (Customs and Excise), 51
    Richards Packaging Inc v Deputy Minister of National Revenue, 52
fresh garlic from China, on ruling for, 387
general rules, application of
    Calego International Inc v Deputy Minister of National Revenue, 87
    Coloridé Inc v Deputy Minister of National Revenue (Customs and Excise), 88
identical goods, meaning of
    R & H Products Ltd v Deputy Minister of National Revenue (Customs and Excise), 37
    Triple-A Specialty Co v Deputy Minister of National Revenue (Customs and Excise), 37
materials used or consumed, value of
    Algo Group Inc v Canada (Deputy Minister of National Revenue), 30–31
payments, non-dutiable
    Nike Canada Ltd v Canada (Deputy Minister of National Revenue), 32
    Triton Industries Ltd v Canada (Deputy Minister of National Revenue for Customs and Excise), 32
price paid or payable must be ascertainable
    Canada (Deputy Minister of National Revenue) v Toyota Canada Inc, 19–20
purchaser in Canada
    Brunswick International (Canada) Ltd v Canada (Deputy Minister of National Revenue), 21
    Canada (Deputy Minister of National Revenue) v Mattel Canada Inc, 19

Canadian Admiral Corporation v
Deputy Minister of National
Revenue (Customs and Excise),
18–19
purchaser and vendor not related
Nu Skin Canada Inc v Canada
(Deputy Minister of National
Revenue), 24
tariff classifications, competing
Accessories Machinery Ltd v Canada
(Deputy Minister of National
Revenue, Customs and Excise),
182
Arctic Cat Sales Inc v Deputy Minister of National Revenue, 152–53
Black & Decker Canada Inc v Deputy
Minister of National Revenue for
Customs and Excise, 161–62
Calego International Inc v Deputy
Minister of National Revenue,
167–68
Canada (Deputy Minister of National
Revenue) v Mattel Canada Inc,
378
Deputy Minister of National Revenue
for Customs and Excise v
Androck Inc, 108
Deputy Minister of National Revenue
v Ferguson Industries Ltd, 52, 82,
180–81
Éditions Panini du Canada Ltée v
Deputy Minister of National
Revenue for Customs and Excise,
109–10
EM Plastic & Electric Products Ltd
v Deputy Minister of National
Revenue, 206–7
Flora Manufacturing & Distributing
Ltd v Deputy Minister of National Revenue, 98
Formica Canada Inc v Deputy Minister of National Revenue, 207

GL&V/Black Clawson-Kennedy v
Deputy Minister of National
Revenue, 188
Hilary's Distribution Ltd v Deputy
Minister of National Revenue, 221
Nokia Products Limited v Deputy Minister of National Revenue, 188
Oriental Trading (MTL) Ltd v Deputy
Minister of National Revenue, 160
Prins Greenhouses Ltd v Deputy Minister of National Revenue, 187
Regal Confections Inc v Deputy Minister of National Revenue, 92, 103
Robert Gustas v Deputy Minister of
National Revenue, 292
Rollins Machinery Ltd v Deputy Minister of National Revenue, 106
Sanyo Canada Inc v Deputy Minister
of National Revenue, 143–44
Sport Dinaco Inc v Deputy Minister
of National Revenue, 153
Thinkway Trading Corporation v
Deputy Minister of National
Revenue, 175
Toys "R" Us (Canada) Ltd v Deputy
Minister of National Revenue, 173
Trudell Medical Marketing Limited
v Deputy Minister of National
Revenue, 175
Uvex Toko Canada Ltd v Deputy Minister of National Revenue, 196
Windsor Wafers, Division of Beatrice
Foods v Deputy Minister of
National Revenue, 191–92
Yves Ponroy Canada v Deputy Minister of National Revenue, 97
Zellers Inc v Deputy Minister of National Revenue, 103
tariff items, interpretation of
Deputy Minister of National Revenue
(Customs and Excise) v Macmillan & Bloedel (Alberni) Ltd, 82

Index

Tribunal, filing an appeal with the
GFT Mode Canada v Canada (Deputy Minister of National Revenue), 50
value, computed
Patagonia International, Inc v Canada (Deputy Minister of National Revenue), 40
Designated Provisions (Customs) Regulations, penalty for violations, 61–62, 68. *See also* Administrative determinations and appeals, enforcement
Duties and taxes, evasion of
non-declaration of goods, 2
smuggling, 2
undervaluation, 2
Duties of customs. *See also* Customs Tariff; Tariff rate quotas and import permits
ad valorem rate, 78
Duties Relief Program, 77
Duty Deferral Program, 77
duty-free allowances, 77
rate of duty, 76–77, 81

England, remaining customs laws from
Merchant Shipping Acts, 1
European Free Trade Association (EFTA) states, refund of duties on goods imported from, 55
Exchequer Court. *See also* Canadian International Trade Tribunal, appeals to
Carter, Macy & Co v Canada, 228
Deputy Minister of National Revenue (Customs and Excise) v Ferguson Industries Ltd, 52, 82, 180–81. *See also* Deputy Minister of National Revenue, Customs and Excise, tariff classifications, competing early cases, 73
Federal Court, predecessor to, 51
Gosselin v Canada, 61. *See* also Administrative determinations and appeals, enforcement

Marun v Canada, 71–72
Sandness v Canada, 61. *See also* Administrative determinations and appeals, enforcement
Excise Act, 2001. *See also* Goods, valuation of imported
ad valorem, 16
adjustments, 40
deductions, 35
duties and taxes, levying of, 77
tobacco, 275, 276
refund of duties, 55
Excise Tax Act, 35, 40, 77, 78, 391
section 280, 70. *See also* Administrative determinations and appeals, enforcement
excise taxes, 278
Export Act, 412–14. *See also* Importers, requirement of permits for goods
intoxicating liquor, export of, 413–14
prohibition of export, 413
section 2, duties imposed under, 413
section 3, duties imposed under, 413
Export and Import Permits Act (EIPA), 80, 267–68, 269, 288. *See also* Importers, requirement of permits for goods
establishment of lists
Area Control List (ACL), 401
Automatic Firearms Country Control List (AFCCL), 401–2, 409
Export Control List, 399–401, 437
Export Permits Regulations (EPR), 399, 407
Import Control List (ICL), 402–6. *See also* Agricultural Marketing Programs Act
Import Permits Regulations (IPR), 399
export and import permits and certificates, 407–10
amendment, suspension, cancellation, and reinstatement, 410
export permits, 407

557

general import or export permits,
    408–9
import and export certificates,
    409–10
import permits, 408
international import certificates, 410
permit to import access quantity,
    409
permits that are required, 407
prohibited firearms and weapons,
    409
objectives, 397–99
offences and penalties, 410–12
    R v Marstar Trading International
        Inc, 411
    R v Martin, 411
    R v Oakes, 411
    R v Wulff, 411
Export and Import of Rough Diamonds
    Act (EIRDA), 425–28
    definition of "rough diamond," 426
    Kimberley Process Certification
        Scheme, 425–26
    offences (sections 8–14, 36–40),
        427–28
    punishment (section 41), 428
    trade regulation, 426–27
        export control (sections 7, 9, 13), 426
        import control (sections 9, 14, 16),
            426–27
        in-transit shipment (section 17), 427
    regulations, 427
Exporters of Processing Services (EOPS)
    program, 281–82
Exporter's Statement of Origin. See
    Canada Border Services Agency
    (CBSA), accounting and payment of
    duties, required documentation

Fair market value, 16. See also Goods,
    methods of valuation
Fair trade, 77

Farm Products Marketing Agencies Act,
    402. See also Export and Import
    Permits Act (EIPA), establishment of
    lists, Import Control List (ICL)
Federal Court of Appeal rulings
    AAi.FosterGrant of Canada Co v Canada
        (Customs and Revenue Agency), 21
    Abbott Laboratories, Ltd v Canada (Min-
        ister of National Revenue), 44–45
    Arctic Cat Sales Inc v Deputy Minister
        of National Revenue, 152–53
    Avrecan International Inc v Canada
        (Deputy Minister of National Rev-
        enue, Customs and Excise, 34. See
        also Goods, methods of valuation,
        adjustments to transaction value
        of goods
    Canada v Sun Parlor Advertising
        Company, 73. See also Administra-
        tive determinations and appeals,
        enforcement
    Canada (Customs and Revenue Agency)
        v Suzuki Canada Inc, 83. See also
        World Trade Organization (WTO)
    Canada (Deputy Minister of National
        Revenue) v Toyota Canada Inc,
        19–20
    Capital Garment Co v Canada (Deputy
        Minister of National Revenue), 30.
        See also Goods, methods of valu-
        ation, adjustments to transaction
        value of goods
    CB Powell Ltd v Canada (Border Servi-
        ces Agency), 44–45.
    Clothes Line Apparel, division of
        2810221 Canada Inc v Canada
        (Border Services Agency), 28, 34–35.
        See also Goods, methods of
        valuation
    Deputy Minister of National Revenue
        for Customs and Excise v Androck
        Inc, 108

Index

Doyon v Canada (Attorney General), 68–70
El Khoury v Canada (Minister of National Revenue, Customs and Excise), 67. See also Administrative determinations and appeals
Ingredia SA v Canada, 70–75
Jockey Canada Co v Canada (Minister of Public Safety and Emergency Preparedness), 50. See also Canadian International Trade Tribunal, appeals to
Kearns & McMurchy Inc v Canada, 75
McGregor v Canada (Minister of National Revenue, Customs and Excise), 67. See also Administrative determinations and appeals
Nike Canada Ltd v Canada (Deputy Minister of National Revenue), 31–32
Nu Skin Canada Inc v Canada (Deputy Minister of National Revenue), 24
Pacific Shower Doors (1995) Ltd v Canada (Canadian International Trade Tribunal), 48. See also Administrative determinations and appeals, payment of duties and taxes before appeal
Patagonia International, Inc v Canada (Deputy Minister of National Revenue), 40–41. See also Goods, methods of valuation, adjustments to transaction value of goods
Richards Packaging Inc v Deputy Minister of National Revenue, 52. See also Canadian International Trade Tribunal, appeals to
Sable Offshore Energy Inc v Canada (Customs and Revenue Agency), 53. See also Canadian International Trade Tribunal, appeals to

Sable Offshore Energy Inc v Commissioner of the Canada Customs and Revenue Agency, 89–90
Sherson Marketing Corporation v Canada (Deputy Minister of National Revenue) cases, 27, 52. See also Goods, methods of valuation, adjustments to transaction value of goods
Simms Sigal & Co Ltd v Canada (Customs and Revenue Agency), 26–27. See also Goods, methods of valuation, adjustments to transaction value of goods
United Parcel Service Canada Ltd v Canada (Minister of Public Safety and Emergency Preparedness), 68–70
Utex Corporation v Canada (Deputy Minister of National Revenue), 26. See also Goods, methods of valuation, adjustments to transaction value of goods
Federal Courts Act, 44–45, 53, 70, 75, 340, 361–62, 371–73, 377, 382, 383, 385, 394, 423. See also Administrative determinations and appeals, determination of value of duty, tariff classification, and origin; Canadian International Trade Tribunal, appeals to
Feeds Act, 439–40
Fertilizer's Act, 439–40
Financial Administration Act, 284. See also Customs Tariff, Duties Relief Programs, other duties relief programs
Firearms Act, 287–88
Food and Drugs Act, 439–40, 445, 472
Form A—Certificate of Origin, 12. See also Canada Border Services Agency (CBSA), accounting and payment of duties, required documentation

Form B255, 12. *See also* Canada Border Services Agency (CBSA), accounting and payment of duties, required documentation
Free and Secure Trade (FAST) Commercial Driver Program, 13
Free on Board (FOB), 35–36
Free trade agreements (FTAs), 11–12, 225
Free Trade Partner Certificate, 11–12. *See also* Canada Border Services Agency (CBSA), accounting and payment of duties, required documentation

General Agreement on Trade and Tariffs (GATT 1994)
    Article VI, anti-dumping and countervailing duties, 301, 302–3, 315
    Article XIX, 259
    Canada's obligations under, 243, 247, 329
GATT Subsidies Agreement, 301
General Rules for the Interpretation of the Harmonized System. See also International Convention on the Harmonized Commodity Description and Coding System (HS Convention); *Customs Tariff*, Schedule to
    application of, 79–80, 86–87, 111, 136, 207, 286
    Canadian Rules, 85–86, 295–96, 136
        Rule 1, 104–5, 112, 139, 145, 174, 176, 203–4
    Compendium of Classification Opinions and the Explanatory Notes to the HS, 79–80, 81, 82–83. *See also* World Customs Organization (WCO)
    Canada (Customs and Revenue Agency) v Suzuki Canada Inc, 83
        Rule 1, 131
        Rule 2, 123, 124, 195–96
        Rule 3, 101, 142–43, 164, 184
    Customs Tariff, as part of, 80–82
    prohibited goods, 285–86
    Rule 5, 296
    Rules 1–6, outline of, 82–86, 294–95
    tariff classification appeals, 81
    tariff classification disputes, 91, 92, 93, 99, 100, 101
        Rule 1, 91–93, 99–100, 101, 108, 110, 113–16, 117, 119, 120, 122, 126, 131, 132, 135, 138, 140, 144–46, 149, 156, 161–62, 165–67, 169, 177, 179, 183, 198
        Rule 2, 114, 115, 123
        Rule 3, 99, 100, 115, 132, 137, 142–43, 148, 158–61, 168, 183, 204, 207
        Rule 6, 104–5, 112, 122, 129, 139, 140, 156, 167, 172, 174, 176, 177, 179, 203
    tariff items, interpretation of, 82
    Tribunal, classification decisions of the, 88
Gold and Silver Marking Act. See also *Precious Metals Marking Act*
    application of marks (sections 3–4), 483
    offences and criminal penalties (section 10), 484
    other marks (sections 3–5), 484
Goods, abandoned and unclaimed, 7
    designated place of safekeeping for, 7
    disposal costs for, 7
Goods, classification of, 79–84. *See also General Rules for the Interpretation of the Harmonized System*
Goods, failure to report, 3–4
    exceptions, 4. *See also* Tariff items, 9813.00.00 and 9814.00.00
    Hoang v Canada (Minister of National Revenue), 4–5
    Kong v Canada, 4
    Proceeds of Crime Act, section 12, 5

R v Cook, 4
Time Data Recorder International Ltd v Canada (Minister of National Revenue), 4
Tourki v Canada (Minister of Public Safety and Emergency Preparedness), 5
Goods, marking of, 229
  regulations, 43–44
  requirements, 43
Goods, methods of valuation, 16–17
  adjustments to transaction value of goods
    assists, 30–31
    commissions 26–30
    deductions, 35–36
    no adjustment, 36
    residual method of valuation, 43
    royalties and licence fees, 31–32
  goods abroad, value for duty of work on the, 16
  goods, removed and subsequently returned, 16, 78
  goods in Iceland, Norway, Switzerland, or Liechtenstein, repairs or alterations made to, 16
  price paid or payable, 19–20
  purchaser and vendor not related, 23–24
  purchaser in Canada, 20–23
    purchaser in Canada, sale for export to, 18
  transaction value, 17–18, 76
    computed value, 40–41
    deductive value, 38–40
    identical goods, of, 36
    similar goods, of, 38
  transaction value method, 15
Goods, movement of
  Customs Act, section 19(3), 5
  warehouses, to, 5
Goods, obligation to report, 2–3

Goods, release of, 6
  after interim accounting, 6
  imported by courier or mail, 6–7
  prior to accounting and payment of duties, 6
Goods, valuation of imported, 15
  ad valorem, 16
  ethno-cultural exemption, 16
  goods exceeding duty-free exemption, 16
Goods and Services Tax (GST) and Harmonized Sales Tax (HST), 78
  Canadian goods returned after being exported, on, 281
  relief from, 276, 278, 279, 282
  Value of Imported Goods (GST/HST) Regulations, 279–80, 281
Governor in Council
  powers concerning CCCT, 236
  powers concerning GPT, 234
  powers concerning LDCT, 235
  powers concerning TRQ, 235, 236, 240, 241

Harmonized Sales Tax (HST). *See* Goods and Services Tax (GST) and Harmonized Sales Tax (HST)
Hasselwander test, 288
Health of Animals Act. *See also* Importers, requirement of permits for goods
  exportation, 469–71
  regulatory provisions (sections 69–71), 469–71
  statutory provision, veterinarian's certificate (section 19), 469
Health of Animals Regulations, 451
  offences, violations, and penalties, 471–72
  criminal offences (sections 65–68), 471
  permits and licences (section 160), 471
  regulatory regime (sections 7–62)

Part II: general provisions, germ-plasm, and regulated animal (sections 7–9), 453–55
Part III: animal products (section 34), 455–56
Part IV: animal byproducts and animal pathogens (sections 40–53), 456–61
Part V: fodder (section 54), 462
Part VI: packing material, beehives, and beeswax (sections 55–57), 462–63
Part VII: quarantine of imported animals (sections 58–62), 466
Part XI: veterinary biologics (sections 121, 122), 463
Part XII: transportation of animals (sections 136–59), 466–68
Part XIV: products of rendering plants (sections 2, 167, 170, 171), 463–64
Part XVI: aquatic animals (sections 190, 191), 464–65
statutory prohibitions (sections 14–18), 451–53
Health Canada, 11. *See also* Canada Border Services Agency (CBSA), accounting and payment of duties, required documentation

Importers, requirement of permits for goods, 7–8
Industrial Hemp Regulations, 441. *See also Controlled Drugs and Substances Act*
International Convention on the Harmonized Commodity Description and Coding System (HS Convention), 79, 82. *See also Customs Tariff*; Duties of customs
General Interpretative Rules. *See General Rules for the Interpretation of the Harmonized System*, application of

Harmonized Commodity Description and Coding System (HCDCS), 79–80
International Valuation Agreement, 23
Invoices, 10. *See also* Canada Border Services Agency (CBSA), accounting and payment of duties, required documentation
Canada Customs Invoice (CCI), 10
commercial, 10

Licences, Brokers
carriers and courier companies, necessity of for, 8
importers and exporters for business, necessity of for, 7
people and businesses for private conveyances, necessity of for, 8
persons conducting business with customs, necessity of for, 8
requirements for obtaining, 7–8
Livestock and Livestock Products Act. *See Health of Animals Act*
Low value shipments, 12. *See also* Canada Border Services Agency (CBSA), accounting and payment of duties, required documentation

Minister of Finance
anti-dumping duties, report on to, 348, 349
COLT rate, power to extend, 239
countervailing duty, report on to, 348
CRT rate, power to extend, 239
CT rate, power to extend, 238
global emergency measures, 245
goods, power to change description of, 80
"Israel or another *CIFTA* beneficiary" and "imported from Israel or another *CIFTA* beneficiary," power to define the expressions, 241

NAFTA benefits, suspension of, 384
PT rate, power to extend, 240
rate of duty when order ceases to
 have effect, 258
review on request of, 367–68
surtax order on agricultural goods,
 253–54
tariff entitlement, power to extend,
 238, 239, 240
tariff item, power to renumber, 80
TRQ rate, power to extend, 240
UST and MT rates, power to extend,
 238

Narcotic Control Regulations, 441, 445,
 447. See also Controlled Drugs and
 Substances Act
New Brunswick Court of Appeal
 Down East Toyota v Canada (Minister
  of National Revenue, Customs and
  Excise), 67. See also Administra-
  tive determinations and appeals
North American Free Trade Agreement
 (NAFTA). See Tariff agreements and
 accords, NAFTA

Ontario Court of Appeal
 Kelly v Palazzo, 59. See also Administra-
  tive determinations and appeals,
  enforcement
 R v Cook, 4
Organisation for Economic Co-oper-
 ation and Development (OECD)
 Transfer Pricing Guidelines for Multi-
  national Enterprises and Tax
  Administrations, 23

People's Republic of China
 "action," meaning of, 269
 dumped footwear from, 364
 dumping and subsidizing by, 331
 exporter, 246–247

Fresh Garlic Originating in or Exported from the People's Republic of
 China, 362, 387
goods originating in, 405–6
market disruption and trade diversion
 by, safeguard measures against,
 243
oil country tubular goods, investigation into, 334–37. See also Special
 Import Measures Act (SIMA), section 20 process investigations
Protocol on the Accession of the People's
 Republic of China, 244. See also
 World Trade Organization (WTO),
 World Trade Organization Agreement
Special Import Measures Regulations
 (SIMR), 309. See also Special Import Measures Act (SIMA), Special
 Import Measures Regulations
 (SIMR)
SUREBONDER® glue guns, manufacturing of, 139
surtax on goods originating from, 269
women's waterproof plastic footwear
 from, 357
Pest Control Products Act
 export control (sections 33 and 67), 474
 import control (sections 6 and 7),
  473–74
 penalties and punishment (sections 6
  and 68), 475
 Pest Control Product Export Control
  List, 474
 Pest Control Products Regulations, 473
 Pest Management Regulatory Agency
  (PMRA), 472
Plant Protection Act
 exportation (sections 55–60), 480–81
 certificates (section 55), 480
 export of grain by vessel (section
  58), 481

export permit, (section 56) 481
import and export control, 476–77
   regulatory provisions (section 47), 477
   statutory provisions (section 7), 476–77
importation
   declaration (section 39), 479
   import for special purposes (section 43), 480
   packaging and labeling (section 41), 479
   permits and phytosanitary certificates (sections 29, 30–37), 477–79
   prohibiting entry (section 42), 480
   treatment of processing (section 38), 479
offences and violations (sections 48–51), 482
   administrative monetary penalties, 482
   offences, 482
Plant Protection Regulations, 476
Plant Quarantine Act. *See Plant Protection Act*
Precious Metals Marking Act, 43
Precursor Control Regulations, 441. *See also Controlled Drugs and Substances Act*
Proceeds of Crime (Money Laundering) and Terrorism Financing Act (Proceeds of Crime Act), 2–3

Reporting goods. *See* Goods, obligation to report

Sale of Goods Act, 18
Smuggling, 2, 72–73. *See also* Administrative determinations and appeals, enforcement; *Criminal Code of Canada*, prohibited goods; *Customs Tariff*, Prohibited Goods

Softwood Lumber Agreement, 368–69, 397
Softwood Lumber Products Agreement, 406–7, 414. *See also Export and Import Permits Act (EIPA)*, establishment of lists, Import Control List (ICL); *Export Act*
Softwood Lumber Products Export Charge Act, 2006 (SLPCA), 406–7, 414. *See also Export and Import Permits Act (EIPA)*, establishment of lists, Import Control List (ICL); *Exports Act*
Special Import Measures Act (SIMA), 48, 77, 78, 259, 266
   anti-dumping, countervailing, and provisional duties, liability for, 314–23
   imposition of duties (sections 3–8), 314–15
   liability to pay (section 3(1)), 315–23
   CBSA action on final determination, order, or finding. *See* Canadian Border Services Agency (CBSA), dumping and subsidies, investigations into
Customs Tariff, 300–1
disputes resolved by WTO
   dairy products, 370–71
   European Union beef hormones ban, 369–70
   softwood lumber, 368
dumping, 301–3
   insignificant margin (sections 30.1 and 30.2), 302
   margin of (section 2(1)), 302
   meaning of (section 2), 301–2
   negligible volume (section 2(1)), 302
export price (sections 24–28), 311–13
general provisions,
   definition of "importer in Canada," 386, 391–93

disclosure of confidential information (sections 82–83), 395
judicial review: application to Federal Court of Appeal (section 77), 393–95
rulings, 387–91
goods or duties levied under, 35, 40
ICL to reinforce decisions of the Tribunal, use of, 402
investigations and inquiries
  complaint, filing a, 325–26. *See also* World Trade Organization (WTO), *World Trade Organization Agreement, Agreement on Subsidies and Countervailing Measures*
  determination of injury, dumping, or subsidizing, 327–31, 337–39
  investigation by CBSA, initiation and notice of, 326–27
  proceedings/inquiry, termination of, 353
  Tribunal, duties of and guidance to (sections 42(3) to (6)), 339
  Tribunal, preliminary inquiry by the, 327–28. *See also* Tariff agreements and accords, *Canada-Chile Free Trade Agreement (CCFTA)*
  Tribunal must advise CBSA, 352–53
  Tribunal's order or finding, 339
NAFTA dispute settlement (section 77)
  binational panel decisions, 374–80
  binational panel review, 372–74
  extraordinary challenge proceedings, 381–82
  orders and decisions of panel and committee, 382
  special committee, appointment of, 382–85
  stay of proceedings, 382–85
normal value (section 2(1)), 305–11

Pacific Shower Doors (1995) Ltd v Canada (Canadian International Trade Tribunal), decision under, 48
public interest inquiries (section 45), 347–48
  iodinated contrast media, 349–51
  prepared baby foods, 349
  refrigerators, dishwashers, and dryers from the United States, 351–52
purpose of, 299–301
review of orders and findings of injury (sections 76–77)
  expiry review, 365–66
  further reviews, 364
  goods of Chile, 371
  interim orders, 363–64
section 20 process investigations
  oil country tubular goods (The People's Republic of China), 334–37
  Polysio insulation board (United States), 332–34
section 98 and compliance with GATT Subsidies Agreement, 301. *See also General Agreement on Trade and Tariffs (GATT 1994)*
Special Import Measures Regulations (SIMR), 305, 309, 348, 379
subsidizing, 302–5
  financial contribution, meaning of (section 2(1.6), 303
  meaning of (section 2(1)), 302
  subsidies, non-specific and specific, 304
  subsidy, amount of (sections 27–36), 305
  subsidy, non-actionable, 303–4
  subsidy, prohibited, 304–5
Tribunal, appeals to the, 356–60. *See* Canadian International Trade Tribunal, appeals to

Aluminart Products Limited v President of the Canada Border Services Agency, 360–61
Cobra Anchors Co Ltd v President of the Canada Border Services Agency, 358–59
M & M Footwear Inc v Commissioner of the Canada Customs and Revenue Agency, 357–58
Toyota Tsusho America Inc v President of the Canada Border Services Agency, 359–60
Tribunal, injury inquiry by, 337–40
    fresh tomatoes exported from the United States, 342–43
    grain corn exported from the United States, 343
    greenhouse bell peppers exported from the Netherlands, 344–45
    Polysio insulation board exported from the United States, 345–47
    steel fuel tanks exported from China and Taipei, 341–42
    steel grating exported from China, 344
    wood venetian blinds and slats from Mexico and China, 340–41
Statutory Instruments Act, 254, 384
Supreme Court Act, 53. See also Canadian International Trade Tribunal, appeals to
Supreme Court of Canada rulings
    Accessories Machinery Ltd v Canada (Deputy Minister of National Revenue, Customs and Excise), 182
    Asea Brown Boveri Inc v Commissioner of the Canada Customs and Revenue Agency, 189–90. See also Tariff items, 85.04
    Canada v Bureau, 72–73. See also Administrative determinations and appeals, enforcement
    Canada (Deputy Minister of National Revenue) v Mattel Canada Inc, 19, 32–34, 52, 378
    Canadian Admiral Corporation v Deputy Minister of National Revenue (Customs and Excise), 18–19
    Cherry Stix Ltd v President of the Canada Border Services Agency, 19
    Comité Paritaire de l'Industrie de la Chemise v Potash, 58
    Deputy Minister of National Revenue v Ferguson Industries Ltd, 52, 82, 180–81
    Deputy Minister of National Revenue (Customs and Excise) v Macmillan & Bloedel (Alberni) Ltd, 82
    Industrial Acceptance Corp v Canada, 62. See also Administrative determinations and appeals, enforcement
    Little Sisters Book and Art Emporium v Canada (Minister of Justice), 54, 293
    Martineau v Canada (Minister of National Revenue), 64. See also Administrative determinations and appeals, enforcement
    R v Jarvis, 58
    R v Ling, 58
    R v Mason, 63. See also Administrative determinations and appeals, enforcement
    R v Monney, 60
    R v Oakes, 74–75. See also Administrative determinations and appeals, enforcement
    R v Simmons, 59
    R v Therriens, inconsistency with decisions, 60
    Shell Canada Ltd v Canada, 21

Tariff agreements and accords. See also Customs Tariff, Tariff treatment

Australia Tariff (AUT), 12, 225, 230, 236. *See also* Canada Border Services Agency (CBSA), accounting and payment of duties, required documentation; Tariff agreements and accords, British Preferential Tariff (BPT)

British Preferential Tariff (BPT), 230. *See also* Tariff agreements and accords, Australia Tariff (AUT); Tariff agreements and accords, New Zealand Tariff (NZT)

Canada-Chile Free Trade Agreement (CCFTA), 12-13, 230, 238, 256, 328, 371, 404. *See also* Customs Tariff, Special Measures, Emergency Measures, and Safeguards, goods from a free trade partner, surtaxes on

Chile Tariff (CT), 238, 406

Canada-Columbia Free Trade Agreement (CCOFTA), 230, 238-39, 403; *See also* Customs Tariff, Special Measures, Emergency Measures, and Safeguards, bilateral emergency measures

Canada-Costa Rica Free Trade Agreement (CCRFTA), 12-13, 230, 239, 257-58, 406. *See also* Canada Border Services Agency (CBSA), accounting and payment of duties, required documentation

Costa Rica Tariff (CRT), 239, 257-58

Canada-European Free Trade Association Free Trade Agreement (CEFTA FTA), 241

countervailing measures, application of, 315

Canada-Israel Free Trade Agreement (CIFTA), 11-12, 55, 240-41. *See also* Warehouses, access to by border services officers

Canada-Israel Agreement Tariff (CIAT), 241

Canada-Jordan Economic Growth and Prosperity Act, 242

Jordan (JT) Tariff, 230, 242, 263-64

Canada-Panama Free Trade Agreement (CPAFTA), 230, 242-43

Panama Tariff (PAT), 243, 264-65

Canada-Peru Free Trade Agreement (CPFTA), 230, 240, 260, 403

Peru Tariff (PT), 240, 260. *See also* Customs Tariff, Special Measures, Emergency Measures, and Safeguards, goods from a free trade partner, surtaxes on

Canada-US Free Trade Agreement. *See* Tariff agreements and accords, NAFTA

CARICOM member countries (ongoing agreements), 230

Commonwealth Caribbean Countries Tariff (CCCT), 12, 225, 230, 233, 235-36. *See also* Canada Border Services Agency (CBSA), accounting and payment of duties, required documentation

European (non EU) countries
Iceland (IT), 230, 241, 258, 260
Norway (NT), 230, 241, 258, 260
Switzerland-Liechtenstein Tariffs (SLT), 230, 241, 242, 258, 260

General Preferential Tariff (GPT), 12, 225, 230, 233-35, 266. *See also* Canada Border Services Agency (CBSA), accounting and payment of duties, required documentation; *See also* Customs Tariff, Tariff treatment, General Preferential Tariff (GPT)

General Tariff (GT), 224-25, 231-32

Honduras Tariff, 230

Least Developed Country Tariff (LDCT), 12, 225, 226, 230, 233, 234–35. *See also* Canada Border Services Agency (CBSA), accounting and payment of duties, required documentation; *Customs Tariff*, Origin of Goods and Marking

Most-Favoured-Nation Tariff (MFNT), 12, 225, 231–32. *See also* Canada Border Services Agency (CBSA), accounting and payment of duties, required documentation; *Customs Tariff*, Special Measures, Emergency Measures, and Safeguards, bilateral emergency measures; World Trade Organization (WTO), *World Trade Organization Agreement*

General Preferential Tariff (GPT) treatment, 230

MFNT Rules of Origin Regulations, 225

rate, 260, 262, 263, 264–67

NAFTA. *See also Customs Tariff*, Special Measures, Emergency Measures, and Safeguards, goods from a free trade partner, surtaxes on countries, 340, 367, 403

dispute settlement, 371–85. *See also Special Import Measures Act (SIMA)*, NAFTA dispute settlement (section 77)

marking imported goods from countries part of, 43–44

Mexico Tariff (MT), 237, 406

Mexico-US Tariff (MUST), 237, 406

panel proceedings, 316–17. *See also Special Import Measures Act (SIMA)*, anti-dumping, countervailing, and provisional duties, liability for

preferential tariff treatment, 12, 14, 218, 225, 228–29, 230, 245

provisions relating to the imposition and application of anti-dumping and countervailing duties, 315. *See also Special Import Measures Act (SIMA)*, anti-dumping, countervailing, and provisional duties, liability for

Rules of Origin Regulations, 226–27. *See also Customs Tariff*, Origin of Goods and Marking

Rules of Procedure, 375–76

US Tariff (UST), 237, 406. *See also Customs Tariff*, Special Measures, Emergency Measures, and Safeguards, bilateral emergency measures

New Zealand Tariff (NZT), 12, 225, 230, 236. *See also* Canada Border Services Agency (CBSA), accounting and payment of duties, required documentation; Tariff agreements and accords, British Preferential Tariff (BPT)

Tariff Board. *See also* Canadian International Trade Tribunal

Dominion Engineering Works Ltd v A B Wing Ltd, 51

General Supply Co of Canada v Deputy Minister of National Revenue (Customs and Excise), 51

R & H Products Ltd v Deputy Minister of National Revenue (Customs and Excise), 36–37

Triton Industries Ltd v Canada (Deputy Minister of National Revenue for Customs and Excise), 31–32

Tariff items

40.16, 106–7, 110

63.07, 114, 115, 120–22, 130–31, 184–85

85.04, 138–39, 183–84, 189

2202.90.90, 93, 95, 137

8520.90.90, 145–46, 192–94

Index

9503.00.90, 164–67, 168–70
9813.00.00 and 9814.00.00, 4, 281. *See also Criminal Code of Canada*, firearms, and prohibited weapons
9898.00.00, 81, 287, 292
9899.00.00, 54, 81, 293
renumbering, 80–81
Tariff rate quotas and import permits, 11, 77, 80, 402. *See also* Canada Border Services Agency (CBSA), accounting and payment of duties, required documentation
Temporary Importation (Excise Levies and Additional Duties) Regulations, 279. *See also Customs Tariff*, Duties Relief Programs, other duties relief programs
Textile Labelling Act, 43, 484–87
exemptions, 486–87
offences and penalties (sections 3, 4, 5, 12–13), 487
prescribed consumer textile article, 487
prohibition (section 3), 485
regulatory requirements (section 5), 485–86
Textile Labelling and Advertising Regulations, 485
Transportation costs, 35–36. *See also* Goods, methods of valuation, adjustments to transaction value of goods

Universal Postal Convention
Letter Post Regulations, Form RE 601, 61. *See also* Administrative determinations and appeals, enforcement
US Department of Commerce (US DOC), 368–69. *See also Special Import Measures Act (SIMA)*, disputes resolved by WTO

Valuation for Duty Regulations, 18, 20, 21, 22
section 3, 24
Value of Imported Goods (GST/HST) Regulations, 279–80, 281. *See also Customs Tariff*, Duties Relief Programs, other duties relief programs

Warehouses
access to by border services officers, 8–9
CBSA memoranda, regulations, and policies for, 8
licences for. *See* Canada Border Services Agency (CBSA), licences, warehouse
Wild Animals and Plant Protection Regulation of International and Interprovincial Trade Act (WAPPRIITA). *See also* Importers, requirement of permits for goods
classification of wild fauna and flora, 415
Convention on International Trade in Endangered Species of Wild Fauna and Flora (CITES), 414–15
exemptions (sections 15–17), 416–17
import and export (section 6), 415
interprovincial transport (section 7), 416
issue of permits, 417–18
limitations and restrictions, 417
possession (section 8)
WAPPRIITA Regulations, 415
section 10, 417–18
section 13, 416
section 14, 417
section 17, 417
section 18, 417
World Customs Organization (WCO), 79, 92–93, 161. *See also General Rules for the Interpretation of the Harmonized System*

569

World Trade Organization (WTO)
Appellate Body, 368–70. *See also Special Import Measures Act (SIMA)*, disputes resolved by WTO
International Valuation Agreement, adoption of, 23
members, 269
World Trade Organization Agreement, 77, 229–30, 266, 269, 315, 367, 403, 405. *See also Customs Tariff*, Tariff treatment; Fair trade
Agreement on Agriculture, 254, 304, 371, 404

Agreement on Safeguards, 249, 258–59
Agreement on Subsidies and Countervailing Measures, 315, 332, 339
Agreement on Textiles and Clothing, 402
Agreement on Trade-related aspects of Intellectual Property Rights, 475
Anti-dumping Agreement, 374–75, 380
World Trade Organization Agreement Implementation Act, 77

About the Author

Mohan Prabhu worked as a senior counsel with the Canadian Department of Justice prior to his retirement, and in that capacity gained experience in regulatory matters, especially in the fields of bankruptcy, environment, and customs and excise. He was the architect of the federal administrative monetary penalties system adopted in 1995, first by Agriculture and Agri-Food Canada and subsequently by Revenue Canada (Customs and Excise), Environment Canada, and other federal departments.

Prior to joining the federal government, he taught law in Toronto and Saskatoon.

Dr Prabhu was the editor of the *Annotated Customs Act* from 1991 to 2012, and of the chapter on Customs and Excise Laws of Canada in the *Canadian Encyclopedic Digest (Ontario)* from 1993 to 2004.

Mohan Prabhu holds undergraduate and graduate degrees from the University of Bombay; an LLM with distinction from the University of London, England; and a doctorate of law from the University of Ottawa. He was called to the bars in India, England, and Canada, from which he has now retired. He was awarded the rank of Queen's Counsel in 1990.